Interviewing Strategies for Helpers

A Guide to Assessment, Treatment, and Evaluation

Interviewing Strategies for Helpers

A Guide to Assessment, Treatment, and Evaluation

William H. Cormier
L. Sherilyn Cormier

West Virginia University

Brooks/Cole Publishing Company,
Monterey, California
A Division of Wadsworth, Inc.

Printed in the United States of America

10   9   8   7   6   5   4

Library of Congress Cataloging in Publication Data

Cormier, William H.
    Interviewing strategies for helpers.

    Bibliography: p.518
    Includes index.
    1. Helping behavior.   2. Interviewing.   I. Cormier,
Louise S.   II. Title.
BF637.H4C67   158'.3   78-12849
ISBN 0-8185-0282-7

Acquisition Editor: *Claire Verduin*
Manuscript Editor: *Beth Luey*
Production Editor: *Joan Marsh*
Interior Design: *Jamie S. Brooks*
Cover Design: *Ruth Scott*
Illustrations: *John Foster*
Typesetting: *David R. Sullivan Company*

To:
Doc and Leona and Bill and Edith

Preface

Helping is a systematic and a spontaneous process that requires a repertory of effective behaviors on the part of the helper. *Interviewing Strategies for Helpers* describes and models a variety of skills that may be used by helpers. These skills and strategies are designed to be used within the context of a helping interview.

There are three major emphases of this book: assessment, treatment, and evaluation. The first part of the book describes verbal and nonverbal behaviors that may be used in the assessment stage of helping. The second part of the book presents a number of different treatment strategies that can be used to facilitate client action and behavior change. Two additional chapters illustrate procedures for conducting process and outcome evaluations of helping. These evaluation chapters clearly support our responsibility as helpers not only to implement our skills but also to assess their impact.

In part, the usefulness of this book may lie in its comprehensive coverage of helping skills. Also, the format of the book is designed to provide valuable learning experiences that promote skill acquisition and application. Each chapter includes a brief introduction, chapter objectives, content material sprinkled with model examples, learning activities and feedback, a post evaluation, and a role-play interview assessment. The book can be completed by individuals on a self-instructional basis or within an organized course or in-service training. Identifying some ways to use this format may enhance the acquisition of the content. Chapter 1 describes the content and format of the book in greater detail. Before reading anything else in this book, we urge you to read Chapter 1.

We appreciate the helpful suggestions of Richard Bednar, University of Kentucky, Gary Belkin, Long Island University, Barry Edelstein, West Virginia University, Marvin Goldfried, State University of New York at Stony Brook, Dwight Goodwin, San Jose State University, John Horan, Pennsylvania State University, George Iglesias, Pima Community College, William Stilwell, III, University of Kentucky, Robert Wrenn, University of Arizona, and Geoffrey Yager, University of Cincinnati, who reviewed the manuscript. We are grateful to Robert Marinelli of West Virginia University for his comments and for his assistance in field-testing portions of the manuscript.

We express warm appreciation to our typist and friend, Anne Drake. And, finally, we are thankful for the instructive feedback provided by our students who participated in the field-testing of this book.

William H. Cormier
L. Sherilyn Cormier

Contents

Verbal Communication 49

Listening Responses 61

Action Responses 77

Sharing and Teaching Responses 94

Interview Discrimination 116

Chapter 1
About This Book

Picture yourself as a helper. A middle-aged, distressed woman has just walked into your office, keeping an appointment to see you. The client doesn't know what to expect from you, and you really don't know too much about this person. She is sitting in front of you now. You become aware that she seems to be sizing you up and trying to decide how much to tell you. The client may be wondering: What kind of person is this counselor? Why is this someone I can trust? Is this person competent enough to handle my concerns?

Likewise, you may be thinking to yourself: What is the first thing I am going to do? What types of things am I going to say? What does the client want to be able to do as a result of counseling? How am I going to help with this? How will I know whether I have helped this person?

We expect that the concern with these questions will vary among the users of this book. Some of you may feel apprehensive about what you're getting into or how much potential you feel you have for counseling. Others of you may feel more comfortable with the helping process and with yourselves. Many of you may recognize a need to sharpen or add to your repertory of counseling skills.

To formulate some responses to these questions, we have designed this book to help you acquire counseling skills systematically. The book is organized in modular chapters with intermittent learning activities, feedback, model examples, and evaluations. Over the past several years, this book has been field-tested with students, paraprofessionals, and practicing counselors. The format and content of the chapters reflect these users' comments and data from empirical evaluations.

Self, Skills, and Process Development

We believe counselors should have training experiences in three major areas: self-development, skill development, and process development. Self-development involves professional growth and self-evaluation. Certain qualities you have as a person may enhance or detract from your counseling. The objective of self-development is for you to identify some of your attitudes and behaviors that may facilitate or interfere with a helping relationship. Your self-image, your values, and your expectations help or hurt your capacity to establish a counseling relationship. In our opinion, counselor qualities of warmth, respect, and empathic understanding are necessary, but often not sufficient, for therapeutic change. We feel your effectiveness as a helper can be increased if, in addition to being a "warm fuzzy," you have some skills and strategies that you can use with a variety of client problems.

Skill development consists of any experience that helps you acquire counseling techniques and develop your own counseling-interview style. The purpose of skill development is to help you learn some possible procedures and strategies for helping people to change. However, this does not necessarily mean that what you do will facilitate client change.

Process development involves discovering ways to monitor and evaluate your behavior and the client's behavior during the counseling process. The goal of process development is for you to make continuous observations of your behavior and to discriminate its effects during counseling. Evaluation occurs before, during, and after a particular counseling intervention. It provides data about the kinds of things the client is doing after counseling that he or she was not doing before or at the beginning of counseling. Process development is a way to assess the level of impact that your helping relationship and strategies may have on the client.

Purpose of the Book

We hope that, in this book, you will find training experiences that facilitate personal growth, develop your counseling skills, and provide ways for you to evaluate your counseling. Personal growth is the most elusive and the most difficult to define of these three areas. It is beyond the scope of this book to focus primarily on self-development. You may explore and evaluate yourself as you go through certain parts of the book, particularly Chapter 2. We also encourage you to seek out additional experiences in which you can receive feedback from others about yourself, your strengths, and some behaviors that may interfere with counseling. These experiences might consist of individual or classroom activities and feedback, growth groups, and personal counseling. At the risk of repeating ourselves, it is well documented that a counselor's warmth, empathy, and positive regard can contribute to client change. We feel that your demonstration of these relationship conditions will enhance the way you perform the skills and strategies presented in this book.

We created the book with three specific purposes. First, we think it will help you acquire a repertory of counseling interview skills and strategies. The book focuses on *interview* skills and strategies as used in a helping relationship. It is directed (but not restricted) to applying skills within a counselor-client dyadic relationship. Some of the skills and strategies may be used appropriately in counseling groups, as well. There are an almost infinite number of counseling techniques, but we have included only the ones that are used most commonly and have some empirical basis or rationale. We should caution you that many of the research studies cited in this book were conducted as analogues—that is, in simulated counseling settings—and the results of an analogue study may not generalize to actual counseling situations. Therefore, we suggest that you regard the research results presented as tentative rather than final.

Our second purpose is to assist you in identifying the potential applicability of many counseling strategies for different client problems. As Krumboltz and Thoresen (1976) point out, a variety of useful counseling methods is available for different problem areas. When you finish the book, we hope you will be able to select and use appropriate counseling strategies when confronted with a depressed client, an anxious client, a nonassertive client, and so forth.

Finally, we hope to provide you with some ways to monitor and evaluate your behavior and the client's behavior during counseling. The recent emphasis on accountability requires each of us to explore the results of our helping activities more closely. Evaluation of counseling also assesses the extent to which the therapeutic goals are achieved.

Content of the Book: An Overview

An overview of the helping process as described in the remaining chapters of this book is presented in Table 1-1. In reviewing this table, you may note some flow and interrelationship among three major stages of the helping-

Table 1-1. Summary of Three Stages of the Helping Process and Related Skills and Chapters

Assessment	*Treatment*	*Evaluation*
2. Ingredients of an Effective Helping Relationship	14. Selecting Helping Strategies	8. Interview Discrimination
3. Nonverbal Communication	15. Common Elements of Strategy Implementation	13. Evaluation of Helping Processes and Outcomes
4. Verbal Communication	16. Symbolic Modeling, Self-as-a-Model, and Participant Modeling	
5. Listening Responses	17. Emotive Imagery and Covert Modeling	
6. Action Responses	18. Cognitive Modeling and Thought-Stopping	
7. Sharing and Teaching Responses	19. Cognitive Restructuring and Stress Inoculation	
9. The ABCs of Defining the Problem	20. Meditation and Muscle Relaxation	
10. Defining the Problem with an Interview Assessment	21. Systematic Desensitization	
11. Selecting Goals: A Reciprocal Decision-Making Process	22. Self-Management Programs and Self-Monitoring	
12. Defining Goals	23. Stimulus Control, Self-Reward, and Self-Contracting	

interview process: assessment, treatment, and evaluation.

Chapters 2 through 7 and 9 through 12 describe some verbal and nonverbal interview responses that may be used in the assessment stage of helping. This initial helping stage involves establishing an effective helping relationship, developing an open channel of counselor-client communication, obtaining relevant client information, defining client problems and concerns, and establishing counseling goals. The assessment stage is concerned with this question: What are the client's problems and what does the client want to change?

The treatment stage of helping involves applying therapeutic strategies to assist the client in resolving problems and in achieving the desired changes. Chapters 14 through 23 describe the process of strategy selection and illustrate how a number of different counseling strategies may be used to facilitate client action. Strategies are not needed for every client; some may achieve their purpose in seeking counseling by relating and communicating with another human being. For other clients, additional processes and procedures may be needed. In this book, each strategy is presented separately—for illustration only. We do not mean to suggest that only a single counseling procedure is employed at one time with a client. In practice, it is more common for the counselor and client to use several methods simultaneously or in combination. For example, anxiety-related problems have been treated by social modeling, assertion training, desensitization, and some self-management procedures. The research documentation available for using any of these strategies for anxiety management can aid you in deciding which strategies may be more useful.

The counseling strategies selected should be used to help the client resolve the defined problem behaviors and achieve the stated goals. However, once a strategy is selected, the counselor cannot assume that the client will use it consistently or that it will contribute to the desired changes. The evaluation stage of helping involves systematic monitoring of the application of strategies and of the client's goals. It is essential to evaluate the direction and degree of desired client change as measured by a "before" and "after" counseling comparison, but this is not enough. In addition, a monitoring of your behavior and the client's behavior is useful at different points during counseling. Chapters 8 and 13 present ways to conduct process and outcome evaluations of helping.

Format of the Book

We have attempted to use a learning format that helps you to demonstrate and measure your use of the counseling competencies presented in this book. Each chapter includes a brief introduction, chapter objectives, content material interspersed with model examples, activities, and feedback, a post evaluation, and a role-play interview assessment. People who have been involved in field-testing this book have found that using these activities has helped them to get involved and to interact with the content material. You can complete the chapters by yourself or in a class. If you feel you need to go over an exercise several times, do so! If part of the material is familiar, jump ahead. Throughout each chapter, your performance on the learning activities and self-evaluations will be a clue to the pace at which you can work through the chapter. To help you use the book's format to your advantage, we will explain each of its components briefly.

Objectives

As we developed each chapter, we had certain goals in mind for the chapter and for you. For each major topic, there are certain concepts and skills to be learned. We feel the best way to communicate this is to make our intentions explicit. After a short chapter introduction, you will find a section called "Objectives." The list of objectives describes the kinds of things that can be learned from the chapter. Using objectives for learning is similar to using goals in counseling. The objectives provide cues for your "end results" and serve as benchmarks for you to assess your progress. As you will see in Chapter 12, an objective or goal contains three parts:

1. the behavior, or what is to be learned or performed
2. the level of performance, or how much or how often to demonstrate the behavior
3. the conditions of performance, or the circumstances or situations under which the behavior can be performed.

Part 1 of an objective refers to what you should learn or demonstrate. Parts 2 and 3 are concerned with evaluation of performance. The evaluative parts of an objective, such as the suggested level of performance, may seem a bit hard-nosed. However, there is evidence that setting objectives with a fairly high mastery level results in more improved performance (Johnston & O'Neill, 1973; Semb, Hopkins, & Hursh, 1973). In this book, the objectives are stated at the beginning of each chapter so you know what to look for and how to assess your performance in the activities and self-evaluations. If you feel it would be helpful to see some objectives now, take a look at the beginning of Chapter 3.

Learning Activities

Learning activities that reflect the chapter objectives are interspersed throughout each chapter. These learning activities, which are intended to provide both practice and feedback, consist of model examples, exercises, and feedback. There are several different ways you can use the learning activities. Many of the exercises suggest that you write your responses. Your written responses may help you or your instructor check the accuracy and specificity of your work. Take a piece of paper and actually write the responses down. Or you may prefer to work through an activity covertly and just think about your responses.

Some exercises instruct you to respond covertly by imagining yourself in a certain situation, doing certain things. We feel that this form of mental rehearsal can help you prepare for the kinds of counseling responses you might use in a particular situation. Covert responding does not require any written responses. However, if it would help you to jot down some notes after the activity is over, go ahead. You are the best person to determine how to use these exercises to your advantage.

Another kind of learning activity involves a more direct rehearsal than the written or covert activities. These "overt rehearsal" exercises are designed to help you apply your skills in simulated counseling sessions with a role-play interview. The role-play activities involve three people or roles: a counselor, a client, and a consultant. Each team should trade roles so that each person can experience the role-play from these different perspectives. One person's task is to serve as the counselor and practice the skills specified in the instructions. A second person, the client, will be counseled during the role-play.

We give one word of caution to whoever takes the client role. Assuming that "counselor" and "client" are classmates, or at least not close friends or relatives, each of you will benefit more when in the counselor's seat if the "client" shares a real concern. These concerns do not have to be issues of life or death. Often someone will say "I won't be a good client because I don't have a problem." It is hard to imagine a person who has no concerns. Maybe your role-play concern will be about a decision to be made, a relationship conflict, some uneasiness about a new situation, or feeling sorry for or angry with yourself. Taking the part of a client in these role-play exercises may require that you first get in touch with yourself.

The third person in the role-play exercise is the "consultant." The consultant has three tasks to accomplish. First, this person should observe the process and identify what the client does and how the counselor responds. When the counselor is rehearsing a specific skill or strategy, the consultant can also determine the strengths and limitations of the counselor's approach. Second, the consultant can provide consultation at any point during the role-play if it might facilitate the experience. Such consultation can occur if the counselor gets stuck or if the consultant perceives that the counselor is practicing too many nonhelpful behaviors. The third and most important task is to provide feedback to the counselor regarding his or her performance. The person who role-played the client also may wish to provide feedback.

Giving helpful feedback is itself a skill that is used in some counseling strategies (see Chapter 15). The feedback that occurs following the role-play should be considered just as important as the role-play itself. Although everyone involved in the role-play will receive feedback after serving as the counselor, it is still sometimes difficult to "hear" negative feedback. Sometimes the receptiveness to feedback will depend on the way the consultant presents it. We encourage you to make use of these opportunities to practice giving feedback to another person in a constructive, useful manner. Try to make your feedback specific and concise. Remember, the feedback is to help the counselor learn more about the role-play; it should not be construed as the time to analyze the counselor's personality or life-style. Some guidelines for giving feedback are presented in a learning activity in Chapter 2.

Another learning activity involves having people learn the strategies as partners or in small groups by teaching one another. We suggest you trade off teaching a strategy to your partner or the group. Person A might teach covert modeling to Person B, and then Person B will teach Person A muscle relaxation. The "student" can be checked out in role-play. Person B would check out on covert modeling (taught by A), and Person A would demonstrate the strategy learned from Person B. This method helps the teacher learn and teach at the same time. If the "student" does not master the skills, additional sessions with the "teacher" can be scheduled.

The Role of Feedback in Learning Activities. Most of the chapter learning activities are followed by some form of feedback. For example, if a learning activity involves identifying positive and negative examples of a counseling conversational style, the feedback will indicate which examples are positive and which are negative. We also have attempted in most of our feedback to give some rationale for the responses. In many of the feedback sections, several possible responses are included. Our purpose in including feedback is not for you to find out how many "right" and "wrong" answers you have given in a particular activity. The responses listed in the feedback sections should serve as a guideline for you to code and judge your own responses. With this in mind, we would like you to view the feedback sections as something that provides information and alternatives. We hope you are not put off or discouraged if your responses are different from the ones in the feedback. We don't expect you to come up with identical responses; some of your responses may be just as good as or better than the ones given in the feedback. Space does not permit us to list a plethora of possibly useful responses in the feedback for each learning activity.

Post Evaluation

A post evaluation can be found at the end of each chapter. Each consists of questions and activities related to the knowledge and skills to be acquired in the chapter. Because you respond to the questions after completing a chapter, this evaluation is called *post*; that is, it assesses your level of performance *after* receiving instruction. The evaluation questions and activities reflect the conditions specified in the objectives. When the conditions ask you to identify a response in a written statement or case, take some paper to write down your responses to these activities. However, if the objective calls for demonstrating a response in a role-play, the evaluation will suggest how you can assess your performance level by setting up a role-play assessment. Other evaluation activities may suggest you do something or experience something to heighten your awareness of the idea or skill to be learned.

The primary purpose of the post evaluation is to help you assess your competencies after completing the chapter. One way to do this is to check your responses with those provided in the feedback at the end of each post evaluation. If there is a great discrepancy, the post evaluation can shed light on those areas still troublesome for you. You may wish to improve in these areas by reviewing parts of the chapter, redoing the learning activities, or asking for additional help from your instructor or colleague.

Role-Play Evaluation

In actual counseling, you must demonstrate your skills orally—not write about them. To help you determine the extent to which you can apply and evaluate your skills, role-play evaluations are provided at the end of most chapters. Each role-play evaluation consists of a structured situation in which you are asked to demonstrate certain skills as a counselor with a role-play client. Your performance on the role-play interview can be assessed by using the role-play checklist at the end of the chapter. These checklists consist of steps and possible responses associated with a particular strategy. The checklist should be used only as a guideline. You should always adapt any helping strategy to the client and to the particular demands of the situation.

There are two ways to assess your role-play performance. You can ask your instructor, a colleague, or another person to observe your performance using the checklist. Your instructor may even schedule you periodically to do a role-play "check-out" individually or in a small group. If you don't have anyone to observe you, assess yourself. Audio-tape your interview and rate your performance on the checklist. Also, ask your client for feedback. If you don't reach the criterion level of the objective on the first try, you may need some extra work. The following section explains the need for additional practice.

Additional Practice

You may find some skills more difficult to acquire the first time around than others. Often people are chagrined and disappointed when they do not demonstrate the strategy as well as they would like on their first attempt. We ask these individuals whether they hold similar expectation levels for their clients! You cannot quickly and simply let go of behaviors you don't find useful in counseling and acquire others that are more helpful. It may be unrealistic to assume you always will demonstrate an adequate level of performance on *all* the evaluations on the first go-around. Much covert and overt rehearsal may be necessary before you feel comfortable with skill demonstration in the evaluations.

Some Cautions about Using This Format

Although we believe the format of this book will promote learning, we want you to consider several cautions about using it. As you will see, we have defined the skills and strategies in precise and systematic ways to make it easier for you to acquire and develop the skills. However, we do not intend for our definitions and guidelines to be used like cookbook instructions. Perhaps our definitions and categories will give you some methodology for helping. But do not be restrained by this, particularly in applying your skills in the interview process. As you come to feel more comfortable with a strategy, we hope you will use the procedure creatively. Technical skills are not sufficient in counseling unless accompanied by inventiveness (Frey, 1975, p. 23), and "therapeutic guidelines cannot substitute for the clinical sensitivity and ingenuity of the therapist" (Goldfried & Goldfried, 1975, p. 114).

Also, remember that counseling is a complex process composed of many interrelated parts. Although different counseling stages, skills, and strategies are presented in this book in separate chapters, in practice there is a meshing of all these components. As an example, the relationship does not stop or diminish in impor-

tance when a counselor and client begin to define problems, establish goals, or implement strategies. Nor is evaluation something that occurs only when counseling is terminated. Evaluation involves continuous monitoring throughout the counseling interaction. Even obtaining a client's commitment to use strategies consistently and to monitor their effects may be aided or hindered by the quality of the relationship and the degree to which client problems and goals have been defined clearly. In the same vein, keep in mind that most client problems are complex and multifaceted. Successful counseling may involve changes in the client's feelings, observable behavior, beliefs, and cognitions. To model some of the skills and procedures you will learn, we have included cases and model dialogues in most chapters. These are intended to illustrate one example of a way in which a specific procedure can be used with a client. However, the cases and dialogues have been simplified for demonstration purposes, and the printed words may not communicate the sense of flow and direction that is normally present in counselor-client interchanges. Again, with actual clients, you will probably encounter more dimensions to the relationship and to the client's concerns than are reflected in the chapter examples.

Our third concern involves the way you approach the examples and practice opportunities in this book. Obviously, reading an example or doing a role-play interview is not as real as seeing an actual client or engaging in a live counseling interaction. However, some practice is necessary in any new learning program. Even if the exercises seem artificial, they probably will help you learn counseling skills. The structured practice opportunities in the book may require a great deal of discipline on your part, but the degree to which you can generalize your skills from practice to an actual counseling interview may depend upon how much you invest in the practice opportunities. One more word on such practice. Our Western culture regards practice as useful because "practice makes perfect." We prefer the Eastern concept—"practice makes different." Practice does not make perfect because people aren't intended to be perfect. However, practice may result in a change within ourselves, in our ideas, attitudes, beliefs, and actions. Practice can help all of us transform ourselves into more competent helpers.

Options for Using the Book

We have written this book in its particular format because each component seems to play a unique role in the learning process. But we are also committed to the idea that each person must determine the most suitable individual method of learning. With this in mind, we suggest a number of ways to use this book. First, you can go through the book and use the entire format in the way it is described in this chapter. If you do this, we suggest you familiarize yourself carefully with the format as described here. If you want to use this format but don't understand it, it is not likely to be helpful. Another way to use the book is to use only certain parts of the format in any combination you choose. You may want to experiment initially to determine which components seem especially useful. For example, you might use the post evaluation but not complete chapter learning activities. Finally, if you prefer a "straight" textbook format, you can read only the content of the book and ignore the special format. Our intent is for you to use the book in whatever way is most suitable for your learning strategies.

One Final Thought

As you go through the book, you undoubtedly will get some feel for the particular ways to use each strategy. However, we caution you against using this book as a prescriptive device, like medicine handed over a counter automatically and without thought or imagination. We are discovering that no one method of learning is equally useful for all people (McKeachie, 1976; Snow, 1974). Similarly, one counseling strategy may not work well for all clients. As your counseling experience accumulates, you will find that one client does not use a strategy in the same way, at the same pace, or with similar results as another client. In selecting counseling strategies, it is helpful to be guided by the documentation concerning the ways in which the strategy has been used. But it is just as important to remember that each client may respond in an idiosyncratic manner to any particular approach. Mahoney and Mahoney (1976) emphasize that counseling is a "personalized science, in which each client's problems are given due recognition for their uniqueness and potential complexity" (p. 100). Finally, remember that most anybody can learn and perform a skill in a rote and mechanistic manner. But not everyone shows the qualities of sensitivity and understanding that give the skills a human touch.

Suggested Readings

Self, Skills, and Process Development

Dyer, W. W., & Vriend, J. *Counseling techniques that work.* Washington, D.C.: American Personnel and Guidance Association, 1975. Chap. 1, Components of effective counseling, 17–28.

Content of the Book

Egan, G. *The skilled helper: A model for systematic helping and interpersonal relating.* Monterey, Calif.: Brooks/Cole, 1975. Chap. 2, An overview of the developmental model of helping, 28–54.

Krumboltz, J. D., & Thoresen, C. E. (Eds.). *Counseling methods.* New York: Holt, Rinehart & Winston, 1976. Part 1, The strategy of counseling, 2–25.

Format of the Book

Cormier, L. S., & Cormier, W. H. Developing and implementing self-instructional modules for counselor training. *Counselor Education and Supervision,* 1976, *16,* 37–45.

Cormier, W. H., Cormier, L. S., Zerega, W. D., & Wagaman, G. L. Effects of learning modules on the acquisition of counseling strategies. *Journal of Counseling Psychology,* 1976, *23,* 136–141.

Hartley, J., & Davies, I. Preinstructional strategies: The role of pretests, behavioral objectives, overviews and advance organizers. *Review of Educational Research*, 1976, *46*, 239–265.

McKeachie, W. J. Psychology in America's bicentennial year. *American Psychologist*, 1976, *31*, 819–833.

Robin, A. L. Behavioral instruction in the college classroom. *Review of Educational Research*, 1976, *46*, 313–354.

Chapter 2
Ingredients of an Effective Helping Relationship

Not too long ago, one of our students was commenting on his progress in becoming a counselor. His comments ran something like this: "You know, I feel a lot less inhibited. I used to think that in order to be a good counselor I couldn't be myself. Now I realize that, with the skills I have, I can use them and still be myself, and it works out a lot better." In our opinion, this person had discovered the magic combination of being able to integrate his counseling skills into his own personal style, something that was comfortable for him.

What happens in the counseling process involves a host of variables; many things happen for both client and counselor. We are inclined to think that a good counseling relationship is like any good interpersonal relationship and has some amount of "chemical bonding" to it. In other words, the process has a flow and direction with some degree of harmony. In watching scores of interviews by counselors in training, we are always struck by a difference in some interviews. Some flow so well; others seem like such a struggle, with so much tension and such a sense of urgency. Most counselors seem to possess basic skills, but there is something about the way some of them use and implement the skills that gives a very different feeling to their interviews. We feel the difference lies in the counselor's style. Style may be something about yourself you bring to counseling, something that is elusive and difficult to mea-

sure but that adds an essential quality to your counseling skills.

This distinctive difference was summarized beautifully by a very talented actress who did some coached client role-plays for us. After portraying the same client role for about 50 counselors, she had this to say:

> You can tell almost instantly if someone's really listening to you. You can tell by the way they look and respond. Some people like this make you think—"Gee, maybe I'll tell them something really important." Other people are only interested in procedure or in getting their point across [P. Murphy, 1976].

In our opinion, effective relationships are those in which counselors are able to demonstrate their skills without being preoccupied with those skills or themselves.

Objectives

This chapter is intended to raise your level of consciousness about yourself. There are three general objectives:

1. The chapter may help you identify some aspects of yourself that could facilitate or interfere with a positive counseling relationship. Exploration of yourself will include identify-

ing some prevailing feelings and thoughts about yourself, your values, and your expectations for clients.

2. The chapter may help you discriminate and communicate the three facilitative conditions of positive regard, genuineness, and empathy.
3. The chapter is designed to sensitize you to the way in which you deliver or use your skills; we refer to this as your "counseling style." Your style has to do with your ability to relate to a person, not just a procedure, and your ability to prevent your own values and feelings from interfering in an interview.

There is no post evaluation for this chapter. In a sense, the entire chapter is an experience in which you will be getting in touch with where you are right now. The experiences provided in the remainder of this book all can be considered as further opportunities for you to engage in an effective relationship and to integrate your counseling style with your newly acquired skills. Also, there are few operational definitions in this chapter and only minimal guidelines for correct responses to the learning activities. To some degree, this reflects the rather elusive quality of counseling-relationship ingredients. The subjective flavor of this chapter also is a projection of our desire to avoid defining too rigorously the parameters of a relationship that, in practice, will always be defined somewhat idiosyncratically by each counselor-client dyad.

Components of an Effective Relationship

Most people agree that a positive relationship is an important factor in counseling (Rimm & Masters, 1974; Rogers, 1951). However, there are not many studies that indicate which relationship variables contribute most to desired therapeutic outcomes (Morganstern, 1976). Some evidence suggests that counselors who provide high levels of three relationship conditions known as *empathy, positive regard,* and *genuineness* are able to enhance client self-exploration (Carkhuff, 1969a, 1969b).

On an intuitive basis, we consider the capacity to understand, convey respect, and be oneself to be important factors in creating and maintaining a positive counseling relationship. We also recognize that the ability to be involved in an effective interpersonal interaction is influenced by feelings and attitudes about ourselves, by our values, and by our expectations for clients. Our self-images, our values, and our expectations can enhance or detract from the counseling process. If we cannot identify our feelings, attitudes, values, and demands, we may be unable to establish the type of counseling relationship we hope might be best for the client.

Self-Image

Our attitudes about ourselves can significantly influence the way we behave. People who have negative views of themselves will "put themselves down" and will either seek out or avoid types of interactions with others that confirm their negative self-image. This has serious implications for counselors. If we don't feel competent or valuable as people, we may communicate this attitude to the client. Or, if we don't feel confident about our ability to counsel, we may inadvertently structure the counseling process to meet our own self-image problems or to confirm our negative self-pictures.

All of our feelings and thoughts influence the way we handle certain things in the counseling relationship. Very strong feelings and attitudes about ourselves may significantly influence our behavior with clients. For instance, a counselor who is very sensitive to rejection may be unduly careful not to offend a client, or may avoid confronting a client when confrontation could be helpful. A counselor who has trouble dealing with negative feelings may structure the counseling interaction so that negative feelings are never "on the agenda."

We have identified three potential self-image problem areas: competence, power, and intimacy. These three areas and the possible feelings, attitudes, and behaviors associated with them are depicted in Table 2-1. The table also describes how these self-image areas could affect one's behavior in counseling interactions.

Table 2-1. Effects of Self-Image on Counseling Interaction

Potential Problem Area and Unresolved Feelings and Needs	Attitude about Self	Possible Counseling Behaviors
COMPETENCE Incompetence Inadequacy	1. Pollyanna; overly positive—fearful of failing	Structures counseling to maintain Pollyanna attitude, avoiding conflicts by: 1. discounting negative feedback 2. giving "fake" feedback 3. avoiding or smoothing over "heavy stuff"
Fear of failure Fear of success	2. Negative; overly self-critical—fearful of succeeding	Structures counseling to maintain negative self-image by: 1. avoiding positive interactions 2. discounting positive feedback 3. giving self overly negative feedback 4. making goals and expectations too high 5. making self-deprecating or apologetic comments
	3. Not masculine enough or not feminine enough	Structures counseling to make self feel more secure as a male or female by: 1. overidentifying with or rejecting very masculine or very feminine clients 2. seducing clients of opposite sex 3. overreacting to or misinterpreting both positive and negative reactions from male and female clients
POWER Impotence Control Passivity Dependence	1. Omnipotent—fearful of losing control	Structures counseling to get and stay in control by: 1. persuading client to do whatever counselor wants 2. subtly informing client how good or right counselor is 3. dominating content and direction of interview 4. getting upset or irritated if client is resistant or reluctant
Independence Counterdependence	2. Weak and unresourceful—fearful of control	Structures counseling to avoid taking control by: 1. being overly silent and nonparticipatory 2. giving client too much direction, as in constant client rambling 3. frequently asking client for permission to do or say something 4. not expressing opinion; always referring back to client 5. avoiding any other risks

Table 2-1. Effects of Self-Image on Counseling Interaction (continued)

Potential Problem Area and Unresolved Feelings and Needs	Attitude about Self	Possible Counseling Behaviors
	3. Life-style converter	Structures counseling to convert client to counselor's beliefs or life-style by: 1. promoting ideology 2. getting in a power struggle 3. rejecting clients who are too different or who don't respond 4. "preaching"
INTIMACY Affection Rejection	1. Needing warmth and acceptance—fearful of being rejected	Structures counseling to make self liked by: 1. eliciting positive feelings from client 2. avoiding confronting or offending client 3. ignoring negative client cues 4. doing things for client—favors and so on
	2. Needing distance—fearful of closeness, affection	Structures counseling to maintain distance and avoid emotional intimacy by: 1. ignoring client's positive feelings 2. acting overly gruff or distant 3. maintaining professional role as "expert"

Competence

Your feelings of personal adequacy and professional competence can influence your covert and overt behavior in counseling interactions. Feelings of incompetence and inadequacy can be described as either fear of failure or fear of success. A counselor who is afraid of failure may approach counseling with an overly positive "Pollyanna" attitude. The fear of failure can be interfering if the counselor structures counseling to avoid conflicts. The counseling interaction may remain superficial because issues and negative topics are pushed under the table.

Other people may maintain a negative picture of themselves by being afraid of success and by avoiding successful situations and interactions. A counselor who fears success may structure counseling to maintain or confirm such a negative self-concept. This counselor tends to discount positive feedback and to have expectations that are out of reach.

Concerns about one's adequacy as a male or a female also can enter into the counseling relationship. Counselors who do not feel comfortable with themselves as men or women may behave in ways that add to their security in this area. For example, a counselor could promote his or her masculinity or femininity by overidentifying with or rejecting clients of the same sex, seducing clients of the opposite sex, and overreacting to or misinterpreting some client cues.

Power

Unresolved feelings about oneself in relation to power and control may include impotence, passivity, dependence, and counterdependence. There are several ways that power can be misused in counseling. First, a counselor who fears being impotent or weak, or who is afraid to give up control, may try to be omnipotent. For this person, counseling is manageable only when it is controllable. Such a counselor may use a variety of maneuvers to stay in control, including persuading the client to do what the counselor wants, getting upset or defensive if a client is resistant or hesitant, and dominating the content and direction of the interview. The counselor who needs to control the interview may be more likely to engage in a power struggle with a client.

In contrast, a counselor may be afraid of power and control. This counselor may attempt to escape from as much responsibility and participation in counseling as possible. Such a counselor avoids taking control by giving too much direction to the client and by not expressing opinions. In other words, risks are avoided or ignored.

Another way that unresolved power needs can influence counseling is seen in the "life-style converter." This person has very strong feelings about the value of one particular life-style. Such a counselor may take unwarranted advantage of the influence processes in a helping relationship by using counseling to convert the client to that life-style or ideology. Counseling, in this case, turns into a forum for the counselor's views and pet peeves.

Intimacy

A counselor's unresolved intimacy needs also can significantly alter the direction and course of counseling. Generally, a counselor who has trouble with intimacy may fear rejection or be threatened by closeness and affection. A counselor who is afraid of rejection may behave in ways that meet the need to be accepted and liked by the client. For example, the counselor may avoid challenging or confronting the client for fear the client may be "turned off." Or the counselor may subtly seek positive client feedback as a reassurance of being valued and liked. Negative client cues also may be ignored because the counselor does not want to hear expressions of client dissatisfaction.

A counselor who is afraid of intimacy and affection may create excessive distance in the relationship. The counselor may avoid emotional intimacy in the relationship by ignoring expressions of positive feelings from the client. Or the counselor may behave in a gruff, distant,

or aloof manner and relate to the client through the "professional role."

Self-Image Learning Activity

Instructions:

The following learning activity may help you explore some of your feelings and attitudes about yourself and possible effects on your counseling interactions. The activity consists of a Self-Rating Checklist divided into the three areas of competence, power, and intimacy. We suggest you work through each section separately. As you read the items listed for each section, think about the extent to which the item accurately describes your behavior *most* of the time (there are always exceptions to our consistent behaviors). If an item asks about you in relation to a client and you haven't had much counseling experience, try to project yourself into the counselor's role. Check the items that are most descriptive of you. Try to be as honest with yourself as possible. After completing each section, refer to the Learning Activity Reaction that follows the checklist.

Self-Rating Checklist

Check the items that are most descriptive of you.

I. *Competence Assessment*

_____ 1. Constructive negative feedback about myself doesn't make me feel incompetent or uncertain of myself.

_____ 2. I tend to put myself down frequently.

_____ 3. I feel fairly confident about myself as a helper.

_____ 4. I often am preoccupied with thinking that I'm not going to be a competent counselor.

_____ 5. When I am involved in a conflict, I don't go out of my way to ignore or avoid it.

_____ 6. When I get positive feedback about myself, I often don't believe it's true.

_____ 7. I set realistic goals for myself as a helper that are within reach.

_____ 8. I believe that a confronting, hostile client could make me feel uneasy or incompetent.

_____ 9. I often find myself apologizing for myself or my behavior.

_____ 10. I'm fairly confident I can or will be a successful counselor.

_____ 11. I find myself worrying a lot about "not making it" as a counselor.

_____ 12. I'm likely to be a little scared by clients who would idealize me.

_____ 13. A lot of times I will set standards or goals for myself that are too tough to attain.

_____ 14. I tend to avoid negative feedback when I can.

_____ 15. Doing well or being successful does not make me feel uneasy.

II. *Power Assessment*

_____ 1. If I'm really honest, I think my counseling methods are a little superior to other people's.

_____ 2. A lot of times I try to get people to do what I want. I might get pretty defensive or upset if the client disagreed with what I wanted to do or did not follow my direction in the interview.

_____ 3. I believe there is (or will be) a balance in the interviews between my participation and the client's.

_____ 4. I could feel angry when working with a resistant or stubborn client.

_____ 5. I can see that I might be tempted to get some of my own ideology across to the client.

_____ 6. As a counselor, "preaching" is not likely to be a problem for me.

_____ 7. Sometimes I feel impatient with clients who have a different way of looking at the world than I do.

_____ 8. I know there are times when I would be reluctant to refer my client to someone else, especially if the other counselor's style differed from mine.

_____ 9. Sometimes I feel rejecting or intolerant of clients whose values and life-styles are very different from mine.

_____ 10. It is hard for me to avoid getting in a power struggle with some clients.

III. *Intimacy Assessment*

_____ 1. There are times when I act more gruff than I really feel.

_____ 2. It's hard for me to express positive feelings to a client.

_____ 3. There are some clients I would really like to be my friends more than my clients.

_____ 4. It would upset me if a client didn't like me.

_____ 5. If I sense a client has some negative feelings toward me, I try to talk about it rather than avoid it.

_____ 6. Many times I go out of my way to avoid offending clients.

_____ 7. I feel more comfortable maintaining a professional distance between myself and the client.

_____ 8. Being close to people is something that does not make me feel uncomfortable.

_____ 9. I am more comfortable when I am a little aloof.

_____ 10. I am very sensitive to how clients feel about me, especially if it's negative.

_____ 11. I can accept positive feedback from clients fairly easily.

_____ 12. It is difficult for me to confront a client.

Learning Activity Reaction: Applications to Your Counseling

1. For each of the three assessment areas you can look over your responses and determine the areas that seem to be OK and the areas that may be a problem for you or something to watch out for. You may find more problems in one area than another.

2. Do your "trouble spots" seem to occur with mostly everyone, or just with certain types of people? In all situations or some situations?

3. Compare yourself now to where you might have been four years ago or where you may be four years from now.

4. Identify any areas you feel you could use some help with, from a colleague, a supervisor, or a counselor.

Values and Helping

The word *value* stands for something we prize, regard highly, or prefer. Values are our feelings or attitudes about something and our preferred actions or behaviors. As an example, take a few minutes to think of (and perhaps list) five things you love to do. Now look over your list to determine how frequently and consistently you actually engage in each of these five actions. Your values are indicated by your frequent and consistent actions (Raths, Harmin, & Simon, 1966). If you say you value spending time with friends but you hardly ever do this, then other

---

activities and actions probably have more value for you.

The affective education movement has created a great deal of interest in a process called "values clarification"—activities in which people identify and sort out actual values, ideal values, and conflicting values (Simon, Howe, & Kirschenbaum, 1972). We are introducing the concept of values clarification in this chapter because the counselor's values inevitably affect the counseling process. As D. Smith and J. Peterson (1977) observe, there is a growing recognition that "value neutrality on the part of the helping person is an impossibility" (p. 310). Your values are more likely to be imposed upon a client if you are not aware of them.

Obviously, not all of our values have an impact on the helping process. For example, the counselor who values sailing can probably work with a client who values being a landlubber without any problem. However, values that reflect our ideas about "the good life," morality, ethics, life-style, roles, interpersonal living, and so forth have a greater chance of entering into the helping process. The very fact that we have entered a helping profession suggests some of our values. As discussed in Chapter 11, there may be times when a referral is necessary because of an unresolved and interfering value conflict with a client. For example, a counselor who views rape as the most terrible and sexist act a person can perform might have difficulty counseling a person accused of rape. This counselor might tend to identify more with the rape victim than with the client. From an ethical viewpoint, if a counselor is unable to promote and respect the welfare of a client, a referral may be necessary (American Personnel and Guidance Association, 1961; American Psychological Association, 1977).

There are other times in the counseling process when our values affect helping, not because they conflict with the client's values, but because they restrict or limit the client. In these instances, our values are getting in the way of helping the person reach her or his potential. Restricting or delimiting values are reflected in such areas as our expectations for different clients, our beliefs about change, and our values about an "ism"

such as sexism, racism, culturism, or ageism. One of *our* values is the need for counselors to be aware of values that might prevent the client from developing his or her potential. We have acted on this value by including some ways to help you examine your values about a number of "isms" and about your expectations for client change.

Stereotypical Values

There is legitimate concern about the possible limiting effects of counselor stereotyping in the helping process. Maslin and Davis (1975) define *stereotyping* as ascribing characteristics to a person on the basis of presumed knowledge about a group to which the person belongs (p. 87). E. J. Smith (1977) asserts that stereotypes "are the conventions that people use for refusing to deal with one another on an individual basis" (p. 390). Stereotyping in counseling may occur when the counselor projects his or her biases on the client or applies cultural and sociological characteristics of a particular cultural group "indiscriminately to all members" of that group (p. 391).

One of the most damaging kinds of stereotyping has to do with sex roles. There is some evidence that, during the helping process, many counselors communicate the stereotypical attitudes toward sex roles of our Western culture (Broverman, Broverman, Clarkson, Rosenkrantz, & Vogel, 1970). In other words, some counselors may attempt to influence male and female clients to behave according to stereotypical concepts of masculinity and femininity portrayed in our culture. Male clients may be reinforced for being strong, independent, and unemotional, whereas female clients are told it is more "healthy" to be less assertive, more passive, dependent, and "soft." Our sex-role values also may be used inappropriately in counseling even when our biases do not reflect the traditional male and female roles. Using nontraditional sex-role values to urge a nonworking mother to work is another example of limiting the client's choices. Okun (1976) suggests that sexist counseling occurs whenever the counselor employs her or his own "sex role ideology" as a basis for helping (p. 189).

Sexism is not the only area in which our values may dominate the helping process. Our biases can interfere when counseling people with handicaps and disabilities, people of limited abilities, and people of different cultures, races, and socioeconomic levels. E. J. Smith (1977) points out that stereotypical counseling treatment of Blacks occurs whenever the counselor applies assumptions and research findings about Black clients in a general, nonidiosyncratic manner. Smith adds that many of the proverbial conclusions about counseling Black clients—such as Blacks have poor self-concepts, Black clients are nonverbal, or Black clients only profit from counseling that is highly structured and action-oriented—may be more myths than realities and may reflect White Anglo-Saxon interpretations and values. Okun (1976) observes that another common form of stereotypical counseling involves ageism, when we convey "our own beliefs and values about what a person can or should do at different ages" (p. 193). A counselor who becomes aware that his or her limiting expectations or stereotypical values are interfering with the helping process has the responsibility to modify the stereotypes or refer the client to another helper.

In some cases, a counselor may be unaware of tendencies toward "ism" counseling because of lack of opportunities to counsel different kinds of clients. For example, if you have never worked with an older person, a handicapped person, or a person of another culture, perhaps you have never confronted your values about these clients. The following learning activity may give you a chance to simulate doing so.

Learning Activity: Personal Values

Descriptions of six different clients are presented in this learning activity. If you work through this activity by yourself, we suggest you imagine yourself counseling each of these clients. Try to generate a very vivid picture of yourself and the client in your mind. If you do this activity with a partner, you can role-play the counselor while your partner assumes the part of each client as described in the six examples. As you imagine or role-play the counselor, try to notice your feelings, attitudes, values, and behavior during the visualization or role-play process. After *each* example, stop to think about or discuss these questions:

1. What attitudes and beliefs did you have about the client?
2. Were your beliefs and attitudes based on actual or presumed information about the client?
3. How did you behave with the client?
4. What values are portrayed by your behavior?

There are no right or wrong answers. A reaction to this learning activity can be found after the client descriptions.

Client 1
This client is a young woman who is having financial problems. She is the sole supporter of three young children. She earns her living by prostitution and pushing drugs. She states that she is concerned about her financial problems but can't make enough money from welfare or from an unskilled job to support her kids.

Client 2
The client is an older man (age 60) who is approaching retirement. He has been working most of his life as a furniture salesperson. He has a high school diploma and has not been in school since he was 18 years old. Now he feels that he wants to go to college and earn a degree.

Client 3
You have been assigned a client who is charged with rape and sexual assault. The client, a male, tells you that he is not to blame for the incident because the victim, a woman, "asked for it."

Client 4
This client is concerned about general feelings of depression. Overweight and unkempt, the client is in poor physical condition and smokes constantly during the interview.

Client 5
The client is a middle-aged woman on welfare. She says she was raped and as a result gave birth to a child. She is torn between trying to keep this baby and giving it up.

Client 6
The client is a 12-year-old boy who recently lost a leg in an automobile accident. He was a strong swimmer before the accident; he wants to continue his swim-

---

ming now so he can eventually make the high school swimming team. He wants to know your opinion about this decision.

Reaction to Learning Activity on Personal Values

Perhaps your visualizations or role-plays revealed to you that you may have certain biases and values about sex roles, age, cultures, race, physical appearance, and rape. Some of your biases may reflect your past experiences with a person or an incident. Most people in the helping professions agree that some of our values are communicated to clients, even unintentionally. Try to identify any values or biases you hold now that could communicate disapproval to a client or could keep you from "promoting the welfare" of your client. With yourself, a peer, or an instructor, work out a plan to reevaluate your biases or to help you prevent yourself from imposing your values on clients.

Expectations for Clients

Counselor expectations can affect both the course and the outcome of the counseling process. One of the major types of counselor expectations that affects counseling is a "prognostic" expectation—that is, the counselor's attitudes about the anticipated degree of client progress (A. P. Goldstein, 1962, p. 111). A counselor's belief that a client has the potential to change can be a significant factor in the degree of client change that actually occurs. In our helping role, we often communicate our expectations to clients, even inadvertently. Thus, it is important to examine our expectations for different clients and also to be aware of the ways in which we may send messages about our expectations. If, as helpers, we communicate some positive expectations (although not overly optimistic ones), this may help the client. Communicating a low expectation level could affect the client's progress adversely. Sometimes, without being aware of it, we may change our expectations to "fit" the client. Lorion (1974) notes that some counselors tend to "give up" on certain clients

—for example, by regarding a low-income client as "untreatable." He suggests that the high attrition rate of low-income clients in counseling may result from such biases becoming known to the clients during therapy. Similarly, the counselor may perceive minority clients as resistant or passive because their behavior does not meet the counselor's expectations. Such misperceptions may cause the counselor to blame the client for "lack of progress" or may result in premature termination (Sue & Sue, 1977). Some people have speculated that a counselor's communication of middle-class values and expectations may be a significant factor in the underutilization of helping services by minority clients (D. W. Sue, 1977b). All of us may find ourselves modifying our expectations for change depending upon the client. We should examine our own values about the possibility of change for clients of different races, cultures, ages, sexes, socioeconomic levels, and physical, intellectual, and social resources to prevent our expectations from limiting the client's capacity to change. The following learning activity may help you confront some of your expectations for clients.

Learning Activity: Expectations

Take a few minutes to respond to the following questions. There are no right or wrong answers.
1. What is your "gut-level" reaction to the statement "Anyone can change"?
2. How do you feel about people's capacities to make choices?
3. Personalize the above two questions with an *I* ("I can change"; "I can choose"). How do you feel about your own capacity to change and to choose? Can you recall times when you rationalized your way out of changing or lowered expectations or standards for yourself?
4. Take a fantasy trip for a few minutes. Try to go through this set of questions by relaxing, closing your eyes, and actually imagining yourself in the situation. Try to picture yourself, other people, and the room in your mind. Imagine what you would say and how you would feel.
   a. First of all, you are counseling your "preferred

client," any client of your choice. What would this client be like? Picture your preferred client in your mind. What does the client look like? Is the client attractive? Male or female? Verbal or nonverbal? Socially assertive or nonassertive? What is the client's age? Culture? Race? Life-style? Socioeconomic level? Religious preference?

Imagine you are talking about the client's concerns. Try now to get in touch with your feelings about this client. Also try to tune in to your expectations for change for this client. How "successful" do you see this client being in counseling?

b. Now, fade your preferred client away in your mind and picture yourself counseling a client whom you would not like to counsel. Get a firm picture of this client in your mind. Now examine your feelings as you talk with this client. What are your expectations for this person?

c. Now you have a different client. You are counseling an older man (age 55) who has been on welfare all his life. He lives in a rundown area of town. He has no family, although he has fathered many children. Imagine your feelings as you're talking with this client. What are your expectations for his capacity to change and grow?

d. Try to assess the totality of your responses to this imagery activity. Did your preferred client differ from the other two clients? How did your feelings differ in working with each of the three clients? Did you notice whether your honest expectations for change varied among clients?

If you are aware that your feelings and expectations seem to vary among clients, you are probably not alone. There is some evidence that just descriptive information about a client tends to sway a counselor's ratings of client acceptability and attractiveness and the counselor's own expectations (A. P. Goldstein, 1971).

There also is some justifiable concern that many of us approach helping with a middle-class code of ethics and life-style as our basis for helping. Our middle-class code is reflected in the fact that most counselors select as the preferred client someone who displays a middle-class syndrome. Many counselors would describe their preferred client by the acronym

YAVIS—young, attractive, verbal, intelligent, and successful (A. P. Goldstein, 1971; Schofield, 1964). Yet, as Sue and Sue (1977) observe, this preference may discriminate against clients from minority groups or lower socioeconomic levels (p. 421). Counseling, which has grown out of Western culture, has generally been a middle-class activity. As Sue and Sue assert, "The counselor must guard against possible misinterpretation of behaviors and be aware that many aspects of counseling may be antagonistic to the values held by the client" (p. 427).

Counselor preferences for clients may pose other reasons for concern in addition to the kinds of values they reflect. If our feelings for some clients are negative, our capacity to demonstrate the fundamental relationship conditions of respect and positive regard may be restricted.

Facilitative Relationship Conditions

Rogers's (1951) early conclusions about the importance of certain facilitative conditions in the counseling relationship have had a great deal of impact on the helping professions. Rogers, Carkhuff (1969a, 1969b), Gordon (1970), Egan (1975), and others have described the effects of counselor-initiated relationship conditions. There is general agreement that three important relationship factors are those we mentioned earlier: positive regard, congruence or genuineness, and empathic understanding.

Positive Regard

Positive regard may be described as the counselor's acceptance of the client without conditions or reservations. The experience of having positive regard for a client may be defined by certain thoughts and feelings, such as "I feel good when I'm with this person," "I like this person," or "I don't feel bothered or uncomfortable about what this person is telling me." Positive regard and acceptance can be conveyed through the use of minimal verbal responses, nonjudgmental verbal messages, and nonverbal attending (Gordon, 1970). As discussed in Chapter 7, positive regard can be shared verbally with the client through sharing responses such as immediacy. Verbal sharing responses to communicate positive regard might include "I really feel good about our talks together," "I have very good feelings for you," or "Right now I'm aware of having warm feelings for you."

It is unrealistic to assume that we will always have positive feelings for all our clients. As mentioned earlier in this chapter, we may tend to feel more positive toward preferred clients. But it is important for each of us to be aware of our feelings about clients and to think about the meaning of these feelings for ourselves and our clients. For example, one of our students had difficulty in feeling accepting of a particular role-play client. The client perceived the student counselor's discomfort. In expressing her feelings, the counselor remarked, "I guess I have trouble relating to traditional women, which was what I perceived my client to be." Rogers (1967) indicates that, in most cases, our negative feelings for a client somehow relate to ourselves, our own concerns, and, of course, our values. In the example just given, the counselor could examine what it is about herself that sets off negative feelings for "traditional women." If these feelings continue to block the relationship, she may decide to discuss this with the client or with a supervisor. If it is very difficult to have any positive feelings for a client, a referral to another counselor may be necessary.

Genuineness

Genuineness means being oneself without being phony or playing a role. Although most counselors are trained professionals, a counselor can convey genuineness by being human and by collaborating with the client. A counselor who uses his or her training and knowledge to come across as "the expert" may project role behavior and may hinder development of self-responsibility in the client. Genuineness also implies that the counselor is congruent, that the counselor's actions and words match her or his feelings. For instance, in the example just mentioned, the counselor would be congruent if she labeled her feelings of discomfort with this client. However, if she denied these feelings yet still gave out cues of discomfort or nonacceptance, she would be presenting a facade or being incongruent. The incongruent counselor is likely to send mixed messages to the client —which is confusing and could prevent progress in the relationship.

In counseling, genuineness can be defined as being aware of your feelings and communicating verbal and nonverbal cues that "match." You can express genuine feelings in the interview by describing your feelings—for example, "I'm aware right now that I've been having trouble accepting what you're telling me. I guess I see you as pushing me to decide for you and I feel uncomfortable with that."

Rogers (1957) notes that being genuine does not mean verbalizing every thought to the client. He suggests the counselor should express negative feelings to the client if the feelings are persistent or if they severely interfere with the counselor's capacity to communicate empathy or positive regard.

Empathy

Empathy may be described as the ability to understand people from their frame of reference rather than your own. Responding to a client empathically may be "an attempt to think *with*, rather than *for* or *about* the client" (Brammer & Shostrom, 1968, p. 180). For example, if a client says, "I've tried to get along with my father but it doesn't work out. He's too hard on me," an empathic response would be something like "You feel discouraged about your unsuccessful attempts to get along with your father." In contrast, if you say something like "You ought to try harder," you are responding from your frame of reference, not the client's. Krumboltz and Thoresen (1976) suggest that one of the primary therapeutic functions of empathy is that it conveys that both counselor and client are working "on the same side" (p. 199).

Both Carkhuff (1969a) and Egan (1975) distinguish between two types of empathic responding. At an interchangeable (Carkhuff) or a primary (Egan) level of empathy, the counselor attempts to understand what the client says explicitly. The counselor communicates empathic understanding at about the same level of intensity as expressed by the client's verbal and nonverbal message. Egan suggests that the primary level of empathy is used mostly during the first stage of counseling to help clients explore themselves (p. 30). The second kind of empathy, referred to as additive empathy (Carkhuff) or as advanced empathy (Egan), conveys understanding at a deeper and more intense level. In additive or advanced empathy, the counselor tries to understand what the client implies and leaves unstated, or the nature of the client's deficit (Egan, pp. 77–78; Carkhuff & Pierce, 1975, p. TG5). According to Egan, advanced empathy is used mostly during the second stage of helping to facilitate client self-understanding and during the third stage to bring about client action (p. 30).

Carkhuff and Pierce (1975) define effective helper communication with a Discrimination Inventory that assesses "Level 1" to "Level 5" counselor responses. Level 3 is considered to be the minimally acceptable response. Level 3 responses on this scale correspond to Carkhuff and Pierce's concept of interchangeable empathy and Egan's (1975) concept of primary-level empathy; Level 4 corresponds to additive (Carkhuff, 1969a) or advanced empathy (Egan) and Level 5 represents facilitating action. The scale can be used either to discriminate among levels of responses or to rate levels of counselor communication. Here is an example of a verbal empathic response at each level of Carkhuff and Pierce's Discrimination Inventory.

Client: I've tried to get along with my father, but it doesn't work out. He's too hard on me.
Counselor at Level 1: I'm sure it will all work out in time [reassurance and denial].

or
You ought to try harder to see his point of view [advice].

or
Why can't you two get along? [question].
Level 1 is a question, reassurance, denial, or advice.
Counselor at Level 2: You're having a hard time getting along with your father.
Level 2 is a response to only the *content* or cognitive portion of the client's message; feelings are ignored.
Counselor at Level 3: You feel discouraged because your attempts to get along with your father have not been very successful.
Level 3 has understanding but no direction; it is a reflection of feeling and meaning based on the client's explicit message. In other words, a Level 3 response reflects both the feeling and the situation. In this response, "You feel discouraged" is the reflection of the feeling and "because of not getting along" is the situation.
Counselor at Level 4: You feel discouraged because you can't seem to reach your father. You want him to let up on you.
Level 4 has understanding and some direction. A Level 4 response identifies not only the client's feelings, but the client's deficit that is implied. In a Level 4 response, the client's deficit is personalized, meaning the client owns or accepts responsibility for the deficit, as in "You can't reach" in this response.
Counselor at Level 5: You feel discouraged because you can't seem to reach your father. You want him to let up on you. One step could be to express your feelings about this to your father.
A Level 5 response contains all of a Level 4 response plus at least one action step the person can take to master the deficit and attain the goal. In this example, the action step is "One step could be to express your feelings about this to your father."

One way to define empathy is through verbal statements by the counselor that reflect the client's feelings (Uhlemann, Lea, & Stone, 1976). However, empathy also is conveyed by such nonverbal behaviors as direct eye contact, a forward-leaning body position, facing the client (Haase & Tepper, 1972), and an open-arm position (Smith-Hanen, 1977). These and other nonverbal behaviors and their effects on the counseling interaction will be explored in Chapter 3.

Learning Activities for Facilitative Conditions

Activity One: Discrimination Exercise

Using the description of Carkhuff and Pierce's (1975) Discrimination Inventory on **page 24**, decide whether each of the following counselor responses belongs in:

Level 1—No understanding, no direction. Counselor response is a question, a denial or reassurance, or advice.

Level 2—No understanding, some direction. Counselor response highlights only *content* of client's message; feelings are ignored.

Level 3—Understanding present; direction absent. Counselor responds to both *content* or meaning and *feelings*.

Level 4—Both understanding and direction present. Helper responds to client feelings and identifies deficit.

Level 5—Understanding, direction, and action present. Counselor response includes all of Level 4 plus one action step.

After rating each response, explain your choice. An example is provided at the beginning of the activity. Feedback can be found after the learning activities.

Example

Client: I've become burned out with teaching. I've thought about changing jobs, but you know it's hard to find a good job now.

Counselor response 1: Teaching is no longer too satisfying to you."
This response is: *Level 2*. Because: *Response is only to the content or the situation of teaching. Client's feelings are ignored.*

Practice Statements

1. Client: I've always wanted to be a doctor, but I've been discouraged from this.
   Counselor: Oh, I'm sure this is something you could do if you really wanted to.
   This response is:
   Because:
2. Client: I've had such a rough semester. I don't know what I got myself into. I'm not sure where to go from here.
   Counselor: You feel perturbed about the way your semester turned out and confused because of this.
   This response is:
   Because:
3. Client: My teacher always picks on me.
   Counselor: Why do you suppose she picks on you?
   This response is:
   Because:
4. Client: I'm bored with my job. It's getting to be the same old thing. But what else is there to do?
   Counselor: You feel dissatisfied with your job because of the routine. You can't find anything in it that really turns you on. You want to find some more appealing work. One step is to list the most important needs a job meets for you and to identify how those needs could be met by certain jobs.
   This response is:
   Because:
5. Client: I don't understand why this accident happened to me; I've always led a good life; now this.
   Counselor: You feel resentful because you can't explain why this sudden accident happened to you. You want to at least figure out some reason that might make it seem more fair.
   This response is:
   Because:
6. Client: My parents are getting a divorce. I wish they wouldn't.
   Counselor: You feel upset because your parents are divorcing.
   This response is:
   Because:
7. Client: It just seems like each year goes by without our being able to have children.
   Counselor: You feel discouraged because you can't seem to get pregnant. You want to have a child very much.
   This response is:
   Because:
8. Client: I'm caught in the middle. I'm not able to move into public housing unless my husband leaves for good. But I'd also want my husband to continue to come and live with me at least some of the time.
   Counselor: Moving into public housing might prevent you and your husband from living together.

This response is:
Because:

9. Client: It's been hard for me to adjust since I've retired. The days seem so empty.

Counselor: You feel useless because of all the time on your hands now. You can't find a way to fill up your days. You want to find some meaningful things to do. One step is to think of some ways you can continue using your work interests even though you are no longer employed.

This response is:
Because:

Activity Two: Responding Exercise

After you have checked your answers with the feedback, go back over the previous exercise. For every counselor statement (except those that were rated at Level 4 or 5), take some paper and write an example of a response that would be rated at Level 4 (both understanding and direction; response identifies client's feelings and deficit). The first one is completed for you as an example. Check your responses with those given in the feedback at the end of the activities.

Example

Counselor response 1 could be rewritten, since it is only Level 1. A Level 4 response would be: "You feel concerned [client's feelings] because you can't get support for your desire to be a doctor [client's deficit]. You want some approval from others for this choice."

Activity Three: Attending, Responding, and Feedback Exercise

This activity is designed to help you rate the effectiveness of helper responses on the Carkhuff and Pierce (1975) inventory. You will need two to five other people to complete this activity. (If you do not have access to a group of other people, you can substitute this activity: Complete a helping interaction that you can audio-tape. Rate your responses on the tape from Level 1 to Level 5 using the Carkhuff and Pierce [1975] Discrimination Inventory on p. 24).

Step 1: Description of a concern

Using a small-group format (approximately six per group), each person writes a personal concern on a slip of paper. The concern doesn't have to be a "big" one, but it should be real. It might be something like "I'm feeling uneasy with being observed," "I'm worried about being evaluated in the program," "I can't find a part-time job and I need the money," or "I'm having trouble getting along with someone."

Step 2: Counselor-counselee dyadic interactions

Each person should have one turn as the counselee and one turn as the counselor. Beginning with one counselor-counselee dyad, these two people should sit in the middle of the circle, with the remainder of the group seated around them.

The counselor-counselee dyad should engage in a 10-minute interaction. During this interaction, the counselee should present and describe her or his concern (step 1) to the counselor. Try to express what it is like for you to have this concern and how it makes you feel. The counselor's task is to listen and respond to the counselee in an *understanding* manner. This can be achieved in several ways:

1. Suspend judgment. Avoid evaluating and agreeing or disagreeing with client statements.
2. Avoid asking questions or giving advice.
3. Respond verbally to the counselee's feelings (affective message) about the concern. Use a statement that identifies the counselee's *feelings* such as "You feel _____" and the *content* of the situation "because _____" (Level 3).
4. Try to identify the deficit present in the person's message and some directions she or he wants to pursue. Use statements such as "You feel _____ because you can't _____ and you want _____" (Level 4).*
5. Check out the accuracy of your messages by listening for a confirmation from the counselee (for example, "That's right"), or asking the counselee whether your message is accurate (for example, "Does this fit for you?").

Step 3: Counselor ratings using Carkhuff and Pierce's Discrimination Inventory

After the 10-minute interaction, the other group members should rate the counselor's

---

*We do not suggest you go beyond Level 4 to Level 5, because identifying action steps in a short helping interaction such as this would be premature and possibly inaccurate because of limited information.

level of communication on the Discrimination Inventory that follows. Each observer can show the completed rating sheet to the counselor. (This step should not take longer than 5 minutes.)

Step 4: Delivery of feedback to counselor

One of the observers should volunteer to deliver feedback to the counselor. This feedback should summarize the counselor's performance on the inventory. The feedback should describe specific examples of times when the counselor did and did not respond with understanding. The person giving the feedback should attempt to follow the five guidelines for effective feedback found in the Feedback Rating Scale (p. 25). (This step should not take longer than 5 minutes.)

Step 5: Ratings of the feedback

After the feedback has been given, the remainder of the group should rate the way this person delivered the feedback, using the Feedback Rating Scale. Everyone can show the completed copy of scale to this person. (This step should not take more than 5 minutes.)

Step 6: Recycling

After one dyad has completed the interaction and the feedback exercise is over, Steps 2–5 should be recycled until each person has had a turn to be the counselor, the counselee, and the feedback giver.

Discrimination Inventory*

Level 1.0 response

This response has no understanding and no direction. The usual form is a question, empty reassurance, or denial of the helpee's position.

Level 2.0 response

This response has no understanding and some direction. The form is usually some type of general advice.

Level 3.0 response

This response has understanding but no direction. It is a reflection of feeling and reason for feeling. It fits the format "You feel _____ because _____."

Level 4.0 response

This response has understanding and some di-

*From The Art of Helping: Trainer's Guide, by R. Carkhuff and R. Pierce. Copyright 1975 by Human Resource and Development Press. Reprinted by permission.

rection. The response identifies the helpee's deficit, the goal which flows from this deficit, and the helpee's feelings because of the deficit. The format is "You feel _____ because you can't _____ and you want _____."

Level 5.0 response

This response contains understanding and specific direction. The response contains all that is contained in the Level 4.0 response plus at least one explicit step for overcoming the deficit and reaching the goal. The format is "You feel _____ because you can't _____ and you want _____. One step is _____."

Activity Four: Self-Expression Exercise

This activity is designed to help you feel comfortable in verbalizing your feelings about a client. Read over the client descriptions on pp. 17–18. Try to get in touch with how you would feel with each person (positive, negative, or both). Then verbalize your feelings aloud. For example, if you feel warmly toward the client you might say something like "Right now I feel very good about you." If something about the client is bothering you, own your feelings by beginning your statement with an "I" message, such as "I feel concerned about your self-neglect. It bothers me to see you not taking care of yourself." If possible, you may want to do this activity with another person to compare your responses with those of someone else. An example is completed for you for Client 1.

Example for Client 1

This client is a young woman who is having financial problems. She is the sole supporter of three young children. She earns her living by prostitution and pushing drugs. She states that she is concerned about her financial problems but can't make enough money from welfare or from an unskilled job to support her kids.

1. "I can sense your feelings of frustration now and I feel supportive of whatever you choose to do to solve your financial concerns."

or

2. "I'm aware I'm feeling concerned right now about the possible consequences of the ways you're using to make money."

Feedback Rating Scale*

Name of Feedback Giver _____ Name of Rater _____

1. Was the feedback descriptive rather than evaluative?
            Yes   No
2. Was the feedback specific rather than general?
            Yes   No
3. Was the feedback directed toward something the person could change?
            Yes   No
4. Was the feedback well-timed? (Given soon after the situation)
            Yes   No
5. Was the feedback checked with the person to insure close communication?
            Yes   No

Feedback for Learning Activities for Facilitative Conditions

Activity One: Discrimination Exercise

Counselor response 1 is at Level 1—no understanding and no direction. The response is a denial of client's concern and a form of advice.

Counselor response 2 is at Level 3—understanding is present; direction is absent. Responds to client's feelings (you feel perturbed) and to content or situation (about the semester).

Counselor response 3 is at Level 1—no understanding, no direction. Response is a question and ignores both the content and feelings of client's message.

Counselor response 4 is at Level 5—understanding, direction, and action are all present. Response tunes in to client's feelings, identifies client's deficit, and identifies one

action step (one step is to list the important needs a job meets).

Counselor response 5 is at Level 4—understanding and direction. Both client's feelings (you feel resentful) and client's deficit (you can't explain why) are included in counselor's response.

Counselor response 6 is at Level 3—understanding is there; no direction. Counselor responds to client's feelings (you feel upset) and to the content or situation (your parents are divorcing).

Counselor response 7 is at Level 4—understanding and direction. Response reflects client's feelings (you feel discouraged) and identifies her deficit (you can't seem to get pregnant).

Counselor response 8 is at Level 2—some direction but no understanding. Response is only to content of client's message; feelings are ignored.

Counselor response 9 is at Level 5—understanding, direction, and action are all there. Response picks up client's feelings and deficit, and identifies one possible action step (one step is to think of some ways).

Activity Two: Responding Exercise

1. A Level 4 response for counselor statement 2 is: "You feel perturbed [feelings] because you can't figure out what exactly happened to you this semester [deficit]. You want to be able to decide what to do next."
2. A Level 4 response for counselor statement 3 is: "You feel upset [feelings] because you can't get out from under the teacher's nose [deficit]. You want her to stop singling you out."
3. This counselor statement is OK as is because it is Level 5.
4. This counselor statement is OK as is because it is Level 4.
5. An example of a Level 4 response for counselor statement 6 is: "You feel upset [feelings] because you can't stop your parents from divorcing [deficit]. You want to be able to keep them together."
6. This is OK as is because it is Level 4.

*From *Reading Book: Laboratories in Human Relations Training,* by the National Training Laboratories Institute for Applied Behavioral Science. Copyright 1969 by the NTL Institute for Applied Behavioral Sciences. Reprinted by permission.

7. An example of a Level 4 response for counselor statement 8 is: "You feel torn [feelings] because you can't decide which of these things you want more [deficit]. You want to be able to move into public housing and have your husband to be able to live with you, too."
8. This is already at Level 5.

Your Helping Style

One of the most difficult parts of learning counseling skills seems to be trusting the skills to work and not being preoccupied with your own performance. We are reminded of a story in *Time* (November 29, 1976) about the conductor of the Berlin Philharmonic, Herbert Von Karajan. When asked why he didn't rely more on entry and cutoff cues in conducting a large orchestra, he replied, "My hands do their job because they have learned what to do. In the performance I forget about them." (p. 82).

Preoccupation with yourself, your skills, or a particular procedure reduces your ability to relate to and be involved with another person. At first, it is natural to focus on the skill or strategy because it is new and feels a little awkward or cumbersome. But once you have learned a particular skill or strategy, the skills will be there when you need them. Gradually, as you acquire your repertory of skills and strategies, you should be able to change your focus from the procedure to the person. The way you implement and deliver your skills or your counseling style is just as important as having

the skills. For this reason, we have included a Helping-Style Checklist at the end of this chapter. We use this checklist periodically throughout the book, suggesting that you be rated or rate yourself on your style as well as your demonstration of skills and strategies.

For some people, style may be more of a problem than skills. Some individuals experience so much discomfort or anxiety surrounding counseling interactions that their potential for relating is inhibited. We agree with Perls (1970) that much of our performance anxiety is "stage fright" (p. 16). It is created by our anticipation and constant mental rehearsal of what might happen to us in our next check-out or our next interview. In some instances, anxious thoughts may be accompanied by body and muscular tension. If this is the case for you, you may find the relaxation strategies described in Chapter 20 to be useful. If your anxious feelings are precipitated by catastrophic and self-defeating thoughts, you might be able to benefit from thought-stopping (Chapter 18), cognitive restructuring (Chapter 19), or stress inoculation (Chapter 19). If you are thinking of yourself as a poor counselor, the covert-modeling procedure described in Chapter 17 may help you change your self-visualizations.

Finally, there is the old but true adage that as soon as you *try* to make something happen, the opposite effect is achieved. If you try too hard to relax, you may only increase your tension. As summarized by another artist, Frederica Von Stade, "Always looking for the magic traps you. . . . Ironically, when you forget about putting out the magic, it happens" (*Time*, December 6, 1976, p. 101).

Helping-Style Checklist

Instructions for using this checklist:
1. Conduct a 15-minute role-play interaction in which you take the part of the helper.
2. Try to establish an effective relationship with the helpee. Be yourself and become involved with the helpee.
3. After the interaction, have the helpee (and possibly also an observer) assess your relating style using the Helping-Style Checklist.

4. From the feedback you receive, identify aspects of your counseling-relationship style that seem positive.
5. Identify any aspects that may interfere with the development of an effective counselor-client relationship. Work out a plan to help you change these limitations to strengths.

_____ 1. To what extent does the counselor display comfortable, nonanxious behaviors with the client and with the subject areas discussed?

1	2	3	4	5
Not at all	Minimally	Somewhat	A great deal	Most always

_____ 2. To what extent does the counselor refrain from persuading the client to accept her or his values and expectations?

1	2	3	4	5
Not at all	Minimally	Somewhat	A great deal	Most always

_____ 3. To what extent does the counselor prevent his or her personal needs for topic selection and control of the interview from dominating or interfering with the session?

1	2	3	4	5
Not at all	Minimally	Somewhat	A great deal	Most always

_____ 4. To what extent does the counselor refrain from communicating (verbally or nonverbally) disapproval or judgment to the client?

1	2	3	4	5
Not at all	Minimally	Somewhat	A great deal	Most always

_____ 5. To what extent is the counselor focused on the client rather than the skills or the procedure?

1	2	3	4	5
Not at all	Minimally	Somewhat	A great deal	Most always

_____ 6. To what extent is the counselor's delivery of the ·skills spontaneous and nonmechanical?

1	2	3	4	5
Not at all	Minimally	Somewhat	A great deal	Most always

_____ 7. To what extent is the client likely to come back to see this counselor?

1	2	3	4	5
Not at all	Minimally	Somewhat	A great deal	Most always

Suggested Readings

Self-Image and Counseling Style

Okun, B. F. *Effective helping: Interviewing and counseling techniques.* North Scituate, Mass.: Duxbury Press, 1976. Chap. 3, Communication skills, 40–69.

Passons, W. R. *Gestalt approaches in counseling.* New York: Holt, Rinehart & Winston, 1975. Chap. 4, Present-centeredness and awareness, 45–74; Chap. 9, Approaches to feelings, 183–214.

Stevens, B. *Don't push the river.* Lafayette, Calif.: Real People Press, 1969.

Stevens, J. O. *Awareness: Exploring, experimenting, experiencing.* Lafayette, Calif.: Real People Press, 1971.

Values and Expectations

Broverman, I., Broverman, D., Clarkson, F., Rosenkrantz, P., & Vogel, S. Sex-role stereotypes and clinical judgments of mental health. *Journal of Consulting and Clinical Psychology,* 1970, 34, 1–7.

Goldstein, A. P. *Therapist-patient expectancies in psychotherapy.* New York: Pergamon, 1962.

Ivey, A., & Gluckstern, N. *Basic influencing skills: Participant manual.* Amherst, Mass.: Microtraining Associates, 1976. Workshop 8, Integration of skills: What is your style? 160–206.

Okun, B. F. *Effective helping: Interviewing and counseling techniques.* North Scituate, Mass.: Duxbury Press, 1976. Chap. 8, Issues affecting helping, 182–203.

Simon, S., Howe, L., & Kirschenbaum, H. *Values*

clarification. New York: Holt, Rinehart & Winston, 1972.

Smith, D., & Peterson, J. Counseling and values in a time perspective. *The Personnel and Guidance Journal,* 1977, *55,* 309–318.

Sue, D. W. Counseling the culturally different: A conceptual analysis. *The Personnel and Guidance Journal,* 1977, *55,* 422–425.

Sue, D. W., & Sue, D. Barriers to effective cross-cultural counseling. *Journal of Counseling Psychology,* 1977, *24,* 420–429.

Facilitative Relationship Conditions

Bayes, M. Behavioral cues of interpersonal warmth. *Journal of Consulting and Clinical Psychology,* 1972, *39,* 333–339.

Egan, G. *The skilled helper: A model for systematic helping and interpersonal relating.* Monterey, Calif.: Brooks/Cole, 1975.

Egan, G. *Interpersonal living: A skills/contract approach to human-relations training in groups.* Monterey, Calif.: Brooks/Cole, 1976.

Gazda, G. M. *Human relations development: A manual for educators.* Boston: Allyn & Bacon, 1973. Chap. 8, Perceiving and responding with empathy, 70–78; Chap. 9, Perceiving and responding with respect, 79–86; Chap. 10, Perceiving and responding with warmth, 87–94.

Haase, R. F., & Tepper, D. Nonverbal components of empathic communication. *Journal of Counseling Psychology,* 1972, *19,* 417–424.

Okun, B. F. *Effective helping: Interviewing and counseling techniques.* North Scituate, Mass.: Duxbury Press, 1976. Chap. 2, The helping relationship, 16–39; Chap. 4, Stage 1: The relationship stage, 70–90.

Rogers, C. R. *On becoming a person.* Boston: Houghton Mifflin, 1961.

Truax, C. B., & Mitchell, K. M. Research on certain therapist interpersonal skills in relation to process and outcome. In A. Bergin & S. Garfield (Eds.), *Handbook of psychotherapy and behavior change: An empirical analysis.* New York: Wiley, 1971.

Chapter 3
Nonverbal Communication

Nonverbal behavior plays an important role in our communication and relationships with others. In communicating, we tend to emphasize the spoken word. Usually much of the meaning of a message, 65 percent or more, is conveyed by our nonverbal behavior (Birdwhistell, 1970). M. L. Knapp (1972) defines nonverbal behavior as "all human communication events which transcend spoken or written words" (p. 20). Of course, many nonverbal behaviors are interpreted by verbal symbols. Nonverbal behavior is an important part of counseling because of the tremendous amount of information it communicates (Sullivan, 1954).

Counselors can learn much about a client by becoming sensitized to the client's nonverbal cues. Also, the counselor's nonverbal behavior has a great deal of impact on the client. One of the primary kinds of client verbal messages dealt with in counseling—the affective message—is highly dependent on nonverbal means of communication. Ekman and Friesen (1969a) have noted that much of the information that can be gleaned from words of patients is derived from their nonverbal behavior (p. 88). Schutz (1967), in his book *Joy: Expanding Human Awareness*, has stated that the "close connection between the emotional and the physical is evident in the verbal idioms that have developed in social interaction. Feelings and behavior are expressed in terms of all parts of the body, of body move-

ment, and of bodily functions" (pp. 25–26). Schutz provided a list of some of these terms which associate the physical with the emotional: "lost your head, chin up, hair-raising, get it off your chest, no backbone, tight-fisted, hard-nosed, butterflies in the stomach, broken-hearted, stiff upper lip, eyebrow lifting, sweat of your brow, stand on your own feet, tight ass, choke up, and shrug it off"—to name a few (pp. 25–26).

Three dimensions of nonverbal behavior with significant effects on communication are *kinesics, paralinguistics,* and *proxemics.* Body motion, or kinesic behavior, includes gestures, body movements, facial expressions, eye behavior, and posture (M. L. Knapp, 1972, p. 5). Associated with the work of Birdwhistell (1970), kinesics also involves physical characteristics that remain relatively unchanged during a conversation, such as body physique, height, weight, and general appearance. In addition to observing body motion, counseling involves identifying nonverbal vocal cues called paralanguage—the "how" of the message. Paralanguage includes voice qualities and vocalizations (Trager, 1958). Silent pauses and speech errors also can be considered part of paralanguage (M. L. Knapp, p. 5). Also of interest to counselors is the area of proxemics (E. T. Hall, 1966)—that is, one's use of social and personal space. As it affects the counseling relationship, proxemics involves the size of the room, seating arrangements, and distance between counselor and client.

Objectives

1. From a list of client descriptions and nonverbal client behaviors, describe one possible meaning associated with each nonverbal behavior. The criterion level for this objective is eight out of ten accurate responses.
2. In an interview situation, identify at least six different nonverbal behaviors of the person with whom you are communicating. Describe the possible meanings associated with these behaviors. The nonverbal behaviors you identify may come from any one or all of the categories of kinesics, or body motion; paralinguistics, or voice qualities; proxemics, or room space and distance; and the person's general appearance.
3. Describe in writing at least five out of six desired counselor nonverbal behaviors from a list of six nonverbal channels of communication.
4. Demonstrate seven out of nine desirable counselor nonverbal behaviors in a role-play interview.
5. Identify at least four out of five occasions for responding to client nonverbal behavior in an interview.

Client Nonverbal Communication

An important part of a counselor's repertory is the capacity to discriminate various nonverbal behaviors of clients and their possible meanings. Recognizing and exploring client nonverbal cues is important in counseling for several reasons. First of all, clients' nonverbal behaviors are clues about their emotions. Even more generally, nonverbal behaviors are part of clients' expressions of themselves. As Perls (1973) states, "Everything the patient does, obvious or concealed, is an expression of the self" (p. 75). Much of a client's nonverbal behavior may be obvious to you but hidden to the client.

Passons (1975) points out that most clients are more aware of their words than of their nonverbal behavior (p. 102). Exploring nonverbal communication may give clients a more complete understanding of their behavior.

Nonverbal client cues may represent more "leakage" than do client verbal messages (Ekman & Friesen, 1969a). Leakage is the communication of messages that are valid yet are not sent intentionally. Passons (1975) suggests that, because of this leakage, client nonverbal behavior may portray the client more accurately than verbal messages (p. 102). He notes that "nonverbal behaviors are generally more spontaneous than verbal behaviors. Words can be selected and monitored prior to being emitted. . . . Nonverbal behaviors, on the other hand, are not as easily subject to control" (p. 102).

M. L. Knapp (1972) points out that nonverbal and verbal behavior are interrelated (p. 9). It is helpful to recognize the ways nonverbal cues support verbal messages. Knapp identifies six such ways:

1. Repetition: The verbal message is to "go to your room"; the finger pointing to the room is a nonverbal repeater.
2. Contradiction: The verbal message is "I like you" communicated with a frown and an angry tone of voice. Some evidence suggests when we receive a contradictory verbal and nonverbal message that we tend to believe the nonverbal one.
3. Substitution: Often a nonverbal message is used in lieu of a verbal one. For example, if you ask someone "How are you?" and you get a smile, the smile substitutes for a "very good today."
4. Complementation: A nonverbal message can complement a verbal message by modifying or elaborating the message. For example, if someone is talking about feeling uncomfortable and they begin talking faster with more speech errors, these nonverbal messages add to the verbal one of discomfort.
5. Accent: Nonverbal messages can emphasize verbal ones and often heighten the impact of a verbal message. For example, if you are communicating verbal concern, your mes-

sage may come through stronger with nonverbal cues such as furrow of the brows, frown, or tears. The kind of emotion one conveys is detected best by facial expressions. The body conveys a better description of the intensity of the emotion (Ekman, 1964; Ekman & Friesen, 1967).

6. Regulation: Nonverbal communication helps to regulate the flow of conversation. Have you ever noticed that when you nod your head at someone after they speak, the person tends to keep talking? But if you look away and shift in body position, the person may stop talking, at least momentarily. Whether or not we realize it, we rely on certain nonverbal cues as feedback for starting or stopping a conversation and for indicating whether the other person is listening [pp. 9–12].*

Identifying the relationship between the client's verbal and nonverbal communication may yield a more accurate picture of the client, the client's feelings, and the concerns that have led the client to seek help. Also, the counselor can detect the extent to which the client's nonverbal behavior and verbal behavior match or are congruent. Frequent discrepancies between the client's expressions may indicate lack of integration or some conflict (Passons, 1975).

Nonverbal behavior has received a great deal of attention in recent years in newspapers, magazine articles, and popular books. These publications may have value in increasing awareness of nonverbal behaviors. However, the meanings that have been attached to a specific behavior may have become oversimplified. It is important to note that the meaning of nonverbal behavior will vary from person to person. For example, water in the eyes may be a sign of happiness and glee for one person; for another, it may mean anger, frustration, or trouble with contact lenses. A person who has a lisp may be dependent; another may have a speech impediment. Twisting, rocking, or squirming in a

seat might mean anxiety for one person, and a stomach cramp for someone else. Also, nonverbal behaviors of one culture may have different or even opposite meanings in another culture. O. M. Watson (1970) reports significant differences between cultures in contact and noncontact nonverbal behaviors (distance, touch, eye contact, and so on). As an example, in some cultures, avoidance of eye contact is regarded as an indication of respect. We simply caution you to be careful not to assume that nonverbal behavior has the same meaning or effect for all.

Table 3-1 is an Inventory of Nonverbal Communication. It presents some possible categories of nonverbal behavior in kinesics, paralinguistics, and proxemics, and the *probable* or *possible* meanings associated with each behavior for each region of the body. Also, a general category of autonomic responses is included. Remember, the effect or meaning of each nonverbal behavior we have presented is very tentative; these meanings will vary from person to person and culture to culture. We present some possible meanings only to help increase your awareness about different behaviors, not to make you an expert on client feelings by using an inventory to generalize meanings applicable to all clients. Any client nonverbal behavior must be interpreted with respect to both the antecedents of the behavior and the counselor's reaction that follows the behavior. This complex interrelationship between client verbal and nonverbal messages and counselor responses is described in further detail in Chapter 8. To show you the importance of interpreting the meaning of nonverbal behavior within a given context, we present various counselor-client interaction descriptions to accompany the nonverbal cues and possible meanings in this inventory.

Kinesics

Eyes. Eye contact can indicate expressions of feeling or willingness for interpersonal exchange. Lack of eye contact or looking away may

*Adapted from *Nonverbal Communication in Human Interaction* by Mark L. Knapp. Copyright © 1972 by Holt, Rinehart & Winston, Inc. Used by permission of Holt, Rinehart & Winston.

Table 3–1. Inventory of Nonverbal Communication

Nonverbal Dimensions	Behaviors	Description of Counselor-Client Interaction	Possible Effects or Meanings
KINESICS *Eyes*			
_____	Direct eye contact	Client is Anglo-American. Client has just shared concern with counselor. Counselor responds; client maintains eye contact.	Readiness or willingness for interpersonal communication or exchange; attentiveness
_____	Lack of sustained eye contact	Client is Anglo-American. Each time counselor brings up the topic of client's family, client looks away.	Withdrawal or avoidance of interpersonal exchange; or respect or deference
		Client is a Mexican-American who demonstrates intermittent breaks in eye contact while conversing with counselor.	Respect or deference
		Client mentions sexual concerns, then abruptly looks away. When counselor initiates this topic, client looks away again.	Withdrawal from topic of conversation; discomfort or embarrassment; or preoccupation
_____	Lowering eyes—looking down or away	Client talks at some length about alternatives to present job situation. Pauses briefly and looks down. Then resumes speaking and eye contact with counselor.	Preoccupation
_____	Staring or fixation on person or object	Counselor has just asked client to consider consequences of a certain decision. Client is silent and gazes at a picture on the wall.	Preoccupation; possibly rigidity or uptightness
_____	Darting eyes or blinking rapidly— rapid eye movements; twitching brow	Client indicates desire to discuss a topic yet is hesitant. As counselor probes, client's eyes move around the room rapidly.	Excitation or anxiety; or wearing contact lenses
_____	Squinting or furrow on brow	Client has just asked counselor for advice. Counselor explains role and client squints, and furrows appear in client's brow.	Thought or perplexity; or avoidance of person or topic
		Counselor suggests possible things for client to explore in difficulties with parents. Client doesn't respond verbally; furrow in brow appears.	Avoidance of person or topic
_____	Moisture or tears	Client has just reported recent death of father; tears well up in client's eyes.	Sadness; frustration: sensitive areas of concern

Table 3–1. Inventory of Nonverbal Communication (continued)

Nonverbal Dimensions	Behaviors	Description of Counselor-Client Interaction	Possible Effects or Meanings
		Client reports real progress during past week in marital communication; eyes get moist.	Happiness
————	Eye shifts	Counselor has just asked client to remember significant events in week; client pauses and looks away; then responds and looks back.	Processing or recalling material; or keen interest; satisfaction
————	Pupil dilation	Client discusses spouse's sudden disinterest and pupils dilate.	Alarm; or keen interest
		Client leans forward while counselor talks and pupils dilate.	Keen interest; satisfaction
Mouth			
————	Smiles	Counselor has just asked client to report positive events of the week. Client smiles, then recounts some of these instances.	Positive thought, feeling, or action in content of conversation; or greeting
		Client responds with a smile to counselor's verbal greeting at beginning of interview.	Greeting
————	Tight lips (pursed together)	Client has just described efforts at sticking to a difficult living arrangement. Pauses and purses lips together.	Stress or determination; anger or hostility
		Client just expressed irritation at counselor's lateness. Client sits with lips pursed together while counselor explains the reasons.	Anger or hostility
————	Lower lip quivers or biting lip	Client starts to describe her recent experience of being raped. As client continues to talk, her lower lip quivers; occasionally she bites her lip.	Anxiety or sadness
		Client discusses loss of parental support after a recent divorce. Client bites her lip after discussing this.	Sadness
————	Open mouth without speaking	Counselor has just expressed feelings about a block in the relationship. Client's mouth drops open; client says he or she was not aware of it.	Surprise; or suppression of yawn—fatigue
		It has been a long session. As counselor talks, client's mouth parts slightly.	Suppression of yawn—fatigue

Table 3–1. Inventory of Nonverbal Communication (continued)

Nonverbal Dimensions Behaviors	Description of Counselor-Client Interaction	Possible Effects or Meanings
Facial Expressions		
_____ Eye contact with smiles	Client talks very easily and smoothly, occasionally smiling; maintains eye contact for most of session.	Happiness or comfortableness
_____ Eyes strained; furrow on brow; mouth tight	Client has just reported strained situation with a child. Then client sits with lips pursed together and a frown.	Anger; or concern; sadness
_____ Eyes rigid, mouth rigid (unanimated)	Client states she or he has nothing to say; there is no evident expression or alertness on client's face.	Preoccupation; anxiety; fear
Head		
_____ Nodding head up and down	Client just expressed concern over the status of his or her health; counselor reflects client's feelings. Client nods head and says "That's right."	Confirmation; agreement; or listening, attending
	Client nods head during counselor explanation.	Listening; attending
_____ Shaking head from left to right	Counselor has just suggested that client's continual lateness to sessions may be an issue that needs to be discussed. Client responds with "No" and shakes head from left to right.	Disagreement; or disapproval
_____ Hanging head down, jaw down toward chest	Counselor initiates topic of termination. Client lowers head toward chest, then says he or she is not ready to stop the counseling sessions.	Sadness; concern
Shoulders		
_____ Shrugging	Client reports that spouse just walked out with no explanation. Client shrugs shoulders while describing this.	Uncertainty; or ambivalence
_____ Leaning forward	Client has been sitting back in the chair. Counselor discloses something about herself or himself; client leans forward and asks counselor a question about the experience.	Eagerness; attentiveness, openness to communication

Table 3–1. Inventory of Nonverbal Communication (continued)

Nonverbal Dimensions	Behaviors	Description of Counselor-Client Interaction	Possible Effects or Meanings
_____	Slouched, stooped, rounded or turned away from person	Client reports feeling inadequate and defeated because of poor grades; slouches in chair after saying this. Client reports difficulty in talking. As counselor pursues this, client slouches in chair and turns shoulders away from counselor.	Sadness or ambivalence; or lack of receptivity to interpersonal exchange. Lack of receptivity to interpersonal exchange
Arms and Hands			
_____	Arms folded across chest	Counselor has just initiated conversation. Client doesn't respond verbally; sits back in chair with arms crossed against chest.	Avoidance of interpersonal exchange or dislike
_____	Trembling and fidgety hands	Client expresses fear of suicide; hands tremble while talking about this.	Anxiety or anger
		In a loud voice, client expresses resentment; client's hands shake while talking.	Anger
_____	Fist clenching to objects or holding hands tightly	Client has just come in for initial interview. Says that he or she feels uncomfortable; hands are clasped together tightly.	Anxiety or anger
		Client expresses hostility toward boss; clenches fists while talking.	Anger
_____	Arms unfolded—arms and hands gesturing in conversation	Counselor has just asked a question; client replies and gestures during reply.	Accenting or emphasizing point in conversation; or openness to interpersonal exchange
		Counselor initiates new topic. Client readily responds; arms are unfolded at this time.	Openness to interpersonal exchange
_____	Rarely gesturing, hands and arms stiff	Client arrives for initial session. Responds to counselor's questions with short answers. Arms are kept down at side.	Tension or anger
		Client has been referred; sits with arms down at side while explaining reasons for referral and irritation at being here.	Anger
Legs and Feet			
_____	Legs and feet appear comfortable and relaxed	Client's legs and feet are relaxed without excessive movement while client freely discusses personal concerns.	Openness to interpersonal exchange; relaxation

Table 3–1. Inventory of Nonverbal Communication (continued)

Nonverbal Dimensions	Behaviors	Description of Counselor-Client Interaction	Possible Effects or Meanings
	Crossing and uncrossing legs repeatedly	Client is talking rapidly in spurts about problems; continually crosses and uncrosses legs while doing so.	Anxiety; depression
	Foot-tapping	Client is tapping feet during a lengthy counselor summary; client interrupts counselor to make a point.	Anxiety; impatience—wanting to make a point
	Legs and feet appear stiff and controlled	Client is open and relaxed while talking about job. When counselor introduces topic of marriage, client's legs become more rigid.	Uptightness or anxiety; closed to extensive interpersonal exchange
Total Body	Facing other person squarely or leaning forward	Client shares a concern and faces counselor directly while talking; continues to face counselor while counselor responds.	Openness to interpersonal communication and exchange
	Turning of body orientation at an angle, not directly facing person, or slouching in seat	Client indicates some difficulty in "getting into" interview. Counselor probes for reasons; client turns body away.	Less openness to interpersonal exchange
	Rocking back and forth in chair or squirming in seat	Client indicates a lot of nervousness about an approaching conflict situation. Client rocks as this is discussed.	Concern; worry; anxiety
	Stiff—sitting erect and rigidly on edge of chair	Client indicates some uncertainty about direction of interview; sits very stiff and erect at this time.	Tension; anxiety; concern
PARALINGUISTICS *Voice Level and Pitch*	Whispering or inaudibility	Client has been silent for a long time. Counselor probes; client responds, but in a barely audible voice.	Difficulty in disclosing
	Pitch changes	Client is speaking at a moderate voice level while discussing job. Then client begins to talk about boss and voice pitch rises considerably.	Topics of conversation have different emotional meanings
Fluency in Speech	Stuttering, hesitations, speech errors	Client is talking rapidly about feeling uptight in certain social situations; client stutters and makes some speech errors while doing so.	Sensitivity about topic in conversation; or anxiety and discomfort

Table 3–1. Inventory of Nonverbal Communication (continued)

Nonverbal Dimensions	Behaviors	Description of Counselor-Client Interaction	Possible Effects or Meanings
	Whining or lisp	Client is complaining about having a hard time losing weight; voice goes up like a whine.	Dependency or emotional emphasis
	Rate of speech slow, rapid, or jerky	Client begins interview talking slowly about a bad weekend. As topic shifts to client's feelings about herself or himself, client talks more rapidly.	Sensitivity to topics of conversation; or topics have different emotional meanings
	Silence	Client comes in and counselor invites client to talk; client remains silent.	Reluctance to talk; or preoccupation
		Counselor has just asked client a question. Client pauses and thinks over a response.	Preoccupation; or desire to continue speaking after making a point
		A Chinese client talks about his or her family. Pauses; then resumes conversation to talk more about same subject.	Desire to continue speaking after making a point
Autonomic Responses	Clammy hands, shallow breathing, sweating, pupil dilation, paleness, blushing, rashes on neck	Client discusses the exciting prospect of having two desirable job offers. Breathing becomes faster and client's pupils dilate.	Arousal—positive (excitement, interest) or negative (anxiety, embarrassment)
		Client starts to discuss sexual concerns; breathing becomes shallow and red splotches appear on neck.	Anxiety, embarrassment
PROXEMICS *Distance*	Moves away	Counselor has just confronted client; client moves back before responding verbally.	Signal that space has been invaded; increased arousal, discomfort
	Moves closer	Midway through session, client moves chair toward helper.	Seeking closer interaction, more intimacy
Position in Room	Sits behind or next to an object in the room, such as table or desk	A new client comes in and sits in a chair that is distant from counselor.	Seeking protection or more space

Table 3–1. Inventory of Nonverbal Communication (continued)

Nonverbal Dimensions	Behaviors	Description of Counselor-Client Interaction	Possible Effects or Meanings
_____	Sits near counselor without any intervening objects	A client who has been in to see counselor before sits in chair closest to counselor.	Expression of adequate comfort level

signal withdrawal, embarrassment, or discomfort (Exline & Winters, 1965). People who generally avoid eye contact may nevertheless make eye contact when they seek feedback. Also, eye contact signals a desire to pause in the conversation or to say something (M. L. Knapp, 1972). The more shared glances there are between two people, the higher the level of emotional involvement and comfort. An averted gaze may serve to hide a person's feeling ashamed of expressing a particular feeling that is seen as culturally or socially taboo (Exline & Winters). Any kind of reduced eye movement, such as staring or fixated eyes, may signal rigidity or preoccupation in thought (Singer, 1975). Darting or rapid eye movement may mean excitation, anger, or poorly fitting contact lenses. Moisture or tears in the eye may have contrasting emotional meanings for different people. Eye shifts—away from the counselor to a wall, for example—may indicate that the client is processing or recalling material (Singer). Also, the dilation of the pupils, which is an autonomic (involuntary) response, may mean alarm, satisfaction, or keen interest.

Some behaviors of the eyes and their conjectured meanings are presented in Table 3-1; however, these meanings must be viewed idiosyncratically for each client. Direct eye contact may be interpreted differently across cultures. Anglo-Americans use eye contact as a way of determining whether someone is paying attention. Yet M. L. Knapp (1972) points out that Navajos may interpret a great deal of direct eye contact as hostile,. because they rely more on peripheral vision. For some Mexican-Americans and Japanese, instances of avoiding eye contact may be interpreted as respect (Sue & Sue, 1977). Sue and Sue conclude that it could be extremely hazardous for a counselor automatically to conclude that lack of eye contact from a client indicates "inattentiveness, rudeness, aggressiveness, shyness, or low intelligence" (p. 426).

Mouth. Smiles are associated with the emotions of happiness or joy about some thought, feeling, or action. Tight lips may mean stress, frustration, hostility, or anger. Lower-lip quivering or biting lips may connote anxiety or sadness. An open mouth without speaking can indicate surprise or difficulty in talking (see Table 3-1).

Facial Expressions. The face of the other person may be the most important stimulus in an interaction, because it is the primary communicator of emotional information (Ekman, Friesen, & Ellsworth, 1971). Most of the time, the face conveys multiple emotions (Ekman & Friesen, 1969b). For example, one emotion may be conveyed in one part of the face and another in a different area. It is considered rare for one's face to express only a single emotion at a time. More often than not, the face depicts a blend of varying emotions.

Different facial areas express different emotions. Happiness and surprise may be conveyed through the lower face (mouth and jaw region) and the eye area, whereas sadness is conveyed with the eyes. The lower face and brows express anger and disgust, and fear is usually indicated by the eyes (M. L. Knapp, 1972). Although it is hard to "read" someone by facial cues alone, these cues may support other nonverbal indexes of emotion within the context of an interview. The facial expressions listed in Table 3-1 are combinations of the mouth and eye regions.

Head. The movements of the head can be a rich source for interpreting a person's emotional or affective state. The head held erect, facing the other person in a relaxed way, indicates receptivity to interpersonal communication. Nodding the head up and down implies apparent confirmation or agreement. Shaking the head from left to right may signal disapproval or disagreement. Shaking the head with accompanying leg movements may connote anger. Holding the head rigidly may mean anxiety or anger, and hanging the head down toward the chest may reflect disapproval or sadness. See Table 3-1 for an outline of these five behaviors and their associated meanings.

Shoulders. The orientation of the shoulders may give clues to a person's attitude about interpersonal exchanges. Shoulders leaning forward may indicate eagerness, attentiveness, or receptivity to interpersonal communication. Slouched, stooped, rounded, or turned-away shoulders may mean that the person is not receptive to interpersonal exchanges. This posture also may reflect sadness or ambivalence. Shrugging shoulders may mean uncertainty, puzzlement, ambivalence, or frustration.

Arms and Hands. The arms and hands can be very expressive of an individual's emotional state. Arms folded across the chest may signal avoidance of interpersonal exchange or reluctance to disclose. Anxiety or anger may be reflected in trembling and fidgety hands or clenching fists. Arms and hands that rarely gesture and are stiffly positioned may mean tension, anxiety, or anger. Relaxed, unfolded arms and hands gesturing during conversation can signal openness to interpersonal involvement or accentuation of points in conversation. The autonomic response of perspiration of the palms may reflect anxiety or arousal.

Legs and Feet. If the legs and feet appear comfortable and relaxed, the person may be signaling openness to interpersonal exchange. Shuffling feet or a tapping foot may mean that the person is experiencing some anxiety or impatience, or wants to make a point. Repeatedly crossing and uncrossing legs may indicate anxiety, depression, or impatience. A person who appears to be very "controlled" or to have "stiff" legs and feet may be uptight, anxious, or closed to an extensive interpersonal exchange (see Table 3-1).

Total Body. Body movements and body posture can be very indicative of emotion. Rocking back and forth in a chair, squirming in the seat, or stiffness reflected in sitting erectly or rigidly in or on the edge of a chair may mean tension, anxiety, concern, or worry. Body orientation at an angle, not facing the person directly in the interview, or slouching in the seat may mean unwillingness for an interpersonal exchange. Leaning forward in a relaxed manner and facing the other person in the interview squarely indicates possible openness to interpersonal communication or eagerness in seeking interpersonal involvement.

To reiterate, it is most important to remember that the conjectured meanings we have presented and abstracted for areas of the body may not have much meaning unless viewed within the context of the individual, the relationship (or interview), and the topics of conversation. Also, body cues must be perceived in conjunction with verbal behaviors and paralinguistic cues.

Paralinguistics

Paralanguage, or paralinguistic cues, can provide a wealth of information about a person's emotional states and attitudes. As you may recall, paralanguage refers to *how* the message is delivered. Some of these vocal cues include voice level, pitch, and fluency of speech.

Voice Level and Pitch. Voice level refers to the volume of speech, whereas pitch refers to intonation. A person who speaks in whispers or at an almost inaudible level may have difficulty in self-disclosing or discussing a sensitive topic. Irregular changes in pitch or louder pitch may mean that sensitive (emotional) topics are being discussed. Changes in voice level and pitch should be interpreted along with accompanying changes in topics of conversation and changes in other nonverbal behaviors.

Voice level may vary among cultures. Sue and Sue (1977) point out that Americans typically have louder voice levels than people of other cultures. In counseling a client from a different cultural background, an American counselor should not automatically conclude that a client's lower voice volume indicates weakness or shyness (Sue & Sue, p. 427).

Fluency in Speech. Fluency in speech refers to hesitations, stuttering, and speech errors. Hesitation and speech errors may indicate a person's sensitivity about topics in conversation. For example, a person may be speaking quite fluently in an interview, and then suddenly, after a shift in the topic, the person's speech becomes halting and tentative. Shifts in topics or content also may result in changes in the rate or rhythm of speech. Sue and Sue (1977) caution counselors to remember that directness in conversation is affected by cultural values. In some cultures, indirectness in speech is regarded as "a prized art," not as a sign of evasiveness (p. 427).

Autonomic Responses

Autonomic responses can provide excellent indexes or cues to a person's emotional state. For example, clammy hands, shallow breathing, sweating, pupil dilation, paleness, blushing, or rashes on the neck may provide cues about anxiety, excitement, keen interest, anger, fear, or embarrassment. These kinds of autonomic responses usually indicate some kind of arousal—which may be positive or negative, depending on the specific cues, the context of the conversation, and the preceding client messages.

Proxemics

Proxemics refers to the concept of environmental and personal space (E. T. Hall, 1966). As it applies to a counseling interaction,

proxemics includes utilization of space relative to the counseling room, arrangement of the furniture, seating arrangements, and distance between counselor and client. Proxemics also includes a variable that seems to be very important in any human interaction—territoriality. Many people are possessive not only of their belongings but of the space around them. In counseling, space and territoriality are affected by several aspects of the physical environment. For example, a smaller counseling room can inhibit verbal productivity in interviewees (Haase & DiMattia, 1976), and conducting an interview in a public area can reduce the level of interviewee self-disclosure (Holahan & Slaikeu, 1977). A client may communicate anxious feelings, an increased level of arousal, or infringement on personal space by certain reactions to the physical environment. For example, a client who moves back or does not move closer may be indicating a need for more space. The client's comfort level also may be detected from the seating position he or she chooses. A client who needs protection may sit behind a desk or a table; a client who feels fairly comfortable may take a chair closer to the counselor. Also, non-Anglo clients, such as some Latin Americans, Africans, and Indonesians, may feel more comfortable conversing at less distance (Sue & Sue, 1977).

---

body might behave in terms of movement or posture. Also, indicate what your voice level and pitch would be like, and how fluent your speech might be. After someone portrays one emotion for all regions of the body and aspects of speech, other members of the group can share how their nonverbal behaviors might differ with respect to the same emotion.

Ways of Responding to Client Nonverbal Behavior

The counselor can use the nonverbal and verbal behavior of the client in several different ways in the ongoing interview. Passons (1975) has described five ways a counselor can respond overtly or covertly to the nonverbal behavior of a client:

1. Ascertain the validity or congruence between the client's verbal and nonverbal behavior;
2. Note or respond to discrepancies or mixed verbal and nonverbal messages;
3. Respond to or note nonverbal behaviors when the client is silent or not speaking;
4. Distract or interrupt the client by focusing on nonverbal behaviors; and
5. Note changes in client nonverbal behavior which have occurred in an interview or over a series of sessions [pp. 103–105].

Congruence between Behaviors

The counselor can determine whether the client's verbal message is congruent with his or her nonverbal behavior. An example of congruence is the client who expresses confusion about a situation accompanied by squinting of the eyes or furrow of the brow. Another client may say "I am really happy with the way things have been working since I've been coming to see you," which is correlated with eye contact, relaxed body posture, and a smile. The counselor can respond in one of two ways to congruence between the client's verbal and nonverbal behaviors. A counselor might make a *mental* note of the congruence in behaviors. Or the coun-

selor could ask the client to explain the meaning of the nonverbal behaviors. For example, the counselor could ask: "While you were saying this is a difficult topic for you, your eyes were moist, your head was lowered, and your hands were fidgety. I wonder what that means?"

Mixed Messages

The counselor can observe the client and see whether what the client is saying and the client's nonverbal behavior are mixed messages. Contradictory verbal and nonverbal behavior would be apparent with a client who says, "I feel really [pause] excited about the relationship. I've never [pause] experienced anything like this before," while looking down and leaning away. The counselor has at least three options for dealing with a verbal and nonverbal discrepancy. The first is to note mentally the discrepancies between what the client says and the nonverbal body and paralinguistic cues with which the client delivers the message. The second option is to describe the discrepancy to the client, as in this example: "You say you are excited about the relationship, but your head was hanging down while you were talking, and you spoke with a lot of hesitation." (Other examples of confronting the client with discrepancies can be found in Chapter 6.) The third option is to ask the client, "I noticed you looked away and paused as you said that. What does that mean?"

Nonverbal Behavior during Silence

The third way a counselor can respond to the nonverbal behavior of the client is during periods of silence in the interview. Silence does not mean that nothing is happening! Again, the counselor should remember that silence has different meanings from one culture to another. In some cultures, silence is a sign of respect, not an indication that the client does not wish to talk more (Sue & Sue, 1977). Also, as these authors point out, "silence by many Chinese and Japanese is not a floor-yielding signal inviting others to pick up the conversation. Rather, it may indicate a desire to continue speaking after making a particular point" (p. 427). The counselor can focus on client nonverbal behavior during silence by noting the silence mentally, by describing the silence to the client, or by asking the client about the meaning of the silence.

Changing the Content of the Interview

It may be necessary with some clients to change the flow of the interview, because to continue on the same topic may be unproductive. Also, changing the flow may be useful when the client is delivering a lot of information or is rambling. In these instances, the counselor can distract the client from the verbal content by redirecting the focus to the client's nonverbal behavior.

For "unproductive" content in the client's messages, the counselor might say, "Our conversation so far has been dwelling on the death of your brother and your relationship with your parents. Right now, I would like you to focus on what we have been doing while we have been talking. Are you aware of what you have been doing with your eyes, your head, and your hands?"

Such counselor distractions can be either productive or detrimental to the progress of therapy. Passons (1975) suggests that these distractions will be useful if they bring the client in touch with "present behavior." If they take the client away from the current flow of feelings, the distractions will be unproductive (p. 105). Passons also states that "experience, knowledge of the counselor, and intuition" all contribute to the counselor's decision to distract or interrupt the client (p. 105).

Client Changes in Nonverbal Behavior

For some clients, nonverbal behaviors may be indexes of therapeutic change. For example, at the beginning of counseling, a client's arms may be folded across the chest. Later, the client may be more relaxed, with arms unfolded and hands gesturing during conversation. At the ini-

tial stages of counseling, the client may blush, perspire, and exhibit frequent body movement during the interview when certain topics are discussed. Later in counseling, these nonverbal behaviors may disappear and be replaced with a more comfortable and relaxed posture. Again, depending on the timing, the counselor can respond to nonverbal changes covertly or overtly.

The way the counselor chooses to respond to nonverbal client behavior will depend on several factors, including the client, how well the client-counselor relationship is established, the topic under discussion, and the extent to which the counselor previously has responded to client nonverbal behavior.

Learning Activity: Responding to Client Nonverbal Cues

The purpose of this activity is to practice verbal responses to client nonverbal behaviors. One person portrays a client (1) giving congruent messages between verbal and nonverbal behavior; (2) giving mixed messages; (3) being silent; (4) rambling and delivering a lot of information; and (5) portraying a rather obvious change from the beginning of the interview to the end of the interview in nonverbal behavior. The person playing the counselor responds verbally to each of these five portrayals. After going through all of these portrayals with an opportunity for the role-play counselor to respond to each, switch roles. During these role-plays, try to focus primarily on your responses to the other person's nonverbal behavior.

Counselor Nonverbal Communication

As a counselor, it is important for you to pay attention to your nonverbal behavior for several reasons. First, some kinds of counselor nonverbal behavior seem to contribute to a facilitative relationship; other nonverbal behaviors may detract from the relationship. Also, the degree to which clients perceive you as interpersonally attractive and as having some expertise is associated with effective nonverbal skills (L. D. Schmidt & S. R. Strong, 1970). A counselor who is perceived as attractive and as having some expertise is likely to be more influential in the counseling process (S. R. Strong & D. N. Dixon, 1971).

Also, the impact of a counselor's nonverbal behavior on the client is a significant factor in the therapy process and outcome. The counselor's nonverbal behavior influences the quality and the type of interview interaction. A recent study found that some counselor nonverbal behaviors can produce different quantities of client verbal messages, such as self-referent statements and expressions of affect (Hackney, 1974).

The effects of counselor nonverbal behavior in conjunction with verbal messages also have some consequences in the relationship, particularly if they are mixed or incongruent. Such mixed messages can be confusing to the client. For example, suppose that a counselor says to a client, "I am really interested in how you feel about your parents" and the counselor's body is turned away from the client with arms folded across the chest. The effect of this inconsistent nonverbal counselor message on the client could be quite potent. In fact, a negative nonverbal message mixed with a positive verbal one may have greater effects than the opposite (positive nonverbal and negative verbal). As Gazda (1973) points out, "when verbal and nonverbal messages are in contradiction, the helpee will usually believe the nonverbal message" (p. 89). Negative nonverbal messages are communicated by infrequent eye contact, body position rotated 45° away from the client, backward body lean (from waist up leaning back), legs crossed away from the client, and arms folded across the chest (Graves & Robinson, 1976; Smith-Hanen, 1977). The client may respond to inconsistent counselor messages by increasing interpersonal distance and may view such messages as indicators of counselor deception (Graves & Robinson, 1976). Also, mixed messages may reduce the extent to which the client feels psychologically close to the counselor and perceives the counselor as genuine.

Most of the evidence regarding the effects of counselor nonverbal behavior has come from analogue research. As you may recall from Chapter 1, the results of analogue research may not always generalize to actual counseling interactions. With this in mind, the nonverbal counselor behaviors that seem to be most important include expressions of regions of the eyes and face, head-nodding and smiles, body orientation and posture, some vocal cues, and physical distance between the counselor and client. The Checklist of Counselor Nonverbal Behaviors at the end of this chapter may help you identify some important nonverbal responses. However, we caution you not to try to apply these behaviors to yourself in a rigid way; this may only increase your tension—and your nonverbal expression of it.

Eye Contact

In Western culture, eye contact is an indication that the counselor is paying attention (Ivey, 1971). Eye contact may be a powerful way of communicating empathy (Haase & Tepper, 1972). Looking away or shifting your eyes may communicate disinterest or preoccupation to the client. People tend to use more eye contact when they have positive feelings for someone. However, persistent eye contact, such as a steady gaze of more than 10 seconds (staring), is likely to make a client anxious and could be interpreted as a sign of hostility (Knapp, 1972). As a counselor, you want to maintain eye contact with a client without staring.

Facial Expression

A blank, expressionless facial appearance seems to have little effect on a client's verbal behavior. Counselor head nods and smiles used in combination seem to reinforce the client's verbal behavior (Hackney, 1974) and appear to be related to the client's perception of the counselor's helpfulness (D'Augelli, 1974). Nods and smiles indicate an affiliative attitude and a more positively perceived relationship (Fretz, 1966).

Body Orientation and Posture

A body orientation facing the client and a forward body lean toward the client convey liking and empathy (Haase & Tepper, 1972; La-Crosse, 1975). A forward body lean (from waist up while seated) may be the most significant factor in communicating empathy (Haase & Tepper). A sideways or angular body orientation may indicate a counselor's negative attitudes (Fretz, 1966; Graves & Robinson, 1976). Also, a rigid sitting position and arms folded across the chest may project an unwillingness to become involved in interpersonal exchange or may be interpreted as a cold and nonempathic cue (Smith-Hanen, 1977). Facing the client with a slight forward lean in a genuinely relaxed manner may communicate that you feel very comfortable.

Paralinguistics

The paralinguistic cues mentioned in connection with client nonverbal communication also may apply to the counselor. For example, halting speech patterns or speech errors may confuse and frustrate the client. Also, speech punctuated with many "uhs" or with asking several questions at one time may convey counselor discomfort.

Distance

The degree of comfort a client experiences in the relationship also may be related to the distance between the two seats (counselor and client). A distance of between 3 feet and 5 feet or between 1 and 1½ meters seems to produce more client comfort and verbal productivity. Less comfort and verbal productivity are reflected at more extreme distances of around 2 feet "close up" and 9 feet "far apart," or at ½ and 2½ meters (Knight & Bair, 1976; G. L. Stone & C. J. Morden, 1976). However, remember that these reported effects of distance have been explored primarily with Anglo clients and could vary with clients of different cultural backgrounds.

Size of Room

The size of the room also influences client verbal behavior and possibly level of arousal. A larger room seems to encourage expression of self-referent statements, whereas a smaller room appears to inhibit such statements (at least in analogue research) (Haase & DiMattia, 1976).

Learning Activity: Counselor Nonverbal Communication

The purpose of this activity is to have you experience the effects of different kinds of nonverbal behavior. You can do this in dyads or groups or outside a classroom setting.
1. Observe the response of a person you are talking with when:
   a. You look at the person or have relaxed eye contact.
   b. You don't look at the person consistently; you avert your eyes with only occasional glances.
   c. You stare or gaze at the person.
   Obtain a reaction from the other person about your behavior.
2. With other people, observe the effects of varying conversational distance. Talk with someone at a distance of (a) 2 feet or ½ meter, (b) 4 feet or 1 meter, and (c) 8 feet or 2 meters. Observe the effect these distances have on the person.
3. You also can do the same kind of experimenting with your body posture. For example, contrast the effects of body positions in conversation: (a) slouching in seat, leaning back, and turning away from the person, compared with (b) facing the person, with a slight lean forward toward the person (from waist up), and with body relaxed.

Learning Activity: Integrating Chapter Material

The purpose of this activity is to apply the material presented in this chapter in an interview setting. Using the Checklist of Counselor Nonverbal Behaviors at the end of the chapter, observe a counselor and determine how many behaviors listed on the checklist she or he demonstrates. Or role-play with another person and have a role-play client or an observer rate your nonverbal behaviors on the checklist. Also, in the same role-play, see whether you can identify the client's nonverbal behaviors, paralinguistics, or autonomic responses. See if you can use the nonverbal behaviors of the role-play client for any or all of the following: (1) validation between verbal and nonverbal behaviors, (2) identification of mixed messages, (3) picking up nonverbal behaviors during role-play client silences, (4) interruption of the role-play client by focusing on nonverbal behavior, and (5) identification of changes in client's nonverbal behavior. Have an observer or role-play client determine whether you responded to one or more of these occasions, either by pointing out the nonverbal behavior or by asking the client its meaning.

Summary

The focus of this chapter has been on client and counselor nonverbal communication. Nonverbal behavior in an interview occurs in conjunction with verbal messages. "Verbal and nonverbal communication should be treated as a total and inseparable unit" (M. L. Knapp, 1972, pp. 8–9). The importance of nonverbal communication in counseling is illustrated by the trust that both counselor and client place in each other's nonverbal messages. Nonverbal behavior may be a more accurate portrayal of our real selves. M. L. Knapp points out that some nonverbal behaviors are very "spontaneous" and cannot easily be "faked" (p. 9). Nonverbal behavior adds significantly to our interpretation of verbal messages. As Argyle (1969) suggests, some of the most important evidence about human interactions highlights the ways that nonverbal communication interacts with verbal behavior (pp. 70–71). As an example, the effects of distance between counselor and client may vary, depending on whether the counselor gives accepting verbal feedback or neutral feedback (Greene, 1977). With this in mind, we will shift our attention in Chapter 4 to verbal communication in counseling.

Post Evaluation

Part One

Describe briefly one possible effect or meaning associated with each of the following ten client nonverbal behaviors. Judge the meaning of the client nonverbal behavior from the client description presented. If you wish, write your answers on a piece of paper. Feedback follows the evaluation. The criterion level of performance for Objective 1 is to make eight out of ten accurate identifications.

Client Nonverbal Behavior	Client Description
1. Direct eye contact	Client has shared concern with counselor and has maintained eye contact while doing so.
2. Staring or fixated on person or object	Counselor has asked client to think about possible options. Client pauses and gazes fixedly at the ceiling.
3. Tight lips (pursed together)	Client has just expressed concern and irritation over being improperly evaluated in a class. Purses lips together while explaining this.
4. Shaking head from left to right	Counselor has just interpreted reasons for client's feeling of failure. Client responds by shaking head from left to right.
5. Slouched in chair; turned away from counselor	Client has just reported that her continual attempts to find her runaway child have not had any result. As she says this, she is sitting in a slouched position and her body is turned away from the counselor.
6. Trembling, fidgety hands	Client expresses fear of losing job; hands tremble as client reveals this.
7. Foot-tapping	During a lengthy counselor response,

Client Nonverbal Behavior	Client Description
	client continually taps feet on floor; then abruptly enters into verbal exchange.
8. Whispering	Client begins to bring up a sensitive topic; voice pitch lowers to a whisper.
9. Silence	Counselor has just made a point. Client pauses for a minute with a reflective look, then responds verbally.
10. Rash on neck, faster breathing	Client discusses the anticipation of approaching birth of a child; rash appears on client's neck and breathing rate quickens.

Part Two

Conduct a short interview and see how many client nonverbal behaviors of kinesics (body motion), paralinguistics (voice qualities), proxemics (space), and general appearance you can identify. Describe the possible effects or meanings associated with each behavior you identify. A consultant might observe you, and you can confer about which nonverbal behaviors you identified and which you missed. Objective 2 states that you should be able to identify at least six different nonverbal behaviors of another person.

Part Three

Describe the desired nonverbal behavior for a counselor with respect to the following: eye contact, head movements, facial expression, body orientation, paralinguistics, proxemics. According to Objective 3, you should be able to identify accurately at least five out of six appropriate nonverbal channels of communication for the counselor.
1. Eye contact:
2. Head movements:
3. Facial expression:
4. Body orientation and posture:
5. Paralinguistics—voice quality:
6. Proxemics—distance:

Part Four

For Objective 4, in a role-play interview, demonstrate at least seven out of nine counselor nonverbal behaviors which appear optimal in facilitating the client-counselor relationship. Use the Checklist of Counselor Nonverbal Behaviors at the end of the chapter to assess your performance.

Part Five

As you probably recall, there are five occasions for responding to client nonverbal behavior. These include:
a. evidence of congruence between the client's verbal and nonverbal behavior
b. a client's "mixed" or discrepant verbal and nonverbal message
c. client's use of silence
d. changes in client's nonverbal cues
e. focusing on client's nonverbal behavior to change or redirect the interview.
Identify which of these five occasions are presented in the following client descriptions. The criterion level for Objective 5 is four out of five accurate identifications.
1. The client says that your feedback doesn't bother him; yet he frowns, looks away, and turns away.
2. The client has paused for a long time after your last question.
3. The client has flooded you with a great deal of information for the last 5 minutes.
4. The client says she feels angry about having to stay in the hospital. As she says this, her voice pitch gets louder, she clasps her hands together, and frowns.
5. The client's face was very animated for the first part of the interview; now the client's face has a very serious look.

Feedback for Post Evaluation

Part One

Some of the possible meanings of these client verbal behaviors are:
1. This client's direct eye contact probably indicates the client is *comfortable* and *willing* to engage in an interpersonal exchange.
2. This client's staring at the ceiling after the counselor's question probably indicates the client is *preoccupied.*
3. In this example, the client's tight lips seem to be an expression of *anger or irritation.*
4. The client's head-shaking after the counselor's interpretation may suggest *disagreement* with the interpretation.
5. The client's body position as she talks about her child indicates *sadness, discouragement.*
6. In this case, the client's trembling hands seem to reflect *tension or anxiety* associated with the idea of a possible loss of employment.
7. The client's foot-tapping reflects *agitation or impatience.*
8. The *whispering* voice level of this client may mean that the person is *anxious or having trouble in disclosing* about this topic.
9. In this case, the silence appears to be a time for the client to *think* before responding verbally to the counselor.
10. This client's breathing rate and neck rash appear to be signs of *positive arousal* associated with anticipation of approaching childbirth.

Part Two

Check with your consultant for feedback or use Table 3-1 to recall which nonverbal behaviors you identified.

Part Three

Check your descriptions of the desirable counselor nonverbal behaviors with the ones listed in the Checklist of Counselor Nonverbal Behaviors at the end of the chapter.

Part Four

You or your consultant can determine which desirable nonverbal behaviors you exhibited as a counselor using the Checklist of Counselor Nonverbal Behaviors.

Part Five

The five possible occasions for responding to client nonverbal cues as reflected in the post-evaluation examples are:
1. Responding to a client's mixed message; in this case the client's frown, break in eye contact, and shift in body position contradict the client's verbal message.
2. Responding to client silence; in this example, the client's pause indicates silence.
3. Responding to client nonverbal behaviors to redirect the interview focus—in this example, to "break up" the flood of client information.
4. Responding to congruence in client verbal and nonverbal messages; in this case, the client's nonverbal behaviors "match" her verbal report of feeling angry.
5. Responding to changes in client nonverbal cues—in this example, responding to the change in the client's facial expression.

Checklist of Counselor Nonverbal Behaviors

Instructions: Determine whether the counselor did or did not demonstrate the desired nonverbal behaviors listed in the right column. Check "yes" or "no" in the left column to indicate your judgment.

Demonstrated Behaviors		Desired Behaviors
Yes	No	
___ 1. Eyes	___	*Eye contact*—Maintained persistent eye contact without gazing or staring.
___ 2. Head nods	___	*Facial expression*—Punctuated interaction with occasional head nods.
___ 3. Smiles	___	*Mouth*—Punctuated interaction with occasional smiles.
___ 4. Facing client	___	
___ 5. Leaning forward	___	*Body orientation and posture*—Faced the other person, slight lean forward (from waist up), body appeared relaxed.
___ 6. Relaxed body	___	
___ 7. Completed sentences	___	*Paralinguistics*—Completed sentences without "uhs" or hesitations in delivery, asked one question at a time, did not ramble.
___ 8. Smooth delivery—no speech errors	___	
___ 9. Distance	___	*Distance*—Seats of counselor and client were between 3 feet, or 1 meter, and 5 feet, or 1½ meters apart.

COMMENTS:

Suggested Readings

Client Nonverbal Communication

Gazda, G. M. *Human relations development: A manual for educators.* Boston: Allyn & Bacon, 1973.
Hall, E. T. *The hidden dimension.* Garden City, N.Y.: Doubleday, 1966.
Knapp, M. L. *Nonverbal communication in human interaction.* New York: Holt, Rinehart & Winston, 1972.
Sue, D. W., & Sue, D. Barriers to effective cross-cultural counseling. *Journal of Counseling Psychology*, 1977, 24, 420–429.

Ways of Responding to Client Nonverbal Behavior

Knapp, M. L. *Nonverbal communication in human interaction.* New York: Holt, Rinehart & Winston, 1972.
Passons, W. R. *Gestalt approaches in counseling.* New York: Holt, Rinehart & Winston, 1975.

Counselor Nonverbal Communication

Graves, J. R., & Robinson, J. D. Proxemic behavior as a function of inconsistent verbal and nonverbal messages. *Journal of Counseling Psychology*, 1976, 23, 333–338.
Greene, L. Effects of verbal evaluative feedback and interpersonal distance on behavioral compliance. *Journal of Counseling Psychology*, 1977, 24, 10–14.
Hackney, H. Facial gestures and subject expression of feelings. *Journal of Counseling Psychology*, 1974, 21, 173–178.
LaCrosse, M. B. Nonverbal behavior and perceived counselor attractiveness and persuasiveness. *Journal of Counseling Psychology*, 1975, 22, 563–566.
Smith-Hanen, S. S. Effects of nonverbal behaviors on judged levels of counselor warmth and empathy. *Journal of Counseling Psychology*, 1977, 24, 87–91.
Stone, G. L., and Morden, C. J. Effect of distance on verbal productivity, *Journal of Counseling Psychology*, 1976, 23, 486–488.

Research in Counseling Nonverbal Communication

Brown, D., & Parks, J. Interpreting nonverbal behavior: A key to more effective counseling: Review of literature. *Rehabilitation Counseling Bulletin*, 1972, 15, 176–184.
Gladstein, G. Nonverbal communication and counseling/psychotherapy: A review. *Counseling Psychologist*, 1974, 4, 34–57.

Chapter 4
Verbal Communication

If you were to analyze the interviews of a counselor, you would find that counselor behavior consists of verbal responses, nonverbal behavior, and strategies or action plans. Counselors use many different verbal and nonverbal responses. Generally, verbal responses can be categorized by their purpose and function in an interview. For example, Ivey and Gluckstern (1974, 1976) describe verbal counselor skills as attending and influencing. Carkhuff, Pierce, and Cannon (1977) label counselor helping skills as attending, responding, personalizing, and initiating. Hackney and Cormier (1979) identify counselor verbal behavior as discriminative stimuli used to elicit cognitive and affective client content. Egan (1975) defines verbal skills by stages of a developmental model: attending (prehelping), primary empathy (stage I), advanced empathy, confrontation, immediacy, and self-disclosure (stage II).

Most of us use certain types of verbal responses in our everyday conversations. However, if we identify the types of responses we use most often in our casual talk, we might find that they differ from some of the desirable counseling "talk." Counselor interview behavior differs from social conversation. For example, much of our conversation with friends consists of asking and answering questions, expressing opinions, and giving information. Can you imagine what it would be like to see clients all day and only give information? Yet beginning counselors often find themselves stuck in coming up with other responses until they can expand their verbal response repertoire (Palisi & Ruzicka, 1974). This chapter may help you identify some ways in which verbal counselor behavior can contribute to the focus and direction of a counseling interview.

Objectives

1. To discriminate accurately between at least eight out of ten positive and negative written examples of counseling conversational style and give a rationale for your identifications.
2. To identify accurately the subject, verb, and time focus in four out of six counselor responses and in four out of six client responses using a written dialogue.
3. To conduct a 15-minute role-play interview and analyze it according to the focus of your verbal responses and the focus of the client's responses.

Counseling Conversational Style

Most beginning helpers tend to respond verbally to clients in the same way they talk to their friends and families. It is very common for helpers to spend time in their first interviews asking questions, offering advice, or analyzing the client's problem. Even more experienced counselors seem to use probing as a frequent response mode (Spooner & Stone, 1977). Most beginning counselors put a great deal of pressure on themselves to probe for the "right" information about the client or to offer the "best" solution for the client's presenting concerns. This experience occurs in the initial phases of skill training for two reasons. First, beginning counselors often haven't considered the possible effects of their usual conversational style in a counseling interaction. Also, many helpers initially don't know what to say in lieu of expressing their opinions, asking questions, or giving advice. The first step in learning some appropriate counselor verbal responses is to discriminate types of conversational style that generally are *not* helpful in counseling interactions—especially if such responses are used frequently.

The major reason some types of response don't get the "green light" for counseling is that they interfere with some of the general objectives of counseling. Talking extensively about superficial topics or about the counselor's problems, and expressing judgment, threats, or intolerance usually do not encourage clients to talk about themselves or to share personal, often very private topics with someone else, especially when the counselor is an "unknown."

The following list summarizes nine types of conversational style that are *not* generally appropriate for a counseling interaction because they can interfere with the objectives of counseling.

1. Cocktail party "chitchat." Assuming the client has a reason to see you, there are more important things to discuss than the weather, politics, or sports.
2. Expressions of judgment, blame, and criticism. Here is an example:
   > Client: The day just hasn't gone my way. Nothing has worked out for me.
   > Counselor: You just sound like you got out of bed on the wrong side today.
3. "Dear Abby" expressions of advice or preaching, such as "You should" or "You ought to."

4. Patronizing expressions and expressions of sympathy, such as "I really feel sorry for you," or "I'm sure I can make you feel better."
5. Cajoling, threatening, or arguing: "You'd better do this for your own good," or "I think your reaction is uncalled for because. . . . "
6. Expressions of intolerance and rigidity, such as "There's only one right way to approach this," or "After you retire, you may have difficulty doing that."
7. Overanalyzing, overinterpreting, or intellectualizing: "I think what you've got is a case of real bad jealousy because you've never worked through this developmental conflict."
8. "Stacking" questions—that is, asking several questions at once: "How do you feel about it; is it that you're upset? What happens to make you feel this way? Could you tell me?"
9. Extensive self-disclosure, especially sharing your own problems: "I've been doing a lot of thinking about myself as we're talking. I, too, have had some bad feelings about myself. For instance. . . . "

Learning Activities: Counseling Conversational Style

I. This activity consists of six client verbal statements, followed by three possible counselor responses. Read each client statement carefully; then select the *one* counselor response that seems most helpful. Give a rationale for your choice, explaining why your selected response may be appropriate *and* why the two you did not select seem inappropriate. The first one is completed for you as an example. Feedback can be found after the activity on page 53.

Example

1. Client: All my life I've wanted to be a doctor. Now I can't get into medical school because of their damn quotas.
   Counselor: a. That really is a shame.
           b. You should try to challenge this policy.
           c. You feel pretty upset about being

excluded from something you've always wanted to do.

The most helpful response is c, because the counselor reflects the client's feelings without agreeing or disagreeing. Response a is not helpful because it is only sympathizing, and b is advice-giving and implies that the counselor also disagrees with the quota policy.

Practice Statements

2. Client: You bet I'm upset about being in this hospital. It's not me who's crazy, it's my whole family. They are really messed up.
   Counselor: a. Well, it's up to me to be the judge of that.
   b. You don't think it's fair that you're the one who is here.
   c. But being here can be good for you.
3. Client: I just feel so down on myself. Nothing I do goes right.
   Counselor: a. You aren't aware of anything you do that you feel is OK?
   b. It seems as if this is the result of your being constantly compared to your sister.
   c. I really can't believe everything has gone so badly.
4. Client: Why don't the kids want to play with me? I'm always a loner. They don't like me.
   Counselor: a. Well, maybe you haven't really tried to get along with them.
   b. Let's talk about it and maybe that will make you feel better.
   c. You'd really like to be involved with the other kids.
5. Client: I just hate it here. This is the worst prison I've ever been in. It's a rat hole, stinking, filthy place. No one deserves to be here regardless of what they've done.
   Counselor: a. You feel that neither you nor anyone else should have to tolerate the poor conditions in this prison.
   b. What did you expect? I mean, where have you been before? How was that so different?
   c. Mmmm, boy, isn't it gorgeous outside today?
6. Client: I've almost been raped several times. There have been some close calls. Now I find it hard not to be suspicious of most men.
   Counselor: a. I know exactly what you mean. I have those feelings, too. It makes it very hard for me to be around some men . . . well, just last week . . . .
   b. Men basically are just power hungry.
   c. Your close calls with rape are making it hard for you to trust men now.

II. Engage in several role-play helping interactions. Let a "consultant" observe your interactions—or audio-tape them. After each interaction, analyze or obtain feedback about your overall conversational style. To what extent did you avoid the nine "pitfalls" listed on p. 50? Were there any pitfalls that were consistently troublesome for you? If so, try to be aware of how you can avoid these areas in your conversations for the next few weeks.

Counselor Verbal Focus

The patterns of counselor verbal and non-verbal communication seem to have some rather specific effects on client behavior and vice versa. In any dyadic relationship, each person influences both the content and the level of the other person's communication. In counseling, the client will be affected by the direction and focus reflected in the counselor's verbal behavior. For example, if the counselor maintains a *content* focus, the client is likely to talk primarily about content or factual information. If the counselor shifts to a feeling or *affective* focus, the client also is likely to begin talking more about feelings. A *behavioral* style seems to increase client talk about goals and action steps more than an affective verbal style (Lavelle, 1977).

Ivey and Gluckstern (1976) identify six focus clusters that may be reflected in a counselor's verbal responses. These focus clusters are usually indicated by the *subject* of the sentence:

1. Focus on client (indicated by subject "you").
2. Focus on counselor (indicated by subject "I").
3. Focus on others (indicated by subject "they" or name of other person[s]).

4. Focus on relationship or group (indicated by subject "we").
5. Focus on topic (indicated by a noun such as grades, happiness, family, friends, anxiety, etc.).
6. Focus on cultural-environmental context or CEC (indicated by words specifying social, cultural, or environmental factors) [pp. 54–56].

Although the first five of these focusing areas are commonly used in counseling, a CEC focus reflects a more recent emphasis. The CEC focus suggests differences in cultural and environmental influences on clients and acknowledges that, in some cases, the individual's concerns can be a direct result of cultural and environmental problems (Ivey & Gluckstern, 1976).

Within all of these (and other) focus areas, the counselor's verbal responses also may reflect an affective, behavioral, or cognitive focus. An affective focus explores client feelings, a behavioral focus identifies visible client behaviors, and a cognitive focus examines the client's thoughts and ideas. You can often identify these three focus areas by the *verb* of the sentence. For example, a clue to identifying the affective focus is the use of the verb *feeling,* as in "You are feeling very upset." The behavioral focus may be suggested by the verbs *doing, acting,* or *behaving,* as in "What are you doing about this?" A cognitive focus is revealed by such verbs as *thinking* or *telling yourself,* as in "What are you telling yourself or what are you thinking about when you're in this situation?" An examination of the verb focus can determine whether a counseling session is directed toward exploring the client's feelings, actions, or thoughts.

The six categories of subject focus and the three areas of verbal focus can be stated in the past, present, or future time focus. The time focus is indicated by the *verb tense* of the sentence. For instance, "I feel anxious" suggests the present tense and reflects the person's current anxiety. "I felt anxious" is in the past tense, indicating previous anxious feelings. "I will feel anxious" suggests the client anticipates that some anxious feelings will occur in a future situation or at a future time. Often it is helpful for a counselor to determine whether most of a session was spent in exploring past, present, or future client concerns. Passons (1975) cautions that too much focus on the past or future may indicate an avoidance of the present. The categories of subject, verb, and time focus are summarized graphically in Figure 4-1.

The following examples may help to clarify the concept of verbal focusing:

Client: I'm having a conflict about working and not being at home with my children.

1. Counselor with a *client* (subject)—*cognitive* (verb)—*present* (time) focus: You find yourself thinking about being at work rather than at home.

    In this response, the client subject focus is reflected in "You find yourself." The cognitive focus is indicated by "thinking about," and the present time focus is indicated by the present tense of the verb, "find."
2. Counselor with a *client* (subject)-*affective* (verb)-*present* (time) focus: You're feeling concerned about being at work when your children are at home without you.
3. Counselor with a *mixed* focus (*client-counselor* [subject]-*affective-behavioral* [verb]-*past-present* [time] focus): I did something similar when my children were at home, and I know this situation worried me at times. What specific feelings do you have about it?
4. Counselor with a *mixed* focus (*client-others* [subject]-*behavioral* [verb]-*present-past* [time] focus): The situation poses a conflict for you although it is something that others have done successfully.
5. Counselor with a *group* (subject)-*behavioral* (verb)-*future* (time) focus: Perhaps this is an area we will explore together and see what you can do.
6. Counselor with a *topic* (subject)-*cognitive* (verb)-*present* (time) focus: Being a working mother is not always easy—there are lots of things to think about.

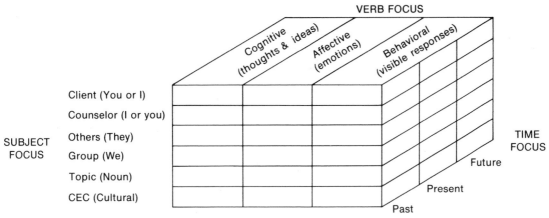

Figure 4-1. Areas of Verbal Focus

7. Counselor with a mixed focus (CEC [*subject*]–*cognitive-behavioral* [verb]–*past* [time] focus): This is a type of conflict that many women have faced because of the ideas our culture has given us about what women should and shouldn't do.

We are presenting the concept of counselor verbal focus in some detail because of the effects of the counselor's verbal behavior on the client. For instance, in the preceding example, perhaps you can see the many different directions the interview could take depending on the particular subject, verb, and time focuses.

It is important for a counselor to be aware of the various focus areas reflected in a given interview. Often, after an interview, a counselor will complain that "the interview didn't go anywhere." A focus analysis of this interview might reveal that the interview did lack direction because the counselor constantly shifted from one subject focus to another. As another example, a counselor might note that an interview seemed more like a "bull session" than a counseling session. An exploration of this interview might indicate that the verb focus was primarily content or cognitive; the affective and behavioral focuses were missing. Counselor verbal behavior does produce significant and different effects on client behavior (Lavelle, 1977). This relationship between counselor and client behavior is examined in the next section.

Feedback for Counseling Conversational Style

Client 2: Response b is the most helpful because the counselor reflects the client's perceptions about being in the hospital. Response a is an expression of judgment, and c could be interpreted as cajoling the client.

Client 3: Response a is the most appropriate: the counselor does not deny the client's feelings of inadequacy yet tries to explore whether the client is aware of anything that is OK. Response b is not helpful because it is over-analyzing or overinterpreting; c could be patronizing and could be seen by the client as judgmental.

Client 4: Response c is the most helpful because the counselor reflects the client's desired goal. Response a might be both a judgment and advice. Response b offers sympathy —but without understanding of the client's feelings or situation.

Client 5: Response a is the most appropriate: the counselor conveys understanding of the client's opinion about the prison. Response b sounds judgmental and also involves stacking questions. Response c ignores the client's complaint and focuses on irrelevant chitchat.

Client 6: Response c is the best: the counselor conveys understanding about the client's present suspicions of men. Response a is inappropriate because the counselor uses self-disclosure to shift the focus to the counselor. Response b is really an expression of

> rigidity and intolerance. Inadvertently, this counselor is reinforcing the client's generalizations about men.

Learning Activities: Using Focus

I. *Counselor Focus Identification*

In the following list, examples of different counselor responses are presented. For each response, determine whether the subject focus is *primarily* client, counselor, group, others, topic, or cultural-environmental context (CEC); whether the verb focus is affective, cognitive, or behavioral; and whether the time focus is past, present, or future. The first counselor response is completed for you as an example. You may wish to write your identifications on a sheet of paper. Feedback is presented following the activity on page 55.

Example

1. Counselor: It sounds like one part of you feels confident about yourself and another part feels apprehensive.
   Subject focus: client ("you")

   Verb focus: affective ("feels confident; feels apprehensive")

   Time focus: present (present tense of "feels")

Practice Statements

2. Counselor: What are you thinking about when you feel scared?
   Subject focus:
   Verb focus:
   Time focus:
3. Counselor: Breaking away from a secure relationship is often a very hard thing for a person to do.
   Subject focus:
   Verb focus:
   Time focus:
4. Counselor: There have been times when I've thought about what might happen if I would break out on my own.
   Subject focus:
   Verb focus:
   Time focus:
5. Counselor: Maybe what we will do here together will help.

Subject focus:
Verb focus:
Time focus:
6. Counselor: Part of the difficulty you may feel in making the break is contributed by our society, which puts so much emphasis on couples, togetherness, etc.
   Subject focus:
   Verb focus:
   Time focus:
7. Counselor: Part of your concern seems to be centered around what you will do after the divorce.
   Subject focus:
   Verb focus:
   Time focus:

II. To experience a change of focus and its effects, try varying verbal focus areas in some of your own conversations. Choose a focus (you, the other person, a topic, and so on) and stick with it for a while. How does the other person respond? Then change your focus and observe the effects on the conversation and the other person's responses.

Mutual Influence of Counselor-Client Verbal Behavior

"The helper cannot help but influence the helpee" (Ivey & Gluckstern, 1976, p. iii). In any relationship, and especially a helping one, there is a mutuality of influence. In counseling, a *functional* relationship seems to exist between the counselor's and client's verbal behavior. What the counselor says and does has certain effects on the client (Auerswald, 1974; Auld & White, 1959; Frank & Sweetland, 1962; Highlen & Baccus, 1977; Lavelle, 1977; Salzinger, 1969; Truax, 1966). Also, client responses may influence the counselor's behavior (Bandura, 1969; Carkhuff & Alexik, 1967; Lichtenberg & Hummel, 1976).

The counseling interaction can be described as a chain, with each counselor expression and each client expression representing a link. The chain is continuous, indicating that the actual counseling encounter consists of a long sequence of behaviors of both counselor and client (Hertel, 1972). Each expression of either counselor or client in this chain elicits some type of response from the other person. This response has an effect on the expression that immediately *preceded* it and on the expression that will immediately *follow* it as well as on expressions that occur later in the session. (Bandura, 1969; Lichtenberg & Hummel, 1976). Verbal responses of both counselor and client may have *three* particular kinds of influence upon each other: a reinforcing influence, a punishing influence, and a cueing or signaling influence. Some counselor responses seem either to maintain or to increase certain types of client responses; client responses also seem to maintain or increase the frequency of certain counselor responses. This is the reinforcing influence (Lichtenberg & Hummel, 1976, p. 310). In contrast, counselor responses can also decrease the frequency of certain types of client responses, just as some client responses can decrease the number or type of certain counselor-response classes. Such responses have a punishing effect on the responses of the other person. Finally, counselor responses seem to "cue" particular client responses, just as client responses prompt certain counselor ones (Hill & Gormally, 1977). In other words, particular client responses are more or less predictable following certain counselor responses, and vice versa (Lichtenberg & Hummel, p. 312). This is the *cueing* influence that counselor and client verbal behavior exert upon each other; one verbal response cues another response and heightens the possibility that a particular kind of response will follow. With the exception of the first and last responses in an interchange, each counselor and client verbal response serves as either a reinforcing (S^R) or punishing stimulus (S^P) *and* as a discriminative or cueing stimulus (S^D).

This pattern is illustrated in Table 4-1. In reading the dialogue, observe two things: first, the reinforcing (S^R) or punishing (S^P) effects, and second, the cueing (S^D) influence of the counselor's and client's responses.

Implications of Mutual-Influence Process for Verbal Counseling Skills

The mutual-influence process in counseling has some important implications for learning and using counseling skills. One implication

is that the effects of each counselor response will influence a client in different ways at different times. Also, the effects of counselor responses may vary from client to client. As a result, it is impossible on an a priori basis to come up with "right" and "wrong" systems of helping. In any actual counseling session, no *single* counselor response can be judged good or bad. A counselor can use many different responses and

Feedback for Using Focus

2. Subject focus is *client*, as indicated by the subject "you."
   Verb focus is *cognitive*, indicated by "thinking."
   Time focus is *present*—use of present tense, indicated in "are" and "feel."
3. Subject focus is *topic*—"breaking away from a relationship."
   Verb focus is *behavioral*, indicated by "to do."
   Time focus is *present*—use of present tense, indicated by "breaking away" and "is."
4. Subject focus is *counselor*, indicated by the subject "I."
   Verb focus is *cognitive*, indicated by "thought about."
   Time focus is *past*, indicated by past tense in "thought" and "have been."
5. Subject focus is *group*, indicated by "we."
   Verb focus is *behavioral*, indicated by "do."
   Time focus is *future*, indicated by the future tense in "will do" and "will help."
6. Subject focus is *cultural-environmental context* (CEC), indicated by "society."
   Verb focus is *affective*, indicated by "feel."
   Time focus is *present*—use of present tense as in "may feel."
7. Subject focus is *client*, indicated by "you."
   Verb focus is *behavioral*, indicated by "do."
   Time focus is *future*, indicated by future tense in "will do."

focuses to facilitate helping and to assist a client in attaining desired goals. For this reason, it is important that counselors learn how to use a *variety* of skills and strategies. Chapters 5, 6, and 7 will assist you in building a broad repertory of verbal interview responses.

A second implication of the influence process is that neither counselor nor client verbal behavior operates independently. To some extent, both counselor and client statements interrelate and control each other (Hertel, 1972, p. 424). The relationship between client and counselor verbal behavior suggests some degree of "lawfulness" to the counseling process. This makes it possible to hypothesize about some "immediate" and "distant" consequences of the interactions (Lichtenberg & Hummel, 1976, p. 314). Recognizing the role, influence, and lawfulness of the process, another important counselor task is to use a response with some purpose in mind. Indiscriminate, haphazard counselor verbal behavior has much less effect on a client than systematic, planned responses (Barnabei, Cormier, & Nye, 1974). Everything we communicate as counselors should be used with some rationale. Chapters 5, 6, and 7 also will help you identify some intended purposes for various verbal interview responses.

A third implication of the mutual-influence process is that what we speculate might happen in an interview may or may not be verified in the actual interview. More specifically, what we *intend* a response to accomplish may not always be achieved (Hill & Gormally, 1977). The intended purposes of using a particular response will, in some cases, differ from its actual effects. For example, a counselor may use a confrontation like "You say you feel happy but you look sad" to get the client to identify the discrepancy between verbal and nonverbal behavior. The counselor's intended effect may or may not be the actual effect. The client may confirm that this discrepancy exists. However, the client may instead deny the discrepancy or go on talking and ignore the confrontation. As a counselor, it is important for you to be able to identify how your counseling behavior actually does affect the client and vice versa. We refer to this skill as *discrimination*, meaning your ability to identify and differentiate between the intended and the actual effects of your behavior on a client. You will discover more about the discrimination process in Chapter 8.

Classification of Verbal Interview Responses

The verbal responses presented in Chapters 5, 6, and 7 were defined operationally in studies of counselor interview communications (Zimmer & Anderson, 1968; Zimmer & Park, 1967; Zimmer, Wightman, & McArthur, 1970). These variables "define characteristics of counselor responses and are thought to cut across varying theoretical orientations" (Zimmer & Pepyne, 1971, p. 442). Based on adaptations of these operationally defined variables, we have placed each response into one of four categories: (L) listening responses, (A) action responses, (S) sharing responses, and (T) teaching responses. Although the acronym for our classification system spells LAST, we're sure that this does not forecast accurately the future development of other such systems. The responses we have selected are not an exhaustive list. Other responses can be used, although the ones presented in these chapters are more common verbal counseling-interview behaviors.

The responses have been classified into one of these four categories (LAST) according to the purpose and function specified in the response definitions, although categories may overlap somewhat. The classification begins with the listening response category, because hearing and recalling messages are prerequisites of effective action, sharing, and teaching skills. We agree with Carkhuff's (1972) comment that listening "lays the base" for helping (p. 86) and with Egan's (1975) assumption that attending (prehelping) and responding with primary-level empathy (Stage I) precede advanced empathy, self-disclosure, confrontation, and immediacy (Stage II) and action programs (Stage III). We do not assume, however, that the remainder of the classification system suggests the order in which a counselor should use these verbal responses. We have no evidence to suggest that the order of sharing responses and action responses has any differential effects on clients (Barnabei et al., 1974). What we do know is that all counselor behavior has significant and different effects on client behavior. We suggest that you not confine

Table 4-1. Illustration of Possible Reinforcing, Punishing, and Cueing Effects of Counselor and Client Verbal Interview Behavior

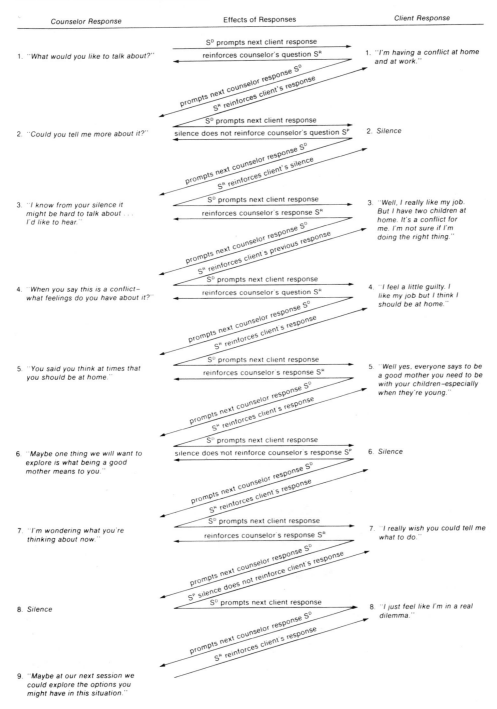

Counselor Response	Effects of Responses	Client Response
1. "What would you like to talk about?"	S^D prompts next client response / reinforces counselor's question S^R	1. "I'm having a conflict at home and at work."
	prompts next counselor response S^D / S^R reinforces client's response	
2. "Could you tell me more about it?"	S^D prompts next client response / silence does not reinforce counselor's question S^P	2. Silence
	prompts next counselor response S^D / S^R reinforces client's silence	
3. "I know from your silence it might be hard to talk about . . . I'd like to hear."	S^D prompts next client response / reinforces counselor's response S^R	3. "Well, I really like my job. But I have two children at home. It's a conflict for me. I'm not sure if I'm doing the right thing."
	prompts next counselor response S^D / S^R reinforces client's previous response	
4. "When you say this is a conflict— what feelings do you have about it?"	S^D prompts next client response / reinforces counselor's question S^R	4. "I feel a little guilty. I like my job but I think I should be at home."
	prompts next counselor response S^D / S^R reinforces client's response	
5. "You said you think at times that you should be at home."	S^D prompts next client response / reinforces counselor's response S^R	5. "Well yes, everyone says to be a good mother you need to be with your children—especially when they're young."
	prompts next counselor response S^D / S^R reinforces client's response	
6. "Maybe one thing we will want to explore is what being a good mother means to you."	S^D prompts next client response / silence does not reinforce counselor's response S^P	6. Silence
	prompts next counselor response S^D / S^R reinforces client's response	
7. "I'm wondering what you're thinking about now."	S^D prompts next client response / reinforces counselor's response S^R	7. "I really wish you could tell me what to do."
	prompts next counselor response S^D / S^P silence does not reinforce client's response	
8. Silence	S^D prompts next client response	8. "I just feel like I'm in a real dilemma."
	prompts next counselor response S^D / S^R reinforces client's response	
9. "Maybe at our next session we could explore the options you might have in this situation."		

yourself to using these responses in some predetermined order, but that you retain spontaneity in your interviews.

Post Evaluation

Part One: Counseling Conversational Style

In the following list, label each counselor response as a positive (+) or a negative (−) example of a counseling conversational style. For each of your labels, give a reason why you consider the response to be helpful or unhelpful. Check your responses with those given in the feedback at the end of the evaluation. The first response is completed for you as an example. According to Objective 1, you should be able to identify accurately at least eight out of ten examples.

1. Client: I just can't seem to fit my study time in with all my other activities.

Example Counselor Response

    Counselor: You really ought to learn to manage your time better.
    This is an inappropriate response because it sounds like judgmental advice-giving.
2. Client: (Silence.)
    Counselor: What do you think of all this snow?
3. Client: I just wish I had never gotten involved with her.
    Counselor: You seem to feel pretty upset right now.
4. Client: School is just a drag.
    Counselor: You'll never get anywhere with an attitude like that.
5. Client: I'm pregnant.
    Counselor: How do you think you'll handle this? I mean, do you think you can do something? What will you do?
6. Client: I've really got a problem with my roommate.
    Counselor: Can you tell me more about it?
7. Client: It's up to my wife to use birth control —not up to me.
    Counselor: That's a male point of view for you.
8. Client: I'm very anxious around men.
    Counselor: You probably have this anxiety because of an unresolved Oedipal conflict.
9. Client: (Silence.)
    Counselor: I can see that it's hard for you to talk about this now.

10. Client: This may sound silly, but I'm scared to death to fly in an airplane.
    Counselor: I've got that problem, too. I've had it for several years. What happened to me was. . . .

Part Two: Counselor-Client Focus Identification

A brief counselor-client dialogue is presented in Table 4-2. For each counselor response and each client response, identify the type of (1) subject focus (client, counselor, others, group, topic, cultural), (2) verb focus (affective, behavioral, or cognitive), and (3) time focus (past, present, or future). The first one is completed as an example. Feedback follows the evaluation. Try to identify accurately at least four out of six counselor responses and four out of six client responses (Objective 2).

Part Three: Interview-Focusing

Objective 3 asks you to conduct and audio-tape a 15-minute role-play interview. Then analyze your interview according to the focus of your responses and the focus reflected in the client responses. Try to determine whether the subject focus centered on the client, yourself, others, both of you, a certain topic, or cultural-environmental concerns. Did the majority of the interview focus on thoughts, feelings, behaviors or all three of these? What time focus (past, present, future) was reflected in your session?

Part One

See if you were able to identify accurately eight out of ten responses (Objective 1).

2. This response is inappropriate because the counselor focuses on the weather, not the client. Talking about the weather is "chitchat."
3. This response is OK as is because the counselor tries to understand the client's feelings.
4. This response is inappropriate because it is judgmental and evaluative.
5. This is not a helpful response because several questions are asked at once—stacking questions.
6. This response is OK; the counselor invites the client to talk more about the problem situation.
7. This response is negative—an expression of intolerance by the counselor.
8. This is an example of overanalyzing and overinterpreting.
9. This is OK as is; the counselor communicates understanding of the client's discomfort.
10. Looks here like the counselor is going to use self-disclosure too extensively for an appropriate response.

Part Two

See if you accurately identified the focus areas for at least four out of six counselor responses and four out of six client responses (Objective 2).
Client 1: Subject focus is client or self ("I"), verb

Table 4-2. Counselor-Client Focus Identification

Counselor Response	Focus Area		Client Response	Focus Area	
1. "How long have you felt upset about this?"	Subj.	client (you)	1. "About a year. I feel worse now."	Subj.	client (I)
	Verb	affective		Verb	affective
		(felt upset)			(feel worse)
	Time	past (felt)		Time	present
					(feel worse now)
2. "What are you thinking about at these times?"	Subj. Verb Time		2. "Well, just that I don't think I ever succeed."	Subj. Verb Time	
3. "I know for myself that can make me feel discouraged."	Subj. Verb Time		3. "I try hard but I never do as much at work as I should."	Subj. Verb Time	
4. "So your work problems are created by the amount that you do—not the quality of your work?"	Subj. Verb Time		4. "Right. I think what I do is fine—but it's not enough. I don't like to compete to begin with."	Subj. Verb Time	
5. "So there's a lot of competition in your work and this competition affects how much work you do."	Subj. Verb Time		5. "Right . . . and I don't feel good about competition."	Subj. Verb Time	
6. "How do you think this affects your work specifically?"	Subj. Verb Time		6. "I feel rattled and pressured with it."	Subj. Verb Time	

focus is affective ("feel worse"), and time focus is present, indicated by present tense of "feel."

Counselor 2: Subject focus is client ("you"), verb focus is cognitive ("thinking"), and time focus is present, indicated by present-tense verb "are thinking."

Client 2: Subject focus is client or self ("I"), verb focus is cognitive ("think"), and time focus is present, suggested by present tense in "don't think" and "succeed."

Counselor 3: Subject focus is counselor ("I"), verb focus is affective ("feel"), and time focus is present ("feel").

Client 3: Subject focus is client or self ("I"), verb focus is behavioral ("do"), and time focus is present ("try," "do").

Counselor 4: Subject focus is topic ("work problems"), verb focus is behavioral ("do"), and time focus is present ("do").

Client 4: Subject focus is client or self ("I"), verb focus is behavioral ("do"), and time focus is present ("do," "is").

Counselor 5: Subject focus is topic ("competition"), verb focus is behavioral ("do"), and time focus is present, as indicated by present tense of verbs.

Client 5: Subject focus is client or self ("I"), verb focus is affective ("feel good"), and time focus is present ("don't feel").

Counselor 6: Subject focus is client ("you"), verb focus is cognitive ("think"), and time focus is present ("think").

Client 6: Subject focus is client or self ("I"), verb focus is affective ("feel rattled"), and time focus is present ("feel").

Part Three

What was the primary subject focus of your interview? What was the major verb focus of your session? The time focus?

Suggested Readings

Counseling Conversational Style

Hackney, H., & Cormier, L. S. *Counseling strategies and objectives* (2nd ed.). Englewood Cliffs, N.J.: Prentice-Hall, 1979. Chap. 3, Recognizing communication patterns.

Wolberg, L. R. *The technique of psychotherapy* (2nd ed.). New York: Grune & Stratton, 1967, 584–590.

Counselor Verbal Focus

Ivey, A., & Gluckstern, N. *Basic influencing skills.* North Amherst, Mass.: Microtraining Associates, 1976. Workshop 3, The concept of focus, 52–65.

Lavelle, J. Comparing the effects of an affective and a behavioral counselor style on client interview behavior. *Journal of Counseling Psychology*, 1977, 24, 173–177.

Mutual Influence of Counselor-Client Behavior

Barnabei, F., Cormier, W., & Nye, L. Determining the effects of three counselor verbal responses on client verbal behavior. *Journal of Counseling Psychology*, 1974, 21, 355–359.

Lichtenberg, J. W., & Hummel, T. Counseling as stochastic process: Fitting a Markov chain model to initial counseling interviews. *Journal of Counseling Psychology*, 1976, 23, 310–315.

Chapter 5
Listening
Responses

Listening is a prerequisite for all other counseling responses and strategies. Listening should precede whatever else is done in counseling. When a counselor fails to listen, the client may be discouraged from self-exploring, the wrong problem may be discussed, or a strategy may be proposed prematurely.

We define listening as involving three processes: receiving a message, processing a message, and sending a message. These three processes are illustrated in Figure 5-1.

Each client message (verbal or nonverbal) is a stimulus to be received and processed by the counselor. After a client sends a message, the counselor receives it. Reception of a message is a covert process; that is, we cannot see how or what the counselor receives. Failure to receive all of the message may occur when the counselor stops attending.

Once a message is received, it must be processed in some way. Processing also is covert, because it goes on within the counselor's mind and is not visible to the outside world —except, perhaps, for the counselor's nonverbal cues. Processing includes thinking about the message and pondering its meaning. Errors in processing a message accurately often occur when counselors' biases or blind spots prevent them from acknowledging parts of a message or from interpreting a message without distortion. Counselors may hear what they want to hear instead of the actual message sent.

The third process of listening involves the verbal and nonverbal messages sent by a counselor. Sometimes a counselor may receive and process a message accurately but may have difficulty sending a message because of lack of skills. Fortunately, you can learn to use listening responses to send messages. Problems in sending messages can be more easily corrected than errors in the covert processes of receiving and processing messages. We hope that you are already able to receive and process a message without difficulty. Of course, this is a big assumption! If you think your own covert processes in listening are in need of further development, this may be an area you will need to work on by yourself or with someone else.

This chapter is designed to help you acquire four verbal listening responses that you can use to send messages to a client: clarification, paraphrase, reflection, and summarization.

Objectives

1. Using a written list of counselor responses, be able to identify accurately the different types of counselor listening responses (clarification, paraphrase, reflection, summarization).
2. From a written list, identify at least one in-

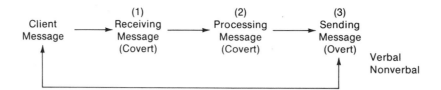

Figure 5-1. Three Processes of Listening

tended purpose of each of the four listening responses.

3. From a list of three client statements, write an example of each of the four listening responses for each client statement.

4. In a 15-minute role-play interview or a conversation in which you function as a listener, demonstrate at least two accurate examples of *each* of the four listening responses.

Listening Is a Prerequisite

We consider listening responses to be the foundation of the entire counseling process. If you conceptualize counseling and each interview as having a beginning, a middle, and an end, then attending and listening are the predominant counselor behaviors for the beginning part, or the first stage, of counseling. Listening also plays a major role in the beginning part of every interview.

One of the difficulties encountered in listening is to achieve a reasonable balance between too much and too little listening. If listening is the only tool used in counseling, the sessions will probably lack direction. However, if the counselor fails to listen, the sessions may be overly structured—at the client's expense. Egan (1975) points out that counselors who move into facilitating action too quickly are satisfying more of their own needs than those of the client (p. 232).

Four Listening Responses

As we mentioned in the beginning, this chapter will present four kinds of listening responses: clarification, paraphrase, reflection,

and summarization. *Clarification* is a question, often used after an ambiguous client message. It starts with "do you mean that . . ." or "are you saying that . . ." along with a repetition or rephrasing of all or part of the client's previous message. Similar to a clarification is the *paraphrase,* defined as a rephrasal of the content part of the message, which describes a situation, event, person, or idea. In contrast, *reflection* is a rephrasing of the client's feelings, or the affect part of the message. Usually the affect part of the message reveals the client's feelings about the content; for example, a client may feel *discouraged* (affect) about not doing well in a class (content). *Summarization* is an extension of the paraphrase and reflection responses that involves tying together and rephrasing two or more different parts of the message.

To illustrate these four responses, a client message is presented with an example of each:

Client, a 35-year-old widow, mother of two young children: My whole life fell apart when my husband died. I keep feeling so unsure about my ability to make it on my own and to support my kids. My husband always made all the decisions for me. Now I haven't slept well for so long and I'm drinking more heavily—I can't even think straight. Besides, I've put on 15 pounds. I look like a witch. Who would even want to think of hiring me the way I am now?

Counselor clarification: Are you saying that one of the hardest things facing you is to have enough confidence in your ability to make the decisions now alone?

Counselor paraphrase: Since your husband's death you have all the responsibilities and decisions on your shoulders.

Counselor reflection: You feel concerned about your ability to shoulder all the family responsibilities now.

Counselor summarization: Now that your husband

has died, you're facing a couple of things that are very difficult for you right now . . . handling the family responsibilities, making the decisions, and trying to take better care of yourself.

Table 5-1 presents the definitions and the intended or hypothesized purposes of the four counselor listening responses of clarification, paraphrase, reflection, and summarization. The counselor responses may not have the same results for all clients. For example, a counselor may find that reflecting feelings prompts some clients to discuss feelings, whereas other clients may not even acknowledge the counselor's statements (Highlen & Baccus, 1977; Hill & Gormally, 1977). The point is that we are presenting some "modal" intentions for each counselor listening response; there are exceptions. The counselor responses will achieve their intended purposes most of the time. However, other dynamics within an interview may yield different client outcomes. Also, the effects of these verbal messages may vary depending on the nonverbal cues sent along with the message. As you may recall from Chapter 4, it is helpful to have some rationale in mind for using a response. Keep in mind, however, that the influence a response has on the client may not be what you intended to achieve by selecting it. The guidelines in Table 5-1 should be used tentatively, subject to modification by particular client reactions.

The next three sections will describe the listening responses and will present model examples of each skill. Opportunities to practice each skill and receive feedback follow the examples.

Listening for Accuracy: The Clarification Response

The clarification response may be defined as a question beginning with "do you mean that . . ." or "are you saying that . . ." along with a rephrasing of all or part of the client's previous message. The clarification may be used to make the client's previous message explicit and to confirm the accuracy of your perceptions about the message. A clarification is appropriate for any occasion when you aren't sure whether you understand the client's message and you need more elaboration. A second purpose of clarification is to check out what you heard of the client's message. Ivey and Gluckstern (1974) point out that too often counselors "charge ahead without stopping to check out whether or not they have really heard what the helpee has to say" (p. 26). In this case, the counselor often makes assumptions and draws conclusions about the client that are somewhat distorted or premature. Particularly in the beginning stages of counseling, it is important to verify client messages before jumping to quick conclusions. The following example may help you see the value of the clarification response.

Student: I wish I didn't have to be in those group activities you do in class. They seem so silly to me.
Teacher: Why don't you like my class?
Student: I didn't say I didn't like the class. As a matter of fact, it is one of my better ones, but I don't think I learn as much in these activities as when I work alone.

In this example, the teacher "shot from the hip" and drew a quick conclusion from the initial message that turned out to be inaccurate. The conversation might have gone differently had the teacher used a clarification prior to assuming that the student didn't like the class:

Student: I wish I didn't have to be in those group activities you do in class. They seem so silly to me.
Teacher: Are you saying you don't see any purpose to the group activities we do in class?
Student: No, I really don't. I don't think I learn as much in these activities as when I work alone.

In this case, the clarification helped both people to establish exactly what was being said. Neither the teacher nor the student had to rely on assumptions and inferences that were not explored and confirmed. The skilled counselor uses clarification responses to determine the accuracy of the messages as they are received and processed.

Table 5-1. Definitions and Intended Purposes of Counselor Listening Responses

Response	Definition	Intended Purpose
Clarification	a question beginning with "do you mean that" or "are you saying that" plus a rephrasing of the client's message	1. to encourage more client elaboration 2. to check out the accuracy of what you heard the client say
Paraphrase (responding to content)	a rephrasing of the content of the client's message	1. to help the client focus on the content of his or her message 2. to highlight content when attention to feelings is premature or self-defeating
Reflection (responding to feelings)	a rephrasing of the affective part of the client's message	1. to encourage the client to express more of his or her feelings 2. to have the client experience feelings more intensely 3. to help the client become more aware of the feelings that dominate him or her
Summarization	two or more paraphrases or reflections that condense the client's messages or the session	1. to tie together multiple elements of client messages 2. to identify a common theme or pattern 3. to interrupt excessive rambling

Learning Activity: Clarification

In this learning activity, you are presented with three client practice statements. Each statement is longer than the preceding one. Starting with client statement 1, read the statement carefully; then verbalize or write an example of a clarification response. You may wish to take some paper and jot down your responses.

An example of the clarification response precedes the statements for you to complete. Feedback is given after the activity, so you can check yourself after completing a clarification for each client practice statement (see p. 66).

Example

Client, a 15-year-old high school student: My grades have really slipped. I don't know why; I just feel so down about everything.

1. Counselor clarification: Are you saying [or "do you mean"] that your poor grades are one reason you feel down—but there are other reasons, too?

or

2. Counselor clarification: Do you mean [are you saying] that feeling down has contributed to your poor grades?

Now respond to the following three client messages with a clarification of your own.

Client Practice Statements

Client 1, a fourth-grader: I don't want to do this dumb homework anyway. I don't care about learning these math problems. Girls don't need to know this anyway.

Client 2, a middle-aged man: I'm really discouraged with this physical disability now. I feel like I can't do anything the way I used to. Not only has it affected me in my job, but at home. I just don't feel like I have anything good to offer anyone.

Client 3, an older person: The company is going to make me retire even though I don't want to. What will I do with myself then? I find myself just thinking over the good times of the past, not wanting to face the future at all. Sometimes retirement makes me so nervous I can't sleep or eat. My family suggested I see someone about this.

Listening for Content and for Affect: Paraphrasing and Reflecting

In addition to clarifying the accuracy of client messages, the counselor needs to listen for information revealed in messages about significant situations and events in the client's life—and the client's feelings about these events. Each client message will express (directly or indirectly) some information about client situations or concerns and about client feelings or emotions. The portion of the message that expresses information or describes a situation or event is referred to as the content, or the cognitive part, of the message. The cognitive part of a message includes references to a situation or event, people, objects, or ideas. Another portion of the message may reveal how the client feels about the content; expression of feelings or an emotional tone is referred to as the affective part of the message (Hackney & Cormier, 1979). Generally the affect part of the verbal message is distinguished by the client's use of an affect or feeling word such as *happy, angry*, or *sad*. However, clients also may express their feelings in less obvious ways, particularly through various nonverbal channels of communication.

The following illustrations may help you distinguish between the content and affective parts of a client's verbal message.

Client, a 6-year-old first-grader: I don't like school. It isn't much fun.

The first sentence ("I don't like school") is the affect part of the message. The client's feelings are suggested by the words "don't like." The second sentence ("It isn't much fun") is the content part of the message because it refers to a situation or an event in this child's life—not having fun at school.

Here is another example:

Client, a 20-year-old woman: How can I tell my boyfriend I want to break off our relationship? He will be very upset. I guess I'm afraid to tell him.

In this example, the first two sentences are the content because they describe the situation of wanting to break off a relationship. The third sentence, the affect part, indicates the client's feelings about this situation—being *afraid* to tell the boyfriend of her intentions.

See if you can discriminate between the content and affective parts of the following two client messages:

Client 1, a young man: I just can't satisfy my wife sexually. It's very frustrating for me.

In this example, the content part is "I can't satisfy my wife sexually." The affect part, or the client's feelings about the content, is "It's very *frustrating* for me."

Client 2, an institutionalized man: This place is a trap. It seems like I've been here forever. I'd feel much better if I weren't here.

In the second example, the statements referring to the institution as a trap and being there forever are the content parts of the message. The statement of "feeling better" is the affect part.

The skilled counselor tries to listen for both content and affect parts of client messages because it is important to deal with significant situations or relationships *and* with the client's feelings about the situations. As you may recall from Chapter 4, responding to cognitive or affective messages will direct the focus of the session in different ways. At some points, the counselor will respond to content by focusing on events, objects, people, or ideas. At other times, the counselor will respond to affect by focusing on the client's feelings and emotions. Generally, the counselor can respond to content by using a paraphrase and can respond to affect with a reflection.

Paraphrase. A paraphrase is a restatement or rephrasing of the content portion of the client's message using your own words. Paraphrasing may be considered synonymous with responding to content. The paraphrase is likely to draw the client's attention to the content of the message, and one purpose of the paraphrase is to help the client think about or focus on the situation, person, object, or idea more clearly. Sometimes a counselor may choose to paraphrase the cognitive message rather than reflect the affective message because of timing. In some instances, a counselor may feel that it is premature or would be overwhelming for the client to attend to intense affect at that time. In other cases, the counselor may determine that the client's expression of affect is chronic and self-defeating, as in the "poor me" game. Rather than focusing on the affective message, the counselor could paraphrase the content part of the message.

Learning to paraphrase involves recalling the message, identifying the content part of the message, and responding to the content by rephrasing it in your own words. Think of this in a three-step sequence:

1. Attend to and recall the client's message by restating it to yourself (covertly).
2. Identify the content part of the message (covertly). Ask yourself "What is the situation, object, person, or idea expressed in this message?"
3. Translate the content part of the message into your own words, and verbalize this to the client in the form of a paraphrase.

Try out this three-step sequence in the following example:

Client: I don't want no damn job that I don't like. I just need to get the check every month. I can't get the kind of work I need and it don't pay that much anyway.

1. Recall and restate this message to yourself.
2. Identify the content part of the message ("I just need to get the check"; "I can't get the kind of work I need"; "it don't pay that much").

Feedback: Clarification

Listed below are two possible clarification responses you might use to respond to each of the three client practice statements. Check to see whether your clarification is similar—your wording will probably be different from the words of these responses. Determine whether your clarification is a question beginning with "Do you mean" or "Are you saying" plus a rephrasing of some part of the client's previous message.

For client statement 1: "Do you mean [or are you saying] that you don't think math is too important to you?"

or

"Are you saying you don't like math or that you don't think girls need to learn it?"

In this statement you can use the clarification to check out what is contributing to the student's dislike of math problems.

For client statement 2, you can use clarification to determine the extent to which the disability has affected the client's self-concept:

"Are you saying that your whole attitude about yourself has changed as a result of your disability?"

or

"Do you mean that you really see yourself differently now than before?"

For client statement 3, use a clarification to explore the client's perceptions of life after retirement:

"Do you mean that you fear the good times are over once you retire?"

or

"Are you saying that it is easier to think about living in the past than in the future?"

3. Take the content portion of the message and translate it into your words; now say this aloud in the form of a paraphrase ("You'd rather get your monthly check than do work that doesn't suit you or pay enough").

Practice this three-step sequence in the following learning activity.

In this activity, read and recall each message. Then identify the content part of the message. Finally, translate the content into your own words and verbalize or write an example of a paraphrase. An example is provided for you. Check your responses with those in the feedback that follows on p. 68.

Example

Client 1, a 15-year-old student: My grades have really slipped. I don't know why; I just feel so down about everything.
Counselor paraphrase: You aren't sure of the reasons for getting poorer grades recently.

Now respond to the three client messages with your own examples of the paraphrase response.

Client Practice Statements

Client 1, a fourth-grader: I don't want to do this dumb homework anyway. I don't care about learning these math problems. Girls don't need to know this anyway.
Client 2, a middle-aged man: I'm really discouraged with this physical disability now. I feel like I can't do anything the way I used to. Not only has it affected me in my job, but at home. I just don't feel like I have anything to offer anyone.
Client 3, an older person: The company is going to make me retire even though I don't want to. What will I do with myself then? I find myself just thinking over the good times of the past, not wanting to face the future at all. Sometimes retirement makes me so nervous I can't sleep or eat. My family suggested I see someone about this.

Reflection of Feeling. You have just learned that the paraphrase is used to restate the cognitive part of the message. Although the paraphrase and the reflection of feeling are not mutually exclusive responses, the reflection of feeling is used to rephrase the *affective* part of the message, the client's emotional tone. The reflec-

tion of feeling is similar to responding to feelings (Carkhuff, 1972) or to conveying primary or basic empathy (Egan, 1975). Here are two examples that may illustrate the difference between a paraphrase and a reflection of feeling.

Client: Everything is humdrum. There's nothing new going on, nothing exciting. All my friends are away. I wish I had some money to do something different.
Counselor paraphrase: With your friends gone and no money around, there is nothing for you to do right now.
Counselor reflection: You feel bored with the way things are for you right now.

Note the counselor's use of the affect word *bored* in the reflection response to tune into the feelings of the client created by the particular situation.

The reflection has three intended purposes. First, it can encourage clients to express more of their feelings (both positive and negative) about something. Second, the reflection may help clients experience feelings more intensely in order to become aware of unfinished situations. The third purpose of a reflection is to help clients become more aware of any feelings that dominate them.

One of the major problems facing the counselor in using a reflection of feeling is the timing, or the point at which the reflection is used, and the effect on the client. When you use a reflection response, you are responding to —and therefore may be reinforcing—the client's feelings. Reflecting feelings often encourages the client to focus on affect (Highlen & Baccus, 1977). You must discriminate when it may be helpful for the client to express feelings, or when attending to feelings might only reinforce the client's tendency to feel depressed or victimized.

Reflecting feelings involves recalling the message, identifying the affect part of the message, and verbally reflecting the client's feelings using your own words. You can identify the affect part of the message—by finding the affect words. Generally a client's feelings can be categorized from one of three major affect categories: anger, affection, and fear (Hackney & Cormier, 1979). Identifying the affect words may require you to build your vocabulary of feeling words. A list of commonly used affect words is presented in Table 5-2 (see also Carkhuff, Pierce, & Cannon, 1977, p. 86; Egan, 1975, pp. 23–33; Gazda, 1973, pp. 163–167).

Sometimes a client may not express feelings directly by using an affect word, but will express feelings indirectly or subtly. Usually a counselor can identify an indirect expression of client feelings by identifying *how* the message is expressed. As you may remember from Chapter 3, nonverbal cues such as body posture, facial expression, and tone of voice are important indicators of client emotions. If you have trouble identifying an obvious affect word in the message, think to yourself "How does this person feel?" Try to imagine what it would be like to be this person. Imagine how you would feel. How do the people feel in the following three messages?

Client 1: I'm really ready to sock him in the face the next time he mouths off.

Perhaps you described these feelings as angry, irritated, or mad.

Client 2: Why do I always have to get picked on? I'm always having to justify why I do something.

Imagine how this person feels. Did you imagine puzzled, defensive, irritated—maybe some of all three.

Client 3: You can imagine how I felt when I discovered my wife was going out on me. What should I do—leave—confront her—beat her?

This person probably feels angry, upset, resentful, and confused.

After you identify the affect part of the message, think of another word you could use to reflect the feeling. The affect word you use in your reflection should say no more and no less than what is expressed by the client. Carkhuff, Pierce, and Cannon (1977) refer to this as an *interchangeable response* (p. 76). Sometimes you

---

Feedback: Paraphrase

See whether your responses are similar to the ones provided here. Is your paraphrase a rephrasal of the *content* part of the message—using your own words?
For client statement 1: "You don't think it's too important for girls to be able to do math."
or
"You're saying that as a girl you don't need to learn math."
In this example, you are paraphrasing the cognitive part of the message: the client's opinion about math for girls.

For client statement 2: "Everything seems different than it used to—especially how you see yourself in work and at home—even how you feel about yourself."
or
"Your view of yourself is different now than it used to be."
This paraphrase zeroes in on the situation the disability creates rather than the client's feelings about it.

For client statement 3: "You're wondering what your life will be like after retirement."
or
"Facing retirement means a lot of changes for you."
The paraphrase is used to focus on the event of retirement rather than how the client feels about the event.

---

may find two or more different feelings in the client's message, so your reflection may contain two different affect words. Then respond directly to the client by verbally reflecting her or his feelings, starting the sentence with words like "you feel . . ." or "you feel . . . and . . . ."

To summarize, the steps in using reflection are:

1. Recall and restate the client's message covertly.
2. Identify the affect part of the message by looking for one or more affect words used by the client or for nonverbal affect cues.

Table 5-2. List of Commonly Used Affect Words

Happiness	Sadness	Fear	Uncertainty	Anger
Happy	Discouraged	Scared	Puzzled	Upset
Pleased	Disappointed	Anxious	Confused	Frustrated
Satisfied	Hurt	Frightened	Unsure	Bothered
Glad	Despairing	Defensive	Uncertain	Annoyed
Optimistic	Depressed	Threatened	Skeptical	Irritated
Good	Disillusioned	Afraid	Doubtful	Resentful
Relaxed	Dismayed	Tense	Undecided	Mad
Content	Pessimistic	Nervous	Bewildered	Outraged
Cheerful	Miserable	Uptight	Mistrustful	Hassled
Thrilled	Unhappy	Uneasy	Insecure	Offended
Delighted	Hopeless	Worried	Bothered	Angry
Excited	Lonely	Panicked	Disoriented	Furious

3. Translate the client's affect words into your words at about the same level of intensity.
4. Verbally reflect the client's feelings in statement form, starting with words like "you feel . . . ."

Try the steps in using reflection with this example:

Client: I don't want no damn job that I don't like. I'm satisfied just to get the check every month. I can't get the kind of work I need and it don't pay that much anyway.

1. Recall and restate this message to yourself.
2. Identify the affect message by looking for affect words ("don't like" and "satisfied"), or nonverbal affect cues.
3. Translate the client's affect words into ones of your own at the same level of intensity. For instance, "a job I don't like" might be translated as "an unpleasant job." "I'm satisfied" might be translated as "I'm pleased."
4. Verbally reflect the client's feelings: "You don't want a job that's unpleasant and, besides, you feel pleased to get the monthly check."

Sometimes counselors wonder about the wording of a reflection response. A reflection is defined not by beginning your response with "you feel" but by reflecting back the emotional part of the message with *appropriate affect words*. Often a counselor will identify any response as a reflection if it begins with "you feel" or "you feel that." Keep in mind that just beginning a response with "you feel" does not ensure it can be defined as a reflection. A counselor who says "You feel that your grades are slipping" has only described the content or the situation, *not* the client's feelings about it. You can vary your own style in reflecting by not always relying on the same wording for a reflection response.

Start listening for the affective part of the messages of people in your life. Sometimes when you reflect the feeling of a friend, the entire conversation takes a shift. Try it!

Learning Activity: Reflection

In this activity, develop reflections that accurately reflect the client's *feelings* about a certain situation or event. Check your reflections with the ones that follow in the feedback on p. 71. An example is given first.

Example

Client 1, a 15-year-old high school student: My grades have really slipped. I don't know why; I just feel so down about everything.

Counselor reflection: You're feeling *discouraged* [affect message] *about your grades and some other things, too* [content].

Client 1, a fourth-grader: I don't want to do this dumb homework anyway. I don't care about learning these math problems. Girls don't need to know this anyway.

Client 2, a middle-aged man: I'm really discouraged with this physical disability now. I feel like I can't do anything the way I used to. Not only has it affected me in my job, but at home. I just don't feel like I have anything good to offer anyone.

Client 3, an older person: The company is going to make me retire even though I don't want to. What will I do with myself then? I find myself just thinking over the good times of the past, not wanting to face the future at all. Sometimes retirement makes me so nervous I can't sleep or eat. My family suggested I see someone about this.

Listening for Themes: Summarization

Usually, after a client has expressed several messages or has talked for a while, her or his messages will suggest certain consistencies or patterns that we refer to as *themes*. Themes in client messages are expressed in topics to which the client continually refers or brings up in some way. The counselor can identify themes by listening to what the client repeats "over and over and with the most intensity" (Carkhuff et al., 1977). The themes indicate what the client is trying to tell us and what the client needs to focus on in the counseling sessions. The counselor can respond to client themes by using a summarization response.

The primary purpose of the summarization is to tie together or link multiple elements of client messages. In this case, summarization can serve as a good feedback tool for the client by creating meaning from vague and ambiguous messages. A second purpose of summarization is to identify a common theme or pattern that

*It would be helpful to hear these statements on an audio-tape so you could use the person's paralinguistic cues as an aid to identifying emotions.

becomes apparent after several messages, or sometimes after several sessions. Occasionally, a counselor may summarize to interrupt a client's incessant rambling.

A summarization may be defined as a collection of two or more paraphrases or reflections that condenses the client's messages or the session. In using a summarization, "a helper attends to the helpee's verbal and nonverbal statements over a period of time (e.g., three minutes to a complete session or even several sessions). The helper then selects out critical dimensions of the helpee's statements and behavior and restates them for the helpee as accurately as possible" (Ivey & Gluckstern, 1974, p. 48).

A summarization may represent collective rephrasings of either cognitive or affective data. Many summarization responses will include references to both cognitive and affective messages, as in the following two examples:

1. Client, an eighth-grader: Well, I don't know if change is possible unless I really want to. I know that I will never completely want to. But at the same time I feel that I am going to have to. I want to change my image to some people and to some people I don't care. I just want to change my image to people I know.
   Counselor summarization: You feel *torn*. You think you need to change, but sometimes you feel *reluctant* to do so [summarization of emotion]. You're most interested in changing your image and then only to people you know [summarization of cognitive content].
2. Client, a middle-aged man trying to fight alcoholism: I know drinking doesn't really help me in the long run. And it sure doesn't help my family. My wife keeps threatening to leave. I know all this. It's hard to stay away from the booze. Having a drink makes me feel relieved.
   Counselor summarization: You're aware of some of the ways that drinking is not very helpful to you [summarization of content], yet you feel better, less overwhelmed after a drink [summarization of affect].

A summarization also may identify a theme or pattern in the client's messages that becomes apparent to the helper over time. For example, suppose you have been counseling a young man who, during the last three sessions, has made repeated references to homosexual relationships, yet has not really identified this issue intentionally. You could use a summarization to identify the theme from these repeated references by saying something like: "I'm aware that during our last few sessions you've spoken consistently about homosexual relationships. Perhaps this is an issue for you we might want to focus on."

As another example, suppose in one session a client has given you several descriptions of different situations in which she feels concerned about how other people perceive her. You might discern that the one theme common to all of these situations is the client's need for approval from others or "other-directedness." You could use a summarization such as this to identify this theme: "One thing I see in all three of the situations you've described, Jane, is that you seem quite concerned about having the approval of the other people. Is this accurate?"

Steps in Summarizing. Summarizing builds on the previous listening responses you have learned, since it is a linking of several cognitive or affective messages or themes. Summarization involves these four steps:

1. your covert recall of the client's message
2. your identification of cognitive and affective parts of the message or of a common theme in the messages
3. your rephrasal of the messages or of the theme
4. your verbal summarization of the message or themes.

Use the summarization steps with this example:

Client: I don't want no damn job that I don't like. I'm satisfied just to get that check every month. I can't get the kind of work I need and it don't pay that much anyway.

1. Recall and restate this message to yourself covertly.
2. Identify whether there is a cognitive part of

Feedback: Reflection

See if your reflections are similar to these. Does each of your responses contain an affect word that is interchangeable with the one in the client's message?

For client statement 1: "You sound as if you feel a little *resentful* about having to do math problems you don't like."

or

"Perhaps you're feeling *annoyed* about having to learn something that isn't important to you."

This reflection focuses on how the client feels about having to do something she doesn't like or value.

For client statement 2, reflect the client's feelings about himself and his disability:

"You seem to feel *useless* to others and *down* on yourself now."

or

"You're feeling *unhappy* with yourself—and the way the disability has affected you."

For client statement 3: "The thought of retirement makes you feel *nervous* now and *worried* about what the future will be like for you."

or

"You feel very *concerned* about what your life will be like after you retire."

The reflections focus on the person's present nervousness and anticipatory worry.

the message (in this case, "I can't get the kind of work I need and it don't pay that much anyway"), and identify whether there is an affective part of the message ("I don't want no damn job that I don't like. I'm satisfied just to get that check every month").
3. Rephrase the cognitive and/or affective parts of the message in your head in a way that summarizes or connects the message.
4. Verbalize your summarization ("You're more satisfied to get your check than to take an unpleasant job [summarization of affect], especially when the job doesn't pay much

or isn't suited for you [summarization of content].")

Learning Activity: Summarization

Try out your own summarization responses in this learning activity. Feedback follows on p. 73.

Example

Client 1, a 15-year-old high school student: My grades have really slipped. I don't know why; I just feel so down about everything.
Counselor summarization: You're uncertain about why your grades have slipped, although you are aware that you are feeling depressed about things in general.

Client Practice Statements

Client 1, a fourth-grader: I don't want to do this dumb homework anyway. I don't care about learning these math problems. Girls don't need to know this anyway.
Client 2, a middle-aged man: I'm really discouraged with this physical disability now. I feel like I can't do anything the way I used to. Not only has it affected me in my job, but at home. I just don't feel like I have anything good to offer anyone.
Client 3, an older person: The company is going to make me retire even though I don't want to. What will I do with myself then? I find myself just thinking over the good times of the past, not wanting to face the future at all. Sometimes retirement makes me so nervous I can't sleep or eat. My family suggested I see someone about this.

Summary

Listening is a prerequisite for other verbal responses (action, sharing, and teaching) used in helping. Listening also lays the foundation for treatment strategies and evaluation. Yet beginning counselors usually find listening to be one of the most difficult skills to acquire—and even more difficult to implement in an interview. Two factors can make it difficult for a helper to use listening responses with clients actively and consistently. First, the helper may not really see the value or the importance of listening. Also, the helper's reception of messages may be blocked by distractions and preoccupation with oneself. We often hear these questions: "What good does all this do? How does just rephrasing client messages really help?" In response, we will reiterate the rationale for using listening responses in counseling.

1. Listening to clients is a very powerful reinforcer and may strengthen clients' desires to talk about themselves and their concerns. Not listening may prevent clients from sharing relevant information (Morganstern, 1976, p. 63).
2. Listening to a client first may mean a greater chance of responding accurately to the client in later stages of counseling such as problem-solving (Carkhuff et al., 1977). By jumping to quick solutions without laying a foundation of listening, you may inadvertently ignore the primary problem or propose inadequate and ill-timed action steps.
3. Listening encourages the client to assume responsibility for selecting the topic and focus of an interview. Not listening may meet your needs to find information or to solve problems. In doing so, you may portray yourself as an expert rather than a collaborator. Simply asking a series of questions or proposing a series of action steps in the initial phases of helping can cause the client to perceive you as the expert and can hinder proper development of client self-responsibility in the interview.

Some counselors can articulate a clear rationale for listening but nevertheless cannot listen in an interview because of certain blocks that inhibit effective listening. Some of the most common blocks to listening include:

1. The tendency to judge and evaluate the client's messages

2. The tendency to stop attending because of distractions such as noise, the time of the day, or the topic
3. The temptation to respond to missing pieces of information by asking questions
4. The temptation or the pressure put on yourself to solve problems or find answers
5. The preoccupation with yourself as you try to practice the skills. This preoccupation shifts the focus from the client to you and actually reduces rather than increases your potential for listening.

Effective use of listening responses requires you to confront these blocks head on. Too often a counselor will simply get discouraged and not listen because it is too difficult. Start slowly and work with each listening response until you feel comfortable with it. As you accumulate counseling experience and confidence, you can listen with greater ease and facility. As you go through the remainder of this book and add to your repertory of skills, we hope that you will treat listening responses as a permanent fixture.

Post Evaluation

Part One

This part is designed for you to assess your performance on Objective 1. Using the written list of client statements and counselor responses, take a sheet of paper and identify each of the counselor listening responses. If you identify 9 out of 12 responses correctly, you have met this objective. You can check your answers with those provided in the feedback that follows the evaluation. The first item is completed as an example.

1. Client: Sometimes I feel like I'm going to flunk out.

Example Counselor Response

a. "You feel pretty concerned about this." (*This type of response is reflection.*)
b. "Are you saying you have some evidence that gives you this feeling?" (*What type of response is this?*)

Feedback: Summarization

How similar are your summarization responses to these? Do your summarizations tie together at least two different parts of the client's message?

For client 1: "You don't like having to do the math problems. You don't think they're important to learn, especially for a girl."

This summarization brings together the client's feelings and opinions about math.

For client 2: "You're noticing a real difference in your life since your disability. It has affected you at home, at work, and generally just made you feel discouraged about yourself."

This response ties together the ways in which the disability affects the client.

For client 3: "Now that it seems like the company is going to force you to retire, you're dreading the thought. It's easier for you to think about the past than to anticipate what the future may bring."

In this example, summarization is used to focus on the client's present situation and tie it to implications for the future.

2. Client: I don't think I can make our next appointment.
   a. "As of now you aren't planning to come in next week."
   b. "Are you saying that you don't think you need to come next week?"
3. Client: I just don't want anyone else to know this.
   a. "You are concerned that someone else may find out."
   b. "You'd rather keep this to yourself."
4. Client: I think that all men are interested in is power.
   a. "Are you saying you've had some unpleasant experiences with men?"
   b. "The way you see it, men are power-hungry."
5. Client: I don't want my husband to make demands on me. I want to make my own decisions.
   a. "You feel that there is no reason for your husband to make demands. You'd rather be independent of his demands."

b. "As far as your husband is concerned, you prefer for him to let you make your own
decisions."
6. Client: I don't think you have enough experience
to really help me.
a. "You feel doubtful about my ability to help
you."
b. "You think my lack of experience may interfere
with my ability to help you."

Part Two

This part is related to Objective 2 of this chapter. For
each of the four listening responses, select the most
appropriate intended purpose of each response from
the following list:
a. to identify client feelings
b. to focus on a situation or event
c. to confirm the accuracy of your perceptions
d. to identify a dominant theme
Feedback is provided at the end of the evaluation.

Listening Responses

Clarification:
Paraphrase:
Reflection:
Summarization:

Part Three

Three client statements are presented. Objective 3
asks you to verbalize or write an example of each of
the four listening responses for each client statement.* Feedback is given at the end of the evaluation. The first one is completed as an example.

Client 1, a beginning teacher: My classroom is a mess.
I can't handle those problem kids. The principal
is breathing down my neck to keep more order
and I'm not even sure how important order is.

Example Counselor Response

Clarification: *"Are you saying that you're unsure
yourself about how much order you need or
want in your class?"*

*These three client messages can be put on audio-tape
with pauses between statements. Instead of reading the
message, you can listen to the message and write or verbalize your responses during the pause.

Paraphrase:
Reflection:
Summarization:

Client 2, an elementary school student: That teacher
doesn't like me. She always picks on me. She
won't change. I just think she's dumb. I get mad
whenever she picks on me.
Clarification:
Paraphrase:
Reflection:
Summarization:

Client 3, a 50-year-old man: I hate to get up and go to
work anymore. I'm tired of the same old
routine. It's a big game. There isn't any value to
what I do. But it's my father-in-law's business
and it would create a big family scene if I
quit—he's too old now to handle the business
himself.
Clarification:
Paraphrase:
Reflection:
Summarization:

Part Four

This part of the evaluation gives you a chance to
demonstrate the four listening responses. Objective 4
asks you to conduct a 15-minute role-play interview
where you use at least two examples of the four listening responses. Your consultant can observe your
performance or you can assess yourself from an
audio-tape of the interview. Try to select a listening response to use when you have a specific
purpose in mind. Remember, in order to listen, it is
helpful to:
a. refrain from making judgments
b. resist distractions
c. avoid asking questions
d. avoid giving advice
e. stay focused on the client.

Part One

1. a. Reflection
   b. Clarification
2. a. Paraphrase
   b. Clarification
3. a. Reflection
   b. Paraphrase
4. a. Clarification
   b. Paraphrase
5. a. Summarization
   b. Paraphrase
6. a. Reflection
   b. Paraphrase

Part Two

Clarification.   c. confirm accuracy
Paraphrase.   b. focus on situation
Reflection.   a. identify client feelings
Summarization.   d. identify dominant theme

Part Three

Here are some examples of possible listening responses. See if yours are similar:

Client statement 1:
1. Clarification: "Are you saying you're under more pressure from the principal than yourself to keep order in your class?"
2. Paraphrase: "There seems to be a lot of pressure on you—from your principal and from yourself—to straighten things out in your classroom."
3. Reflection: "You feel *frustrated* about your classroom—and *torn* between what your principal wants and what you think may be best."
4. Summarization: "Your classroom is havoc and you're having a tough time with problem kids. At the same time, you're feeling pressure from your principal about keeping order. Even so you wonder at times how important an orderly classroom is."

Client statement 2:
1. Clarification: "Are you saying that you think your teacher picks on you because she doesn't like you?"
2. Paraphrase: "You're faced with a teacher who doesn't seem to like you and continually picks on you."
3. Reflection: "You feel *resentful* about being picked on by your teacher."
4. Summarization: "You've got this teacher who doesn't seem to like you. She picks on you and this makes you mad. Besides that, you don't think she'll ever change."

Client statement 3:
1. Clarification: "Do you mean that you feel it's up to you to carry on the family business?"
2. Paraphrase: "Your job doesn't have much appeal to you, but the rest of your family seems to have a lot of investment in it for you."
3. Reflection: "You really *dislike* your job but perhaps you also feel *obliged* to your family to continue with it."
4. Summarization: "Work has become a chore for you. It's lost its meaning. But you think since it's your father-in-law's business there would be a big family hassle if you quit."

Part Four

You or your consultant can determine when you use listening responses simply by marking down each time you demonstrate a clarification, a paraphrase, a reflection, and a summarization. Also, try to determine whether your responses are accurate or inaccurate according to the definitions for each type of response listed below:

Listening Response Definitions

To receive an *A* for accuracy
1. the *clarification*:
   a. is in the form of a question
   b. starts with "do you mean that . . ." or "are you saying that . . ."
   c. restates or rephrases the client's message
2. the *paraphrase*:
   a. is in the form of a statement
   b. rephrases the *content* part of the client's message
   c. rephrases or translates the client's message into the counselor's words
3. the *reflection*:
   a. is in the form of a statement

b. rephrases the *affective* part of the client's
      message
   c. translates the client's message into the
      counselor's words
4. the *summarization*:
   a. is a statement of at least two client messages
      or a theme that has been repeated during a
      5-minute or longer time period
   b. translates the client's messages into the
      counselor's words

Suggested Readings

Carkhuff, R. R., Pierce, R. M., & Cannon, J. R. *The art of helping III.* Amherst, Mass.: Human Resource Development Press, 1977.

Danish, S., & Hauer, A. *Helping skills: A basic training program.* New York: Behavioral Publications, 1973.

Hackney, H., & Cormier, L. S. *Counseling strategies and objectives* (2nd ed.). Englewood Cliffs, N.J.: Prentice-Hall, 1979.

Highlen, P. S., & Baccus, G. K. Effect of reflection of feeling and probe on client self-referenced affect. *Journal of Counseling Psychology,* 1977, 24, 440–443.

Ivey, A., & Gluckstern, N. *Basic attending skills: Participant manual.* Amherst, Mass.: Microtraining Associates, 1974.

Perez, J. *The initial counseling contact.* Boston: Houghton Mifflin, 1968.

Chapter 6
Action
Responses

Listening responses involve responding primarily to client messages from the client's point of view or frame of reference. There are times in the counseling process when it is legitimate to move beyond the client's frame of reference and to use responses that include more counselor-generated data and perceptions. These responses, which we have labeled *action responses*, are active rather than passive and reflect a counselor-directed more than a client-centered style. Action responses are based as much on the counselor's perceptions and hypotheses as on the client's messages and behavior. There are four such action responses: probe, ability-potential responses, confrontation, and interpretation. The general purpose of action responses, according to Egan (1975), is to help clients see the need for change and action through a more objective frame of reference (p. 228).

Objectives

1. With a written list of counselor responses, be able to identify accurately at least six out of eight examples of the four counselor action responses.
2. Using a written list, describe at least one intended purpose of each of the four action responses.

3. With a written list of three client statements, write an example of each of the four action responses for each client statement.
4. In a 20-minute role-play interview, demonstrate at least one accurate example of each of the four action responses. Also, use at least the first 5 minutes of the interview for listening responses.

Action Responses and Timing

The most difficult part of using action responses is the timing, the point at which these responses are used in the interview. As you recall from Chapter 5, some helpers tend to jump into action responses before listening and establishing rapport with the client. Listening responses generally reflect clients' understanding of themselves. In contrast, action responses reflect the *counselor's* understanding of the client. Action responses can be used a great deal in the interview as long as the counselor is careful to lay the foundation with attending and listening. The listening base can heighten the client's receptivity to a counselor action message. If the counselor "lays on" his or her opinions and perceptions too quickly, the client may respond with denial, defensiveness, or even with dropping out of counseling.

Four Action Responses

We have selected four action responses to describe in this chapter: the probe, ability-potential response, confrontation, and interpretation. A *probe* is an open-ended question beginning with "what," "how," "who," "when," or "where." An *ability-potential response* is a statement that points out or describes the client's current potential for doing something. A *confrontation* is a description of a client discrepancy or distortion. An *interpretation* is a possible explanation for the client's behavior.

Look at the way these four action responses differ in this illustration:

Client, a 35-year-old widow, mother of two young children: My whole life fell apart when my husband died. I keep feeling so unsure about my ability to make it on my own and to support my kids. My husband always made all the decisions for me. Now I haven't slept well for so long and I'm drinking more heavily—I can't even think straight. Besides, I've put on 15 pounds. I look like a witch. Who would even want to think of hiring me the way I am now?

Counselor probe: What makes you think of yourself as not being able to make it on your own?

or

How do you think you could handle the situation?

Counselor ability-potential response: I know it seems hard for you to think of yourself as being able to make the decisions, but you did take the initiative to come here. That indicates you have the capacity to make some decisions about your future.

Counselor confrontation: It seems that you're saying two things—first that you aren't sure of your ability to work and support your family, but also that you're almost making it hard for someone else to see you as employable by some of the things you're doing, such as drinking and putting on weight.

Counselor interpretation: It's possible that your drinking heavily and not sleeping well are ways to continue to avoid accepting the responsibility of making decisions for yourself.

Table 6-1 describes the definitions and intended purposes of these four action responses. Remember, these intended purposes are pre-sented only as tentative guidelines, not as "the truth." The remainder of the chapter will describe and present model examples of these four skills. You will have an opportunity to practice each skill and receive feedback about your responses.

Probes

A probe may be defined as an open-ended question beginning with "what," "how," "when," "where," or "who." It may be understood best when compared with a closed approach to interviewing. Closed questions start with "are you," "do you," "can you," and so forth. Consider the following example:

Open: *"What* can you tell me about your close relationships?"

Closed: *"Are* you married or single? *Do you* get along with your spouse?"

Who is to structure the interview is an important consideration in asking questions. Probes are centered around concerns of the *client* rather than around concerns of the counselor for the client (Ivey & Gluckstern, 1974, p. 17). By using closed questions, the counselor often leads the client to topics of interest only to the counselor. For instance, in the previous example, asking "Are you married or single?" could be interpreted as an indication of the counselor's vested interest in knowing whether the client is single or attached. The question also assumes that the client is either married or single; other life-styles are excluded. Sometimes questions dealing with age, religion, or marital status have discriminatory connotations. In answering the open-ended question "What can you tell me about your close relationships?" the client will decide what pertinent information to provide to the counselor. If you need to obtain factual information about the client's marital status, an example of a probe would be: "What is your present marital status?"

Open-ended questions provide room for clients to express themselves without the imposed categories and values of the counselor. An open question gives clients an opportunity to explore themselves with the counselor's sup-

Table 6-1. Definitions and Intended Purposes of Counselor Action Responses

Response	Definition	Intended Purpose
Probe	open-ended question beginning with what, how, when, where, or who	1. to begin an interview 2. to encourage client elaboration or to obtain information 3. to elicit specific examples of client's behaviors, feelings, or thoughts
Ability-potential response	statement that points out client's current potential for doing something	1. to encourage client who lacks initiative or self-confidence to do something 2. to expand client's awareness of personal strengths 3. to point out a potentially helpful client action
Confrontation	description of client discrepancy or distortion	1. to identify client's mixed or distorted messages 2. to explore other ways of perceiving client's self or situation
Interpretation	possible explanation of or association among various client behaviors	1. to identify the relationship between client's implicit messages and behaviors 2. to examine client behavior from alternative view or with different explanation 3. to add to client's self-understanding as a basis for client action

port. Also, a probe elicits much more information and elaboration from the client than a closed question. Closed questions usually can be answered in a few words or with a simple yes or no, and the client may give a minimal answer or only limited information. Open-ended questions often result in more elaboration by the client, perhaps because such questions usually prompt an answer (Hill & Gormally, 1977, p. 96).

Probes have a number of purposes in different counseling situations (Hackney & Cormier, 1979; Ivey & Gluckstern, 1974). Some of these are:

1. Beginning an interview. ("What would you like to discuss today?")
2. Encouraging the client to express more information. ("What else can you tell me about this?")
3. Asking for expressions of feeling from the client. ("What are you feeling as you're discussing this?")
4. Eliciting examples of specific behavior so that the counselor can understand better the conditions contributing to the client's problem. ("What are you doing in that situation? What are you thinking in that situation?")

As you will see in Chapter 10, probes are used as a major tool for obtaining information during the problem-identification process.

You might be wondering whether there is a reason we did not include "why" as a way to begin a probe. YES! Although there is nothing really wrong with asking "why," in our opinion it serves no useful purpose. You can obtain the same information by asking "what." For instance, if you want a client to notice that she or he is avoiding your question, "What are you doing now?" can be used instead of "Why are you avoiding my question?" Sometimes you may be inclined to ask a "why" question to have a client explain behavior or offer a reason for doing something. In most cases, the reason is either very obvious or so obscure that the client wouldn't be able to tell you. As an example, one counselor asked an overweight client in an initial interview session "Why are you heavy?" The client replied "Because I eat too much." The counselor followed this with "Why do you think you eat so much?" and the client laughed and said "Well, I like food." At this point, the counselor was stuck. The client had confirmed an obvious reason for eating a lot—a reason that was not irrational, since most folks do appreciate food. There are other reasons why the client was overweight, but these were too obscure for the client to identify in an initial session. "Why" questions also can make a client defensive. An occasional client may think that asking "why" is demanding an explanation or justification of behavior.

Learning Activity: Probe

Try out some probes of your own in this activity. An example is completed for you. Feedback is presented after the activity on p. 81.

Example

Client, a 15-year-old high school student: My grades have really slipped. I don't know why; I just feel so down about everything.
Counselor probe: *What* else do you think you feel down about?
or
How long have you been feeling this way?
or
When are some times you feel down?
or
Where are you when you feel most depressed?
or
Who are you with when you feel depressed?

Client Practice Statements

Client 1, a fourth-grader: I don't want to do this dumb homework anyway. I don't care about learning these math problems. Girls don't need to know this anyway.

Client 2, a middle-aged man: I'm really discouraged with this physical disability now. I feel like I can't do anything the way I used to. Not only has it affected me in my job, but at home. I just don't feel like I have anything good to offer anyone.
Client 3, an older person: The company is going to make me retire even though I don't want to. What will I do with myself then? I find myself just thinking over the good times of the past, not wanting to face the future at all. Sometimes retirement makes me so nervous I can't sleep or eat. My family suggested I see someone about this.

Ability-Potential Responses

In an ability-potential response, "the counselor points out and refers to the client's current potential for entering into a defined activity" (Zimmer & Pepyne, 1971, p. 442). An ability-potential response is a supportive response in which the counselor recognizes verbally the client's potential or capability for doing something. Ability-potential responses are similar to what Kanfer and Phillips (1969) describe as "instigation therapy," the "systematic use of daily suggestions and assigned tasks in the patient's daily environment" (p. 452). There are three intended purposes of an ability-potential response. First, it may be used to encourage a client who wants to do something but lacks the initiative, drive, or self-confidence to begin. Second, the ability-potential response can expand the client's awareness of personal strengths or positive qualities. Third, from the counselor's point of view, the ability-potential response may point out an action the counselor determines would be helpful, even though the client has not considered such an action. Usually a client will perceive an ability-potential response as "stroking" and will feel encouraged or reinforced by it. However, an occasional client may have difficulty accepting the intent of the statement, particularly if the client tends to discount positive feedback. A counselor should be careful in such instances not to push the client to accept or to agree with the response.

Here are some examples of ability-potential responses:

1. As encouragement for an older woman who has been staying at home for 20 years and is uneasy about trying out new options, an ability-potential response could be: "You've been very successful in your home and child-rearing tasks. These are successes you can build on to explore some new options."
2. As a description of overlooked strengths for a client who is unaware of his or her ability to communicate in an articulate manner, an ability-potential response might be: "You seem to do very well in communication with others. I've noticed how articulate you are in our conversations."
3. As a description of a possible action a student could take to resolve a difficulty in class, an ability-potential response could be: "You say it's important to you to do well in Mrs. Jones's class. I believe you can use your determination about this to help—possibly first by talking to her and finding out what you need to do to work things out."

Cautions to Consider. There are several times when an ability-potential response may not be helpful or appropriate. First, keep in mind that such a response is used to encourage clients to consider their potential. However, it is not intended to counter a client's *frequent* self-defeating comments. For instance, if a client continually says "I'm really not very good with people," an ability-potential response of "You're really OK—I know things you do very well with people" may only reinforce this client's tendency to make self-deprecating statements. Before using the ability-potential response, the counselor needs to discriminate whether this response will reinforce the client's action-seeking behavior or the client's feelings of inadequacy. If a counselor uses an ability-potential response and discovers that the client's self-defeating comments still recur frequently, this would be an additional cue that the response is not having the intended effect. At this point, the counselor would probably refrain from using an additional ability-potential response in order to avoid further reinforcement

---

of the client's negative self-statements.

Second, describing the client's potential implies that the counselor in some way can or does evaluate the client's potential or skills. Therefore, such responses should be used only when the counselor has some basis for recognizing the client's capacity to pursue a desired action or activity. It would be a mistake to use the ability-potential response only to raise false hopes or to offer insincere reinforcement or encouragement.

Finally, the counselor should not use an ability-potential response simply as a pep talk or a band-aid to smooth over or discount the client's real feelings of discouragement. Probably these feelings first should be reflected and clarified. The counselor should reserve the use of the ability-potential response for times when the client has indicated a readiness for action but is hesitant to jump in "head first" without some prior encouragement.

After reading the example of an ability-potential response, try out your own responses to the three client practice statements. Feedback is provided after the activity on p. 83.

Example

Client, a 15-year-old high school student: My grades have really slipped. I don't know why; I just feel so down about everything.

Counselor ability-potential response: You realize that you are capable of pulling your grades up if you want to—and if your other feelings become less interfering.

This response attempts to provide encouragement to the client about the grade difficulty.

Client Practice Statements

Client 1, a fourth-grader: I don't want to do this dumb homework anyway. I don't care about learning these math problems. Girls don't need to know this anyway.

Your ability-potential response might suggest potential action the client could consider.

Client 2, a middle-aged man: I'm really discouraged with this physical disability now. I feel like I can't do anything the way I used to. Not only has it affected me in my job, but at home. I just don't feel like I have anything good to offer anyone.

Your ability-potential response might focus on the client's personal strengths.

Client 3, an older person: The company is going to make me retire even though I don't want to. What will I do with myself then? I find myself just thinking over the good times of the past, not wanting to face the future at all. Sometimes retirement makes me so nervous I can't sleep or eat. My family suggested I see someone about this.

Your ability-potential response might focus on the client's strengths.

Confrontation

A confrontation is a verbal response in which the counselor describes some discrepancy or distortion apparent in the client's message and behavior. Egan (1975) describes confrontation as "a responsible unmasking of the discrepancies, distortions, games, and smoke screens the client uses to hide both from self-understanding and from constructive behavioral change" (p. 158).* Frequently clients exhibit inconsistent or mixed messages in an interview. In many cases, the client is unaware of the mixed message and does not realize the conflict he or she is experiencing. One purpose of a confrontation is to point out the discrepancy and to help the client explore each part of the mixed message. At other times, the client may present distorted behavior or messages. The client who does not want to face up to something may distort her or his view of it. To the client, this distortion represents reality. To an outsider with different needs and experiences, less distorted views are possible. A counselor can confront the client with the distortion. In this case, the purpose of the confrontation is to help the client become more aware of the distortion and to explore other ways of perceiving the situation. The confrontation goes beyond what the client has said and introduces the counselor's point of view. However, such a confrontation should be based on facts, not opinions.

Confrontation for a Distorted Message. The counselor can confront a client's distorted perceptions by (1) describing them *and* (2) indicating one or more alternative ways the client might see himself or herself or the situation. For example, a mother who does not want to face the fact that her only son, who has joined a commune, didn't live up to her expectations may say her son is "mentally ill." Perceiving her son as sick is easier for her than realizing he did something she didn't expect or want of him. The

*This and all other quotations from this source are from *The Skilled Helper: A Model for Systematic Helping and Interpersonal Relations*, by G. Egan. Copyright © 1975 by Wadsworth, Inc. Reprinted by permission of the publisher, Brooks/Cole Publishing Company, Monterey, California.

counselor can use a confrontation to present another way for the mother to view the situation: "You see your son as a sick person because he joined a commune [description of client's present perceptions], yet it could be that his behavior is a sign of independence and growth on his part [alternative perception]." In this confrontation, the counselor is describing the mother's view of her son and also is pointing out a possible alternative way of seeing the situation—or, in this case, her son. As another example, a client who has difficulty accepting himself may conclude that none of his peers like him or that all his peers reject him. It may be hard for this client to see that, because of his own behavior, he rejects and avoids his peers. A counselor could confront this client's perception of the situation by saying something like: "You believe that none of your classmates like you and that none of them want anything to do with you [client's present perception], yet you've said you go out of your way to avoid them. Perhaps by doing so you are in fact rejecting them [alternative perception]."

In addition to pointing out client distortions, the counselor can confront apparent or stated inconsistencies in the client's behavior. These inconsistencies may be referred to as "mixed messages."

Confrontation for Mixed Messages. There are many instances within an interview in which a client says or does something that is inconsistent. For example, a client may say she doesn't want to talk to you because you are a male but then goes ahead and talks to you. In this case, the client's verbal message is inconsistent with her actual behavior. This is an example of an inconsistent or mixed message. The purpose of using a confrontation to deal with a mixed message is to describe the discrepancy or contradiction to the client. In many cases, the client is only vaguely aware of the conflict before the counselor points it out. In describing the discrepancy, it is often most helpful to use a confrontation that presents *both* parts of the discrepancy. As presented in the examples that follow, counselor confrontations are clearer when the confrontation includes the "you

---

Feedback: Ability-Potential Responses

For client statement 1: "Perhaps you could learn the math problems more easily if you decided it was important to you."

This ability-potential response refers to the student's potential capacity to learn math.

For client statement 2: "Although you feel discouraged with your disability, you still have all the personal qualities you had before the accident."

This ability-potential response focuses on the client's abilities and yet acknowledges the client's feelings of discouragement.

Client statement 3: "You're presently having a tough time thinking about retirement, but all the skills you have now you'll still have to pursue things after retirement."

This ability-potential response points out that the client's present capabilities will still exist and can be used after retirement.

---

said—but look" conditions of the mixed message (Hackney & Cormier, 1979) or "On the one hand, this is happening; on the other hand, there is this."

Four major types of mixed messages and accompanying descriptions of counselor confrontations are presented as examples:

1. *Verbal and Nonverbal Behavior:*
   a. The client says "I feel comfortable" (verbal message) and at the same time is fidgeting and twisting his or her hands (nonverbal message).
   Counselor confrontation: You say you feel comfortable, but you're also fidgeting and twisting your hands.
   b. The client says "I feel happy about the relationship being over—it's better this way" (verbal message) and is talking in a slow, low-pitched, unemotional voice (nonverbal message).
   Counselor confrontation: You say you're happy it's over, but from the way your

voice sounded as you talked I wonder if you have some other feelings, too.

2. *Verbal Messages and Action Steps or Behaviors:*
   a. The client says "I'm going to call her" (verbal message) but reports the next week that he or she did not make the call (action step).
   Counselor confrontation: You said you would call her, but as of now you haven't done so.
   b. The client says "Counseling is very important to me" (verbal message) but calls off the next two sessions (behavior).
   Counselor confrontation: Several weeks ago you said how important counseling is to you, yet I'm aware that you called off our last two meetings.

3. *Two Verbal Messages* (Stated Inconsistencies):
   a. The client says "He's sleeping around with other people, too. I don't feel bothered [verbal message 1], but I think our relationship should mean more to him than it does [verbal message 2]."
   Counselor confrontation: First you say his behavior is OK with you, but now you're saying it also bugs you that your relationship is not as important to him as it is to you.
   b. The client says "I really do love little Georgie [verbal message 1], although he often bugs the hell out of me [verbal message 2]."
   Counselor confrontation: You seem to be aware that much of the time you love him, and yet at other times you feel very irritated toward him, too.

4. *Two Nonverbal Messages* (Apparent Inconsistencies):
   a. Client is smiling (nonverbal message 1) and crying (nonverbal message 2) at the same time.
   Counselor confrontation: You're smiling and also crying at the same time.
   b. Client is looking directly at counselor (nonverbal message 1) and has just moved chair back from counselor (nonverbal message 2).
   Counselor confrontation: You're looking at me while you say this, yet you also just moved away.

Effects. Most helping professionals agree that the general purpose of confrontation is to help the client engage in self-awareness and self-exploration, but the research support for the effects of confrontation on self-exploration is not conclusive. A study by Kaul, Kaul, and Bednar (1973) does not support a generalized notion that confrontation always leads to increased client self-exploration. These authors suggest that the relationship is complicated, difficult to measure, and may vary with different clients. Carkhuff (1972) states that an effective confrontation should result in additional information. However, the effects of confrontation, like the effects of any other counselor response, will vary with each counselor-client interaction.

Ground Rules. Because confrontation can have very powerful effects, counselors should use this response cautiously, with a few ground rules in mind. First, getting the client to examine motives and perceptions can be accomplished best by a confrontation that is a *description* instead of a judgment or evaluation of the client's message and behavior. A confrontation can result in a defensive client reaction when the counselor judges or coerces the client to change. Egan (1975) concludes that a confrontation viewed as an attack "for the client's own good" serves no useful purpose in a helping relationship (p. 157). He suggests that, in using the confrontation, "the motive of the counselor should be to help the client, not to be right, not to punish, to get back at the client, or to put him in his place" (p. 166).

In describing the distortion or discrepancy, the confrontation should cite a *specific example* of the behavior rather than make a vague inference. A poor confrontation might be: "You want people to like you but your personality turns them off." In this case, the counselor is making a general inference about the client's personality and also is implying that the client must undergo a major "overhaul" in order to get along with others. A more helpful confrontation would be: "You want people to like you, but your frequent remarks about yourself seem to get in the way and turn people off."

Also, before a counselor attempts to confront a client, rapport and trust should be established. Johnson (1972) states that confrontation probably should not be used unless you, the counselor, are willing to maintain or increase your involvement in or commitment to the counseling relationship. Some counselors, regardless of the status of the counseling relationship, may sprinkle their counseling style with liberal doses of critical, negative messages. Egan (1975) suggests that someone who specializes in confrontation may be a destructive person who isn't too adept at her or his chosen specialty (p. 171). At the other extreme, some counselors may be so uncomfortable with anything other than positive communication or "good news" that they totally avoid using confrontation even with long-term clients. The primary consideration is to judge what your level of involvement seems to be with each client and adapt accordingly. The stronger the relationship, the more receptive the client may be to a confrontation.

The *timing* of a confrontation is very important. Since the purpose is to help the person engage in self-examination, try to offer the confrontation at a time when the client is likely to use it. The perceived ability of the client to act upon the confrontation should be a major guideline in deciding when to confront (Johnson, 1972, p. 160). In other words, before you jump in and confront, determine the person's attention level, anxiety level, desire to change, and ability to listen.

It is also a good idea not to overload the client with confrontations that make heavy demands in a short time. The rule of "successive approximations" suggests that people learn small steps of behaviors gradually more easily than trying to make big changes overnight. Initially, you may want to confront the person with something that can be managed fairly easily and with some success. Carkhuff (1972) suggests that two successive confrontations may be too intense and should be avoided.

Client Reactions. Sometimes counselors are afraid to confront because they are uncertain how to handle the client's reactions to the confrontation. Even clients who hear and acknowledge the confrontation may be anxious or upset about the implications. Generally, a counselor can expect four different types of client reaction to a confrontation: denial, confusion, false acceptance, or genuine acceptance.

In a denial of the confrontation, the client does not want to acknowledge or agree to the counselor's message. A denial may indicate that the client is not ready or tolerant enough to face the discrepant or distorted behavior. Egan (1975) lists some specific ways the client might deny the confrontation:

1. discredit the counselor (for example, "How do you know when you don't even have kids?"),
2. persuade the counselor that his or her views are wrong or misinterpreted ("I didn't mean it that way"),
3. devaluate the importance of the topic ("This isn't worth all this time anyway"),
4. seek support elsewhere ("I told my friends about your comment last week and none of them had ever noticed that") [pp. 169–170].

At other times, the client may indicate confusion or uncertainty about the meaning of the confrontation. In some cases, the client may be genuinely confused about what the counselor is saying. This may indicate that your confrontation was not concise and specific. At other times, the client may use a lack of understanding as a smokescreen—that is, as a way to avoid dealing with the impact of the confrontation.

Sometimes the client may seem to accept the confrontation. Acceptance usually is genuine if the client responds with a sincere desire to examine her or his behavior. Eventually such clients may be able to catch their own discrepancies and confront themselves. But Egan (1975) cautions that false acceptance also can occur, which is another client game. In this case, the client verbally agrees with the counselor. However, instead of pursuing the con-

Action Responses

frontation, the client agrees only to get the counselor to leave well enough alone.

There is no "set" way of dealing with client reactions to confrontation. However, a general rule of thumb is to go back to the client-oriented listening responses of paraphrase and reflection. A counselor can use these responses to lay the foundation before the confrontation and return to this foundation after the confrontation. The sequence might go something like this:

Counselor: You seem to feel concerned about your parents' divorce [reflection].
Client: Actually, I feel pretty happy—I'm glad for their sake they got a divorce (said with low, sad voice) [mixed message].
Counselor: You say you're happy, yet the way your voice sounds you seem unhappy [confrontation].
Client: I don't know what you're talking about, really [denial].
Counselor: I sense that what I just said has upset you [reflection].

Learning Activity: Confrontation

Read the following example of a confrontation. Then respond with your own confrontation responses to the three client practice statements. Feedback follows the activity on p. 87.

Example

Client, a 15-year-old high school student: My grades have really slipped. I don't know why; I just feel so down about everything.
Counselor confrontation: You've indicated you don't know why your grades have slipped, but you also have suggested that one reason has to do with your feeling so down about things.
or
You say you have no idea as to why your grades have slipped, but you seem to see this as a result of feeling so down about things in general.

Here the counselor is describing two inconsistent verbal messages: one is that the client doesn't know why the grades have slipped; the other is an indication that the client has a reason in mind.

Client Practice Statements

Client 1, a fourth-grader: I don't want to do this dumb homework anyway. I don't care about learning these math problems. Girls don't need to know this anyway.
Client 2, a middle-aged man, smiling: I'm really discouraged with this physical disability now. I feel like I can't do anything the way I used to. Not only has it affected me in my job, but at home. I just don't feel like I have anything good to offer anyone.
Client 3, an older person: The company is going to make me retire even though I don't want to. What will I do with myself then? I find myself just thinking over the good times of the past, not wanting to face the future at all. Sometimes retirement makes me so nervous I can't sleep or eat. My family suggested I see someone about this.

Interpretation

Interpretation is a skill that involves understanding and communicating the meaning of a client's messages. In making interpretive statements, the counselor provides clients with a fresh look at themselves or with another explanation for their attitudes or behaviors (Ivey & Gluckstern, 1976). According to Brammer and Shostrom (1968), interpretation involves "presenting the client with an *hypothesis* about *relationships* or *meanings* of attitude behaviors for the client's consideration" (p. 268). Interpretive responses can be defined in a variety of ways (Brammer & Shostrom, 1968; Ivey & Gluckstern, 1976; Levy, 1963). An interpretation may vary to some degree according to your own theoretical orientation and frame of reference because, in part, it is a process of *imposing meaning* on events" (Brammer & Shostrom, 1968, p. 241).

We define an interpretation as a counselor statement that makes an association among various client behaviors or presents a possible explanation of a client's behavior (including the client's feelings or affect, thoughts or cognitions, and observable actions). An interpretation differs from the listening responses (paraphrase, clarification, reflection, summarization) in that it deals with the *implicit* part of a message—the part the client does not talk about explicitly or directly. As Brammer and Shostrom (1968) note, when interpreting, a counselor will often verbalize "material which the client may have felt only vaguely" (p. 279). Our concept of interpretation is similar to what Egan (1975) refers to as "advanced accurate empathy," which is a tool to help the client "move from the less to the more." In other words, "if the client is not clear about some issue, or if he speaks guardedly, then the helper speaks directly, clearly, and openly" (p. 147).

A major purpose of interpretation is to identify relationships between clients' explicit and implicit messages and behaviors. Another purpose of interpretation is to help clients examine their behavior from a different reference point or with a different explanation. A third purpose is to add to client self-understanding or insight when the counselor believes such insight will help clients achieve desired changes.

Here are several examples that may help you understand the nature of the interpretation response more clearly:

Client 1, a young woman: Everything is humdrum. There's nothing new going on, nothing exciting. All my friends are away. I wish I had some money to do something different.
Counselor interpretation: It seems as if you need friends or money to make your life enjoyable.

or

It's hard for you to find personal satisfaction in your life without friends or money to help you out.

or

I wonder whether you feel that other people are more responsible than yourself for making your own life enjoyable?

In this example, the counselor uses interpretation to point out that the client is more dependent on things or other people than on herself for making her life meaningful. In other words, the counselor is describing a possible association or relationship between the client's explicit feel-

ings of being bored and the client's implicit behavior of depending on others to alleviate the boredom. The counselor hopes that this explanation will give the client an increased understanding of herself that she can use to create meaning and enjoyment in her life.

Here is another example:

Client, a middle-aged man: I just don't like to work with some of the other sales personnel. They don't take their job as seriously as I do—it's hard for me to work with people who do just enough work to get by.

Counselor interpretation: Perhaps you're saying that you have trouble getting along with people who don't live up to your expectations.

or

Do you suppose that you have a tendency to impose your own work standards on other people?

or

It's possible that getting down on your co-workers for their lower standards is one way you use to feel good about yourself.

In this example, the wording and intent of all three interpretations vary slightly; one is just as right as the others. In all three responses, the counselor attempted to point out some relationship between the client's expectations of himself and of others. Again, such an interpretation should be used to help the client make the desired changes in himself or in his work situation. The particular wording and thrust of an interpretation will depend on the timing, the client, and the context in which the interpretation is offered.

Effects. Generally, an interpretation encourages the client to engage in greater self-understanding. Auerswald (1974) reported that, in a low-structured initial counselinglike interview, the use of interpretation significantly increased the proportion of client self-referenced affective statements. However, at least one study found that client levels of self-exploration decreased following interpretive statements by the counselor (Bergman, 1951). Brammer and Shostrom (1968) observe that the ultimate test of an effective interpretation is whether "it facilitates behavior change in the desired direction" (p. 268). Like the confrontation response, an interpretation can appear to be "strong stuff" to

the client. The effects of interpretation may vary among clients, depending on their readiness to deal with implicit messages and on their motivation to change. The counselor may facilitate the positive effects of interpretation by using the response cautiously and by keeping some basic ground rules in mind.

Ground Rules. An interpretation may be the one counselor activity that helps a client to face rather than defend or avoid a conflict or problem. However, the potential contribution of an interpretation depends somewhat on the counselor's ability to use such responses effectively and at advantageous times. There are several ground rules to consider in deciding to use interpretation. First, be careful about timing. The client should demonstrate some degree of readiness to explore or examine himself or herself before you use an interpretation. Generally, an interpretation response is reserved for later rather than initial sessions, since some data must be gathered as a basis for an interpretive response. Also, the typical client requires several sessions to become accustomed to the type of material discussed in counseling. The client's receptiveness to your interpretation may be greater if she or he is not ill at ease with the topics being explored and shows some readiness to accept the interpretive response. As Brammer and Shostrom (1968) note, a counselor usually does not engage in interpreting until the client has gained some awareness and understanding of the subject of the intended interpretation (p. 285).

Timing of an interpretation within a session is also important. Generally, an interpretation is more helpful in the initial or middle phases of an interview, so that the counselor and client have sufficient time to work through the client's reaction. If the counselor suspects that the interpretation may produce anxiety or resistance, it may be a good idea to postpone it until the beginning of the next session. Generally, the greatest problem in timing is the danger of interpreting something that is too painful or difficult for the client to face at that time (Brammer & Shostrom, 1968, p. 286). As Helner and Jessell (1974) observe, in using interpretation, a counselor "should realize that he is running the risk of placing the counselee in a defensive position to the extent that he may become angry and resistant so as to either jeopardize the counseling process or result in premature termination" (p. 480).

A second ground rule is to make sure your interpretation is based on the client's actual message rather than your own biases and values projected onto the client. This requires that you be aware of your own blind spots. As an example, if you have had a bad experience with marriage and are biased against people getting or staying married, be aware of how this could affect the way you interpret client statements about marriage. If you aren't careful with your values, you could easily advise all marital-counseling clients away from marriage, which might not be in the best interests of some of them. As Ivey and Gluckstern (1976) state, "psychological imperialism" must be avoided—especially in the use of an interpretation (p. 135). Try to be aware of whether you are interpreting to present helpful data to the client or only to show off your expertise. Make sure that your interpretation is based on sufficient data.

A third ground rule in using interpretation effectively concerns the way in which the counselor phrases and offers the statement to the client. An interpretation should be offered tentatively. The counselor can say something like "I wonder if," "it's possible that," "perhaps," or "maybe" to avoid presenting the interpretation in an absolute manner. Following an interpretation, check out the accuracy of your interpretive response by asking the client whether your message fits. Returning to a clarification is always a useful way to determine whether you have interpreted the message accurately.

Client Reactions. There are many ways clients may react to an interpretation, ranging from acceptance to strong protest. The client who genuinely accepts and learns from the interpretation usually indicates so by some cue, such as a recognition sign or an elaboration. The counselor should be alert to those occasional clients whose acceptance seems more passive and may simply be an attempt to please the counselor. Another client may reject or protest the interpretation—signaled by an attack on the statement, withdrawal, or avoidance (Helner & Jessell, 1974). It is difficult to know whether the protest means that the interpretation is off base or that it is so close to home that the client protests its validity. Often a counselor can respond to a protest initially by reflecting the client's feelings and, at a later time, reiterating the interpretation with more data—provided the counselor feels it is still valid. However, Brammer and Shostrom (1968) caution against blindly repeating an interpretive response without carefully reexamining the content and the nature of the supporting evidence.

Learning Activity: Interpretation

Read the example and then respond to the three client practice statements with your own interpretations. Feedback follows the activity on p. 90.

Example

Client, a 15-year-old high school student: My grades have really slipped. I don't know why; I just feel so down about everything.
1. Counselor interpretation: Your feelings of being down are affecting the way you're performing.
   This interpretation makes an association between the client's feelings and behavior.
2. Counselor interpretation: It seems like you're ready to give up. I wonder if it would be easier to do that than to try to work things out.
   This interpretation presents a possible explanation for the client's behavior.

Client Practice Statements

Client 1, a fourth-grader: I don't want to do this dumb homework anyway. I don't care about learning these math problems. Girls don't need to know this anyway.
Client 2, a middle-aged man: I'm really discouraged with this physical disability now. I feel like I

can't do anything the way I used to. Not only has it affected me in my job, but at home. I just don't feel like I have anything good to offer anyone.

Client 3, an older person: The company is going to make me retire even though I don't want to. What will I do with myself then? I find myself just thinking over the good times of the past, not wanting to face the future at all. Sometimes retirement makes me so nervous I can't sleep or eat. My family suggested I see someone about this.

Summary

Listening responses reflect clients' perceptions of their world. Action responses provide alternative ways for clients to view themselves and their world. A change in the client's way of viewing and explaining things may be one indication of positive movement in counseling. According to Egan (1975), counselor statements that move beyond the client's frame of reference are a "bridge" between listening responses and specific change programs (p. 132). To be used effectively, action responses require a great deal of counselor concern and judgment. In an actual interview, these responses must be used flexibly, sensitively, and in the context of a client's nonverbal cues as well as verbal messages.

Post Evaluation

Part One

Using the following written statements for completion of Objective 1, you should be able to identify at least six out of eight counselor action responses. The first one is completed as an example. Feedback is provided after the evaluation.

1. Client: Sometimes I feel like I'm going to flunk out.

   #### Example Counselor Response
   a. "When do you usually feel this way?" (This type of response is probe.)
   b. "You do have the capacity to make good grades if you choose to do this." (What type of response is this?)

2. Client: I don't think I can make our next appointment because I want to go in town shopping that day.
   a. "You're saying that shopping is important for you to do next week, but you also seem to regard counseling as necessary for you, too."
   b. "How do you see that shopping would benefit you more than our session?"
3. Client: I think all men are interested in is power.
   a. "You seem to be talking about all men on the basis of your experiences with a few men. I'm wondering if your experiences really mean that all men are like the ones you've encountered."
   b. "What has happened to make you think this?"
4. Client: I don't want my husband to make demands on me. I want to make my own decisions.
   a. "You do have the potential to make your own decisions with or without your husband's demands."
   b. "I wonder—if your husband didn't make demands, would you be any more likely to be independent?"

Part Two

To test yourself on Objective 2, use the list of purposes of action responses to select one intended purpose for each action response. Feedback can be found at the end of the evaluation.
a. to point out a potentially helpful action the client could take
b. to begin an interview
c. to identify a client's distorted message
d. to identify the relationship between the client's explicit and implicit messages and behaviors

Action Responses

Probe:
Ability-potential response:
Confrontation:
Interpretation:

Part Three

For each of the following client statements, Objective 3 asks you to verbalize or write an example of each of the four action responses.* The first one is completed for you. Feedback follows the evaluation.

*These client messages can be put on audio tape so you can verbalize or write your responses after hearing the client statement.

Client 1, a beginning teacher: My classroom is a mess. I can't handle those problem kids. My principal is breathing down my neck to keep more order and I'm not even sure how important order is.

Example Counselor Response

> Probe: *"What are your feelings now about this situation?"*
> Ability-potential response:
> Confrontation:
> Interpretation:

Client 2, an elementary school student: That teacher doesn't like me. She always picks on me. She won't change. I just think she's dumb. I get mad whenever she picks on me.
Probe:
Ability-potential response:
Confrontation:
Interpretation:

Client 3, a 50-year-old man: I hate to get up and go to work anymore. I'm tired of the same old routine. It's a big game. There isn't any value to what I do. But it's my father-in-law's business and it would create a big family scene if I quit—he's too old now to handle the business himself.
Probe:
Ability-potential response:
Confrontation:
Interpretation:

Part Four

Conduct a 20-minute role-play interview. After using listening responses for the first 5 or 10 minutes, demonstrate at least one accurate example of each of the four action responses. You or your consultant can assess your performance live or with an audio tape.

Feedback: Interpretation

For client statement 1: "Could it be that you're using the fact you're a girl as one good reason to quit math?"

In this interpretation, the counselor points out a possible explanation for the student's desire not to learn math.

For client statement 2: "I wonder if you're allowing your disability to interfere with your ability to cope."
This interpretation makes an association between the client's disability and resulting feelings and behaviors.

or

"Is it possible that your disability has become an excuse for withdrawing?"
This interpretation offers a possible explanation of the client's withdrawal.

For client statement 3: "It seems that living in the past is safer and more secure for you than facing the future."

This interpretation offers a possible explanation for the client's present anxiety about retirement.

Feedback: Post Evaluation

Part One

1. a. Probe
   b. Ability-potential response
2. a. Confrontation
   b. Probe
3. a. Confrontation
   b. Probe
4. a. Ability-potential response
   b. Interpretation

Part Two

Probe. b. begin an interview
Ability-potential response. a. point out helpful action
Confrontation. c. identify distorted message
Interpretation. d. identify relationship between explicit and implicit messages and behaviors

Part Three

Some possible action responses for client statement 1:

> Probe: "What do you value most for your class?"
>
> > or
> >
> > "How do you think having order helps?"
> >
> > or
> >
> > "When do you feel most pressured to keep order?"
>
> Ability-potential response: "You seem to have enough strength to decide for yourself how you want your classroom to be."
>
> Confrontation: "You're saying on the one hand that your class is a mess, but on the other hand you're indicating that classroom order isn't of that much value to you."
>
> Interpretation: "Perhaps it's harder to accept your principal's request for control when you don't feel in control yourself."

Possible action responses for client statement 2 are:

> Probe: "What do you do that your teacher doesn't like?"
>
> > or
> >
> > "How else does your teacher act around you?"
> >
> > or
> >
> > "When are some other times you think your teacher doesn't like you?"
>
> Ability-potential response: "Maybe there is something you could do to make this class better for you."
>
> Confrontation: "You seem to have your mind made up that your teacher has it in for you, but do you think there are things you do in class that upset her?"
>
> Interpretation: "Is it easier to believe your teacher picks on you because she doesn't like you than to think of anything you do that might irritate her?"

For client statement 3:

> Probe: "What would you really like to be doing?"

> > or
> >
> > "How do you think your work helps *you*?"
> >
> > or
> >
> > "When does your work bother you most?"
>
> Ability-potential response: "You do seem to recognize there are some other kinds of work you could do."
>
> Confrontation: "You're saying that you're really bored with your work, but also that you're reluctant to quit because of being hassled for doing so."
>
> Interpretation: "There are a lot of risks in quitting this business. I wonder whether you use your family's attitude as a source of support for not taking these risks."

Part Four

You or your consultant can determine when you use the action responses by marking down each time you demonstrate a probe, an ability-potential response, a confrontation, and an interpretation. Try to determine whether your responses are accurate or inaccurate according to the definitions for each type of response listed below:

Action Response Definitions

To receive an *A* for accuracy:

1. The *probe* must be a question that begins with "what," "how," "when," "where," or "who."
2. The *ability-potential response* must be a statement identifying (a) the client's strength or positive potential (b) for doing something or taking some action.
3. The *confrontation* may be (a) a descriptive statement of a client contradiction or mixed message, or (b) an identification of an alternative way of viewing or perceiving something the client distorts.
4. The *interpretation* should describe an association among various client behaviors, or provide a possible explanation for the client's behaviors.

Suggested Readings

Probes

Hill, C. E., & Gormally, J. Effects of reflection, restatement, probe, and nonverbal behaviors on client affect. *Journal of Counseling Psychology*, 1977, 24, 92–97.

Ivey, A., & Gluckstern, N. *Basic attending skills: Participant manual*. Amherst, Mass.: Microtraining Associates, 1974. Session II, Open invitation to talk, 16–23.

Ability-Potential Responses

Hackney, H., & Cormier, L. S. *Counseling strategies and objectives*. (2nd ed.). Englewood Cliffs, N.J.: Prentice-Hall, 1979. Chap. 10, Discrimination between cognitive and affective communications.

Kanfer, F. H., & Phillips, J. S. A survey of current behavior therapies and a proposal for classification. In C. M. Franks (Ed.), *Behavior therapy: Appraisal and status*. New York: McGraw-Hill, 1969.

Confrontation

Berenson, B. G., & Mitchell, K. M. *Confrontation: For better or worse*. Amherst, Mass.: Human Resource Development Press, 1974.

Egan, G. *The skilled helper: A model for systematic helping and interpersonal relating*. Monterey, Calif.: Brooks/Cole, 1975. Confrontation, 156–172.

Johnson, D. *Reaching out: Interpersonal effectiveness and self-actualization*. Englewood Cliffs, N.J.: Prentice-Hall, 1972. Chap. 9, Constructive confrontation, 159–170.

Interpretation

Auerswald, M. C. Differential reinforcing power of restatement and interpretation on client production of affect. *Journal of Counseling Psychology*, 1974, 21, 9–14.

Brammer, L. M., & Shostrom, E. *Therapeutic psychology: Fundamentals of actualization counseling and psychotherapy*. Englewood Cliffs, N.J.: Prentice-Hall, 1968. Chap. 9, Interpretation techniques, 267–297.

Egan, G. *The skilled helper: A model for systematic helping and interpersonal relating*. Monterey, Calif.: Brooks/Cole, 1975. Advanced accurate empathy, 134–150.

Helner, P. A., & Jessell, J. Effects of interpretation as a counseling technique. *Journal of Counseling Psychology*, 1974, 21, 475–481.

Ivey, A., & Gluckstern, N. *Basic influencing skills: Participant manual*. Amherst, Mass.: Microtraining Associates, 1976. Workshop 6, Interpretation, 106–139.

Levy, L. H. *Psychological interpretation*. New York: Holt, Rinehart & Winston, 1963.

Chapter 7
Sharing and Teaching Responses

Recent directions in counseling have suggested two predominant types of counselor responses in addition to the listening and action responses presented in the last two chapters. One direction emphasizes the mutuality of the counseling relationship. Counselors can contribute to mutual communication by using responses that reveal something about themselves as people—about their experiences, thoughts, feelings, or beliefs. We call such self-revelation "sharing" responses. These responses also are referred to as "you-me" talk (Egan, 1975, p. 178) or as "direct mutual communication" (Ivey & Gluckstern, 1976, p. 140). The sharing responses presented in this chapter include self-disclosure and immediacy.

In addition to the skills of self-expression, the tools of influencing, structuring, and directing are becoming a more accepted part of a helper's repertory. Because counseling is a learning process, we have included a section on verbal responses that can be used explicitly to influence and to inform. These "teaching" responses include instructions, verbal setting operations, and information-giving.

Objectives

After completing this chapter, here are the things you should be able to do:

1. From a written list, identify at least eight out of ten examples of counselor sharing responses and teaching responses.
2. Using a written list, select one intended purpose of each counselor sharing and teaching response.
3. Using written counseling situations, write two accurate examples of counselor sharing responses and two accurate examples of counselor teaching responses.
4. Conduct at least one 15-minute role-play interview in which you integrate your style (Chapter 2), nonverbal behaviors (Chapter 3), the listening responses (Chapter 5), the action responses (Chapter 6), and the sharing and teaching responses of this chapter. You can analyze your responses using the Interview Inventory at the end of the chapter.

Sharing Responses

Counselors use two skills that involve more sharing or giving than many other responses. We call these responses *self-disclosure* and *immediacy* (see Table 7-1). Both involve counselor self-expression and usually contain content that refers to the counselor, the client, or emotions of either counselor or client (Crowley & Ivey, 1976). The use of sharing responses may lend some mutuality to the helping process, enabling the client to see the counselor as an active human being who also has legitimate feel-

Table 7-1. Definitions and Intended Purposes of Counselor Sharing Responses

Response	Definition	Intended Purpose
Self-disclosure	counselor verbal sharing of information about himself or herself	1. to provide open, facilitative counseling atmosphere 2. to increase clients' perceived similarity between themselves and the counselor and to reduce role distance 3. modeling: to increase clients' disclosure level 4. to influence clients' perceived or actual behavioral changes
Immediacy	description of current counselor feelings about self, about client, and significant relationship issues	1. to bring covert feelings or unresolved relationship issues into the open for discussion 2. to provide immediate feedback about counselor and client feelings and aspects of the relationship as they occur in the session

ings and ideas. Both self-disclosure and immediacy can be effective tools as long as they are expressed in a sincere and genuine way.

Self-disclosure and immediacy are skills that clients can use in interpersonal relationships outside counseling. As Egan (1975) indicates, these kinds of skills "belong to life and not just to the helping process" (p. 133). When a counselor uses sharing responses in interviews, these responses are being modeled for clients. As the counselor continues to use sharing responses, clients may start to apply these skills in their own relationships.

Self-Disclosure

Self-disclosure may be defined as any information counselors convey about themselves to their clients (Cozby, 1973). Typically, counselors may choose to reveal something about themselves through verbal sharing of such information. Self-disclosure is not confined to verbal behavior, of course. As Egan (1976) points out, we always disclose information about ourselves through nonverbal channels and by our actions even when we don't intend to (p. 55). This section, however, will focus on the

purposeful use of verbal disclosure as a counselor sharing response.

Although all self-disclosures reveal information about oneself, the type of information disclosed can vary. As displayed in Figure 7-1, the content of a self-disclosure can be categorized as demographic or personal (Simonson, 1976) and as positive or negative (Hoffman-Graff, 1977).

In demographic disclosures, the counselor talks about nonintimate events. In personal disclosures, the counselor reveals more private, personal events (Simonson, 1976). Examples of demographic self-disclosure would be "I had some discouraging times during my school work also" or "At first I had thought I didn't want children; then I changed my mind, so we had them." A personal self-disclosure could mean saying something like "Well, I don't always feel loving toward my children. There are times when I feel pretty angry with them and just want some peace and quiet"; or "I think it's pretty natural to have very warm feelings for your close friends. There are times when I've been a little scared of my deep feelings for my friends, too."

Also, a counselor's self-disclosure may be positive or negative. Positive self-disclosure

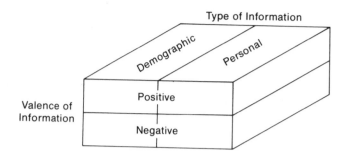

Figure 7-1. Possible Content of Self-Disclosive Information

reveals personal strengths, coping skills, or positive successful experiences; negative self-disclosure provides information about personal limitations or unsuccessful or difficult experiences (Hoffman-Graff, 1977, p. 189). In a positive self-disclosure, a counselor might say "I'm really a task-oriented person. When I decide to do something, I usually work at it until it's finished"; or "It's important to me to try to be as honest with people as possible. If people upset me, I try to be open with them about this." In a negative self-disclosure, one might tell a client "I also tend to have trouble expressing opinions—I sort of see myself as wishy-washy a lot of the time"; or "When I recall my own high school days, they were filled with anxiety. I always wondered why I was never too well liked by the other kids."

There are several purposes for using self-disclosure with a client (see Table 7-1). Counselor self-disclosure may generate an open and facilitative counseling atmosphere. In some instances, a disclosive counselor may be perceived as more empathic and warm than a nondisclosive counselor (Halpern, 1977). Counselor disclosure can reduce the role distance between a counselor and client (Egan, 1975). Counselor self-disclosure also can be used to increase the disclosure level of clients (Thase & Page, 1977), to bring about changes in clients' perceptions of their behavior (Hoffman-Graff, 1977), and possibly even to influence actual client behavior change (Hoffman & Spencer, 1977). However, not everyone agrees that counselor self-disclosure is always therapeutic or professional (Polansky, 1967).

Effects. The effects of counselor self-disclosure seem to vary with counselors and with situational variables. For example, one study found that counselors who disclosed about their background did facilitate more disclosure by participants (Simonson, 1976); yet another study concluded that self-disclosure of the counselor's background did not have such effects (Savitsky, Zarle, & Keedy, 1976). Other mixed results were reported by Hoffman-Graff (1977), who found that subjects rated interviewers who disclosed personal weaknesses higher on empathy and regard than interviewers who disclosed strengths. However, another study failed to replicate these results (Hoffman & Spencer, 1977).

Other evidence suggests that, in appropriate amounts and at appropriate times, self-disclosure can be beneficial. For instance, counselor self-disclosure may increase the perceived similarity between the client and the counselor and may make the client regard the counselor more favorably (Giannandrea & Murphy, 1973; Jourard & Friedman, 1970; Mann & Murphy, 1975). Use of counselor self-disclosure also seems to have a modeling effect. The interviewer's disclosure level may increase (or decrease) the interviewee's disclosure level (Halpern, 1977; Mann & Murphy, 1975; Thase & Page, 1977). Since most individuals tend to disclose less about more intimate topics, the counselor's ability to generate client disclosure may be especially important for counseling. As Thase and Page point out, a counselor's use of self-disclosure as a modeling tool can facilitate client self-exploration and disclosure, which, in turn, may affect the process and outcome of therapy (p. 39). Counselor disclosure also can reduce the role distance between counselor and client (Egan, 1975, p. 152). One study found that, following interviewer disclosure, the subjects perceived the interviewer more as a person than as an expert (K. C. Murphy & Strong, 1972). We believe that self-disclosure does have a place in counseling but should be used with discretion. Some of the ground rules for use of self-disclosure are considered in the next section.

Ground Rules. There are several ground rules that may help a counselor decide what, when, and how much to disclose. One ground rule relates to the "breadth," or the cumulative amount of information disclosed (Cozby, 1973, p. 75). Most of the evidence indicates that a moderate amount of disclosure has more positive effects than a high or low level (Giannandrea & Murphy, 1973; Mann & Murphy, 1975; Simonson, 1976). Some self-disclosure may indicate a desire for a close relationship and may increase the client's estimate of the helper's trustworthiness (Levin & Gergen, 1969). Counselors who disclose very little could add to the role distance between themselves and their clients. At the other extreme, too much disclosure may be counterproductive. The counselor who discloses too much may be perceived as lacking in discretion, being untrustworthy (Levin & Gergen), seeming self-preoccupied (Cozby), or needing assistance. A real danger in overdisclosing is the risk of being perceived as needing therapy as much as the client.

Another ground rule to consider concerns the duration of self-disclosure, or the amount of time used to give information about yourself (Cozby, 1973, p. 75). A long self-disclosing statement may be useful if your intent is to generate more client disclosure about a certain topic. Jourard and Jaffe (1970) pointed out that subjects disclosed more about a topic when the topic discussion was preceded by increases in the duration of the interviewer's disclosure about the topic. Of course, extended periods of counselor disclosure will consume time that could be spent in client disclosure. As one per-

son reveals more, the other person will necessarily reveal less (Levin & Gergen, 1969). From this perspective, some conciseness in the length of self-disclosive statements seems warranted.

A third ground rule to consider in using self-disclosure concerns the depth or intimacy of the information revealed (Cozby, 1973, p. 75). You should attempt to make your statements similar in content and mood to the client's messages. Ivey and Gluckstern (1976) refer to this similarity as "parallelism," meaning that the counselor's self-disclosure is closely linked to the client's statements (p. 86). For example:

Client: I just feel so down on myself. My husband is so critical of me and often I think he's right. I really can't do much of anything well.
Counselor (parallel): There have been times when I've also felt down on myself, so I can sense how discouraged you are. Sometimes, too, criticism from a male has made me feel even worse, although I'm learning how to value myself regardless of critical comments from my husband or a male friend.
Counselor (nonparallel): I've felt bummed out, too. Sometimes the day just doesn't go well.

A counselor can alter the depth of a self-disclosure by adapting the content of the information revealed. For instance, if a client discloses about a nonintimate event, a demographic counselor disclosure may be more appropriate than a personal disclosure. Or, if the client is discussing a negative experience, a negative counselor disclosure will be more similar than a positive disclosure. In fact, a positive counselor disclosure following client expression of negative feelings (or vice versa) can inhibit rather than expand the client's communication. Imagine how insensitive it would sound if a counselor said "I'm very happy today. Of course I consider myself to be a very optimistic person" after a client had just revealed feelings of sadness or depression. Generally, the counselor can achieve the desired impact of self-disclosure as long as the depth or content of the information is not grossly discrepant from the client's messages and behavior.

In using self-disclosure, a counselor should be very aware of the effects it produces in the interview. There is always a danger of accelerating self-disclosure to the point where the counselor and client spend time swapping stories about themselves or playing "I've got one to top that." This effect does not reflect the intended purposes of self-disclosure.

In addition to being cognizant of the actual effects of self-disclosure, counselors should be aware of their motivation for using the response in the first place. Self-disclosure is appropriate only when you can explain how it may benefit the client. Counselors who are unaware of their own biases and vulnerabilities may self-disclose because they identify too much with a client or a topic area. Other helpers may self-disclose simply to reduce their anxiety level in the interview. As with all other counselor behavior, self-disclosure should be structured to meet the client's needs.

We have defined counselor self-disclosure as information counselors reveal about themselves. The next sharing response, immediacy, can be considered a special kind of disclosure that involves sharing feelings and experiences as they occur within the counseling process.

Learning Activities: Self-Disclosure

I. Respond to the following three client situations with a self-disclosing response. Make sure you reveal something about yourself. It might help you to start your statements with "I." Also, try to make your statements similar in content and depth to the client messages and situations. Feedback is provided following the exercise on p. 99, and an example is given first.

Example

The client is having a hard time stating specific reasons for seeking counseling. Your self-disclosing statement: "I'm reluctant at times to share something that is personal about myself with someone I don't know; I know it takes time to get started."

Now use your self-disclosure responses:

1. The client is feeling like a failure because nothing seems to be going well."
   Your self-disclosure:

2. The client is hinting that he or she has some concerns about sexual performance but does not seem to know how to introduce this concern in the session.
   Your self-disclosure:
3. The client has started to become aware of feelings of anger for the first time and is questioning whether such feelings are legitimate or whether something is wrong with him or her.
   Your self-disclosure:

II. In a conversation with a friend or in a group, use the skill of self-disclosure. You may wish to use the questions below as "starters." Consider the criteria listed in the feedback to assess your use of this response.

Preference Survey

1. What things or activities do you enjoy doing most?
2. What things or activities do you dislike?
3. What things or activities do you try to avoid?
4. When you're feeling down in the dumps, what do you do to get out of it?
5. What things or people do you think about most?
6. What things or people do you avoid thinking about?

Immediacy

Immediacy refers to a counselor verbal response describing something *as it occurs* within a session. Usually, the counselor reflects upon a current, "here and now" aspect of (1) some thought or feeling within the counselor, (2) some thought or feeling about the client, or (3) some aspect of the relationship. The verbal expression of immediacy may incorporate a combination of other verbal responses such as reflection, interpretation, summarization, confrontation, and self-disclosure. Here are some examples of these three categories of immediacy.

1. Counselor immediacy: the counselor reveals his or her own thoughts or feelings in the counseling process as they occur "in the moment":
   "I'm glad to see you today."
   "I'm sorry, I am having difficulty focusing. Let's go over that again."

2. Client immediacy: the counselor provides feedback to the client about some client behavior or feeling as it occurs in the interview:

> "You're fidgeting and seem uncomfortable here right now."

> "You're really smiling now—you must be very pleased about it."

3. Relationship immediacy: the counselor reveals feelings or thoughts about how he or she experiences the relationship:

> "I'm glad that you're able to share that with me."

> "It makes me feel good that we're getting somewhere today."

Egan (1975) points out that expressions of immediacy regarding a relationship may be about single "here and now" transactions or about the overall quality of the relationship, represented by the sum of many individual interactions (p. 201). Expressions of counselor immediacy may include comments about specific situations, patterns of the counseling relationship, or both. For example, a counselor might note one instance of apparent client discomfort and give feedback about this to the client by saying something like: "Just now you seem concerned about mentioning this to me." Or the counselor may notice that the client has spent most of one session playing the "yes, but" game and use immediacy to reflect on the fact that this has occurred repeatedly in the session: "I'm aware that just in the last 30 minutes several times you have not really accepted some of my statements. I'm wondering what may be going on."

Two purposes of immediacy were described in Table 7-1. One purpose is to bring out in the open something that you feel about yourself, the client, or the relationship that has not been expressed directly. Generally, it is assumed that covert or unexpressed feelings about the relationship may inhibit effective communication or may prevent further development of the relationship unless the counselor recognizes and responds to these feelings. This may be especially important in the case of negative feelings. As Eisenberg and Delaney (1977) note, "when stress occurs in the rela-

Feedback: Self-Disclosure

I. Here are some possible examples of counselor self-disclosure for these three client situations. See whether your responses are *similar*; your statements will probably reflect more of your own feelings and experiences. Are your statements fairly concise? Are they similar to the client messages in content and intensity?

1. "I, too, have felt down and out about myself at times."

> or

"I can remember especially when I was younger feeling very depressed if things didn't turn out the way I wanted."

2. "For myself, I have sometimes questioned the adequacy of my sexual performance."

> or

"I find it hard sometimes to start talking about really personal topics like sex."

3. "I can remember when I used to feel pretty afraid of admitting I felt angry. I always used to control it by telling myself I really wasn't angry."

> or

"I know of times when some of my thoughts or feelings have seemed hard for me to accept."

II. *Self-Disclosure Assessment*

1. What was the amount of your self-disclosure in relationship to the amount of the other person's—low, medium, or high?
2. What was the *total* amount of time you spent in self-disclosure?
3. Were your self-disclosure statements similar in content and depth to those expressed by the other person?
4. Did your self-disclosure detract from or overwhelm the other person?

tionship between the client and counselor, it is generally more adaptive to deal openly with the stress than to avoid dealing with it" (p. 203). In this way, immediacy may bridge the gap between what is directly and covertly expressed in the relationship.

A second purpose of immediacy is to generate discussion or to provide feedback about some aspects of the relationship or the interactions as they occur. This feedback may include verbal sharing of the counselor's feelings or of something the counselor sees going on in the interactive process. Immediacy is not used to describe every passing counselor feeling or observation to the client. But when something happens in the counseling process that influences the client's feelings toward counseling, then dealing openly with this issue has high priority. Usually it is up to the counselor to initiate discussion of unresolved feelings or issues (Eisenberg & Delaney, 1977, p. 202). Immediacy can be a way to begin such discussion and, if used properly, can strengthen the counselor-client relationship.

Ground Rules. There are several rules to consider in using immediacy effectively. First, the counselor should describe what she or he sees *as it happens.* If the counselor waits until later in the session or until the next interview to describe a feeling or experience, the impact is lost. Also, feelings about the relationship that are discounted or ignored may build up and eventually be expressed in more intense or distorted ways. The counselor who puts off using immediacy to initiate a needed discussion runs the risk of having unresolved feelings or issues damage the relationship. Second, to reflect the "here and nowness" of the experience, any immediacy statement should be in the present tense—"I'm feeling uncomfortable now," rather than "I just felt uncomfortable." This models expression of current rather than past feelings for the client. Also, when referring to your feelings and perceptions, own them or take responsibility for them by using the personal pronouns *I, me,* or *mine,* as in "I'm feeling concerned about you now" instead of "You're making me feel concerned." Expressing your current feelings with "I" language communicates that you are responsible for your feelings and observations, and this may increase the client's receptivity to your immediacy expressions. Finally, as in using all other responses, the counselor should consider timing. Using a lot of immediacy in an early session may be overwhelming for some

clients. If a counselor uses immediacy and senses that this has threatened or scared the client, then the counselor should decide that the client is not yet ready to handle these feelings or issues. Also, not every feeling or observation a counselor has needs to be verbalized to a client. The session does not need to turn into a "heavy" discussion, nor should it resemble a confessional. Generally, immediacy is reserved for initiating exploration of the most significant or most influential feelings or issues. Of course, a counselor who never expresses immediacy may be avoiding issues that have a significant effect on the relationship.

___

Learning Activities: Immediacy

I. For each of the following client stimuli, write an example of a counselor immediacy response. Feedback can be found on p. 102, and an example has been completed.

Example

The client has come in late for the third time and you have some concern about this.
Immediacy response: "I'm aware that you're having difficulty getting here on time, and I'm feeling uncomfortable about this."

Now use immediacy in the following three situations:

1. Tears begin to well up in the client's eyes as he or she describes the loss of a close friend.
   Your immediacy response:
2. The client stops talking whenever you bring up the subject of his or her academic performance.
   Your immediacy response:
3. The client has asked you several questions regarding your competence and qualifications.
   Your immediacy response:

II. In a conversation with a close friend or in a group, use the sharing skill of immediacy. If possible, tape the conversation for feedback—or ask for feedback from the friend or the group. You should consider the criteria listed in the feedback in assessing your use of immediacy. You may wish to use the topics listed in the following Relationship Assessment Inventory as topics for discussion using immediacy.

1. To what extent do we really know each other?
2. How do I feel in your presence?
3. How do you feel in my presence?
4. What areas do I have trouble sharing with you?
5. What is it about our relationship that makes it hard to share some things?
6. Do we both have a fairly equal role in maintaining our relationship or is one of us dominant and the other passive?
7. How do we handle power and conflict in the relationship? Is one of us consistently "top dog" or an "underdog"?
8. Do we express or avoid feelings of warmth and affection for each other?
9. How do our concepts of our sex roles affect the way we relate to each other?
10. How often do we give feedback to each other—and in what manner is it given?
11. How do we hurt each other?
12. How do we help each other?
13. Where do we want our relationship to go from here?

Teaching Responses

If you assume that most clients come to you out of concern or dissatisfaction with themselves, their relationships, or their environment, then counseling becomes a process of change. Change means that clients learn new ways to deal with themselves, others, or environmental situations. By helping clients learn and change, the counselor assumes the role of a teacher. The counselor may teach clients new behaviors, new awareness, or new perceptions—or how to teach themselves (see Chapters 22 and 23 on self-management strategies).

Many people regard teaching as a function that can be carried out by anyone, without any prerequisite skills or prior thought and experience. But there is no reason to believe that haphazard teaching skills, or haphazard counseling skills, will have any specific desirable results. Because of the importance of the teaching role in counseling, we have included a section describing three verbal responses associated

with teaching and learning: instructions, verbal setting operations, and information-giving (see Table 7–2). These responses are often not found in counselor training programs, but they are used frequently in actual helping sessions. There is an increasing recognition that some amount of teaching has a legitimate role in the overall counseling process.

Instructions

Instructions consist of one or more statements in which the counselor instructs, directs, or cues the client to do something. Instructions also may be referred to as directions (Ivey & Gluckstern, 1976) or coaching (McFall & Lillesand, 1971). The instructions may encourage the client to do something, either within or outside the interview, regarding her or his thoughts, feelings, or overt actions. Whether used within or outside the interview, instructions have both influencing and informational effects. Instructions should help to encourage and influence a person to respond in a certain way and should also provide information that helps a client perform a certain task. Instructions can be used as guidelines to help a person acquire, strengthen, weaken, or eliminate a behavior. These purposes of instructions are summarized in Table 7-2.

Occasionally, instructions may precede or accompany modeling strategies and rehearsal procedures. In these instances, instructions are used to provide sufficient information for the client to observe a model or to practice a task. Sometimes instructions alone are enough to help a client do something in a specified way. In other words, simply telling a client how to do something may be sufficient. In one study in which persons were taught to respond empathically, the students learned as much from instructions as they did from modeling and rehearsal when their performance was assessed by a written task (Stone & Vance, 1976). Instructions may be a very useful strategy when the goal is to help a person acquire a new response (Stone & Vance, 1976).

Instructions are probably most effective when the instructive statements contain three elements: (1) what to do, (2) how to do it, and (3) the do's and don't's of performing. Telling a client *specifically* what and how to do something will probably be more helpful than a vague instructive statement such as "do that again." Specific, concise instructions seem to be more effective than general or lengthy instructions (Doster, 1972; McGuire, Thelen, & Amolsch, 1975; Stone & Gotlib, 1975). Also, some evidence indicates that a person can discriminate between good and poor responses when both the "do's" and "don't's" for the response are included in the instructions (Stone & Gotlib, 1975; Stone & Vance, 1976).

Table 7-3 gives some examples of counselor instructions that contain the three components of *what, how,* and *do's and don't's.*

Ground Rules. A counselor should remember that simply giving an instruction does not mean that the client will understand it or will carry it out. There are several ways to determine whether the instruction is understood and to encourage a client to follow through. First, after giving instructions, check to see whether the person really understands what you are directing her or him to do. One way to do this is to ask the person simply to repeat what you said. Second, instructions are more likely to be carried out if they contain an exhortation for the person to attend to or use the instructions (Whalen, 1969). For example, in addition to describing the response, the instructions might include a suggestion to pay close attention and to think about using the instructions in the future.

Schwartz and Goldiamond (1975) indicate that clients are more likely to follow instructions if the instructions are linked to positive or rewarding consequences (p. 30). In other words, instructions may be used more effectively if the client is positively reinforced for following them (Thomas, 1971). Such encouragement can be as simple as a head nod, a smile, or an "I'm glad you were able to _____."

One final caution about using instructions in the helping process: there are many ways in which instructions can be worded. "You should do something" is very dogmatic and sounds like a drill sergeant. Wording more useful for a

helper could be "I'd like you to" or "I'd appreciate it" or "I think it would help if." Instructions, like any counseling response, will have more impact with a "motivated" client. The next section will describe how to use a verbal setting operation to help clients understand and use the processes of helping.

Verbal Setting Operation

A setting operation is an activity that attempts to predispose someone to view a situation or an event in a certain way beforehand. As

---

Feedback: Immediacy

I. Here are some expressions of immediacy. See how these compare to yours.

  1. "At this moment you seem to be experiencing this loss very intensely."
     or
     "I'm sensing now that it is very painful for you to talk about this."
  2. "Every time I mention academic performance, like now, you seem to back off."
     or
     "I'm aware that, during this session, you stop talking when the topic of your grades comes up."
  3. "You seem to be questioning now how qualified I am to help you."
     or
     "I'm wondering if it's difficult right now for you to trust me."

  Are your immediacy responses in the present tense? Do you "own" your feelings and perceptions by using "I feel" rather than "You're making me feel"?

II. *Immediacy Assessment*
  1. Did you express something personal about your feelings, the other person's feelings, or the relationship?
  2. Were your immediacy statements in the present tense?
  3. Did you use "I," "me," or "mine" when referring to *your* feelings and perceptions?
  4. Did you express immediacy as your feelings occurred within the conversation?

Table 7-2. Definitions and Intended Purposes of Counselor Teaching Responses

Response	Definition	Intended Purpose
Instructions	One or more statements in which the counselor tells the client 1. what to do 2. how to do it 3. do's and don't's of performing	1. to influence or give cues to help client respond in a certain way 2. to provide information necessary for acquiring, strengthening, or eliminating a response
Verbal setting operation	A statement describing 1. rationale about counseling and/or treatment 2. potential value of counseling and/or treatment for client	1. to motivate client to use counseling and/or treatment 2. to help client understand the purposes of counseling or treatment
Information-giving	Verbal communication of data or facts	1. to identify alternatives 2. to evaluate alternatives 3. to dispel myths

Table 7-3. The "What," "How," and "Do's" and "Don't's" of Counselor Instructions

Instructions	In the Interview	Outside the Interview (Homework)
What to do	"Now, tell me what you will say to him."	"Record the thoughts that you are having before you talk in front of the group."
How to do	"When you say this, pretend that I'm your husband—look at me and maintain eye contact with me while you say it."	"Write the thoughts that you are having before you talk on a note card or a piece of paper and bring them in next week."
Do's and Don't's	"Say it in a strong, firm voice. Don't speak in a soft, weak voice. Look at me while you say it, don't look away."	"Remember, record these thoughts before you speak in front of the group. Don't record them after you have given your talk."

an example, imagine that you are traveling on an airplane that develops landing-gear trouble. Now imagine that the person sitting next to you, a veteran traveler, says: "Don't worry, I've had this happen a lot. It usually only means that the landing-gear light is out on the pilot's control panel." This kind of statement might have a different effect on you than if your seatmate goes into hysterics about a possible plane crash. In each case, the way you view the plane's difficulty may be different.

The same phenomenon occurs in learning and counseling. For example, if you enroll in a completely automated course for the first time, your "set" toward the course may vary, depending on the rationale and instructions you receive about this method of learning. There is some evidence that performance may be enhanced when one is provided with a rationale and detailed instructions regarding the learning process (Hartley & Davies, 1976; Snow, 1974). In other words, "situations of optimum learning require a great deal of preparation" (D. Hawkins, 1966, p. 6).

Similarly, much of the process and outcome of counseling is influenced by the client's attitudes and beliefs upon entering and engaging in therapy. Many clients experience counseling as a new and anxiety-producing situation. The client's receptiveness toward counseling may be increased when you make use of verbal setting operations at the beginning of the counseling process and as it continues. A verbal setting operation for counseling consists of two parts: a description of the rationale or purpose of counseling and treatment, and an overview of counseling for the client. A verbal set should reflect an optimistic rather than a pessimistic flavor. However, such a statement should not be unrealistic. Remember, you are only trying to express your positive beliefs in the power of change—not trying to persuade the client to buy a used car!

Two specific kinds of verbal setting operations are used in counseling. One type consists of a rationale and an overview of various treatment strategies used in helping. This kind of verbal set is described in more detail in Chapter 15. A second type consists of an overview of the counseling process. This setting operation is typically provided to clients in an intake or initial interview. It is an attempt to motivate the client to pursue counseling. A description and examples of this kind of verbal setting operation are provided in the following section.

Helping-Process Overview. At the beginning of counseling, most clients know little about what counseling does or should involve. Some clients may even have mixed emotions about the benefits of counseling and may adopt a "wait and see if it's worth it" attitude. One way to increase a client's initial receptiveness toward counseling is to create a set about what goes on in counseling and how the client might experience it. A. P. Goldstein (1975) refers to this as "role expectancy structuring" (p. 19). Goldstein

(1962) also feels that initial structuring should focus upon and clarify counselor and client role expectations—and that this type of structuring should be "detailed, deliberate, and repeated" (p. 121).

Several reasons for providing a new client with an initial set about the counseling process are summarized in Table 7-2. A verbal set used at the time of intake may motivate a client to continue to pursue counseling. As Krause (1966) points out, a discussion of the benefits and costs of therapeutic treatment may strengthen a client's decision to come back after an initial interview. An initial verbal setting operation also may prevent the client from entering counseling with misconceptions or misinformation. Goldstein (1975) suggests that some initial structuring about counseling may prevent negative feelings in the client resulting from lack of information about what to expect (p. 19). Misleading information about therapy may have a detrimental effect on therapeutic outcomes (S. B. Miller, 1972). An initial set about counseling may help both the counselor and client understand each other's expectations for counseling. Goldstein (1962) indicates that mutually shared expectations about the roles of the counselor and client are crucial in establishing realistic therapeutic expectations. Incompatible role expectations or very negative client expectations may have a detrimental effect on the relationship (Ziemelis, 1974). To summarize, clients who receive an initial orientation about the helping process are more likely to pursue therapy (Krause), to stay in therapy longer, and, from responses to various indexes, to benefit more from counseling (Goldstein, 1973).

Although many words can be used to describe counseling to a client, here is one example of a verbal set used to provide structure for an incoming client:

Overview of counseling: "I believe it would be helpful if I talked first about what counseling may involve. We will spend some time talking together—to find out first the kinds of things concerning you and what you want to do about these concerns. Then we'll work as a team to help you find ways to work on these concerns.

Sometimes I may ask you to do some things on your own outside the session."

Purpose of counseling: "The talks we have may help you feel relieved and will help you understand yourself. The action plans you'll carry out—with my assistance—can help you learn to do things you'd like to do in the situations that are of concern to you."

After providing a set, you can check out the person's understanding of counseling by asking for a description of his or her expectations.

Checking out client's expectations: "How does this fit with your ideas and hopes about counseling?"

A verbal setting operation about the counseling process or about counseling strategies is, in a sense, a way of giving information to the client about counseling and its components. Information-giving as a counselor response also may be very important at other points in the counseling process.

Information-Giving

There are many times in the counseling interview when a client may have a legitimate need for information. For instance, a client who reports being abused by her husband may need information about her legal rights and alternatives. A client who has recently become physically disabled may need some information about employment and about life-style adaptations such as carrying out domestic chores or engaging in sexual relationships. As E. C. Lewis (1970) observes, in these kinds of cases the lack of information contributes to the clients' problems. Until such clients obtain relevant data, they may be restricted in dealing with their problems and goals constructively (p. 135). The counselor can help by recognizing the client's need for information and providing the data or directing the client to find the facts. Withholding of information that might result in a client's making a poor choice because of lack of data or misinformation is unethical and unhelpful.

We define information-giving as the verbal communication of data or facts about experiences, events, alternatives, or people. As summarized in Table 7-2, there are three intended purposes of information-giving in counseling. First, information is necessary when the client does not know her or his options. Giving information is a way to help the client identify possible alternatives. As Gelatt, Varenhorst, Carey, and Miller (1973) suggest, a "person's choices are increased if he can create new alternatives based on information" (p. 6). For example, you may be counseling a pregnant client who says she is going to get an abortion because it is her only choice. Although she may decide eventually to pursue this choice, she should be aware of other options before making a final decision. Information-giving also is helpful when a client is not aware of the possible outcomes of a particular choice or plan of action. Giving information can help the client evaluate different choices and actions. For example, if the client is a minor and is not aware that she must have her parents' consent for an abortion, this information may influence her choice. Information-giving also can be useful to correct invalid or unreliable data, or to dispel a myth. In other words, information-giving may be necessary when the client is misinformed about something. For example, a pregnant client may decide to have an abortion based on the erroneous assumption that an abortion also is a means of subsequent birth control.

The ability to generate and select from a variety of alternatives or responses may be viewed as a necessary part of effective problem-solving (D'Zurilla & Goldfried, 1971), competence (Goldfried & D'Zurilla, 1969), or generally healthy functioning (Spivack, 1973). Identifying and evaluating alternatives requires that a person be able to gather and use information. Recent studies have indicated that certain client populations, such as disturbed children (Shure & Spivack, 1972) and psychiatric patients (Platt & Spivack, 1972), are generally deficient in problem-solving skills partly because they lack information necessary to generate suitable alternatives.

Ground Rules. E. C. Lewis (1970) observes that information should be a tool for counseling, not an end in itself. As a tool, information-giving is generally considered to be appropriate when the need for information is directly related to the client's concerns and goals and when the presentation and discussion of information are used to help the client achieve these goals (p. 135).

To use information-giving appropriately, a counselor should consider three major guidelines. These cover when to give information, what information is needed, and how the information should be delivered. Table 7-4 summarizes the "when," "what," and "how" guidelines for information-giving in counseling. The first guideline, the "when," involves recognizing the client's need for information. If the client does not have all the data or has invalid data, a need exists. At this point, the counselor turns to the "what" of information-giving by identifying what kinds of information the client can use and where the information can be found. However, the counselor should not impose information on the client, who ultimately is responsible for deciding what information to use (Lewis, 1970, p. 135). In some cases, the information should be presented sequentially; the client may need to know some things before finding out others. In the interview itself, the actual delivery of information, the "how" of information-giving, is crucial. The information should be discussed in a way that makes it "usable" to the client and encourages the client to "hear and apply" the information (Gazda, Walters, & Childers, 1975, p. 172).

To be effective, information must be well timed. The client should indicate receptivity to the information before it is delivered. As Lewis (1970) observes, a client may ignore information if it is introduced too early (p. 135). Also, information should be presented objectively. Don't leave out facts simply because they aren't pleasant. Watch out, too, for information overload. Most people are not "bionic" and can't assimilate a great deal of information in "one shot." Limit the amount of information presented at any one time. Be aware that some information also has an emotional impact, and ask for and discuss the client's reactions to the information. Note how the client's biases affect the way the

information is received. Also, try to determine when it's time to stop dealing with information. Continued information-giving could reinforce a client's tendency to avoid taking action (Gelatt et al., 1973). Finally, make sure you have the facts straight. If you aren't sure of your data, say so! Validate any information you give to clients with other sources. Better yet, encourage clients to seek out the information for themselves. A counselor should not be a walking encyclopedia, and clients may learn more from seeking information than from having it handed to them (Lewis, p. 136).

Consider the use of information-giving in the following example. Suppose you are counseling a woman whose doctors have advised her to have a mastectomy because of breast cancer. Among other things, the client expresses concern about public reactions to her "deformity" after the operation. This concern may be a cue that the client needs information about a prosthesis and special clothing. The counselor might say something like: "I'm wondering if you're aware of the availability of certain things you can use so that you don't feel conspicuous about your body in public. If not, we can talk about these things." Such information should be given when this client is willing to hear it. Before giving the information, verify your facts with another reliable source. After presenting the information initially, encourage the client to seek out data for herself about the availability of possible clothing and a prosthesis. Also, be aware that this is an emotional issue. Ask the client: "How do you feel now that you know this is available?" Recognize, too, that in this case the client's biases and fears about losing a breast may affect her receptivity to the information. This also should be explored.

Learning Activities: Teaching Responses

I. The following examples of counselor teaching responses include instructions, verbal setting operations, and information-giving. Identify the type of teaching response in each of the following statements using the letters I = instructions, SO =

Table 7-4. The "When," "What," and "How" of Information-Giving in Helping

When—Recognizing Client's Need for Information	What—Identifying Type of Information	How—Delivery of Information in Interview
1. Identify information presently available to client. 2. Evaluate client's present information—Is it valid? data-based? sufficient?	1. Identify kind of information useful to client. 2. Identify possible reliable sources of information. 3. Identify any sequencing of information (option A before option B).	1. Wait for client cue of readiness; don't give information prematurely. 2. Present all the relevant facts; don't protect client from negative information. 3. Limit amount of information given at one time; don't overload. 4. Ask for and discuss client's feelings and biases about information. 5. Know when to stop giving information so action isn't avoided. 6. Validate information with other sources for accuracy.

setting operation, and IG = information-giving. Feedback is provided at the end of the exercise. The first one is completed as an example.

Example

1. "There are four things we will work on together. First, we'll identify why you came for counseling. Next, we will want to develop and establish some counseling goals. This will provide some direction and purpose for where we are going. We will then use some techniques or strategies to help you achieve the goals. And last, we will monitor or evaluate our progress in achieving these goals." *(The type of response is SO.)*

Practice Statements

2. "I would like you to use this relaxation tape every night this week just before you go to sleep. Get in a comfortable position and use it when you aren't likely to be interrupted."
3. "Initially, it might help if we discussed what counseling is and what it can offer you. You and I will first try to determine what it is you would like counseling to do for you. Based on that, we will work together to help you resolve your concerns."
4. "Your voice is too loud—you are still coming across a little aggressively. Try this again and soften the tone of your voice."

5. "Just because you are confined to a wheelchair now doesn't mean that you can't learn to do many of your usual activities by yourself. There are ways that we can help you learn how to be mobile in your chair and do things sitting down instead of standing up."
6. "Having someone to talk to usually helps you feel relieved. Also, counseling can help you learn to do what you want to do—or can help you learn to cope with things that are now difficult for you."
7. "Your arm is not relaxed. Just relax. Let the tension flow out of your body."
8. "I want you to become immersed in your imagining this situation. Visualize the sensation and details of your imagery."
9. "Military academies are no longer restricted to men. If you're interested in pursuing a military career and have good grades, you can apply to any of the academies. The number of females being admitted is increasing each year."

II. We suggest that you use a situation in which you teach something to someone else to demonstrate the three teaching responses: instructions, verbal setting operations, and information-giving. You can assess your performance by audio-taping your teaching. Use the criteria listed in the feedback as guidelines to rate your teaching.

The following list may give you an idea of how you could demonstrate these three responses to teach something to someone else.

Teaching Topics

1. Teach a skill you've already learned in this book, such as nonverbal attending, reflecting, and probing. Give a "set" about your teaching and provide instructions and information about the skill.
2. Teach someone how to do part of your favorite hobby, such as taking a photograph, baking bread, handling the tiller on a boat, assuming the beginning position for skiing, or learning the musical alphabet.
3. Teach something to a small child, such as tying shoes, learning new words, dressing oneself, or using an alarm clock.

Integrating Your Verbal and Nonverbal Skills and Style in the Interview

Up to this point, you have learned a great many skills—all as separate pieces. For example, in Chapter 2, you assessed your relationship and helping style. In Chapter 3, you learned the important components of counselor nonverbal behavior. In Chapter 4, you explored all the possible focus areas of your interviews. Chapters 5 and 6, as well as this chapter, presented different verbal responses to use in your helping repertory. In part four of the post evaluation, you will have an opportunity to put together all these skills and use them appropriately in an interview context. We urge you to work through this part of the post evaluation several times —until you feel quite comfortable with your style and satisfied with your ease at integrating your nonverbal and verbal interview behaviors. Your successful completion of the remainder of the book will hinge on your capacity to use effectively what you've learned up to now.

Also, none of the responses you've acquired at this point should be used randomly. Counseling is not a haphazard process. As we have stressed, a counselor should have a hypothesized or intended purpose in mind when using any particular response. However, what the counselor expects to happen in using a response may not always occur in an actual interview. The counselor should recognize or discriminate whether the counseling response achieved the intended purpose from the resulting client messages. The process of discriminating counselor responses and client messages is described and modeled in the next chapter.

Post Evaluation

Part One

Using the following written list, identify the type of counselor response according to whether it is an example of self-disclosure, immediacy, instruction, verbal setting operation, or information-giving. Write your identification on a piece of paper. The first one is completed as an example. Objective 1 is accomplished if you have eight out of ten accurate identifications. Check your answers with those given in the feedback that follows the evaluation.

1. Client: I often feel as if someone is going to hurt me.

Example

   Counselor: Just sit back now and think specifically about this. Try to tell me when you feel this way.
   (This response is an *instruction*.)
2. Client: How are you going to vote?
   Counselor: In the past I've voted Democratic; now I'm undecided so I'm not able to say for sure.
3. Client: Well, I'm not worried about walking alone at night because I've been told there've been no rapes on our campus.
   Counselor: Well, there are times other than at night when rape occurs. There have been three reported rapes on this campus so far this semester during the day.
4. Client: I'm looking for a part-time job. One employer wants a résumé. What's that?
   Counselor: A résumé is a summary of your school courses, activities, and any work or volunteer experience you've had. It's a way to describe your experiences and qualifications that might help you get a particular kind of job.
5. Client: I've told you what bothers me. Now what do you think is the reason?

Feedback: Teaching Responses

I. Counselor responses 2, 4, 7, and 8 are examples of instructions. These responses indicate what, how, and/or the do's and don'ts of something the client is asked to do or perform. Examples of a verbal setting operation are 1, 3, and 6. These statements explain the purpose and value of counseling. Statements 5 and 9 are examples of information-giving responses.

II. *Teaching-Response Assessment*

A. *Instructions*
1. Were your instructions specific and detailed?
2. Were your instructions brief and concise?
3. Did your instructions include
   a. *What* to do?
   b. *How* to do it?
   c. *Do's and don'ts* of doing?
   d. Suggestion to attend to the instructions for future use?
4. Did you check to see whether the person understood the instructions?
5. Did you reinforce the person after she or he followed the instructions?

B. *Verbal Setting Operations*
1. Did you provide a verbal set about your teaching or about what the person would do by
   a. providing a rationale?
   b. describing an overview of the process?
2. Did you ask the person about her or his expectations for what would be learned?

C. *Information-Giving*
1. Did you identify the type of information needed by the person?
2. Did you check your facts with at least one other reliable source?
3. Did you deliver both positive and negative data, if warranted?
4. Did you attempt to limit the amount of information you gave at one time?
5. Did you discuss the client's reactions to the information?

D. *Summarize your use of teaching responses.*
   I used the teaching responses with:
   The purpose of my teaching session was:

The things that went well in my teaching were:
The things I need to work on are:
The person I taught felt _____ about it.

Counselor A: I'm having a tough time now telling you all the reasons—I'm feeling a little concerned that you're seeing me as an answer giver.
Counselor B: Actually counseling does not always give you specific answers. It does help you explore some possible things contributing to your concerns.

6. Client: I think I'm the most awful person in the world.
   Counselor A: The one thing that comes to my mind is that some of the things we do in counseling may help you to look at yourself differently.
   Counselor B: What I'd like you to do this week is to list all the times you feel this way. Then bring in the list next week.

7. Client: I don't like having to meet here. It's such a drab place.
   Counselor A: I guess I'm wondering right now how you feel about me.
   Counselor B: Tell me how this seems to interfere during our sessions.

Part Two

For Objective 2, use the list below to select one intended purpose for each of the sharing and teaching responses that follow. Feedback can be found after the evaluation.

Intended Purpose of Responses
a. to dispel myths or correct misinformation
b. to help the client understand the purpose of counseling
c. to provide immediate feedback about aspects of the counseling relationship or about counselor-client feelings
d. to tell the client how to perform a certain response or activity
e. to provide an open, facilitative counseling atmosphere

Sharing and Teaching Responses
Self-disclosure:
Immediacy:
Instructions:

Verbal setting operations:
Information-giving:

Part Three

This part of the post evaluation presents various simulated counseling situations. Your task, as stated in Objective 3, is to respond to each situation and write two accurate examples of self-disclosure, immediacy, instructions, verbal setting operations, and information-giving. Feedback is provided following the post evaluation. In order to process this activity most effectively, we suggest that you first *imagine* your responses covertly. You may even feel like whispering a response or saying a response aloud first to "try it on." Then write the response that seems most comfortable for you.

Respond to these two situations with immediacy:

Situation 1: The client is trying to get you to "guess his feeling." He states he has a certain feeling but won't disclose what it is. You become aware you are being conned into the "guessing game" and decide to share your feelings about it.
Immediacy:
Situation 2: You are working with a client who is asking for suggestions. You have given several for consideration, to which the client replies "Yes, but." After this has just occurred again, you decide to share your perceptions.
Immediacy:

Respond to these two situations with self-disclosure:

Situation 1: You are leading a problem-solving group in a high school. The members are spending a lot of time talking about the flack they get from their parents but are not sharing feelings about this. You decide to do some self-disclosing to facilitate the members' sharing of feelings.
Self-disclosure:
Situation 2: You are counseling a client who is almost ready to flunk out because of poor grades. The client states that he doesn't know of anyone who ever flunked out of school and "made it" after that. Since this happened to you, you decide to share this.
Self-disclosure:

Now write an example of each counselor teaching response (instructions, verbal setting operations, and information-giving) for the following two client situations:

Client situation 1: A fourth-grade girl is referred to you by her teacher because she (according to the teacher) talks incessantly and does not listen. The girl indicates to you that she is not sure why the teacher referred her to you. You have difficulty in getting her to hear what you are saying. (1) Can you instruct her in how to listen? (2) You suggest how counseling might help her to control her "talking out" all the time; give a verbal set for this. (3) Give information that may help her understand the reason the teacher referred her to you.
Instructions:
Verbal setting operation:
Information-giving:

Client situation 2: A 58-year-old man who is having difficulty getting it together since his wife died comes to you for counseling. He has difficulty in discussing his concern or problem with you. Also, he is not clear about your role as a counselor and what counseling might do for him. He seems to feel that you can give him some advice or possibly a tranquilizer. (1) What instructions might you give him to help him talk to you? (2) What verbal set might you give him about counseling? (3) What information might you share about your counseling role and functions?
Instructions:
Verbal setting operation:
Information-giving:

Part Four

In order to have an opportunity to integrate your skills, conduct at least one role-play interview that is approximately 15 minutes long. You may want to consider this role-play as an initial helping interview. Your objective is to use as many of the verbal responses (listening, action, sharing, and teaching) and the nonverbal behaviors as seem appropriate within this time span. Also, give some attention to the quality of your relationship and your helping style. Try to regard this as an opportunity to get involved with the person in front of you and not as just another practice. If you feel some discomfort in using your verbal and nonverbal skills then you may wish to do several more interviews with this goal in mind. Use the Interview Inventory at the end of the chapter to assess your interview. You may wish to copy the Inventory or superimpose a piece of paper over the Inventory for your ratings.

Feedback: Post Evaluation

Part One

1. Instructions
2. Self-disclosure
3. Information-giving
4. Information-giving
5. A. Immediacy
   B. Verbal setting operation
6. A. Verbal setting operation
   B. Instructions
7. A. Immediacy
   B. Instructions

Part Two

Self-disclosure.   e. open, facilitative atmosphere
Immediacy.   c. immediate feedback
Instructions.   d. how to perform
Verbal setting operation.   b. purpose of counseling
Information-giving.   a. dispel myths

Part Three

For immediacy:
1. "I'm realizing that we're doing something now that has gone on for the last 15 minutes. You report you have a feeling and I just asked you for the fifth time what it was. I'm feeling concerned about spending our time this way."
2. "I'm aware that you just told me all the reasons why this idea wouldn't work. I'm wondering if we could look at what's going on now—I make a suggestion and you explain why it won't help."

For self-disclosure:
1. "Several people just said that one problem of concern to some of you is the flack you get from your parents. I noticed you talked about how they hassle you, but no one said how you feel about this. I can remember times when I felt I got so much unfair flack that I felt very resentful even of having parents. At least at that time. I don't feel that way now, but I did before."
2. "I guess maybe it might be helpful for you to know one person who flunked out and did go back and made it—that's me. I really partied in college and flunked out after my sophomore

year. After several years of working, I went back and did the rest of my undergraduate and graduate work. I guess I was more ready then to work."

Possible counselor teaching responses for client situations 1 and 2 are:

Client situation 1
  Instructions: "Can you tell me what we were just talking about?" (Instructs the client what to do.)
      or
  "When you listen you can't talk; otherwise you won't hear what the other person is saying. Try to think about what the person is saying." (Instructs on do's and don't's of listening and talking.)
  Verbal setting operation: "If you are concerned about what you do in this class, our talks together can help you decide to continue what you're doing or to change some things." (Explains the purpose of counseling.)
  Information-giving: "The reason your teacher told me she wanted us to talk is because she feels you talk too much in her class. How do you feel about this?" (Informs the girl of the reason for the referral.)

Client situation 2
  Instructions: "Tell me about what has happened to you since the death of your wife." (Instructs client to give information.)
  Verbal setting operation: "People have found that counseling can turn their lives around somewhat. But I cannot tell you what to do—we can work together. I do not do magic, but with your help and energy I am confident that we can find some things that will help you." (Describes purpose of counseling.)
  Information-giving: "I can give you some information about your options, but I am not a fortuneteller or advice giver. Also, I don't have a medical degree and therefore can't give you medication." (Informs client of limitations of counselor's role and function.)

Part Four

You can rate your own interview or have a rater use the Interview Inventory that follows. If you are using audio tape, you will be able to rate only your verbal responses. If you have a video tape or if the rating is live, both verbal and nonverbal behavior can be scored. Follow the instructions on the Interview Inventory for the ratings. After all the ratings are completed, you may want to look at your ratings in the light of these questions.

1. Examine the total number of the verbal responses you used in each category. Did you use responses from each category with the same frequency? Did most of your responses come from one category? Did you seem to avoid using responses from one category? If so, why?
2. What do your totals indicate about your theoretical biases? For example, a predominance of listening and sharing responses would be associated with a client-centered or experiential approach; using a lot of action and teaching responses might reflect more Gestalt, rational-emotive, Adlerian, or behavioral frameworks.
3. Was it easier to integrate the verbal responses or the nonverbal skills?
4. Which nonverbal skills were easiest for you to demonstrate? Which ones did you find most difficult to use in the interview?
5. To what extent does your quantitative rating seem related to your qualitative rating? Did you find one more difficult than another?
6. What aspects of your helping style seem to be assets for you? What parts are problems for you?
7. What do you see that you have learned about your counseling interview behavior so far? What do you think you need to improve?

Interview Inventory

Interview No. _____ Counselor _____ Client _____ Rater _____

Instructions for rating: There are two parts to this rating form—a quantitative and a qualitative scoring. The quantitative scoring involves obtaining a frequency count of the types of verbal and nonverbal responses made by the counselor. For each counselor statement, indicate the type of verbal and nonverbal response made. At the end of the interview, tally the number of responses associated with each response category. The qualitative rating involves a subjective judgment by a rater or by the client (or both) about aspects of the counselor's style. After observing the interview for each of the seven items, circle the number (1 to 5) that best represents your judgment about the counselor during most of the interview. Comments can be added at the bottom of the rating sheet.

Qualitative Rating of Helping Style

1. To what extent was the counselor comfortable with the client and with the subject areas discussed?

1	2	3	4	5
Not at all	Minimally	Somewhat	A great deal	Most always

2. To what extent did the counselor refrain from imposing values and expectations on the client?

1	2	3	4	5
Not at all	Minimally	Somewhat	A great deal	Most always

3. To what extent did the counselor prevent personal needs from dominating or interfering with the session?

1	2	3	4	5
Not at all	Minimally	Somewhat	A great deal	Most always

QUANTITATIVE RATING OF RESPONSES

Total	10	9	8	7	6	5	4	3	2	1	Counselor Statement No.		
											Clarification	Listening	Verbal Responses
											Paraphrase		
	·										Reflection of Feeling		
											Summarization		
											Probe	Action	
											Ability Potential		
											Confrontation		
											Interpretation		
											Self-Disclosure	Sharing	
											Immediacy		
											Instructions	Teaching	
											Setting Operation		
											Information-giving		
											Initiates Eye Contact	Eyes	Nonverbal Behavior
											Breaks Eye Contact		
											Head Nods	Face	
											Smiles		
											Body Facing Client	Body	
											Body Turned Away		
											Body Lean Forward		
											Body Lean Backward		
											Body Relaxed		
											Body Tense		
												Paralinguistics	
											Completed Sentences		
											Broken Sentences, Speech Errors		

4. To what extent did the counselor refrain from communicating disapproval or judgment to the client?

 1   2   3   4   5

 Not at all Minimally Somewhat A great deal Most always

5. To what extent was the counselor focused on the person rather than the procedure or the practice?

 1   2   3   4   5

 Not at all Minimally Somewhat A great deal Most always

6. To what extent was the counselor's delivery of the skills spontaneous and nonmechanical?

 1   2   3   4   5

 Not at all Minimally Somewhat A great deal Most always

7. How likely is the client to come back to see this counselor again?

 1   2   3   4   5

 Not at all Minimally Somewhat A great deal Most always

General comments from rater or from client:

Suggested Readings

Self-Disclosure

Cozby, P. C. Self-disclosure: A literature review. *Psychological Bulletin*, 1973, *79*, 73–91.

Egan, G. *Interpersonal living: A skills/contract approach to human-relations training in groups.* Monterey, Calif.: Brooks/Cole, 1976. Chap. 3, The skill of self-disclosure, 38–63.

Hoffman, M. A., & Spencer, G. P. Effect of interviewer self-disclosure and interviewer-subject sex pairing on perceived and actual subject behavior. *Journal of Counseling Psychology*, 1977, *24*, 383–390.

Ivey, A., & Gluckstern, N. *Basic influencing skills: Participant manual.* Amherst, Mass.: Microtraining Associates, 1976. Workshop 5, Self-disclosure: Feelings and thoughts, 74–105.

Jourard, S. M. *The transparent self* (Rev. ed.). New York: Van Nostrand Reinhold, 1971.

Mann, B., & Murphy, K. C. Timing of self-disclosure, reciprocity of self-disclosure, and reactions to an initial interview. *Journal of Counseling Psychology*, 1975, *22*, 304–308.

Simonson, N. The impact of therapist disclosure on patient disclosure. *Journal of Counseling Psychology*, 1976, *23*, 3–6.

Thase, M., & Page, R. A. Modeling of self-disclosure in laboratory and nonlaboratory interview settings. *Journal of Counseling Psychology*, 1977, *24*, 35–40.

Immediacy

Egan, G. *Interpersonal living: A skills/contract approach to human-relations training in groups.* Monterey, Calif.: Brooks/Cole, 1976. Chap. 11, Immediacy: Direct, mutual talk, 200–214.

Ivey, A., & Gluckstern, N. *Basic influencing skills: Participant manual.* Amherst, Mass.: Microtraining Associates, 1976. Workshop 7, Direct-mutual communication, 140–159.

Instructions

Ivey, A., & Gluckstern, N. *Basic influencing skills: Participant manual.* Amherst, Mass.: Microtraining Associates, 1976. Workshop 4, Directions, 66–73.

McFall, R. M., & Lillesand, D. V. Behavior rehearsal with modeling and coaching in assertive training. *Journal of Abnormal Psychology*, 1971, *77*, 313–323.

McGuire, D., Thelen, M., & Amolsch, T. Interview self-disclosure as a function of length of modeling and descriptive instructions. *Journal of Consulting and Clinical Psychology*, 1975, *43*, 356–362.

Stone, G., & Gotlib, I. Effects of instructions and modeling on self-disclosure. *Journal of Counseling Psychology*, 1975, *22*, 288–293.

Thomas, E. J., O'Flaherty, K., & Borkin, J. Coaching marital partners in family decision making. In J. D. Krumboltz & C. E. Thoresen (Eds.),

Counseling methods. New York: Holt, Rinehart & Winston, 1976.

Verbal Setting Operations

Coe, W. C., & Buckner, L. G. Expectation, hypnosis, and suggestion methods. In F. H. Kanfer & A. P. Goldstein (Eds.), *Helping people change.* New York: Pergamon Press, 1975.

Goldstein, A. P. *Therapist-patient expectancies in psychotherapy.* New York: Pergamon Press, 1962.

Rosen, G. M. Therapy set: Its effects on subjects' involvement in systematic desensitization and treatment outcome. *Journal of Abnormal Psychology,* 1974, *83,* 291–300.

Information-Giving

D'Zurilla, T. J., & Goldfried, M. R. Problem solving and behavior modification. *Journal of Abnormal Psychology,* 1971, *78,* 107–126.

Gazda, G., Walters, R., & Childers, W. *Human relations development: A manual for health sciences.* Boston: Allyn & Bacon, 1975. Chap. 17, Responding with information, 171–180.

Gelatt, H., Varenhorst, B., Carey, R., & Miller, G. *Decisions and outcomes: A leader's guide.* Princeton, N.J.: College Entrance Examination Board, 1973.

Lewis, E. C. *The psychology of counseling.* New York: Holt, Rinehart & Winston, 1970. Chap. 7, Some issues in counseling: Diagnosis, information, and records, 128–148.

Chapter 8
Interview Discrimination

One of the most important processes the counselor engages in during counseling is *discrimination*. We define discrimination as differential responding in different counseling situations. Discrimination involves the ability to distinguish, or tell apart, two or more behaviors, concepts, events, objects, or feelings. The ability to discriminate is a prerequisite for making decisions about counseling behaviors. As you may recall from Chapter 4, a counselor can use a variety of potentially helpful responses in an interview. The decision about which response to use is based upon two types of discriminations or judgments a counselor makes within an interview. The first involves identifying the purposes of the counseling interview and of the counselor's responses. The second discrimination requires assessing the effects of the selected responses and strategies on client responses and outcomes. In other words, the counselor must be able to differentiate which client responses seem to achieve the counselor's intended purposes and which do not. This information gives the counselor an evaluative basis for selecting the next strategy or response in the interview.

Objectives

The overall purpose of this chapter is to help you learn to make discriminations about your interview behavior and its effects on clients during role-play or "in vivo" interviews.

1. In a 15-minute audio-taped role-play interview, implement the three parts of interview discrimination: (1) identify the purpose of your responses, (2) select and implement a response based on your purpose, and (3) identify whether the client response does or does not achieve your intended purpose.
2. Using the audio tape of your interview, make a written interview typescript analysis including: (1) the purpose of your responses, (2) your actual responses, (3) the client's responses, and (4) an identification of whether the client responses were related to your purposes or distracted from your purposes.

Three Parts of Interview Discrimination

Interview discrimination is a self-evaluation process that occurs continuously throughout a counseling session. The counselor makes hundreds of decisions about the intended purposes of the interview and of his or her responses, selects a response, judges the resulting client response, and selects another response that may be very similar or very different from the counselor's preceding response. The pattern of previous counselor and client responses helps the counselor to determine the direction and focus of the interview and also to select and evaluate future responses. The important point is that a particular counselor response or strategy must be judged for effectiveness on the basis of the subsequent client responses (both verbal and nonverbal). When one response or strategy does not achieve its intended purpose, the counselor uses discrimination to identify and select another response or strategy that is more likely to achieve the desired results or focus.

These three parts of the counselor interview discrimination process are illustrated in Figure 8-1.

Purposes of Interview Discrimination

There are several reasons why interview discrimination is important. First of all, interview discrimination helps the counselor explore the degree to which counselor and client behaviors are functionally related—that is, to what extent the counselor's responses achieve their intended purposes in the interview. The counselor can use discrimination to recognize and judge the effects of his or her behavior on each client. An interview discrimination may prevent a counselor from blindly asserting that this response or that message is helpful or unhelpful. "Right" or "wrong" counselor behavior cannot really be determined a priori, because the effects of counselor responses will vary with each client.

A second purpose of interview discrimination is to give the counselor a rationale for selecting each response. The counselor's responses can be selected according to the continuous interview analysis rather than from standardized response modes or predetermined theoretical biases.

Finally, making some discriminations about the client's behavior may increase the counselor's understanding of the client and may indicate some possible future directions for the interview. For example, after one or more interviews, your mental notes and assessments may suggest patterns or themes in the client's communication. You may note that the client seems to be returning to an issue of control or independence. Or you may be aware that the client's selection of topics reflects certain priority areas for the client to explore or avoid (Hackney & Nye, 1973, p. 27). For instance, you may be aware that you have received a lot of messages about the client's mother but not about the father. The information from this discrimination may tell you that one direction that needs exploration in future sessions involves the client's relationship with her or his father.

A Cognitive Map for the Interview

This section demonstrates how to apply the three parts of interview discrimination to your actual or "in vivo" counseling interviews.

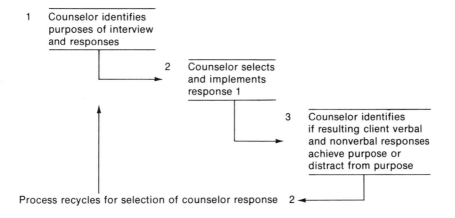

Figure 8-1. Three Parts of Counselor Interview Discrimination

Our intent is to show you a way to *think* about or *process* what happens to you and your client in the interview. Up to this point, most of this book has focused on helping you acquire overt and visible skills. However, there is more to counseling competence than the mastery and demonstration of skills and techniques. Effective implementation of these skills is enhanced by your capacity to judge when to use skills, how to use them, and what happens when you do use them. Because of the number of possible alternatives and directions that could be pursued in any given session, it is impossible to give you precise directions for when and how you should use a given skill or strategy with a client. In lieu of providing you with a recipe that inevitably would not work with all clients, we are suggesting a plan to help you decide when to use the skills and how to assess the effects of these skills with clients. We refer to this plan as drawing a *cognitive map* for your interviews. In this context, a cognitive map can be thought of as your plan for how to get where you want to go in the interview.

Two Directions for Your Cognitive Map

There are two primary things for you to think about as you go through an interview. First, as you hear each client statement, think about whether it is related to the ongoing purpose of the interview or whether it distracts from the interview purpose. For example, one of the primary purposes of an initial counseling interview is to encourage the client to talk. As counseling goes on, the counselor attempts to help the client talk about himself or herself (Hackney & Nye, 1973, p. 27). Therefore, in an initial interview, you may ask the client to talk about his or her concerns or to discuss the reasons for seeking counseling. If the client responds by sharing these topics with you, you can decide that these responses contributed to the purpose of the interview. However, if the client is continually silent or talks about unrelated events and people, you can conclude that these client responses distracted from the ongoing purpose of this interview.

As another illustration, suppose that the interview purpose is to help the client identify some action steps to reach her or his stated goal of "expressing feelings more frequently." In this example, goal-related client statements are those that indicate the client has thought of an action step or will consider one. In contrast, "distracting" client statements are those that avoid dealing with action steps or that suggest the client won't or can't try a particular alternative. Client responses can also be communicated nonverbally. If, for example, one purpose of the interview is to reduce the client's discomfort, and the client continually sends nonverbal messages of tension, you can conclude that this purpose has not yet been achieved. So the first assessment you make "in your head" is to decide whether the client response (which may be verbal, nonverbal, or both) is goal-related or distracting from the purposes of the interview.

The second part of your cognitive map is drawn after you determine whether the client message is goal-related or distracting. Based on this judgment, your map should help you select and use future responses that you believe will achieve your intended purpose. These discriminations can help you decide whether you need to continue or to change responses or strategies following off-base or distracting client verbal or nonverbal responses. If you get client responses that are goal-related, you may decide that your responses are on target. But if you note several client statements that are distracting, you may need to analyze your previous responses. Perhaps a change in your responses is necessary. For example, if the interview purpose is "identifying covert behaviors associated with the client's problem," after you determine that a client's response is distracting, you must select another response that you believe is more likely to help the client identify covert behaviors. Or, when the interview purpose is "to identify some action steps," suppose you suggest something that the client indicates won't work. After determining that this is a distracting client response, you will need to formulate and use an alternative response. Your next response may suggest another action step the client is more likely to try out—or it may focus on the client's reluctance to pursue an action step. Regardless of what your next response is, the important point is that you can identify a purpose or direction, assess whether the resulting client responses are related to that purpose, and select alternative responses with a rationale in mind.

These assessments should be made covertly, "in your head," for each client and for each interview. As you will see in the remaining chapters of this book, a cognitive map is useful for every interview in the counseling process. For example, in helping the client to define problems (Chapters 9 and 10), the counselor needs to pursue some very specific kinds of information. During the problem-definition process, you will need to assess the type and amount of information you receive from the client. Your assessment will help you decide how long to stay with one focus and when to move on to another area. Effective implementation of all counseling skills requires use of a plan or a cognitive map when your skills are in action.

Generating a cognitive map during an interview will be modeled for you in a short dialogue of an initial counseling interview. We will assume that the goals or purposes of this initial interview are to encourage the client to talk, to talk about himself, and to specify his reasons for seeking counseling. In this dialogue, each counselor verbal response is preceded by what the counselor is thinking, the counselor's *cognitive map*. Therefore, both the counselor's mental notes about the client's preceding verbal and nonverbal responses and the counselor's plans for the next response are included.

The length of what the "counselor thinks" is exaggerated in the following dialogue because we have attempted to give you a variety of examples of what the counselor might be thinking.

Counselor-Client Dialogue with a Cognitive Map

Interview purpose: To find out why the client came to see me today.

1. Counselor: What would you like to talk about today?
   Client (in an "edgy" voice): I sure had a tough time getting into this office today. You'd think that a new building that has the rehab office in it would get rid of these things that make it tough for people like me in wheelchairs to get in and out of the buildings.
   Counselor thinks: *I don't think he came to see me to complain about structural barriers to the handicapped. My first question really didn't get much of why he is here. Better check again and focus on what he wants to see me about. For my next response I'll reflect his feelings of discomfort that I picked up from his tone of voice and ask more directly about his concerns.*
2. Counselor: Getting in and out of buildings in your wheelchair is awkward for you. Is that what you're concerned with or something else?
   Client: Well, it's not so much getting around in my wheelchair. As a matter of fact, I can maneuver myself really well. It's more that people insist on helping me. Like today, three people wanted to help me.
   Counselor thinks: *OK, the client is talking a little more about himself. My last response seemed to help him start to identify a concern. However, he didn't really say how other people's help is a problem for him—or how it bothers him. So I believe next I'll ask him to focus on his feelings when people do help.*
3. Counselor: I'd like you to describe how you feel when people try to help you.
   Client: What do you mean "how I feel"?
   Counselor thinks: *From his response, he either is very reluctant to get into his feelings or he isn't aware of his feelings. If it's the latter, it might help to show him what I mean by a feeling. I'll give some examples of a feeling in my next response by self-disclosing.*
4. Counselor: Well, sometimes when I feel capable of doing something myself, and someone insists on doing it for me, I feel frustrated and resentful.
   Client (voice pitch goes up, voice gets louder): Well, how could you know how it would feel to be in a wheelchair like I am?
   Counselor thinks: *My example only seemed to make the client avoid verbal expression of his feelings more. But, based on his nonverbal response here plus the way he complained when he came in, I believe he does have some strong feelings about himself and his disability. Perhaps they're too intense for him to handle now. I believe I'll respond to his question and then direct the focus back to his expressed concern of having too much help.*

5. Counselor: I can't really know your feelings. I can only tell you how I feel when someone wants to give me help I don't need or want. I guess that having people help you is something you've had to face ever since you've been in a wheelchair.

Client (voice continues to be loud): You bet it is. I feel so damn dependent. I want to tell people to bug off although I don't want to hurt their feelings. Their intentions are good.

Counselor thinks: *That's the most I've gotten from the client. It's the first indication he's willing to explore the situation. The issue seems to be related to dependence and being in control. He's letting people help him; he doesn't want to hurt their feelings; he may be having some assertiveness problems. Seems, too, like he's bottled up some anger. However, I'm just speculating now and this is premature; I'll stick with his stated feelings of dependence for now.*

6. Counselor: You mentioned feeling dependent. Are you saying that being in a wheelchair and having people help you are two things that make you feel dependent?

Client: Yeah. Being in a wheelchair is bad enough. But when people treat you as if you're disabled and weak, it's worse.

Counselor thinks: *I'm still picking up some feelings of resentment and anger, but they're very covert. He is continuing to talk about dependency, so my last response seemed to continue this focus. The client does seem ready to explore himself in relationship to dependence and his disability. I'll try to tie together how the dependency affects him in my next response.*

7. Counselor: Having people act as if you aren't capable of doing things on your own makes you feel worse. You'd like for others to realize you are fairly independent. I guess, too, that being treated by others as if you're dependent and weak might affect the way you see yourself.

Client (avoids eye contact): Oh, how so?

Counselor thinks: *From the lack of eye contact and the client's brief verbal message, I believe either my response was unclear or he isn't ready to look at his self-image yet. I'll go in the back door by asking the client to describe what has happened in some situations where he has felt dependent.*

8. Counselor: Well, I'm not sure. Maybe you could tell me what seems to happen in a situation where people are too solicitous.

Interview Typescript Analysis

Sometimes it is useful to test out your cognitive map by exploring the discriminations you actually made in an interview. One way to do this is with a written typescript analysis of the interview. Using an audio tape of your session, you can analyze very specific parts of the interview by identifying, in writing, the purpose of your responses (as you recall), your actual responses, and the client's verbal and nonverbal responses. From this typescript, you can assess whether each client response was goal-related or distracting. You also can identify areas in the interview where you made these discriminations, as well as times when you failed to notice client responses that were distracting or off-base.

An interview analysis is also useful for seeing the totality, or the Gestalt, of an interview. The analysis may help you realize all the multiple directions that could be pursued and the variety of responses that could be used in an interview. A written interview analysis also may point out patterns or themes that may be difficult to identify during the interview. For example, a close look at an interview reveals that it is not one continuous unit but a series of "islands and hiatuses" (Hackney, Ivey, & Oetting, 1970, p. 343). According to these authors, an island is one topic or a series of related topics, and at the end of an island there is a pause, referred to as the hiatus. The hiatus seems to be a point where the counselor and client take time out to decide whether to continue with the same topic or introduce different topics. The typescript analysis can show clearly whether one topic is continued and when new topics or directions are introduced. An interview analysis also may show that the client avoided feelings or topics at certain times. This is apparent in client responses 3, 4, and 5 of Table 8-1, a typescript analysis of the dialogue you just read.

Before reading the interview analysis, you may wish to note the column headings at the top of Table 8-1. These headings represent ways to categorize counselor and client interview behavior in order to identify the relationship between the counselor behavior and resulting client responses. Based on the purpose of the interview (column 1), and on the purpose of a response (column 2), the counselor makes a response (column 3), which is followed by a client response (column 4). In doing the typescript analysis, the counselor determines whether or not each client response achieved the purposes stated in columns 1 and 2. If so, the counselor lists it as goal-related; if not, it is listed as distracting (column 5). Based on this assessment and on the overall purpose of the session, the counselor develops and lists a plan for the next response (column 6). The plan for one's next response should be directly related to the purpose or focus of the interview, and the description of the plan (column 6) should be directly reflected in the purpose of the next response (column 2). Use this explanation now to read and analyze the sample typescript in Table 8-1.

Table 8-1. An Interview Typescript Analysis

1 Purpose of Interview	2 Purpose of Response	3 Counselor Response	4 Client Verbal and Nonverbal Responses	5 Client Response Goal-Related	Distracting	6 Plan for Next Response
To get client to talk: a. about specific reasons for counseling b. about self	1. to find out why client came for counseling	"What would you like to talk about today?"	"I sure had a tough time getting in today." (Goes on to complain about the building. Voice sounds edgy.)		Didn't tell me why he's here.	Continue to pursue his reasons for counseling by asking him more directly what is his concern.
	2. to find out why client came for counseling (same as 1)	"Getting in and out of buildings in your wheelchair is awkward for you. Is that what you're concerned with or something else?"	"It's not so much getting around as it is that people insist on helping me."	Starts to specify one concern —having too much help.		Focus on concern of being helped and client's *feelings* about this.
	3. to help client identify his feelings related to being helped	"I'd like you to describe how you feel when people help you."	"What do you mean 'how I feel'?"		Didn't express feelings about being helped.	Model what a feeling is by use of self-disclosure.

Table 8-1. An Interview Typescript Analysis (continued)

1 Purpose of Interview	2 Purpose of Response	3 Counselor Response	4 Client Verbal and Nonverbal Responses	5 Client Response Goal-Related	Distracting	6 Plan for Next Response
	4. to model a feeling to help client get in touch with his feelings	"Well, sometimes when I feel capable of doing something myself and someone insists on doing it for me, I feel frustrated and resentful."	"Well, how could you know how it would feel to be in a wheelchair like I am." (Voice pitch goes up and voice gets louder.)		Didn't verbally express feelings about being helped; nonverbals still suggest some resentment.	Drop feelings for now. Go back to subject of having people help, as it seems safer for client to talk about. Will come back to feelings later.
	5. to focus on issue of being helped	"I can't know your feelings. . . I guess that having people help you is something you've had to face ever since you've been in a wheelchair."	"You bet it is. I feel so damn dependent. I want to tell people to bug off although I don't want to hurt their feelings."	Focus of being helped is achieved. Also, client did express feelings, something I was striving for earlier, perhaps too early.		Stick with his feelings of being dependent.
	6. to get client to continue to talk about being dependent.	"Are you saying that being in a wheelchair and having people help you are two things that make you feel dependent?"	"Yeah. Being in a wheelchair is bad enough. But when people treat you as if you're disabled and weak it's worse."	He continues to talk about dependence on others.		Relate client's feelings of dependency to self-image.

Table 8-1. An Interview Typescript Analysis (continued)

1 *Purpose of Interview*	2 *Purpose of Response*	3 *Counselor Response*	4 *Client Verbal and Nonverbal Responses*	5 *Client Response* *Goal-Related*	*Distracting*	6 *Plan for Next Response*
	7. to have client identify how feeling dependent affects self-image	". . . being treated by others as if you're dependent might affect the way you see yourself."	"Oh, how so?" (Avoids eye contact.)	Client avoided verbal response and eye contact.		Drop self-image and explore more about situations that make client feel dependent; go back to self-image later when client may be more ready to discuss it.
	8. to have client describe situation in which he gets too much help and feels dependent	"Maybe you could tell me what seems to happen in a situation where people are too solicitous and you feel dependent."				

Learning Activity: Interview Typescript Analysis

Instructions: This learning activity consists of a short typescript of a counselor-client dialogue. Read the dialogue carefully. For each of the six client responses, decide whether the response did or did not achieve the intended purposes of the counselor's response (as listed on the typescript). Give a rationale for your decision. Feedback follows on p. 125.

Purpose of Interview	*Purpose of Response*	*Counselor Response*	*Client Verbal and Nonverbal Responses*	*Client Response* *Goal-Related*	*Distracting*
To get client to talk: 1. about reasons for counseling 2. about self	1. Find out why client came for counseling 2. Find out why client came for counseling	1. "I'm wondering why you're here to see me." 2. "I know sometimes it's hard to talk about this."	1. Silence (looks down). 2. "Well, I've been upset lately. It's hard to talk without getting upset."	1. ____ because or ____ because 2.	

Purpose of Interview	Purpose of Response	Counselor Response	Client Verbal and Nonverbal Responses	Client Response Goal-Related	Distracting
3. Find out why client came for counseling related to being upset	3. "I can see that it's difficult for you. You say you've been feeling upset recently?"		3. "Yes. Well, my husband died about 6 months ago. I've been having trouble pulling myself together." (Tears well up.)	3.	
4. To help client identify more about feeling upset	4. "You seem to be pretty upset just thinking about it."		4. "Yes—it was so unexpected. I was so dependent on Joe. Now I can't stand the loneliness. It's depressing."	4.	
5. To have client expand on her loneliness concern	5. "So you're concerned not only about his sudden death— but how lonely you feel now that he's gone."		5. "Yes. I never had many other friends. I didn't work. I'm having trouble reaching out. I just don't feel like it, though I ought to."	5.	
6. To have client identify or confirm her mixed message in her previous response	6. "So part of you is saying you should make contact with others— another part of you is holding back."		6. Silence and then— "Well. . . ."	6.	

A written typescript analysis of an interview (or of a portion of a session) is a useful way to see the pattern between counselor and client behavior. Specifically, the analysis can help the counselor identify the three types of interview discriminations we have proposed in this chapter: (1) identifying the purpose of the interview and of your responses, (2) identifying goal-related and distracting client responses, and (3) selecting alternative responses. In the post evaluation at the end of this chapter, you are asked to complete a typescript analysis such as the one presented in Table 8-1 for an interview you conduct. This is a time-consuming task. However, our students have consistently reported that it has been one of their most productive learning experiences. We hope you also will find the benefits of this task to outweigh the time demands.

Interview Discrimination and Evaluation of Counseling

According to Dyer and Vriend (1975), counseling competence can be defined as the use of "informed judgment which helps a counselor to make accurate assessments of client reality data." Counselor competence involves both the selection and initiation of behaviors which effect a helping interaction in a purposeful way (p. 21). As an analysis of the ongoing counseling process, interview discrimination provides a basis for the counselor's selection of responses that are purposeful, not haphazard. Interview discrimination also is a way for the counselor to assess the direction of a counseling session and to identify the immediate results of counselor interview responses. However, this is a "micro" counseling evaluation which is not sufficient unless accompanied by a "macro" assessment of counseling. Ultimately, the results of counseling must be assessed by what the client does outside the interview. Evaluation procedures for determining the overall effects of counseling are presented in Chapter 13.

Post Evaluation

1. Conduct a 15-minute audio-taped role-play of an initial interview. Use as your general purpose of the interview "encouraging the client to talk, and to talk about himself or herself." During the interview, try to discriminate between client responses that do and do not contribute to this general purpose and to the intended purposes of your responses. Use your discriminations to help you make a plan or a cognitive map for your future responses in the interview.
2. Using the audio tape of the interview, verify your discriminations by making a written analysis of (1) the purpose of your responses, (2) your responses, (3) the client's responses, and (4) identification of whether the client responses were related to your purposes or distracted from your purposes. You can use the sample typescript analysis in Table 8-1 as a guide.

There is no feedback for this evaluation because it is done "in vivo." We suggest you check your typescript analysis yourself or with another person, or give it to your instructor for feedback.

You may wish to consider these questions in assessing your typescript analysis:

1. Did you find that you tended to use responses

Feedback: Interview Typescript Analysis

1. Client response 1 is probably distracting because the client didn't identify any reason for being there.
2. Although this response is a little vague, the client did identify one feeling that perhaps prompted her to seek counseling—feeling upset. This could be considered goal-related.
3. This is quite goal-related since the client identifies a past and a present concern.
4. This is very goal-related. Client confirms counselor's response ("Yes") and identifies other present feelings—dependency, loneliness, depression.
5. This is also goal-related. Client identifies another concern—making contact.
6. This is perhaps distracting—client does not identify or confirm her mixed message.

---

randomly, or to use unhelpful responses when you had no clear purpose or rationale in mind?
2. What patterns do you see between your responses and client responses? Look for continuity or change in focus and topic.
3. Does your analysis indicate whether you did or did not discriminate between goal-related and distracting client responses during the interview and make adjustments in your behavior as necessary?
4. For each client response you identify as distracting, what did you do immediately after this in your interview? Where did this lead? You may wish to rethink some of the responses you actually used and, in the last column of the analysis (plans for next response), identify some alternative plans and responses you could have used.

Suggested Readings

Hackney, H., Ivey, A., & Oetting, E. Attending, island and hiatus behavior: Process conception of counselor and client interaction. *Journal of Counseling Psychology*, 1970, 17, 342–346.
Lichtenberg, J. W., & Hummel, T. J. Counseling as stochastic process: Fitting a Markov chain model to initial counseling interviews. *Journal of Counseling Psychology*, 1976, 23, 310–315.

Chapter 9
The ABCs of Defining the Problem

Institutionalized patient: Why are people always out to get me?

Student: I can't ever talk to my mom. What a hassle.

Disabled person: Ever since I've had this automobile accident and had to change jobs, I don't seem to be able to get it together.

Older person: I never feel like I can do anything well anymore. And I feel so depressed all the time.

These client statements are representative of the types of concerns that clients bring to counselors every day. One thing these clients and others have in common is that their initial problem presentation is often vague and filled with emotion. A counselor can translate vague client problems into specific problem statements by using certain skills associated with problem definition and assessment. This chapter presents a conceptual framework a counselor can use to define and analyze client problems. Chapter 10 demonstrates a way for the counselor to implement this framework in the interview setting.

What Is Problem Definition?

Problem definition, also referred to as assessment, consists of one or more procedures and tools used to collect and process information from which the entire counseling program is developed. The ultimate purpose of problem definition is to make the best decision regarding an effective counseling approach or strategy for each client. The information obtained during the problem-definition process should help to answer this well-thought-out question: "What treatment, by *whom,* is most effective for *this* individual with *that* specific problem and under *which* set of circumstances?" (Paul, 1967, p. 111). Engaging in problem definition can help both counselor and client discover what is or is not happening in the client's environment. This information is a prerequisite for selecting effective counseling strategies or action plans.

Although a thorough definition of the problem is a prerequisite for planning the course of counseling, assessment should not stop after the initial problem has been defined. It should be carried out continuously during counseling in order to make any necessary changes in treatment plans and to base treatment plans on data rather than intuition (Kanfer & Phillips, 1970).

Objectives

After completing this chapter, you should be able to identify, in writing, using a simulated client case:

1. the client's problem behaviors
2. whether the problem behaviors are overt or covert
3. the antecedent conditions
4. the consequences
5. the way in which each consequence influences the problem behaviors.

Reasons for Problem Definition

Let's consider some reasons why problem definition is such an important starting point in counseling. Perhaps you can think of many reasons for accurate problem definition; here are four of the most important. First of all, problem definition can help the counselor and client identify the presenting problem and determine whether it represents all or only part of the client's real concerns. Sometimes a client refrains from presenting all the problems initially to test the counselor. Other clients may omit describing parts of the problem that they do not readily recognize. The counselor who is committed to conducting a thorough problem assessment may be able to identify client concerns that are not revealed explicitly. Another important reason for engaging in problem definition is to ensure that the counseling process is structured to meet the *client's* needs. Counselors who fail to determine or to deal with a client's problem may be using counseling to make themselves feel comfortable or to work out their own concerns. A third significant reason for accurate problem definition is to eliminate ambiguity and to clarify the client's specific purpose for seeking help. Unless the client's expectations are clarified, the counselor may propose good solutions for the wrong problem. Specifying client problems accurately is the basis for formulating the goals of counseling (see Chapters 11 and 12). The problem behaviors defined in an initial analysis serve as a baseline or starting point from which a client's progress toward the goal behaviors can later be assessed. Finally, problem definition is a way to evolve a consistent view of the problem for both counselor and

client. One way to conceptualize client problems is presented in the next section.

Conceptualizing Client Problems

Depending on their theoretical orientation, counselors may view client problems in different ways. One approach some counselors take is to use the client's history and information to label the client according to some predetermined diagnostic category such as "deviant," "manic-depressive," "schizophrenic," or "neurotic." Clients also may be labeled according to their scores on standardized tests. On the basis of these tests, a counselor may conclude that the client is "introverted," "moody," or "withdrawn." Other counselors may use a generalized approach to problem identification by assuming that one client's problem statement has the same meaning as another client's. For instance, the counselor may consider one client's report of "I feel depressed" to mean the same thing as another client's report of depression.

These approaches to problem conceptualization often are not very useful for several reasons. First, diagnostic categories and standardized test labels are probably not reliable or valid for all clients. Also, diagnostic labels may bias the way in which the client is treated. For example, children who are labeled "below average," "slow," or "unmotivated" are sometimes treated differently (and more negatively) than children who are tagged with positive labels. Institutionalized patients who are labeled "manic-depressive" or "schizophrenic" may be treated by the staff as if they are sick, irresponsible, and unable to change. This phenomenon has been documented even in cases where the institutionalized patients were, in fact, mentally healthy volunteers (Rosenhan, 1973). Labels such as *disruptive* or *moody* represent hypothetical constructs that are abstract and may overlook any relationship to overt behavior patterns. As Krumboltz and Thoresen (1969) note, "too often labels are prematurely attached to a behavior . . . without carefully determining how the person and others act before and after the behavior occurs" (p. 261).

Viewing the Problem Operationally

We suggest another way to view client problems that defines the client's present problem behaviors and some contributing problem conditions. This approach has been referred to as defining the problem *operationally*. An operational problem definition functions like a measure, a barometer, or a "behavioral anchor." Operational definitions indicate some very specific problem behaviors; they do not infer vague traits or labels from the client's problem statement. These two different approaches to problem conceptualization were contrasted by Mischel (1968): "The emphasis is on what a person does in situations rather than on inferences about what attributes he *has* more globally" (p. 10).

Consider the following example of a way to view a client's problem operationally. In working with the "depressed" client, we would try to define precisely what the client means by *depressed* in order to avoid any misinterpretation of this self-report feeling statement. Instead of viewing the client's problem as "depression," we would attempt to specify some problem thoughts, feelings, actions, and situations that are associated with the client's depression. We would find out whether the client experiences certain physiological changes during depression, what the client is thinking about while depressed, and specific activities and behaviors that occur during the depressed periods. With this client, our operational definition of the initial problem statement of "feeling depressed" might be:

a. constant thoughts that "I am a failure"
b. school experiences of failure; specifically, poor grades and few friends
c. lack of energy, evidenced by staying in bed and cutting classes occasionally.

After defining the client's problem behaviors operationally, we would try to discover how these behaviors are influenced by the client's environment.

Problem Behavior as Learned Behavior

Another assumption we use in viewing client problems is that behavior is learned and influenced by things about the client and the client's environment. In other words, behavior does not occur in a vacuum. It is related to what is or is not happening within ourselves (our internal environment) or outside ourselves (our external environment). Our behavior is influenced by certain visible or overt events (verbal, nonverbal, motoric responses) and by less visible, covert events (thoughts, images, physiological and affective states) that precede and follow many of our behaviors. These overt and covert events can maintain, increase, decrease, start, or eliminate a given behavior at any time. From this perspective, client problem behavior is learned and influenced by certain events and is not symptomatic of some underlying conflict or pathological state. This is a very important concept in problem definition and involves performing a functional analysis of the client's behavior and environment. This analysis rests on the ABC model of behavior described in the next section.

The ABC Model of Behavior

One way to identify the relationship between problem behavior and environmental events is by the ABC model (Goldiamond, 1965; Goodwin, 1969; Mahoney & Thoresen, 1974; Thoresen & Mahoney, 1974). The ABC model of behavior suggests that the behavior (B) is influenced by events that precede it, called antecedents (A), and by some types of events that follow behavior, referred to as consequences (C). An antecedent (A) event is a cue or signal that can inform a person of how to behave in a situation. A consequence (C) is defined as an event that strengthens or weakens a person's behavior. Note that these definitions of antecedents and consequences suggest that an individual's behavior is directly related to or influenced by certain events. Problem definition in counseling focuses on identifying the particular antecedent and consequent events that influence or are functionally related to the client's defined problem behavior.

As a very simple example of the ABC model, consider a behavior (B) that most of us engage in frequently—talking. Our talking behavior usually is occasioned by certain cues, such as starting a conversation with another person or being asked a question. These are examples of antecedents (A) that encourage our response of talking. Our talking behavior may be maintained by the verbal and nonverbal attention we receive from another person, which is a very powerful positive consequence, or reinforcer. We may talk less when the person's eye contact wanders, or when he or she tells us more explicitly that we've talked enough. These are negative consequences (C), or punishment, that decrease our talking behavior.

Overt and Covert Behavior

Overt behavior includes any visible event in the client's environment or something visible that the client is doing or demonstrating. For example, suppose two elementary school children are referred to a counselor. One child reports that the other child really "bugs" him, and similarly the other tells the counselor that he feels "picked on." The problem descriptions by these two children are ambiguous and really do not describe what each child is doing to the other. The counselor might ask one child "What do you do to Sam?" and ask a similar question of the other child. In this example, the identified overt behaviors might include such things as hitting, pulling hair, verbal attacks, or sarcastic comments.

Covert behaviors include events that are not visible to someone else, such as thoughts, feelings, images, and physiological states of which an individual is aware. Some covert behaviors a client might describe are illustrated in the following example. A client reports feelings of anxiety, associated physiological responses such as frequent headaches, stomach-aches, and rapid heartbeat, and repetitive anxiety-producing thoughts. Since the counselor cannot see such covert events, it is imperative for the client to describe specific feelings and thoughts that are associated with the problem. With this client, the counselor could say "Describe your anxious feelings to me" or could ask "What are some examples of these repetitive thoughts?" A covert behavioral description is obtained only after the client has identified the specific feelings and physiological states and has defined the repetitive thoughts, such as "worrying about beating my children."

Antecedents

Antecedents do not influence behavior automatically but may elicit certain emotional and physiological responses or may occasion the occurrence of some other responses. The influence that antecedents have on our behavior may vary with each of us. Also, a person may respond differently to antecedents at various times. In attempting to identify the antecedents of a problem behavior, the counselor and client will explore where and when the problem behavior usually occurs. Typically, a problem behavior is elicited by specific cues or events that precede the behavior itself. For example, our eating behavior often is elicited by such cues as going past a restaurant, visiting the grocery store, walking by the refrigerator, or thinking about the good taste of a chocolate ice cream cone.

In many clinical cases, it is not so easy to pinpoint specific antecedent events that occur *right before* or are simultaneous with the problem. Other antecedent conditions may have occurred some time before the problem began. These conditions may no longer even exist but still might be contributing to the problem—if they still have an effect on the client. For example, three years ago a person may not have been admitted to medical school. Now, three years later, when the person is applying to dental school, he or she is haunted by the experience and feelings of failure that were brought about by the previous event, even though the event has long since ended and is not an ongoing part of the person's life.

There are two important reasons for identifying antecedents of problem behavior during the problem-definition process. First, knowledge of the antecedents can give the counselor and client information about the times and situations when the problem behavior is likely to occur. Second, often a change in an antecedent can alter the client's problem behavior in the desired direction. Similarly, knowledge of the events that *follow* the problem behavior and maintain it can be used in the counseling plan.

Consequences

The consequences of a behavior are only those things that exert some influence on the behavior, that are functionally related to the behavior. In other words, not everything that follows a behavior is automatically considered a consequence. For example, suppose you are counseling an overweight woman who tends occasionally to go on eating binges. She reports that, following a binge, she feels guilty, regards herself as even more unattractive, and tends to suffer from insomnia. Although these events are results of her eating-binge behavior, they are not consequences unless in some way they directly influence her binges, either by maintaining or decreasing them. In this case, other events that follow the eating binges may be the real consequences. For instance, perhaps her binges are maintained by the enjoyment or anxiety reduction she gets from eating; perhaps they are temporarily decreased when someone else, such as her husband, notices her behavior and reprimands her for it.

Consequences are categorized as positive or negative. Positive consequences can be referred to technically as *rewards* or *reinforcers;* negative ones can be labeled *punishers.* By definition, positive consequences (rewarding events) will maintain or increase the behavior. In contrast, negative consequences (punishing events) will weaken or decrease it. As an example, the overweight woman may maintain her eating binges

because of the feelings of pleasure she receives from eating (a positive reinforcing consequence). Or, her eating binges could be maintained because they allow her to escape from or avoid an anxiety-producing or boring situation (negative reinforcing consequence). In contrast, her husband's reprimands or sarcasm may, at least temporarily, reduce her eating binges (punishing consequence). Like antecedents, the consequences will always vary with clients. Things that maintain or weaken a problem behavior for one client may be quite different from influential events for another person.

Another way to distinguish between positive and negative consequences has been suggested by Mahoney and Thoresen (1974). They note that a counselor can determine the value a consequence may have for a client by discovering whether the client will work to produce or avoid the *consequence* (not the behavior itself). They state that, if a person "will work to produce or prolong a certain consequence, then we are justified in calling it positive. On the other hand, if he will work to avoid or terminate it, then it is negative" (p. 5). In the example of the overweight woman, the counselor might try to determine whether the client tries to produce pleasurable feelings from eating and prolong avoidance of an anxiety-producing or boring situation. Similarly, the counselor might check to see whether the woman attempts to avoid her husband's reprimands or sardonic comments.

Consequences may play a significant role in influencing some behaviors and a minimal role in others. Consequences also may be immediate, delayed, or both. For instance, our overweight client expressed some immediate consequences of her eating binge, such as pleasurable sensations and reduction of anxiety or boredom. Delayed consequences of her binge behavior could include added excess pounds, changes in her physical appearance, and potential hazards to her health. As another example, consider a male client who does not engage in some social activities because of anxiety or fear about interacting with other people. The immediate consequences maintaining his behavior may include feeling relieved at escaping a dreaded situation and receiving attention for his "problem" from a friend or roommate. Delayed consequences could include effects on all his social interactions, resulting in a lack of opportunities to develop his social skills and to create important interpersonal relationships. In these two examples, the problem behavior is often hard to change, because the immediate consequences make the person feel better in some way. As a result, the problem behavior is reinforced, even if the delayed or long-term consequences are unpleasant. In other words, in these examples, the client "values" the behavior that he or she is attempting to eliminate.

Overt and Covert ABCs

The ABC model for viewing behavior is not always so simple when applied to actual client problems. In addition to visible events, the cognitive and affective processes within an individual also can be antecedents or consequences. Likewise, the behavior itself can be an overt, visible action or a less visible cognitive, affective, or physiological activity that goes on within the client.

An overt event is any visible action of the client or of someone in the client's environment. An environmental situation also can be classified as an overt event. In contrast, a covert process represents a "private event" (Skinner, 1953)—that is, some internal activity of a person that is not directly visible to someone else. Covert events include cognitive responses—the client's thoughts, beliefs, and images. Emotions, feelings, or affective states are other examples of covert events. However, a person's "feeling" is usually the result of the way she or he thinks about or labels something. For instance, if we feel depressed after a close friend terminates our friendship, our feeling of depression is a result of our labels or beliefs about the situation (for example, "I'm not good enough; my friend rejected me"). Physiological responses also are typically classified as covert because having an "upset stomach" or a "pounding heart" is not usually obvious to an outside observer.

The ABC model is complicated a little more in defining client problems because, for any given problem, a number of different combinations of overt and covert As, Bs, and Cs can exist. Mahoney (1974, p. 77)* has listed eight possible ways in which overt (O) and covert (C) As, Bs, and Cs can interact in a problem situation:

Antecedents	Behavior	Consequences
O	O	O
O	O	C
O	C	O
O	C	C
C	O	O
C	C	O
C	O	C
C	C	C

Several examples of overt and covert ABCs of client problems may help to illustrate this model. Suppose the client's problem behavior has been defined as talking very loudly in the classroom. This behavior, a visible event, is overt. Perhaps it is elicited whenever the teacher leaves the room—an overt antecedent—and maintained by subsequent peer laughter—an overt consequence. As another example, consider a client who reports frequent negative thoughts about himself or herself—a covert problem behavior. These thoughts are elicited by a covert antecedent—episodes of anxiety described by the client as "feeling panicked, with a nauseous pit in my stomach." The negative self-thoughts might result in aversive or unpleasant self-images such as "I'm sick" or "There's something wrong with me" or "I can't make it, so I won't try." These covert consequences, although unpleasant, could maintain the client's negative self-thoughts. Also, these thoughts might be maintained by additional overt or visible consequences including peer or family attention in the form of verbal support (such as "Oh, you're really OK" or "You really can do it").

*Adapted from *Cognition and Behavior Modification*, by M. J. Mahoney. Copyright 1974 by Ballinger Publishing Co. Used by permission.

To assist you in conceptualizing client problems from an ABC model, we have provided a case illustration followed by two practice cases for you to complete. The conceptual understanding you should acquire from this chapter will help you actually define client problems with an interview assessment, described in Chapter 10.

An ABC Model Case

To assist you in identifying the overt and covert ABCs of a client problem, the following hypothetical case is presented. Extensions of this case will be used as illustrations in remaining chapters of the book.

The Case of Joan

Joan is a 15-year-old student who is completing her sophomore year at a local high school where she is presently taking a college-preparatory curriculum. Her initial statement in the first counseling session is that she is "unhappy" and feels "dissatisfied" with this school experience but feels unable to do anything about it. Upon further clarification, Joan reveals that she is unhappy because she doesn't think she is measuring up to her classmates and that she dislikes being with these "top" kids in some of her classes, which are very competitive. She reports particular concern in one math class which she says is composed largely of "guys" who are much smarter than she is. She states that she thinks about the fact that "girls are so dumb in math" rather frequently during the class. She reports that, as soon as she is in this class, she gets anxious and "withdraws." She states sometimes she gets anxious just thinking about the class. When asked what she means by "withdrawing," she says she sits by herself, doesn't talk to her classmates, and doesn't volunteer answers or go to the board. Often, when called upon, she says nothing. As a result, she reports, her grades are dropping. Also, she states that her math teacher has spoken to her several times about her behavior and has tried to help her do better. However, Joan's nervousness in the class has resulted in her cutting the class whenever she can find any reason.

Also, she has almost used up her number of excused absences from school. She states that her fear of competitive academic situations has been a problem since junior high, when her parents started to compare her to other students and put "pressure" on her to do well in school so she could go to college. When asked how they "pressure" her, she said they constantly talk to her about getting good grades and, whenever she doesn't, they lash out at her and withdraw certain privileges like her allowance. She reports that, during this year, since the classes are tougher and more competitive, school is more of a problem to her and she feels increasingly anxious in certain classes, especially math. Joan also states that sometimes she thinks she is almost failing on purpose to get back at her parents for their pressure. Joan reports that all of this has made her dissatisfied with school and she has questioned whether she wants to stay in a college-prep curriculum. She states that she has considered switching to a work-study curriculum so she could learn some skills and get a job after high school. However, she says she is a very indecisive person and does not know what she should do. Also, she is afraid to decide this because if she changed curriculums, her parents' response would be very negative. Joan states that she cannot recall times when she has ever made a decision without her parents' assistance. She feels they have often made decisions for her. She states that her parents have never encouraged her to make decisions on her own, because they say she might not make the right decision without their help.

Analysis of Case

Problem Situations

First of all, there are two related but distinct problem situations for Joan. Her "presenting" problem is that she feels anxious in certain competitive classes in school. She identifies math class as the primary problem class. Second, she is having difficulty making a decision about the type of curriculum she should pursue. More generally, another problem is that she considers herself indecisive in most situations. The analysis of this case will explore Joan's problem behaviors and the antecedents and consequences for each of these two problem areas.

Analysis of School Problem

1. *Problem Behaviors*
   Joan's problem behaviors at school include
   a. self-defeating labeling of her math class as "competitive" and of herself as "not as smart as the guys."
   b. sitting alone, not volunteering answers in math class, not answering the teacher's questions or going to the board, and cutting class.
   Her self-defeating labels are a covert behavior; her sitting alone, not volunteering answers, and cutting class are overt behaviors.
2. *Antecedent Conditions*
   Joan's problem behaviors at school are elicited by anxiety regarding certain "competitive" classes, particularly math. Previous antecedent conditions would include verbal comparisons about Joan and her peers made by her parents and verbal pressure for good grades and withholding of privileges for bad grades by her parents. Note that these antecedent conditions do not occur at the same time. The antecedent of the anxiety in the "competitive" class occurs in close proximity to Joan's problem behaviors. However, the verbal comparisons and parental pressure began several years ago.
3. *Consequences*
   Joan's problem behaviors at school are maintained by
   a. an increased level of attention to her problems by her math teacher.
   b. feeling relieved of anxiety through avoidance of the situation that elicits anxiety. By not participating in class and by cutting class, she can avoid putting herself in an anxiety-provoking situation.
   c. her poorer grades, possibly, because of two "pay-offs." (1) If her grades get too low, she may not qualify to continue in the college-prep curriculum. This would be the "ultimate" way to avoid putting herself in competitive academic situations that elicit anxiety. (2) The lowered grades also could be maintaining her problem behaviors because she labels the poor grades as a way "to get back at" her parents for their pressure.

Analysis of Decision-Making Problem

1. *Problem Behaviors*
   The problem behavior can be described as not making a decision for herself—in this case, regarding a curriculum change. Depending on the client, problems in making decisions can be either a covert or an overt problem. In people who have the skills to make a decision but are blocking themselves because of their "labels" or "internal dialogue" about the decision, the problem behavior would be designated as covert. In Joan's case, her indecisive behavior seems based on her past learning history of having many decisions either made for her or made with parental assistance. The lack of opportunities she has had to make choices suggests she has not acquired the skills involved in decision-making. This would be classified as an overt problem.
2. *Antecedent Conditions*
   Joan's previous decision-making history is the primary antecedent condition. This consists of (1) having decisions made for her, and (2) a lack of opportunities to acquire and use the skills of decision-making.
3. *Consequences*
   The consequences that seem to be maintaining her problem behavior of not deciding include
   a. getting help with her decisions, thereby avoiding the responsibility of making a choice
   b. anticipation of parental negative reactions (punishment) to her decision-making through her "self-talk"
   c. absence of positive consequences or lack of encouragement for any efforts at decision-making in the past
   d. in the specific decision of a curriculum change, her low grades which, if they get too bad, may help her avoid making a curriculum decision by automatically disqualifying her from the college-prep curriculum.

Learning Activity: ABCs of Problem Definition

To help you in conceptualizing a client's problem from the ABC model, the following two cases are provided. We suggest that you work through the first case completely before going on to the second one. After reading each case, by yourself or with a partner, respond to the questions following the case. Then check your responses with the feedback.

The Case of Ms. Weare and Freddie

Ms. Weare and her 10-year-old son, Freddie, have come to counseling at the referral of Family Services. Their initial complaint is that they don't get along with each other. Ms. Weare complains that Freddie doesn't dress by himself in the morning and this makes her mad. Freddie complains his mother yells and screams at him frequently. Ms. Weare agrees she does this, especially when it is time for Freddie to leave for school and he isn't dressed yet. Freddie agrees he doesn't dress himself and points out he does this just to "get Mom mad." Ms. Weare states this has been going on as long as she can remember. She states that Freddie gets up and usually comes down to breakfast not dressed. After breakfast, Ms. Weare always reminds him to dress and threatens him that she'll yell or hit him if he doesn't. Freddie usually goes back to his room where, he reports, he just sits around until his mother comes up. Ms. Weare waits until 5 minutes before the bus comes and then calls Freddie. After he doesn't come down, she goes upstairs and sees that he's not dressed. She reports she gets very mad and yells "You're dumb. Why do you just sit there? Why can't you dress yourself? You're going to be late for school. Your teacher will blame me since I'm your mother." She also helps Freddie dress. So far, he has not been late, but Ms. Weare says she "knows" he will be if she doesn't "nag" him and help him dress. Upon further questioning, Ms. Weare states that this does not occur on weekends, only on school days. She states that, as a result of this situation, she feels very nervous and edgy after Freddie leaves for school, often not doing some necessary work because of this. Asked what she means by "nervous" and "edgy," she reports that her body feels tense and jittery all over. She

reports that, since Freddie's father is not living at home, all the child-rearing is on her shoulders. Ms. Weare also states that she doesn't spend much time with Freddie at night after school.

Respond to these questions. Feedback is on p. 135.
1. What problem behavior(s) does Freddie demonstrate in this situation?
2. Is each problem behavior you have listed overt or covert?
3. What problem behavior(s) does Ms. Weare exhibit in this situation?
4. Is each problem behavior you have listed overt or covert?
5. List one or more antecedent conditions that seem to bring about Freddie's problem behavior(s).
6. List one or more antecedent conditions that seem to bring about Ms. Weare's problem behavior(s).
7. List one or more consequences that influence Freddie's problem behavior(s). After each consequence listed, identify how the consequence seems to influence his behavior.
8. List one or more consequences that seem to influence Ms. Weare's behavior. After each consequence listed, identify how the consequence seems to influence her behavior.

The Case of Mr. Phyle

Mr. Phyle is a middle-aged man who has recently been admitted to a hospital psychiatric ward because of displaying inappropriate sexual behavior in public; specifically, Mr. Phyle was seen exposing himself to his female neighbors. Since his admittance to the ward, he has occasionally attempted to expose himself, usually in the presence of female staff members or visitors. Typically, the visitors, in particular, have responded by screaming, gasping, running away, or looking shocked. The staff have tended to react by reprimanding Mr. Phyle or by sending him back to his room. Mr. Phyle reports to his therapist that he continues to expose himself because it makes him feel like "a worthwhile person." He reports that it is the one thing he feels he can do successfully. In addition to this, Mr. Phyle continually makes derogatory statements about himself and has indicated that he sees himself as unattractive and unsuccessful. He reports that he always feels unattractive around women and has never been able to establish a relationship in which a woman responded to him positively. Moreover, his few attempts at relating to women sexually have "bombed" miserably; the women have refused his advances. Now Mr. Phyle reports that he tries to avoid getting involved with women on any basis—interpersonal, physical, or other.

Respond to these questions. Feedback is on p. 136.
1. What problem behaviors does Mr. Phyle demonstrate?
2. Is each problem behavior you have listed overt or covert?
3. List one or more antecedents that seem to elicit Mr. Phyle's problem behaviors.
4. List one or more consequences that appear to influence the problem behaviors. Describe how each consequence seems to influence the behavior.

Summary

The development of counseling goals and the selection of counseling strategies can be facilitated by defining the client's problem behaviors and the antecedent and consequent contributing conditions. These ABCs can be overt or covert. The conceptualization presented in this chapter for defining client problems can be applied in the interview. During the interview, the counselor gathers information that is used to specify and delineate the problem. The next chapter describes and illustrates counselor leads used to define a client's problem in the interview.

Post Evaluation

Read the case description of Mr. Brown that follows and then answer the following questions:

1. What are the client's problem behaviors?
2. Are the problem behaviors overt or covert?
3. What are the antecedent conditions of Mr. Brown's concern?

Feedback for the Case of Ms. Weare and Freddie

1. Freddie's problem behavior is sitting in his room and not dressing for school.
2. This is an overt behavior since it is visible to someone else.
3. Ms. Weare's problem behaviors are: (1) feeling mad and (2) yelling at Freddie.
4. (1) Feeling mad is a covert behavior, since feelings can only be inferred. (2) Yelling is an overt behavior that is visible to someone else.
5. Receiving a verbal reminder and threat from his mother at breakfast elicits Freddie's behavior.
6. Ms. Weare's behavior seems to be cued by a 5-minute period before the bus arrives on school days.
7. Two consequences seem to influence Freddie's problem behavior of not dressing for school. (1) He gets help in dressing himself; this influences his behavior by providing special benefits. (2) He gets some satisfaction from seeing that his mother is upset and is attending to him. This seems to maintain his behavior because of the control he exerts over his mother and the attention he gets. According to the case description, he doesn't seem to get much attention at other times from his mother.
8. The major consequence that influences Ms. Weare's behavior is that she gets Freddie ready on time and he is not late. This appears to influence her behavior by helping her avoid a situation where she or someone else would consider her to be a poor mother.

4. What are the consequences of the problem behaviors?
5. Describe the way in which the consequences influence the problem behaviors.

Answers to these questions are provided after the case description.

The Case of Mr. Brown

A 69-year-old man, Mr. Brown, came to counseling because he felt his performance on his job was "slipping." Mr. Brown had a job in a large automobile company. He was responsible for producing new car designs. Mr. Brown revealed that he noticed he started having trouble about 6 months ago, when the personnel director came in to ask him to fill out retirement papers. Mr. Brown, at the time he sought counseling, was due to retire in 9 months. (The company's policy made it mandatory to retire at the age of 70.) Prior to this incident with the personnel director and to the completion of the papers, Mr. Brown reported, everything seemed to be "OK." He also reported that nothing seemed to be changed in his relationship to his wife or family. However, on some days at work, he reported having a great deal of trouble completing any work on his car designs. When asked what he did instead of working on designs, he said, "worrying." The "worrying" turned out to mean that he was engaging in constant repetitive thoughts about his approaching retirement, such as "I won't be here when this car comes out" and "What will I be without having this job?" Mr. Brown stated there were times when he spent almost an entire morning or afternoon "dwelling" on these things and that this seemed to occur mostly when he was alone in his office actually working on a car design. As a result, he was not turning in his designs according to the specified deadline. Not meeting his deadlines made him feel more worried. He was especially concerned that he would "blow" his previously established reputation in the eyes of his colleagues and superiors who, he felt, always could have counted on him "to get the job done." He was afraid that his present behavior would jeopardize the opinion others had of him, although he didn't report any other possible "costs" to him. In fact, Mr. Brown indicated it was his immediate boss who suggested, after several talks and after-work drinks, that he see a counselor. The boss also indicated the company would pay for Mr. Brown's counseling. Mr. Brown indicated that his boss has not had any noticeable reactions to his missing deadlines, other than reminding him and being solicitous, as evidenced in the talks and after-work drinks. Mr. Brown reported that he enjoyed this interaction with his boss and often wished he could ask his boss to go out to lunch with him. However, he stated these meetings had all been at his boss's request. Mr. Brown felt somewhat hesitant about making the request himself. In the last 6 months, Mr. Brown had never received any sort of reprimand for missing deadlines on his drawings. Still, he was concerned with maintaining his own sense of pride about his work, which he

Feedback for the Case of Mr. Phyle

1. There are two main problem behaviors for Mr. Phyle: (1) exposing himself and (2) self-deprecating thoughts (negative self-thoughts).
2. Exposing himself is an overt behavior—obviously visible to others! His negative self-thoughts are covert.
3. Both problem behaviors appear to be elicited by the presence of women, which is the major antecedent. Another antecedent, although not so immediate, involves his past relationship history with women, which he regards as unsuccessful.
4. The exposing behavior appears to be influenced by two consequences: (1) the attention Mr. Phyle receives from staff and visitors following his self-exposing incidents, and (2) the image of himself as a "worthwhile" person that he describes occurs after an exposing incident.

felt might be jeopardized since he'd been having this trouble.

Feedback: Post Evaluation

1. Mr. Brown's self-reported problem behaviors include worry about retirement and not doing work on his automobile designs.
2. Worrying about retirement is a covert behavior. Not doing work on designs is an overt behavior.
3. One antecedent condition occurred 6 months ago, when the personnel director conferred with Mr. Brown about retirement and papers were filled out. This is an overt antecedent. The personnel director's visit seemed to elicit Mr. Brown's worry about retirement and not doing his designs. A covert antecedent is Mr. Brown's repetitive thoughts about retirement, getting older, and so on.
4. The consequences include Mr. Brown's not meeting his deadlines, worrying about losing his reputation, and receiving extra attention from his boss.
5. Mr. Brown's problem behaviors appear to be maintained by the consequence of being ex-

cused from not meeting his deadlines with only a "reminder." He is receiving some extra attention and concern from his boss, whom he values highly.

Suggested Readings

Conceptualizing Client Problems

Goldfried, M. R., & Davison, G. C. *Clinical behavior therapy.* New York: Holt, Rinehart & Winston, 1976. Chap. 2, 18–36.

Krumboltz, J. D., & Thoresen, C. E. (Eds.). *Counseling methods.* New York: Holt, Rinehart & Winston, 1976. Pt. 1, 2–25.

Rosenhan, D. L. On being sane in insane places. *Science,* 1973, *179,* 250–258.

Swensen, C. H. *An approach to case conceptualization.* Boston: Houghton Mifflin, 1968.

ABC Model of Behavior

Cone, J. D., & Hawkins, R. P. (Eds.). *Behavioral assessment: New directions in clinical psychology.* New York: Brunner/Mazel, 1977.

Goldiamond, I. A constructional approach to self control. In A. Schwartz & I. Goldiamond, *Social casework: A behavioral approach.* New York: Columbia University Press, 1975. Chap. 3, 67–130.

Hersen, M., & Bellack. A. (Eds.). *Behavioral assessment: A practical handbook.* New York: Pergamon Press, 1976.

Mahoney, M. J. *Cognition and behavior modification.* Cambridge, Mass.: Ballinger, 1974.

Mahoney, M. J., & Thoresen, C. E. (Eds.). *Self control: Power to the person.* Monterey, Calif.: Brooks/Cole, 1974. Chap. 1, 3–19.

Thoresen, C. E., & Mahoney, M. J. *Behavioral self control.* New York: Holt, Rinehart & Winston, 1974.

Chapter 10
Defining the Problem with an Interview Assessment

There are many ways to help clients define problems, including completion of surveys and questionnaires, direct observation, self-monitoring, and the interview. The interview, if used efficiently, can be a very important assessment tool. As Kanfer and Grimm (1977) note, the purpose of a problem-assessment interview is to develop hypotheses about factors influencing the client's problems and possible change strategies (p. 8). There are at least three possible advantages of the interview method of problem definition. First, the client can become more involved than in other methods, and this involvement may reinforce the client's desire to change. Second, an interview assessment can provide important information that may help the client and counselor to identify problems and contributing conditions. Finally, the interview may help the client learn something about the counselor's approach in problem-solving methods. As Linehan (1977) notes, sometimes a change in the client's conceptualization of the problem can be therapeutic in itself (p. 36).

This chapter illustrates and describes some particular counselor verbal responses or "leads" used to define a client's problem in the assessment interviews. The leads presented in this chapter reflect the ABC model of behavior described in the previous chapter and also our own preference for problem definition with clients.

However, our task in synthesizing problem-definition leads has been assisted by the interview descriptions of Kanfer and Grimm (1977), Kanfer and Saslow (1969), Meichenbaum (1976), Morganstern (1976), Schwartz and Goldiamond (1975), and Wolpe (1976). This chapter and other chapters in this book describe interview leads that, in applied settings, are likely to elicit certain kinds of client information. However, as Morganstern observes, little research on the effects of interview procedures has been conducted. The leads suggested in this chapter are supported more by practical considerations than by empirical data. As a result, the counselor will need to be very attentive to the effects produced by using these questions with each client. In addition to learning what types of problem-definition leads to use, the counselor will need to discriminate the kinds of client responses to these leads, as suggested in Chapter 8.

Objectives

1. With a written counselor-client dialogue, identify accurately 18 out of 23 examples of the counselor leads associated with the seven categories of problem definition.
2. Select a problem behavior to self-monitor; use a behavior log to self-record the behavior,

its frequency or duration, and its antecedents and consequences.

3. Demonstrate 12 out of 14 of the leads of problem definition in a 30-minute role-play interview using the Problem-Definition Interview Checklist at the end of the chapter. You can have a consultant sit in and rate your performance or you can evaluate yourself from an audio tape of the interview.

When Does Problem Definition Occur?

With most clients, the problem-definition process begins after one or several initial interviews. Remember, before probing for a lot of information, your first task is to establish rapport and trust, and to open channels of communication. This will take at least one and usually several sessions with a client. We feel it is better to move a little more slowly at the beginning than to rush through the process with only the thought of accomplishing your agenda. Our own problems with clients have occurred mostly when, in trying to be more expedient, we have minimized the time and effort required to establish an effective relationship.

Once the relationship allows for more counselor input and direction, the counselor can start to obtain the information associated with the seven categories of problem definition. However, don't be misled into viewing each phase of counseling as independent of other processes. Maintaining a positive relationship during problem definition is just as important as it is at the beginning of counseling. Also, the counselor will continue to use all the relationship, nonverbal, and verbal skills presented earlier in this book. Think of it this way: in problem definition, you are simply *supplementing* your basic skills with some specific leads designed to obtain certain kinds of information. Many of your leads will consist of open-ended questions or probes. However, even a problem-definition interview should not disintegrate into a question-and-answer or an interrogation session. You can obtain information and give the information some meaning through

other verbal responses such as summarization, clarification, confrontation, and reflection. The model dialogue later in this chapter will illustrate how some of the previous verbal leads you have learned are used to help define the problem in an interview.

Problem Definition: What Does the Counselor Need to Know?

In helping a client define a problem, many counselors wonder exactly what they need to pursue to find out about the problem. We like Morganstern's (1976) response to this question: the counselor should attempt to find out "everything that is relevant to the development of effective, efficient, and durable treatment interventions" and, from an ethical standpoint, "no more" (p. 52). Morganstern points out that there is a serious ethical question "regarding the legitimacy of inquiry into diverse aspects of a client's life, however interesting they may be to the therapist or to the client himself, when such content is irrelevant to treatment" (p. 53).

As we suggested in Chapter 8, everything you do or say in the interview should have a purpose. Moreover, the purpose should be related to the goals of the helping process rather than to your own curiosity. Peterson (1968) indicates that, because counselors often ask questions with no purpose or only a vague purpose in mind, perhaps as much as 75% of the material usually covered in interviews could be eliminated at no great loss.

Seven Categories for Defining Problems

To help you acquire the skills of problem-definition interview leads, we have divided these leads into seven content categories. Each category represents a particular area of information to be acquired and processed in the interview. The ABC model of conceptualizing client problems described in Chapter 9 is reflected in these interview leads. These seven categories are illustrated and defined briefly in the following list and also are summarized in the Interview Checklist at the end of the chapter.

1. Explanation of problem-definition *purpose*—presentation of rationale for problem definition to the client
2. Identification and selection of *problem concerns*—leads to help client (a) identify general concerns, (b) set priorities and select concerns, and (c) pinpoint situations that are part of concern
3. Identification of *present problem behaviors*—leads to help client identify overt (visible) and covert (not visible) behaviors that compose the problem
4. Identification of *antecedent* contributing conditions—leads to help client identify overt and covert events that precede and cue problem behaviors
5. Identification of *consequent* contributing conditions—leads to help client identify events that follow and influence problem behaviors
6. Identification of *client coping skills*—leads to help client identify past and present coping or adaptive behavior
7. Identification of *problem intensity*—leads or client self-monitoring to identify (a) extent of problem, (b) degree of problem severity, and (c) frequency or duration of problem behaviors

The first two categories—explanation of the purpose of problem definition and identification and selection of problem concerns—are a logical starting place. First, it is helpful to give the client a rationale or purpose for problem definition before gathering information. Following this, some time must be spent in helping the client to identify and select problems to explore. Before the problems can be analyzed, the client has to identify the problem areas.

The other five categories follow problem selection. After the counselor and client have identified and selected the problems to work on, these five categories of counselor leads are used to define and analyze parameters of the problem. The counselor may find that the order or pattern of using problem-definition leads varies

among clients. A natural sequence will evolve in each interview, and the counselor will want to use the leads associated with these content categories in a pattern that fits the flow of the interview. This variation in the order in which leads are used is legitimate—as long as the counselor explores all the pertinent information. The amount of time and number of sessions required to obtain this information will vary with problems and with clients. It is possible to complete assessment in one session, but with some clients, three or four assessment interviews may be necessary. A complete analysis of the problem may go beyond "first appearances" in counseling (Morganstern, 1976, p. 53). Although the counselor may devote several interviews to problem definition, the information-gathering and hypothesis-testing that go on do not automatically stop after these few sessions. Some degree of problem assessment continues throughout the entire therapy process (Linehan, 1977).

Explanation of Problem-Definition Purpose

In explaining the purpose of problem definition, the counselor gives the client a rationale for defining the problem. The intent of this first category of problem definition is to give the client a "set," or an expectation, of what will occur during the interview and why problem definition is important to both client and counselor. One way the counselor can communicate the purpose of problem definition is: "Today I'd like to focus on some concerns that are bothering you most. In order to find out exactly what you're concerned about, I'll be asking you for some specific kinds of information. This information will help both of us to identify what you'd like to work on in counseling. How does this sound to you?" Following the rationale, the counselor should look for some confirmation or indication that the client understands the importance of defining problems. If client confirmation or understanding is not forthcoming, the counselor may need to provide more explanation before proceeding to other areas.

Identification and Selection of Problem Concerns

Identification and selection of problem concerns can be defined as the use of open-ended counselor leads to help the client identify general concerns, to set priorities and select concerns, and to describe all the situations that are part of the concern. Problem identification and selection also is a way to establish who is the appropriate client. In some cases, a client may attribute the problem or the undesired behavior to an event or to another person. For instance, a student may say, "That teacher always picks on me. I can never do anything right in her class." Although another person may be involved in the client's problem (such as the teacher in this example), both counselor and client should realize that only the individual who seeks direct assistance is identified as the client. This is the only person who can take the responsibility for working out the problem. The counselor's assistance will be directed toward the identified client, although, in some cases, interviews or consultation with significant people in the client's environment may be warranted (Linehan, 1977). Three categories of leads are associated with identifying and selecting problem concerns: general problem situations, selection of the problem, and pinpointing the problem.

General Problem Situations. The first part of identification and selection of problem concerns is referred to as "general problem situations." The purpose of these leads is to have the client describe all the problem areas he or she currently faces. As Kanfer and Grimm (1977) point out, rarely does a client present only a single problem or only one undesirable behavior pattern (p. 9). The primary question to be answered by general-problem leads is "What is the range of client concerns?" These global leads are used to get the "whole picture" of the client's situation. This global approach is analogous to listening to all kinds of music before focusing on one or two kinds that you really enjoy. In other words, it's helpful to explore a range of problems and situations before focusing on what to deal with. If a general-problem exploration is omitted, some of the client's concerns may never be elicited or discussed.

Examples of general-problem leads are:

"What are your concerns in your life now?"
"Could you describe some of the things that seem to be bothering you?"
"What are some present stresses in your life?"
"What situations are not going well for you?"

Following the use of general-problem leads, the counselor should look for the client's indication of some general areas of concern or things that are troublesome for the client or difficult to manage. An occasional client may not respond affirmatively to these leads. Krumboltz and Thoresen (1976) point out that sometimes a client may have a "vested interest" in not identifying a problem or may come in with a "hidden agenda" that is not readily disclosed (p. 29). In these cases, the counselor may need to use a different approach than verbal questioning to elicit problem statements. For example, Lazarus (1969, p. 21) has recommended the use of an "Inner Circle" strategy to help a client disclose problem areas.* The client is given a picture like this:

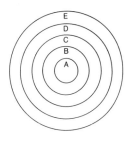

The counselor points out that topics in circle A are very personal, whereas topics in circle E are more or less public information. The counselor can provide examples of types of topics likely to be in an A circle, such as sexual concerns, feelings of hostility, marriage problems, and dishonesty. These examples may encourage the

*From "The Inner Circle Strategy: Identifying Crucial Problems," by A. Lazarus. In *Behavioral Counseling: Cases and Techniques,* edited by John D. Krumboltz and Carl E. Thoresen. Copyright © 1969 by Holt, Rinehart & Winston, Inc. Reprinted by permission of Holt, Rinehart & Winston.

client to disclose personal concerns more readily. Sometimes the counselor may be able to obtain more specific problem descriptions from a client by having the client role-play or act out a typical problem situation. Another client might provide more information by describing a fantasy or visualization about the problem. This last method has been used by Meichenbaum (1976), who asks the client "to run a movie through your head" in order to recall various aspects of the problem (p. 151).

Selection of the Problem. Many clients will refer to general problem areas in the very first counseling interview, and discussion of general areas of concern may be interwoven throughout the first few interviews. After the client describes all of her or his concerns, the counselor and client will need to select the problems that best represent the client's purpose for seeking counseling. The primary question to be answered by selection-of-problem leads is "What is the specific problem situation the client chooses to start working on?" Karoly (1975) points out that the selected target for change is sometimes difficult for a client to identify. Generally, a selected problem area represents something that is "harmful" to the person's safety, "disruptive" of the person's emotions, or "damaging" to the person's effectiveness (p. 205). The selection of the problem is the client's responsibility, although the counselor may help with the client's choice. If the client selects a problem that severely conflicts with the counselor's values, a referral to another counselor may be necessary. Otherwise, the counselor may inadvertently or purposefully block the discussion of certain client problem areas by listening selectively to only those problems that the counselor can or wants to work with (Kanfer & Grimm, 1977). As an example, a counselor who is strongly opposed to abortions may discourage or ignore discussion of this alternative in counseling a pregnant client.

Selection-of-problem leads are very useful in cases where the client presents multiple problems (which is typical). If the client has described several types of problems, selection-of-problem leads may help the client to set

priorities. The client may want to begin with the problem that is most distressing or with the concern that has the best chance of being solved or managed (Karoly, 1975, p. 205). Often it is overwhelming for a client to tackle three or four problems simultaneously. Goldfried (1976a) recommends that the counselor and client establish problem priorities by asking the following question about each presenting problem: "What are the consequences of my *not* doing anything therapeutically to handle this particular problem?" As he notes, "depending on the severity of the consequences associated with ignoring—at least temporarily—each of the different presenting problems, one can obtain a clearer picture as to what is most important" (p. 319).

Consider these examples of selection-of-problem leads:

"Which bothers you most—_____ or _____?"
"Of these three concerns you mentioned, which is the most stressful for you?"
"Rank-order in terms of *stress* the three concerns you mentioned."
"Which of these concerns is most pressing to you now?"
"Rank the three concerns you mentioned in the order you would like to work on them."
"Tell me which of these problems you think you could learn to manage most easily or successfully."

The counselor may need to continue using these types of leads until the client has set priorities and has selected a problem to work on initially. Keep in mind, though, that the problem selected as the target for focus often changes as counseling progresses. For example, a client initially may indicate a desire to improve his or her grades. A month later, the client may decide that another concern is more pressing and is, in fact, contributing to the lower grades.

Pinpointing the Problem. The third part of identification and selection of problem concerns involves pinpointing the problem. *Pinpointing* refers to checking out manifestations of the selected problem at other times, in other situations, or with other people. The counselor is looking for a client response that will identify whether the problem is confined to one type of situation at one time or is exhibited in many different situations. For instance, a client's selected problem may be "trying to reduce the pressure I put on myself to perform well in school." The counselor could use pinpointing leads to determine whether the client pressures himself or herself in other kinds of performance situations in addition to school.

Some examples of pinpointing leads are:

"In what other situations has this happened?"
"What are some other times you feel this way?"
"Can you recall other times this has been a problem for you?"
"What is another example of when this has happened?"
"Does the same thing happen with other people or in other situations?"
"Has anything like this happened to you before or in other circumstances?"
"What kinds of other situations bother you in this way?"

The counselor will need to use pinpointing leads until the extent to which the client's problem occurs in one or more situations is determined.

Identification of Overt and Covert Problem Behaviors

After identifying and selecting the client's problem, it is necessary to determine some specific overt and covert behaviors that occur during the problem situation. In other words, if a client states "I'm having trouble in my work," we would want to identify the client's actions, thoughts, and feelings that occur during the problem work situations. For instance, without further exploration it would be difficult to know whether the client's work problems resulted primarily from an overt action such as lack of skills, from a covert response such as thinking about herself or himself as inadequate or incompetent, or from both. Or perhaps the client's "work trouble" may be a result of specific events in the work environment. As you may recall from our discussion in Chapter 9, specifying overt and covert behaviors is a way to define

the problem in operational terms. The primary client responses to be given by overt and covert problem-behavior leads are examples of events, actions, thoughts, feelings, images, dreams, and physiological states that occur during the problem situations.

Leads for Overt Problem Behaviors. Some examples of counselor leads used to identify environmental events and overt client behaviors are:

"Describe what happens in this situation."
"What are some things that go on in your _____ environment that bother you?"
"What do you mean when you say you're 'having trouble at work'?"
"What are you doing when this occurs?"
"How does _____ behave toward you in this situation?"
"How do you do _____?"
"What do you do when this happens?"
"What effect does this situation have on your behavior?"

The counselor should continue to use such leads until the client's overt behavior and the environmental events that compose the problem are specified.

Leads for Covert Problem Behaviors. Some counselor leads used to identify covert behavior are:

"How do you feel about this?"
"What kinds of feelings do you have when this happens?"
"What about the feeling you have _____; is it the same or different?"
"What do you mean by feeling 'depressed'?"
"What reaction do you have when _____?"
"What are you thinking when this happens?"
"Can you describe what kinds of thoughts seem to make you feel more _____?"
"When you say you feel defeated, what picture of yourself do you see?"
"What do you notice goes on inside you when you feel anxious?"

Meichenbaum (1976) points out that it is important to identify both the presence and absence of the client's covert behaviors. First, the counselor can look for specific thoughts and feelings that are present in the client's repertory and seem to interfere with the client's ability to behave in desirable ways. Second, the counselor can determine whether certain thoughts or feelings are missing from the client's repertory that, if present, would lead to more desired overt responses (p. 149). Until these two questions can be answered, the counselor and client probably have not obtained all the information about covert problem behaviors.

Identification of Antecedents

You may recall from Chapter 9 that there are usually certain things that happen before or after a problem that contribute to it. In other words, people are not born feeling depressed or thinking of themselves as inadequate. Other events may contribute to the problem by serving as a pay-off that maintains the problem behaviors, thoughts, or feelings. Much of the problem-definition process consists of exploring events that precede or cue the problem (antecedents) and things that happen after the problem (consequences) that, in some way, influence or maintain it.

To review our previous discussion of the ABC model, remember that antecedents and consequences may be overt and covert. Also, antecedents and consequences are likely to be different for each client. Antecedents represent external or internal events that elicit or cue the problem behaviors. Some antecedents may occur immediately before the problem; other antecedents may have taken place a long time ago.

Leads to Identify Antecedents. In assessing antecedents, you are looking for client responses that specify any overt and covert events that seem to cue or bring about the problem. In other words, you are trying to determine when the problem started, what was happening then, and whether the problem seems to occur at certain times or places or following certain events, thoughts, or feelings. For example, if a client

reports recent feelings of depression, what was going on in the client's life when these feelings appeared? And, on a daily basis, are there certain people, activities, thoughts, or images that seem consistently to bring about these depressed feelings? The counselor and client should continue to explore antecedents until this sort of information is determined.

Some examples of leads to obtain information about *overt* antecedents are:

"What do you think started this?"
"You say this happened _____ ago?"
"I'm interested in the moment you first experienced this."
"What do you mean this started 'recently'?"
"What things seemed to lead up to this?"
"What was happening in your life when you first started to notice this?"
"What do you think made you _____?"
"Can you recall the first time this happened?"
"Can you think whether certain events, situations, or activities seem to 'set off' this problem?"
"What usually happens right before this problem?"

Some examples of leads to obtain *covert* antecedents are:

"How would you say you felt before this happened?"
"Did you ever feel this way at any other time in your life?"
"Can you say what made you anxious?"
"When was the first time you felt this way (or this happened)?"
"What do you recall feeling like just before this occurs?"
"What are you usually thinking about before this happens?"

Identification of Consequences

In assessing consequences, you are trying to determine overt and covert events that seem to influence (by maintaining, increasing, or decreasing) the problem behavior. For example, if a client reports feeling depressed, do certain things happen after these depressed periods that seem to maintain or even strengthen the person's depression? Does the client receive extra attention or special consideration from being depressed that he or she does not get when feeling happy? Or does the client continue to feel depressed because he or she can use the depression to avoid or escape something? Are there certain events or thoughts that follow the depressed feelings and seem to increase or decrease them? These are all questions to consider in assessing the role of consequences in the client's behavior.

Leads to Identify Consequences. Some leads to use to identify *overt* consequences include:

"What do you do after this and how does this affect _____?"

"What happens after this? How does this affect _____?"

"Has your problem ever given you any special consideration or extra advantage?"

"Have you ever gotten out of anything or avoided something as a result of your problem?"

"Do you notice anything that happens afterwards that you try to prolong or to produce?"

"How has your problem jeopardized you?"

"What seems to stop this?"

"Can you recall anything that has happened afterwards that decreases _____?"

"Do you notice anything that occurs afterwards that you try to stop or avoid?"

Leads to identify *covert* consequences include:

"What are you thinking about after this and how does this affect _____?"

"How do you usually feel after this occurs? Do these feelings seem to strengthen or weaken _____?"

"Can you recall any thoughts or feelings that make the problem better or worse?"

"When do you usually stop feeling this way?"

"Are there certain thoughts or feelings that you experience afterwards that either strengthen or weaken the problem?"

"Are there certain feelings or thoughts that go on after _____ that you try to prolong?"

"Are there certain feelings or thoughts that go on after _____ that you try to stop or avoid?"

The counselor and client will need to explore thoroughly the role of consequences in the problem behavior. The counselor should continue to pursue this information until the counselor and client can identify overt and covert events that maintain (or strengthen) and weaken the problem behaviors.

Identification of Client Coping Skills

All too often as counselors we promote clients' negative pictures of themselves and their environment by inquiring about and focusing on only deficits, stresses, or problems. Swensen (1968) emphasizes that almost everyone, even people with multiple problems, can offer some evidence of assets, resources, or coping skills. As Swensen notes, anything that demonstrates creative, constructive, or responsible behavior is an indication of strength (p. 25).

The primary purpose of a coping-skills assessment is to help the client identify examples of coping or self-enhancing behaviors that pertain to the defined problem situations. These leads may help the client to see a more balanced picture of his or her environment and to be more aware of the positive, of available personal resources, and of coping and adaptive behaviors. Information obtained from strengths assessment can be used to identify capabilities and resources that the client may be able to use in the next stage as part of the counseling treatment program. Also, the information obtained from these leads can help the client and counselor contrast the present problem situations with other past or present times when the client has been coping successfully. A coping-skills assessment should determine the way in which the client has previously dealt with problem behaviors and how successful these past attempts have been. This assessment also can explore how much self-control the client seems to possess, the ways in which the client typically deals with setbacks, and the extent to which the client relies on himself or herself or on others for encouragement and approval (Meyer, Liddell, & Lyons, 1977, p. 127).

Some examples of leads to assess strengths and coping skills are:

"In the past, how have you dealt with or mastered this or other problems?"

"You say this has been a problem for you for the last 3 months. What was it like before that time?"

"Tell me how you coped before this came up in your life."

"Give me some examples of some positive things going on in your life now."

"Describe a situation or a time when this concern does not usually interfere."

"Describe some things you feel you do adequately or successfully."

"What kinds of resources do you have that might help you deal with this concern?"

"What are some examples of ways you might cope with this concern?"

"Can you think of some things to think about during this situation to help you manage or deal with it?"

The counselor should continue to assess the client's past and present coping skills until the client is able to describe some potential resources, strengths, or coping behaviors. However, as Schwartz and Goldiamond (1975) point out, many clients may be "thrown" by strengths questions because "their vision, understandably, is blocked by the overwhelming presence of the problems" (p. 86). These clients may need instructions, information-giving, or counselor self-disclosure in order to identify strengths and coping behaviors. If these direct leads still do not result in client identification of strengths, the interview leads may need to be supplemented by a structured strengths activity (see Canfield & Wells, 1976; Dyer, 1978).

The information obtained from a coping-skills assessment also can be used as a clue about the problem intensity. If the stresses and deficits severely outweigh the client's coping skills, then the problem may be quite intense and interfering to the client.

Identification of Problem Intensity

It is also useful to determine the intensity or severity of the problem. In other words, you want to check out how much the problem is affecting the client and the client's daily functioning. If, for example, a client says "I feel anxious," does the client mean a little anxious or

very anxious? Is this person anxious all the time or only some of the time? And does this anxiety affect any of the person's daily activities, such as eating, sleeping, or working? There are three kinds of intensity to assess: the extent of the problem, the degree of problem intensity, and the frequency (how often) or duration (how long) of the problem.

Extent of the Problem. One way the counselor can assess the problem intensity is to explore the extent or pervasiveness of the problem. A problem that is more intense may be exhibited in a variety of situations and may occur most of the time. The counselor can explore the extent of the problem by asking the client to describe where and when the problem usually occurs. Consider these example leads:

"Where does this happen?"

"In what situations or places does this occur?"

"When does this happen?"

"At what time does this occur?"

"Does this happen all the time or only sometimes?"

In assessing the extent of the problem, you are trying to obtain specification of places and times that the problem is noticeable to the client.

Degree of Problem Intensity. Often it is useful to obtain a client's subjective rating of the degree of discomfort, stress, or intensity of the problem. The counselor can use this information to determine how much the problem affects the client and whether the client seems to be incapacitated or immobilized by it. To assess the degree of problem intensity, the counselor can use leads similar to these:

"You say you feel anxious. On a scale from 1 to 10, with 1 being very calm and 10 being extremely anxious, where would you put your feeling?"

"How strong is your feeling when this happens?"

"How has this interfered with your daily activities?"

In assessing degree of intensity, you are looking for a client response that indicates how strong or how interfering the problem seems to be.

Frequency or Duration of Problem Behaviors. In asking about frequency and duration, your purpose is to have the client identify how long (duration) or how often (frequency) the problem behaviors occur. Data about how long or how often the problem occurs *before* a counseling strategy is applied are referred to as *baseline data.* Baseline data provide information about the *present* extent of the problem. Baseline data also can be used later to compare the extent of the problem before and after a counseling strategy has been used.

Some examples of leads to assess the frequency and duration of the problem behavior include:

"How often does this happen?"
"How many times does this occur?"
"How long does this feeling usually stay with you?"
"How much does this go on, say, in an average day?"

Some clients can discuss the frequency or duration of the problem behavior during the interview rather easily. However, many clients may be unaware of the number of times the problem occurs or how much time it occupies. Most clients can give the counselor more accu-rate information about frequency and duration by engaging in self-monitoring of the problem behaviors with a written log. The ways in which logs can be used to supplement the interview data are discussed later in this chapter.

A review of these seven categories of prob-lem definition can be found in Table 10-1. This table may help you conceptualize and sum-marize the types of data you will seek during problem-definition interviews.

The Limitations of Interview Leads in Problem Definition

According to Lazarus (1973), "faulty prob-lem identification . . . is probably the greatest impediment to successful therapy" (p. 407). As we mentioned earlier in this chapter, the ABC model for viewing client problems is reflected in the problem-definition leads presented in this chapter. The leads are simply a tool the coun-selor can use to elicit certain kinds of client in-formation. They are designed to be used as a guide or road map to provide some direction for the problem-definition interviews. However, the leads alone are an insufficient basis for prob-

Table 10-1. Review of Seven Problem-Definition Categories

I. Explanation of problem-definition purpose
II. Identification and selection of problem concerns
    A. General areas of concern
    B. Selection of concerns
    C. Pinpointing related situations
III. Identification of present problem behaviors (B)
    A. Overt behaviors
    B. Covert behaviors
IV. Identification of antecedent contributing conditions (A)
    A. Overt and covert antecedents
    B. Past and immediate antecedents
V. Identification of consequent contributing conditions (C)
    A. Overt and covert consequences
    B. Positive and negative consequences
    C. Immediate and delayed consequences
VI. Identification of client coping skills
VII. Identification of problem intensity
    A. Extent of problem
    B. Degree of problem intensity
    C. Frequency or duration of problem behaviors

} ABC model

lem definition, because they represent only about half of the process at most—the counselor responses. The other part of the process is reflected by the responses these leads generate from the client. A complete problem definition includes not only asking the right questions but also synthesizing and integrating the client responses.

The ABC model may give the counselor a basis for integrating the client responses into a meaningful scheme. After obtaining all the information, the counselor and client should be able to generate some ideas about the relationship between the client's problem behaviors and contributing conditions. The interview leads you will learn in this chapter are overt responses; however, you will also need to use your own cognitions to process and synthesize the data you receive from the client. Helping clients define problems depends not only on using some appropriate interview leads but also on being able to take the client data and put it all together. It is not easy to turn random, isolated pieces of information into a synthesized picture with themes, patterns, and interrelationships. You will have to recall, summarize, discriminate, and think through all the messages you receive from a client in the interview. Perhaps the following model dialogue will display the relationship between the counselor's overt problem-definition leads (these are numbered) and the counselor's covert processing of the client data (in italics).

Model Dialogue: The Case of Joan

To assist you in identifying how these problem-definition leads are used in an interview, a dialogue of the case of Joan (Chapter 9) is given. An explanation of the counselor's lead and the counselor's rationale for using it are given in italics before each lead.

Counselor response 1 is a verbal set, to explain to the client the purpose of problem definition.
1. Counselor: Joan, you mentioned last week you were unhappy and dissatisfied with school. Today, if you feel this is still what's on your

mind, I'd like to ask you some questions about this so we can get an idea of what's going on. This will help us to know what we can do about your concerns. How does this sound?
   Client: Fine with me. What do you want to know?
Counselor response 2 is a general-problem lead for identification and selection of problem concerns. The counselor uses this lead to help Joan identify the range of her concerns.
2. Counselor: Well, in talking about your school problems, what about the situation bothers you?
   Client: Well, I'm having trouble in some of my classes. There's too much competition. I feel the other kids are better than I am. I've thought about changing from this college-prep program to the work-study program, but I don't know what to do. I don't like to make decisions anyway.
Counselor response 3 is a selection-of-problem lead that the counselor uses to try to help Joan clarify and rank the two problems she just mentioned: the class competition and the decision-making problem. This is part of identification and selection of problem concerns.
3. Counselor: You've just mentioned two different things that are bothering you—your competitive classes and having trouble making decisions, especially the one about your curriculum. Which of these two problems bothers you more?
   Client: I'm not really sure. I'm concerned about having trouble in my classes. But sometimes I think if I were in another type of curriculum I wouldn't be so tense about these classes. But I'm sort of worried about deciding to do this.
Counselor response 4 is a clarification. The counselor wants to see whether the client's interest in work-study is real or a way to avoid the present problem.
4. Counselor: Do you see getting in the work-study program as a way to get out of your present problem classes, or is it a program that really interests you?
   Client: It's a program that interests me. I think sometimes I'd like to get a job after high school instead of going to college. But I've been thinking about this for a year and I can't decide what to do. I'm not very good at making decisions on my own.
Counselor response 5 is a summarization and an instruction. The counselor goes back to the two problem areas mentioned in general-problem identification. Note that the counselor does not draw explicit attention to the client's last self-deprecating statement.

5. Counselor: Well, your two concerns of your present class problems and of making this and other decisions are somewhat related. Maybe we could explore both concerns—and then talk later about what you want to work on.

Client: That's fine with me.

Counselor response 6 is a lead to identify some present problem behaviors related to Joan's concern about competitive classes. Asking the client for examples can elicit specificity about what does or does not occur during the problem situation.

6. Counselor: OK, what is an example of some trouble you've been having in your most competitive class?

Client: Well, I withdraw in these classes. I've been cutting my math class. It's the worst. My grades are dropping, especially in math class.

Counselor response 7 is an intensity lead regarding the extent of the problem to see whether the client's concern occurs at other times or other places.

7. Counselor: Where else do you have trouble—in any other classes, or at other times or places outside of school?

Client: No, not outside of school. And, to some degree I always feel anxious in any class because of the pressure my parents put on me to get good grades. But my math class is really the worst.

Counselor response 8 is a lead to help the client identify overt problem behaviors in math class.

8. Counselor: Describe what happens in your math class that makes it troublesome for you.

Client: Well, it's a harder class for me to start with. I have to work harder to do OK. In this class I get nervous whenever I go in it. So I withdraw.

Client's statement of "I withdraw" is vague. So counselor response 9 is another overt-problem-behavior lead to help the client specify what she means by withdrawing. Note that, since the counselor did not get a complete answer to this after response 8, the same type of lead is used again.

9. Counselor: What do you do when you withdraw?

Client: Well, I sit by myself, I don't talk or volunteer answers. Sometimes I don't go to the board or answer when the teacher calls on me.

Now that the client has identified certain overt behaviors associated with the problem, the counselor will use a covert-problem-behavior lead to find out whether there are any predominant thoughts or feelings the client has during the math class.

10. Counselor: What are you generally thinking about in this class?

Client: What do you mean—am I thinking about math?

The client's response indicated some confusion. The counselor will have to use a more specific covert-problem-behavior lead, along with some self-disclosure, to help the client respond more specifically.

11. Counselor: Well, sometimes when I'm in a situation like a class, there are times when my mind is in the class and other times I'm thinking about myself or about something else I'm going to do. So I'm wondering if you've noticed anything you're thinking about during the class?

Client: Well, some of the time I'm thinking about the math problems. Other times I'm thinking about the fact that I'd rather not be in the class and that I'm not as good as the other kids.

The client has started to be more specific, and the counselor thinks perhaps there are still other thoughts going on. The counselor uses another covert-problem-behavior lead in response 12 to pursue this.

12. Counselor: What else do you recall you tell yourself when you're thinking that you're not as good as other people?

Client: Well, I think that I don't get grades that are as good as some other students. My parents have been pointing this out to me since junior high. And in the math class I'm one of four girls. The guys in there are really smart. I just keep thinking how can a girl ever be as smart as a guy in a math class? No way. It just doesn't happen.

The client identifies more specific covert problem thoughts and also suggests two possible antecedents—parental comparison of her grades, and cultural stereotyping (girls shouldn't be as good in math as boys). The counselor's records show that the client's test scores and previous grades indicate that she definitely is not "dumb" in math. The counselor in the next few responses will focus on these and on other possible antecedents, such as the nervousness the client mentioned earlier.

13. Counselor: You know, Joan, earlier you mentioned that you get nervous about this class. When do you notice that you feel this way—before the class, during the class, or at other times?

Client: Well, right before the class is the worst. About 10 minutes before my English class ends—it's right before math—I start thinking about the math class. Then I get nervous and feel like I wish I didn't have to go. Recently, I've tried to find ways to cut math class.

The counselor still needs more information about how and when the nervousness affects the client, so 14 is another antecedent lead.

---

14. Counselor: Could you tell me more about when you feel most nervous and when you don't feel nervous about this class?

    Client: Well, I feel worst when I'm actually walking to the class and the class is starting. Once the class starts, I feel better. I don't feel nervous about it when I cut it or at other times. However, once in a while, if someone talks about it or I think about it, I feel a little nervous.

The client has indicated that the nervousness seems to be more of an antecedent than a problem behavior. Also, she has suggested that cutting class is a consequence that maintains the problem because she uses this to avoid the math class that brings on the nervousness. The counselor realizes at this point that the word nervous *has not been defined and goes back in the next response to a* covert-problem-behavior *lead to find out what Joan means by* nervous.

15. Counselor: Tell me what you mean by the word *nervous*—what goes on with you when you're nervous?

    Client: Well, I get sort of a sick feeling in my stomach and my hands get all sweaty. My heart starts to pound.

Next the counselor will use an intensity lead to determine the degree of intensity of nervousness.

16. Counselor: How strong is this feeling—a little or very?

    Client: Before class, very strong—at other times, just a little.

The client has established that the nervousness seems mainly to be exhibited in physiological behaviors and is more intense before class. The counselor will pursue the relationship between the client's nervousness and overt and covert problem behaviors described earlier to verify the nervousness as an antecedent. *Another* antecedent *lead is used next.*

17. Counselor: Which seems to come first—feeling nervous or not speaking up in class—or thinking about other people being smarter than you?

    Client: Well, the nervousness. Because that starts before I get in the class.

The counselor will summarize *this pattern and confirm it with the client in the next response.*

18. Counselor: Let's see. So you feel nervous—like in your stomach and hands—before class and when math class starts. Then during class, on days you go, you start thinking about not being as smart in math as the guys and you don't volunteer answers or don't respond sometimes when called on. But after the class is over you don't notice the nervousness so much. Is that right?

    Client: That's pretty much what happens.

The counselor has a clue from the client's previous comments that there are other antecedents in addition to nervousness that have to do with the client's problem behavior—such as the role of her parents. The counselor will pursue this in the next response, using an antecedent *lead.*

19. Counselor: Joan, you mentioned earlier that you have been thinking about not being as smart as some of your friends ever since junior high. When do you recall you really started to dwell on this?

    Client: Well, probably in seventh grade.

The counselor didn't get sufficient information about what happened to the client in the seventh grade, so another antecedent *lead will be used.*

20. Counselor: Well, what things seemed to happen then when you began to compare yourself to others?

    Client: Well, my parents said when you start junior high your grades become really important in order to go to college. So for the last three or four years they have been telling me some of my grades aren't as good as other students. Also if I get a "B" they will withhold a privilege like my allowance.

The counselor has no evidence of actual parental reaction but will work with the client's report at this time, since this is how the client perceives parental input. If possible, a parent conference should be arranged at a later date with the client's permission. The counselor wants to pursue the relationship between the parents' input and the client's present behavior to determine whether parental reaction is eliciting part of Joan's present concerns and will use a lead to identify this as a possible antecedent.

21. Counselor: How do you think this reaction of your parents relates to your present problems in your math class?

    Client: Well, since I started high school they have talked more about needing to get better grades for college. And I have to work harder in math class to do this. I guess I feel a lot of pressure to perform—which makes me withdraw and just want to hang it up. Now of course my grades are getting worse, not better.

The counselor, in the next lead, will paraphrase *Joan's previous comment.*

22. Counselor: So your parents' pressure seems to draw out pressure in you.

    Joan: Yes, that happens.

In response 23, the counselor will explore another possible antecedent *that Joan mentioned before—thinking that girls aren't as good as boys in math.*

23. Counselor: Joan, I'd like to ask you about some-

thing else you mentioned earlier. You said one thing that you think about in your math class is that you're only one of four girls and that as a girl you're not as smart in math as a boy. Can you see what makes you think this?

Client: I'm not sure. Everyone knows or says that girls have more trouble in math than boys. Even my teacher. He's gone out of his way to try to help me because he knows it's tough for me.

The client has identified a possible consequence of her problem behavior as teacher attention. The counselor will pick up on this later. First, the counselor is going to respond to the client's response that "everyone" has told her this thought. Counselors have a responsibility to point out things that clients have learned from stereotypes rather than actual data, as is evident in this case from Joan's records. Counselor will use confrontation in the next response.

24. Counselor: We can deal more with this later, but it's evident to me from your records that you have a lot of potential for math. Yet you've learned to think of yourself as less capable, especially less capable than guys. This is a popular idea that people throw around in our culture. But in your case I don't see any evidence for it.

Client: You mean I really could do as well in math as the guys?

Counselor response 25 consists of an interpretation to help the client see the relationship between overt and covert behaviors.

25. Counselor: I don't see why not. But lots of times the way we act or how we perform in a situation is affected by how we think about the situation. I think some of the reason you're having more trouble in your math class is that your performance is hindered a little by your nervousness and by the way you put yourself down. These are things we can work on in counseling. But first there are still some other things we need to find out.

The counselor is going to go back now to pursue possible consequences that are influencing the client's problem behavior. The next response is a lead to identify consequences.

26. Counselor: Joan, I'd like to go back to some things you mentioned earlier. For one thing, you said your teacher has gone out of his way to help you. Would you say that your behavior in his class has gotten you any extra attention or special consideration from him?

Client: Well, certainly extra attention. He's talked to me more frequently. He doesn't get upset either when I don't go to the board.

Counselor response 27 will continue to explore the teacher's behavior as a possible consequence.

27. Counselor: Do you mean he may excuse you from board work?

Client: For sure. I think he almost expects me not to come up with the answer.

The teacher's behavior may be maintaining the client's overt problem behaviors in class by giving extra attention to her for her problems and by excusing her from certain work. A teacher conference may be necessary at some later point. The counselor, in the next two responses, will continue to use other leads to identify possible consequences.

28. Counselor: What do you see you're doing right now that helps you get out of putting yourself through the stress of going to math class?

Client: Do you mean something like cutting class?

29. Counselor: I think that's perhaps one thing you do to get out of the class. What else?

Client: Nothing I can think of.

The client has identified cutting class as one way to avoid the math class. The counselor in the next response will suggest another consequence that the client had mentioned earlier but not as a way to get out of the stress associated with the class. The counselor will suggest this relationship but in a tentative interpretation that is "checked out" with the client in the next three responses:

30. Counselor: Also, Joan, you told me earlier that your grades were dropping in math class. Is it possible that, if these grades—and others —drop too much, you'll automatically be dropped from these college-prep classes?

Client: That's right.

31. Counselor: I'm wondering whether one possible reason for letting your grades slide is that it is almost an automatic way to get out of these competitive classes.

Client: How so?

32. Counselor: Well, if you became ineligible for these classes because of your grades, you'd automatically be out of this class and others that you consider competitive and feel nervous about. What do you think about that?

Client: I guess that's true. And then my dilemma is whether I want to stay in this or switch to the work-study program.

In the next response, the counselor uses summarization and ties together the effects of "dropping grades" to math class and to the earlier expressed concern of a curriculum-change decision. The counselor also uses a lead to help the client identify present coping skills.

33. Counselor: Right. And letting your grades get

too bad will automatically mean that decision is made for you, so you can take yourself off the hook for making that choice. We didn't really talk about that today, but we could discuss that concern at our next session. Right now I'm thinking we've been talking a lot today about some things that aren't going too well for you. Before our session is over I'd like to spend a little time on some things that are going well for you. Could you tell me about some things in school now that you feel you're handling well?

Client: I'm involved in the French Club and in cheerleading. I enjoy these. And I'm doing well in English class.

In response 34, the counselor will pick up on these "pluses" and use another coping-skills lead to have the client identify particular ways in which she handles positive situations, especially her English class.

34. Counselor: So there are some things about school that are going OK for you. You say you're doing well in your English class. What can you think of that you do or don't do to help you perform well in this class?

Client: Well, I go to class of course regularly. And I guess I feel like I do well in reading and writing. I don't have the hangup in there about being one of the few girls.

35. Counselor: So maybe you can see some of the differences between your English and math classes—and how you handle these. Next week we can discuss this some more and also your concern about decision-making.

(Session is concluded until next week.)

Learning Activities: Problem-Definition Leads

I. The following activity is designed to assist you in identifying problem-definition leads in an interview. You are given a counselor-client dialogue of the case of Ms. Weare and Freddie (Chapter 9). This dialogue consists of an interview with the mother, Ms. Weare. For each counselor response, your task is to identify and write down the type of problem-identification lead used by the counselor. You may find it helpful to use the Interview Checklist at the end of the chapter as a guide for this learning activity. There may be more than one example of any given lead in the dialogue. Also, other basic verbal interview responses are included. Feedback follows on p. 155.

Dialogue with Ms. Weare and Counselor

1. Counselor: Hello, Ms. Weare. Could you tell me about some things going on now that are concerning you?

   Client: Not too much. Family Services sent me here.

2. Counselor: So you're here just because they sent you—or is there something bothering you?

   Client: Well, they don't like the way I treat my kid, Freddie.

3. Counselor: What do you think about the way you treat Freddie?

   Client: Well, I yell at him a lot. I don't like to do that but sometimes he gets me so mad. I don't like to, but he needs to learn.

4. Counselor: So there are times when you get real mad at Freddie and then you yell at him. You don't like to do this, but you see it as a way to help him learn right and wrong.

   Client: That's it. I don't like to, but there are times when he needs to know something. Like yesterday, I bought him new pants and he came home from school with a big hole in them. Now I just don't have money to keep buying him new pants.

5. Counselor: You just mentioned the incident with Freddie's pants. What are some other things that happen with Freddie that you get mad about?

   Client: Every morning. Freddie's in fifth grade now. But he still doesn't dress himself in the morning. I want to be a good mother and get him to school on time, and he tries to be late. He waits around not getting dressed.

6. Counselor: Any other times you can remember getting mad?

   Client: Well, not too long ago he was playing outside and broke a window. I got mad then. But that doesn't happen every day like his not getting dressed does.

7. Counselor: So one thing that really bothers you is in the morning. Could you tell me exactly what does happen each morning at your house?

   Client: Well, I call Freddie to get up and tell him to dress before he comes down for breakfast. He comes down all right—in his pajamas. I warn him after breakfast to get ready. Usually about 5 minutes before the bus comes, I'll go up. He'll just be sitting in his room! He's still not dressed. I'll yell at him and then dress him so he's not late.

8. Counselor: And your main feeling at this point is that you're mad. Anything else?

Client: No, just very mad.

9. Counselor: And what exactly do you do when you go upstairs and he's not dressed?

Client: I yell at him. Then I help dress him.

10. Counselor: What kinds of things do you usually say to him?

Client: I tell him he's dumb and he's going to be late for school, and that I have to make sure he won't be.

11. Counselor: You mentioned this happens in the morning. Does this situation go on every morning or only some mornings?

Client: Just about every morning except weekends.

12. Counselor: When did these incidents seem to begin?

Client: Ever since Freddie started going to school.

13. Counselor: How does this situation seem to be interfering for you?

Client: Well, Freddie is too old not to get dressed by himself. He shouldn't need my help.

14. Counselor: OK, now let's go back over this situation. You told me you remind Freddie every morning to get dressed. He never dresses by breakfast. You remind him again. Then, about 5 minutes before the bus comes, you go upstairs to check on him. When do you notice yourself starting to feel mad or to think about the situation?

Client: I think about it as soon as I realize it's almost time for the bus to come and Freddie isn't down yet. Then I feel mad.

15. Counselor: And what exactly do you think about right then?

Client: Well, that he's probably not dressed and that if I don't go up and help him he'll be late. Then I'll look like a bad mother if I can't get my son to school on time.

16. Counselor: So in a sense you actually go help him out so he won't be late. How many times has Freddie ever been late?

Client: Never.

17. Counselor: You believe that helping Freddie may prevent him from being late. However, your help also excuses Freddie from having to help himself. What do you think would happen if you stopped going upstairs to check on Freddie in the morning?

Client: Well, I don't know, but I'm his only parent. Freddie's father isn't around. It's up to me, all by myself, to keep Freddie in line. If I didn't go up and if Freddie was late all the time, his teachers might blame me. I wouldn't be a good mother.

18. Counselor: Of course, we don't *really* know what would happen if you didn't go up and yell at him or help him dress. It might be so different for Freddie after the first day or two he would dress himself. It could be that he thinks it's easier to wait and get your help than to dress himself. He might think that by sitting up there and waiting for you to help, he's getting a special advantage or attention from you.

Client: You mean like he's getting a favor from me?

19. Counselor: Sure. And when we find a way to get a favor from someone we usually do as much as we can to keep getting the favor. Ms. Weare, I'd like to ask you about something else. Do you think maybe that you see helping Freddie out as a way to avoid having Freddie be late and then not having someone blame you for this?

Client: Sure. I'd rather help him than get myself in hot water.

20. Counselor: OK, so you're concerned about what you think might happen to you if he's late. You see getting him ready on time as a way to prevent this from happening.

Client: Yes.

21. Counselor: Earlier you said you were more concerned about the situation because you thought Freddie was old enough to dress by himself. How do you usually feel after these incidents?

Client: Well, it upsets me.

22. Counselor: OK, you feel upset. Do these feelings seem to make you want to continue or to stop helping Freddie?

Client: Probably to stop. I get worn out. Also, sometimes I don't get my work done then.

23. Counselor: So helping Freddie so he won't be late and you won't be blamed sort of makes you want to keep on helping him. Yet when you feel upset and worn out afterwards, you're tempted to stop helping. Is this right?

Client: I guess that could be true.

24. Counselor: Ms. Weare, we've been talking a lot about some problem situations you've had with Freddie. Could you tell me about some times when the two of you get along OK?

Client: Well, on weekends we do. Freddie dresses himself whenever he gets up. I sleep later.

25. Counselor: What happens when the two of you do things together?

Client: Sometimes I'll take him shopping with me. And we eat all our meals together. Usually this is pleasant. He can be a good boy and I don't scream all the time at him.

26. Counselor: So you realize it is possible for the two of you to get along. How do you feel about my talking with you again and with Freddie to work this out?
    Client: That's OK.

II. In order to incorporate the interview leads into your verbal repertory, we suggest you try a role-play interview of the case of Ms. Weare (Chapter 9) or the case of Mr. Phyle (Chapter 9) with a triad. One person can take the part of the client; another can be the counselor; and the third person can be the consultant. The consultant can use this dialogue or the Interview Checklist at the end of the chapter as a guide (see pp. 159–162).

Client Self-Monitoring

The data given by the client in the interview can be supplemented by client self-monitoring outside the interview. Self-monitoring may be defined as the process of observing specific things about oneself and one's interaction with others and the environment. In using self-monitoring as a problem-assessment tool, the client is asked to record her or his observations in writing. These written recordings can be entered on a log (Schwartz & Goldiamond, 1975) or a daily record sheet. Clients who cannot write or small children can use a golf wrist counter, a timer or watch, pictures, or stars in lieu of a written record.

One purpose of client self-monitoring is to help the counselor and client gain information about the problem in real-life settings. Another purpose is to validate the accuracy of the client's oral reports during the interviews. As Linehan (1977) points out, sometimes the client's interview description is not a complete report of the events that occur, or the way that the client describes the events differs from the way the client actually experiences them (p. 45). Client self-monitoring of problem situations and behaviors outside the interview should add more accuracy and specificity to the information

discussed in the interview. As a result, client self-monitoring may accelerate treatment and enhance the client's expectations for change (Shelton & Ackerman, 1974, p. 7).

As we mentioned earlier, a client can record observations on some type of written record or log. Two types of logs can be used for different observations a client might make during problem definition. A *descriptive log* can be used to record data about identification and selection of problem concerns. A *behavior log* can be used to record information about the problem behaviors and the antecedents and consequences.

Descriptive Logs

In an initial session with a client, a simple descriptive or exploratory log can be introduced to find out what is going on with the client, where, and when (Schwartz & Goldiamond, 1975). Such a descriptive log could be set up as shown in Figure 10-1. The descriptive log is extremely useful when the client has difficulty identifying problem concerns or pinpointing problem situations. However, once the problem concerns have been identified and selected, a counselor and client may find that a behavior log is helpful as an interview adjunct for defining the ABCs of the problem.

Behavior Logs

The ABCs of problem definition and the intensity of the problem can be clarified with client self-monitoring of the problem behaviors, the contributing conditions, and the frequency or duration of the problem behavior. All of this information can be recorded in a behavior log, which is simply an extension of the descriptive log. An example of a behavior log for our client, Joan, is presented in Figure 10-2.

In a behavior log, the defined problem behaviors are listed at the left. The client records the date, time, and place when these behaviors occur. To record contributing conditions, the client is instructed to record those behaviors and events that occur before and after the prob- lem behaviors. This information helps to estab- lish a pattern between the problem behaviors, things that cue or elicit the problem behaviors, and activities that maintain, strengthen, or weaken the problem behaviors.

The client also is asked to observe and record how long (duration) or how often (fre- quency) the problem behaviors occur. Determin- ing the level of the present problem serves as a baseline—that is, the rate or level of the problem *before* any counseling interventions have been started. The baseline is useful initially in helping establish the direction and level of change de- sired by the client. This information, as you will see in Chapter 12, is essential in establishing client goals. And, as counseling progresses, these baseline data may help the client compare progress during and near the end of counseling to progress at the beginning of counseling (see Chapter 13).

Uses of Logs

The success of the written logs may de- pend upon the client's motivation to keep a log as well as upon the instructions and training given to the client about the log. Four guidelines may increase the client's motivation to engage in self-monitoring:

1. Establish a rationale for the log, such as: "We need a written record in order to find out

Page _____ of _____

DAILY RECORD SHEET

Date	Time	Place	Activity	People	Observed Behavior

Figure 10-1. A Descriptive Log

For   Joan

Week of Nov. 6–13

(Problem Behaviors) Behavior Observing	Date	Time	Place	(Frequency/ Duration) Number or Amount	(Antecedents) What Precedes Behavior	(Consequences) What Follows Behavior
1. Thinking of self as not as smart	Mon. Nov. 6	10:00 A.M.	Math class	IIII	Going into class, know have to take test in class	Leaving class, being with friends
	Tues. Nov. 7	10:15 A.M.	Math class	IIII IIII	Got test back with a "B"	Teacher consoled me
	Tues. Nov. 7	5:30 P.M.	Home	IIII II	Parents asked about test. Told me to stay home this weekend	Went to bed
	Thurs. Nov. 9	9:30 A.M.	English class	II	Thought about having to go to math class	Got to math class. Had substitute teacher
	Sun. Nov. 12	8:30 P.M.	Home	III	Thought about school tomorrow	Went to bed
2. a. Not volunteering answers	Tues. Nov. 7	10:05 A.M. 10:20	Math class	II	Felt dumb	Nothing
b. Not answering teacher questions	Thurs. Nov. 9	10:10 A.M. 10:20 10:40	Math class	III	Felt dumb	Nothing
c. Not going to board	Thurs. Nov. 9	10:30 A.M.	Math class	I	Teacher called on me	Nothing
	Fri. Nov. 10	10:10 A.M. 10:35 A.M.	Math class	II	Teacher called on me	Nothing
	Thurs. Nov. 9	10:45 A.M.	Math class	I	Didn't have a substitute teacher	Nothing
	Fri. Nov. 10	10:15 A.M.	Math class	I	Teacher asked girls to go up	Teacher talked to me after class
3. Cutting class	Wed. Nov. 8	9:55 A.M.	School	1 hour	Didn't want to hassle class or think about test	Cut class. Played sick. Went to nurse's office for an hour

Figure 10-2. Example of Behavior Log

what is going on. This will help us make some decisions about the best way to handle your problem." A client is more likely to keep a log if he or she is aware of a purpose for doing so.

2. Provide specific, detailed instructions regarding how to keep the log. The client should be told *what, how, when,* and for *how long* to record. The client should be given an example of a model log to see how it may look. Providing adequate instructions may increase the likelihood that the client will record data on the log consistently and accurately.

3. Adapt the type of log to the client's ability to do self-monitoring. At first, you may need to start with a very simple log that does not require a great deal of recording. Gradually, you can increase the amount of information the client observes and records. If a client has trouble keeping a written log, a substitute can be used, such as a tape recorder, golf wrist counter, or, for children, gold stars or pictures. Schwartz and Goldiamond (1975) point out that even clients who seem "out of contact" with themselves are able to keep a log if they are not overwhelmed with entries and if attention to their entries is given promptly (p. 106).

4. Involve the client in discussing and analyzing the log within the interview. At first, the counselor can begin by putting together "hunches" about patterns of problem behavior and contributing conditions. As counseling progresses, the client can take a more active role in analyzing the log. Increasing the client's involvement in analyzing the log should serve as an incentive to the client to continue the time and effort required to collect the data.

The counselor should remember that the process of client self-monitoring can be reactive. In other words, the very act of observing oneself can influence and affect that which is being observed. This reactivity may affect the data reflected in the log. However, the reactivity can be helpful in the overall counseling program. There are times when self-monitoring is used deliberately as a change strategy to increase or decrease a particular behavior (see Chapter 22).

The data obtained from client self-monitoring are used not only during the problem-definition process but also in establishing client goals. During problem-definition sessions, the self-monitoring data will help the client and counselor to determine the ABCs of the problem. The baseline data will be the starting place for the discussion of desired counseling outcomes (see Chapters 11 and 12).

Post Evaluation

Part One

Use the counselor-client dialogue (Mr. Brown) that follows. Objective 1 asks you to identify in writing leads of questions associated with the 7 categories of defining the problem. Other counselor verbal responses from previous chapters also may be included. You can take some paper to write your responses. Answers follow the evaluation.

1. Counselor: I'm glad to see you today. I'm wondering if you could tell me some things that seem to be bothering you most right now.
   Client: Well, I just don't seem to be as productive in work now as I used to be. I guess that's a sign I'm getting old.

2. Counselor: What seems to be bothering you most—your work problems or thinking about getting old?
   Client: Well, I'm not sure, although I guess my thinking about getting older and having to retire gets in my way when I'm working on some projects at work.

3. Counselor: Has anything like this ever happened to you before—or in other circumstances?
   Client: No, it's been a recent thing. I've always been excited about my work and have met my deadlines. But lately I'm not finishing projects on time.

4. Counselor: You've been talking about how thinking of getting older and retiring interferes with your work projects. Does the same thing happen in other situations?
   Client: No, not really. I mean things at home are going on as usual. Of course I'm not retiring from home, I'm retiring from work.

5. Counselor: You seem pretty concerned about your retirement.

   Client: Yes. Well, I just am not sure what I'll do with myself after I retire. Work has always been a big part of my life. It's hard to imagine not working.

6. Counselor: What do you find yourself thinking about retirement that bothers you the most?

   Client: Well, I find myself thinking that soon someone else will be taking my place; that after I retire I won't be of use to anyone or maybe even to myself. Then I start thinking about how people you've known all your life forget you and forget your achievements when you're old and at home all the time.

7. Counselor: So you're concerned about not being able to carry on with your important achievements and also perhaps anxious about being forgotten for what you've done.

   Client: I guess so. I don't like to admit it, but I guess I do want to be remembered for some of the things I've done with the company.

8. Counselor: You say you find yourself thinking about retirement mostly at work. What are you usually doing when this occurs?

   Client: Well, it seems to be worse when I'm working alone in my office—particularly when I'm starting on a new design project. That's when I seem to get bogged down—soon after I start working on the project.

9. Counselor: Could you describe exactly what happens in this type of situation—as best as you can recall?

   Client: Well, there are some days when the boss asks me to work on or look over a particular car design. I'll take the plans and start to look at them and think about the pros and cons. Then it seems I start thinking about the fact that, when this car comes out, I won't be here. I get stuck for a while then and just don't do any more on the project.

10. Counselor: Have you ever experienced anything like this before? If so, how were you able to solve the problem?

    Client: There have been times when I might have been preoccupied with something, but it was never as persistent as what I'm experiencing now. I guess I just forgot about my problems by losing myself in my work.

11. Counselor: You said earlier that this problem started fairly recently. What do you mean by recently?

    Client: Well, I can't remember this being a problem over a year ago.

12. Counselor: Can you recall the first time you noticed that you were thinking about retirement and got bogged down at work?

    Client: Well, last spring the personnel director came in and gave me some company forms to fill out that had to do with retirement. Then it hit home.

13. Counselor: How did you feel before this incident with the personnel director?

    Client: OK. I guess I had never really thought that much about retiring before that. When I did, it would be a momentary thing. It certainly never interfered with my work. Now it sticks with me.

14. Counselor: What is going on at work that seems to bring on these periods of not working on your designs?

    Client: Well, it seems to happen mostly when I'm alone in my office, actually with a design in front of me. That's when I start thinking. It doesn't seem to happen much when I'm doing other kinds of work.

15. Counselor: You say you've missed some deadlines. What has happened as a result of this?

    Client: Not much. The boss has reminded me a couple of times.

16. Counselor: You mean, in a sense you've been excused from the deadlines?

    Client: I guess so. Nothing has happened to me because of it. As a matter of fact, my boss has gone out of his way to be understanding.

17. Counselor: How has he done this?

    Client: Well, by talking to me and taking me out for a drink. He even offered for the company to pay for my therapy—he knew this is important to me.

18. Counselor: Do you see this as your getting some special consideration from having this problem?

    Client: Possibly so. I never thought about it that way, but I enjoy these conversations with my boss. However, they're at his request. I'd like to ask him for some type of interaction, but I always wait until he initiates it.

19. Counselor: Well, we've been talking about your boss's reaction to your problem. What about you—how do you feel after you miss a deadline?

    Client: Lousy, quite depressed.

20. Counselor: And what are you thinking about after this happens?

    Client: Mainly that I'm going to blow my reputation by doing this.

21. Counselor: When you do think about retirement,

how long do these thoughts stay with you?

Client: 'Til someone comes in or until I go out of my office—or possibly until I get home at night.

22. Counselor: How have these thoughts interfered with anything else in your job—or in your life?

Client: Well, they really haven't. I don't think about it at home—I don't get distracted with it there.

23. Counselor: So you notice these problem thoughts occurring mainly at work, especially when you're alone. Are you aware of any other times or places that these thoughts crop up?

Client: No, not really.

Part Two

Use a behavior log such as Figure 10-2 to self-monitor a problem behavior. Objective 2 asks you to log the behavior, the frequency or duration of its occurrence, and antecedents and consequences. For this to be most effective, keep the log for a week or more.

Part Three

Objective 3 asks you to demonstrate at least 12 out of 14 of the leads associated with problem identification in a 30-minute role-play interview. Use the Interview Checklist that follows the feedback to assess your performance on an audio tape or have a consultant check your performance. Also, you should be rated on your style as you go through the interview. Use the Helping-Style Checklist at the end of the chapter.

Feedback: Post Evaluation

Part One

1. General problem: identification and selection of problem concerns
2. Selection of problem: identification and selection of problem concerns
3. Pinpointing problem: identification and selection of problem concerns
4. Pinpointing problem: identification and selection of problem concerns
5. Reflection of feeling
6. Present problem behavior: covert behavior
7. Summarization
8. Present problem behavior: overt behavior
9. Present problem behavior: overt behavior
10. Identification of coping skills
11. Antecedent: contributing conditions
12. Antecedent: contributing conditions
13. Antecedent: contributing conditions
14. Antecedent
15. Consequences
16. Consequences
17. Probe
18. Consequences
19. Consequences
20. Consequences
21. Intensity: duration of problem behavior
22. Intensity: degree of problem
23. Intensity: extent of problem

Part Three

Use a consultant or an audio tape to assess your performance in the role-play interview. If you do not demonstrate 12 out of 14 of the leads, you may wish to do another interview.

Interview Checklist for Defining the Problem

Instructions: Determine which of the following leads or questions were demonstrated by the counselor. Check each counselor question demonstrated. Also check if the client answered the content of the counselor's question. Some examples of counselor leads are provided in the right column.

CHECKLIST Counselor's Question	Client's Answer	Examples of Counselor Leads
I. *Purpose of problem definition* _____ 1. Counselor tells client what they are going to do.	_____ (Client confirms understanding)	"I am going to ask you a lot of questions so that we can get a picture of what is going on. Getting an accurate picture about your concern (or problem) will help us later to decide what we can do about it. Your input about your most important concern will help us later. How does that sound?"
II. *Identification and selection of problem concerns* _____ 2. General problem	_____ (General)	"What is your primary concern?" "What would you like to talk about today?" "How could you describe some of the things that are really bothering you now?" "What are some present concerns (stresses) in your life?" "What is it about the situation that bothers you?"
_____ 3. Selection of problem	_____ (Check if the client answered most of the clarification questions.)	"Which one of these concerns do you feel that you would like to focus on first?" "Of the three concerns that you mentioned, which one is most stressful?" "Rank-order in terms of stress the three concerns you mentioned." "Which one of these things we have discussed do you see as having the best chance of being conquered?"
_____ 4. Pinpointing problem	_____ (Check if the client answered most of the questions.)	"Recall and tell me other times this has been a problem for you." "In what other situations has this happened?" "Has anything like this ever happened to you before—or in any other situation?" "Does the same thing happen with other people or situations?"
III. *Present problem behavior* _____ 5. Overt behaviors	_____ (Overt)	"Describe what happens in this situation." "What are you doing when this occurs?" "What did you mean when you said that you are not communicating?" "What did you do when this happened?" "How do you do _____?" "How does _____ act toward you then?"

Counselor's Question	Client's Answer	Examples of Counselor Leads
____ 6. Covert behaviors	____ (Covert)	"How do you feel about this?" "What kinds of feelings does this situation give you?" "Tell me what you mean by the word *depressed*." "How would you describe your feelings?" "What are your thoughts while this is going on?" "What feeling did this situation give you?" "Describe what kinds of thoughts made you feel more anxious." "What reactions do you have when _____?" "What goes on inside you when _____?"
IV. *Antecedent contributing conditions* ____ 7. Overt	____ (Overt)	"What were things like before you had this concern?" "How long ago did this happen?" "When and where was the first time this happened?" "How do you see those events related to your present concern?" "What things that happened seemed to lead up to this?" "What do you mean this started recently?" "What do you think made you _____?"
____ 8. Covert	____ (Covert)	"Did you ever feel this way at any other time in your life?" "How would you say you felt before this happened?" "When was the first time you felt this way?" "What are your thoughts before this thing happens?" "Can you say what made you anxious or think that way?" "How do you feel right before this happens?"
V. *Consequences* ____ 9. Overt	____ (Overt)	"What did you do after this happened?" "What happened after this?" "What happened when you stopped doing _____?" "Has your concern or problem ever produced any special advantages or considerations for you?" "As a consequence of your concern, have you gotten out of or avoided things or events?" "What can you do to stop this?"

Counselor's Question	Client's Answer	Examples of Counselor Leads
_____ 10. Covert	_____ (Covert)	"What were you thinking about after it happened?" "How did you feel after? How does this affect _____?" "How did the experience change your feelings?" "When did you stop feeling (or thinking) this way after it happened?" "Can you recall any thoughts or feelings that made the problem better or worse?"
VI. *Coping skills* _____ 11. Client coping skills and resources	_____ (Strengths)	"Describe a situation when this concern (or problem) is not interfering." "In the past, how did you master or deal with this or other problems?" "What skills do you have now that might help you manage this concern?"
VII. *Intensity of problem* _____ 12. Extent of problem	_____ (Where and _____ when)	"Does this happen all the time or only sometimes?" "When does this happen?" "Where does this happen?"
_____ 13. Degree of intensity	_____ (Degree or severity)	"How strong was your _____ at this time?" "You say sometimes you feel *very anxious*. On a scale from 1 to 10, with 1 being very calm and 10 being very anxious, where would you put your feelings?" "How has this interfered with other areas of your life?"
_____ 14. Frequency and duration of problem behaviors	_____ (Frequency or duration)	"How much does this go on in a typical day?" "How long does this _____ stay with you?" "How often (or how much) does this occur?"

OTHER SKILLS

Yes _____ 15. The counselor evidenced other verbal responses (such as reflection, summarization, confrontation) in addition to open-ended questions.

No _____   _____ Comments of consultant

          _____

Yes _____ 16. Most of the information given to the counselor by the client was remembered or recalled accurately by the counselor.

No _____   _____ Comments of consultant

          _____

Helping-Style Checklist

1. To what extent are you comfortable as a counselor with the client and with the subject areas discussed?

1	2	3	4	5
Not at all	Minimally	Somewhat	A great deal	Most always

2. To what extent do you refrain from imposing your values and expectations on the client?

1	2	3	4	5
Not at all	Minimally	Somewhat	A great deal	Most always

3. To what extent do you prevent your personal needs from dominating or interfering with the session?

1	2	3	4	5
Not at all	Minimally	Somewhat	A great deal	Most always

4. To what extent are you flexible and able to adapt your style to the person?

1	2	3	4	5
Not at all	Minimally	Somewhat	A great deal	Most always

5. To what extent are you focused on the person and the process rather than on the procedure or yourself?

1	2	3	4	5
Not at all	Minimally	Somewhat	A great deal	Most always

6. To what extent are you spontaneous and nonmechanical in the delivery of your skills?

1	2	3	4	5
Not at all	Minimally	Somewhat	A great deal	Most always

7. Based on your helping style, how likely would the client be to come back and see you or to refer a friend to you?

1	2	3	4	5
Not at all	Minimally	Somewhat	A great deal	Most always

Suggested Readings

Seven Categories for Defining the Problem

Goldfried, M. R., & Davison, G. C. *Clinical behavior therapy*. New York: Holt, Rinehart & Winston, 1976. Chap. 3, 37–54.

Kanfer, F. H., & Grimm, L. G. Behavioral analysis: Selecting target behaviors in the interview. *Behavior Modification*, 1977, *1*, 7–28.

Kanfer, F. H., & Saslow, G. Behavioral diagnosis. In C. M. Franks (Ed.), *Behavior therapy: Appraisal and status*. New York: McGraw-Hill, 1969.

Linehan, M. Issues in behavioral interviewing. In J. D. Cone & R. P. Hawkins (Eds.), *Behavioral assessment: New directions in clinical psychology*. New York: Brunner/Mazel, 1977.

Meichenbaum, D. A cognitive-behavior modification approach to assessment. In M. Hersen & A. S. Bellack (Eds.), *Behavioral assessment: A practical handbook*. New York: Pergamon Press, 1976.

Morganstern, K. P. Behavioral interviewing: The initial stages of assessment. In M. Hersen & A. S. Bellack (Eds.), *Behavioral assessment: A practical handbook*. New York: Pergamon Press, 1976.

Schwartz, A., & Goldiamond, I. *Social casework: A behavioral approach*. New York: Columbia University Press, 1975. Chap. 3, 67–130.

Wolpe, J. *Theme and variations: A behavior therapy casebook*. New York: Pergamon Press, 1976.

Chapter 11
Selecting Goals: A Reciprocal Decision-Making Process

Pause for a few minutes to answer the following questions to yourself or with someone else.

1. What is one thing you would like to change about yourself?
2. Suppose you are successful in accomplishing this change. How would things be different for you?
3. How feasible is this change?
4. What are some of the risks—to you or others—of this change?
5. What would be your pay-offs for making this change?
6. If someone were to help you make this change, would you foresee any conflict in ideas or values you might have with this helper, based on your responses to the first five questions?

These six questions reflect the process of selecting goals in counseling. Perhaps thinking through or discussing them alerted you to the implications of trying to define and work toward some desired change. After defining the client's problem, the counselor and client should determine the desired outcomes or goals. Counseling goals give direction to the counseling process and minimize the ambiguity created by vague theoretical or therapeutic purposes. Goals can serve as milestones that may provide continuous indications of client progress and of the effectiveness of the counseling interventions.

Selecting counseling goals is a highly interactive process between the counselor and the client. The client usually determines the outcome goals of counseling. However, the counselor's input is essential in helping the client identify the desired results of counseling in clearly defined, visible goal statements. This chapter will explain the purpose of counseling goals and will describe and give examples of the decision-making procedures involved in selecting them. This chapter is designed to help you acquire some interview leads to use for selecting client goals and to assist you in identifying some probable client responses to your leads.

Objectives

1. Using a written dialogue, identify accurately 11 out of 14 counselor leads associated with the six categories of selecting goals.
2. Demonstrate 5 of the 6 leads for selecting goals with a role-play client in a 20-minute interview. A consultant can sit in, or you can assess your own performance by taping it. Use the Interview Checklist at the end of the chapter to evaluate your interview.

Purposes of Goals

Goals have three important purposes in counseling. First, they represent some directions for counseling. Clearly defined goals reflect the specific areas of client concern that need most immediate attention (Hill, 1975). Establishing goals can clarify the client's initial expectations of counseling (D. L. Smith, 1976). Goals may help both counselor and client anticipate more precisely what can and cannot be accomplished through counseling (Krumboltz, 1966). Without goals, counseling may be "directionless" or may be based more on the theoretical biases and "personal preferences" of the counselor than on the needs of the client (Bandura, 1969, p. 70). Some clients may go through counseling without realizing that the sessions are devoid of direction or are more consistent with the counselor's preferences than the client's needs and aims. However, in other aspects of our lives, most of us would be very aware of analogous situations. If we boarded an airplane destined to a place of our choice, and the airplane went around in circles or the pilots announced a change of destination that they desired, we would be upset and indignant.

A second purpose of goals is to have some basis for selecting and using particular counseling strategies and interventions. The changes the client desires will, to some degree, determine the kinds of action plans and treatment strategies that can be used with some likelihood of success. Without a specific identification of what the client wants from counseling, it is almost impossible to explain and defend one's choice to move in a certain direction or to use one or more counseling strategies. Without goals, the counselor may use a particular approach without any "rational basis" (Bandura, 1969, p. 70). Whether the approach will be helpful or not is left to chance rather than choice.

A third and most important purpose of goals is their role in an outcome evaluation of counseling. Goals can indicate the difference between what and how much the client is able to do now and what and how much the client would like to do in the future. With the ultimate goal in mind, the counselor and client can monitor progress toward the goal and compare progress before and after a counseling intervention. These data provide continuous feedback to both counselor and client (Smith, 1976). The feedback can be used to assess the feasibility of the goal and the effectiveness of the intervention. The role of well-defined outcomes in evaluation of counseling has been summarized very aptly by Bandura (1969):

> When desired outcomes are designated in observable and measurable terms, it becomes readily apparent when the methods have succeeded, when they have failed, and when they need further development to increase their potency. This self-corrective feature is a safeguard against perpetuation of ineffective approaches, which are difficult to retire if the changes they are supposed to produce remain ambiguous [p. 74].*

An Overview of Selecting and Defining Goals

The sequence of selecting and defining goals is presented in Figure 11-1, which represents the following steps in this process.

Selecting Goals

1. The counselor explains the purpose of goals.
2. The counselor asks the client to specify what change or goal is desired as a result of counseling.
3. The counselor and client explore the feasibility of the desired goal.
4. The counselor and client identify any risks associated with the goal.
5. The counselor and client describe advantages of the goal.
6. The counselor and client must make a decision. Based on the information obtained about client-stated goals, they select one of the following alternatives: to continue counseling, to reconsider the client's goals, or to seek a referral.

*This and all other quotations from this source are from *Principles of Behavior Modification*, by Albert Bandura. Copyright © 1969 by Holt, Rinehart & Winston, Inc. Reprinted by permission of Holt, Rinehart & Winston.

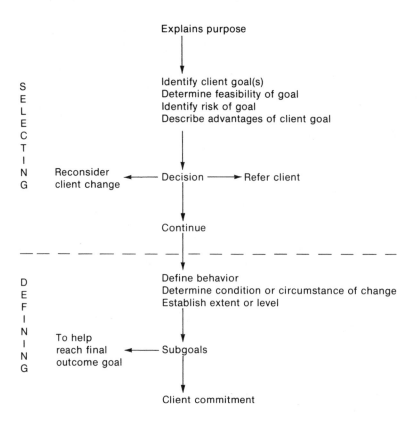

Explains purpose

S
E
L
E
C
T
I
N
G

Identify client goal(s)
Determine feasibility of goal
Identify risk of goal
Describe advantages of client goal

Reconsider client change ← Decision → Refer client

Continue

- -

D
E
F
I
N
I
N
G

Define behavior
Determine condition or circumstance of change
Establish extent or level

To help reach final outcome goal ← Subgoals

Client commitment

Figure 11-1. Selecting and Defining Goals

The process of selecting goals may also involve values clarification between the client and the counselor.

As illustrated in Figure 11-1, defining goals occurs after the goals have been selected and agreed to by both counselor and client. This process includes five steps.

Defining Goals

1. The counselor and client define the overt and covert behaviors associated with the goal.
2. The counselor and client determine the circumstances or conditions of change.
3. The counselor and client establish the level or extent to which the goal behavior is to occur.
4. The counselor and client arrange subgoals sequentially.

5. The counselor obtains the client's commitment to work toward the goals.

The counselor can facilitate the development of counseling goals by using leads in the interview that are directed toward selection and definition of goals. The leads associated with selecting goals are presented in this chapter, and Chapter 12 describes the leads to be used in defining goals. The interview leads associated with the six content categories of selecting goals as depicted in Figure 11-1 are presented in the next section. Examples of these leads are provided, and more can be found in the Interview Checklist at the end of the chapter. These leads are merely suggested examples. You can provide examples that are equally good or better for each category.

Interview Leads for Selecting Goals

Purpose of Goals

The first step in selecting goals consists of a rationale given to the client about goals. The statement should describe goals, the purpose of having them, and the client's participation in the goal-setting process. The counselor's intent is to convey the importance of having goals, as well as the importance of the client's participation in developing them. An example of what the counselor might say about the purpose of goals is: "We've been talking about these two areas that bother you. It might be helpful now to discuss how you would like things to be different. We can develop some goals to work for during our sessions. These goals will tell us what you want as a result of counseling. So today, let's talk about some things *you* would like to work on."

After this explanation, the counselor will look for a client response that indicates understanding. If the client seems confused, the counselor will need to explain further the purposes of goals and their benefits to the client.

Identification of Client Goals

After describing the purpose of goals, the counselor asks the client to select areas to work on during counseling. In most cases, the counselor attempts to move the focus from discussion of the client's problems to specification of changes the client would like to make that might alleviate or eliminate the problems. The counselor tries to give the client the responsibility for deciding what she or he wants to have happen as a result of counseling.

What Does "Change" Mean? The notion of change is implicit in any client statement of desired outcomes. We assume that, in most cases, clients have come to a counselor because of dissatisfaction or concern about themselves, their relationships, or certain situations in their lives. For example, Gottman and Leiblum (1974) suggest that clients enter counseling with a "per-

formance discrepancy"; in some way or in some situation, the client is performing in a manner that needs to be changed. The performance discrepancy is represented by the difference between the client's perception of current functioning and the client's expectations of alternative ways of functioning (p. 25). Most clients' desired counseling goals will reflect something *different* about themselves or their life-styles. The desired differences may be overt behaviors or situations, covert behaviors, or combinations of both. The goals clients select may be directed at eliminating something or increasing something; but, in all cases, the change is expected to be an improvement over what currently exists (Srebalus, 1975, p. 415). Client goals based on a performance discrepancy reflect a typical definition of change cited by Srebalus as movement from one state of being to another (p. 416). This concept of change indicates a discrepancy between what the client is doing now and what the client wants to accomplish. These changes may result from developmental changes, counseling interventions, or both. Srebalus suggests that some clients may want to change some aspects of their lives but maintain other things the way they are. In these cases, the counseling sessions may be oriented toward identifying and describing things that are going well for the client in addition to modifying unsatisfying situations and behaviors.

Regardless of the client's expectations for counseling, we hope that the counselor is responsive to the client's selection of goals—even if these goals do not reflect the counselor's theoretical biases or personal preferences. This sort of responsiveness has been defined very appropriately by Gottman and Leiblum (1974): "If he [the client] wants help in accepting his homosexuality, do not set up a treatment program designed to help him find rewards in heterosexuality. Respect for your client implies respect for his diagnosis of his needs and wishes" (p. 64).*

*This and all other quotations from this source are from *How to Do Psychotherapy and How to Evaluate It: A Manual for Beginners*, by John Mordechai Gottman and Sandra Risa Leiblum. Copyright © 1974 by Holt, Rinehart & Winston, Inc. Reprinted by permission of Holt, Rinehart & Winston.

Interview Leads to Elicit Client Goals. Examples of some leads the counselor can use to elicit goal statements from the client are:

"Suppose some distant relative you haven't seen for a while sees you after counseling. What would be different then from the way things are now?"
"Assuming we are successful, what would you be doing or how would these situations change?"
"What do you expect to accomplish as a result of counseling?"
"How would you like counseling to benefit you?"

The counselor's purpose in using these sorts of leads is to have the client identify some desired outcomes or results of counseling. The counselor is looking for some verbal indication of the results the client expects. If the client does not know of desired changes or cannot specify a purpose for engaging in counseling, some time should be spent in exploring this area before moving on. The counselor can assist the client in selecting goals in several ways: by assigning homework ("Make a list of what you can do now and what you want to do one year from now"), by using imagery ("Imagine being someone you admire. Who would you be? What would you be doing? How would you be different?"), by additional questioning ("If you could wave a magic wand and have three wishes, what would they be?"), or by self-report questionnaires or inventories such as the Behavioral Self-Rating Checklist (BSRC) developed by Cautela and Upper (1975). This checklist asks the client to indicate which of 73 adaptive overt and covert behaviors the client needs to learn in order to function more effectively (Cautela & Upper, 1976, p. 91).

Feasibility of Goals

Although it is generally the client's responsibility to select goals, the counselor can help the client evaluate the feasibility of achieving the goals and the possible consequences or implications of change. This exploration enables the client to make more informed choices. In examining the feasibility of goals, the counselor is trying to help the client determine how realistic the client's goals are.

What Is a Feasible Goal? The feasibility of a goal is usually related directly to the degree of control the client has in the situation and the resources available to the client for goal achievement. For example, suppose you are counseling an 8-year-old girl whose parents are getting a divorce. The child says she wants you to help her convince her parents to stay married. This goal would be very difficult for the child to attain, since she has no responsibility for her parents' relationship. Or imagine that you are counseling someone whose goal is to make a basketball team this year, even though she or he has never played basketball. This person may not have the resources or requisite skills to meet this goal in the next three months.

In exploring the feasibility of goals, the counselor should be careful not to overestimate or underestimate the client's potential. There are many things a person can do if he or she is determined. A man can become a woman or vice versa, a person with a prosthetic leg can become a swimming star, and a peanut farmer can attain high political office.

Interview Leads for Feasibility of Goals. To help the client determine the feasibility of goals, the counselor can say something like:

"How much control do you have over this situation?"
"What would you have to do to reach this goal?"
"How feasible is it for you to be able to _____?"

The intent of these leads is to have the *client* assess the degree to which a goal can be attained in a realistic way and within a practical amount of time. The counselor is looking for a response that indicates the client has some evidence the goal is realistic and can be attained in a reasonable time and manner. If the client selects a goal and considers it feasible, but the counselor does not agree, the counselor and client will have to decide either to pursue this goal, to negotiate a reconsidered goal, or to refer the client to another helper, as we shall discuss shortly.

Risks of Client Goals

During the process of goal selection, the counselor and client will explore various alternatives and some of their probable consequences (Bandura, 1969). Because change is viewed as an improvement over one's current situation, we often assume that change has only positive consequences. But many changes desired by clients may have some negative consequences, either for the client or for significant others in the client's environment. For example, for a woman who decides to stop working in order to be at home, some negative consequences might include loss of income and loss of daily contact with other people. Or a client who wants to be more assertive may risk termination of some relationships with people who have trouble dealing with the client's "new" behavior.

Leads for Risks of Goals. The counselor uses leads to have the client consider some risks or side effects that could accompany the desired change. Some examples of leads the counselor might use to explore the risks of change are:

"What might be some possible risks of doing this?"
"How would your life be changed if this happened?"
"What are some possible disadvantages of going in this direction?"
"What are some negative consequences this change might have for you—or for others?"
"How will this change limit or constrain you?"

The counselor is looking for some indication that the client has considered the possible risks associated with the goal. If the client discounts the risks or cannot identify any, the counselor can use immediacy or confrontation to point out some disadvantages. However, the counselor should be careful not to persuade or coerce the client to pursue another alternative simply because the counselor believes it is better. As Eisenberg and Delaney (1977) note, "It is one thing to help a person be aware of the consequences of the choice he or she has made and another thing to persuade the client to prefer another alternative" (p. 202).

Advantages of Client Goals

If change is desired, it is almost always because the client believes the change will improve or enhance his or her current situation in some way. Most clients can readily identify some positive consequences associated with their desired changes. Nevertheless, it is still a good idea with all clients to explore positive consequences of the change for at least three reasons: to determine whether the advantages the client perceives are indicative of actual benefits; to point out other possible advantages to the client or to others that have been overlooked; and to strengthen the client's incentive to change.

Interview Leads for Advantages of Goals. Some examples of leads used to explore advantages of client change are:

"What do you see as the benefits of this change?"
"Who would benefit from this change and how?"
"What are some positive consequences that may result from this change?"
"What are some advantages of attaining this goal?"

In using these leads, the counselor is looking for some indication that the client is selecting a goal based on the positive consequences the goal may produce. If the client overlooks some advantages, the counselor can describe them to add to the client's incentive to change.

If the client is unable to identify any benefits of change for herself or himself, this may be viewed as a signal for caution. Failure to identify advantages of change for oneself may indicate an attempt to change at someone else's request. Further exploration may indicate that another person is a more appropriate client, or that other goals may need to be selected.

Decision Point

The process of developing goals to this point has involved the client as the primary agent in choosing goals. The counselor's role has been secondary and confined primarily to helping the client explore the feasibility, risks, and advantages of change. At this point in the process, the primary issue for the counselor is whether she or he can help the client attain the selected goals. Most people agree that this is one of the biggest ethical and, to some extent, legal questions the counselor faces during the helping process (Bandura, 1969; Gottman & Leiblum, 1974; Krumboltz, 1966; Morganstern, 1976).

The counselor and client will need to choose whether to continue with counseling and pursue the selected goals, to continue with counseling but reevaluate the client's initial goals, or to refer the client to another counselor. This decision, which always has to be made on an individual basis, should consider the client's goals and the counselor's skills and values. We offer the following ideas as food for thought in this area. First of all, as much as possible, be responsive to the *client's* requests for change (Gottman & Leiblum, 1974, p. 64). Also, if you have a *major* reservation about pursuing the selected goals, a referral might be more helpful to the client (Gottman & Leiblum, p. 43).

Major Reservations of a Counselor. A counselor might have several reservations or limitations that would affect this decision point. One possible major reservation for you, the counselor, is any previous difficulty you have had in working with similar clients. Your own unresolved conflicts in the area the client wants to pursue may block successful counseling. Other reservations may surface when your values are not compatible with those reflected in the client's choice of goals. When goals pose harm to the client or others, you may decide it would be ethically irresponsible to help the client pursue them. You also might have some reservations if the client insists that you use a technique that data suggest is ineffective or harmful, or if the client insists on a treatment approach that is beyond your skill level or the realm of counseling. Finally, you may feel counseling would not help when the contributing problem conditions are outside the client's control or when the client is unwilling to change these factors.

Three Kinds of Choices. We see three kinds of choices that could be made at this decision

point: to continue with the client and pursue the client's selected goals, to continue with the client but reevaluate the goals, or to refer the client to another counselor.

If the client selects goals and neither you nor the client has any major reservations, you will probably decide to continue with counseling to help the client attain her or his goal. You might summarize this to the client as in the following example: "You stated that you want to do _____ as a result of counseling. You seem to be willing and able to change the factors that are part of this problem. The benefits of this change for you seem to outweigh the disadvantages." After this point, assuming the client confirms this statement, the counselor and client will move on to defining the goal (see Chapter 12).

In other cases, you may decide to continue with the client on the basis of some reevaluation of the client's selected goals. Morganstern (1976) observes that there may be times when it would be difficult to accept the client's goals without offering "re-education." For example, if the client wants to have a child and cannot identify any risks or disadvantages posed by this choice, the counselor may point out some constraints. Or, if a client chooses as her or his goal "I want to be just exactly like my best friend," the counselor might point out the difficulty in achieving this goal. In reconsidering the client's goal, the counselor might say something like: "I can't help you be just like your best friend, because each of us is a little different from everyone else. Our differences are what make us unique. If there is something about yourself you'd like to work on, I can help with that."

Reevaluation of the client's goals is a very sticky issue. Bandura (1969) observes that a redefinition of the client's goal by the counselor, especially "unilateral redefinition," is a prevailing but "largely ignored ethical issue" (p. 103). Bandura recommends that, when initiating reevaluation or redefinition of the client's goals, the counselor should make this path explicit to the client. Also, the counselor should inform the client that such comments are based on information *and* on the counselor's own belief system (p. 103). Reevaluation of client goals should be pursued only "with the understanding and consent of the client" who is "free to exert 'counter-control'—that is, to challenge, refute, or refuse to comply with the therapist's suggestions" (Gottman & Leiblum, 1974, p. 68). The counselor's influence in reconsideration should be explicit, not implicit, open rather than disguised.

Referral may be appropriate in any of the following cases: if the client wants to pursue a goal that is incompatible with your value system; if you are unable to be objective about the client's concern; if you are unfamiliar with or unable to use a treatment requested by the client; or if you would be exceeding your level of competence in working with the client. Referral may be a better choice than continuing to work with the client in the midst of serious limitations or reservations. Referral is a way to provide an alternative counseling experience and, we hope, one that will leave the client with a positive impression of counseling.

In deciding to refer a client, the counselor does have certain responsibilities. From the initial counseling contacts, the counselor and client have entered into at least an unwritten contract. Once the counselor agrees to counsel a client, he or she "assumes a degree of loyalty and responsibility for the outcomes of therapy" (Van Hoose & Kottler, 1977, p. 82). In deciding to terminate this "contract" by a referral, the referring counselor can be considered legally liable if the referral is not handled with due care (Dawidoff, 1973). Due care implies that "when referral is undertaken the referring therapist has the responsibility for ascertaining the appropriateness of the referral, including the skill of the receiving therapist. Furthermore, he should provide the receiving therapist with information sufficient to enable him to give proper help to the client. It is also important that the therapist attempt to follow up on the status of his client's well-being" (Van Hoose & Kottler, p. 83).

Learning Activity: Decision Point

To give you practice in thinking through the kinds of decisions you may face in the goal-setting process, you may want to use this learning activity.

The exercise consists of four hypothetical situations. In each case, assume that you are the counselor. Read through the case. Then sit back, close your eyes, and try to imagine being in the room with the client and being faced with this dilemma. How would you feel? What would you say? What would you decide to do, and why?

There are no "right" or "wrong" answers to these cases. You may wish to discuss your responses with another classmate, a coworker, or your instructor.

Case 1
You are counseling an 18-year-old male client. The client says he has been very depressed lately. After analysis of the problem, you discover the client has been depressed since he discovered his girlfriend had an abortion. She had not consulted him about this. However, your client feels that, since he was partially responsible for her pregnancy, he is now responsible for her abortion. He feels that it is a "sin" to have an abortion, and he feels like a "murderer." He states that he wants your help in giving him the courage to take his own life as retribution for killing this unborn child. What do you do?

Case 2
You are counseling a fourth-grader. You are the only counselor in this school. One day you notice this boy seems to be all bruised. You inquire about this. After much hesitation, the child blurts out that he often is singled out on his way home by two big sixth-grade "bullies" who pick a fight, beat him up for a while, and then leave him alone until another time. Your client asks you to forget this information. He begs you not to say or do anything for fear of reprisal from these two bullies. He states he doesn't want to deal with this in counseling since he has come to see you about something else. What do you do?

Case 3
You are a counselor working in a vocational-rehabilitation agency. One of your clients has lost his last three jobs. After making some inquiries, it seems apparent that your client is a good worker but has been fired because of a sloppy appearance, including such things as wearing torn and dirty clothes to work, not shaving or cutting his hair, and reportedly having a smell that "even your best friend won't tell you about." In discussing this, he states that

he will work with you on some things he can do to keep jobs in the future. However, he states he doesn't want to deal with his appearance, because he does not feel that one's appearance helps or hinders one's work skills. What do you do?

Case 4

You are working in a large college counseling center. A 25-year-old woman comes in to see you. She is a grad student in engineering and is on a work-free fellowship to receive her doctorate. She states that she is fed up with graduate school. She has considered leaving for a while to get a job. However, she has not done this because she would lose her lucrative fellowship and probably would not be eligible to get it if she returned at a later time. She states that her goal is to make some decision about what she should do. In discussing alternative courses of action, she states that she could (1) continue as is and suffer through her work, (2) continue but try to change her attitude or parts of her environment, or (3) drop out of the program. After talking, she decides to continue without any changes—just to stay in misery. She states she would like to continue to see you for a while to ventilate her feelings to someone. You are aware of your feeling that she has made the wrong decision. What do you do?

Model Dialogue: The Case of Joan

To help you see how the leads for selecting goals are used with a client, the case of Joan, introduced in Chapter 9, is continued here as a dialogue. This dialogue is presented in two different counseling sessions, both directed toward selection of goals. Each counselor response is prefaced by an explanation (in italics) of what type of response is being used.

Session 1

In response 1, the counselor starts out with a "recap" of the last session as a review.

1. Counselor: Joan, last week we talked about some of the things that are going on with you right now that you're concerned about. What do you remember that we talked about?
    Client: Well, we talked a lot about my problems in school—like my trouble in my math class. Also, about the fact that I can't decide whether or not to switch over to a voca-

tional curriculum—and if I did my parents would be upset.

In response 2, the counselor will move from problem definition to goal selection. Response 2 will consist of an explanation about goals and the purpose of goals.

2. Counselor: That's a good summary. We've been talking about a couple of these areas that bother you. Today it might be helpful to talk about how you would like things to be different. We'll call these changes our goals—which means where you feel you are right now and what you'd like to work on in counseling. How does that sound?
    Client: That's OK with me. I mean, do you really think there are some things I can do about these problems?

The client has indicated some uncertainty about possible change. The counselor will pursue this in response 3 and indicate more about the purpose of goals and possible effects of counseling for this person.

3. Counselor: You seem a little uncertain about how much things can be different. To the extent that you have some control over a situation, it is possible to make some changes. Depending on what kind of changes you want to make, there are some ways we can work together on this. It will take some time on your part, too. How do you feel about this?
    Client: OK. I'd like to get out of the rut I'm in.

In response 4, the counselor will explore the ways in which the client would like to change. The counselor will use a lead to identify client goals.

4. Counselor: What kinds of changes would you like to make that would be of some benefit to you?
    Client: Well, I'd like to feel less pressured in school, especially in my math class.

The client has identified one possible goal. The counselor will pursue others in responses 5, 6, and 7 with other leads to help Joan identify possible goals.

5. Counselor: OK, that's one thing you'd like to be different. Any others?
    Client: Well, I'd like to make some decisions for myself for a change.

6. Counselor: OK, so two things you'd like to work on are feeling less pressured now in your math class and learning to make some decisions on your own. Is that about it, or can you think of any other situations you'd like to work on?
    Client: Well, I guess it's related to making my own decisions, but I'd like to decide whether to stay in this curriculum or switch to the vocational one.

7. Counselor: So you're concerned also about mak-

ing a special type of decision about school that affects you now.

Client: That's right. But I'm sort of afraid to because I know if I decided to switch, my parents would have a terrible reaction when they found out about it. I guess I was hoping if I did decide to switch you could tell them for me.

The client is alluding to possible side effects (risk) of making this decision. The counselor will explore these in response 8, using a lead to identify risks of change.

8. Counselor: It sounds like you're concerned about this decision because you're anticipating a real negative reaction from your folks if you did decide to switch.

Client: Oh, boy, you know it. But I was thinking if you broke the news to them and possibly even told them that you advised me to switch, it would make it a lot easier for me.

In response 9, the counselor explores the client's concern about talking to her folks as another possible goal and as a risk to making decisions, and clarifies what the counselor's role permits.

9. Counselor: You know, I can sense how hard it seems to you right now to talk to your folks about this kind of issue. Maybe that's another thing we could work on. It's something we need to talk about today. What will be the effects—both positive and negative—of these changes? You seem to be saying this might be a risk you'd take in making this decision. Maybe it would be. If so, we can work on how you'll deal with it. But I don't feel comfortable in handling the risk for you by telling your folks you acted on my advice.

Client: (Silence.)

The client didn't give any overt reaction to the counselor; in response 10, the counselor will respond to the client's silence.

10. Counselor: You seem to be thinking about what I've just said.

Client: (More silence.)

Still no overt comment. The counselor will try to reflect the client's present feelings in response 11.

11. Counselor: Possibly you're a little let down. This is something you hoped I would do for you; now you hear I won't do this.

Client: I guess I'm not sure I see why it would be a problem for you.

In response 12, the counselor will explain the rationale for his or her behavior and relate it to risks of change.

12. Counselor: That's a good question. What I'm thinking about this is that you're telling me you haven't had many chances to make decisions.

You'd like to be able to make your own choices. Sometimes, in making choices, there are risks. If, in this choice, I step in and handle the risk or do away with it, I'm taking away part of the choice from you. So, to me, doing this for you would not be a way of helping you learn to make choices on your own.

Client: (Silence, with set look on face.)

In response 13, the counselor will reflect the client's evident nonverbal reaction.

13. Counselor: You still seem to be upset with what I'm saying.

Client: I understand what you mean, but I'd still like you to do it. If I decided to switch, I'd like to know that you had guaranteed me you would tell my folks.

The counselor has made a decision about the basis on which he or she can and cannot continue with the client in pursuit of this goal and makes this known in response 14.

14. Counselor: And that's something I won't guarantee you. I can and will help you learn how to make choices—and how to deal with the risks of a choice like this one. But I don't feel comfortable working together on this choice if you want me to guarantee you that I'll tell your folks. That's not something I can do.

Client: (Silence.)

The counselor interprets silence as the need for the client to think. Response 15 responds to this need for time and puts some choice for future sessions on the client.

15. Counselor: I know this is an important issue to you. If you can accept what I can and can't do for you and want to work together on the other things you mentioned, we can. Maybe you'd like to think it over and come back in a day or two and tell me what you'd like to do.

Session 2

1. Counselor: Joan, I'm glad to see you today. It's been almost a week since our last talk. What kinds of things have you been thinking over?

Client: Well, I guess I was a little mad when we talked last week. But I thought about what you said, and I guess I wanted to cop out. I guess I was expecting you to help me cop out, but since that's one of my problems it wouldn't be right.

In responses 2 and 3, the counselor will probe the theme of copping out.

2. Counselor: How do you see copping out as one of your problems?

Client: Well, like we talked about a while back, I try to get out of situations that bother me.

3. Counselor: You mean like cutting math class because you feel nervous there?

Client: Yes.

In response 4, the counselor will focus on learning how to handle situations differently and goes back to identifying the goal or what the client wants to change.

4. Counselor: Well, you're using this sort of copping out as your present way of coping with the problem. What we need to do is to figure out other, more helpful ways of coping with your concerns. Did you do any more thinking about things you'd like to work on?

Client: Well, my math class is a pretty big problem. And of course making this decision—and decisions in general.

In response 5, the counselor uses a lead to pursue the advantages of one goal, dealing with math class.

5. Counselor: OK, let's take a look at these things. For instance, being able to go to your math class and feel comfortable there, and being able to give answers, and so forth. How would doing these things help you?

Client: Well, just by feeling better. Feeling less worried about having to compete. And probably my grades would get better.

In response 6, the counselor asks about possible risks of this change.

6. Counselor: OK. Those are some ways that making these changes would benefit you. In what way might these changes be risky or have any negative effects for you?

Client: I'm not sure.

The client didn't identify any negative consequences. The counselor remembers that one of the client "pay-offs" in math class is increased teacher attention. In responses 7, 8, 9, and 10, the counselor will explore how this might change or be a risk if the client achieves the goal.

7. Counselor: When we talked earlier, you mentioned your teacher had been helping you quite a bit and seemed to excuse you when you didn't go to the board. What do you think his reaction would be after you start to do things differently and respond more in his class?

Client: Well, I think he would be surprised. I'm not sure he thinks I've got it in me to do these things.

8. Counselor: What about the amount of attention he gives to you now—and will give to you in the future if you accomplish this?

Client: Well, he never pays that much attention

to kids who do pretty well—unless it's someone who's really, really good. He sort of holds someone like that up to the rest of the class. But I doubt if he'd be as concerned about me as he is right now if I started to do better work. He wouldn't have any reason to talk to me individually.

9. Counselor: And how do you think you'd feel about that, now that you're more or less accustomed to being singled out?

Client: I don't really care that much about that.

10. Counselor: OK, so you don't see that as a way that your changing in math class might hurt you?

Client: No, not really.

In response 11, the counselor explores the possibility of risks from reactions of Joan's peers in class.

11. Counselor: Joan, what about the other students. How would they react if you started to participate more?

Client: I don't really think they care one way or the other.

In response 12, the counselor explores the feasibility of this goal for the client.

12. Counselor: OK, how feasible do *you* think it is to make some of these changes in math class?

Client: Well, at first I didn't think I could. But after seeing my test scores, I realize I must have some ability.

In response 13, the counselor will explore another area of the client goal—decision-making.

13. Counselor: OK, let's talk for a little while now about the other area of concern—learning to make decisions on your own. You've said you haven't had many opportunities to do this, or haven't been encouraged to do this. Is that still the way you see it?

Client: Yes.

In responses 14 and 15, the counselor asks the client to explore the feasibility of this goal.

14. Counselor: How do you feel about your potential for starting to make decisions on your own?

Client: Well, I think I should be able to. Most of my friends can.

15. Counselor: What might get in the way of your learning to do this?

Client: Well, I'm not sure how to go about it. And I back off because of how my parents react.

In response 16, the counselor tries to determine whether the client sees her parents' reaction as making the goal unrealistic or as a possible side effect or risk of the change.

16. Counselor: Making a good decision involves

learning some skills we can work on together. But your parents' reaction—do you see it as something that blocks your decision-making or as a side effect of actually making the decision?

Client: I guess it's more a possible side effect —something that might be a problem after I've actually made a decision.

In responses 17 and 18, the counselor explores how her parents' reaction seems to be a side effect or risk of this change for Joan.

17. Counselor: What about their reaction is a problem for you?

    Client: I'm not sure. I guess I try not to talk to them about anything controversial.

18. Counselor: Do you mean that if something controversial comes up you leave the scene?

    Client: Right. So I'm not used to talking to them and I'm not sure how to approach them.

In response 19, the counselor not only identifies the pattern of problem behavior for the client, but also reiterates how this can be changed as a possible goal.

19. Counselor: I see a similarity here. Like your math class—when something comes up with your parents that's touchy, your usual response is to leave, to get out of the situation. It's your way of coping now. It's OK, but it doesn't give you any experience in handling this kind of thing. Possibly this would need to be something we would work on.

    Client: Yeah, you're right. I guess I weasel my way out of a lot of things.

In responses 20 and 21, the counselor reinforces the idea of learning alternative ways to cope and pursues the advantages of this change or goal for the client.

20. Counselor: That's the way you've learned to handle some situations you don't like or don't feel comfortable with. We can work on other ways of handling these situations. Now, we've been talking about some risks of making your own decisions. How could learning to make decisions help you?

    Client: Well, mainly through making me feel like I can make some good decisions on my own. I think it would increase my self-confidence. And I wouldn't just wait around until it was too late to make a choice.

21. Counselor: OK, those are some good reasons for working on this area. Learning these skills should help you with the decision you're worried about now—in terms of your curriculum.

    Client: Yeah, I hope so.

In responses 22 and 23, counselor and client identify possible areas to be maintained, not changed.

22. Counselor: You know, we've been talking about some areas you'd like to change. What about anything in your life right now you'd like to just keep the way it is?

    Client: Well, my friendships. I do have some really close friends.

23. Counselor: So this is an area where you'd like to just keep on doing the things you're presently doing with your friends.

    Client: Yeah.

The counselor verbalizes the decision to continue counseling and to pursue these goals in the next response.

24. Counselor: Our time is almost up. I am thinking that we have some goals which are realistic and will have some positive effects for you. We can continue discussing these goals in more detail next week. Perhaps you'd like to summarize the changes you'd like to see for yourself.

Learning Activity: Selecting Goals

In the following client-counselor dialogue of the case of Ms. Weare and Freddie, for each counselor response, identify and write down the type of goal-selection lead used by the counselor. You may wish to use the Interview Checklist for Selecting Goals at the end of the chapter as a guideline. Feedback is on p. 177.

Dialogue with Ms. Weare and Counselor

1. Counselor: Ms. Weare, today we want to find out what changes you would like to make for yourself in trying to help Freddie. We will try to develop some goals so that we can see whether what we do in our meetings is helping you. How does this sound?

    Client: I guess that's OK.

2. Counselor: What changes in yourself would you like to see in helping Freddie, if we are successful?

    Client: I want to stop helping him get dressed in the mornings.

3. Counselor: You have been dressing Freddie most of his life. What would you have to do in order to stop yourself from dressing him?

    Client: Well, instead of going upstairs and helping him, I could stay downstairs and do my chores.

4. Counselor: That's fine. What else would you need to do to make this change?

Client: Maybe tell him that it is his job to dress himself, and if he misses the school bus, I am not going to write a note.

5. Counselor: That's a good idea. What do you think might be some good things that might happen for you and Freddie by not helping him get dressed?

Client: Lots. I won't have to yell and worry about him. I could get my chores done.

6. Counselor: What about for Freddie? How would your change help him?

Client: A boy his age should be able to dress himself.

7. Counselor: OK, what are some possible bad things or some possible disadvantages of not helping Freddie get dressed?

Client: Things are bad enough as it is, although he might be late for school. Then we could both get in trouble.

8. Counselor: So you see that one thing that could happen is that Freddie might be late. Of course, as we talked about last week, we don't know if this would happen. Perhaps if he were late once or twice and realized you were serious about not helping him, he would decide to get dressed on time.

Client: I suppose so. I threaten not to help him, but I never follow through. I guess being late a couple of times probably wouldn't be a big thing.

9. Counselor: You've said you want to stop helping Freddie get dressed in the morning. That's one big thing we can work on in our meetings. You also mentioned that your change—not helping him get dressed—could have a big pay-off for you and Freddie. From my point of view, doing this sounds good. How does it sound to you?

Client: Fine.

Summary: Selection of Goals

The primary purpose of *selecting* goals is to convey to the client the responsibility and participation she or he has in contributing to the results of counseling. Without active client participation, counseling may be doomed ultimately to failure, resembling little more than a benevolent dictatorship. The selection of goals should reflect client choices. The counselor's

role is primarily to use leads that facilitate the client's goal selection. However, some value judgments by both counselor and client may be inevitable during this process. If the client selects goals that severely conflict with the counselor's values or that exceed the counselor's level of competence, the counselor may decide to refer the client or to renegotiate this goal. If counselor and client agree to pursue the selected goals, these goals must be defined clearly and specifically. The process of defining outcome goals is described in the next chapter.

Post Evaluation

I. Using the counselor-client (Mr. Brown) dialogue, Objective 1 asks you to identify 11 out of 14 of the counselor leads or questions associated with the six categories of selecting goals. Other verbal responses from previous chapters may also be included. You may wish to write your responses on a piece of paper. Feedback follows the post evaluation on p. 178.

1. Counselor: For the time we have together today, we want to find out how you would like things to be different with respect to your retirement. We want to develop some goals. The goals will give us something we can work toward, and they will help us monitor our progress. What the goals will be should be your decision on what is important for you. How does this sound?

Client: Yeah, that's fine. I'm not sure how we can do this.

2. Counselor: Let's start by finding out what you would like to do differently with respect to your thoughts and feelings about retirement.

Client: That's easy. I wish I didn't have to retire. All my problems would be solved if I could keep my job. You know—I guess I wouldn't have any worries if I could just keep working and keep on doing what I am doing.

3. Counselor: How possible is that with the company you are working for?

Client: I'm not sure that I know what you mean.

4. Counselor: Does your company allow people to work after the mandatory retirement age?

Client: Oh, heavens no. Mandatory retirement at

age 70 is one thing my company enforces. They require people to retire at age 70—and they go out and hire younger people at a much lower salary.

5. Counselor: So staying on with your company isn't a real possibility. You don't have any control over that situation.

   Client: Yeah—that's right. It's really unfortunate.

6. Counselor: I wonder if you could get similar kinds of work with another company—possibly on a part-time basis.

   Client: I don't think I would like that. It wouldn't be the same after being with this company for over 40 years. Come to think of it, I wouldn't want to work with *any* other company, even part time. It would be like starting over.

7. Counselor: Working for another company wouldn't be the same after being with your company.

   Client: That's right. Being with the same group for so long—you know the people and the routine. It's like a big family.

8. Counselor: Mr. Brown, we have talked about how unrealistic it would be to remain with your company and your feelings about going with another company even on a part-time basis. I now wonder what are some realistic changes you might want to happen now, while you're still in your job situation.

   Client: Well, I guess one thing is that I would like to do my work better while I am on the job.

9. Counselor: That sounds good. What are some other changes that you would like to see happen?

   Client: Let me think for a minute. (Pause.) I would like to be able to initiate social contacts with my boss. Another thing is that I want to feel less worried about retirement.

10. Counselor: Which of the three changes you mentioned—wanting to do better work, wanting to be able to initiate social contacts with your boss, or wanting to feel less worried about retirement—seems most important for you to work on first?

    Client: I think that, if I could feel better and stop worrying about retirement, that would really be good.

11. Counselor: That sounds good, and changing your worrying is something you can have control over. What do you think would be the positive results of this change?

    Client: Well, possibly spending more time on my

Feedback: Selecting Goals

1. Explanation of purpose of goals
2. Identification of client goal
3. Feasibility of goal
4. Feasibility of goal
5. Advantages of goal
6. Advantages of goal
7. Risks of goal
8. Risks of goal
9. Decision to continue with client's selected goal

---

work and meeting my deadlines. Also, I guess I could be more creative—my mind wouldn't be cluttered with thoughts about retirement.

12. Counselor: What might be some possible risks or disadvantages of feeling less worried about retirement?

    Client: I don't know if this would happen, but I could stop thinking about retirement altogether. I guess there is a difference between thinking about something and worrying about it. I cannot think of anything bad that would come from stopping worrying.

13. Counselor: That's a real good point. There is a difference between worrying and thinking about something. You've stated that you want to worry less about retirement as a result of our sessions together. As you have pointed out, there are some pay-offs or benefits for doing this. Also, there don't appear to be any adverse things that could happen because of this change. Do you think this is accurate?

    Client: I agree.

14. Counselor: Well, the change you would like to achieve for now is to worry less about retirement. This is a goal we can work on together. It's something that is feasible for you, and there would be a lot of advantages for you if you could worry less.

    Client: That's right. Now when do we start?

II. Demonstrate 5 of the 6 leads associated with selecting goals in a 20-minute role-play interview. Audio-tape the interview or have a consultant check out your interview using the Interview Checklist for Selecting Goals at the end of the chapter.

Interview Checklist for Selecting Goals

Instructions: Determine which of the following leads or questions were demonstrated by the counselor. Check each counselor question demonstrated. Also, check if the client answered the content of the counselor's question. Some suggested examples of counselor leads and questions are provided next to each item of the checklist.

Checklist	Examples of Counselor Leads and Questions
I. *Purpose of goals*	
___ 1. Counselor explains purpose of goals to client.	"Today we want to find out how you would like things to be different with respect to your concern. For this, we will try to develop some goals. The goals will give us something to strive for. Goals will also help us to monitor our progress in counseling. What the goals should be is up to you to decide. How does this sound to you?"
___ Client response (Indicating client confirmation, agreement, or request for clarification)	
II. *Identification of client goals*	
___ 2. Counselor focuses on how client wants to be different or would like things to change.	"Suppose a distant relative whom you have never met sees you after your changes. Describe what he or she would see you doing—how would you be different?" "Imagine what would be different about you (or the situation). What would you (or the situation) be like?" "How do you see yourself being different?" "Assuming that we are successful, what will you be doing after these changes have occurred?" "What are some realistic changes in that situation for you?"

Checklist	Examples of Counselor Leads and Questions

___Client response (Indicating desired changes. If client "doesn't know," counselor assigns homework for client, uses imagery, questioning, or checklists to discover what changes client desires.)

III. *Feasibility of goal*

___ 3. Counselor probes about how feasible (realistic) the changes are for client.

"How much control over the situation do you have to make this happen?"

"What would you have to do to make this be different?"

"What are your personal strengths, or what resources do you have, to help change take place?"

___Client response (Indicating that client has some control over desired changes so that change is feasible. If change is not within client's control, see Step 6.)

IV. *Risks of goal*

___ 4. Counselor gives leads to determine possible risks, disadvantages, or adverse consequences for client change.

"What might be some possible risks of doing this?"

"Are you aware of any side effects or adverse consequences this change may have for you—or someone else?"

"What are some possible disadvantages, if any, of going in this direction?"

___Client response (Some indication of client's awareness of negative consequences, if there seem to be any. If client does not confirm any and counselor sees some, refer to Step 6.)

V. *Advantages of goal*

___ 5. Counselor determines possible benefits or advantages of client change.

"What might be some advantages of this change—for you and for someone else?"

"Have you thought about how this change might benefit you or _____?"

"What would be the positive results of this change?"

___Client response (Some indication that client has decided to change because of advantages she or he sees rather than changing at someone else's request. If client doesn't indicate any advantages of the change for himself or herself, see Step 6.)

VI. *Decision point*

___ 6. Based on the information obtained in 2, 3, 4, and 5, counselor makes a decision to do one of the following:

a. continue with client
   ___Client response (confirmation)

a. "You stated you want to do _____ as a result of counseling. This seems to be something you can change. There don't seem to be any side effects to doing this. You realize this will help you and your family."

Checklist	_Examples of Counselor Leads and Questions_
b. reconsider client goals ___Client response (client reconsideration of perceptions about goals, feasibility of goals, or possible advantages or disadvantages of goals)	b. "You say you'd like to get your parents back together. I'm not too sure that this is your responsibility, since they have to work out their relationship in some way. So this may not be too feasible for you. Maybe we could look at the effects this situation has on you." "You say it would help your husband if you did this. What about yourself? If not, maybe there's something you'd like to do that will have some benefits for you, also."
c. refer client ___Client response (exploration of referral)	c. "This is not something I feel I can really help you with. I'd like to suggest that you see _____, who is more qualified in this area than I am. Of course, I'd like to check in with you and find out how things are going in the future."

Suggested Readings

Purposes of Goals

Bandura, A. _Principles of behavior modification._ New York: Holt, Rinehart & Winston, 1969. Chap. 2, Value issues and objectives, 70–117.

Hill, C. A process approach for establishing counseling goals and outcomes. _The Personnel and Guidance Journal,_ 1975, 53, 571–576.

Krumboltz, J. D. Behavioral goals for counseling. _Journal of Counseling Psychology,_ 1966, 13, 153–159.

Smith, D. L. Goal attainment scaling as an adjunct to counseling. _Journal of Counseling Psychology,_ 1976, 23, 22–27.

Client Goals

Gottman, J. M., & Leiblum, S. R. _How to do psychotherapy and how to evaluate it._ New York: Holt, Rinehart & Winston, 1974. Chap. 5, Set objectives of initial change efforts, 47–63.

Srebalus, D. J. Rethinking change in counseling. _The Personnel and Guidance Journal,_ 1975, 53, 415–421.

Feasibility of Goals

Hosford, R., & de Visser, L. _Behavioral approaches to counseling: An introduction._ Washington, D.C.: American Personnel and Guidance Press, 1974. Chap. 4, Formulating counselor goals, 64–76.

Risks and Advantages of Goals

Bandura, A. _Principles of behavior modification._ New York: Holt, Rinehart & Winston, 1969. Chap. 2, Value issues and objectives, 70–117.

Decisions about Goal Selection

Bandura, A. _Principles of behavior modification._ New York: Holt, Rinehart & Winston, 1969. Chap. 2, Value issues and objectives, 70–117.

Gottman, J. M., & Leiblum, S. R. _How to do psychotherapy and how to evaluate it._ New York: Holt, Rinehart & Winston, 1974. Chap. 5, Set objectives of initial change efforts, 47–63.

Krumboltz, J. D. Behavioral goals for counseling. _Journal of Counseling Psychology,_ 1966, 13, 153–159

Morganstern, K. P. Behavioral interviewing: The initial stages of assessment. In M. Hersen & A. Bellack (Eds.), *Behavioral assessment: A practical handbook.* New York: Pergamon Press, 1976.

Van Hoose, W., & Kottler, J. *Ethical and legal issues in counseling and psychotherapy.* San Francisco: Jossey-Bass, 1977.

Chapter 12
Defining Goals

As you did with the questions at the beginning of the last chapter, pause for a few minutes to answer the following questions. You may want to refresh your memory by glancing at the questions on the first page of Chapter 11. If you like, share the answers to these questions with someone else.

1. What would you be doing and/or thinking as a result of a change you would like to make for yourself?
2. In what situations do you want to be able to do this?
3. How much or how often would you like to increase or decrease _____?
4. Looking at what you're doing now and where you'd like to be—are there some steps along the way to get from here to there? If so, rank them in an ordered list from "easiest to do now" to "harder to do."
5. How willing are you to do the work involved to reach your goal?

Once the counselor and client have agreed to continue counseling on the basis of the client's selected goals, they begin the process of defining these goals. The five questions to which you just responded reflect the steps of defining goals in counseling. Two basic guidelines were suggested by Krumboltz (1966) in one of the first articles to describe counseling goals. First, the goal should be stated for each client individually. Second, the goal should be stated in terms of visible outcomes. These two guidelines help to ensure that the process of developing counseling goals is highly individualized and that the goals will be observable. Observable counseling goals may be referred to as *outcome goals*, because they reflect the desired outcomes or end product of counseling. A well-defined outcome goal includes three parts: behavior, condition, and level. The behavior specifies *what* the client will do, the condition indicates *where* this will be done, and the level indicates *how much* or *how often* this will be done.

Objectives

1. Imagine a situation about you or your life that you would like to change. Imagine an outcome goal that represents change for you in this situation. Specify the overt and covert behaviors associated with the goal, the conditions of change, and the level of change. If you imagine any subgoals, arrange these in a hierarchy. Give a rationale for the order of the subgoals in terms of sequencing or difficulty.
2. Using a written dialogue, identify accurately 14 out of 17 counselor leads associated with the five categories of defining goals.
3. Demonstrate 4 out of 5 leads associated with

defining goals in a 20-minute interview with a role-play client, using the Interview Checklist for Defining Goals at the end of the chapter. Also, try to maintain a facilitative counseling style with the items on the Helping-Style Checklist rated at 3.0 or above.

Defining Goals: An Overview

The process of defining goals illustrated in part of Figure 11-1 is presented in Figure 12-1. It includes five steps:

1. defining the goal behavior
2. determining the conditions under which the goal behavior is to occur
3. establishing the level or extent of the goal behavior
4. identifying and sequencing subgoals
5. obtaining an oral or written client commitment for working toward the goal

Most clients will select more than one goal. Ultimately, it may be more realistic for the client to work toward "attainment of a variety of specific objectives rather than a single, omnibus outcome" (Bandura, 1969, p. 104). For example, in our model case, Joan has selected five out-come goals: decreasing the number of times she cuts math class from two to zero per week, increasing her participation in math class to three times per class session, developing positive thoughts about her ability to do math to at least two during math class, acquiring decision-making skills, and maintaining her present friendships and her present friendship behaviors (see Joan's goal chart on p. 194).

At first, it is useful to have the client specify all the desired goals. However, to tackle several outcome goals at one time would be unrealistic. The counselor should ask the client to choose one of the outcome goals to pursue first. After selecting an initial outcome goal to work toward, the counselor and client can define the three parts of the goal and identify subgoals. This chapter will introduce some counselor leads used to help the client define the outcome goals of counseling and will present some probable responses that indicate client responsiveness to the leads. Some suggested examples of counselor leads are also presented in the Interview Checklist for Defining Goals at the end of the chapter.

Interview Leads for Defining Goals

Defining the Behavior of an Outcome Goal

The behavior of an outcome goal describes what the client (whether an individual, group member, or organization) is to *do* as a result of counseling. This part of an outcome goal defines the specific behavior the client is to perform. Some examples of a behavior include reducing one's weight, asking for help from a teacher, verbal sharing of positive feelings about oneself, or thinking about oneself in positive ways. As you can see, both overt and covert behaviors can be included in this part of the outcome goal as long as the behavior is defined by what it means for each client. Defining goals behaviorally makes the goal-setting process specific, and specifically defined goals are more likely to create incentives and guide performance than vaguely stated intentions (Bandura & Simon, 1977, p. 178).

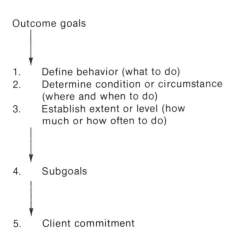

Outcome goals

1. Define behavior (what to do)
2. Determine condition or circumstance (where and when to do)
3. Establish extent or level (how much or how often to do)

4. Subgoals

5. Client commitment

Figure 12-1. Defining Goals

Interview Leads for Defining Goal Behavior. Some leads a counselor can use to identify the behavior part of a goal are:

"When you say you want to _____, what do you see yourself doing?"

"What could I see you doing or thinking as a result of this change?"

"You say you want to be more self-confident. What things would you be thinking and doing as a self-confident person?"

It is important for the counselor to continue to pursue these leads until the client can define the overt and covert behaviors associated with the goal. This is not an easy task, for most clients talk about changes in vague or abstract terms. If the client has trouble specifying behaviors, the counselor can help with further instructions, information-giving, or by self-disclosing a personal goal.

Another way to obtain behavioral goal descriptions suggested by Hill (1975) is to use the Counseling Outcome Inventory (COI). In using the COI, the client is asked to list some characteristics, qualities, or descriptions that are important to the client to acquire or to demonstrate. Then, for each of these descriptors, the client is asked to list one or more actual behaviors of this quality, referred to by Hill as "behavioral anchors" (p. 573). For instance, the vague descriptor of "self-confidence" might be translated into a behavioral anchor of "making fewer negative self-statements"; the descriptor "be more attractive" might be translated into the behavioral anchors of "lose 10 pounds" and "smile more often." The COI procedure helps to make the outcome goals observable and also helps to develop goals that are stated meaningfully for different clients.

Defining the Conditions of an Outcome Goal

The second part of an outcome goal specifies the condition—that is, the *situation* or *circumstances* where the behavior will occur. This is an important element of an outcome goal for both the client and the counselor. The condi-tion suggests a particular *person* with whom the client may perform the desired behaviors, or a particular *setting*. Specifying the conditions of a behavior also helps to ensure that the behavior occurs only in desired settings or with desired people and does not generalize to undesired settings. This idea can be illustrated vividly. For example, a woman may wish to increase the number of positive verbal and nonverbal responses she makes toward her husband. In this case, time spent with her husband would be the condition or circumstances in which the behavior occurs. However, if this behavior generalized to include all men, it might have some negative effects on the very relationship she is trying to improve.

Interview Leads for the Condition of a Goal. Some examples of leads used to determine the conditions of the outcome goal include:

"Where would you like to do this?"

"In what situations do you want to be able to do this?"

"Where and when do you want to do this?"

"Who would you be with when you do this?"

"In what situations is what you're doing now not meeting your expectations?"

The counselor is looking for a response that indicates where or with whom the client will make the change or perform the desired behavior. If the client gives a noncommittal response, the counselor may suggest client self-monitoring to obtain these data. The counselor also can use self-disclosure and personal examples to demonstrate that a behavior may not be appropriate in all situations.

Defining a Level of Change

The third element of an outcome goal specifies the level or *amount* of the behavioral change. In other words, this part describes *how much* the client is to do or to complete in order to reach the desired goal. The level of an outcome goal serves as a barometer that measures the extent to which the client will be able to perform the desired behavior. For example, a man may state that he wishes to decrease cigarette-smoking. The following week, he may report that he did a better job of cutting down on cigarettes. However, unless he can specify how much he actually decreased smoking, both he and the counselor will have difficulty determining how much the client really completed toward the goal. In this case, the client's level of performance is ambiguous. In contrast, if the client had reported that he reduced cigarette-smoking by two cigarettes per day in one week, his level of performance could be determined easily. If his goal was to decrease cigarette-smoking by eight cigarettes per day this information would help to determine progress toward the goal.

As with the behavior and condition parts of an outcome goal, the level of change always should be established individually for each client. The amount of satisfaction derived from goal attainment often depends on the level of peformance established (Bandura & Simon, 1977, p. 178). A suitable level of change will depend on such factors as the present level of the problem behavior, the present level of the desired behavior, the resources available for change, the client's readiness to change, and the degree to which other conditions or people are maintaining the present level of problem behavior. Hosford and de Visser (1974) point out that such factors often make the level of a goal the most difficult part to define.

As an example, suppose a client wants to increase the number of assertive opinions she expresses orally with her husband. If she now withholds all her opinions, her level of change might be stated at a lower level than that defined for another client who already expresses some opinions. Also, if the client's husband is accustomed to her refraining from opinion-giving, this might affect the degree of change made, at least initially. The counselor's and client's primary concern is to establish a level that is manageable, that the client can attain with some success. Occasionally the counselor may encounter a client who always wants to achieve more change than is desirable or even possible. As Krumboltz and Thoresen (1976) note, progressively raising levels of change has a limit (p. 105). These authors suggest that, in such cases, the counselor must avoid reinforcing the client's perfectionistic goal statements (p. 104).

Leads to Identify the Level of Change. Here are some leads you can use to help identify the client's desired extent or level of change:

"How much would you like to be able to do this compared to how much you're doing it now?"
"How often do you want to do this?"
"From the information you obtained during self-monitoring, you seem to be studying only about an hour a week now. What is a reasonable amount for you to increase this without getting bogged down?"
"You say you'd like to lose 40 pounds. Let's talk about a reasonable amount of time this might take and, to start with, what amount would be easy for you to lose just in the next 3 weeks."

The counselor is looking for some indication of the present and future levels of the desired behavior. This level can be expressed by either the number of times or the amount the client wants to be able to do something. In some cases, an appropriate level may be only one, as in the case of a client whose outcome goal is to make one decision about a job change. The counselor can help the client establish an appropriate level of change by referring to the self-monitoring data collected during problem definition. If the client has not engaged in monitoring, this is another point where it is almost imperative to have the client observe and record the present amounts of the problem behavior and the goal behavior. This information will give some idea of the present level of behavior, referred to as the base-rate or baseline level. As you may recall from Chapter 10, a client's data-gathering is very useful for defining problems and goals and for monitoring progress toward the goals.

Level as an Indicator of Type and Direction of Change. The level of change reflected in an outcome goal specifies both the direction and type of change desired. In the example of the client who wants to be more assertive, if the client's present level of the desired behavior is zero, then the goal would be to acquire some assertive skills. When the base rate of a behavior is zero, or when the client does not seem to have certain skills in her or his repertory, the goal is stated as acquiring a behavior. If, however, the client wants to improve or increase something that she or he can already do (but at a low level), the goal is stated as increasing a behavior. In contrast, if the client is doing too much of something and wants to lower the present level, the goal is stated as decreasing a behavior and possibly, later on, eliminating it from the client's repertory. Sometimes, when the client wants to eliminate something, she or he wishes to replace whatever is eliminated with a more appropriate or self-enhancing behavior. For instance, a client trying to lose weight may desire to eliminate junk-food snacks and replace these with low-calorie snacks. This client's goal is stated in terms of "restructuring" something about her or his environment—in this case, the type of snack eaten. Although this is an example of restructuring an overt behavior, restructuring can be cognitive as well. For example, a client may want to eliminate negative or self-defeating thoughts about difficulty in taking tests and replace these with positive or self-enhancing thoughts about the capacity to perform adequately in test-taking situations.

In some instances, the level of a goal may reflect maintenance or preservation. As you recall from our discussion of client change in the last chapter, not all goals will reflect a discrepancy between the client's present and future behavior. Some goals may be directed toward maintaining a desired or satisfying situation or response. Such goals may be stated something like "to maintain my present amount (3 hours daily) of studying," "to maintain the present balance in my life between work on weekdays and play on weekends," "to maintain the positive communication I have with my spouse in our daily talks," or "to maintain my present level (two a day) of engaging in relaxation sessions." A maintenance goal suggests that the client's present level of behavior is satisfying and sufficient, at least at this particular time. A maintenance goal may help to put things in perspective by acknowledging the areas of the client's life that are going well.

To summarize, the level of change stated by the outcome goal usually will reflect one of these five categories:

1. a response increment
2. a response decrement
3. a response acquisition
4. a response restructuring
5. a response maintenance

If you recall that most clients have more than one outcome goal, then perhaps you've already realized that more than one of these five directions of change may be reflected in the client's objectives. In our model case of Joan, her goal of not cutting class reflects a response decrement. The goal of achieving more class participation consists of response increments, since Joan's log shows some present (even though minimal) level of this behavior. Her goal of developing positive thoughts about her ability to do math involves restructuring her present negative thoughts. Since Joan doesn't make decisions now and hasn't learned the decision-making skills, her goal of learning decision-making skills consists of response acquisition. A fifth goal Joan has is to maintain her current friendships and to continue to demonstrate the behaviors that make her a good friend (see Joan's goal chart on p. 194).

The direction and level of change defined in the client's goals are prerequisites for selecting appropriate counseling strategies. For example, self-monitoring (see Chapter 22) is used differently depending on whether it is applied to increase or to decrease a response. One counseling strategy might be used appropriately to help a client acquire responses; yet another strategy may be needed to help a client restructure some responses. It is very important for the counselor and client to spend sufficient time on specifying the level of the goal, even if this process seems very elusive and difficult.

Defining and Sequencing Subgoals

Each of us can probably recall times when we were expected to learn something so fast that the learning experience was overwhelming and produced feelings of frustration, irritation, and discouragement. The change represented by counseling goals can be achieved best if the process is gradual. Any change program should be organized into an "orderly learning sequence" that guides the client through small steps toward the ultimate desired behaviors (Bandura, 1969, p. 74). In defining goals, this gradual learning sequence is achieved by breaking down the ultimate goal into a series of smaller goals called *subgoals*. The subgoals usually are arranged in a hierarchy, with the client completing subgoals at the bottom of the ranked list before the ones near the top. Although an overall outcome goal can provide a "general directive" for change, the specific subgoals may determine a person's immediate activities and degree of effort in making changes (Bandura & Simon, 1977, p. 178). As these authors note, "by focusing on the distant future, it is easy to put off efforts at change in the present. . . . Exercising control over behavior in the present increases the likelihood that desired futures will be realized" (p. 179).

For some reason, it seems difficult to realize that effective client change must consist of well-planned, sequenced activities in order to achieve encouraging results. Yet, if we think of the way we have learned other skills, this concept of small steps of change does not seem so foreign. Most of us, at age 14, didn't know how to operate a car, but by age 16 we had learned how to steer, brake, turn, and park. In a short time, some of us also have changed from nonskiers to skiers and nonsailors to sailors. Such change was often accomplished because the ultimate goal was analyzed and sequenced for us into small subtasks.

Bandura (1969) suggests that the sequencing of goals into smaller subgoals is more likely to produce the desired results for two reasons. First, the completion of subgoals may keep failure experiences to a minimum. Completing subgoals successfully will encourage the client and will help maintain the client's motivation to change (p. 75). K. M. Jeffery (1977) found that progressively increasing subgoals sustained a high level of client motivation even when the overall outcomes were difficult to attain. Second, arranging the ultimate goal into subgoals

may give the client greater control over achieving the desired outcomes (Bandura, 1969, p. 75).

Building a Hierarchy of Subgoals. Not all outcome goals need to be broken down into subgoals. However, most should be arranged into subgoals if there is a series of tasks that must be completed to attain the desired results. Generally, this series of tasks can be arranged in a hierarchy according to complexity, sequencing, or both (Gagné, 1970). For example, a client's goal can be arranged in a series of subgoals from the least complex or least difficult to the most complex or most difficult. Or the subgoals can be arranged according to what tasks must come before others. The arrangement of subgoals in order of complexity or sequencing is based on a learning principle called *shaping*. Shaping helps someone learn a small amount at a time, with appropriate reinforcement or encouragement for each task completed successfully. Gradually, the person learns the entire amount or achieves the overall result through these day-to-day learning experiences that successively approximate the overall outcome.

The time between the subgoals will depend, to some extent, on the nature of the client's goals and the client's capacity for managing certain subgoals during a set time period. However, as Schwartz and Goldiamond (1975) observe, "it is always better to err on the side of conservatism and make the subgoal steps too small" (p. 119). It is easier to make adjustments to maximize successful attainment of subgoals than to have to make adjustments that attempt to minimize failure. However, in any case where the subgoals are not met, the counselor and client should analyze what went wrong and what can be done more successfully in the future. When the subgoals are met, they become part of the client's current repertory that can be used in additional change efforts toward the terminal goals (Schwartz & Goldiamond, p. 117).

Distant versus Immediate Subgoals. Much of the usefulness and effectiveness of subgoals may depend on whether the subgoals established are distant or immediate. Recent evidence indicates that immediate, daily subgoals may be more potent than weekly, distant subgoals (Bandura & Simon, 1977). In this study, obese clients who devised or used immediate subgoals stated on a *daily* basis reduced their food consumption and lost even more weight than their goals specified. In contrast, clients who adhered to distant subgoals stated on a *weekly* basis rarely attained these subgoals, achieved only small reductions in food consumption, and lost no weight. This study also found that some people who were assigned distant or weekly subgoals abandoned them and substituted daily or more immediate subgoals. In other words, clients may have a natural inclination to establish immediate goals for themselves. In developing subgoals, the counselor should encourage each client to set and use subgoals daily.

Perhaps an example will help to clarify the process of developing subgoals with a client. Suppose you are working with a person who wishes to lose 40 pounds. Losing 40 pounds is not a goal that anyone can accomplish overnight or without small requisite changes along the way. First of all, the person will need to determine a reasonable weekly level of weight loss, such as 1 to 2 pounds. Next, you and the client will have to determine the tasks the client will need to complete in order to lose weight; these tasks can be stated as daily subgoals that the client can strive to carry out each day.

After discussing the degree of difficulty and the sequencing of three subgoals, the client's hierarchy might look like this:

Terminal goal: to lose 40 pounds over 12 months
Weekly goal: to lose 1 pound
Daily subgoals (arranged in order of difficulty and sequencing):

1. Increase time spent in eating first helpings at dinner by 10 minutes by chewing food slowly, putting fork down between bites, carrying on a conversation.
2. Decrease second helpings at dinner by refusing them.
3. Increase amount of daily exercise in walking by 20% per day.
4. Increase physical feelings of relaxation while

at home by engaging in two 15-minute periods of muscle relaxation per day.
5. Increase positive thoughts about yourself as a thinner person at home and at work by three a day. (Think like a thin person.)
6. Decrease snacks on junk food at work by one a day; substitute with celery or low-calorie snacks.

Note that all the subgoals are stated in the same way as the terminal outcome goal—with the definition of the behaviors to be changed, the level of change, and the conditions or circumstances of change. Also note that, in this case, both overt and covert behaviors are included in the subgoals list. A comprehensive change program usually involves changes in the client's thoughts and feelings, as well as in overt behaviors and environmental situations.

After the subgoal hierarchy has been established, the client selects at least one subgoal, and possibly two or three, to carry out during the week. For the first few weeks, one or two subgoals might be sufficient to complete daily. As the weeks go on, the client can continue with these, modify them, or add others as necessary. All the future modifications and rearrangement of the subgoal hierarchy depend on the way the client meets the subgoals and on the effectiveness of the counseling strategies employed.

Interview Leads to Establish Subgoals. To help the client identify subgoals, the counselor can use the following kinds of questions:

"What are some steps you'll need to take to get to your goal?"
"How could we order these steps to maximize your success in reaching your goal?"
"Let's think of the steps you need to take to get from where you are now to where you want to be —and arrange them in an order from what seems easiest to you to the ones that seem hardest for you."
"Can you think of some things you need to do before some other things as you make progress toward your goal?"

The counselor is looking for an indication from the client of some steps the client may need to take in order to reach the ultimate goal. The counselor also is seeking the client's input in ordering these steps, either by sequencing or complexity. If the client leaves out some necessary subgoals or suggests an ordering of subgoals with large gaps, the counselor may need to suggest some additional steps or some reordering of the subgoal hierarchy.

Commitment and Contract

After the goals have been selected and defined, the counselor will begin selecting counseling strategies to meet the client's goals. At this point, the counselor should elicit some commitment from the client to do the work necessary for goal attainment. The counselor can ask for an oral or written statement of commitment from the client. Although an oral commitment is useful, a written contract between counselor and client makes the process more explicit. The written commitment contract specifies the agreements made about the selected goals and the methods and homework that will be used to achieve them. The contract helps to eliminate any ambiguity associated with expectations for counseling and indicates to the client that her or his role is active rather than passive (Gottman & Leiblum, 1974, p. 44).

Interview Leads to Obtain Client Commitment. Some leads the counselor can use to elicit client commitment are:

"Your goals will take some work. How willing are you to do this?"
"Let's list your goals in writing in a contract. My signature will indicate my efforts at helping you reach your goals; your signature will indicate your commitment to reaching these goals."

The counselor is looking for some indication that the client is willing to pursue the stated goals through the counseling sessions and the homework used outside the sessions.

In some instances, the counselor may detect client hesitation or resistance toward making a commitment, such as the client who asks "How long will this take?" or indicates "I'm not sure what I can do about the situation." Resistance can be defined as "a description of certain kinds of overt or covert verbalizations and actions made by the client, and not an explanation of lack of progress" (Gottman & Leiblum, 1974, p. 6). Clients may indicate hesitation or resistance for a variety of reasons, including:

1. The client is testing out the counselor's level of support and competence.
2. The client may be concerned about the counselor's expectations and methods of change.
3. The client may have a vested interest in not changing.
4. The client may be concerned about the change but may be receiving a lot of pay-offs for not changing.

If resistance occurs, the counselor will have to consider all these alternatives and deal with the resistance accordingly. As Gottman and Leiblum caution, "There may not be one secret to unlock the riddle of the client's resistance to change" (pp. 102–103).

In most cases, resistance should be discussed openly. If it is ignored, further blocks in the counseling relationship may be created. A counselor might say "You seem surprised this may take some time" or "You seem hesitant about committing yourself to work on this right now." In doing so, the counselor will check out the client's readiness to continue with the counseling contract at this time.

Resistance may not be evident at this point in counseling but may occur during later sessions, when the client is actually working on change. The counselor will need to deal with any evidence of client resistance or blocking whenever it appears. In some cases, the client may be dissatisfied with the goals or the consequences produced by the changes. For these reasons, the goals of counseling can never be viewed as fixed and permanent, without need of modification or revision. The commitment contract can always be changed to reflect revised outcome goals and subgoals.

Are Well-Defined Outcome Goals Worth It?

You may be thinking something like "How necessary is it to go to all this trouble to be so specific about a goal? Why can't you just get a rough idea of what clients want out of counseling and go from there?" We have asked ourselves the same questions. And we have found an almost universal reluctance to obtain specificity about the behavior, condition, and level of a client's goal, almost as if this means imposing something on a client that is either superfluous or too structured. We have no firm answers to these questions. We will point out that there may be times when it seems almost impossible to obtain specifics from a particular client about parts of an outcome goal. In our own counseling, if clients are occasionally unable or unwilling to be this specific, we give them this "right to be." However, we have needed to distinguish between times when we failed to define goals specifically because of the client's needs and times when we rationalized our way out of going to the trouble to do so. One of us was at a loss when, after eight sessions, a client asked "What changes do you think I've made so far —and to what extent?" The one who was counselor recounts the situation:

I had difficulty in responding because we had discussed desired changes only very loosely. I had not bothered to go to the trouble to define the goals specifically. When I tried to analyze the way I had let this slip by, I recalled I did so on the grounds that this client would benefit more from a less structured approach to counseling. Now, when faced with this question that I couldn't really answer, it was hard to justify what actual benefit this really had for this particular person. We spent the next several sessions going over some desired changes, level of changes, and ways to monitor the changes. The situation made me do some rethinking. I had been tuning in so much to what I felt would be helpful for this person that I may have failed to perceive what really would have contributed to the person's desired changes.

Learning Activity: Outcome Goals

We have found that the most difficult part of developing goals with a client involves specifying the three parts of the outcome goal. We believe the reason is that the concept is foreign to most of us and difficult to internalize. This is probably because, in our own lives, we think about small, very mundane goals. With more complex goals, we still don't assess the specific overt and covert behaviors to be changed, where and with whom change will occur, and the extent of the change. When writing this section, we thought over some of the "goals" we had discussed in our own lives over the past week. They went like this:
1. To make a decision when we'll invite _____ over to dinner.
2. To decide on our travel plans for Christmas.
3. We need to do more exercise than we're doing.
4. We need to be more scheduled on our writing during this month.

Goals 1 and 2 are rather simple decisions. Goals 3 and 4 represent some desired changes, but they are pretty vague! What kind of exercise? Where? How much more? and so on. We decided to try to come up with a learning activity that will help you create some *personal* meaning from these three parts of an outcome goal. If you feel comfortable with this, you are more likely to help a client define her or his goals. We suggest the following activity.
1. During the next week, keep a log of all the decisions you need to make and any changes you're considering.
2. After each decision and change you note in your log, try to identify:
   a. What you'll be doing (overt behavior) and thinking and feeling (covert behavior) as a result of this change
   b. Where, when, and with whom you want to do this (conditions of change)
   c. How much or how often you want to do this (level of change)

Model Dialogue: The Case of Joan

The dialogue for the case of Joan is continued in this chapter to help you see how the leads for defining goals are used with a client. The first two sessions for selecting goals were presented in the last chapter. We pick up with the third session. As in the last chapter, each counselor response is prefaced by an explanation of what the counselor is going to do in the next response.

Session 3

1. Counselor: Joan, let's talk today some more about the areas you've indicated you'd like to change—your problems in your math class and your difficulty in making decisions. Let's start first with one area and try to find out exactly what you want to change. Which area?
   Client: My math class.
   In response 2, the counselor will ask the client to specify desired <u>overt behaviors of the goal</u>.
2. Counselor: OK, let's think about some of the problems we've talked about in your math class. You say you want to do better in math class. I'd like you to tell me the kinds of things you'd like to be able to do in your math class that would help you do better in it.
   Client: Well, I should go to class more. I shouldn't be cutting it. And I should participate more—I just sit there lots of times when I could be talking or going to the board.
   In response 3, the counselor will pursue <u>goal behaviors</u> that would indicate participation.
3. Counselor: By *participating* do you mean the kinds of things we talked about that you observed in your log—volunteering answers, answering questions, going to the board?
   Client: Yeah, those kinds of things.
   In response 4, the counselor explores <u>covert behaviors</u> associated with the goal.
4. Counselor: OK. What would you need to think about in order to do better in your math class?
   Client: Well, I'd like to think that I'm not so dumb. And that even being a girl I can still do math all right.
   In response 5, the counselor pursues <u>conditions</u> associated with the goal.
5. Counselor: OK, you've said before that these things you want to change are problems for you in your math class. Are there any other situations where you'd like to be able to do these things?
   Client: No, not really. I mean there is some competition in all my classes, but I only really clam up in my math class.
   In response 6, the counselor will <u>summarize parts of the goal</u> that have been described so far: overt and covert behaviors and conditions of the goal.
6. Counselor: OK, so we're talking about your

being able to attend class and participate more, such as volunteering answers, answering when the teacher calls on you, and going to the board. Also, thinking of your ability to do math well—mainly during or right before or after the time of your math class at school.
   Client: That's it.
   In responses 7 and 8, the counselor will explore present and desired <u>levels</u> of the behaviors associated with the goal, starting first with <u>class attendance</u>. The client's log is used to find out baseline data or the present level of problem behavior.
7. Counselor: I'd like to talk about the degree to which you'd like to be able to change these things. I think it might be helpful if we looked at the log you've been keeping for the last two weeks.
   Client: Sure, here it is. I carry it with me, 'cause I mark it mostly in math class.
8. Counselor: OK, let's take these things one at a time. For instance, reducing the number of times you cut class. According to your logs, you seem to be cutting class one or two times a week. How much would you like to decrease this?
   Client: I don't want to cut it at all.
   In response 9, the counselor will write down the goal on a chart as it is completed (behavior, description, level). Present and desired <u>levels</u> of other goal behaviors are included in responses 9 and 10. (A copy of Joan's goal chart is included at the end of this dialogue.)
9. Counselor: OK, so if we put this down on our chart, we'll be saying you'd like to reduce the number of times you cut math class from two (at most) a week to none at all. OK, now let's talk about some of the things involved in your participation in class. How much do you seem to participate now—say during each class?
   Client: Oh, usually not more than once during the class, at the most.
10. Counselor: OK, let's take a look at your log here. It looks like there are usually a couple of times during each class when you refrain from participating—by not volunteering answers, or not going to the board, or not answering Mr. _____'s questions. Yet you aren't saying that you don't participate at all.
    Client: No, I usually try to make myself say something once during the class or during every other class.
    In response 11, the counselor asks the client about the desired <u>level</u> of participation.
11. Counselor: Well, if you do participate a little

now, how much do you think you could increase your participation?

Client: Oh, I'd like to participate about two or three times for each class.

In responses 12 and 13, the counselor suggests a lower initial level, working up gradually to a higher level in order to maximize the client's chances for success.

12. Counselor: OK, that might be something we could work toward eventually. Maybe, since your present level of participation is low, we could start with something a little smaller, like say at least one time during each class meeting. How does that sound?

    Client: Not too hard.

13. Counselor: OK, that's good. You've got the idea. It's hard to make giant steps all at once, so we'll work on midget steps at first. So if we put this on your chart it might be, "To increase number of times you participate orally in math class to at least one during each class—and eventually up to three for every class."

    In response 14, the counselor uses a probe to check out the client's reaction to the goals.

14. Counselor: How do you feel about all of this so far?

    Client: Well, it helps me feel like maybe I can improve at least a little.

    In responses 15, 16, and 17, the counselor will explore present and desired levels of restructuring the client's thoughts about her ability to do math.

15. Counselor: OK, let's take another look at your log and the number of times you found yourself thinking about yourself as not being very smart in math. What can you see from your log?

    Client: Well, this seems to be a big problem for me. It can vary from a couple of times to, well, a lot. One day I counted eight different times. That day I got a test back with a "C" on it. On weekends I don't seem to think about this so much. My mind's on other things.

16. Counselor: Well, it seems like during the week, anyway, you might be thinking these thoughts around four times a day. Does this seem to go on during your entire math class or only during parts of it? Or at any other times?

    Client: Actually, pretty much throughout the class. When I logged it, I would try to stop it but I found myself drifting back to it anyway.

17. Counselor: What do you think would be a reasonable amount to try to change these thoughts, at least to start with?

    Client: Well, I don't know. I mean I've been thinking about being dumb in math for a while.

    The counselor picks up some degree of difficulty the

client thinks she may have in reaching this goal and uses this as a cue to start slowly and be gradual with the level of change, as indicated in responses 18 and 19.

18. Counselor: So you're saying this seems hard for you to change. Perhaps to begin, maybe just try to build up the number of times you think positive thoughts about your ability to two per math class. How does that sound?

    Client: Do you think that's enough?

19. Counselor: Well, probably for now. Eventually, we can work on almost totally replacing your negative thoughts about your ability with positive thoughts. Right now we seem to be saying that we need to work on increasing the number of positive thoughts you have about your ability to do math to at least two per class for right now. OK, let's take a look at your chart here. We've got three main things here to work on that you feel would indicate doing better in math—not cutting class, increasing your participation in class, and learning to change the way you think about yourself in relation to math. How do you feel about this?

    Client: OK. I guess I'm wondering how exactly to go about doing this.

    In response 20, the counselor will explain subgoals and start to identify subgoals associated with the outcome goal of not cutting class.

20. Counselor: Good question. I think it would help if we could take a look at the kinds of things you need to be doing to reach the goals—like some things you could do during math class this week, next week, and so forth. We could call these subgoals or action steps that will help you get where you want to be, but on a gradual basis. For instance—not cutting class. I think we talked about this a couple of weeks ago. What do you think is a reason you cut class now?

    Client: Well, I don't like class. It makes me feel bad about myself and my ability to compete. And I get real nervous when I think about going to math class.

    In responses 21, 22, and 23, the subgoal of decreasing nervousness is explored. (Note that the behavior, level, and condition of this subgoal are established. If you recall from Joan's case in Chapter 10, the nervousness was one antecedent that cued her cutting class and her low level of participation, so decreasing it would be an important prerequisite for achieving these two outcome goals.)

21. Counselor: OK, so one of the things we might need to do first is to work on decreasing your nervousness before and during math class.

How do you think this would help you in terms of not cutting math class?

Client: A lot. I know there are some times I cut class more than others because I dread going and I get a sick feeling in the bottom of my stomach.

22. Counselor: OK, so on your chart here under this goal we can put down that we'll work first on decreasing your nervous feeling about class. By this we mean decreasing the sick feelings you get in your stomach. How nervous do you get now, say, on a scale from 1 to 100, with 1 being not nervous at all and 100 being very nervous?

Client: Oh, about a 50, in the middle, but at some points it's higher, maybe a 70.

23. Counselor: How much would you like this to go down on this scale?

Client: Maybe to a 25. That wouldn't be too bad.

In responses 24 and 25, counselor and client will ex-plore subgoals associated with the outcome goal of increasing Joan's oral participation.

24. Counselor: OK, we can put this down on your chart as a subgoal—meaning this is one thing you'll have to do first in order to help you reach your goal of not cutting math class. Now, about working on your participation in class—what are some things you could accomplish during your math classes for this?

Client: Well, some of the things I put in my log.

25. Counselor: OK, let's take a look at some of these. There are three types of participation here: volunteering answers, answering when the teacher asks you questions, and going to the board. Anything else you can think of that might be a step toward more participation?

Client: No, not right now.

In response 26, the counselor will ask the client to rank-order these three subgoals in order of difficulty.

26. Counselor: Well, I'm wondering if we could ar-range these three things in an order, starting with the one thing that seems easiest for you to do and ending with the one that seems hardest for you.

Client: Well, it would be easiest for me to answer when the teacher calls on me. Going to the board would be in the middle. Volunteering on my own would be the worst. I feel pretty unsure about that.

In response 27, the counselor will elicit more subgoals from Joan.

27. Counselor: OK, let's put these on your chart under this goal in the order you just mentioned. Anything else you can think of that might help you in your participation?

Client: Well, just thinking of my ability to do math in more positive ways could help.

In response 28, the counselor will ask about subgoals associated with this goal Joan has just mentioned.

28. Counselor: OK, so this other goal we've talked about is also important—developing some posi-tive thoughts about your ability to do well in math. What kinds of things can you see that you need to do in order to replace your negative thoughts about your ability with some more positive thoughts?

Client: Well, I'll have to have more confidence in my ability.

The client's response of having confidence is vague. Remember, the overt and covert behaviors of each sub-goal must be defined. In responses 29, 30, and 31, the counselor will pursue the definition of confidence and follow up on what steps would be involved.

29. Counselor: OK, what would you be doing or thinking that would give you more confidence?

Client: Well, I guess I should rely more on my own opinion. Maybe I shouldn't talk so much to my math teacher and parents about it.

30. Counselor: You mean you think you should stop conversations about your ability in math with other people like your teacher and parents?

Client: Yes, because they downgrade my ability and I tend to believe them.

31. Counselor: OK, that's one thing. Anything else you can think of?

Client: No, not really.

The counselor is aware of other possible substeps that the client did not mention and will discuss these in responses 32, 33, and 34.

32. Counselor: I have a suggestion.

Client: OK.

33. Counselor: In terms of developing your own opinion of your math ability, it might help to break this down into a couple of different parts. The first step is to learn to stop yourself when you realize you're putting yourself down. Then you can learn some more positive things you could think about. How does that sound?

Client: Pretty good. Is that hard?

34. Counselor: Well, it takes some work, but it's not impossible. It's similar to changing a habit. OK, we can put these three subgoals down on your chart—stopping conversations, stopping nega-tive thoughts, and developing and using posi-tive thoughts about your math class. You know, our time is about gone for today. We didn't discuss your other two goals—learning some decision-making skills and maintaining your friendships. We could do that next week. I'm

wondering what your reaction is to our talk today?

Client: Well, I think we got some stuff I could do. Of course, it seems like a lot.

In responses 35, 36, and 37, counselor and client will pursue the client's level of commitment toward goals.

35. Counselor: Yes, if you look at everything, it does seem like a lot. That's why we break it down into smaller steps. Of course, even the steps will take some time and work for you to accomplish. How do you feel about this?

Client: Well, I'd like to try. I have some confidence from talking with you that there are some things I can do.

36. Counselor: Perhaps it would be a good idea if we both signed your chart as a way to commit ourselves toward working on these goals—at least for now. Then any time you feel like your goals need changing we may want to go back and change them. Do you see what I mean?

Client: Sure. It will be what we have agreed to now, anyway.

37. Counselor: Right. So we can sign this to indicate our agreement to work toward these goals. Then I'll see you next week.

Joan's Goal Chart

Behavior	Condition	Present Level	to Desired Level	Subgoals
Outcome Goal 1				
To reduce absences	in math class	1–2 per week	0 per week	1. To decrease nervousness about math class from an intensity of 50 to an intensity of 25
Agreed to on ___Nov. 14___ (date)				
by ___J. B.___ and by ___S. T.___				
(Joan's initials)	(Counselor's initials)			
Outcome Goal 2				
To increase verbal participation	in math class	1 per every other class	1. 1 per class initially up to 2. 3 per class	1. To answer teacher's questions 2. To go to board 3. To volunteer answers
Agreed to on ___Nov. 14___				
by ___J. B.___ and by ___S. T.___				
Outcome Goal 3				
To develop positive thoughts about ability to do well in math	in math class	0 per class	1. 2 per class initially and up to 2. only positive thoughts during entire class	1. Stop conversations about lack of ability 2. Stop dwelling on negative thoughts 3. Identify negative thoughts and replace with positive thoughts
Agreed to on ___Nov. 14___				
by ___J. B.___ and by ___S. T.___				
Outcome Goal 4				
To acquire some decision-making skills	for myself for school-related decisions	no evident skills	at least half the skills involved in making a decision	
Outcome Goal 5				
To maintain present things I'm doing (being loyal, keeping promises, being helpful)	with friends		same as present level	

Learning Activity: Defining Goals

The following client-counselor dialogue continues the dialogue with Ms. Weare presented in the last chapter. For each counselor response, identify, on a piece of paper, the type of goal-defining lead used by the counselor. You may wish to use the Interview Checklist for Defining Goals at the end of the chapter as a guideline. Feedback follows on p. 197.

Dialogue with Ms. Weare and Counselor

1. Counselor: We know generally what you want to change and what the goal will be. Let's try to define it a little more. You say what you want to do is not help Freddie get dressed in the morning.
   Client: Yeah! That's right.
2. Counselor: When would you do this—every morning or just every school day?
   Client: It's not a problem on weekends—he dresses himself. So it would just be the days he goes to school.
3. Counselor: Last time we were together, you said that you help Freddie every school day. How much would you like to decrease helping him?
   Client: I don't want to help him at all. He's too big for that.
4. Counselor: So you would like to eliminate the number of times you help dress him from every morning before school to no mornings?
   Client: That's right.
5. Counselor: Then, you'd like to decrease the number of times you help Freddie get dressed on school mornings from five to zero. I wonder if there are some things or steps you could take that would help you accomplish this?
   Client: One thing I could do is explain to Freddie that he has to dress in the morning, and I won't come up and help him. I could put an alarm clock in his room and tell him that he has got to get up himself.
6. Counselor: That is a good idea. What other things could you do?
   Client: I can't think of any.
7. Counselor: What about just not going upstairs to help him get dressed 5 minutes before the bus comes?

   Client: Yeah, I like that. But what if I don't go up before the school bus comes? He'll be late.
8. Counselor: Well, you could agree not to take him to school if he misses the bus and not to write an excused-absence note for him.
   Client: Oh, I see. If he misses the school bus, that's his problem.
9. Counselor: Exactly. Also, while you are doing your chores downstairs, you could think about how much and how quickly you are able to get things done without interruption and without being hassled.
   Client: I never thought of it that way, but I guess I could do that.
10. Counselor: One other thing or subgoal might be helpful. Can you think of something you might need to do in terms of talking to the people at school about this?
    Client: Well, I could call Freddie's teacher and let her know what is going on so she might expect him to be late at least once or twice.
11. Counselor: OK—letting her know what might happen even if it doesn't. That might help you feel better about this. Could you tell me the steps we have discussed that you will take to stop helping Freddie get dressed?
    Client: Well, telling Freddie about the new rules, not going upstairs when the bus comes, thinking about how much more pleasant it is to do my chores without interruption. (Pauses.) Not taking Freddie to school or not writing absence notes, and talking with his teacher.
12. Counselor: That's great. Now if we put these steps in an order of which one to do first, second, and so forth, what would you start with?
    Client: First, I should probably talk to his teacher, because I'm afraid of her reaction if I don't help him and he's late.
13. Counselor: That's a good start. I think you'd feel better about carrying out your actions knowing she knew what was happening. So, assuming you've told her, what would be the best thing to do next?
    Client: Well, telling Freddie.
14. Counselor: OK, and then what?
    Client: Well, probably just making myself stay downstairs so I don't go up.
15. Counselor: How could you help yourself to do that?
    Client: I guess by just doing my work.
16. Counselor: Yes, and as you're doing your chores, that could be a time to think about how

great it is to do these without feeling has-sled. Now what will you do if Freddie is late?

Client: I will just go ahead and work. But I won't write him a note of excuse. I think the teacher will like that.

17. Counselor: So, if we put these things in order, we've got talking to the teacher first, talking to Freddie, staying downstairs and doing chores in the morning, thinking about not being hassled, and not writing Freddie an excuse or taking him to school if he's late. Which ones could you do this week?

Client: I think a talk with his teacher and a talk with Freddie would help.

18. Counselor: That sounds like a good start. You know we've talked about a lot of things today. Sometimes it's easier to talk about doing something than it is to carry it out. How willing do you feel to carry out these plans?

Client: Well, I know it will be tough. But it's pretty bad, my helping my 10-year-old son like this. I will definitely plan to talk to his teacher this week.

19. Counselor: That's great. Maybe we could put these action steps in writing and sign them with our initials indicating agreement. Of course, we can always change these later on if we need to.

Flexibility of Goals

Goal-setting is a dynamic and flexible process. "Decisions about objectives are not irrevocable" (Bandura, 1969, p. 103). Goals may change or be redefined substantially as counseling progresses (Thompson & Wise, 1976). For example, a client's initial outcome goal may be to make one decision (behavior and level) about whether to go to college and report the decision to the counselor (condition). However, in the process of counseling, the client's goal may change to initiating three discussion sessions (behavior and level) with his parents (condition) in response to their continuous pressure on him to attend college. Once the person begins to change in a certain direction, the actual con-

sequences of the change may lead to modification of the initial goals. Changes that the client perceived originally as feasible may turn out to be unrealistic. Moreover, as Bandura points out, at different points during the counseling process, some "previously ignored areas of behavioral functioning may become more important" (p. 104).

For these reasons, the outcome goals should always be viewed as temporary and subject to change. Bandura (1969) recommends that, in order to retain "flexibility in the selection, sequencing, and timing of objectives," initially selected objectives should be regarded as provisional at least until the client has a chance to try out some new behaviors and to experience their actual consequences (pp. 103–104). As an example, perhaps you are working with a client who is having marital problems. The client's initial goal may be to work out a separation. The goal of separation should be considered as a trial, for the protection of all parties involved. In the process of separation, your client may decide to go ahead with a permanent separation or to reestablish the marriage relationship. If, for some reason, you have a vested interest in the client's pursuing one or the other direction, you may block the client from modifying the original goals. With this in mind, the counselor should assess periodically the client's reactions to the changes being made. Client "resistance" at later stages in counseling may be the client's way of stating that the original goals need to be modified or redefined. The counselor who is committed to counseling to meet the client's needs will remember that, at any stage, the client always has the prerogative of changing or modifying directions. If the counselor is "highly sensitive to feedback from resultant changes," any or all parts of the original goal may be reevaluated and modified (Bandura, p. 104).

The flexibility required in modifying outcome goals also should be a part of the interview process for defining goals. Do not get so bogged down in checking off the interview categories that you lose touch with the client. As you become more comfortable in defining outcome goals, we hope you do not become encapsulated by the procedure. Remember, there is much more to counseling than carrying out a procedure in an assembly-line fashion.

Post Evaluation

Part One

Objective 1 asks you to imagine that you have a real or hypothetical problem for which you select a counseling outcome goal. Try to imagine what you would be doing (thoughts, feelings, or actions) in making this change. Also, picture the circumstances in which you would be performing your desired goal. Think of how much or how often you would want to do this behavior. Imagine some things that you would do (subgoals) to help you reach your outcome goal. Assuming that you cannot achieve the goal immediately, what do you imagine to be some actions or small steps that you could do daily to facilitate progress toward your goal? Sequence these subgoals or arrange them in order of importance: Which subgoal would you do first? Why?

Part Two

Using the following counselor-client (Mr. Brown) dialogue, Objective 2 asks you to identify in writing 14 out of 17 counselor leads or questions associated with the five categories of defining goals. Other verbal responses from previous chapters also may be included. You may want to refer to the Interview Checklist at the end of the chapter for some suggested examples of leads.

Recall from the last chapter that Mr. Brown's selected goal was to worry less about retirement. This dialogue will focus on helping Mr. Brown define this goal by behavior, level, and condition.

1. Counselor: If this is the change you want to work on first, I think it would be helpful for us to specify our goal a little more. For example, what would you be thinking about in order to feel less worried about retirement?
   Client: Well, I would not think as often about such things as "when this car comes out on the market, I won't be with the company anymore."
2. Counselor: These thoughts are interfering or self-defeating because you become preoccupied with them. It would help you if you could decrease them.

Feedback: Defining Goals

1. Behavior of goal
2. Condition of goal
3. Level of goal
4. Summarization of goal
5. Subgoals
6. Subgoals
7. Subgoals
8. Subgoals
9. Subgoals
10. Subgoals
11. Subgoals
12. Hierarchy of subgoals
13. Hierarchy of subgoals
14. Hierarchy of subgoals
15. Hierarchy of subgoals
16. Hierarchy of subgoals
17. Hierarchy of subgoals
18. Commitment
19. Commitment

   Client: It sure would—so that I could feel better and think of work or more pleasant things about retirement.
3. Counselor: Where is it most important for you to be able to do this?
   Client: You know, at work. As we discovered the last time, I don't worry about retirement when I am at home or other places outside the office. It's just when I am at the office alone thinking about the car designs which I have developed—this is the place that seems to spark off worrying about retirement.
4. Counselor: So being alone at the office is really the only place where you feel you need to be able to do this.
   Client: Yes, it isn't a problem for me in any other place.
5. Counselor: You remember when you counted the number of times you were alone at the office that you spent worrying about retirement?
   Client: Yeah, sure.
6. Counselor: How much time or what amount of time did you waste worrying about retirement?
   Client: About a couple of hours a day.
7. Counselor: How much would you like to decrease

the amount of time you are preoccupied or worry about retirement?

Client: Well, I'm not sure. I guess it would be nice not to be worried or preoccupied at all, but maybe that's not too realistic. I am sure I'll think about it sometimes while I'm at work.

8. Counselor: That's right, but remember you said that you wanted to work toward decreasing the *self-defeating* or negative thoughts about retirement, *not* just thoughts of retirement.

Client: I think maybe decreasing bad thoughts which distract me from what I am doing to about—say from around 2 hours to—say an hour.

9. Counselor: How reasonable does this amount sound for you to start with?

Client: Well, maybe it would be easier to try for an hour and a half at first.

10. Counselor: So what we have established as our goal is to decrease self-defeating thoughts about retirement when you are alone in your office. We also said that we would want to start by decreasing the time that you spend worrying about retirement from 2 hours to about an hour and a half. Does that sound like what we agreed you want your goal to be?

Client: Exactly!

11. Counselor: You know, Mr. Brown, I have been thinking that it might be helpful for us to think of some specific steps you could take to accomplish your goal.

Client: I am not sure I know what you mean.

12. Counselor: For example, to help us work toward decreasing self-defeating thoughts, we might have a subgoal or an action step which would be something you could accomplish each day this week. For instance, every time in your office when you are alone and start to have one of these self-defeating thoughts about retirement, you could get up and go out of your office briefly. What do you think of that as a possible action step?

Client: Oh, I see what you are talking about. That's a good idea that might keep me from continuing to think negatively so much.

13. Counselor: What else could you do?

Client: I'm not sure. Maybe instead of not working at all on a design I could try to get so much done each day.

14. Counselor: I believe that might be another good way to complete some work. How would that help you decrease your worrying?

Client: I think by helping me realize I've got to get at least some amount of work done each day.

15. Counselor: Working on these subgoals will take a little effort. How willing are you to do this?

Client: I can do both of these things rather easily.

Part Three

With a role-play client in a 20-minute interview, Objective 3 asks you to demonstrate 4 out of 5 leads associated with defining goals. Use a consultant to check your performance, or check your own performance by audio-taping it. Use the Interview Checklist for Defining Goals after the feedback as a guideline. During the interview, try to maintain a facilitative counseling style, as measured by ratings of 3.0 or above on the Helping-Style Checklist on p. 200.

Feedback: Post Evaluation

Part One

What answers can you provide for the following questions:

What was the thought, feeling, or action (behavior) of your outcome goal?

Under what condition (with whom or in what situation) did you want to perform the behavior?

How frequently or how much (level) was your outcome goal behavior to be performed?

Did you have subgoals? If yes, what rationale did you have for arranging your subgoals in an order or hierarchy? Were most of your subgoals immediate or daily ones?

Part Two

1. Specifies behavior of outcome goal
2. Specifies behavior of outcome goal
3. Determines condition of outcome goal
4. Determines condition of outcome goal
5. Level of outcome goal
6. Level of outcome goal
7. Level of outcome goal
8. Behavior of outcome goal

Interview Checklist for Defining Goals

Instructions: Determine which of the following leads or questions were demonstrated by the counselor. Check each counselor question or lead demonstrated. Also, check if the client answered the content of the counselor's question. Example counselor leads and questions are provided next to each item of the checklist. These are only suggestions—be alert to other responses used by the counselor.

Checklist	*Examples of Counselor Leads and Questions*

I. *Specify client's goal behavior*

___ 1. Counselor clarifies goal by specifying what client will do. Helps client to define the goal in *behaviors*.

"You say you want to change. What do you want to do?"

"What could I see you doing or thinking after this change?"

"You're saying you'd like to be more self-confident. What things would you be doing as a self-confident person?"

___Client response (Specification of overt and/or covert behaviors associated with goal. If client has trouble, may need to give client model of personal descriptions and associated behaviors.)

II. *Determine conditions of goal*

___ 2. Counselor asks about conditions or circumstances in which change can occur.

"Who would you be with when you do this?"

"Where would you like to have this happen?"

"In what situations do you want to be able to do this?"

"Where and when do you want to be able to do this?"

___Client response (Identification of situations or circumstances under which change will occur. If client doesn't know, counselor can use client monitoring to get data, or modeling to show client an example of what counselor means.)

III. *Level of goal*

___ 3. Counselor asks about how much (duration) or how often (frequency) goal behavior will occur.

"How much would you want to do this?"

"How often do you want to increase (or decrease) this?"

"Let's take a look at the data you got in monitoring. Right now you seem to be studying about 3 hours a week. How much would you like to increase that by next week?"

___Client response (Indication of desired level of change; counselor can help client here by use of baseline data. If no data, can have client self-monitor present level of behavior.)

IV. *Subgoals*

___ 4. Counselor and client arrange daily subgoals in hierarchy. Counselor provides leads to "order" goals in potentially successful sequence. (This step is not required if there is only one outcome goal without related subgoals.)

"Let's take the distance between what you're doing now and what you want to be doing. Let's think of all the steps in between and list these in order, starting with the step you think is easiest for you to accomplish now."

"To do all of what you want to accomplish at once is a lot. Let's break down your desired changes into subgoals. As you work on one or two each day during the week, you'll be doing things to reach your overall goal."

"How could we order some things you need to do for this goal to maximize being successful?"

___Client response (If subgoals, client helps to develop these by specifying workable increments of change.)

V. *Commitment*

___ 5. Counselor asks for a verbal commitment to pursue the goal. An oral or written contract is agreed upon.

"This will take some work. How willing are you to do this?"

"Let's list what we've talked about today in writing. What kind of commitment do you have to really work on this?"

"Perhaps it would be helpful if we put down these goals in a contract —what you're going to do and what I'll do to help you. This can change later but right now it indicates where we're headed."

___Client response (Indication of client commitment level by oral agreement or signature. If this is not obtained, counselor will need to explore possible reasons and make adjustments.)

Helping-Style Checklist

1. To what extent are you comfortable as a counselor with the clients and with the subject areas discussed?

1	2	3	4	5
Not at all	Minimally	Somewhat	A great deal	Most always

2. To what extent do you refrain from imposing your values and expectations on the client?

1	2	3	4	5
Not at all	Minimally	Somewhat	A great deal	Most always

3. To what extent are you able to prevent your personal needs from dominating or interfering with the session?

1	2	3	4	5
Not at all	Minimally	Somewhat	A great deal	Most always

4. To what extent are you flexible and able to adapt your style to the person?

1	2	3	4	5
Not at all	Minimally	Somewhat	A great deal	Most always

5. To what extent are you focused on the person rather than on the procedure or yourself?

1	2	3	4	5
Not at all	Minimally	Somewhat	A great deal	Most always

6. To what extent are you spontaneous and nonmechanical in delivering your skills?

1	2	3	4	5
Not at all	Minimally	Somewhat	A great deal	Most always

7. Based on your helping style, how willing would this client be to come back and see you?

1	2	3	4	5
Not at all	Minimally	Somewhat	A great deal	Most always

Suggested Readings

Behavior of Goal

Bandura, A. *Principles of behavior modification.* New York: Holt, Rinehart & Winston, 1969. Chap. 2, Value issues and objectives, 70–117.

Hill, C. A process approach for establishing counseling goals and outcomes. *The Personnel and Guidance Journal,* 1975, 53, 571–576.

Mager, R. F. *Preparing instructional objectives.* Palo Alto, Calif.: Fearon, 1962.

Conditions of Goal

Gottman, J. M., & Leiblum, S. R. *How to do psychotherapy and how to evaluate it.* New York: Holt, Rinehart & Winston, 1974. Chap. 5, Set objectives of initial change efforts, 47–63.

Mager, R. F. *Preparing instructional objectives.* Palo Alto, Calif.: Fearon, 1962.

Level of Goal

Gottman, J. M., & Leiblum, S. R. *How to do psychotherapy and how to evaluate it.* New York: Holt, Rinehart & Winston, 1974. Chap. 5, Set objectives of initial change efforts, 47–63.

Hill, C. A process approach for establishing counseling goals and outcomes. *The Personnel and Guidance Journal,* 1975, 53, 571–576.

Hosford, R., & de Visser, L. *Behavioral approaches to counseling: An introduction.* Washington, D.C.: American Personnel and Guidance Press, 1974. Unit 4, Formulating counseling goals, 62–78.

Mager, R. F. *Preparing instructional objectives.* Palo Alto, Calif.: Fearon, 1962.

Defining and Sequencing Subgoals

Bandura, A. *Principles of behavior modification.* New York: Holt, Rinehart & Winston, 1969. Chap. 2, Value issues and objectives, 70–117.

Bandura, A., & Simon, K. The role of proximal intentions in self-regulation of refractory behavior. *Cognitive Therapy and Research,* 1977, 1, 177–193.

Gagné, R., & Briggs, L. *Principles of instructional design.* New York: Holt, Rinehart & Winston, 1974. Chap. 6, Designing instructional sequences, 99–120.

Goldiamond, I. A constructional approach to self control. In A. Schwartz and I. Goldiamond, *Social casework: A behavioral approach.* New York: Columbia University Press, 1975.

Commitment and Contract

Gottman, J. M., & Leiblum, S. R. *How to do psychotherapy and how to evaluate it.* New York: Holt, Rinehart & Winston, 1974. Chap. 4, Negotiate therapeutic contract, 43–46.

Hoopes, M. H., & Scoresby, A. L. Commitment to change: Structuring the goals and ground rules for counseling. In J. D. Krumboltz & C. E. Thoresen (Eds.), *Behavioral counseling: Cases and techniques*. New York: Holt, Rinehart & Winston, 1969.

Flexibility of Goals

Prazak, G. Accountability for counseling programs. In J. D. Krumboltz & C. E. Thoresen (Eds.), *Counseling methods*. New York: Holt, Rinehart & Winston, 1976.

Chapter 13
Evaluation of Helping Processes and Outcomes

A primary part of helping involves monitoring and evaluating the effects of the helping process. We view evaluation as a major component of helping that is just as vital to the conduct of therapy as all the other components. An evaluation of helping provides encouragement to both counselor and client and also indicates the extent to which counseling goals are achieved. As Egan (1975) points out, "tangible results form the backbone of the reinforcement process in counseling. If the client is to be encouraged to move forward, he must see results. Therefore, both counselor and client should be able to judge whether the action program is or is not being implemented, and to what degree, and the results of this implementation" (p. 225).

The remaining chapters contain many references to analogue and clinical research studies that have demonstrated "effective" outcomes resulting from a particular therapeutic strategy applied to certain clinical problems. These studies are examples of experimental research. The experimental designs used in research studies have been described in a variety of sources (Hersen & Barlow, 1976; Huck, Cormier, & Bounds, 1974; Kazdin, 1973b, 1976d). It is not the purpose of this chapter to describe the potential use and relevance of experimental designs. Our objective is to present some practical techniques that a counselor can use to evaluate the process and outcomes of therapy.

Although some of the methodology and schemes for evaluation presented in this chapter are the same as some research designs, the purpose of counseling evaluation is often different from the objectives of experimental research. Empirical research may be considered a quest for causality or "truth." In contrast, a counseling evaluation is more of a hypothesis-testing process (M. B. Shapiro, 1966). The data collected from a helping evaluation are used to make decisions about selection of treatment strategies and about the extent to which a client's stated goals are achieved. M. J. Mahoney (1977c) has summarized the use of data collection in making decisions about helping processes and outcomes:

> The most efficient therapist is sensitively tuned to the personal data of the client. He is not collecting data for the sake of scientific appearances or because that is what is considered proper. . . . The effective therapist uses data to guide his or her own efforts at having an impact, and—regardless of theoretical bias or procedural preference—he adjusts therapeutic strategies in tune with that feedback [p. 241].*

Objectives

1. Given a client case description and description of data-collection and evaluation procedures, identify:

*This and all other quotations from this source are from "Some Applied Issues in Self-Monitoring," by M. J. Mahoney. In J. Cone and R. Hawkins (Eds.), *Behavioral Assessment: New Directions in Clinical Psychology.* Copyright 1977 by Brunner/Mazel Publishers. Reprinted by permission.

a. types of measures used with this client
b. methods of data collection used with this client
c. times of data collection
2. Given examples of client self-monitoring data during baseline, treatment, and post-treatment assessment periods, be able to graph these data and identify trends reflected in the graphs.
3. With yourself, another person, or a client, conduct an outcome evaluation of one real or hypothetical outcome goal, specifying the types, methods, and times of measurement.

Definition and Purpose of Helping Evaluation

In evaluation of helping, the counselor and client monitor and assess change. There are two purposes for conducting an evaluation of helping. The primary purpose is to assess therapeutic outcomes. The evaluation helps the counselor and client to determine the type, direction, and amount of change in behavior (overt and covert) demonstrated by the client during and after therapy. Stated another way, evaluation of the helping process is designed primarily to assess the degree to which the client's desired goals are achieved. A second purpose is to assess the helping process. Specifically, the data collected during counseling can be used to monitor whether a strategy is helping a client in the designated way and whether a client is using the strategy accurately and systematically. Hosford and de Visser (1974) define the evaluation process in helping this way:

> Observations of the client's behavior near the termination point of counseling can easily be compared with the base rate data if the counselor records the same target behavior, in the same way, and for the same period of time as was done during the initial observations. This provides the counselor with an objective measure of the success of his learning interventions. If the data indicate that little or no behavioral

change occurred, the learning strategies should be reevaluted and perhaps changed [p. 81].*

Although an evaluation of helping can yield valuable information about the process and outcome of therapy, it is naturally not so rigorous as an evaluation conducted under carefully controlled experimental conditions. In other words, a counseling evaluation cannot suggest definitively that the client's change resulted *solely* from this or that strategy. The results of counseling may be influenced by factors other than the particular counseling intervention used. These factors, often referred to as nonspecific, or nontreatment, conditions, may contribute to the client's change. In the final analysis, it is difficult to rule out the possible effects of other sources of influence in counseling. Some of the primary nontreatment sources of influence are described in the next section.

Nontreatment Sources of Influence in Counseling

A variety of factors occur in counseling, either independently of or in conjunction with the application of a helping strategy, that may affect counseling outcomes. Some of the most important nontreatment factors include the influence of the counselor and the counseling relationship; demand characteristics; instructions and expectancy set; and the potential reactivity of measurement.

Influence of the Counselor and the Relationship

The chemistry of the client-counselor relationship is reciprocal: client and counselor are mutual sources of influence. Client changes in counseling can result from "nonspecific aspects of attention, suggestion and faith (in the therapist or his techniques) that are common to most interpersonal situations" (Paul, 1966, p. 5). As M. J. Mahoney (1977a) observes, a

*This and all other quotations from this source are from *Behavioral Approaches to Counseling: An Introduction*, by R. E. Hosford and L. A. J. M. de Visser. Copyright 1974 by American Personnel and Guidance Association. Reprinted by permission.

counselor engages in a great deal of persuasive communication to encourage the client to behave, think, or feel differently. To the extent that the client regards the counselor with trust, respect, and regard, the counselor's "power of suggestion" is greatly enhanced. In other words, the reinforcing value of the counselor is increased. Rosenthal, Hung, and Kelley (1977), for instance, found that clients' fear and avoidance could be modified simply by manipulating social-influence factors and the clients' perceptions of the counselor. As we discussed in Chapter 2, certain relationship conditions initiated and displayed by the counselor can motivate the client to change or to behave in certain ways. For example, it is well documented that counselor empathic reflections can influence certain kinds of client verbal behavior in the interview (Merbaum & Southwell, 1965; Truax, 1966).

Demand Characteristics

According to Orne (1969), demand characteristics include any cues that influence a person's perception of his or her role in a particular setting. In counseling, these cues may not only influence a client's perception of his or her role, but may also affect the client's behavior during and between sessions. For example, perceiving that it is very important to complete therapy assignments systematically will probably motivate the client to complete assignments regularly and conscientiously. In this example, the demand characteristic prompts the client to use therapy in a certain way—which may affect the degree and direction of change. Another demand characteristic that may influence counseling outcomes is the client's desire to please the therapist. This may affect the client's behavior in a number of ways, ranging from the degree of improvement the client reports to the investment and "work" she or he conducts during the counseling process. Other factors that can influence counseling outcomes by communicating certain "demands" include instructions and expectancies.

Instructions and Expectancy Set

A client's motivation to change and to work at the change process also is influenced by instructions and belief factors. Clients who receive specific and detailed instructions about counseling or about a treatment strategy may be more likely to use the strategy accurately and to offer unbiased self-reports (Bootzin, 1972; Nicassio & Bootzin, 1974). Also, clients who are given high-demand instructions emphasizing the critical importance of a task or behavior may respond to counseling differently than people who receive low-demand instructions (Bernstein, 1974; Miller & Bernstein, 1972). Martinez and Edelstein (1977) indicate that clients' behavior may fluctuate, depending on the instructions they receive and on the context or situation in which they are seen or evaluated.

Clients who receive suggestions of therapeutic improvement without "formal" treatment may demonstrate a great deal of clinical progress (Kazdin, 1973b). Client expectations regarding the helpfulness of therapy can significantly affect both the course and outcomes of counseling. As J. D. Frank (1961) has indicated, "part of the success of all forms of psychotherapy may be attributed to the therapist's ability to mobilize the patient's expectation of help" (pp. 70–71). If the client views the counselor and the treatment as highly credible, the client's change efforts may be enhanced. Some research has indicated that therapy outcomes are improved after a positive expectancy set has been established for the client (Woy & Efran, 1972).

Reactivity of Measurement

Some of the procedures used to measure client change in counseling may be reactive; that is, the process of measuring or collecting data may itself contribute to client change. Reactivity can be defined as the changes in behavior that occur as a consequence of observing and recording the behavior despite, or in addition to, treatment intervention (Kanfer, 1970, p. 148).

A great deal of reactivity is associated with client self-monitoring measurement techniques (Kanfer, 1970; Lipinski & Nelson, 1974; Nelson, Lipinski, & Black, 1976b). For example, a client may be instructed to observe and record instances of smoking cigarettes or of self-defeating thoughts for 2 weeks at the beginning of counseling, before any treatment strategy is employed. At the end of the 2 weeks, decreases in the client's smoking or self-defeating thoughts may be apparent even though the counselor has not yet implemented specific strategies to help the client reduce these behaviors. Other types of measures of client change, such as standardized tests, questionnaires, and simulated laboratory or role-play measures, also may have reactive qualities (Hughes & Haynes, 1978; Lick & Katkin, 1976; Lick & Unger, 1977). In assessing change, the counselor should be aware of possible reactive properties of the types of measures used to monitor change.

Practically speaking, the influence of the counselor, the demand characteristics associated with counseling, the client's expectancy set, and the reactivity of certain types of measures can be assets for maximizing desired therapeutic changes. However, from an empirical perspective, these factors are potentially confounding sources of influence when one wishes to infer that the selected counseling strategy was the only cause of therapeutic change. In evaluating the effects of counseling, it is important to recognize the potential impact of some of the nontreatment sources of influence we have just described.

Conducting an Outcome Evaluation of Counseling

Figure 13-1 summarizes the major components of an evaluation procedure for monitoring and evaluating the outcomes of counseling. The procedure includes selecting an appropriate type, method, and time of measurement. The counselor is responsible for arranging and explaining the evaluation procedures to the client, who is an active participant in the data-collection process. The model described in Figure 13-1 is not intended to connote that evaluation of counseling is easy or simplistic. Evaluation can be a very complex issue; however, we do not believe its complexity precludes our attempts as helpers to assess therapeutic change.

Type of Measurement

The counselor and client are interested in assessing the degree to which the defined outcome goal or goal behavior has been achieved. Because the client typically monitors the overt and covert goal behaviors, evaluation of counseling outcomes depends upon a clear specification of the behavior, level, and condition of the client's counseling goals (see Chapter 12). A counselor and client may assess one or several goals, depending upon the number of changes they have agreed to during the goal-definition process. The counselor and client should evaluate by sampling the relationships between the target behaviors and specific situations in which these behaviors do or do not occur (Goldfried & D'Zurilla, 1969). Adequate sampling of a variety of situations is required to achieve a valid representation of what is happening in the client's world (Ciminero, 1977).

The goal behaviors are evaluated by having the client assess the amount or level of the defined behaviors. Five ways commonly used to measure the direction and level of change in goal behaviors are verbal self-reports, frequency counts, duration counts, rating scales, and checklists. A client may use one or a combination of these types of measurement, depending on the nature of the goal and the feasibility of obtaining particular data. These measures should be individualized, particularly since they vary in the time and effort they cost the client.

Verbal Self-Report. One way to assess the client's progress toward the goal behavior is to elicit some self-reported verbalizations. The client can provide information about the goal behaviors in response to counselor leads about the nature and extent of the client's behavior, particularly outside the interview. Although client verbal reports have typically not been regarded as the most reliable measure of behavior, "from a purely clinical perspective, measurement that is independent of the patient's report is superfluous" (Tasto, 1977, pp. 153–154). As Tasto asserts:

> In the realm of clinical practice *the operational criteria for the existence of problems are self-reported*

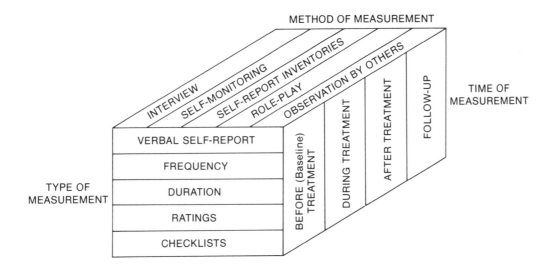

Figure 13-1. A Model of Monitoring and Evaluating Counseling Outcomes

verbalizations. If a patient says there is a problem, then there is a problem. And conversely, when the patient claims there is no problem, then there is no problem. Therapeutic intervention is considered to be progressing to the extent that the patient (and others who may also be involved) report that things are better and, conversely, therapeutic intervention may be considered to be of no value or even harmful as a result of the patient's (and sometimes others') report [p. 154].*

Using the client's verbal reports of progress is an easy and convenient type of measurement—for both counselor and client. Client self-reports may provide useful dimensions of information about the desired outcomes. However, this type of data is often too vague or nonspecific to quantify. For example, a client may report "I'm feeling less uptight now" but may not know how much the anxious feelings have decreased in amount, number, or severity. Because of this, client verbal reports are usually supplemented with some other types of measurement that may produce more specific and quantifiable data.

*From "Self-Report Schedules and Inventories," by D. L. Tasto. In A. Ciminero, K. Calhoun, and H. Adams (Eds.), *Handbook of Behavioral Assessment.* Copyright 1977 by John Wiley & Sons, Inc. Reprinted by permission.

Frequency Counts. Frequency counts reflect the number (how many, how often) of overt or covert behaviors. They involve obtaining measures of each occurrence of the goal behavior. Frequency counts are typically used when the goal behavior is discrete and of short duration. The number of panic episodes experienced or the number of pounds lost are examples of behaviors that can be monitored with frequency counts (Ciminero, Nelson, & Lipinski, 1977, p. 198).

Sometimes frequency counts should be obtained as percentage data. For example, knowing the number of times a behavior occurred may not be meaningful unless data also are available on the number of *possible* occurrences of the behavior. Ciminero et al. recommend that percentage measures be obtained when it is important to determine the number of opportunities to perform the target behavior as well as the number of times the behavior actually occurs. For example, data about the number of times an overweight client consumes snacks might be more informative if expressed as a percentage. In this example, the denominator would reflect the number of opportunities the person had to eat snacks; the numerator would indicate the number of times the person actually did snack. The advantage of percentage scores is that they indicate whether the change is a function of an increase or decrease in the number of opportunities to perform the behavior or an actual increase or decrease in the number of times the response occurs. Thus, a percentage score may give more accurate and more complete information than a simple frequency count. However, when it is hard to detect the available opportunities, or when it is difficult for the client to collect data, percentage scores may not be useful.

Duration Counts. Duration reflects the amount or length of time a particular response or collection of responses occur. Ciminero et al. indicate that duration measurement is appropriate whenever the goal behavior is not discrete and lasts for varying periods (p. 198). Thinking about one's strengths for a certain period of time, the amount of time spent on a task or with another person, the period of time for depressive thoughts, and the amount of time that anxious feelings lasted are examples of behaviors that can be measured with duration counts.

Another type of duration count involves observing the *latency* of a particular response. The number of minutes before falling asleep is an example of a latency response. Another is the amount of time that elapsed before self-disclosing to another person or in a group. Duration and latency measures can be used in combination. For example, a client can record both the latency of self-disclosing responses and the duration of those responses in a group situation. Observing the latency of a response provides useful information about the target behavior even though the data may not always be precise. For example, clients often overestimate sleep latency. If the client can obtain information about response latency using a timer or a clock, then the data are likely to be more accurate.

Frequency counts, percentage scores, and duration counts can be obtained in one of two ways: continuous recording or time-sampling. If the client can obtain data *each time* he or she engages in the goal behavior, then the client is collecting data continuously. Sometimes continuous recording is impossible, particularly when the goal behavior occurs very often or when its onset and termination are hard to detect. In these cases, a time-sampling procedure may be more practical. In time-sampling, a day is divided into equal time intervals—90 minutes, 2 hours, or 2.5 hours, for example. The client keeps track of the frequency or duration of the goal behavior only during randomly selected intervals. In using time-sampling, data should be collected during at least three time intervals each day and during *different* time intervals each day, so that representative and unbiased data are recorded. One variation of time-sampling is to divide time into intervals and indicate the presence or absence of the target behavior for each interval in an "all or none" manner (Mahoney & Thoresen, 1974, p. 31). If the behavior occurred during the interval, a *yes* would be recorded; if it did not occur, a *no* would be noted. Time-sampling is not so precise as continuous recordings of frequency or duration of a behavior. Yet it does provide an estimate of the behavior and may be a useful substitute for high-frequency or nondiscrete target responses (Mahoney & Thoresen).

Rating Scales. The intensity or degree of the goal behavior can be assessed with a rating scale. For example, intensity of anxious feelings can be measured with ratings of 1 (not anxious) to 5 (panic). Cronbach (1970) suggests three ways of decreasing sources of error frequently associated with rating scales. First, the helper should be certain that what is to be rated is well defined and specified in the client's language. For example, if a client is to rate depressed thoughts, the counselor and client specify, with examples, what constitutes depressed thoughts (such as "Nothing is going right for me," "I can't do anything right"). These definitions should be tailored to each client, based on an analysis of the client's problem behavior and contributing conditions. Second, rating scales should be designed so that there is a description for each point on the scale. For example, episodes of anxious feelings in a particular setting can be rated on a five-point scale, with 1 representing little or no anxiety, 2 equal to some anxiety,

3 being moderately anxious, 4 representing strong anxious feelings, and 5 indicating very strong or intense anxiety. Third, rating scales should be unidirectional, starting with zero or one. Negative points or points below zero should not be included. Also, the helper should consider the range of points in constructing the scale. There should be at least four points and no more than seven. A scale of less than four points may limit a person's capacity to discriminate, whereas a scale that includes more than seven points may not be rated reliably by the client because too many discriminations are required.

Checklists. Checklists are similar to rating scales. The basic difference is the type of judgment one makes. On a rating scale, a person can indicate the degree to which a behavior is present; a checklist simply measures the presence or absence of a behavior. Checklists describe a cluster or collection of behaviors that a client may demonstrate. A checklist assesses the client's *capability* "to emit a particular behavior to a given standard under a given condition" (Walls, Werner, Bacon, & Zane, 1977, pp. 79–80). For example, suppose a counselor used either covert or participant modeling as a treatment strategy for teaching a person job-interview skills. The nonverbal and verbal behaviors associated with demonstrating appropriate job-interview skills can be listed on a checklist. If a client demonstrates a specific behavior in a naturalistic or simulated situation, he or she would receive a check on a list for that particular behavior. A checklist also can be used in conjunction with frequency and duration counts and rating scales.

As an evaluative tool, checklists may be very useful, particularly when the reference points on the list are clearly defined and are representative of the particular performance domain being assessed. In the example just given, a checklist of observable job-interview skills could be a useful tool. A list and review of 166 behavior checklists is provided by Walls et al. (1977, pp. 90–146).

Any or all of these five types of measures can be used to assess the magnitude and direction of change reflected in the goal behaviors.

The next section explores how the counselor and client can go about actually collecting data to be used in evaluating helping outcomes.

Learning Activity: Types of Measurement

Read the following client case. Based on the case description, decide which types of measurement you would instruct this client to use while monitoring the target behavior. As a review, there are five primary types of measurement:
1. verbal self-reports—client self-reported verbalizations about progress
2. frequency counts—(1) how often the behavior occurs, or (2) how often the behavior occurs and the number of opportunities available (percentage score)
3. duration counts—how much the behavior occurs
4. rating scales—ratings of intensity, severity, or degree of behavior
5. checklists—presence or absence of behavior

Case Description

The client is a 38-year-old single female who referred herself for counseling because of recurring fears about having cancer. Although the client is in excellent health, over the last two years she has had repeated ruminations about the possibility she may contract cancer. She reports that this concern began after a close friend died suddenly from an undiagnosed cancer condition. The client reports that she has several anxiety attacks per day about this. These can occur both at work and at home. She also reports that some of the attacks are mild, but others are more severe and result in headaches and nausea. Her attacks are centered around thoughts of "worrying that I have or will get cancer and it will be too late to do anything about it." Her goal is to reduce these anxiety-producing ruminations and the concurrent feelings of anxiety and panic.

Based on this description, assume that the client is going to evaluate her anxiety attacks as the outcome measure. If you were her counselor, what type of measures would you have her use to collect data about these attacks? List your choices on a sheet of paper and briefly describe a rationale for each type you suggest. Feedback follows on p. 211.

How to Evaluate: Methods of Measurement

There are at least five methods a counselor and client can use to measure progress toward desired outcomes: interviews, self-monitoring, self-report inventories and survey schedules, role-playing, and observation by others. Any one of these methods or a combination can be used to provide indications of whether or not the desired goal behaviors are being achieved.

Interviews

As we have described in previous chapters, the interview is very useful for gathering data about the client's problems and for defining client goals. The interview also can be used to evaluate informally the degree to which the goal behaviors are achieved. There are at least two ways a helper can use the interview as a measurement method. First, the helper can use open-ended verbal leads to elicit client self-report data about progress toward the desired goals. Specifically, the helper can draw upon some of the leads we suggested for problem and goal definition at a later point in counseling to find out whether progress has been made. The interview leads for determining the intensity of the problem (Chapter 10) and for specifying desired changes (Chapter 11) are particularly appropriate for eliciting client verbal descriptions of therapeutic progress. Presumably, if changes are occurring, the client will indicate that the extent and severity of the problem have decreased as helping strategies are introduced and implemented.

A second way the interview can be used in data collection is to audio-tape randomly selected interview sessions at the beginning, middle, and end points of the helping process. Segments of these tapes or entire sessions can be rated independently by the counselor or by other raters on dimensions of client verbal responses that may be representative of the counseling goals. For example, if the client's goal is to reduce depressed thoughts, defined as thoughts such as "life is rotten," "I'm no good," or "nothing is going well for me," these operationally defined client verbalizations can be scored and rated across taped interviews. Positive statements such as "I'm getting more out of life now," "I'm realizing I'm a worthwhile person," or "good things are starting to happen for me now" also can be scored. As counseling continues, if the client is making progress toward the goal, there should be a decrease across the interview sessions in the negative statements and an increase in the positive statements.

Advantages. The interview is perhaps the easiest and most convenient method of data collection available. It is a relatively "low-cost" measurement method, requiring very little extra time and effort from either counselor or client. It is also a good way to elicit the client's perceptions about the value of the helping process. These perceptions may be especially important in cases where the client believes that therapy is helping (or hurting) although these beliefs are not always supported by quantified data.

Limitations. The interview is the least systematic and standardized way to collect data, however, and the resulting information is often not very precise or specific. For example, the client may be able to report about the duration of change (increase or decrease, positive or negative) but may be unable to indicate the specific level of change (increase or decrease by two per day, 3 hours per week, and so on). Another disadvantage involves the reliability of client verbalizations. If the interview is the only measurement method used, the helper must rely totally on the client's reports of progress. There is always a danger that some clients will report that they feel good or are making desired changes simply to please the counselor (Okun, 1976, p. 161).

Guidelines for Use. The interview method may be more effective as an evaluation tool when used in the following ways:

1. The helper should determine in advance some structured, open-ended leads to elicit client descriptions of progress. These leads should include client indications of the present extent of the problem, the present severity of the problem, and how things are different than they were at the beginning of counseling.
2. These interview leads should be used at several points during the helping process; the helper should use the same leads at each of these "sampling points."
3. Where feasible, the helper should supplement the use of interview leads with ratings of various audio-taped interview segments on dimensions of client goal-related verbal behavior.

Self-Monitoring

Self-monitoring is a process of observing and recording aspects of one's own covert or overt behavior (Kazdin, 1974f). Self-monitoring can be used in the helping process in three different ways: to define client problems (see Chapter 10), to increase or decrease desired target behaviors (see Chapter 22), and to evaluate the effects of helping. The discussion of self-monitoring in this chapter is limited to its role as a measurement method. For the purpose of evaluating goal behaviors, a client uses self-monitoring to collect data about the amount (frequency, percentage, or duration) of the goal behaviors. The monitoring involves not only noticing occurrences of the goal behavior but also recording them with paper and pencil, mechanical counters, timers, or electronic devices (Ciminero et al., 1977).

Advantages. This method has a number of advantages as a way to collect data about client progress toward goal behaviors. Self-monitoring, or an ongoing account of what happens in a person's daily environment, can have more "criterion validity" than some other data-collection procedures (Lick & Unger, 1977). In other words, self-monitoring may produce data that more closely approximate the goals of coun-

---

Feedback: Types of Measurement

At least three types of measures could be used very appropriately with this client to collect data about the goal behavior:
1. Frequency counts of attacks. This information would help determine how many times these attacks occur and, ultimately, whether counseling is helping the client reduce the number of the attacks.
2. Duration counts of attacks. If each attack lasted as long as 30 minutes, this could impede the client's overall functioning.
3. Ratings of severity of attack. Using something like a five- or seven-point scale, she could rate each attack according to its severity. This information would be a clue as to the overall intensity of the attacks. These data also might suggest whether more severe attacks were linked to any specific antecedent conditions.

---

seling than measures such as inventories or standardized instruments. Also, the predictive validity of self-monitoring may be superior to that of other measurement methods, with the exception of direct observation (Mischel, 1968). As McFall (1977b) explains, "the best way to predict an individual's future behavior in a particular situation is to observe his past behavior in that same situation, but the next best way is to simply ask the person how he typically behaves in that situation" (p. 199).* Self-monitoring also can provide a thorough and representative sample of the ongoing behaviors in the client's environment. Also, self-monitoring is relatively objective. McFall notes that it is more objective than informal or verbal self-reports primarily because "it prompts subjects to use a formal structure for their self-observation and reporting" (p. 199). Finally, self-monitoring is flexible. It can be used to collect data on covert and physiological indexes of change as well as more

*This and all other quotes from this source are from "Parameters of Self-Monitoring," by R. McFall. In R. B. Stuart (Ed.), *Behavioral Self-Management: Strategies, Techniques and Outcomes.* Copyright 1977 by Brunner/Mazel, Inc. Reprinted by permission.

---

observable behaviors (Lick & Katkin, 1976, p. 183).

Limitations. Self-monitoring should not be used by clients who cannot engage in observation because of the intensity of their problems or because of medication. Kazdin (1974f) points out that some clients may not monitor as accurately as others. Also, not all clients will agree to engage in self-monitoring (Ciminero et al., 1977). Some clients may resist continuous or quantifiable data collection. Self-monitoring can be a "high-cost" method for the client because of the time and effort required to make such frequent records of the goal behavior. Finally, as an evaluation tool, self-monitoring data are subject to two potential problems: reactivity and reliability.

As we suggested earlier in this chapter, the major problem associated with any self-report measure is its potential reactivity. Simply observing oneself and one's behavior may produce a change in the behavior. However, one can argue that other methods of data collection, such as standardized tests and questionnaires and role-play assessments, are subject to as much reactivity and invalidity as self-report procedures (Lick & Katkin, 1976; Lick & Unger, 1977). Also, as M. J. Mahoney (1977c) notes, the reactive effects of self-monitoring are often "variable" and "short-lived" (p. 243).

Another problem associated with self-monitoring is its reliability, the consistency and accuracy with which the client collects and reports the data. Some have argued that individuals do not collect and report data about themselves in a reliable manner, particularly when they know that no one else will check on their observations (Lipinski & Nelson, 1974; Reid, 1970). The reliability of self-report data seems to be a problem primarily when the target behaviors are subtle or not easily discriminable (Lick & Katkin, 1976).

Both reactivity and reliability can affect the use of self-monitoring as a measurement method. As Nelson (1977) notes, the potential reactivity of self-monitoring should be maximized for therapeutic change yet minimized for evaluation. In using self-monitoring solely as

a helping strategy, there is no real need for reliability. However, for use as a measurement method, accurate reporting of self-monitored data is essential. The next section describes some guidelines that may enhance the accuracy of client self-monitoring as a data-collection method.

Guidelines for Use. There are six guidelines a counselor and client can use to increase the accuracy of self-monitoring as a data-collection procedure. Many of these have been reviewed by McFall (1977b).

1. The behaviors to be observed should be defined clearly so that there is no ambiguity about what is to be observed and reported. Reliability of self-monitoring can be increased if the behaviors to be observed are well defined and easy to discriminate (Lick & Unger, 1977; Simkins, 1971). R. P. Hawkins and R. W. Dobes (1977) suggest three criteria for an adequate response definition: objectivity, clarity, and completeness. For example, a client should be instructed to observe specific responses associated with aggressiveness instead of just recording "aggressive behavior." In this case, the client might observe and record instances of raising one's voice above a conversational tone, hitting another person, or using verbal expressions of hostility. Usually any definition of the target behavior should be accompanied by examples so the client can discriminate instances of the observed behavior from instances of other behaviors.

2. The accuracy of a client's report may be increased by having the client record the target behaviors immediately rather than after a delay (Frederiksen, Epstein, & Kosevsky, 1975).

3. Bootzin (1972) and Nicassio and Bootzin (1974) suggest that increasing the specificity of self-monitoring may offset any potential client biases arising from self-report. The counselor should spell out clearly the procedures for *what, where, when, how,* and *how long* to report the behaviors. McFall (1977b) points out that "the more systematic the SM [self-monitoring] method used, the more reliable and accurate it is likely to be" (p. 200).

4. Reliability of recording can be increased

when clients are trained to make *accurate* recordings (Nelson, Lipinski, & Boykin, 1978). M. J. Mahoney (1977c) recalls that, following his instructions to a client to record her intake of sweets, the client asked: "But what if I get three pieces of candy in my mouth at once, is that one or three responses?" (p. 252). Mahoney thus recommends that clients practice self-monitoring before leaving the session. He advocates the following training sequence:

1. Give explicit definitions and examples of the behavior(s).
2. Give explicit self-monitoring instructions.
3. Illustrate data collection with a sample (model) form—possibly one of your own.
4. Ask the client to repeat the definitions and instructions.
5. Have the client practice or monitor several trial instances you describe [p. 252].

5. Self-monitoring should not be too much of a chore for the client. Sometimes a reluctant client can be encouraged to self-monitor if the demands are minimal (Mahoney, 1977c). A client may be discouraged from self-monitoring or may record inaccurately if required to record many behaviors. The client should self-monitor at least the major goal behavior; other behaviors can be added at the counselor's discretion. Also, clients should not attempt to self-monitor in situations where they are busy with other tasks or responses (Epstein, Webster, & Miller, 1975; Nelson, 1977).

6. The counselor may need to "sell" the client on the importance of the self-recording process and its accuracy, for the client must be motivated to use it. The counselor can point out that accurate self-recording may provide the counselor and client with an awareness of varying parameters of the problem, the possible strategies for treatment, and the extent to which the therapeutic goals are reached. Accuracy of reporting also may be increased if the counselor positively reinforces the client for producing accurate self-monitored data (McFall, 1977b) and if the counselor stresses the personal honesty and integrity of the client in reporting these data (Bornstein, Hamilton, Carmody, Rychtarik, & Veraldi, 1977).

Self-Report Inventories or Survey Schedules

Self-report inventories can focus on the client's reports of specific overt behavior, on fear, on anxiety, and on perceptions of the environment (Goldfried, 1976a). For example, several inventories have been developed for overt or assertive behaviors, such as the Rathus Assertiveness Scale (Rathus, 1973), the College Self-Expression Scale (J. P. Galassi, DeLo, Galassi, & Bastien, 1974), and an Assertion Inventory (Gambrill & Richey, 1975). An example of a fear inventory is the Fear Survey Schedule (Wolpe & Lang, 1964). D. Watson and R. Friend (1969) have developed two anxiety inventories—the Social Avoidance and Distress Scale and the Fear of Negative Evaluation Scale. Moos (1972) has developed questionnaires assessing a person's social environment. Descriptive lists of self-report instruments in these and related areas are reported by Bellack and Hersen (1977), Cautela and Upper (1976), and Tasto (1977). These self-report inventories are used to measure reports of covert or overt behaviors and should be differentiated from inventories designed to measure traits. Self-report inventories can be used to assess the client's progress before, during, and after therapy.

Advantages. Bellack and Hersen (1977) note that self-report inventories are useful in at least two ways: to collect data about a client's overt and covert behaviors, and to obtain data about the person's subjective evaluation of these behaviors (p. 55). As Lick and Katkin (1976) note, inventories are relatively easy to administer, take little time to complete, and can help the counselor and client identify important clinical material (p. 179).

Limitations. One problem of self-report inventories is that they may not measure specific client behaviors or responses. For example, the items in an inventory may not represent specific behaviors of the client in relationship to fear, assertion, depression, or anxiety. Also, the wording of the items on the inventory may be subject to a variety of interpretations (Cronbach, 1970).

Evaluation of Helping Processes and Outcomes

213

Guidelines for Use. In selecting useful self-report questionnaires or inventories, the counselor might be aided by the following guidelines.

1. Select instruments that have been used and validated with more than one population. As Bellack and Hersen (1977) note, "although data derived from studies with the college volunteer subjects are of academic interest, they frequently are of limited value when the assessor is confronted with the clinical situation in an applied setting" (p. 75). However, self-report inventories used in evaluating goal behaviors may not have to be validated beyond the agreement between what a client says he or she does and what actually occurs. For example, selected individual items from the Beck Depression Scale (Beck, 1972), administered daily, provide continuous data about how the individual responds to items related to depression. One does not have to "interpret" or "score" the answers on the scale for comparison with norms.

2. Select inventories in which the wording of the items or questions is objective and is related specifically to the client's concerns. An inventory may have more meaning when the terms reflected in the items are defined explicitly (Bellack & Hersen, 1977, p. 58).

3. Select inventories in which the response choices are, in some way, quantifiable and unambiguous. Words such as *always, seldom,* or *hardly,* or points along a continuum such as "1 to 7," should be clearly defined (Cronbach, 1970).

Role-Play

The role-play procedure consists of scenarios designed by the counselor to evaluate the client's performance of the goal behaviors. For instance, role-play scenes can be created to assess the client's performance in stressful or painful situations, or in specific problem situations, such as a social situation or a parent-child or other relationship interaction (see Nay, 1977). The counselor can have the client take part in role-plays before, during, and after counsel-

ing. Role-play evaluations of the goal behavior may be especially useful as an adjunct to self-monitoring or inventories and survey schedules.

Advantages. A variety of advantages are associated with role-play assessments. First, observing the client's behavior in role-plays within the interview setting may be more convenient and practical than using direct observation in the client's natural environment. Second, role-play assessments or "situational analogues" (McFall, 1977a) can help to avoid ethical problems that might be associated with mishandling of a client's "real-life" performance (McFall, 1977a, p. 153). Also, as Lick and Unger (1977) note, role-play assessments conducted in a laboratory or a counseling session represent an "ideal context" for making "precise, multichannel assessments" of client responses to problem stimuli and provide a rich record of client responses (p. 301).

Limitations. Role-play tests are not without their drawbacks and must be carefully constructed in order to have external validity—that is, to provide accurate data about how the client actually functions in his or her natural environment. Role-play assessments may impose "artificial constraints" on a client (McFall, 1977a, p. 162). The counselor must be aware that a client's performance in even a well-constructed role-play test with a variety of different scenarios or stimulus situations may not correspond to how the client might behave in the actual environment. As Hughes and Haynes (1978) point out, "The relationship between the behaviors observed in naturalistic and structured environments has not been adequately investigated" (p. 445). Also, the client's performance on a role-play test may be affected by the presence of the counselor (or someone else), and by the client's knowledge that he or she is being observed (Lick & Katkin, 1976; Lick & Unger, 1977). The client's degree of ego involvement in the role-play assessment also may affect performance (M. D. Galassi & J. P. Galassi, 1976; Lick & Unger, 1977). Also, the demand characteristics of the role-play situation or the instructions given to the client may influence performance (Martinez & Edelstein, 1977; Orne, 1969).

Guidelines for Use. Three guidelines should be considered if a counselor wishes to use role-play to collect data about goal behaviors.

1. A variety of role-play scenes should be developed as vividly as possible in order to approximate a number of situations in the client's actual environment. The scenes should approximate the real-life situations to which the target or goal behavior is directed. This is important because, in reality, clients have to deal with a variety of stimulus situations requiring responses across different dimensions.

2. The scenes used for the role-play should be developed on the basis of an individual analysis of problematic situations encountered by each client. Lick and Unger (1977) recommend that the counselor have the client identify a series of problem situations that have "maximum relevance" for the client's everyday life (p. 302). The role-play assessments can replicate some of these scenes. Basing the role-play test on an individual analysis helps to ensure that this assessment does not misrepresent or underrepresent the most important dimensions to which the client will respond in the "real world" (Lick & Unger).

3. There should be some degree of standardization in the role-play scenarios used across time. For example, suppose a counselor has developed a variety of scenes to assess a client's assertive behavior of making refusals. In these scenes, the nature of the scene and the responses of the other person in the scene should be standardized or consistent across repeated role measures. This ensures that evaluation of the client's behavior is not based on changes in the nature of the scene or in the behavior of the other person in the scene.

A client's performance in role-play scenarios can be assessed with frequency counts, duration counts, rating scales, or checklists. For example, a counselor may count the number of times the client expresses opinions during the role-play, or the amount of time the client spends in verbal expression of opinions. The client's behavior in role-plays also could be rated on a scale according to the degree of effectiveness or competence. Finally, the presence or absence of a collection of responses can be checked using a behavior checklist.

Observation by Others

A combination of the five procedures of interviewing, self-monitoring, self-report questionnaires, and role-play assessments may be useful in cross-validating the data collected by any one of these approaches. It also has been suggested that data collected from these methods can be verified or correlated with more direct observations made about the client in his or her environment. For example, an observer (the counselor or someone else) can watch the client's performance or demonstration of behaviors in the environment, or the counselor can contact and query significant others in the client's environment who have opportunities to observe the client in various natural situations.

Advantages. In addition to using observation by others to confirm self-report data, there may be times when it is useful to have significant others subjectively rate or evaluate the client's level of functioning, particularly at the end of counseling. This is especially true in cases where clients have altered "negative" behaviors but may still be mislabeled by others in their environment. As Kazdin (1977) indicates:

> The evaluation of behavior by others is important independently of the behaviors that the clients perform after treatment. The problem with many deviant populations is not merely their behavior but how they are perceived by others and perceive themselves. . . . Thus, it is possible that changing behavior of clients will not necessarily alter the evaluations of individuals with whom the target clients have interacted [pp. 446–447].

There may be times when subjective evaluations

by significant others can add important information to the more specific data obtained by client self-monitoring. Other advantages of observation by others include objectivity and reliability.

Limitations. Although using outside observers as another source of data is often feasible, in our opinion it has several disadvantages. First, outside observation poses ethical problems. Before contacting any other person, the counselor must obtain the client's permission and, in contacting observers or significant others, problems of confidentiality may arise. Another major drawback of using observers or of contacting other people is the possibility of communicating mistrust of the client. This could damage the counseling relationship and interventions. Finally, as Lick and Unger (1977) note, unless *trained* observers are used, the reports of other people may suffer from as much discrepancy and bias as client self-report data.

Guidelines for Use. We believe that the counselor should be extremely cautious in using observers or significant others as a source of data about client outcomes. The counselor must always obtain the client's consent before employing others as observers. An alternative might be to have the client bring in representative tape-recorded samples of his or her behavior in the environment. These samples would have to consist of situations in which the client could use a tape-recorder unobtrusively and without violating the rights of others. The client might be unable to tape-record all the clinically important situations encountered in the environment. Still, this method provides data about the client's functioning in the environment and does not pose a threat to the confidentiality and trust necessary for an effective therapeutic relationship.

Regardless of which of these methods is used to collect outcome data, it is important to remember that none of the methods is perfect—and all may suffer from what we refer to as "the invalidity of external validity." In other words, any outcome measure is effective only to the degree that it is tied directly to the clinical criterion or goal behaviors. This point was well stated by Lick and Katkin (1976):

> Clients do not, in our estimation, seek therapy to change responses on questionnaires, physiological and behavioral reactions to imagined animals, or unassertive responses to videotaped unreasonable requests. Regardless of the reliability of such measures or the thoroughness with which they assess behavioral, cognitive, and physiological reactions, they have little *clinical value* as outcome measures unless they correlate highly with a client's reactions to problematic stimuli encountered in the natural environment [p. 182].

Generally, these procedures can be used to collect data on the goal behavior at four different times—before counseling (baseline), during counseling, after counseling, and at follow-up. The next section explores the ways in which data are collected at these four times.

Learning Activity: Methods of Measurement

Read over the client case description on p. 209 again. Assuming you are the counselor for this client:

1. On a sheet of paper list the methods of evaluation you believe to be most appropriate for this case.
2. For each method you select, provide a brief rationale about your choice.
3. For each method you select, write sample instructions you would give to this client about how to use this method. Feedback follows.

When to Evaluate: Time of Measurement

There are several times during which a counselor and client can log progress toward the goal behaviors. Generally, it is important to assess the client's performance before counseling (baseline), during counseling or during application of a counseling strategy, immediately after

Feedback: Methods of Measurement

The method of evaluation that would be most useful for this client is self-monitoring. The behavior to be assessed is primarily covert, and self monitoring lends itself to assessment of covert behavior more readily than role-plays or observation by others. Also, because this client is concerned about a very specific anxiety-provoking situation, most of the structured questionnaires and inventories typically used for fear assessment are too general to be helpful.

The client would be instructed to self-monitor the frequency and severity of the anxiety attacks. Your instructions for this method might go something like this:

"I would like you to get some very specific information this week about these anxiety attacks. I am going to ask you to carry this note card and pencil with you during the week. Whenever you have an anxiety attack—that is, whenever you are thinking about or feeling anxious about the idea of getting cancer—I want you to mark this down with a checkmark on the note card, like this:

Mon	Tues	Wed	Thurs	Fri	Sat	Sun
√						

"Be sure you note even the slightest bit of anxiety. Sometimes the thoughts will lead up to an attack. Also, as you do this, write down the intensity or severity of your attacks, using a five-point scale: 1 would be complete calm and 5 would be complete panic. If, for example, you feel just a little anxious, your number would be 2. If you feel very, very anxious you would select a higher number such as 4 or 5. See—after the check mark, indicate your rating of the intensity of the attack with a number, like this:

Mon	Tues	Wed	Thurs	Fri	Sat	Sun
√ - 4						
√ - 2						
√ - 3						
√ - 4						

"Now, to make sure we're clear on this, could you tell me what you're going to do on this note card this week? . . . OK, let's practice this. Assume you're having an anxiety attack now. You're thinking about having cancer and not knowing it until it's too late. Use the card now to mark these things down."

counseling, and some time after counseling at a follow-up. Repeated measurements of client change may provide more precise data than only two measurement times such as before and after counseling. Limited measurements often reflect "random fluctuation" whereas "frequent and repeated" measurements indicate stability of client change (Chassan, 1962, p. 615).

Baseline or Pretreatment Assessment

Baseline assessment measures the goal behaviors before treatment. The baseline period is a reference point against which therapeutic change in the client's goal behavior can be compared during and after treatment. The length of the baseline period can be 3 days, a week, 2 weeks, or longer. One criterion for the length of the baseline period is that it should be long enough or contain enough data points to serve as a *representative sample* of the client's behavior. Another criterion is that it be long enough to show some stability or *regularity* in the pattern of the behavior. Regularity or stability in behavior can be quite variable; that is, if variability in the data reflects a representative sample of the client's behavior, then these data may be considered stable. For example, suppose a client self-records instances of "eating binges" over 3 weeks. Perhaps there are some days when the client does not engage in binges and other days when there are four or five such episodes. Even though these data may reflect a great deal of variability during the 3 weeks, the data would be considered stable because of the apparent regularity of the target behavior.

Collecting Self-Monitoring Data during Baseline. Typically, during the baseline period, the client is asked to self-monitor instances of the problem and goal behaviors. All the guidelines for using self-monitoring described earlier should be followed at this time. The behaviors to be observed should be defined clearly, and the client should rehearse the process of self-observing and recording. The client will self-monitor the frequency or duration of a behavior and, in some cases, both. For example, suppose a client wants to decrease the number of self-critical thoughts. During the baseline period, the client would be instructed to observe and record (with some device) each time she or he noticed the onset of a self-critical thought. The client would be counting the number, or frequency, of self-critical thoughts.

Typically, the frequency or duration of the observed behavior during baseline can be seen more clearly if it is displayed pictorially or visually. This pictorial display can be accomplished with a graph. Usually, the counselor will be responsible for taking the client's data and displaying it graphically; however, the graph should be shared with the client because of its potential informational value. To make a graph for our example of self-critical thoughts, a counselor would plot the number of self-critical thoughts (1 to 10) along the vertical axis (the ordinate) as a function of the number of days the behavior was observed. The number of days (1 to 14) would be plotted along the horizontal axis (the abscissa). Generally, in graphing baseline data, the observed behavior is plotted along the vertical line and the time (or days) is plotted along the horizontal line.

Graphic display of self-monitored data is very important in evaluation. The client can continue to self-monitor instances of the goal behavior *during* and *after* the application of

counseling strategies. The baseline graph can be compared with the graphs of data collected at these later points to see whether there is evidence of change in the observed behavior. Graphic display of data also is of informational value to the counselor and client, particularly the graph of the baseline data. As mentioned in Chapters 10 and 12, self-monitored baseline data can give clues about the nature and intensity of problem and goal behaviors and contributing problem conditions.

A graph also can provide information about the *relative* stability or instability of the observed behavior. The observed behavior may be stable or unstable over time. If the observed behavior occurs consistently over time—even with increasing or decreasing trends or fluctuations in frequency or duration—it is usually considered stable. Unstable baseline data present more of a problem in evaluation because the irregular fluctuations in the data make comparisons more difficult. However, instability can be an important source of information for problem definition (Chapters 9 and 10) and definition of goal behaviors (Chapters 11 and 12). The instability of baseline data may add new dimensions to the defined problem or may help to refine the goal behaviors.

To demonstrate some of the ways self-monitored baseline data may look pictorially, Figure 13-2 presents five hypothetical baseline graphs for the client who observed the daily number of self-critical thoughts. Graph A illustrates relatively unvarying data. Graph B illustrates an increase in the behavior over the baseline period: the range of the thoughts increases from three on the first day to nine on day 14. The increase might be caused by the reactivity of the self-recording of self-critical thoughts. Another possibility for the increase in Graph B is that greater job or home demands were imposed on the client, causing more self-critical thoughts. The counselor and client should discuss the increasing trend in these thoughts to discover possible contributing factors. Graph C depicts a decreasing trend, from nine thoughts on day 1 to three on day 14. As in Graph B, reactivity or situational demands could have contributed to the decreasing trend. Again, the

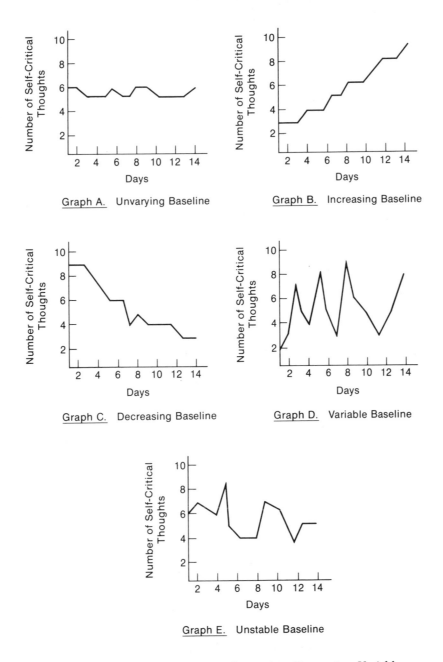

Graph A. Unvarying Baseline

Graph B. Increasing Baseline

Graph C. Decreasing Baseline

Graph D. Variable Baseline

Graph E. Unstable Baseline

Figure 13-2. Graphs of Unvarying, Increasing, Decreasing, Variable, and Unstable Baselines

counselor would query the client about what might have contributed to decreases in these

thoughts. It is also possible for baseline data to reflect a combination of an increasing and decreasing trend or a decreasing and increasing trend. Graph D reveals such variable data. An explanation for these fluctuations in self-critical thoughts might be that more of these thoughts occurred during days on which the client had unsuccessful experiences in his or her environment. A counselor might also discover that, on days in which relatively low numbers of self-critical thoughts occurred (days 1, 2, 4, 7, and 11), the client was at home, faced fewer demands, or reported more "successful" activities.

Graphs A through D could all be considered stable if the data reflected a consistent pattern in each case. In other words, stability of data and trends in data are not mutually exclusive. In contrast, Graph E can be described as unstable because there is no indication of consistent variability, increase, or decrease in the goal behavior. As with the previous graph patterns, the counselor could use the hypothetical data in Graph E to determine contributing factors that might create the varying number of self-critical thoughts. Such discussion can help define the antecedents and consequences of the problem behavior. In some cases, irregular fluctuations in the baseline data may mean that the client is not self-monitoring accurately or regularly—or that another, more important, goal behavior has been overlooked. It is also important to note that stability in goal behavior can be affected by the unit of time in which data are collected and graphed. If the unit of time is expanded, instability in the data will decrease.

Graphs also can be used to display client ratings of problem intensity during the baseline period. Remember that, in addition to self-monitoring the frequency or duration of a behavior, the client can record ratings of the intensity of the behavior. For example, a client might rate the level of anxiety on a five-point scale in addition to noting the number of times anxious feelings occur. When rating intensity, one should attempt to provide anchor points that are not directly related to the problem. If anxious about public speaking, for example, one can use anxiety experienced while climbing stairs or approaching a busy intersection as anchor points. The rationale for providing neutral anchor points is that the client's ratings can be con-

founded by overall reductions in anxiety, thus altering the rating scale. The ratings of the anxiety level can be displayed pictorially in the same way that frequency or duration counts are displayed. The time (days) would be plotted along the horizontal line, with the client's ratings plotted along the vertical line (see Figure 13-3).

Collecting Role-Play Data during Baseline. The counselor may wish to obtain corroborative measures of the client's progress in therapy in addition to data collected from self-monitoring or intensity ratings. Also, self-monitoring may not always be feasible. In such cases, other procedures will have to be employed. For example, consider a male client who lacks social confidence, defined as feelings of anxiety and lack of verbal skills in being able to approach and ask females for dates. It may not be possible to have this client self-report feelings, thoughts, or behaviors in actual situations, because his reported anxiety is so high that he cannot focus on his own behavior.

In this case, the counselor might create several situations in which the client would role-play asking someone for a date. Several role-play scenarios could be used during the baseline period. A checklist used during the role-plays could indicate whether the client demonstrated a particular collection of be-

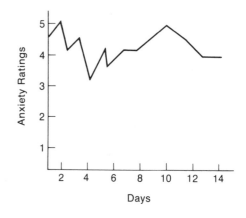

Figure 13-3. Graph of Client Ratings of Anxiety Level during Baseline Period

haviors associated with asking for a date. This topography, or collection, of behaviors is defined in the interview session in which the goals for counseling are established. As you may remember from our discussion of the role-play assessment, the behaviors and scenarios that make up the role-play should be defined on the basis of a situational problem analysis for each client. A checklist or a rating list can be used for each role-play session during the baseline period, and the collection of behaviors the client demonstrates during role-play can be scored. For example, 0 = demonstrated none of the desired behavior associated with asking a female for a date, 10 (or more) = exhibited all the goal behaviors. If the client consistently demonstrates the same behaviors across all of the role-plays, these behaviors may reflect skills already in the client's repertory. Then the focus of counseling should be directed toward the skills that were *not* exhibited during the role-plays.

The data could be plotted on a graph. Assuming that the range for the role-play checklist is 0 to 10, Figure 13-4 illustrates how data from two hypothetical role-play sessions were graphed. The observed behaviors are plotted on the vertical line, with the two role-play times

plotted on the horizontal axis. Note from the graph that the client demonstrated two of the desired behaviors in the first role-play and three in the second one.

Collecting Self-Report Inventory Data during Baseline. The counselor also can administer a self-report schedule or an inventory to a client during the baseline period. For example, with our male client, the Fear of Negative Evaluation (FNE) Scale or the Social Avoidance and Distress (SAD) Scale (D. Watson & R. Friend, 1969) could be used. The scores obtained on each scale each time it was administered during the baseline period can be recorded and graphed. Figure 13-5 presents hypothetical graphs in which this client's scores on the questionnaires are plotted on the vertical lines and the two scale administrations are plotted on the horizontal axes.

It is not always necessary to plot all the baseline data graphically. The counselor can simply keep a record of the client's self-monitored data, role-play checklists, and scores on any self-report schedules or inventories used. However, the graphic display of data has more practical use to the client and also may make progress toward the goal behavior more observable.

A baseline measurement may not be possible with all clients. The client's problem concern may be too urgent or intense to take time to gather baseline data. For example, if a client reports "exam panic" and is faced with an immediate and very important test, the counselor and client would need to start working on reducing the test anxiety at once. In such cases, the treatment or counseling strategy must be applied immediately.

Assessment during Treatment Strategies

According to Cronbach (1975), any evaluator is engaged in monitoring an ongoing operation (p. 126). In counseling, the counselor and client monitor the effects of a designated treatment on the goal behaviors after collecting baseline data and selecting a counseling treatment strategy. The monitoring during the treatment phase of counseling is conducted by

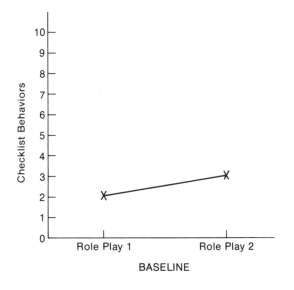

Figure 13-4. A Graph for Role-Play Baseline Data

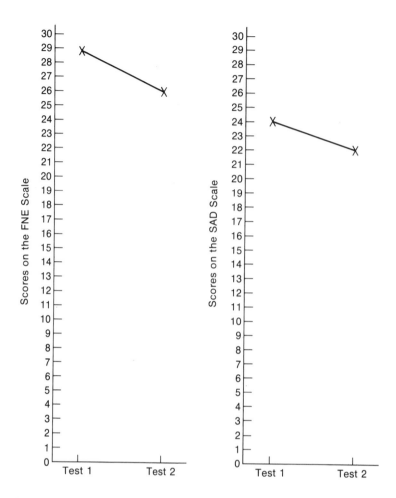

Figure 13-5. Graphs for Baseline Administration of Self-Report Inventories

continuing to collect data about the client's performance of the goal behavior. The same types of data collected during the baseline period are collected during treatment. For example, if the client self-monitored the frequency and duration of self-critical thoughts during the baseline period, this self-monitoring would continue during the application of a helping strategy. Or, if inventories and role-play assessments of the client's social skills were used during the baseline period, these same methods would be used to collect data during treatment. Data collection during treatment is a feedback loop that gives both the counselor and the client impor-

tant information about the usefulness of the selected treatment strategy and the client's demonstration of the goal behavior. Monitoring the goal behavior during treatment is analogous to what Cronbach (1975) calls "short-run empiricism," the idea of taking depth soundings as one moves into unknown waters (p. 126). The data collected during treatment can indicate the need for adjustments in the client's goals or in the treatment plan.

As an example, consider the client who was instructed to self-monitor instances of self-critical thoughts during a baseline period. Before working with any treatment strategies, this client and the counselor would have spent several sessions defining the problem and establishing and defining desired outcome goals. During portions of this time, the client would have been self-monitoring instances of self-critical thoughts; data from the interviews, role-plays, inventories, and observation by others might also have been obtained. After defining the problem and goal behaviors and collecting baseline data, the counselor and client would select and use one or several counseling (treatment) strategies to help the client achieve the designated goal behaviors. For instance, with the client who wanted to decrease self-critical thoughts, the counselor and client might decide to use a thought-stopping procedure (Chapter 18). During the first treatment session, suppose the counselor helped this client learn how to stop instances of these thoughts. Following this session, the client would monitor application of this part of thought-stopping by continuing to observe and record instances of self-critical thoughts. If role-play assessments and self-report inventories had been used during the baseline period, these sources of data also would be used at one or several points during application of the thought-stopping procedure.

Effects of Treatment Measures. Measures of the effects of treatment on the goal behavior can have the same degree of stability or instability as baseline measures (see Figure 13-2). For example, suppose our client continued to monitor instances of self-critical thoughts during and after thought-stopping. Graphs of the effects of the treatment on this behavior might show decreasing, increasing, or variable trends, as depicted in Figure 13-6.

In Graph A, the client's self-observed instances of self-critical thoughts decreased after thought-stopping was applied. Note the decreasing trend in the self-reported thoughts from the end of the baseline or beginning of treatment (day 15) to the last day of treatment (day 22). In this example, the client's goal behavior is changing in the desired direction (a decrease in self-critical thoughts). Such a graph indicates that treatment is having the desired effect. It is likely that the treatment is contribut-

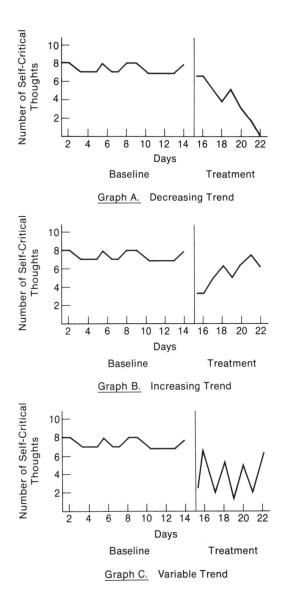

Graph A.   Decreasing Trend

Graph B.   Increasing Trend

Graph C.   Variable Trend

Figure 13-6. Graphs of Decreasing, Increasing, and Variable Trends in Behavior during Treatment Application

ing to the desired change, although nontreatment factors such as the relationship, reactivity, and demand characteristics also may be at work. The counselor and client can discuss the client's reaction to the helping strategies used (in this case, thought-stopping) and to additional factors contributing to the desired change.

In an occasional case, the opposite of the desired effect seems to occur when treatment is applied. In Graph B of Figure 13-6, for example, the client's number of self-critical thoughts increases from the beginning of treatment (day 15) to the last day data were collected (day 22). In this example, the increasing trend does not reflect the desired direction of change in the goal behavior.

When treatment has an unintended effect, several factors may be involved, and the counselor and client should discuss these to determine what might be going on. First of all, the reactivity of the measurement may be creating change in an unintended direction. For example, self-monitoring these thoughts may increase the client's attention to them. Occasionally, a heightened awareness or attention to an undesired behavior may result in an increase (although usually a temporary one) in the behavior. Another possible explanation for a behavior change in an undesired direction concerns the way in which the data are being collected. Perhaps the client is recording inaccurately or is monitoring the wrong behavior. An undesired effect of treatment also may be a function of time. In this case, the client's self-critical thoughts increased during the first week of treatment. A longer time period may achieve a different effect—perhaps these thoughts initially may increase and then decrease 2 to 3 weeks later. Also, it is possible that the nature of the client's problem behavior is contributing to a temporary setback or movement away from the desired goals. For instance, it is not uncommon for clients trying to decrease addictive behaviors to reduce their level of addiction initially—but later during treatment to increase it.

Obtaining an unintended effect of treatment may require that some adjustments be made in the way the client monitors or what the client monitors. Or the counselor may decide to extend the time period during which the treatment is applied. If such adjustments are made and the trend still continues in the undesired direction, then the counselor may conclude that the selected treatment strategy is inappropriate for this client or for the target behavior. Changes in the particular counseling strategy being applied may be warranted. However, the counselor should be careful not to jump to quick conclusions about the ineffectiveness of a strategy and to terminate its use before exploring possible contributing factors.

Sometimes the effects of treatment may not be so clear-cut as those depicted in Graphs A and B. Graph C in Figure 13-6 depicts variability in the goal behavior during treatment application (days 15–22). Such variability may indicate that the client is not using the treatment regularly or accurately or that more time is required for the treatment to have an effect. In some cases, a second procedure or strategy may be needed to contribute to changes in the desired level of the goal behavior. Variability in the goal behavior during treatment also may indicate a need to reexamine and possibly revise the client's goals.

Treatment without a Baseline. Some client problems may be so intense that treatment or a counseling strategy must be applied immediately, without obtaining baseline measures of the goal behavior. In such cases, the client can be instructed to self-monitor during treatment, and inventories or role-play assessments of the goal behavior can be made. For instance, a very depressed client might be instructed to report the number of depressed thoughts per day while the counselor is applying treatment and the client is practicing the procedure. Figure 13-7 is a graph of how this client's self-monitored data of depressed thoughts would appear when treatment is applied without a baseline. Note that the average number of depressed thoughts for this client remained constant during the first 5 weeks of treatment, then decreased during weeks 6 through 10. The counselor and client might have used something like a cognitive-restructuring counseling strategy (Chapter 19) that required some time before the client's depressed thoughts were reduced.

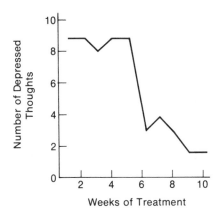

Figure 13-7. Graph of Self-Monitoring Data during Treatment without a Baseline

Posttreatment: Assessment after Counseling

At the conclusion of a counseling treatment strategy or at the conclusion of counseling, the counselor and client should conduct a posttreatment assessment. The purpose of assessing the client's goal behavior at these points is to indicate in what ways and how much counseling has helped the client achieve the desired results. Specifically, the data collected during a posttreatment assessment are used to compare the client's demonstration and level of the goal behavior after treatment with the data collected during the baseline period (before counseling) and during treatment.

The posttreatment assessment may occur at the conclusion of a counseling strategy or at the point when counseling is terminated—or both. For instance, if a counselor is using cognitive restructuring (Chapter 19) to help a client reduce depressed thoughts, the counselor and client could collect data on the client's level of depressed thoughts after they have finished working with the thought-stopping strategy. This assessment may or may not coincide with counseling termination. If the counselor plans to use a second treatment strategy, then data would be collected at the conclusion of the cognitive-restructuring strategy and prior to the use of another strategy, such as anticipation training (Chapter 22). This example is depicted in Figure 13-8. Note that the client continued to self-monitor the number of depressed thoughts for 2 weeks between cognitive restructuring and anticipation training and for 4 weeks after anticipation training, when counseling was terminated. In some cases, the final data point of treatment can serve as the posttreatment assessment.

Ideally, the same types of measures used to collect data before and during counseling should be employed in the posttreatment assessment. For instance, if the client self-monitored depressed thoughts before and during treatment, then, as Figure 13-8 illustrates, self-monitoring data also would be collected during posttreatment assessment. However, if the counselor also had employed questionnaires or structured role-play assessments during the baseline period and treatment, these measures would be used during posttreatment data collection as well.

Follow-Up Assessment

After the counseling relationship has terminated, some type of follow-up assessment should be conducted. A counselor can conduct both a short-term and a long-term follow-up. A short-term follow-up can occur 3 to 6 months after counseling. A long-term follow-up would occur 6 months to a year (or more) after counseling has been terminated. Generally the counselor should allow sufficient time to elapse before conducting a follow-up in order to determine to what extent the client is maintaining desired changes without the counselor's assistance.

There are several reasons for conducting follow-up assessments. First, a follow-up can indicate the counselor's continued interest in the client's welfare. As Okun (1976) observes, follow-up "is a form of recognition that both parties can appreciate in that it can communicate genuine caring and interest" (p. 165). Second, a follow-up provides information that can be used

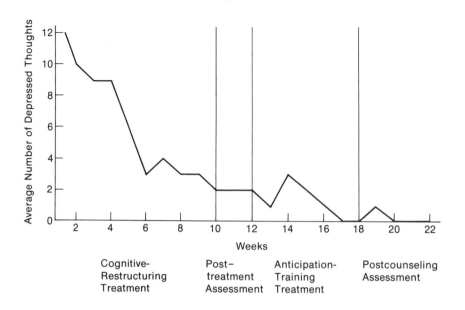

Figure 13-8. Graph of Data of Posttreatment Assessments of One Goal Behavior

to compare the client's performance of the goal behavior before and after counseling. Another important reason for conducting a follow-up is to determine to what extent the client is able to perform the goal behaviors in his or her environment without relying on the support and assistance of counseling. In other words, a follow-up can give some clues about the degree to which the counseling treatment has been effective or has generalized to the client's actual environment. This reflects one of the most important evaluative questions to be asked: Has counseling helped the client to maintain desired behaviors and to prevent the occurrence of undesired ones in some self-directed fashion?

Many practitioners are legitimately concerned about the long-term effects of therapy. Although a short-term follow-up may reflect significant gains, all too often, 6, 9, or 12 months after counseling, the client is back where he or she started. As Bandura (1976a) asserts, the value of a counseling approach must be judged, not only in terms of successful "initial elimination" of a problem behavior, but also in terms of the client's "vulnerability to defensive" or

maladaptive "re-learning" after counseling is over (p. 261).

Both short-term and long-term follow-ups can take several different forms. The kind of follow-up a counselor conducts often depends on the client's availability to participate in a follow-up and the time demands of each situation. Here are some possible ways a follow-up can be conducted:

1. Invite the client in for a follow-up interview. The purpose of the interview is to assess or evaluate how the client is coping with respect to his or her "former" concern or problem. The interview also can involve client demonstrations of the goal behavior in simulated role-plays.
2. Mail an inventory or questionnaire to the client, seeking information about her or his current status in relationship to the original problem or concern. Be sure to include a stamped, self-addressed envelope.
3. Send a letter to the client about the current status of the problem.
4. Telephone the client for an oral report.

These examples represent one-shot follow-up procedures that take the form of a single interview, letter, or telephone call. A more extensive (and sometimes more difficult to obtain) kind of follow-up involves the client's engaging in self-monitoring of the goal behavior for a designated time period, such as 2 or 3 weeks. Figure 13-9 shows the level of depressed thoughts a client self-monitored in a follow-up 6 months after counseling. Note in this graph that the client's level of depressed thoughts 6 months after counseling had remained at the same low level as indicated by the posttreatment assessment. These data suggest that the client has been able to control his or her level of depressed thoughts while functioning in the environment without the counselor's assistance. If the number of depressed thoughts had risen substantially from the postcounseling assessment to the follow-up assessment, this might indicate a need for some additional counseling or a booster treatment. It also could be an indication that, at the end of counseling, the counselor failed to incorporate some treatment or strategy to help the client apply coping skills to manage depressed thoughts in a self-directed manner.

A follow-up in the form of client self-monitoring has some advantages over an interview or telephone call because the data collected are more specific. However, some clients may not be willing or able to collect such data at this point. In lieu of client self-monitoring, an interview, letter, or telephone call is better than no follow-up at all. Also, if possible, the counselor can incorporate structured role-plays and self-report inventories into the follow-up if these measures were used during the previous assessments.

Learning Activity: Times of Measurement

Continue with the client case description found on p. 209 and work through the following questions and instructions. Feedback is provided after the learning activity.

1. Assume that you asked the client to self-monitor and record the frequency and severity of the anxiety attacks for a 2-week (14-day) baseline period. Here are the client's self-recorded baseline data:

Day	Frequency	Average Daily Severity
1	3	1
2	2	5
3	4	2
4	3	3
5	3	5
6	4	1
7	3	2
8	4	5
9	3	1
10	3	4
11	4	3
12	3	2
13	3	4
14	3	.2

Take a piece of paper and plot these data on two graphs. Both should have days as the horizontal axis. The first should show the number of attacks on the vertical axis; the second, the average daily ratings of the severity of attacks.

a. Does the baseline for the number of attacks reflect unvarying, variable, decreasing, or increasing trends? Do the data seem to reflect a regular (stable) or irregular (unstable) pattern?

b. Does the baseline for the severity of attacks indicate unvarying, variable, decreasing, or increasing trends? Are consistent or irregular patterns reflected?

c. What hunches or clues do the baseline data give you about the client or about things to explore with the client?

2. Assume that, after 2 weeks of baseline data collection and four sessions of problem and goal definition, you teach the client, in session 5, the thought-stopping strategy. You work on thought-stopping during sessions 5 through 8. During this time (days 15–42), you ask the client to continue to self-observe and record the frequency and severity of the anxiety attacks. Here are the client's data collected during treatment (thought-stopping):

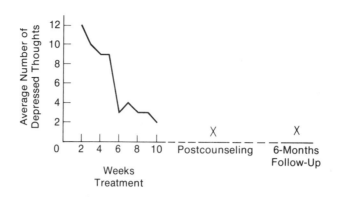

Figure 13-9. Graph of Self-Monitored Follow-Up Data

Day	Frequency	Average Severity Ratings
15	3	1
16	4	5
17	3	4
18	4	3
19	5	1
20	4	4
21	3	3
22	2	1
23	2	2
24	1	4
25	2	5
26	1	1
27	1	2
28	1	4
29	2	3
30	2	2
31	3	4
32	1	1
33	1	5
34	0	1
35	0	1
36	1	2
37	0	1
38	1	5
39	0	1
40	0	1
41	0	1
42	0	1

Plot these data on the same sorts of graphs you used in question 1.

a. What do the data for the number of attacks suggest about the effects of the thought-stopping strategy? Is this an intended or unintended effect?
b. What do the data for the severity of attacks indicate about the effects of the thought-stopping strategy? Is this an intended or unintended effect?
c. As the counselor, what hunches might you draw from these data? What directions would you pursue with this client in counseling?
3. Imagine that, after 4 weeks of thought-stopping, you terminate this strategy and ask the client to continue to self-monitor the frequency and severity of attacks for 2 more weeks (days 43–56). Here are the client's data for this postassessment period:

Day	Frequency	Average Severity Ratings
43	0	1
44	0	1
45	1	5
46	0	1
47	0	1
48	1	4
49	0	1
50	1	5
51	0	1
52	0	1
53	1	3
54	2	1
55	0	1
56	0	1

Plot these data on the same sorts of graphs you used in questions 1 and 2.

a. Compare these data with the data shown on your baseline graphs. To what extent have the client's counseling goals been achieved?
b. Based on these data, would you, at this point, suggest continuing or terminating counseling? If you continue, what direction or plan would you pursue?
c. What factors in your counseling might have contributed to the positive effects of counseling other than your treatment strategy?
d. What kind of one-shot follow-up assessment might you use with this client? When would you initiate follow-up?

Conducting a Process Evaluation of Helping

The data collected from evaluation of helping outcomes should be of practical value to both counselor and client. The evaluation data serve as a feedback loop to help confirm or redefine the selected problem area and the established goals. Also, the data aid the counselor in selecting and using strategies that are likely to help the client. The primary benefit to be realized from an outcome evaluation is the information about the extent to which the client's goals are being achieved.

In addition to the ongoing data collection about outcomes, an evaluation of helping involves some ongoing monitoring of processes. Such a *process evaluation* provides information about the means used to achieve the results —that is, about the specific counseling treatments and any nontreatment factors that may contribute to the outcomes. Both outcome and process evaluation involve continuous data collection during the helping process. The primary difference between these two types of evaluation is in what is monitored. An outcome evaluation assesses the goals, or the dependent variables; a process evaluation monitors the treatment and action strategies, or the independent variables.

A process evaluation helps a counselor to answer the question "What happened, or what did I do, that helped the client achieve the desired outcomes?" Answers to this question —although speculative and tentative—can help the counselor plan future cases and determine how and what important factors might be reproduced in future helping sessions. As Rinn and Vernon (1975) note, "outcome measures generally are not useful for further planning *unless* the intervention technique is quantifiable and its consistent application insured. Thus, the inclusion of process evaluation is mandatory for interpretation of outcome data" (p. 11).

A process evaluation should provide descriptions of three major counseling processes that might contribute to the desired outcomes: the process of each session; the treatment strategies used; and the counselor's behavior and skills. The data to be collected about these three aspects of counseling are described in the following sections.

Description of Sessions

After each session, the counselor should review and record in writing the major focus and activities of the interview. The counselor's notations also might include the counselor's major impressions of the session and any ideas for change and innovation in succeeding sessions (Rinn & Vernon, 1975). Any significant client behavior during the session also should be recorded. Client feedback about the session, whether from a debriefing or unsolicited, can be noted.

The main purpose of noting descriptive information about the sessions is to help the counselor identify nontreatment factors that may enhance or hinder the outcomes. Usually a counselor will assume that change is being achieved by the specific treatment strategy. However, at times, a client may indicate that some small, seemingly insignificant thing the counselor said or did had a great deal of impact. Detailed descriptions of sessions and of the client's behavior during sessions may shed light on other process variables contributing to change. However, sometimes notations about the client should be avoided due to the nature of the problem and potential legal issues.

Feedback: Times of Measurement

1. Here are graphs for the client's baseline data:

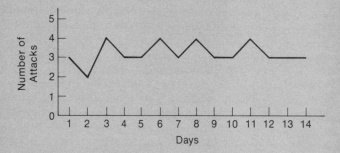

a. These data indicate a relatively unvarying and regular (stable) baseline for the reported frequency of the anxiety attacks. These data might suggest that the attacks are occurring pretty consistently and seem to occur both at work and at home, as the client originally reported.

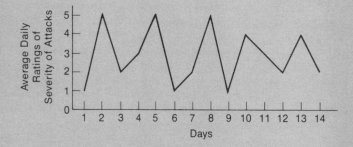

b. These data indicate a relatively variable baseline for the client's average daily ratings of the severity of the attacks. It could be that, with a longer baseline, this variability would be consistent, although it is difficult to determine the relative stability from what you see here. The data do suggest that some of the attacks are very mild, but others are very severe.

c. The counselor and client would need to determine the specific conditions or problem behaviors reflected in the more intense attacks. The counselor also may need to determine whether the client understands the five-point rating scale and is using it accurately.

2. Here are the graphs of the client's data collected during treatment:

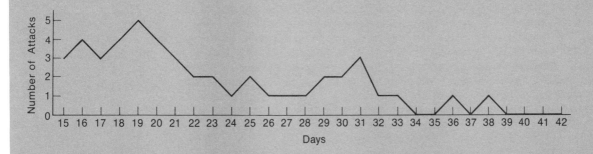

a. These data indicate that, during application of the thought-stopping strategy, the client's number of anxiety attacks did decrease, particularly after the first week of treatment (days 22–42). Clearly, the intended and desired effect was obtained, suggesting that this approach was useful in decreasing and possibly eliminating the anxiety attacks.

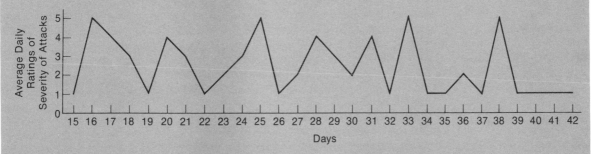

b. These data are variable, indicating that the client's ratings of severity of attacks still range from very mild to very intense. It does not appear that the thought-stopping is reducing the severity of the attacks—at least during this time period. Even though the number of attacks is being reduced, it seems as though the client still rates an attack occurring at the end of this period as pretty severe.

c. This may suggest that another strategy, directed more at the client's felt or experienced distress, is necessary. It also may be an indication that there are times in the "in vivo" setting when the client does not stop the anxiety-producing thoughts but continues to ruminate about them. It may also be a cue that there are some other, unidentified thoughts occurring that are very distressful to the client.

3. Here are the graphs for the client's post-strategy assessment data:

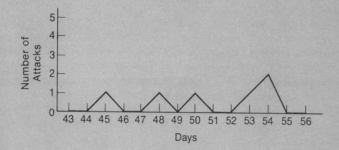

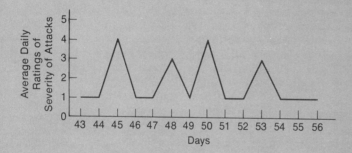

a. These data indicate that the client's goal of decreasing anxiety attacks has been achieved, although when an attack occurs, it still is rated as moderately severe or severe.

b. Because the severity of the attacks still is moderate, counseling might be continued to explore this variable. The counselor and client might focus directly on reducing the client's physiological or cognitive index of severity or stress. Or they might determine whether certain factors that could be resolved or eliminated are contributing to the severity.

c. In addition to the usefulness of thought-stopping, it is possible that nontreatment variables might have contributed to the reduction of the anxiety attacks. The nature of the relationship and such counselor-initiated relationship conditions as empathy and positive regard might have helped to extinguish some of the client's anxiety, particularly in the counseling sessions. If the counselor had provided a positive expectancy set about the thought-stopping strategy, this could have enhanced the client's belief in the possibility of change. Finally, the client's self-monitoring of the anxiety attacks could have had some reactive properties that contributed to the decrease in the attacks.

d. A one-shot follow-up would occur about 3 months after counseling had been terminated. The follow-up could consist of an interview, telephone call, or letter asking the client to report the general incidence and severity of anxiety attacks during this 3-month period.

Description of Treatment Strategies

Because the counseling strategies used do affect the outcomes, it is essential to note some parameters of the strategies used with each client. Sometimes failure to obtain significant changes in the goal behavior over time may be a function of the client's irregular or inaccurate use of treatment rather than the inefficiency or impotence of the particular treatment approach. Monitoring of the treatment strategy is important to determine whether the client is using or practicing the procedure regularly and accurately. In addition to collecting information, client recording of the use of a strategy may create demand characteristics that can encourage a client to use the treatment persistently and systematically.

A process evaluation of the treatment strategies should include:

1. Notations about the specific strategies used,

including the instructions and expectancy set given to the client about each strategy.

2. Notations about the client's use of a strategy. Specifically, each time a client uses or practices a procedure, the client should record (a) the time of day the treatment was used; (b) the location or situation in which the treatment was used; (c) the number of interruptions during use or practice of the treatment; (d) the length of time spent on each use or practice of the treatment; and (e) a description of which parts of the treatment were used or practiced.

3. Client subjective ratings of each strategy while and after the strategy is used. This information is useful because the client's perceptions of the treatment may affect the way she or he uses the strategy.

4. Notations about the cumulative time spent on a strategy within and outside the sessions.

All these data can help the counselor and client assess the usefulness and acceptability of particular treatment strategies. These data can indicate client satisfaction with counseling and the cost-effectiveness of treatment strategies. For example, if the data show that thought-stopping was taught to the client in 30 minutes and achieved the same results as cognitive restructuring, which required three sessions or 90 minutes of therapist time, thought-stopping is the more cost-effective procedure. In addition, the client's ratings of these two procedures may suggest which one he or she perceived as more beneficial or acceptable. The counselor can use these data to detect ways in which the procedures may be helping or blocking achievement of the desired goals.

Description of Counselor's Behaviors and Skills

In addition to evaluating the within-session activities and the focus and use of the treatment strategies, a process evaluation should include some assessment of the counselor's behaviors and skills. As Rinn and Vernon (1975) point out, "a most important aspect of process evaluation is measurement of the therapist's actual abilities 'on the job'" (p. 9). This measurement is important because the skill level of the counselor in conducting sessions and in using strategies can affect outcomes. An evaluation of the counselor's performance might include specifications of skills the counselor performed competently, skills in need of modification, and a plan to alter or reduce skill deficits. A counselor's performance can be analyzed by having a colleague or supervisor sit in and observe the interview or review a tape of the interview (assuming the client has given permission). However, counselors do not always have to rely on others to make these assessments. Counselors should always be able to conduct self-observation and analysis of their own performance and to determine skill strengths and deficits for themselves. As noted in Chapter 8, discrimination of the counselor's interview behavior provides information about the possible relationship between the counselor's behavior and resulting effects on the client.

A System for Recording Evaluation Data

As you can see, conducting thorough process and outcome evaluations of helping can generate a great deal of data. If the data are lost or forgotten, their usefulness is negligible. Therefore, we recommend that a counselor contrive a system to record the process and outcome data as they are collected. A counselor record sheet used to record data from process and outcome evaluations is presented in Figure 13-10. The counselor can use this record sheet during and between sessions for each client.

Figure 13-10. Counselor Record Sheet

Client Name or ID Number _____ Address _____ Phone _____

I. Process evaluation data

Sessions	*Session No.*	
Description of focus and activity of each session	1 2	3 4
Description of client feedback and behavior during session	1 2	3 4
Treatment strategies Description of strategies used, including instructions and set given to client	1 2	3 4
Client's reported use of strategy (time of day, location, length of time, parts of strategy used)	1 2	3 4
Client ratings of strategy	1 2	3 4

Figure 13-10. Counselor Record Sheet (continued)

| Time spent on strategy | 1 | 3 |
| | 2 | 4 |

Counselor's performance

Skills performed at desired level	1	3
Skills in need of alteration		
Plan to modify skill deficits	2	4

II. Outcome evaluation data

		Revisions
Problem behaviors	_____	_____
Counseling goals	_____	_____
Subgoals	_____	_____
	_____	_____

Instructions
for data collection

What data to collect	_____	_____
How to collect data	_____	_____
When to collect data	_____	_____

Client compliance with
data collection
(check which applies:)
_____ a. never collects data
_____ b. occasionally collects data
_____ c. consistently collects data but omits some data
_____ d. consistently collects all pertinent data

Notations or graphs of data	*Baseline*	*During Treatment*	*Posttreatment*	*Follow-Up*
Interview assessment	_____	_____	_____	_____
Inventory scores	_____	_____	_____	_____
Role-play assessments	_____	_____	_____	_____
Self-monitoring	_____	_____	_____	_____
Observation by others	_____	_____	_____	_____

Model Example: The Case of Joan

Throughout this book, we provide model illustrations of processes and strategies with our hypothetical client, Joan. We will now provide sample illustrations of how we could use the process and outcome evaluation procedures described in this chapter with Joan.

Description of Problem and Goal-Definition Sessions

In Chapters 10, 11, and 12, four sessions with Joan were illustrated: session 1 (Chapter 10) was used to define the problem; sessions 2 and 3 (Chapter 11) were devoted to selecting goals; and session 4 (Chapter 12) was used to define Joan's outcome goals for counseling. After each of these sessions, the counselor recorded the description of the session and the defined problems and goals on the Counselor Record Sheet. These sample entries have been filled in on the Counselor Record Sheet for the case of Joan (Figure 13-11) under sessions 1, 2, 3, and 4. Also, the defined problem behaviors, goals, and subgoals are recorded after each respective session.

Selection of Treatment Strategies

In session 4 (Chapter 12), Joan and the counselor decided to work on Joan's goals in the order reflected on Joan's goal chart (and on the Counselor Record Sheet):

1. to reduce absences in math class
2. to increase participation in math class
3. to develop positive thoughts about math ability (reducing self-critical thoughts and increasing positive or coping thoughts)
4. to acquire decision-making skills

In session 5 (Chapter 14), Joan and the counselor explored some of the possible strategies Joan might use to reduce her absences by decreasing her nervousness about math class. A summary of this session has been entered on the Counselor Record Sheet (Figure 13-11).

Baseline Data Collection for Goal 1

Joan's first outcome goal has been defined as "to reduce the number of absences in math class"; the subgoal is "to reduce nervous feelings about math class." The counselor and Joan need to establish what type of data Joan would collect to monitor progress toward this goal. We would recommend that Joan obtain frequency counts of her actual "cuts" of math class, and ratings of the intensity of her nervousness on a scale of 1 (complete calm) to 5 (complete panic) before each math class. Next, the counselor and Joan would determine the methods to be used for data collection—in this case, Joan's self-monitoring. Joan would be instructed to observe and record each time she cut math class and also to record an intensity rating of her nervousness before *each* math class. Note that continuous recording rather than time sampling is being used for these self-monitored behaviors. She could record these data on a log or on note cards. At first she would be instructed to record these data for a baseline period before she and the counselor actually used any strategies to help her obtain this goal. She could collect these data as she and the counselor are defining the problem and goals. This information would be noted on the Counselor Record Sheet under "Instructions for Data Collection" for each goal (see Figure 13-11).

Let's assume that Joan collected 1 week of baseline data on these two behaviors. Her baseline data would look like this:

JOAN'S DATA LOG School Days							
	1	2	3	4	5	6	7
Number of Times Cut Math Class	✓			✓		✓	
Ratings of Nervousness before Math Class	5	2	3	4	1	4	1

First, the counselor would note whether Joan did or did not collect the data—and if so, how consistently and completely she did so. These notations are listed on the Counselor Record Sheet (Figure 13-11) under "Client Compliance with Data Collection."

The counselor could make graphs of these data so Joan could see them visually, and the graphs could be recorded on the Counselor Record Sheet under "Notations or Graphs of Data—Baseline."

According to Joan's baseline data, she cut math class 3 out of 7 days. The data of her nervousness ratings are variable; the high or intense ratings appear to occur on the days she cut class. These data seem to confirm that Joan's nervousness about the class is a major antecedent of her cutting class.

Treatment Strategies and Data Collection for Goal 1

In this book, two primary treatment strategies will be illustrated as possible ways to help Joan reduce her nervousness about math class: stress inoculation (Chapter 19) and systematic desensitization (Chapter 21). Let's assume that Joan and the counselor decided first to use the stress-inoculation strategy. First, we might assume that this strategy was introduced and taught to Joan during sessions 6, 7, and 8; the particular parts of the strategy presented and implemented in each session are noted under "Sessions" and "Treatment Strategies" on the Counselor Record Sheet. Also, the client's rating of the strategy and self-recorded use of it outside the sessions are entered.

Data Collection during Treatment for Goal 1

During the time Joan and the counselor are using stress inoculation, Joan would continue to self-monitor the number of times she cut math class and her ratings of her nervousness before each math class. Assume that Joan reported the following data (shown on p. 237) for 21 school days in which the stress-inoculation strategy was being used:

Looking at the graphs of these data on the Counselor Record Sheet, we can see some decrease in Joan's absences and in her ratings of nervousness, although the data still reflect some variability. There do seem to be more decreases during week 3 of treatment (days 22–28). The counselor might continue to have Joan use stress inoculation for another week or two before deciding whether to continue with stress inoculation or to try another approach. During this time, Joan would continue to self-monitor her ab-

JOAN'S DATA LOG																					
	School Days																				
	8	9	10	11	12	13	14	15	16	17	18	19	20	21	22	23	24	25	26	27	28
Number of Cuts			✓			✓				✓				✓				✓			
Ratings of Nervousness	2	3	4	1	1	3	3	2	1	3	1	1	1	3	3	2	1	2	1	1	1

sences and ratings of nervousness. If these data indicate that her absences and nervousness ratings are definitely decreasing, the counselor probably would not use another strategy. If these data still reflect variability, the counselor at this point probably would decide to implement an alternative strategy, such as desensitization. Again, during the use of the second strategy, Joan would continue to collect data on these two behaviors, as noted on the Counselor Record Sheet for weeks 5–6 (days 29–42).

Posttreatment Data Collection

After application of either the stress-inoculation strategy or desensitization, the counselor would instruct Joan to continue to collect data on the frequency of her absences and the ratings of her nervousness for 1 or 2 weeks. Suppose Joan collected the following data during a 7-day posttreatment assessment period:

JOAN'S DATA LOG							
	School Days						
	1	2	3	4	5	6	7
Number of Cuts							
Ratings of Nervousness	2	2	1	1	1	1	1

Looking at the graphs of these data on the Counselor Record Sheet (Figure 13-11), we see a definite decreasing trend. Comparing these data with the baseline data, Joan and the counselor can note a decrease in the number of absences from 3 (week 1) to 0 (week 7) and a definite decrease in Joan's ratings of nervousness from week 1 (before treatment) to week 7 (posttreatment). The data indicate that Joan has successfully achieved this goal at this point.

Follow-Up Data Collection

About 3 to 6 months after this (or before, if school will be over for the year), the counselor would initiate a follow-up with Joan to discuss her maintenance of change for this goal. The counselor could ask Joan to report orally or to self-monitor frequency of absences from math class. This information would be noted on the Counselor Record Sheet under "Follow-Up."

Summary of Future Sessions and Evaluation of Joan's Additional Outcome Goals

Here is a brief summary of the way the counselor and Joan could collect data to monitor and evaluate Joan's other outcome goals:

Goal 2—to increase participation in math class, defined by (a) volunteering answers; (b) answering when called on; and (c) going to the board to work problems.

What to evaluate: Joan would obtain percentage scores. She would count both the number of opportunities she had to do a, b, and c and the actual number of times she performed these behaviors.

How to evaluate: Joan would obtain percentage scores using self-monitoring. Also, one of Joan's friends and classmates could report percentage scores of these same behaviors.

Figure 13-11. Counselor Record Sheet: The Case of Joan

Client Name or ID No. ___Joan___   Address ___Homeroom 101___ Phone ___

I. Process evaluation data

Sessions   Session No.

	1–3	4–5	6–7	8–9	10–11
Description of focus and activity of each session	1. Explored Joan's concerns about school, competition, apprehension about competition, and difficulty in making decisions 2. Explored feasible goals; Joan is concerned with my not being able to make decisions for her 3. Identified desired changes and advantages, risks and feasibility of these changes	4. Defined goals very clearly—dealing with her math class and her decision-making skills 5. Explained strategies to decrease nervousness about math	6. Described process and rationale of stress inoculation; began to model muscle relaxation and coping skills 7. Most of session devoted to Joan's practice of muscle relaxation and coping skills	8. Practiced applying muscle relaxation and cognitive coping skills in imaginary math-related scenes 9. More of session 8	10. More of session 8 11. Decided to stop with stress inoculation and evaluate
Description of client feedback and behavior during session	1. Willing to discuss problem concerns openly and readily 2. Joan is upset about my not being willing to make decisions for her—she may or may not come back 3. Seemed to take major responsibility now for goals and for her decisions	4. Was eager to participate in defining goals 5. A little hesitant about actual possibility of reducing nervousness	6. Joan accepted rationale rather readily 7. Joan reported good concentration during muscle relaxation	8. Joan had some difficulty with nervousness arising during the practice scenes 9. Joan was able to use relaxation and coping thoughts quite easily in imaginary practice	10. Good practice and concentration by Joan 11. Joan reports nervousness about math is greatly reduced

Treatment strategies	Session No. 1	2	3	4	5	6	7	8	9	10	11
Description of strategies used, including instructions and set given to client	1. Problem definition—ABCs of the problems	2. Selecting goals—discussed desired changes	3. Selecting goals—feasibility, risks, advantages of goals	4. Defined behaviors, levels, and conditions of outcome goals	5. Selection of possible strategies for first major goal and subgoal; instructed Joan to collect baseline data for next 7 school days	6. Stress inoculation: rationale, modeling of muscle relaxation and coping thoughts	7. Stress inoculation: rehearsal of muscle relaxation and coping thoughts	8. Stress inoculation: applied relaxation and coping thoughts to imaginary practice scenes	9. Stress inoculation: Same as 8	10. Stress inoculation: Same as 8	11. Instructed Joan to continue to get frequency counts for next 7 school days
Client's reported use of strategy (time of day, location, length of time, parts of strategy used)	1.	2.	3.	4.	5.	6.	7. Had practiced relaxation 5 times during week	8. Had practiced relaxation 3 times during week	9. Practiced relaxation and coping with scenes 5 times	10. Had practiced relaxation with scenes 4 times	11.
Client ratings of strategy	1.	2.	3.	4.	5.	6.	7. Relaxation rating 6	8. Relaxation rating 6	9. Relaxation rating 7	10. Relaxation rating 2	11. Relaxation rating 7
Time spent on strategy	1. Problem definition—60 min.	2. Selecting goals—30 min.	3. Selecting goals—45 min.	4. Defining goals—60 min.	5. Strategy session—45 min.	6. Stress inoculation—30 min.	7. SI—40 min.	8. SI—30 min.	9. SI—45 min.	10. SI—35 min.	11. Instructions for data collection—15 min.

Counselor's performance	Session No.										
	1	2	3	4	5	6	7	8	9	10	11
Skills performed at desired level	1. Identified ABCs—obtained data from client	2. Initiated discussion of selecting goals—client identified possibilities	3. Good open-ended probes to pursue advantages and risks of goals	4. Obtained specificity about goals	5. Good explanation of strategies	6. Seemed to provide a good model of strategy and skills	7.	8. Was able to give more time for Joan's practice of coping skills	9. A-OK for everything	10. OK	11.
Skills in need of alteration	1.	2. Need to improve use of immediacy, especially in responding to client cues of anger	3.	4. Need to reduce length of some responses—too "windy"	5. Same as above (4). Length is still a problem	6.	7. Need to allow more time for Joan to practice the coping skills	8.	9.	10.	11. Forgot to model for Joan how to collect her data
Plan to modify skill deficits	1.	2. To recognize client nonverbal cues of anger or discomfort more quickly and to use more verbal immediacy at these times	3.	4. To monitor my use of words and stop myself after several sentences or after asking one question	5. Same as above (4)	6.	7. Pause for another minute or so before I start to say something or interrupt her practice	8.	9. Provide examples of data collection at next session; check to see if Joan understands my instructions	10.	11.

Revisions

II. Outcome evaluation data
Problem behaviors
1. School—esp. math class: cuts class, low level of participation, self-defeating thoughts about math ability
2. Evidence of lack of decision-making skills

Counseling goals
Subgoals
1. To reduce absences in math class
   to decrease nervousness about math class

2. To increase participation in math class
   to volunteer answers to questions
   to answer when called on
   to go to board to work problems

3. To develop positive thoughts about math ability
   to stop negative thoughts about math ability
   to increase positive or coping thoughts about math

4. To acquire decision-making skills
   to increase number of identified alternatives
   to increase identification of pros and cons of alternatives

5. To maintain present friendship behaviors

Notations or Graphs of Data

Instructions for Data Collection

What   1. Number of times she cuts math class
          2. Ratings of intensity of nervousness
              about math class

How   Written tallies on log

When   1. Each time she cuts math class
          2. Before each math class

Client Compliance with Data Collection

(Check which applies:)

___a. never collects data
___b. occasionally collects data
___c. consistently collects data but omits
       some data
✓ d. consistently collects all pertinent
       data

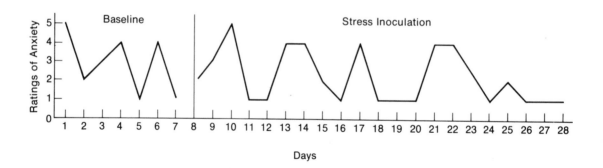

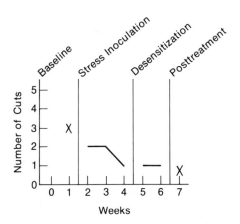

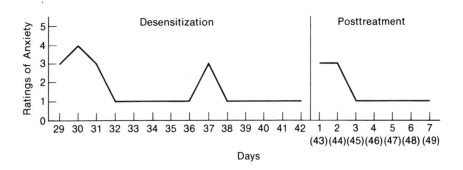

Follow-Up

Five months later, during last month of
school year, Joan reports no cuts and
very little nervousness. Teacher's end-
of-semester written report on students
indicates he believes Joan is doing well
in his class.

When to evaluate: Self-monitored data and observational data collected by a classmate would be gathered during the baseline period, during treatment strategies used to help Joan with this goal, and after treatment. At a later follow-up, Joan could again obtain percentage counts of these three behaviors for 1 or 2 weeks—or simply give an oral report to the counselor about her class participation.

Goal 3—to develop positive thoughts about her ability to do math. Joan's subgoals include reducing self-critical thoughts about her math ability and increasing positive or coping thoughts about her math ability.

What to evaluate: Joan would collect data on the frequency of both self-critical and positive thoughts about her math ability. If she were unable to detect the onset and termination of these thoughts, instead of obtaining continuous data, she could use a time-sampling method such as the "all or none" procedure, where she indicates the presence or absence of the thoughts during predetermined time intervals.

How to evaluate: Since these goal behaviors are covert, self-monitoring would be the most practical method of data collection. Also, the counselor could audio-tape interviews at different points and define and rate Joan's positive and negative verbal statements during these sessions.

When to evaluate: Joan would self-monitor these thoughts for a baseline period, continue to self-monitor while working with strategies, and also self-monitor after the strategies. She could also supply some self-monitored data of these thoughts at a follow-up.

Goal 4—to acquire decision-making skills, defined by (a) increasing the number of possible alternatives Joan can identify, and (b) increasing the number of advantages and disadvantages of each alternative that Joan can identify.

What to evaluate: the frequency of these particular decision-making skills; qualitative ratings of these skills as assessed by a rating scale; and the presence or absence of these skills as assessed by a checklist.

How to evaluate: Frequency of these skills might be obtained by Joan's self-monitoring of these behaviors. Also, the counselor could administer a decision-making-skills inventory to Joan. Qualitative ratings and evidence of the frequency of these skills could be obtained from structured role-play assessments in which Joan is presented with choice situations and is asked to identify all the options and the pros and cons of each.

When to evaluate: Self-monitoring, decision-making inventory, and role-plays would all be done before, during, and after treatments. At follow-up, at least one of these same methods also could be used.

Summary

An evaluation of helping should be performed primarily to meet the needs of the client, rather than the needs of the counselor or the agency. Therefore, the evaluation designs and sequences proposed in this chapter should be adapted for each client. Adapting evaluation to each client requires that, like all other components of the helping process, evaluation be implemented idiosyncratically. In the final analysis, each counselor will need to use his or her own ingenuity to set up and conduct evaluation plans for each client. The flexibility and adaptability that are required in an evaluation of helping can encourage helpers to be creative in seeking information about the effectiveness of helping processes and outcomes.

We believe that most of us feel committed to making the necessary efforts to provide the best possible service we can for each of our clients. To do so, we believe, each of us must feel personally dependent on the collection and availability of data during our helping efforts. As an integral part of the entire counseling process, evaluation should occur for one primary reason—to promote the welfare of our clients.

Post Evaluation

Part One

Objective 1 asks you to use a client case description to identify appropriate types of measurement, methods of measurement, and times of measurement.

Recall that *types* of measurements include (1) client verbal reports, (2) frequency counts (including percentage scores), (3) duration counts, (4) intensity or severity ratings, and (5) checklists of the presence or absence of the goal behavior. *Methods* of measurement include (1) interviews, (2) self-monitoring, (3) self-report inventories, (4) role-play, and (5) observation by others. *Times* of measurement are (1) before treatment, (2) during treatment, (3) immediately after treatment, and (4) follow-up, 3 months to a year after treatment. Now read over the following client case description and respond in writing or covertly to the questions following the case. Feedback follows the evaluation.

The Case of Joe

Joe is 36 years old, married, has two children, and works for a large steel-fabrication plant in a large city. Joe is a production manager and is active in several community and church organizations. He comes to a counselor concerned about his "uptightness" in crowds. After a couple of initial sessions of problem identification, Joe and the counselor define the problem and goals in the following way:

Problem: Setting—Small groups or crowds of people such as meetings at work, church services, waiting in line for a movie or restaurant, or sporting events such as swim meets or baseball games.

Thoughts—Thoughts are generally negative when in these settings. For example, "Wish I didn't have to stand in line—there are too many people," "I have to present this stuff in front of this group—boy, I'll screw up if I'm not careful," "These people are making too much noise."

Feelings—General feelings of tension in these settings—hands sweat, butterflies in stomach, reports heart beating faster.

Behaviors—Performance before groups generally OK, although at times his speech may be faulty (stuttering), but generally no real or obvious anxious behaviors in crowds or small groups other than stuttering occasionally.

Goals: 1. To reduce feelings of tension and discomfort and increase feelings of relaxation in group and crowd situations.
2. To reduce self-defeating thoughts and to increase positive or coping thoughts in group and crowd situations.
3. To reduce any evident stuttering when speaking in front of groups of more than two people.

Following the problem and goal-definition sessions, Joe was instructed to self-monitor his level of tension on a seven-point scale (what), each time (when) he is in a crowd or in a small group, (where) on a note card he can carry in his pocket, and to self-record this tension level for the next 2 weeks (baseline). Joe also was instructed to make a note or count of each time he was aware of a negative or self-defeating thought and of a positive or coping thought about his ability to speak in front of groups. He was instructed to make these tallies also on the note card during the next 2 weeks.

Before deciding on any treatment strategies, the counselor was interested in obtaining a general index of Joe's anxiety over receiving negative evaluations. For this purpose, Joe completed the Fear of Negative Evaluation Scale (FNE) developed by D. Watson and R. Friend (1969). The counselor also structured several role-plays in which Joe was asked to talk informally to six people. These role-plays were audio-taped so that any evidence of Joe's stuttering could be rated.

After these data were collected for 2 weeks, in consultation with Joe, the counselor and client used stress inoculation for 6 weeks. During these 6 weeks and for 2 weeks following, Joe continued to collect data on ratings of his tension level and frequency of self-defeating and coping thoughts in group or crowd situations. Also, after 3 weeks of using stress inoculation and again following the use of this strategy, the counselor readministered the FNE Scale and the structured role-play assessments to Joe. According to the data collected, Joe's tension level and number of self-defeating thoughts had decreased substantially, and his coping thoughts increased. However, Joe's level of stuttering exhibited in the role-plays remained at about the same level. Therefore, the counselor introduced the self-as-a-model strategy to help Joe reduce his stuttering in public-speaking situations. This strategy was used for 4 weeks. After 2 weeks and at the end of these 4 weeks, additional role-play assessments were made. At the end of 4 weeks, Joe's stuttering level in these role-play assessments had decreased over 50%.

Six months after counseling, the counselor contacted Joe by telephone to see how things were going—specifically to see how Joe felt now in talking in front of groups. The counselor also asked Joe to complete the FNE Scale again and sent it to him in the mail with a stamped, self-addressed envelope.

Now respond to these questions.

1. What types of data were collected?
2. What methods of data collection were used?
3. At what specific times were data collected?

Part Two

Objective 2 asks you to graph examples of Joe's self-monitored data and to explain the trends reflected in the graphs. Make a graph of the following data and explain what the trends for the baseline period, for the treatment period, and for the posttreatment period might mean. Feedback follows the evaluation. The tension rating runs from 1 (no tension) to 7 (maximum tension).

Baseline Data		Data Collected during 4 Weeks of Stress-Inoculation Treatment				Data Collected for 2 Weeks after Stress-Inoculation Treatment	
Day	Tension Rating	Day	Tension Rating	Day	Tension Rating	Day	Tension Rating
1	7	15	4	29	3	43	2
2	2	16	5	30	2	44	1
3	4	17	6	31	3	45	2
4	5	18	7	32	2	46	1
5	6	19	5	33	2	47	1
6	6	20	4	34	1	48	2
7	7	21	3	35	1	49	1
8	4	22	4	36	2	50	2
9	7	23	3	37	1	51	1
10	7	24	3	38	1	52	1
11	3	25	4	39	2	53	1
12	5	26	5	40	2	54	1
13	3	27	4	41	2	55	2
14	6	28	3	42	1	56	1

Part Three

Objective 3 asks you to conduct an outcome evaluation with yourself, another person, or a client. You may wish to do so using the following guidelines.

1. Define and give examples of a desired goal behavior.
2. Specify what type of data you or the other person will collect (for example, verbal reports, frequency, duration, ratings, or checklists of the behavior).
3. a. Identify the methods to be used to collect these data (such as interview, self-monitoring, inventories or questionnaires, role-plays, observation or ratings by others).
   b. For *each* method to be used, describe very specifically the instructions you or the client would need to use this method.
4. Collect baseline data on the goal behavior for 1 to 4 weeks; graph these data.
5. Following baseline data collection, implement some treatment strategy for a designated time period. Continue to have data collected during treatment; graph these data.
6. Collect data for 1 to 4 weeks after treatment; graph these data.
7. Compare the three graphs and note what changes have occurred in the goal behavior.

Feedback: Post Evaluation

Part One

1. For the case of Joe, the following types of data were collected:
   a. intensity ratings of Joe's level of tension
   b. frequency counts of self-defeating and coping thoughts about Joe's speaking ability
   c. anxiety rating of Joe's fear of negative evaluation
   d. checklist of presence or absence of Joe's stuttering behavior in public-speaking situations

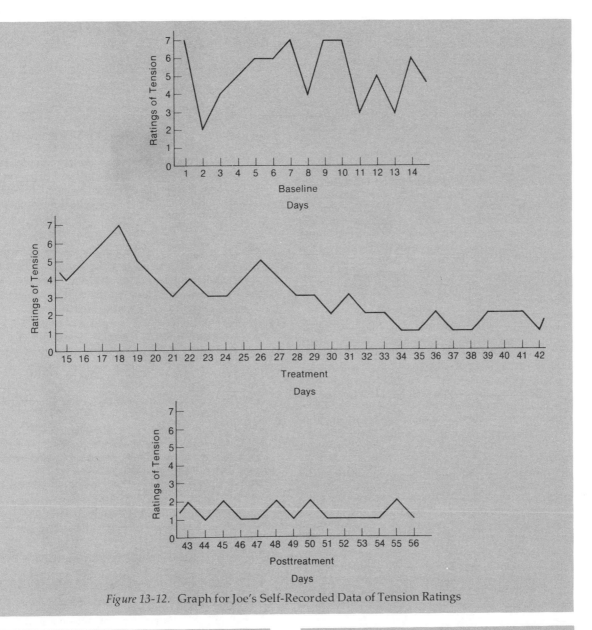

Figure 13-12. Graph for Joe's Self-Recorded Data of Tension Ratings

2. The methods used to collect these data included:
   a. self-monitoring for tension ratings (a above) and for thoughts (b above)
   b. completion of a self-report inventory (Fear of Negative Evaluation Scale) (c above)
   c. structured role-play assessments simulating public-speaking situations (d above)

3. These data were collected at the following times:
   a. 2-week baseline (before treatment)
   b. during stress-inoculation treatment
   c. after stress-inoculation treatment
   d. during self-as-a-model treatment
   e. after self-as-a-model treatment
   f. at a 6-month follow-up

A graph of Joe's baseline, treatment, and post-treatment self-recorded data of tension levels is shown in Figure 13-12. According to these data, Joe's tension level before treatment is variable. During the first 2 weeks of treatment (days 15–28), some variability persists; however, during the last 2 weeks of treatment (days 29–42), there is a decreasing trend in his reported tension level. This trend is maintained in the posttreatment data, which also reflect less variability than the baseline data.

Suggested Readings

Nontreatment Sources of Influence in Counseling

Bernstein, D. A. Manipulation of avoidance behavior as a function of increased or decreased demand on repeated behavioral tests. *Journal of Consulting and Clinical Psychology*, 1974, 42, 896–900.

Lipinski, D., & Nelson, R. The reactivity and unreliability of self-recording. *Journal of Consulting and Clinical Psychology*, 1974, 42, 118–123.

Mahoney, M. J. Cognitive therapy and research: A question of questions. *Cognitive Therapy and Research*, 1977, 1, 5–16.

Nelson, R., Lipinski, D., & Black, J. The relative reactivity of external observations and self-monitoring. *Behavior Therapy*, 1976, 7, 314–321.

Orne, M. T. Demand characteristics and the concept of quasi-controls. In R. Rosenthal & R. Rownow (Eds.), *Artifact in behavioral research*. New York: Academic Press, 1969.

Rosenthal, T. L., Hung, J. H., & Kelley, J. E. Therapist social influence: Sternly strike while the iron is hot. *Behaviour Research and Therapy*, 1977, 15, 253–259.

Conducting an Outcome Evaluation of Counseling

Baer, D. M., Wolf, M. M., & Risley, T. R. Some current dimensions of applied behavior analysis. *Journal of Applied Behavior Analysis*, 1968, 1, 91–97.

Barlow, D., & Hersen, M. Single-case experimental designs: Uses in applied clinical research. *Archives of General Psychiatry*, 1973, 29, 319–325.

Bellack, A. S., & Hersen, M. Self-report inventories in behavioral assessment. In J. D. Cone & R. P. Hawkins (Eds.), *Behavioral assessment: New directions in clinical psychology*. New York: Brunner/Mazel, 1977.

Bornstein, P. H., Hamilton, S. B., Carmody, T. B., Rychtarik, R. G., & Veraldi, D. M. Reliability enhancement: Increasing the accuracy of self-report through mediation-based procedures. *Cognitive Therapy and Research*, 1977, 1, 85–98.

Cautela, J. R., & Upper, D. The behavioral inventory battery: The use of self-report measures in behavioral analysis and therapy. In M. Hersen & A. Bellack (Eds.), *Behavioral assessment: A practical handbook*. New York: Pergamon Press, 1976.

Ciminero, A. R., Nelson, R., & Lipinski, D. Self-monitoring procedures. In A. R. Ciminero, K. S. Calhoun, & H. E. Adams (Eds.), *Handbook of behavioral assessment*. New York: John Wiley, 1977.

Hersen, M., & Barlow, D. *Single case experimental designs: Strategies for studying behavior change*. New York: Pergamon Press, 1976.

Hughes, H., & Haynes, S. Structured laboratory observation in the behavioral assessment of parent-child interactions: A methodological critique. *Behavior Therapy*, 1978, 9, 428–447.

Lick, J. R., & Katkin, E. S. Assessment of anxiety and fear. In M. Hersen & A. Bellack (Eds.), *Behavioral assessment: A practical handbook*. New York: Pergamon Press, 1976.

Lick, J. R., & Unger, T. The external validity of behavioral fear assessment: The problem of generalizing from the laboratory to the natural environment. *Behavior Modification*, 1977, 1, 283–306.

McFall, R. M. Analogue methods in behavioral assessment: Issues and prospects. In J. D. Cone & R. P. Hawkins (Eds.), *Behavioral assessment: New directions in clinical psychology*. New York: Brunner/Mazel, 1977.

McFall, R. M. Parameters of self-monitoring. In R. B. Stuart (Ed.), *Behavioral self-management: Strategies, techniques and outcomes*. New York: Brunner/Mazel, 1977.

Nay, W. R. Analogue measures. In A. R. Ciminero, K. S. Calhoun, & H. E. Adams (Eds.), *Handbook of behavioral assessment*. New York: John Wiley, 1977.

Nelson, R. Methodological issues in assessment via

self-monitoring. In J. D. Cone & R. P. Hawkins (Eds.), *Behavioral assessment: New directions in clinical psychology*. New York: Brunner/Mazel, 1977.

Shapiro, M. B. The single case in clinical-psychological research. *Journal of General Psychology*, 1966, 74, 3–23.

Tasto, D. L. Self-report schedules and inventories. In A. R. Ciminero, K. S. Calhoun, & H. E. Adams (Eds.), *Handbook of behavioral assessment*. New York: John Wiley, 1977.

Walls, R. T., Werner, T. J., Bacon, A., & Zane, T. Behavior checklists. In J. D. Cone & R. P. Hawkins (Eds.), *Behavioral assessment: New directions in clinical psychology*. New York: Brunner/Mazel, 1977.

Conducting a Process Evaluation of Counseling

Kazdin, A. E. Assessing the clinical or applied importance of behavior change through social validation. *Behavior Modification*, 1977, 1, 427–452.

Mahoney, M. J. Cognitive therapy and research: A question of questions. *Cognitive Therapy and Research*, 1977, 1, 5–16.

Rinn, R. C., & Vernon, J. C. Process evaluation of outpatient treatment in a community mental health center. *Journal of Behavior Therapy and Experimental Psychiatry*, 1975, 6, 5–11.

Wolf, M. M. Social validity: The case for subjective measurement or how applied behavior analysis is finding its heart. *Journal of Applied Behavior Analysis*, 1978, 11, 203–214.

Chapter 14
Selecting Helping Strategies

Helping strategies are "modi operandi" or plans of action tailored to meet the specific goals of each client (Hackney & Nye, 1973, p. 102). Strategies, along with an effective counseling relationship, "can powerfully expedite the helpee's feelings, thoughts, or behavior changes" (Okun, 1976, p. 160). In a nutshell, helping strategies represent the procedural plan to help the client get from point A to point B. And, as in traveling from one place to another, no single means of transportation is suitable for all travelers. Hosford and de Visser (1974) explain the emphasis on the variety of counseling strategies this way: "Just as there is no one perfect way to understand the client's problem, so there is no single perfect counseling strategy that fits all situations. Different techniques work differently for different individuals, for different problems, and for different goals" (p. 97).

Tailoring the treatment plan to the client is a move away from the "all-purpose single-method" therapies (Bandura, 1969, p. 89). A. P. Goldstein and N. Stein (1976) charge that, all too often, helpers counsel according to the "one true light" assumption; that is, they assume that their preferred approach is "equally and widely applicable" to most or all clients (p. 3). As a result, these helpers fail to develop treatment plans on the basis of assessment and fail to orient the plan to the desired outcomes (Ban-

dura, 1969; Goldstein & Stein, 1976). Instead, such helpers manage to mold their clients' problems to fit their "brand" of therapy and encourage clients to behave in ways that meet the assumption of this brand (Lazarus, 1971).

In contrast to the all-purpose counseling approach, we advocate the judicious selection of treatment strategies tailored to the individual client. We believe that counselors need to ask themselves constantly "Which treatment strategy, or combination of strategies, will be most effective for this client with these desired outcomes?" (Paul, 1967, p. 111). We realize that this concept is easy to discuss but difficult to practice. Our purpose in this chapter is twofold: to propose some criteria a counselor can use to select treatment strategies, and to describe an interview process in which both counselor and client can be involved in strategy selection.

Objectives

1. List in writing four out of five guidelines that indicate the appropriate timing for introduction of a helping strategy.
2. Using a written dialogue, identify accurately six out of seven counselor leads associated with the five criteria for strategy selection.

Timing of Helping Strategies: Five Guidelines

Many counselors wonder when a helping strategy should be introduced. There is no easy answer, and the answer varies with clients. Sometimes beginning helpers tend to use intervention strategies too quickly and offer premature recommendations or action steps because of their own need to be "helpful." It is impossible (and, in our judgment, inappropriate) to state that "the time" for a strategy is the third, fifth, or eighth session. Nor do we wish to convey the erroneous idea that a treatment procedure *always* will be used with every client. We do believe that a counselor should always attempt to have a plan or a rationale for whatever route is taken. The transition from building a strong relationship and from problem and goal definition to selecting and implementing a counseling procedure is crucial. Eisenberg and Delaney (1977) point out that the timing of this transition is vital to the successful use of a strategy. These authors note that premature use of a procedure can have a "disastrous impact" (p. 145). Although it is hard to define what "premature use" might be in every case, we think that there are a few guidelines to help you make this transition more effectively. The five guidelines you can use to help you judge the timing for a strategy involve the quality of the relationship, the definition of the problem, the development of desired counseling goals, client cues of readiness and commitment, and collection of baseline measures.

Quality of the Relationship

Hackney and Cormier (1979) and Okun (1976) indicate that a counseling strategy may not be effective unless it is used with a strong counseling relationship. When the client begins working with a plan or a procedure, the counselor's support remains vital. Egan (1975) suggests that the client may need even more support at this point, since the change may be painful as well as growth-producing and may involve failure as well as success (p. 227).

How do you know when the relationship is strong enough to provide the support the client will need? Again, this may vary with clients, but here are a few indicators of "quality" in the relationship:

1. The client has given you verbal feedback that you are understanding his or her feelings or concerns accurately.
2. The client has demonstrated a willing (as opposed to reluctant) involvement in counseling through such behaviors as being on time, coming to sessions, completing homework, self-disclosing personal concerns, and sharing feelings with you.
3. The client and the counselor have discussed anything that might deter or impede open communication.
4. You, the counselor, feel comfortable in confronting, disclosing, and using immediacy with this person.

If you sense these conditions in your relationship, it is probably sufficiently well developed to introduce a helping strategy.

Definition of the Problem

It is always premature to suggest a plan of action unless the client's problem has been defined. As soon as you find yourself wanting to suggest some steps the client should take, ask yourself mentally some of these questions:

1. Do I know why the client is here?
2. Is the client's presenting concern all or only part of the entire problem?
3. Do I know the problem behaviors and situations for this person?
4. Can I describe the conditions contributing to the client's problem?
5. Am I aware of the present severity and intensity of the problem?

If you can answer these questions affirmatively, then follow through on your plan. If not, maybe you should check your impulse to move into an action plan until a more thorough assessment has been completed. In some instances, the client also should be given an opportunity to respond to these questions in order to have a role in deciding the appropriate time for introduction of action strategies.

Development of Counseling Goals

If you introduce a strategy before establishing counseling goals, you may be barking up the wrong tree. Because a strategy is a way to promote the goals, clearly specified outcomes are a prerequisite to strategy selection. Be sure that you and the client can describe the desired behavioral outcomes of counseling before you suggest a way to reach them.

Client's Readiness and Commitment

The client's readiness for and commitment to action is the fourth guideline you can use to judge the timing of strategy selection. It is always easier to move slowly and then speed up the process than to move into action plans too quickly and possibly scare or discourage the client from taking further steps. Egan (1975) cautions counselors to "take the client where he is. Never put demands on a client for which he is not sufficiently prepared" (p. 194). For example, clients who are seeking some advice, a panacea, or a quick way to solve their problems probably are not ready for the slow and sometimes painful growth that may be involved in working toward their goals. Clients who have a history of avoidance behaviors may need extra time before being ready to put aside their typical escape or denial patterns. Clients' motivation and incentive to change affect their use of a procedure. A client might indicate readiness to "work" by giving verbal permission, by demonstrating awareness of the positive consequences of change, and by doing at least some covert work or hard thinking between sessions. Sometimes a client's readiness to pursue the outcomes is indicated by a shift in one part of his or her behavior. For example, the client may become more disclosive or may do more initiating in the interview. Another client may demonstrate

readiness for action by starting to assert his or her right to begin the session on time.

Collection of Baseline Measures

As we mentioned in the previous chapter, problem and goal definition are usually accompanied by some baseline data collection, unless the client's concerns are so urgent that immediate intervention is required. Baseline measures, which may include interviews, self-monitoring, self-report inventories, role-plays, and observation by others, can provide valuable information about the nature of the client's concerns and desired goals. Collecting baseline data before implementing strategies is essential in order to determine to what extent the strategies are helping the client.

To summarize, there are no hard and fast rules about moving into the strategy phase of helping. Introduction of a strategy will depend upon the quality of the helping relationship, accurate assessment of the client's problem, establishment of observable counseling goals, client behaviors that indicate readiness for action, and collection of baseline measures.

Criteria for Selection of Strategies

Once you believe the prerequisites for appropriate timing of a strategy have been met, you may be ready to move into the strategy phase of counseling. In our own counseling endeavors, in consultation with our clients, we use some criteria for selecting strategies. Our description of these criteria reflects our own preferences; however, we have been aided by the thoughtful work of Goldfried and Davison (1976), Okun (1976), and Sherman (1973). Five important criteria to consider in selecting helping strategies involve counselor characteristics and preferences, the documentation for strategies, the nature of the client's problem behavior and desired outcomes, client characteristics and preferences, and environmental factors.

In selecting strategies, all five of these criteria should be considered, although perhaps the most important is the nature of the client's problems. Counseling strategies should be used that have the best chance of helping clients resolve their particular concerns most effectively. To a lesser degree, the other four parameters will affect the choice of strategies made by the counselor and client.

To consider these five elements in strategy selection, the counselor and client can use a systematic problem-solving model delineated by Goldfried and Davison (1976). After generating all the possible strategy options, the counselor and client can weigh and rank each procedure according to its possible consequences for the client. Strategies that are most likely to produce positive consequences should be assigned a +; those with neutral outcomes can be given a 0; and those that might be more risky can be assigned a − (Goldfried & Davison, p. 200). The strategies that are most likely to be effective would be selected and used before ones that might not be as helpful.

Counselor Characteristics and Preferences

"The best helper is the one who has the widest repertory of helping skills and who can readily call upon any of these skills to meet the different needs of any client" (Egan, 1975, p. 187). We value the counselor who keeps abreast of new procedures and is adept at using a variety of procedures in the counseling process. We question whether a counselor will be able to function adequately with many clients with only a limited range of skills. To paraphrase Maslow (1966), if your only tool is a hammer, you probably will treat everything as if it were a nail (pp. 15–16). However, our enthusiasm for a multiplicity of treatment strategies does not mean that a helper should abandon principles of human behavior just to offer "the latest thing." Nor do we believe that you should propose a strategy that you know little or nothing about. As Okun (1976) points out, "pretending to be an expert when you're not can backfire and even if it doesn't, it is of questionable ethics" (p. 160). Misrepresenting

yourself and your qualifications to a client also can have serious legal consequences (Van Hoose & Kottler, 1977).

We are suggesting that you use *your* skills as one criterion for judging which strategy may be most appropriate. Your previous use of a procedure and your attitude about it are major factors affecting your preferences. At the same time, don't restrict yourself to your old standbys. Be open to using different techniques—but be aware of when you need supervision or consultation to accompany your testing out a new approach. Don't hesitate to share your preferences with a client. Also, your preferences for strategies may reflect your particular orientation to therapy; this, too, should be shared with the client at the beginning of therapy.

Documentation about Strategies

Varying amounts of data exist for different counseling procedures. All the strategies presented in the remainder of this book have some empirical support. Whether or not a strategy has been documented should be one, but not the only, criterion to consider in deciding whether to use it. The data can help you determine the ways in which the strategy has been used successfully and with what types of client problems. However, don't restrict yourself to past use. Participant modeling (Chapter 16), for example, has been documented most extensively for reduction of fears. We have used it also in helping clients to acquire new skills. There is a great deal of ongoing research assessing the effects of certain counselor behaviors and treatment strategies in producing various kinds of client change. However, as Krumboltz and Thoresen (1976) indicate, we are simply not at the point where we have sufficient data on most strategies to describe which procedure is best for which person with which problem. Therefore, relying only on the available data about a strategy is an insufficient criterion for your decision—at least at this point. It is often useful to point out to the client that procedure X and procedure Y both have been documented to some extent.

Nature of Client Problem and Outcome

The counselor must assume some responsibility for generating suggestions of strategies that are based upon the previous definition of the client's problem. To some extent, the strategies should reflect the nature of the problem behaviors and the desired outcomes. Of course, this requires thorough problem and goal definition, as well as knowledge about the purpose of particular procedures. As an example, if a client wanted to improve grades on tests and the assessment revealed the student didn't study, the counselor would have a basis for suggesting some type of study-skills training. But if the assessment revealed that the client studied frequently but panicked on tests, the counselor would have a basis for suggesting an approach for managing test anxiety, such as desensitization (Chapter 21), cognitive restructuring (Chapter 19), or both.

Client Characteristics and Preferences

In our opinion, the choice of appropriate counseling strategies is a mutual decision in which both counselor and client are actively involved. We believe it is a misuse of the inherent influence of the helping process for the counselor to select a strategy or to implement a treatment plan independent of the client's input. As Frey (1975) has indicated, we believe that the client should be a co-producer, not merely a consumer of services (p. 23). The client's preferences for a treatment plan are important, regardless of the setting in which a person is helped. As Kanfer and Goldstein (1975) point out, a counselor working with institutionalized clients must take special precautions to ensure that the person's civil rights are not violated and that treatment programs are not implemented without client participation and consent (p. 13).

We like the idea of using a menu of strategies, where the client can select from an array of procedures rather than being told that only one item is "being served." In order to help the client make an informed choice, the counselor should give some information about each of the possible treatment strategies. We know of people who are opposed to telling the client about their approach because they feel that an explanation may detract from the procedure's effect. Our own practical experience, as well as some data, indicates otherwise: usually the client's participation is only strengthened when the client has a rationale and an idea of what is going on. Without adequate explanation, an occasional client might be scared away and decide to drop out of counseling (Okun, 1976).

The carelessness exhibited by many helpers in randomly selecting an approach without explicit client understanding and consent has made this part of the helping process very sensitive to legal charges (Van Hoose & Kottler, 1977). Most clients will be swayed by the kind of information the counselor provides about potential treatment strategies, and the kind of information imparted about the nature of problems and potential strategies can have a great deal of impact. If the client questions the counselor's explanation, more elaboration may be necessary. If a counselor does not have the information sought by the client, saying "I don't know" is more helpful than saying nothing. In the latter case, the client may sense your uncertainty anyway and this ambiguity may create anxiety.

We believe the counselor is acting in good faith to protect the client's rights and welfare by providing the following information about strategies, as suggested by Okun (1976):

1. a description of all relevant treatment approaches for this particular client
2. a rationale for each procedure
3. the possible consequences (advantages and risks) of each approach
4. the time and activities involved in each approach

The client should be helped to evaluate the degree of risk involved in any approach and to weigh the risk against the anticipated success. The counselor can assist the client in selecting strategies that are most likely to maximize positive consequences and minimize negative ones (Goldfried & D'Zurilla, 1969). Obviously, a procedure that has a high probability of being successful will be more helpful than one that involves many risks.

In addition to explaining and considering client preferences for treatment strategies, it is helpful to consider any client characteristics that might affect the use of a strategy. Goldfried and Davison (1976) point out that, in some techniques, a client's capacity to report specific examples is very important (p. 27). In other procedures, such as covert modeling (Chapter 17) and desensitization (Chapter 21), the client's capacity to generate and sustain mental images is crucial. The counselor will need to determine whether the client can generate clear and vivid images before using such strategies.

Egan (1975) suggests that the counselor should help the client choose an action plan that is consistent with the client's values and lifestyle (p. 219). The client's values may give either a positive or negative valence to an action strategy. If a strategy runs counter to a client's values, the person's investment in the strategy may be minimal, or the use of the plan may create further problems (pp. 219–220).

Environmental Factors

Certain factors within the counseling environment or the client's environment may affect whether a strategy is practical or impractical. The amount of time you have to spend with a client for each session and for the totality of counseling is one factor to consider in proposing strategies. In time-limited counseling, specific, concrete procedures that are easy to work with are more practical. The nature of your counseling setting may also affect possible procedures. For example, it would be difficult to train a client in deep relaxation (Chapter 20) without a comfortable chair. It may be impossible for the client to leave some settings to carry out any kind of "in vivo" treatment.

The client's environment also is important. Egan (1975) points out that an action plan that may occur in an unbending environment or that may meet with a lot of resistance is not a practical strategy (pp. 221–222). Goldfried and Davison (1976) indicate that the availability of role models and reinforcers in the client's environment also may affect possible strategies. It is not helpful to depend on a procedure that requires a great deal of encouragement from significant others if the client has very few close relationships.

Selecting Combinations of Strategies

It is important to remember that helping strategies are rarely used in isolation. Although the counseling strategies in the remainder of this book are presented one at a time for instructional purposes, in the "real world" these strategies often are used in combination. Also, there can be a great deal of overlap among strategies in the actual implementation.

A variety of strategies is necessary in order to treat the complexity and range of problems presented by a single client. It is just not that common to encounter a client with only one very straightforward concern (such as fear of flying in airplanes) that can be treated successfully with only one strategy (such as systematic desensitization). As M. J. Mahoney (1974) asserts, "unidimensional presenting problems appear to be a myth propagated by research conventions. The average client is not simply snake phobic—he often expresses desires to improve personal adjustment along a wide range of foci" (p. 273).

Because most client problems are multidimensional and controlled by diverse variables, the targets of change usually need to be multiple. Since thoughts, feelings, and external behavior interact and affect one another, the effective helper does not rule out any type of external or internal behavior as an important element for change. Furthermore, increasing evidence indicates a strong correlation between performance changes and cognitive changes. Performance accomplishments in the form of personal mastery experiences can strengthen clients' expectations of personal effectiveness or self-efficacy (Bandura & Adams, 1977; Bandura, Adams, & Beyer, 1977). A well-integrated helping program will employ all the necessary strategies to work with a client's performance skills, cognitive skills, emotional responses, body processes, and environmental factors.

Model Dialogue: The Case of Joan

In this dialogue, the counselor will explore with Joan some of the strategies they could use to work with the first two goals on Joan's goal chart (Chapter 12). Specifically, Joan and the counselor will explore strategies that could help Joan reduce her absences from math class by decreasing her nervousness about it. Each counselor lead will be preceded by a description of what the counselor plans to do in the next response. It might be helpful for you to think of this interview as a subsequent session to the interview in Chapter 12, in which Joan's goals were defined.

In the initial part of the interview, the counselor will summarize the previous session and will introduce Joan to the idea of exploring strategies with a <u>verbal set</u> for strategy selection.

1. Counselor: Last week, Joan, we talked about some of the things you would like to see happen as a result of counseling. One of the things you indicated was pretty important to you was not cutting math class. One of the things that seems to contribute to your cutting the class is your apprehension about it. There are several ways we might deal with your apprehension. I thought today we might explore some of the procedures that may help. These procedures are things we can do together to help you get where you want to be. How does that sound?

   Client: It's OK. So we'll find a way maybe I could be less nervous.

In the second response, the counselor continues with the <u>verbal set</u> and attempts to explain to Joan what strategy selection involves and the importance of Joan's input.

2. Counselor: Yes. One thing to keep in mind is that there are no easy answers and there is not necessarily one right way. What we can do today is explore some ways that are used to help people be less nervous in specific situations, and try to come up with a way that you think sounds workable for you. I'll be giving you some information about these procedures for your input in this decision.

   Client: OK.

In responses 3 and 4, the counselor suggests possible strategies for Joan to consider. The counselor also explains how one strategy, relaxation, is <u>related to Joan's concerns and can help her achieve her goal</u>.

3. Counselor: From my experience, I believe that there are a couple of things that might help you manage your nervousness to the point where you do not feel as if you need to cut math class to avoid feeling nervous about it. First of all, when you're nervous, you're tense. Sometimes when you're tense you feel bad or sick, or just out of control. One thing we could do is to teach you some relaxation methods (Chapter 20). The relaxation can help you learn to identify when you're starting to feel nervous, and it can help you manage this before it gets so strong you just skip class. Does this make sense?

   Client: Yes, because when I really let myself get nervous, I don't want to go. Sometimes I force myself to go, but I'm still nervous and I don't feel like going.

4. Counselor: That's a good point. You don't have the energy or desire to do something you're apprehensive about. Sometimes for some people, just learning to relax and control your nervousness might be enough. If you want to try this first and it helps you be less nervous to the point where you don't cut math class, then that's fine. However, there are some other things we might do also, so I'd like you to know about these action plans, too.

   Client: Like what?

The counselor proposes an additional strategy in response 5 and indicates how this procedure can help Joan decrease her nervousness by <u>describing how it also is related to Joan's problem and goal</u>.

5. Counselor: Well, one procedure has a very interesting name—it's called stress inoculation (Chapter 19). You know when you get a shot like a polio inoculation, the shot helps to prevent you from getting polio. Well, this procedure helps you to prevent yourself from getting so overwhelmed in a stressful situation such as your math class that you want to avoid the situation.

   Client: Is it painful like a shot?

The counselor provides more information about what stress inoculation would involve from Joan in terms of the <u>time, advantages, and risks of the procedure</u>; this information should help Joan assess her preferences.

6. Counselor: No, not like that, although it would involve a little work on your part. In addition to learning the relaxation training I mentioned earlier, you would learn how to cope with stressful

situations—through relaxing your body and thinking some coping kinds of thoughts. When you are able to do this successfully with me, you would start to do this in your math class. Once you learned the relaxation, it would take several sessions to learn the other parts. The advantage of stress inoculation is that it helps you learn how to cope with rather than avoid a stressful situation. Of course, it does require you to practice the relaxation and the coping thoughts on your own, and this takes some time each day. Without this sort of practice, this procedure may not be that helpful.

Client: It does sound interesting. Have you used it a lot?

The counselor indicates some information about the strategy based on the counselor's experience and use of it with others.

7. Counselor: I believe I tend to use it, or portions of it, whenever I think people could benefit from learning to manage nervousness and not let stressful situations control them. I know other counselors have used it and found that people with different stresses can benefit from it. It has a lot of potential if you're in a situation where your nervousness is getting the best of you and where you can learn to cope with the stress.

Client: Well, it sounds OK to me. I do like the idea of the relaxation that you mentioned earlier.

The counselor moves on in response 8 to describe another possible strategy, explains what this involves and how it might help Joan manage her nervousness, and relates the use of the procedure to her problem and goal.

8. Counselor: There's also another procedure called desensitization that is a pretty standard one to help a person decrease anxiety about situations (Chapter 21). It is a way to help you desensitize yourself to the stress of your math class.

Client: Well, how exactly does that work—to desensitize yourself to something?

The counselor explains how this strategy helps Joan decrease her nervousness and explains elements, advantages, and risks of this strategy.

9. Counselor: It works on the principle that you can't be relaxed and nervous at the same time. So, after teaching you how to relax, then you imagine situations involving your math class—however, you only imagine a situation when you're relaxed. You practice this way to the point where you can go to your class without feeling all the nervousness you do now. In other words, you become desensitized. Most of this process is something we would do together in these sessions. This might be easier than

something requiring a lot of outside work on your part.

Client: Does that take a long time? I'd like to get over this fast.

The counselor gives Joan some information about the time involved in the desensitization procedure.

10. Counselor: This may take a little longer than the other two procedures. This procedure has helped a great many people decrease their nervousness about specific situations—like taking a test or flying. Of course, keep in mind that any change plan takes some time.

Client: It sounds helpful.

The counselor points out some of the environmental factors involved in these procedures.

11. Counselor: Another thing I should point out is that all of these procedures will require you to practice on your own once or twice a day. Is that possible?

Client: Sure, as long as it's something I can do at home. I don't know. What do you think will help me most?

In response 12, the counselor indicates his or her preferences and provides information about documentation.

12. Counselor: I'd like us to make the decision together. I feel comfortable with all of these things I've mentioned. Also, these procedures have been found to be pretty effective in dealing with the different fears of many people who are concerned about working on their nervousness in situations so it isn't a handicap.

Client: I'm wondering exactly how to decide where to go from here.

In responses 13 and 14, the counselor guides the client's decision about strategies based on client preferences.

13. Counselor: Well, maybe we could review the action plans I've mentioned and go over them, to see which one you feel might work best for you, at least now. We can always change at a later point. How does that sound?

Client: Good. There's a lot of information and I don't know if I remember everything you mentioned.

14. Counselor: OK. Well, we talked first about relaxation as something you could learn here and then do on your own to help you control the feelings and physical sensations of nervousness. Then we discussed desensitization, which involves using relaxation first but also involves having you imagine the scenes related to your math class. This procedure is something we would work on together, although the re-

laxation requires daily practice from you. The third plan, stress inoculation, involves giving you some skills to use to cope with the stressful situations in your math class. What do you think would be most helpful to you at this point?

Client: I think maybe the relaxation might help since I can practice with it on my own.

Learning Activity: Strategy Selection

Listed here are some examples of counselor leads used with the clients Ms. Weare and Mr. Phyle. These leads are representative of the five criteria of strategy selection: counselor characteristics and preferences, documentation about strategies, the nature of the client's problem and goal, client characteristics and preferences, and environmental factors. These leads are not in any particular order. Read each lead and then take some paper to identify in writing which of the five criteria of strategy selection is represented by each lead. Feedback can be found on p. 259.

1. "Ms. Weare, you've indicated that you're ready to do something other than continuing to help Freddie dress every morning. I'd like to suggest several things you might try to make the situation better. These are all action plans I've used with other parents, and I feel they work quite well based on my experience with them."

2. "Ms. Weare, one of the ways that contracting might help you and Freddie is that each of you agree to do certain things—sort of as an exchange. For instance, Freddie might agree to dress himself in the morning while you agree to sit down and talk to him at night or watch TV with him. This way you don't continue your pattern of helping him every morning but he does get your attention at night."

3. "Contracting has been used effectively with other parents and children as a way to resolve their conflicts and achieve more desirable communication."

4. "We would work out the details of the contract here, but it is something that you and Freddie would need to carry out each day in your home. Of course, one advantage of this is that you are being responsible for giving a solution to this problem, rather than relying on me or someone else."

5. "Mr. Phyle, there are some things we could do to help you improve your relationships with women and reduce your anxiety about relating to women. One thing that might help is to talk over all the situations about this that upset you or make you nervous. Starting with something that is pretty easy to handle, we might practice how you would want to respond in this situation. Then, when you're actually in the situation, you will feel more comfortable and adequate with your approach."

6. "We have found that practicing the way someone wants to respond in difficult situations—first with the help of someone like me, then gradually on your own—will help you respond when you're actually in the situation. We know this plan has worked in other instances like this."

7. "There is another way we could approach this. It involves having you learn to relax while you imagine yourself in these difficult situations. Of course this means that you would need to imagine a situation pretty vividly."

8. "The idea behind this approach is that learning to relax while you're imagining what you fear will help you when you're actually in the fearful situation, so you'll feel relaxed with a woman rather than uncomfortable."

9. "I'm comfortable with both of these approaches. From my point of view either one is workable."

10. "Based on the information you have about these plans, which one sounds like it would be most helpful for you?"

Summary

Most clients will present complex problems with a diverse set of counseling goals. This will require a set of interventions and combinations of strategies designed to work with all the major target areas of a person's functioning. Both counselor and client should be active participants in choosing counseling treatment strategies that are appropriate for the client's problem and desired outcomes. The strategies reflected by the overall treatment plan should be sufficient to deal with all the important target areas of change. After the strategies have been selected, the counselor and client will continue to work together to implement the procedures. Some common elements of strategy implementation are considered in the next chapter.

Post Evaluation

Part One

This part of the evaluation corresponds to Objective 1. See if you can write down at least four guidelines that indicate the appropriate timing for introduction of a counseling strategy. Feedback is found after the evaluation.

Part Two

Listed below are some examples of counselor leads associated with strategy selection. The leads are part of your continuing case dialogue with Mr. Brown. Your task, as stated in Objective 2, is to identify accurately, in writing, at least six of the seven leads associated with the five criteria of strategy selection. You may wish to take a sheet of paper to write your responses. Feedback follows the evaluation.

1. Counselor: Mr. Brown, in terms of working on feeling less worried about retirement, from my experience there are several strategies we might use. One is called thought-stopping, another is called stimulus control, and another is cognitive restructuring. Other possibilities include anticipation training and covert self-modeling. I'm sure these names don't mean much to you, but they are procedures I'm comfortable with and have used before. I'd like to give you some information about them to help you determine which ones might be most suitable for you.
   Client: You're right. I don't know what they mean. I'll just go along with your suggestions.
2. Counselor: Well, let me give you some information about them, because I'd like your input. One thing that might interest you is that all of these procedures have been used successfully with other people who have concerns similar to yours.
   Client: You mean you know these procedures have been used for people who are sort of in the same boat I am?
3. Counselor: That's right. These procedures have been used effectively to help people control and modify their thoughts about a situation.
   Client: What exactly is involved?
4. Counselor: I think it would be helpful if I gave you some information about each of these proce-

dures and then you could decide what sounds best for you. The first thing we might work on is helping you to cut down on the negative thoughts you have about retirement, since these are most interfering to you now. One thing we could try is the thought-stopping procedure I mentioned earlier (Chapter 18). It is something I can teach you quickly in one or two sessions and then you can use it on your own to stop yourself from thinking a lot about these negative things. It is a way to stop yourself from constantly ruminating about retiring. If this doesn't sound reasonable to you, we might try something that has a big name—stimulus control (Chapter 23). What happens in this is that we designate a "worry" time and place. When you're in that place—which in your case would *not* be at work—you can let yourself worry —but only for the designated time and in that place. Now it's also possible to use these strategies together. For example, you could have your worry time and place outside of work. And when you're at work you could use thought-stopping to keep these thoughts from interfering with your work projects.
   Client: Neither of those things sounds too hard. I believe I could do both of them.
5. Counselor: Are you saying you feel like you want to do both of them to start with—or would you like to consider other options?
   Client: These two plans sound OK to me. Can you show me how?
6. Counselor: Sure. Maybe before I do that we should make sure that you can use these procedures easily. For example, is there a place you can think of other than your work that you could

use for a worry place, or would that be hard to find?

Client: Well, what about outside? We have a large yard, and sometimes when I sort of want to be alone, I go out there—or else in my shop.

7. Counselor: OK. That's fine. Both of these procedures are things you can learn in our sessions—but use on your own. That's a real advantage for you. It will require some outside practice from you, but when you need to cut off these thoughts on your own, you'll be able to without relying on me.

Feedback: Post Evaluation

Part One

See if you listed at least four of these five cues for effective timing of strategy introduction:

1. Strong relationship
2. Thorough problem definition
3. Specification of counseling goals
4. Indicators of client readiness
5. Collection of baseline measures

Part Two

1. Counselor characteristics and preferences
2. Documentation about strategy
3. Documentation about strategy
4. Nature of client problem and goals
5. Client characteristics and preferences
6. Environmental factors
7. Client preferences, time and advantages of strategies

Suggested Readings

Selection of Counseling Strategies

Egan, G. *The skilled helper: A model for systematic helping and interpersonal relating.* Monterey, Calif.: Brooks/Cole, 1975. Chap. 6, Action programs, 182–232.

Eisenberg, S., & Delaney, D. J. *The counseling process* (2nd ed.). Chicago: Rand McNally, 1977. Chap. 9, Counseling strategies and methods, 145–182.

Goldstein, A. P., & Stein, N. *Prescriptive psychotherapies.* New York: Pergamon Press, 1976. Chap. 1, Introduction, 3–26.

Humphreys, L., & Beiman, I. The application of multiple behavioral techniques to multiple problems of a complex case. *Journal of Behavior Therapy and Experimental Psychiatry,* 1974, 5, 311–315.

Kiesler, D. J. Experimental designs in psychotherapy research. In A. Bergin & S. Garfield (Eds.), *Handbook of psychotherapy and behavior change: An empirical analysis.* New York: John Wiley, 1971.

Chapter 15
Common Elements of Strategy Implementation

The helping strategies presented in the remainder of this book all share four common elements when used and applied with clients: the verbal set for the strategy, modeling of goal behaviors, rehearsal of goal behaviors, and "in vivo" homework and transfer of training. As you will see in the coming chapters, each strategy is explained to the client with a verbal set in which the counselor provides a rationale for the procedure and an overview of it. Most strategies involve some form of modeling, in which the goal behaviors are demonstrated, live or symbolically. And typically the modeling is followed by some form of rehearsal within the interview, often accompanied by coaching and feedback from the helper. Finally, each strategy includes a transfer-of-training element in which the client engages in homework or self-directed practice in the environment. This chapter will describe the major ways in which these elements are used in implementing helping strategies. The four elements are summarized in the Checklist for Strategy Implementation at the end of the chapter.

Objectives

1. Given a simulated client case, describe how you would apply the four elements of strategy implementation with this client.

2. With a partner, demonstrate the four elements of strategy implementation in a skill-building program.

Verbal Set for Strategy

Before implementing any strategy, the counselor should use a verbal setting operation about the procedure. As you may recall from Chapter 7, a setting operation about a treatment strategy consists of a *rationale* for the procedure and a brief *overview* of its components. After providing a set about the strategy, you should seek the client's willingness to try it out. As with any part of the counseling process, clients should never be forced or coerced into using something without their express commitment. The counselor also should explore whether the client's expectations about change are realistic. Goldfried and Davison (1976) suggest that a client with perfectionistic standards may expect too much change too quickly. The counselor may need to point out that the proposed strategies will not produce miracles and that change is achieved gradually, not suddenly.

In the remaining chapters, examples of a verbal set that might be used to explain each particular strategy to a client are modeled. Here is an example of a counselor providing a verbal set about using modeling and role-play as part of a skill-building program for a young girl who would like to talk more honestly with her best friend.

Counselor: Kathy, you've said you'd like to be able to learn to tell your friend Tammy when she has hurt your feelings, but you aren't sure how to do this. I think I can show you a way to talk to Tammy and then you can pretend that I am Tammy and talk to me about how I have hurt your feelings [overview]. I believe if you can pretend I'm your friend and talk to me about this, then later on you will be able to talk to Tammy the way you want to [rationale]. How does this sound to you? [client's willingness].
Client: OK. We pretend in my class sometimes.
Counselor: So would you like for us to go ahead and try this out?
Client: Sure. It's fine with me.

To summarize, there are three things a counselor can explain in giving the client an adequate verbal set about any counseling strategy: a rationale for the strategy, an overview of the strategy, and a confirmation of the client's willingness to use the strategy.

Modeling

Modeling is a procedure by which a person can learn through observing the behavior of another person. In some instances, modeling alone is used as a counseling strategy to help a client acquire responses or extinguish fears (see Chapter 16). In other cases, modeling is a component of a strategy in which the counselor provides demonstrations of the goal behaviors. Models can be live or symbolic. Live models are people: the counselor, a teacher, a friend, or a peer. As Nye (1973) points out, a counselor can be a live model "by demonstrating a desired behavior and arranging optimal conditions for the client to do the same" (p. 381). Symbolic models can be provided through written materials such as manuals or handbooks, films, audio or video tapes, slide tapes, or photographs. Modeling also can take place by having the client imagine someone performing the target behaviors, as is done in covert modeling (see Chapter 17).

Processes Involved in Modeling

Bandura and Jeffery (1973) claim that there are four processes involved in modeling: attention, retention, reproduction, and motivation. *Attention* refers to the activity of the observer in focusing on what is modeled. For example, it might be very difficult for a client to attend to a model when feeling anxious. In such cases, the counselor may have to introduce relaxation procedures (Chapter 20) before modeling can be used. One way the counselor can facilitate client attention is to cue or instruct the client about what to look for before the model is presented.

Retention refers to symbolic or linguistic coding, cognitive organization, or covert rehearsal of what has been modeled or demonstrated. A counselor can enhance the retention processes by sequencing the presentation of the model in a series of brief modeled scenarios. After the model has been presented, a summarization of what has been demonstrated by the counselor or client may also aid retention.

The third process involved in modeling is *reproduction,* which refers to the ability of the observer to reproduce, rehearse, or practice the modeled behavior.

The last process common to all modeling procedures is *motivation*. A counselor can encourage motivation by giving the client a rationale for using modeling. For example, a counselor might explain how the procedure is applied and the benefits the client might derive from its use. Motivation also can be increased if the client successfully performs the modeled behavior. This can be arranged by practice of small, successful steps. These four processes of attention, retention, reproduction, and motivation overlap. For example, client motivation can be enhanced by successful reproduction of the modeled behavior. These processes may be enhanced by the characteristics of the model and by the presentation of the modeling procedure.

Model Characteristics

The characteristics of the model can be important factors contributing to the success of modeling. The model characteristics described in this section represent the ideal. However, it may not be practical or feasible for the counselor to apply all the ideal characteristics, particularly when the counselor has to be the model or when other live models are used. It is perhaps easier to incorporate these model characteristics into symbolic models (see Chapter 16).

Research indicates that the effects of modeling may be enhanced when there is a great deal of similarity between the model and the client (Bandura, 1971a). The model selected should be like the client in age and sex. Also, the prestige of the model and similarity in cultural and ethnic background and racial origin may have important effects for some clients (Cormier & Cormier, 1975).

A coping model is perhaps better than a mastery model (Kazdin, 1973a, 1974a, 1974b; Meichenbaum, 1971). That is, a model who shows some fear or anxiety, makes errors in performance, and shows some degree of struggle or coping while performing the behavior or activity may be less threatening than a model who comes across flawlessly or perfectly. A client may be able to identify more easily with a coping model, or what Marlatt and Perry (1975) refer to as a "slider" model, who displays gradual improvement during a complex series of modeled behaviors. For example, a phobic client may improve more quickly if timid models gradually attain calmness than if they perform fearlessly at once. Model displays should be tuned to the perspective of the clients and not be beyond their reach. Also, models who share concerns similar to those of the client may contribute a great deal to the success of a modeling procedure. Models who share yet overcome handicaps are therapeutically beneficial when seen by clients as having mutual concerns with similar histories (Rosenthal, 1976).

Repeated demonstrations of the same response are often necessary. As Bandura (1976a) indicates, multiple modeling demonstrations show the client how something can be performed best and also that any feared consequences do not occur (p. 250). Multiple demonstrations can be arranged by having a single model repeat the demonstration or by having several different models demonstrate the same activity or response. For example, one model could demonstrate several times how our client Kathy could talk to her friend, or several models could demonstrate this same activity. The multiple models would be portrayed as possessing characteristics and concerns similar to those of the client (Marlatt & Perry, 1975). The use of multiple models also may increase the generalizability and efficacy of modeling. Multiple models may give more cues to the client and can have greater impact than a single model, because clients can draw upon the strengths of each model.

Remember that, in some cases, a counselor may not be able to use multiple models in an interview setting. The selection of particular model characteristics will be dictated by the parameters of the client's problem and goals, and the individual characteristics of the client. Sometimes the client is the best model (see self-as-a-model, Chapter 16).

Presentation of Live Modeling

When using live modeling in the interview, the model first engages in role reversal; that is, the model plays the part of the client while the client plays the part of a significant other person in the client's environment. It is important to instruct the client to portray this person as realistically as possible. This provides an opportunity for the behaviors to be modeled under conditions that closely resemble the client's extratherapeutic environment. At the same time, it enables the model to identify the kind of person who should be portrayed later in the client's practice sequences. When using live modeling, try to remember that the modeling is a suggestion—not a decision for the client. Encourage the client to adapt the modeling to his or her own style.

Here is an example of a live modeling sequence with the counselor modeling the goal behavior for Kathy:

Counselor: We're going to pretend for a bit. I'd like you to pretend to be Tammy. Just be the way she is and tell me what she says about your clothes. I'm going to pretend to be you. Only instead of biting my lip and being quiet like you tell me you are, I'm going to tell her my feelings are hurt. OK. Now you start as Tammy.

Client (as Tammy, in a jeering voice): You know, Kathy, that dress looks funny on you today. Are those clothes yours or are they hand-me-downs from your sister?

Counselor (as Kathy, silent for a moment, starts to bite lip, then stops herself): No, they're mine. Hey, Tammy, what's the big deal about clothes? We only have so much money. . . . I have hurt feelings when you say something about my clothes like that.

Client (as Tammy): Oh, let's forget it. I'm sorry. Can you come over after school today?

After the demonstration, the client can summarize the main points of the modeled presentation. Also, general guidelines or principles that the client should remember during subsequent practice attempts can be reviewed. These guidelines may help the client code the modeled input in a way that facilitates recall. If the client has trouble summarizing or reviewing, additional modeling may be required before practice attempts are initiated. Also, the client should be encouraged to select for practice only those parts of the modeled demonstration that he or she finds comfortable. For example:

Counselor: OK, Kathy, let's talk about our pretending. Did you feel like you acted the way Tammy does?

Client: Yes. I believe she did feel sorry, too. I don't think she wants to be mean.

Counselor: That's probably right. But as long as you don't say anything, she doesn't know how you feel. What did you see me do?

Client: Well, you started to bite your lip. But it looked like you got brave then and told her your feelings were hurt.

Counselor: Do you think you could say something like I did to Tammy?

Client: Sure, I think so.

Counselor: Well, we can try another pretend, only this time I'll be Tammy and you are yourself. If you see that you forget to say something and start to bite your lip, just stop, take your time, and then tell me in your own words that your feelings are hurt.

To summarize, the counselor should implement modeling with the following guidelines in mind:

1. Instruct the client what to look for before the modeled demonstration.
2. Select a model who is similar to the client and who can demonstrate the goal behaviors in a coping manner.
3. Present the modeled demonstration in a sequence of scenarios that minimize stress for the client.
4. Ask the client to summarize or review what he or she saw after the demonstration.

Typically, modeling of goal behaviors will be followed by practice or rehearsal of these responses. Modeling is used as a necessary precondition for rehearsal when the client's behavioral repertory is deficient or defective, and the goal of rehearsal is *response acquisition*. The rationale for this is very simple: if a person wants to do something but doesn't know how, without a modeled demonstration it would be very difficult to practice the desired behavior. Modeling provides the client with some response choices he or she can use during practices of the goal behaviors.

Rehearsal or Practice of Goal Behaviors

Most strategies involve some form of response practice in which the client rehearses the goal behaviors. Usually these rehearsal attempts follow the sequence in which the goal behaviors have been arranged. The actual practice of each response should be very similar to the situations that occur in the client's environment. As Mischel (1971) asserts, "generalization is enhanced to the degree that the stimulus conditions sampled in treatment are similar to those in the life situation in which the new behaviors will be used" (p. 468). To simulate these situations realistically, the practice attempts should include any necessary props and should portray any other people involved with the client as accurately as possible. This portrayal should include acting out the probable response of this person to the client's goal behavior.

Overt and Covert Rehearsal

The actual rehearsal attempts can be covert or overt. A client can rehearse covertly by imagining and reflecting about the desired response. Or, in overt rehearsal, the client can verbalize and act out the desired behaviors in a role-play scene. Both overt and covert rehearsal have some empirical support (McFall & Twentyman, 1973); the choice depends on the timing, the client, and the desired behaviors. When the target response consists of sexual behaviors or acquisition or discrimination of covert responses, covert rehearsal may be more appropriate. With clients who have difficulty generating and maintaining real-life images, overt rehearsal may be more helpful. With many clients, both covert and overt practice can be used. Initially, it may be useful to have the client engage in covert rehearsal, because it is less visible and may decrease the client's concern about being evaluated by the counselor. Gradually, the client can approximate overt rehearsals, first by verbalizing while practicing covertly and then by acting out the situation in a role-play.

Coaching and Induction Aids

Immediately before a goal behavior is rehearsed, it may help to have the client review covertly or aloud what he or she is going to do and say during the practice. Also, the client's fear of "fouling up" may be decreased if the counselor stops to prompt or coach when the client gets stuck. Coaching consists of giving the client instructions about the general principles for performing the desired behavior effectively. Coaching can provide the cues for the person to make discriminations about the appropriate use of the target responses. The counselor can coach by giving verbal suggestions or by flashing cue cards to the client during practice. If a client has repeated difficulty in rehearsing one particular response, it may be necessary to go back to the previous response. In some cases, additional modeling and coaching may be required, or the order of the rehearsed responses may need rearrangement.

Sometimes a client may have difficulty practicing the desired responses unless the practice attempts are supplemented with *induction aids*, performance or supportive aids arranged by the counselor to assist a client in performing a feared or difficult response. Induction aids are safeguards that are introduced temporarily during initial practice attempts to help clients do what they are too frightened to think about or too hesitant to initiate on their own (Bandura, 1976a, p. 250). Bandura describes the use of induction aids as follows: "During the early phases of treatment, therapists use whatever supplementary aids are necessary to initiate behavioral changes. As treatment progresses, however, the supportive aids and practice controls are gradually removed until clients function effectively without assistance" (p. 251).

Examples of some induction aids adapted from Bandura to be used with practice attempts include:

1. practice with the counselor's (or model) assistance
2. verbal or physical guidance, support, or coaching by the counselor
3. repeated practice of only one activity or response
4. use of graduated time intervals for practice, such as a shorter to a longer duration
5. graduated levels of severity, risk, or threat in a practice situation (low risk to high risk)
6. any arrangement of protective practice conditions to reduce the likelihood of feared or undesired consequences (pp. 250–251).

Induction aids are useful to help clients who cannot perform an activity or behavior by themselves or to assist a client through difficult performances. A client should never be coerced to perform a behavior or engage in a specific activity. However, a client's refusal to practice might indicate a need for help in the form of induction aids, and not necessarily a willingness to stop trying (R. W. Jeffery, 1976, p. 304). If the counselor has difficulty thinking of suitable induction aids, she or he should ask the client to recommend induction aids that would help the client to participate, practice, or engage in the desired activity or behavior in either the interview or the natural setting. The counselor and client can use any induction aids that are necessary to initiate behavioral change and to ensure successful performance. The more aids the counselor can use, the greater the probability of success for treatment. The importance of a wide array of induction aids was demonstrated with phobic, incapacitated clients (Bandura, Jeffery, & Wright, 1974). Bandura (1976a) suggests that the number of supportive aids should be a function of the severity of the client's disabilities or deficits.

Client Self-Directed Practice

As the client becomes able to master the activity or behavior with aids, support, and guidance from the counselor, the coaching or induction aids should be *gradually* withdrawn so that the client performs the activities or behaviors unassisted. Dispense with aids and coaching when clients can perform the desired activities. But remember, encourage the client to practice only what is clearly within the client's *immediate capabilities* and what the client is *willing* to do. The counselor can decide when and how to decrease the amount of coaching and induction aids by relying on such indicators as client performance and verbal feedback. Gradually, clients should be able to rehearse a response directing themselves with self-cueing.

Criteria for Effective Practice

One response in the sequence should be covered adequately before moving on to the next task. The counselor can use three criteria proposed by Lazarus (1966) to determine when a practice attempt has been rehearsed satisfactorily:

1. the client is able to enact the response without feeling anxious
2. the client's general demeanor supports the client's words
3. the client's words and actions would seem

fair and reasonable to an objective onlooker (p. 210).

Also, as Goldfried and Davison (1976) suggest, the client should take an active role in deciding when a scene has been rehearsed sufficiently (p. 147).

In the following dialogue, Kathy and the counselor are starting the practice attempts of the first response on their ordered list:

Counselor: Kathy, let's try another pretending. This time you just be yourself and I'll pretend to be Tammy. Let's just be walking home from school together. Nothing touchy has come up. Now can you tell me what you think you could say if I said something to hurt your feelings—like about your clothes? [review of target response].

Client: Well, I'd think I could just say—"Tammy, I don't think my clothes should matter. But when you say that they do, my feelings are hurt."

Counselor: That's great. I think it would help if you could just go over that for a few minutes using your imagination. Just pretend Tammy makes a remark about your clothes and imagine telling her your feelings are hurt. Then imagine what she would say to you [covert rehearsal].

(Pause)

Counselor: OK, tell me what happened in your imagination.

Client: Well, it was after school. She brought up the Girl Scout banquet and told me she thought I should borrow her dress since our troop decided not to wear our uniforms. I told her I had a dress I wanted to wear and it bothered me when she said something like that. [Pauses.]

Counselor: And then what happened?

Client: Tammy was surprised. She said she was sorry.

Counselor: OK, let's try this out again. This time I'll be Tammy and you be yourself [overt rehearsal].

Counselor (as Tammy): You know, Kathy, I've been noticing that your clothes look like, well, I mean don't you think you should get a new dress for the banquet—or borrow one of mine?

Client: Tammy, we don't have a lot of money right now for clothes. Besides, I'd rather spend my allowance on my bike [somewhat defensively].

Counselor: Let's stop there. Did you say to Tammy what you really wanted to tell her? [counselor coaching].

Client: No, not really. I left out the part about my hurt feelings, didn't I?

Counselor: Yes. You got off to a good start, but you

did leave it out. Sometimes you can remember that part by the words *I feel,* like "I feel hurt or upset when you talk about my clothes." Let's go over it again [counselor coaching and repeated practice of same response].

After several successful practices, the counselor would encourage Kathy to practice the scene without any assistance from the counselor. Then practice would begin with the next response. The rehearsal attempts would continue until each response in the sequence had been completed satisfactorily. At this point, Kathy should be able to demonstrate the desired behaviors in appropriate ways, and any anxiety that was present should be decreased. However, the rehearsal efforts may be of limited value unless accompanied by some form of feedback or analysis of performance.

Feedback

Feedback is a way to observe and evaluate oneself and one's behavior and, under the right circumstances, to initiate corrective action (Melnick, 1973). Feedback that follows rehearsal provides a basis for recognizing successful performance and for recognizing and correcting any problems encountered during practice (Geis & Chapman, 1971, p. 40). Feedback should be designed to help the client improve performance and to recognize desirable and undesirable aspects of her or his rehearsal. For feedback to have a positive effect, it must be used cautiously and with some guidelines. Too much feedback, particularly if it comes from an external source, can be threatening or punishing. Thomas (1977) summarizes the role of feedback in a behavior-change program as follows: "The problem with feedback, then, is that while it generally informs the recipient and sometimes changes his behavior favorably, its behavioral function is uncertain" (p. 95).

According to McKeachie (1976), feedback is most likely to be facilitative if three conditions are met:

1. the person receiving the feedback is motivated to improve

2. the feedback provides an adequate, but not an excessive, dose of information
3. the feedback helps the person to identify or implement other response alternatives (p. 824).

The extent to which these conditions of effective feedback are met will depend upon the type, timing, and amount of feedback used in conjunction with a client's practice sessions.

The following three guidelines can be used to apply feedback in conjunction with a practice effort.

1. Give the client the first opportunity to assess his or her own performance. As Rose (1973) points out, if the client is responsible for a great deal of the feedback, this sensitizes the client to his or her behavior and helps the client to monitor performance between sessions.

2. Verbal assessment (by either the counselor or the client) should be supplemented with a periodic objective assessment, such as a playback of a video or audio tape. Initially a taped playback may seem threatening to a client. But as a client becomes accustomed to being on tape, the playback will not be viewed with apprehension. At first, the counselor and client can go over the playback together. Eventually, the client should be able to take the tape home and evaluate progress alone. The advantage of the taped feedback is that it allows the client to see or hear objective evidence of successive rehearsals with greater refinement of the desired skills. Also, the knowledge of being taped may itself bring about change by activating the client's self-monitoring system (Melnick & Stocker, 1977). If it is impossible to tape record any rehearsal sessions, a substitute playback using role reversal can be used. In this method, the counselor takes the part of the client and attempts to mirror exactly the way in which the client completed the previous rehearsal attempt. This may be more accurate than verbal analysis, which is subject to more distortions and biases.

3. Verbal assessment by the counselor should contain encouragement for some part of the client's practice attempt and some suggestions for how the client might improve or do something differently. Krumboltz and Thoresen

(1976) suggest the use of Homme's "sandwiching" technique for counselor feedback. In this technique, the first part (a slice of bread) is a positive stroke, followed by a suggestion or a criticism (the filling), followed by another positive stroke (the other slice of bread). It is important to give some positive feedback for *each* rehearsal attempt. Don't wait for a perfect performance before giving encouragement. Each successive attempt should be reinforced by the counselor. Gradually, the counselor can reduce the amount of praise given and help clients learn to reinforce themselves for successes. This will help clients learn how to praise themselves after a rehearsal effort. Clients are usually able to do this after a sufficient amount of modeling or coaching has provided a basis for discriminating improved performance.

Here is an example of the counselor and Kathy using feedback after a practice attempt.

Counselor: OK, Kathy, let's stop for a minute. What do you think just happened in our practice?
Client: Well, I did tell Tammy my feelings were hurt. It wasn't as hard as I thought. Uh, well, it's harder to talk to her than to you.
Counselor: So maybe you think a little more practice might be needed. Would you like to listen to the way we sound on this tape?
Client (giggles): Sure.
(Tape is turned on and replayed. Immediately after Kathy has responded with the desired behavior, counselor adds feedback.)
Counselor: Right there, Kathy. I can play this part back again. Notice how you just told Tammy your feelings were hurt—you didn't hem and haw around [stroke]. You may want to speak up a little the next time—hear how soft your voice is [suggestion]. That was a good effort [stroke].
Client: Yeah, I didn't realize I talked softly.
Counselor: You don't seem to usually. Perhaps it was because you're learning something new. What did you hear on the tape that you liked about the way you handled the situation? [cueing Kathy for self-reinforcement].
Client: Well, I liked saying "Tammy, I have hurt feelings." As my older brother says, "Tell it like it is."
Counselor: Yes, you were being honest and yet you were doing it in a way that was not putting down your friend either.

To summarize, rehearsal or practice of the goal behaviors involves the following steps:

1. a review of the target responses to practice
2. covert and/or overt rehearsal attempts of sequenced responses
3. counselor coaching and induction aids during initial practice attempts
4. reduction of coaching and induction aids
5. client self-directed practice of response
6. adequate practice of one response before moving on to another
7. counselor and client feedback, verbal and taped

After the client is able to demonstrate the goal behaviors during practice attempts in the interview, then "in vivo" practice opportunities can be arranged. Typically these take the form of homework tasks that make up a transfer-of-training program.

Homework and Transfer of Training

Facilitating the transfer of behavior from the counseling or training session to the "natural" environment should be an integral part of the helping process. Generalization of desired changes can be achieved by homework assignments that are part of a transfer-of-training program. Homework experiences are arranged by tailoring a transfer-of-training program for each client. In an adequate program, the client's new skills are used first in low-risk situations in the client's natural environment or in any situation in which the client will probably experience success or favorable outcomes. Gradually, the client extends the application of the skills to natural situations that are more unpredictable and involve a greater threat. The particular homework developed and assigned will vary with each client and with the client's desired goal. If the client is learning to express feelings, then the homework would be structured to assist the client in that goal. For a very thorough description of homework activities, the reader is referred to Shelton and Ackerman's (1974) *Homework in counseling and psychotherapy*.

Characteristics of Effective Homework

Whatever the homework assignment is, it should be something clients can instigate by themselves that is likely to meet with some success. Initially, the homework should involve a fairly simple task; gradually more complex situations can be added. Each homework assignment should contain a "do" statement and a "quantity" statement (Shelton & Ackerman, 1974). The "do" statement specifies what the client will do or complete, and the quantity statement tells the client how often the task is to be completed. To increase the probability that the client will carry out the assignment accurately, Rose (1973) suggests that self-directed prompts in the form of cue cards be made up for the client. The client can go over the cue cards just before carrying out the assignment. Both the type of homework assignment and the prompts on the cue cards should be developed in conjunction with the client. A client who has had a major role in selecting and developing the assignment is more likely to complete the homework. In lieu of using cue cards, sometimes the counselor or another person can accompany the client on a homework assignment. Ascher and Phillips (1975) suggest that a trained aide who functions in this capacity can model for the client and also can reinforce the client's progress in the "in vivo" setting.

Self-Monitoring of Written Homework

The client should be encouraged to self-monitor certain aspects of the completed homework. Specifically, the client should record both the use or application of the strategy and some measure of the goal behaviors. Goldfried and Davison (1976) suggest that giving the client a daily log sheet to monitor homework completion has certain demand characteristics that may facilitate the client's written observations (p. 150). Log sheets can be developed that enable the client to gather data germane to each counseling strategy. For example, a log sheet used to record homework associated with muscle relaxation is presented in Chapter 20, and one used for cognitive restructuring can be found in Chapter 19. The data the client collects during homework completion may be used as part of evaluating the overall effects of the counseling strategy, as described in Chapter 13. The counselor also should arrange for an interview or a telephone follow-up after the client has completed some part of the homework.

Here is an example of a homework assignment the counselor developed with Kathy.

Purpose: to help Kathy think about expressing her feelings to Tammy outside the counselor's office (task 1, a simple situation that Kathy can initiate).

Instructions:

"Quantity" statement:
1. Each day (1) before school, (2) after school, and (3) before bed take out the card that says FEELINGS on it (cue card, see Figure 15-1).

"Do" statement:
2. Read over the card. Then sit back, close your eyes, and think about telling Tammy about your hurt feelings.

Self-monitoring statement:
3. Each time you are able to do this and feel OK with it, check this on the "Daily Log" (see Figure 15-1).

Follow-up:
4. At the end of the week, bring the log in to the counselor.

"In vivo" homework in the form of client self-directed practice or independent mastery results in more generalization of behavioral changes, more evidence of coping skills, and enhancement of self-competence levels (Bandura, Jeffery, & Gajdos, 1975). Self-competence or confidence is enhanced more by independent practice, because a client is more likely to attribute the success to his or her own capabilities than to external aids or supports (Bandura et al., p. 142).

Kathy's Cue Card					

Kathy's Cue Card

```
            FEELINGS
"Tammy,  I   feel   hurt
when . . ."
```

Kathy's Homework Log

DAILY LOG					
Times	Mon	Tue	Wed	Thur	Fri
Before school					
During school					
After school					

Figure 15-1. Homework Cue Card and Log

Model Dialogue: The Case of Joan

First, the counselor gives Joan a verbal set about the strategies being used.

1. Counselor: I believe today we can start working on some of the skills involved in making a decision. I think there is a way we could go about doing this that you might find helpful. It involves talking about the skills and practicing the skills in some role-plays. It gives you a chance to practice making decisions without having to worry about what happens. As you feel more skillful about making decisions in this way, it will be easier for you to do so on your own. How does this sound to you?

   Client: Pretty good. It sounds like it might be fun. We act out things in my English class.

The counselor gives an overview of how they will proceed.

2. Counselor: Well, what we'll do is go over one situation at a time. We'll work on the first one until you feel comfortable with it and then move on.

   Client: OK.

The counselor introduces both symbolic and live modeling of the first target response and situation, and gives instructions about what to look for.

3. Counselor: Since there are a couple of skills to work on, let's work on one at a time and then we can practice putting all the skills together later on. I believe that it might be a good idea if you read over this book, *Deciding,** before our

*Gelatt, H., Varenhorst, B., & Carey, R. *Deciding.* Princeton, N.J.: College Entrance Examination Board, 1972.

next session. It will give you a good overview of the decision-making skills. Or, if you prefer, you can come in and watch a filmstrip if you'd rather do that. We'll be starting with how you learn to find all the alternatives in a situation, so perhaps you can pay close attention to that area in the book or the filmstrip. Also, we could go over this today. Let's take a decision about how you spend your time. This time why don't you be your friend, Barbara, and I'll be you. Try to look for how many options I can find in this decision. I'll start out. (as Joan) Say, Barbara, what are you planning to do after school today?

Client (as Barbara): Oh, I've got to go to the store for Mom. Want to come along?

4. Counselor (as Joan): Well, that's a possibility. Actually, I don't have anything I really have to do today after school. I've been thinking all day about what I'm going to do.

Client (as Barbara): Well, what else do you need to do?

Counselor (as Joan): Well, I guess I should go home and work on my English theme. If I don't, I'll have to do it all tomorrow night. But it's so nice outside I'd rather either go out with you or just go shopping.

Client (as Barbara): Well, make up your mind.

Counselor (as Joan): Well, I've got three choices —go with you, go shopping alone, or go home and do my English theme. Of course, those are all things I usually do. I also could go play tennis, go down and watch my little brother's baseball game, stay after school and work on the newspaper, or go see that movie the French Club is showing.

Client (as Barbara): You never usually do those things.

Counselor (as Joan): I know, but I'm trying to think of all my possible options.

Client (as Barbara): Well, why stay after school anyway? If you're going to do that you might as well go home and work on your English theme—that's the safest thing to do.

Counselor (as Joan): Yeah, but I'm not concerned right now about whether or not my choices are good or bad. I'm just trying to think of all my possible choices.

The counselor stops live modeling and coaches Joan on a way to generate different alternatives in a situation.

5. Counselor: OK, Joan, let's stop here. What I was trying to do was to come up with all the ways I could spend my free time that day, if I were you. The idea of generating options is like brainstorming—the more ideas, the better. And you're only trying to *find* options right now, not to evaluate them.

The counselor asks Joan to review what she saw during the modeled demonstration.

6. Counselor: What did you notice about what went on in this role-play?

Client: Well, at first you sounded just like me —doing what is easy or necessary. I usually would either just let Barbara talk me into going with her, or I would probably study. When you started listing all those other ideas it made me realize how automatic my decisions really are.

The counselor asks Joan to review what she is going to try to do during her practice of this situation.

7. Counselor: OK, let's switch roles now. This time let's give you a chance to practice this for yourself. You be yourself and I'll be Barbara. Could you briefly review what it is you're going to try to do during the practice?

Client: Well, I'm not going to make a snap decision. I'm going to hold out and try to come up with as many options as possible. Also, I'm not going to worry whether the ideas sound good or bad.

The counselor asks Joan to practice the scene covertly at first.

8. Counselor: OK, that's great. Sounds like you've got this well in mind. You know I think before we practice this in a role-play, it might be helpful if you went over this situation first in your imagination. Just put yourself in the situation and rehearse thinking about all your options. Do you understand?

Client: Yeah. How long should I do this?

9. Counselor: Spend as much time as you like.

Client: OK. (Closes eyes, pauses for several minutes.)

The counselor cues Joan to report what went on during covert rehearsal.

10. Counselor: Now, tell me what happened.

Client: Well, I didn't tell Barbara right away I'd go with her. I could feel myself holding out longer. But it was still hard to think of some things I don't usually do after school. I did think of going to the library and reading some magazines.

The counselor initiates overt practice with audio-tape recording.

11. Counselor: Well, let's try this in a role-play practice. If it's OK with you, I'll audio-tape this and then we can both listen to a playback.

Client: That's fine. I've never heard myself on tape before so it will be a surprise.

12. Counselor: OK, let's begin. I'll be Barbara and you be yourself now. (as Barbara) Hey, Joan, want to go to the store with me after school?

Client: Well, I'm not sure. I was thinking I should go home and study.

Counselor (as Barbara): Do you have a big test?

Client: No, I just didn't want to get behind. You know though, Barbara, have you ever felt like doing something different?

Counselor (as Barbara): What do you mean?

Client: Well, I was thinking I usually just make snap judgments like this. I usually either go with you or go study. I was trying to think of something different to do.

(Note the counselor's use of the friend's possible response next.)

Counselor (as Barbara): Don't you like to go places with me?

Client: Sure I do. But I was even trying to think of some things we could do together that we don't usually do.

Counselor (as Barbara): Like what?

Client: I'm not sure. Can you think of anything?

Joan has just gotten "stuck" in trying to get her friend to think of options. Counselor stops and asks Joan to report what happened.

13. Counselor (stops): What did you just do there?

Client: I guess I sort of tried to get you to come up with the ideas.

The counselor coaches Joan and initiates overt practice again.

14. Counselor: Right. And I remember you said earlier that you haven't always been happy with

having Barbara make the decisions. Let's pick up there again. (as Barbara) Well, Joan, what kinds of things could we do together?

Client: Well, we could go to the library and read magazines. Or maybe go over to the Art Museum.

Counselor (as Barbara): That's sort of neat.

Client: Or we could go down to the record shop and get a new record.

Counselor (as Barbara): You know that sounds like fun. I guess we just usually do the same things. Maybe it would be fun to try something different.

The counselor asks Joan to give herself feedback.

15. Counselor: OK, let's stop here, Joan. What do you think about what just happened?

Client: Well, it seemed to go better than when I tried to imagine it. I realize I did sort of do my same old trick when you stopped me. After I realized it was up to me, it didn't seem too hard to think of some ideas.

The counselor gives verbal feedback. Note use of "sandwiching"—positive feedback, followed by suggestion, followed by positive feedback. Then the counselor initiates playback feedback.

16. Counselor: You know you were able to come up with three good ideas of things that you and Barbara don't usually do together. At first you did want to shift the decision to her. That's something to work on. But after that it seemed like you were able to think of some alternatives pretty easily. How about listening to the playback?

Counselor plays back the tape and asks Joan to evaluate herself from the playback.

17. Counselor: What did you notice from the playback that you liked about this practice?

Client: Well, I seemed pretty persistent. I wasn't too put off by your comments and I didn't make a snap judgment.

Note that the counselor reinforces Joan's own positive assessment.

18. Counselor: That's right. Even by the end of our practice you had successfully managed not to make an automatic decision.

The counselor assesses the extent to which the scene has been practiced sufficiently.

19. Counselor: What kinds of feelings did you have during this role-play?

Client: I felt pretty comfortable. It wasn't as hard as I thought.

The counselor points out a way in which the target response might need more work and initiates another practice of the same scene.

20. Counselor: You seemed pretty comfortable. I think the main area where you got bogged down was just getting started. Once you got past that point, you really got going. How would you feel about practicing a similar situation again?

Client: I think that would be good.

During the second practice, the counselor instructs Joan to direct herself during practice (withdraws coaching).

21. Counselor: OK, let's go over it again. This time try to direct yourself. If you feel like you're getting stuck, stop and talk yourself through the problem. I'll keep a low profile now.

After the second practice, the counselor encourages Joan to direct herself and initiates playback feedback.

22. Counselor: OK, let's stop. I think it would be a good idea for you to hear the playback. That practice really went smoothly and you didn't need much help from me.

Client: You know, this is sort of fun. Let's hear the tape.

The counselor plays the tape and points out the way in which Joan was able to get herself out of being "stuck."

23. Counselor: Did you notice the way you stopped and got yourself back on the track?

Client: Yeah. I also was able to come up with more ideas that time.

The counselor initiates possible "in vivo" homework.

24. Counselor: Right. I'm wondering if this situation is something that you could initiate with Barbara this week?

Client: Sure. We do a lot of things together after school at least a couple of days a week.

25. Counselor: OK, I'd like to give you a homework assignment. It will be very similar to what we did today, only you'll be carrying it out with Barbara. How does that sound to you?

Client: OK. What exactly will I do?

The counselor gives instructions about homework. Note that Joan has the responsibility for initiating the homework situation.

26. Counselor: Well, I'd like you to initiate a situation with Barbara where you try to discuss different ways you could spend your time. Don't worry about actually deciding what to do. Your main goal is to come up with as many alternatives as possible—let's say at least three different options. Does that sound reasonable to you?

Client: Sure. We did that today.

Counselor specifies a "do" and a "quantity" statement for homework.

27. Counselor: Right. I'll write this down for you on this card—"To initiate a conversation with Bar-

bara in which I identify at least three different ways we could spend our after-school time together."

Counselor and client work out cue cards to help Joan carry out the homework successfully.

28. Counselor: Now, maybe we could list some guidelines for you that we discussed today to help you carry out the homework. We'll call them cue cards—just like they use in the movies to help them remember. What cues would help you carry this out?

    Client: Well, the one thing would be for me to come up with some ideas rather than asking Barbara.

29. Counselor: OK, I'll put down here—"I'll find ideas." What else?

    Client: Mm [thinking].

30. Counselor: What about coming up with as many ideas as possible without evaluating them for now.

    Client: Yes. You mean, don't worry if the idea is good or bad.

31. Counselor: Right. So your second cue can be —"Think of many ideas. Don't evaluate now."

The counselor instructs Joan on keeping written self-monitoring data during the week using log sheets.

32. Counselor: OK, Joan. On these daily record sheets here, take a blank sheet for each day of the week. Every time you complete this assignment, make a check. Also, write the number of ideas *you* found during the discussion. Does that seem clear?

    Client: Yes. Do I bring it back?

The counselor initiates a follow-up.

33. Counselor: Yes. Bring it with you next week at this time and we can see how your assignment worked out. Also, feel free to call me and report on your progress, all right? Next week, we'll go over the next situation on our list that we put together.

    Client: OK, I'll probably call or stop in later on this week.

Learning Activity: Strategy Implementation

This activity consists of examples of counselor responses associated with the four components of strategy implementation for the case of Mr. Phyle. Take some paper and identify in writing which of the four components of strategy implementation is represented by each response. Feedback is on p. 274.

1. "Mr. Phyle, there are several things we'll do to-

day to help you find some ways to approach women. First I'll show you some of the ways you might go about doing this, then I'll ask you to practice this with my help. This will help you gradually learn to be able to do what you now fear. How does that sound?"

2. "I'm going to show you some ways that you might initiate a conversation with a woman. Try to look at the way I approach this person and the things I say [demonstration ensues]."

3. "Now I'd like you just to imagine that you are going up to this woman, looking her directly in the eyes, and greeting her."

4. "Here's how we'll proceed. I'll pretend to be this woman and you just will be yourself. You can then practice initiating a conversation with me. Then we'll stop and talk about how this worked out. We'll go over this several times until you feel comfortable with the practice."

5. "This time let's try this role-play again. Remember to look at me when you say hello."

6. "During this week I'd like you to try first to identify three women you would like to be able to approach."

7. "Can you tell me exactly what you saw me do when I showed you some ways to initiate a conversation with a woman?"

8. "When you have finished this assignment, give me a call and we can see how you're doing."

Summary

Most counseling strategies or action plans involve similar components. The use of any strategy should be prefaced by a verbal set about the procedure. Modeling, rehearsal, feedback, and homework tasks are important ingredients in any therapeutic change program. In addition, the four elements described in this chapter are the components used in all skill-building programs. For example, assertion training consists of modeling assertive skills, practicing assertive skills in simulated conditions with feedback, and practicing these responses in the actual environment. In the following chapters which present various treatment strategies, you will discover the importance of these four components for strategy implementation.

Post Evaluation

Part One

Objective 1 asks you to take a simulated client case and describe how you would apply the four common elements of strategy implementation (verbal set, modeling, rehearsal, homework) with this client.

As you may recall with our client, Mr. Brown, one of his desired counseling goals was to be able to initiate social contacts with his boss. Although Mr. Brown had acquired some reasonably useful social skills, he was hesitant to initiate requests with his boss. In other words, his social skills were inhibited in the presence of his boss. Mr. Brown stated that he felt awkward about initiating a social contact with his boss, although he did initiate such contacts with other people apparently quite successfully and without any discomfort. Based on Mr. Brown's desired goal, as well as this description, describe how you would use the four components of strategy implementation to help Mr. Brown demonstrate social skills with his boss.

Part Two

Objective 2 asks you to demonstrate the four components of strategy implementation in a skill-building program. Here's how you might do this:

1. Ask a partner to select a skill or skills he or she would like to learn. The person might wish to learn to give compliments to others, to initiate a conversation with strangers, or to give constructive feedback, for example.
2. Use modeling, rehearsal, and homework to teach the person the skill. Provide a verbal set to the person about this process.
3. Tape your teaching and rate it using the Checklist for Strategy Implementation, or have a consultant sit in and observe you. This checklist can be found at the end of the chapter.

Feedback: Strategy Implementation

1. Verbal set
2. Modeling (instructions)
3. Rehearsal (covert)
4. Verbal set
5. Rehearsal (coaching)
6. Homework (assignment)
7. Modeling (summarization)
8. Homework (follow-up)

Feedback: Post Evaluation

Part One

1. *Verbal set*
   You might explain to Mr. Brown that this strategy will help him practice the skills he needs in approaching his boss in low-threat situations. You can tell him this involves seeing someone else (like yourself) demonstrate these skills and then having him practice them—first in the interview and then actually with the boss. You might emphasize that this method can help him gain confidence in the skills he needs to approach his boss.
2. *Modeling*
   Beginning with the easiest goal behavior (social skill), you or someone else could model this for Mr. Brown, taking his part while he assumes the role of his boss. You would instruct him about what to look for before the demonstration—which would be portrayed in a coping manner. Following the modeled presentation, you would ask Mr. Brown to summarize what he saw.
3. *Rehearsal*
   Beginning with the easiest goal behavior, you would use a role-play to help Mr. Brown practice this. The enactment of this scene should be as similar to Mr. Brown's actual environment as possible, in order to help Mr. Brown see how his behavior might affect others and to give him practice under conditions that will approximate what he will be involved in in outside counseling. You might ask Mr. Brown to practice the response covertly (in his head) at first, especially if he seems nervous about going over it with you. The reason for this is to reduce some of his concern about having you see and evaluate this initial performance. Gradually, though, you would ask Mr. Brown to shift into an overt rehearsal or an actual enactment of the

response. If Mr. Brown has a tendency to get stuck during the scene, you can prompt him or use cue cards. Also, you could go back to the previous scene. Consistent trouble in Mr. Brown's rehearsals may call for more coaching or for some introduction of induction aids such as joint practice. You would make sure that each response was rehearsed satisfactorily before going on to another one. The decision to move on should be made jointly. Mr. Brown should be able to practice the response without feeling anxious and also be able to demonstrate the target response adequately before moving on. After each practice attempt, you should provide feedback that will help Mr. Brown assess his prior performance. First, you may want to give Mr. Brown an opportunity to assess his own practice. Periodically, a taped playback of the practice would be helpful to provide objective feedback. As the counselor, you want to be sure to encourage Mr. Brown for small indications of improvement as well as to give suggestions for the next practice. Gradually, you should encourage Mr. Brown to direct his own practice attempts and to assess and reinforce himself for a successful rehearsal.

4. *Homework*
Finally, you should assign homework to Mr. Brown that will help him practice the target response outside the sessions. The homework, at first, may consist simply of mental rehearsal. Gradually, Mr. Brown might be assigned tasks in which he initiates a simple social contact with his boss, such as going on a coffee break. The nature of the tasks can be changed as Mr. Brown successfully and comfortably completes requisite tasks. Cue cards might be given to Mr. Brown to help him remember any guidelines for carrying out the homework. Mr. Brown should be instructed to observe his performance while carrying out the homework and to monitor his completion of the homework on log sheets. You should follow up the homework assignments with a face-to-face or telephone check-in.

Part Two

Use the Checklist for Strategy Implementation that follows as a guide to assess your teaching of a skill to a partner.

Checklist for Strategy Implementation

Check to see which of the following steps the counselor used.

I. *Verbal set for strategy*
___ 1. Did the counselor provide a rationale to the client about the strategy?
___ 2. Did the counselor provide an overview of the strategy?
___ 3. Did the counselor obtain the client's willingness to try the strategy?

II. *Modeling of goal behaviors*
___ 4. Were instructions about what to look for in the modeled demonstration given to the client?
___ 5. Did the model demonstrate the goal behaviors in a coping manner?
___ 6. Was the modeled demonstration presented in a series of sequential scenarios?
___ 7. Did the client review or summarize the goal behaviors after the modeled demonstration?

III. *Rehearsal of goal behaviors*
___ 8. Did the counselor ask the client to review the target responses before the practice attempts?
___ 9. Did the client engage in:
___ Covert rehearsal
___ Overt rehearsal
___ Both
___ 10. During initial rehearsal attempts, did the counselor provide:
___ Coaching
___ Induction aids
___ Both
___ 11. Was the amount of coaching and the number of induction aids decreased with successive practice attempts?
___ 12. Did the client engage in self-directed practice of each goal behavior?
___ 13. Was each practice attempt covered satisfactorily before moving on to another goal behavior? (Check which criteria were used in this decision.)
___ the decision to move on was a joint one (counselor and client)
___ the client was able to enact the scene without feeling anxious
___ the client was able to demonstrate the target responses, as evidenced by de-

meanor and words

___ the client's words and actions during the scene would seem realistic to an objective onlooker

___ 14. Did the counselor and client go over or arrange for a taped playback of the rehearsal?

___ 15. Did the counselor provide feedback to the client about the rehearsal? (Check if the counselor's feedback included these elements.)

___ counselor's feedback contained a positive reinforcer statement, a suggestion for improvement, and another positive reinforcer

___ counselor encouraged each successive rehearsal attempt

IV. *Homework and transfer of training*

___ 16. After successful practices in the interview, did the counselor assign rehearsal homework in the client's environment?

___ 17. Did the homework assignment include (check any that apply):

___ situations the client easily could initiate

___ graduated tasks in which the client could gradually demonstrate the target response

___ a "do" statement for the client

___ a "quantity" statement for the client

___ 18. Was the client given self- or other-directed assistance in carrying out the homework through:

___ written cue cards

___ a trained counselor's aide

___ 19. Did the counselor instruct the client to make written self-recordings of both the strategy (homework) and the goal behaviors?

___ 20. Did the counselor arrange for a face-to-face or telephone follow-up after the client's completion of some of the homework?

Suggested Readings

Verbal Set for Treatment Strategies

Coe, W. C., & Buckner, L. G. Expectation, hypnosis, and suggestion methods. In F. H. Kanfer &

A. P. Goldstein (Eds.), *Helping people change*. New York: Pergamon Press, 1975.

Modeling

Bandura, A., & Jeffery, R. W. Role of symbolic coding and rehearsal processes in observational learning. *Journal of Personality and Social Psychology*, 1973, 26, 122–130.

Kazdin, A. E. Covert modeling, model similarity, and reduction of avoidance behavior. *Behavior Therapy*, 1974, 5, 325–340.

Kazdin, A. E. The effect of model identity and fear-relevant similarity on covert modeling. *Behavior Therapy*, 1974, 5, 624–635.

Marlatt, G. A., & Perry, M. A. Modeling methods. In F. H. Kanfer & A. P. Goldstein (Eds.), *Helping people change*. New York: Pergamon Press, 1975.

Rehearsal

Flowers, J. V. Simulation and role playing methods. In F. H. Kanfer & A. P. Goldstein (Eds.), *Helping people change*. New York: Pergamon Press, 1975.

Goldfried, M. R., & Davison, G. C. *Clinical behavior therapy*. New York: Holt, Rinehart & Winston, 1976. Chap. 7, Behavior rehearsal, 136–157.

McFall, R., & Twentyman, C. Four experiments on the relative contributions of rehearsal, modeling, and coaching to assertion training. *Journal of Abnormal Psychology*, 1973, 81, 199–218.

Melnick, J., & Stocker, R. An experimental analysis of the behavioral rehearsal with feedback technique in assertiveness training. *Behavior Therapy*, 1977, 8, 222–228.

Homework and Transfer of Training

Bandura, A.; Jeffery, R. W., & Gajdos, E. Generalizing change through participant modeling with self-directed mastery. *Behavior Research and Therapy*, 1975, 13, 141–152.

Shelton, J. L., & Ackerman, J. M. *Homework in counseling and psychotherapy*. Springfield, Ill.: Charles C Thomas, 1974.

Chapter 16

Symbolic Modeling, Self-as-a-Model, and Participant Modeling

Picture the following series of events. A young girl is asked what she wants to be when she grows up. Her reply: "A doctor, just like my mom." Think of a child who points a toy gun and goes "bang, bang" and says "You're dead" after watching a police program on television. Think of people flocking to stores to buy clothes that reflect the "outdoor" or "leisure look," which has been described and featured in some magazines as the "L. L. Bean look." All these events are examples of a process called imitation, copying, mimicry, vicarious learning, identification, observational learning, or modeling. Marlatt and Perry (1975) define modeling as "the process of observational learning in which the behavior of one individual or group, the model, acts as a stimulus for the thoughts, attitudes, or behavior of another individual who observes the model's performance" (p. 117).

There are several ways people can learn through modeling. A person can acquire new behaviors from live or symbolic modeling. Modeling can help a person perform an already acquired behavior in more appropriate ways or at more desirable times. Modeling also can extinguish client fears. Modeling procedures have been used to help clients acquire social skills, modify verbal behavior, acquire emotional responses, modify study behaviors, modify phobic responses, and treat drug addiction (Marlatt & Perry, 1975). According to Rachman (1972), the clinical significance of modeling lies

in the strength of the procedure to eliminate fearful and undesired behavior and to promote acquisition of desired responses (p. 393).

In this chapter, we present three modeling procedures: symbolic modeling, self-as-a-model, and participant modeling. The steps we present for each procedure should be viewed only as guidelines for application. The creative variation of or departure from a particular procedure is a decision based on the counselor, the client, the nature of the defined concern or problem, the goals for counseling, and the setting in which the problem behavior occurs.

Objectives

1. Develop and try out a script for one symbolic model with a client or a group of clients of your choice. After completing the script, evaluate it on the Checklist for Developing Symbolic Models at the end of the chapter.
2. Given a case description of a client and a counseling goal, describe how the five components of the self-as-a-model strategy could be used with this client.
3. Demonstrate at least 13 out of 16 steps of the self-as-a-model strategy in a role-play interview with a client.
4. Describe how you would apply the four components of participant modeling in a simulated client case.

5. Demonstrate at least 14 out of 17 steps associated with participant modeling with a role-play client.

Symbolic Modeling

In symbolic modeling, the model is presented through written materials, audio or video tapes, films, or slide tapes. Symbolic models can be developed for an individual client or can be standardized for a group of clients. For example, M. L. Russell (1974) used cartoon characters as models to teach decision-making skills to children. These characters were presented in a self-contained set of written materials and a cassette audio tape. Counselors may find that developing a standardized model is more cost-effective because it can reach a greater number of clients. For instance, a school counselor who sees many students with deficits in information-seeking skills could develop one tape that could be used by many of these students.

In this section, we present some suggestions for developing self-instructional symbolic-modeling procedures. A self-instructional model contains demonstrations of the target behavior, opportunities for client practice, and feedback. In developing a self-instructional symbolic-modeling procedure, the counselor will have to consider the following elements: the characteristics of the consumers who will use the model; the goal behaviors to be modeled or demonstrated; the media to be used; the content of the script; and the field-testing of the model. These five steps are summarized in the Checklist for Developing Symbolic Models at the end of the chapter.

Characteristics of Consumers

The first consideration in developing the symbolic model is to determine the characteristics of the people for whom the model is designed. For example, the age, sex, cultural practices, racial characteristics, and problem definitions of the people who will use the procedure should be assessed.

The characteristics of the symbolic model should be similar to those of the people for whom the procedure is designed, as described in Chapter 15. The counselor should also consider the degree of variation that may exist in these characteristics among the users of the symbolic model. Including several different people as models (as in multiple models) can make a symbolic model more useful for a variety of clients. In some instances, former clients may serve as appropriate symbolic models on audio and video tapes. For example, Reeder and Kunce (1976) used ex-addict paraprofessional staff and "advanced" residents of a drug-abuse treatment program as the models for their six video-model scenarios. The models in each scenario displayed a coping attitude while performing the various skills required for achieving the goal behaviors associated with one of six problem areas. For example:

> The model was initially shown as being pessimistic and ineffective in the given problem area. The model would then reflect upon his problem and discuss it with a peer or staff member. Following reflection and discussion, the model would try out new problem-solving behaviors. As the scenarios progressed, the model would progressively display more independence in solving problems, becoming less dependent upon the advice of the others [p. 561].

Goal Behaviors to Be Modeled

The goal behavior, or what is to be modeled, should be specified. A counselor can develop a series of symbolic models to focus on different behaviors, or a complicated pattern of behavior can be divided into less complex skills. For instance, Reeder and Kunce (1976) developed scenarios for their video models for six problem areas: accepting help from others, capitalizing on street skills, job interviewing, employer relations, free-time management, and new life-style adjustment.

Regardless of whether one model or a

series of models is developed, the counselor should structure the model around three questions: What behaviors are to be acquired? Should these behaviors or activities be divided into a sequence of less complex skills? How should the sequence of skills be arranged?

Media

In an attempt to help you acquire counseling skills, we have presented written symbolic models throughout the book in the form of modeled examples, practice exercises, and feedback. Any of these modeled examples could be filmed, audio- or video-taped, or presented on slide tape. The choice of the medium will depend on where, with whom, and how symbolic modeling will be used. Written and audio-taped symbolic models can be checked out for the client and used independently in a school, an agency, or at home. Films and video tapes can be checked out and used independently in a school or an agency, but not in home settings. We have found that audio-taped models (cassettes) are economical and extremely versatile. However, in some instances, audio tapes may not be as effective because they are not visual. Written models can serve as a bibliotherapeutic procedure (reading) by portraying a person or situation similar to the client and the desired goal (Nye, 1973). However, a self-instructional written symbolic model differs from traditional bibliotherapy procedures by including additional components of self-directed practice and feedback. In other words, self-instructional symbolic models can be administered by the client without therapist contact (Glasgow & Rosen, 1978).

Content of the Script

Regardless of the medium used to portray the modeled presentation, the counselor should develop a script to reflect the content of the modeling presentations. The script should include five parts: instructions, modeling, practice, feedback, and a summarization.

Instructions. Instructions should be included for each behavior or sequence of behaviors to be demonstrated. Brief but specific and detailed instructions presented before the model will assist the client in identifying the necessary components of the modeled display (McGuire, Thelen, & Amolsch, 1975). Instructions provide a rationale for the modeling and cues to facilitate attention to the model. The instructions also can describe the type of model portrayed, such as "The person you are going to see or hear is similar to yourself."

Modeling. The next part of the script should include a description of the behavior or activity to be modeled and possible dialogues of the model engaging in the goal behavior or activity. This part of the script should present complex patterns of behavior in planned sequences of skills.

Practice. The effects of modeling are likely to be greater when presentation of the modeled behavior is followed by opportunities to practice. In symbolic modeling, there should be opportunities for clients to practice what they have just read, heard, or seen the model do.

Feedback. After the client has been instructed to practice and sufficient time is allowed, feedback in the form of a description of the behavior or activity should be included. The client should be instructed to repeat the modeling and practice portions again if the feedback indicates some trouble spots.

Summarization. At the conclusion of a particular scenario or series, the script should include a summary of what has been modeled and the importance for the client of acquiring these behaviors.

Field-Testing of the Model

It is a good idea to check out the script before you actually construct the symbolic model from it. You can field-test the script with some colleagues or some people from the target or client group. The language, the sequencing, the model, practice time, and feedback should be examined by the potential consumer before the final symbolic model is designated as ready for use. If at all possible, a pilot program should be designed for the initial use of the symbolic model. For example, M. L. Russell and C. E. Thoresen (1976) validated a written symbolic model on decision-making skills for children by comparing the performance of children who completed the workbook (the model) with children who did not (controls). The resulting data enabled the authors to validate the effectiveness of their written model for teaching decision-making skills to children. Data from the field-testing can be used to make any necessary revisions before the finished product is used with a client.

Learning Activity: Symbolic Modeling

You are working with a Caucasian client in her late 20s who is employed as a salesperson in a local department store. The client's goal at this point is to lose 20 pounds. The client has previously attempted to lose weight unsuccessfully and is now seeking your assistance. One approach you believe might help the client is to portray someone like herself who models some weight-reduction procedures. You decide to select an appropriate person as the model and use this person on an audio-taped symbolic model of weight-reduction procedures.

1. Describe the type of model you would select, including age, sex, race, a coping or mastery model, and concerns presented by the model.
2. Develop an outline for a script you would use for the audio-taped model. Include in the script instructions to the client; a description of the model; a brief example of one modeled scenario, perhaps about one weight-reduction procedure; an example of a practice opportunity; feedback about the practice; and a summarization of the script. Feedback follows on p. 281.

Self-as-a-Model

The self-as-a-model procedure uses the client as the model. The procedure as we present it in this chapter has been developed primarily by Hosford. Hosford and de Visser (1974) have described self-modeling as a procedure in which the client sees himself or herself as the model —performing the goal behavior in the desired manner. The client also practices with a tape. Successful practices are rewarded and errors are corrected. Note that this procedure involves not only modeling, but practice and feedback.

Why have the client serve as the model? As we mentioned in Chapter 15, the literature indicates that such model characteristics as prestige, status, age, sex, and ethnic identification have differential influence on clients (Bandura, 1969, 1971a). For some people, observing another person—even one with similar characteristics—may produce negative reactions (McDonald, 1973). Some people may attend and listen better when they see or hear themselves on a tape or in a movie (Hosford, Moss, & Morrell, 1976). For example, when we perform in front of a video camera or a tape-recorder, we have to admit there is a little exhibitionism and "ham" in each of us.

We have extrapolated five steps associated with the self-as-a-model procedure from Hosford and de Visser (1974). These five components, which are illustrated in the Interview Checklist for Self-as-a-Model at the end of the chapter, are:

1. Verbal set about the strategy
2. Recording the desired behavior on tape
3. Editing the tape
4. Demonstrating with the edited tape
5. Homework: client self-observation and practice

Verbal Set

After the client and counselor have reviewed the problem behaviors and the goal behaviors for counseling, the counselor presents a verbal set for the self-as-a-model procedure to the client. The counselor might say something like this:

> "The procedure we are going to use is based on the idea that people learn new habits or skills by observing other people in various situations [rationale]. The way this is done is that people watch other people doing things or they observe a film or tape of people doing things. What we are going to do is vary this procedure a little by having you observe yourself rather than someone else. The way we can do this is to video tape [or audio tape] your desired behavior and then you can see [hear] yourself on the tape performing the behavior. After that, you will practice the behavior that you saw [heard] on the tape and I will give you feedback about your practice performance. I think that seeing yourself perform and practice these behaviors will help you acquire these skills [overview]. How does this sound to you? [client's willingness]."

Of course, this is only one example of the rationale for the self-as-a-model procedure a counselor might use. A counselor could add, "Seeing yourself perform these behaviors will give you confidence in acquiring these skills." This statement emphasizes the cognitive component of the self-as-a-model strategy: by using oneself as the model, one sees oneself coping with a formerly anxiety-arousing or difficult situation.

Recording the Behavior

The desired goal behaviors are recorded on audio or video tape first. For example, one particular client may need to acquire several different assertion skills, such as expression of personal opinions using a firm and strong voice tone, delivery of opinions without errors in speech, and delivery of the assertive message without response latency (within 5 seconds after the other person's message). For this example, the counselor and client might start with voice tone and record the client expressing opinions

to another person in a firm, strong voice. The counselor might have to coach the client so that at least some portion of the taped message reflects this desired response. The tape should be of sufficient duration that the client will later be able to hear himself or herself expressing opinions in a firm voice throughout several verbal exchanges with the other person. The counselor might have to spend a great deal of time staging the recording sessions in order to obtain tapes of the client's goal behavior. A dry run might be helpful before the actual tape is made.

Sometimes the counselor can instruct clients to obtain recordings of their behavior "in vivo." For example, clients who stutter could be instructed to audio-tape their interactions with others during designated times of the week. We also have suggested such recordings to people who felt incompetent in talking with those of the opposite sex. The advantage of "in vivo" recordings is that examples of the client's actual behavior in real-life situations are obtained. However, it is not always possible or desirable to do this, particularly if the client's baseline level of performing the desired skill is very low. Regardless of whether tapes are made "in vivo" or in the session, the recording is usually repeated until a sample of the desired behavior is obtained.

Editing the Tape

Next, the counselor will edit the audio- or video-tape recordings so that the client will see or hear *only* the appropriate or goal behavior. Hosford et al. (1976) recommend that the "inappropriate" behaviors be deleted from the tape, leaving a tape of only the desired responses. The purpose in editing out the inappropriate or undesired behaviors is to provide the client with a positive, or self-enhancing, model. It is analogous to weeding out the dandelions in a garden and leaving the daffodils. In our example, we would edit out portions of the tape when the client did not express opinions in a strong voice and leave in all the times when the client did use a firm voice tone. For the stutterer, the stuttering portions from the audio tape would be deleted so that the edited tape included only portions of conversations in which stuttering did not occur.

Demonstrating with the Edited Tape

After the tape has been edited, the counselor plays it for the client. First, the client is instructed about what to observe on the tape. For our examples of stuttering and assertion training, the counselor might say, "Listen to the tape and notice that, in these conversations you have had, you are able to talk without stuttering," or "Note that you are maintaining eye contact when you are delivering a message to the other person."

After these instructions, the counselor and client play back the tape. If the tape is long, it can be stopped at various points to obtain the client's reaction. At these points, or after the tape playback, it is important for the counselor to give encouragement or positive feedback to the client for demonstrating the desired behavior.

After the tape playback, the client should practice behaviors that were demonstrated on the tape. The counselor can facilitate successful practice by coaching, rewarding successes, and correcting errors. This component of self-as-a-model relies heavily on practice and feedback.

Homework: Client Self-Observation and Practice

The client may benefit more from the self-as-a-model strategy when the edited tape is used in conjunction with practice outside the interview. The counselor can instruct the client to use a self-model audio tape as a homework aid by listening to it daily. (For homework purposes, the use of a video tape may not be practical.) After each daily use of the taped playback, the client should practice the target behavior covertly or overtly. The client could also be instructed to practice the behavior without the tape. Gradually, the client should be instructed to use the desired responses in actual instances outside the interview setting. Also, the client should record the number of practice sessions and the measurement of the goal behaviors in a log sheet. And, as with any homework assignment, the counselor should arrange for a follow-up after the client completes some portion of the homework.

Model Dialogue of Self-as-a-Model Strategy

To assist you in identifying the steps of a self-as-a-model strategy, the following dialogue is presented with our client, Joan. In this dialogue, the strategy is used to help Joan achieve one of her counseling goals described in Chapter 12, increasing her participation in her math class.

Session 1

In response 1, the counselor provides Joan with a verbal set for the self-as-a-model strategy. One part of her participation, that of volunteering answers to questions, will be worked with using this strategy. Note that the counselor's verbal set includes a rationale and a confirmation of the client's willingness to try the strategy.

1. Counselor: One of the things we discussed that is a problem for you now in your class-participation level is that you rarely volunteer answers or make comments during math class. As we talked about before, you feel awkward

doing this and unsure about how to do this in a way that makes you feel confident. One thing we might try that will help you build up your skills for doing this is called "self-as-a-model." It's sort of a fun thing because it involves not only you but also this tape-recorder. It's a way for you to actually hear how you come across when volunteering answers. It can help you do this the way you want to and also can build up your confidence about this. What do you think about trying this?

Client: Well, I've never heard myself on tape too much before. Other than that, it sounds OK.

In response 2, the counselor responds to Joan's concern *about the tape-recorder and initiates a period of using it so it doesn't interfere with the strategy.*

2. Counselor: Sometimes the tape-recorder does take a little time to get used to, so we'll work with it first so you are accustomed to hearing your voice on it. We might spend some time doing that now. (Joan and the counselor spend about 15 minutes recording and playing back their conversation.)

In response 3, the counselor gives Joan an overview *of what is involved in the self-as-a-model strategy.*

3. Counselor: You seem to feel more comfortable with the recorder now. Let me tell you what this involves so you'll have an idea of what to expect. After we work out the way you want to volunteer answers, you'll practice this and we'll tape several practice sessions. Then I'll give you feedback, and we'll use the tape as feedback. We'll take the one practice that really sounds good to you and you can take that and the recorder home, so you can listen to it each day. Does that seem pretty clear?

Client: I think so. I guess the tape is a way for me to find out how I really sound.

In response 4, the counselor emphasizes the cognitive or coping part *of self-as-a-model.*

4. Counselor: That's right. The tape often indicates you can do something better than you think, which is the reason it does help.

Client: I can see that. Just hearing myself a little while ago helped. My voice doesn't sound as squeaky as I thought.

In this case, the client's verbal participation already has been defined by three behaviors. The one behavior, volunteering answers, will be worked with at this point. The other two can be added later. In response 5, the counselor will coach *Joan on ways to perform this skill.*

5. Counselor: OK, Joan, let's talk about what you might do to volunteer answers in a way that you

would feel good about. What comes to your mind about this?

Client: Well, I just hardly ever volunteer in the class now. I just wait until Mr. _____ calls on me. It's not that I don't know the answer, because lots of time I do. I guess I just need to raise my hand and give out the answer. See, usually he'll say, "OK, who has the answer to this problem?" So all I need to do is raise my hand and give the answer, like 25 or 40 or whatever. I don't know why I don't do it. I guess I'm afraid I will sound silly or maybe my voice will sound funny.

In the next response the counselor uses a clarification *to determine Joan's particular concern about this skill.*

6. Counselor: So are you more concerned with the way you sound than with what you have to say?

Client: I think so.

In response 7, the counselor continues to coach *Joan about ways to perform the desired skill, volunteering answers, and also initiates a* trial practice.

7. Counselor: Well, let's try this. Why don't I pretend to be Mr. _____ and then you raise your hand and give me an answer. Just try to speak in a firm voice that I can easily hear. Maybe even take a deep breath at first. OK? (Counselor turns on tape-recorder.) (As Mr. _____) Who has the answer to this problem?

(Joan raises her hand.)

Counselor (as Mr. _____, looks around room, pauses): Joan?

Client (in a pretty audible voice): 25.

After the dry run, the counselor, in responses 8, 9, and 10, gives feedback *(using tape playback) about Joan's performance of the target behavior.*

8. Counselor: OK, let's stop. What did you think about that?

Client: Well, it wasn't really that hard. I took a deep breath.

9. Counselor: Your voice came across pretty clear. Maybe it could be just a little stronger. OK. Let's hear this on tape. (Playback of tape.)

10. Counselor: How do you feel about what you just heard?

Client: Well, I sound fine. I mean my voice didn't squeak.

In response 11, the counselor initiates tape-recordings *of Joan's demonstration of the skill (volunteering answers). This tape will be edited and used as a modeling tape.*

11. Counselor: No, it was pretty strong. Let's do this several times now. Just take a deep breath and speak firmly. (Practice ensues and is recorded.)

In response 12, the counselor explains the tape-editing process; the tape is edited before their next session.

12. Counselor: OK, I'm going to need to go over this tape before we use it for feedback. So maybe that's enough for today. We can get together next week, and I'll have this tape ready by then. Basically, I'm just going to edit it so you can hear the practice examples in which your voice sounded clear and firm. (Before the next session, the counselor erases any portions of the tape in which Joan's answers were inaudible or high-pitched. Only audible, firm, level-pitched answers left on the tape.)

Session 2

After a brief warm-up period in this session, the counselor instructs Joan about what to listen for in the demonstration with the edited tape playback.

1. Counselor: Well, Joan, I've got your tape ready. I'd like to play back the tape. When I do, I'd like you to note how clearly and firmly you are able to give the answers. (Tape is played.)

2. Counselor: What did you think?
   Client: You're right. I guess I don't sound silly, at least not on that tape.

In response 3, the counselor gives positive feedback to Joan about demonstrating the skill.

3. Counselor: You really sounded like you felt very confident about the answers. It was very easy to hear you.
   Client: But will I be able to sound like that in class?

In response 4, the counselor instructs Joan on how to use the tape as daily homework in conjunction with practice. Note the homework assignment consists of both a "do" and a "quantity" statement.

4. Counselor: Yes, and we'll be working on that as our next step. In the meantime, I'd like you to work with this tape during the week. Could you set aside a certain time each day when you could listen to the tape, just like we did today? Then after you listen to the tape, practice again. Imagine Mr. _____ is asking for the answer. Just raise your hand, take a deep breath, and speak firmly. Do you understand how to use this now?
   Client: Yes, just listen to it once a day and then do another round of practice.

In response 5, the counselor asks Joan to record her use of homework on log sheets.

5. Counselor: As you do this, I'd like you to use these log sheets and mark down each time you do this

homework. Also, rate on this five-point scale how comfortable you feel in doing this before and each time you practice.
   Client: That doesn't sound too difficult, I guess.

In response 6, the counselor encourages Joan to reinforce herself for progress and arranges for follow-up on homework at their next session.

6. Counselor: Well, this recording on your log sheet will help you see your progress. You've made a lot of progress, so give yourself a pat on the back after you hear the tape this week. Next week we can talk about how this worked out and then we'll see if we can do the same type of thing in your classes.

The next step would be to obtain some tape-recorded samples of Joan's volunteering in a class situation. A nonthreatening class in which Joan presently does volunteer might be used first, followed by her trying this out in math class. The biggest problem in this step is to arrange for tape-recorded samples in a way that is not embarrassing to Joan in the presence of her classmates.

Learning Activity: Self-as-a-Model

You may recall from the case of Ms. Weare and Freddie that Ms. Weare wanted to eliminate the assistance she gave Freddie in getting ready for school in the morning. One of Ms. Weare's concerns is to find a way to instruct Freddie about the new ground rules—mainly that she will not help him get dressed and will not remind him when the bus is 5 minutes away. Ms. Weare is afraid that, after she delivers her instructions, Freddie will either pout or talk back to her. She is concerned that she will not be able to follow through with her plan or else will not be firm in the way she delivers the ground rules to him.

Describe how you could use the five components of the self-as-a-model strategy to help Ms. Weare accomplish these four things:
1. deliver clear instructions to Freddie
2. talk in a firm voice
3. maintain eye contact while talking
4. avoid talking down, giving in, or changing her original instructions

Feedback follows.

Feedback: Self-as-a-Model

1. *Verbal set about strategy*

   First, you would explain to Ms. Weare how the self-as-a-model procedure could help her (rationale) and what is involved in the procedure (overview). Then, ask Ms. Weare how she feels about trying this procedure (client's willingness).

2. *Recording the desired behavior*

   According to the case description, there are four things Ms. Weare wants to learn to do in delivering her instructions to Freddie. It would be useful to work on one thing at a time, starting with the one subskill that may be easiest for her, such as maintaining eye contact when she talks to Freddie. After each subskill is worked with separately, she can work on doing all four skills in combination.

   The counselor will probably need to coach Ms. Weare on a successful way to perform the skill before recording her demonstration of it. Also, a dry run may be necessary.

   When the counselor believes Ms. Weare can demonstrate the skill at least sometimes, a video or audio recording will be made. (For eye contact, a video tape would be necessary.) Since Ms. Weare presently is not engaging in these behaviors with Freddie, an in-session tape would be more useful than an "in vivo" tape at this point. The counselor can role-play the part of Freddie during the taping. The taping should continue until an adequate sample of each of the four skills is obtained.

3. *Editing the tape*

   After the tape has been recorded, the counselor will edit it. Only inappropriate examples of the skill would be deleted. For example, instances when Ms. Weare looks away would be erased from the tape. The edited tape would consist only of times when she maintains eye contact. A final tape in which she uses all four skills would consist only of times when she was using the desired skills.

4. *Demonstrating with the edited tape*

   After the edited tape is ready, it would be used for demonstration and practice with Ms. Weare. The counselor would instruct Ms. Weare as to what to look for, then play back the tape. The counselor would give positive feedback to Ms. Weare for instances of demonstrating eye contact and the other three skills. After the playback, Ms. Weare would practice the skill and receive feedback from the counselor about the practice performance.

5. *Homework: Client self-observation and practice*

   After Ms. Weare was able to practice the skills with the counselor, she would use the self-modeling tape as homework. Specifically, you would instruct her to listen to or view the tape on her own if possible. Also Ms. Weare could practice the skills—first covertly and later overtly—with Freddie. This practice could occur with or without the tape. A follow-up should be arranged to check on her progress.

Participant Modeling

Participant modeling consists of modeled demonstration, guided practice, and successful experiences (Bandura, 1976a). Participant modeling assumes that a person's successful performance is an effective means of producing change. Bandura, Jeffery, and Gajdos (1975) indicate that participant modeling is an effective way to provide "rapid reality testing, which provides the corrective experiences for change" (p. 141). By performing successfully a formerly difficult or fearful response, a person can achieve potentially enduring changes in behavior. Participant modeling has been used to reduce avoidance behavior and the associated feelings a person has about fearful activities or situations (Bandura, Blanchard, & Ritter, 1969; Bandura, Jeffery, & Gajdos, 1975; Bandura, Jeffery, & Wright, 1974; G. P. Smith & R. E. Coleman, 1977). For example, imagine an outside house painter who develops acrophobia. Participant modeling could be used to help the painter gradually climb "scary" heights by dealing directly with the anxiety associated with being in high places. In participant modeling with phobic clients, successful performance in fearful activities or situations helps the person learn to cope with the feared situation. There is probably nothing more persuasive than successful performance in feared situations (Bandura, 1969).

Another application of participant modeling is with people who have behavioral deficits or who lack such skills as social communication, assertiveness, child management, or physical fitness. Some of these skills might be taught as preventive measures in schools or community agencies. For example, parents can be taught child-management skills by modeling and practicing effective ways of dealing with and communicating with their children.

There are four major components of participant modeling: a verbal set, modeling, guided participation, and successful experiences (homework). These components are essentially the same whether participant modeling is used to reduce fearful avoidance behavior or to increase some behavior or skill. As you can see from the Interview Checklist for Participant Modeling at the end of the chapter, each component includes several parts. We present a description for each component, followed by a hypothetical counselor-client dialogue illustrating the implementation and use of the participant-modeling strategy. We are indebted to the work of Bandura (1969, 1976a) in our description of this strategy.

Verbal Set

Here is an example of a verbal set the counselor might give for participant modeling:

"This procedure has been used to help other people overcome fears or acquire new behaviors [rationale]. There are three primary things we will do. First, you will see some people demonstrating _____. Next, you will practice this with my assistance in the interview. Then we'll arrange for you to do this outside the interview in situations likely to be successful for you. This type of practice will help you perform what now is difficult for you to do [overview]. Are you willing to try this now? [client's willingness]."

Modeling

The modeling component of participant modeling consists of five parts:

1. The goal behaviors, if complex, are divided into a series of subtasks or subskills.
2. The series of subskills is arranged in a hierarchy.
3. Appropriate models are selected.
4. Instructions are given to the client before the modeled demonstration.
5. The model demonstrates each successive subtask with as many repetitions as necessary.

Dividing the Goal Behaviors. Before the counselor (or someone else) models the behavior to be acquired by the client, it should be determined whether the behavior should be divided. Complex patterns of behavior should be divided into subskills or tasks and arranged by small steps or by a graduated series of tasks in a hierarchy. Dividing patterns of behavior and arranging them in order of difficulty may ensure that the client can perform initial behaviors or tasks. This is a very important step in the participant-modeling strategy, because you want the client to experience success in performing what is modeled. Start with a response or a behavior the client can perform.

One example of dividing behaviors involved in competence training into subskills is assertion behaviors. A counselor and client might decide to divide assertive behavior into three categories: (1) eye contact with the person who is receiving the assertive message; (2) delivery of the assertive message without errors in speech; and (3) delivery of the assertive message without latency (time between the end of the other person's message and the beginning of the client's assertive response).

For our acrophobic house painter, the target behavior might be engaging in house-painting at a height of 30 feet off the ground. This response could be divided into subtasks of painting at varying heights. Each task might be elevated by several feet at a time.

Arranging the Subskills or Tasks in a Hierarchy. The counselor and client then arrange the subskills or subtasks in a hierarchy. The first situation in the hierarchy is the least difficult or threatening; other skills or situations of greater complexity or threat follow. Usually, the first behavior or response in the hierarchy is worked with first. After each of the subtasks has been successfully practiced one at a time, the client can practice all the subskills or tasks. With a nonassertive client, the counselor and client may decide it would be most helpful to work on eye contact first, then speech errors, response latency, and finally all these behaviors at once.

In phobic cases, the content and arrangement of each session can be a hierarchical list of feared activities or objects. According to Bandura (1976a), you would first work with the situation that poses the least threat or provokes the least fear for the client. For our acrophobic house painter, we would begin with a situation involving little height and gradually progress to painting at greater heights.

Selecting an Appropriate Model. Before implementing the modeling component, an appropriate model should be selected. At times, it may be most efficient to use the counselor as the model. However, as you may recall from Chapter 15, therapeutic gains may be greater when multiple models are used who are somewhat similar to the client. For example, phobia clinics have successfully employed participant modeling to extinguish phobias by using several formerly phobic clients as the multiple models.

Prior Instructions to the Client. Immediately before the modeled demonstration, to draw the client's attention to the model, the counselor should instruct the client about what will be modeled. The client should be told to note that the model will be engaging in certain responses without experiencing any adverse consequences. With our nonassertive client, the counselor might say something like "Notice the way this person looks at you directly when refusing to type your paper." With the house painter, the counselor might instruct this client, "Look to see how the model moves about the scaffolding easily at a height of 5 feet."

Modeled Demonstrations. In participant modeling, a live model demonstrates one subskill at a time. Often, repeated demonstrations of the same response are necessary. As Bandura (1976a) indicates, multiple modeling demonstrations show the client how something can be performed best and also that any feared consequences do not occur (p. 250). Multiple demonstrations can be arranged by having a single model repeat the demonstration or by having several different models demonstrate the same activity or response. For example, one model could show moving about on the scaffolding without falling several times, or several models could demonstrate this same activity. When it is feasible to use several models, you should do so. Multiple models lend variety to the way the activity is performed and believability to the idea that adverse consequences will not occur.

Guided Participation

After the demonstration of the behavior or activity, the client is provided with opportunities and necessary guidance to perform the modeled behaviors. Guided participation or performance is one of the most important components of learning to cope, to reduce avoidance of fearful situations, and to acquire new behaviors. People must experience success in using what has been modeled. The client's participation in the counseling session should be structured in a nonthreatening manner aimed at "fostering new competencies and confidence, rather than at exposing deficiencies" (Bandura, 1976a, p. 262).

Guided participation consists of the following five steps:

1. client practice of the response or activity with counselor assistance
2. counselor feedback
3. use of various induction aids for initial practice attempts

4. fading of induction aids
5. client self-directed practice

Each of these steps will be described and illustrated.

Client Practice. After the model has demonstrated the activity or behavior, the client is asked to do what has been modeled. The counselor has the client perform each activity or behavior in the hierarchy. The client performs each activity or behavior, starting with the first one in the hierarchy, until he or she can do this skillfully and confidently. It is quite possible that, for an occasional client, there does not need to be a breakdown of the behaviors or activities. For these clients, guided practice of the entire ultimate goal behavior may be sufficient without a series of graduated tasks.

Our nonassertive client would first practice delivering an assertive message using direct eye contact. When the client was able to do this easily, she or he would practice delivering a message using eye contact while concentrating on making as few speech errors as possible. When the client was able to do this successfully, the next practices would focus on decreasing response latency. Finally, the client would practice delivering assertive messages and simultaneously using direct eye contact, limiting speech errors, and shortening the amount of time between others' responses and his or her replies.

Our house painter would practice moving about on a ladder or scaffolding at a low height. Practices would continue at this height until the painter could move about easily and comfortably; then practices at the next height would ensue.

Counselor Feedback. After each client practice attempt, the counselor provides verbal feedback to the client about his or her performance. There are two parts to the feedback: praise or encouragement for successful practice, and suggestions for correcting or modifying errors. For example, after the nonassertive client delivered a message while attempting to use direct eye contact, the counselor might say,

"That time you were able to look at me while you were talking. You looked away after you finished talking, which did reduce the impact of your message. Your eye contact is definitely improving; let's try it again." Or, with the painter, the counselor might say, "You seem comfortable at this height. You were able to go up and down the ladder very easily. Even looking down didn't seem to bother you. That's really terrific."

Use of Induction Aids during Initial Practice Attempts. As you may recall from Chapter 15, induction aids are performance or supportive aids arranged by the counselor to assist a client in performing a feared or difficult response. Many people consider successful performance to be a good way to reduce anxiety. However, most people are just not going to participate in something they dread simply because they are told to do so. For instance, can you think of something you really fear, such as holding a snake, riding in an airplane or a boat, climbing a high mountain, or getting in a car after a severe accident? If so, you probably realize you would be very reluctant to engage in this activity just because at this moment you read the words *do it.* On the other hand, suppose we were to be there and hold the snake first, and hold the snake while you touch it, and then hold its head and tail while you hold the middle, then hold its head while you hold the tail, and so on. You might be more willing to do this or something else you fear under conditions that incorporate some supportive aids.

With our nonassertive client, the counselor might assist the client in initial practice attempts with verbal cues regarding the desired performance. Repeated practice of one type of assertive behavior also could be used. Graduated time intervals might be another feasible aid: the counselor could arrange for the client to practice short intervals of direct eye contact, followed by longer durations.

To help our acrophobic painter reduce fear of heights, an initial induction aid might be joint practice. If actual practice with a ladder or scaffolding is possible, nothing may be more supportive than having the counselor up on the scaffolding with the painter, or standing directly behind or in front of the painter on a ladder. This also functions as a type of protective aid. Of course, this assumes that the counselor is not afraid of or overwhelmed by heights. In our own experience, the one of us who is the nonacrophobic induces the other (no names mentioned) to climb lighthouses, landmarks, hills, and other such "scenic views" by going first and extending a hand. This type of induction aid enables both of us to enjoy the experience together. As a result, the fears of one person have never interfered with the pleasures of the other, because continued practice efforts with some support have reduced the fear level substantially.

Induction aids can be used in the counseling session, but they also should be applied in settings that closely approximate the natural setting. If at all possible, the counselor or a model should accompany the client into the "field," where the client can witness further demonstrations and can participate in the desired settings. For example, teaching assertive behavior to a client in the interview must be supplemented with modeling and guided participation in the natural setting in which the final goal behavior is to occur. It is doubtful that a counselor would be equipped with scaffolds so that the modeled activities at different heights could be practiced by our acrophobic house painter. The counselor could use covert rehearsal instead of live or overt practice. The point we are making is that the counselor who uses live participant-modeling procedures must be prepared to provide aids and supports that help the client practice as closely as possible the desired goal behavior. If this is not possible, the next best alternative is to simulate those activities as closely as possible in the client's real situation. Induction aids can be withdrawn gradually. With our nonassertive client, the use of four induction aids initially might be gradually reduced to three, two, and one. Or, with the painter, a very supportive aid such as joint practice could be replaced by a less supportive aid such as verbal coaching.

Client Self-Directed Practice. At some point, the client should be able to perform the desired activities or responses without any induction aids or assistance. A period of client self-directed practice may reinforce changes in the client's beliefs and self-evaluation and may lead to improved behavioral functioning. Therefore, the counselor should arrange for the client to engage in successful performance of the desired responses independently unassisted. Ideally, client self-directed practice would occur both within the interview and in the client's natural setting. Our nonassertive client would practice the three desired assertion responses unassisted. The house painter would practice moving on the ladder or scaffolding alone. Client self-directed practice is likely to be superior to therapist-directed practice (G. P. Smith & R. E. Coleman, 1977).

In addition to the application of the participant-modeling procedures in the counseling sessions, facilitating the transfer of behavior from the counseling or training session to the natural environment should be an integral part of counseling or training. Generalization of desired changes can be achieved by success or by reinforcing experiences that occur as part of a transfer-of-training program.

Success or Reinforcing Experiences

The last component of the participant-modeling procedure is success or reinforcing experiences. Clients must experience success in using what they are learning. Also, as Bandura (1976a) points out, psychological changes "are unlikely to endure unless they prove effective when put into practice in everyday life" (p. 248). Success experiences are arranged by tailoring a transfer-of-training program for each client. In an adequate transfer-of-training program, the client's new skills are used first in low-risk situations in the client's natural environment or in any situation in which the client will probably experience success or favorable outcomes. Gradually, the client extends the application of the skills to natural situations that are more unpredictable and involve a greater threat.

Bandura (1976a) describes a possible transfer-of-training program for a nonassertive client:

After the clients have perfected their social skills and overcome their timidity, they accompany the therapist on excursions into the field where they witness further demonstrations of how to handle situations calling for assertive action. The therapist then reduces the level of participation to background support and guidance as the clients try their skills in situations likely to produce favorable results. By means of careful selection of encounters of increasing difficulty, the assertion requirements can be adjusted to the clients' momentary capabilities to bolster their sense of confidence. As a final step in the program, the clients are assigned a series of assertive performance tasks to carry out on their own [pp. 262–263].

To summarize, success experiences are arranged through a program that transfers skill acquisition from the interview to the natural setting. This transfer-of-training program involves the following steps:

1. The counselor and client identify situations in the client's environment in which the client desires to perform the target responses.
2. These situations are arranged in a hierarchy, starting with easy, safe situations in which the client is likely to be successful, and ending with more unpredictable and risky situations.
3. The counselor accompanies the client into the environment and works with each situation on the list by modeling and guided participation. Gradually the counselor's level of participation is decreased.
4. The client is given a series of tasks to perform in a self-directed manner.

Bandura (1976a) concludes that participant modeling achieves results, given adequate demonstration, guided practice, and positive experiences. One advantage of participant modeling is that "a broad range of resource persons," such as peers or former clients, can serve as therapeutic models (p. 249). Bandura also points out that participant modeling helps clients to learn new responses under "life-like conditions." As a result, the problems of transfer of learning from the interview to the client's real-life environment are minimized.

Model Dialogue: The Case of Joan

Here is an example of the use of participant modeling with our client, Joan. The participant modeling will be used to help Joan perform the three behaviors in math class that she typically avoids. The rationale for the counselor responses is set off by the italicized comments that precede each counselor response.

Session 1

In the first response, the counselor will provide a verbal set about the strategy, a rationale, and a brief overview of the procedure.
1. Counselor: This procedure has been of help to other people who have trouble in classroom participation. We'll take each of the ways you would like to participate and either I myself or maybe one of your classmates will show you a way to do this, then help you practice it. At first we'll just practice here. Then gradually you'll try this out in your other classes and, of course, finally in your math class. What do you think about this?
   Client: It's OK with me. It's just something I know I can do but I don't because I'm a little nervous.
The counselor will pick up on Joan's previous response and use it to provide an additional rationale for the participant-modeling strategy.
2. Counselor: And nervousness can keep you from doing something you want. This procedure helps you to learn to do something in small steps. As you accomplish each step, your confidence in yourself will increase and your nervousness will decrease.
   Client: I think that will definitely help. Sometimes I just don't believe in myself.
In response 3, the counselor ignores Joan's previous self-effacing comment. The counselor instead begins with the modeling component by reviewing the ways Joan wanted to increase her participation and the hierarchy of these behaviors.
3. Counselor: You know, last week I believe we found some ways that you would like to increase your participation in math class. And I think we arranged these in an order, starting with the one that you thought was easiest for you now, to the one that was hardest for you. Can you recall these things and this order?
   Client: Yes, I believe it was like this: answering

questions, going to the board, and then volunteering answers.

The counselor asks the client if additional activities need to be added or if the hierarchy order needs to be rearranged.

4. Counselor: OK, after thinking about it for a week, have you thought of any other ways you'd like to participate—or do you think this order needs to be rearranged at all?

   Client: Well, one more thing—I would like to be able to work the problems on my own after I ask Mr. _____ for help. That's where I want to begin. He usually takes over and works the problems for me.

In response 5, the counselor will explore a potential model for Joan and obtain Joan's input about this decision.

5. Counselor: OK, one thing we need to do now is to consider who might model and help you with these activities. I can do it, although if you can think of a classmate in math who participates the way you want to, this person could assist you when you try this out in your class. What do you think?

   Client: Is it necessary to have someone in the class with me? If so, I think it would be less obvious if it were someone already in the class.

The counselor picks up on Joan's discomfort about the counselor's presence in her class and suggests another classmate as the model.

6. Counselor: Well, there are ways to get around it, but it would be more helpful if someone could be there in your class, at least initially. I think you would feel more comfortable if this person were another classmate rather than me. If there is someone you could pick who already does a good job of participating, I'd like to talk to this person and have him or her help during our next sessions. So try to think of someone you like and respect and feel comfortable around.

   Client: Well, there's Debbie. She's a friend of mine and she hardly ever gets bothered by answering Mr. _____'s questions or going to the board. I could ask her. She'd probably like to do something like this. She works independently, too, on her math problems.

The counselor provides a rationale for how Joan's friend will be used as the model so that Joan understands how her friend will be involved. Note that Joan's reaction to this is solicited. If Joan were uncomfortable with this, another option would be explored.

7. Counselor: OK, if you could ask her and she agrees, ask her to drop by my office. If that doesn't work out, stop back and we'll think of something else. If Debbie wants to do this, I'll train her to help demonstrate the four ways you'd like to participate. At our session next week, she can start modeling these things for you. How does that sound?

   Client: OK. It might be kind of fun. I've helped her with her English themes before, so now maybe she can help with this.

The counselor encourages the idea of these two friends providing mutual help in the next response.

8. Counselor: That's a good idea. Good friends help each other. Let me know what happens after you talk to Debbie.

After session 1, Joan stopped in to verify that Debbie would be glad to work with them. The counselor then arranged a meeting with Debbie to explain her role in the participant-modeling strategy. Specifically, Debbie practiced modeling the four participation goals Joan had identified. The counselor gave Debbie instructions and feedback so that each behavior was modeled clearly and in a coping manner. The counselor also trained Debbie in ways to assist Joan during the guided-participation phase. Debbie practiced this, with the counselor taking the role of Joan. In these practice attempts, Debbie also practiced using various induction aids that she might use with Joan, such as joint practice, verbal coaching, and graduated time intervals and difficulty of task. Debbie also practiced having the counselor (as Joan) engage in self-directed practice. Classroom simulations of success experiences also were rehearsed so Debbie could learn her role in arranging for actual success experiences with Joan. When Debbie felt comfortable with her part in the strategy, the next session with Joan was scheduled.

Session 2

In response 1, the counselor gives instructions to Joan about what to look for during the modeled demonstration. Note that the counselor also points out the lack of adverse consequences in the modeling situation.

1. Counselor: It's good to see you today, Joan. I have been working with Debbie and she is here today to do some modeling for you. What we'll do first is to work with one thing you mentioned last week, telling Mr. _____ you want to work the problems yourself after you ask him for an explanation. Debbie will demonstrate this first. So I'll play the part of Mr. _____ and Debbie will come up to me and ask me for help. Note that she tells me what she needs explained, then firmly tells Mr. _____ she

wants to try to finish it herself. Notice that this works out well for Debbie—Mr. _____ doesn't jump at her or anything like that. Do you have any questions?

Client: No, I'm ready to begin. (Modeling ensues.)

Debbie (as model): Mr. _____, I would like some explanation about this problem. I need you to explain it again so I can work it out all right.

Counselor (as Mr. _____): OK, well here is the answer . . .

Debbie (as model, interrupts): Well, I'd like to find the answer myself, but I'd like you to explain this formula again.

Counselor (as Mr. _____): OK, well here's how you do this formula . . . .

Debbie (as model): That really helps. Thanks a lot. I can take it from here. (Goes back to seat.)

After the modeling, the counselor asks Joan to react to what she saw.

2. Counselor: What reactions did you have to that, Joan?

Client: Well, it looked fairly easy. I guess when I do ask him for help, I have a tendency just to let him take over. I am not really firm about telling him to let me finish the problem myself.

The counselor picks up on Joan's concern and initiates a second modeled demonstration.

3. Counselor: That's an important part of it—first being able to ask for additional explanation and then being able to let him know you want to apply the information and go back to your seat and try that out. It might be a good idea to have Debbie do this again—see how she initiates finishing the problem so Mr._____ doesn't take over.

Client: OK.

(Second modeled demonstration ensues.)

In response 4, the counselor asks Joan for her opinion about engaging in a practice.

4. Counselor: How ready do you feel now to try this out yourself in a practice here?

Client: I believe I could.

Before the first practice attempt, the counselor will introduce one induction aid, verbal coaching, from Debbie.

5. Counselor: OK. Now I believe one thing that might help you is to have Debbie sort of coach you. For instance, if you get stuck or start to back down, Debbie can step in and give you a cue or a reminder about something you can do. How does that sound?

Client: Fine. That makes it a little easier.

The first practice attempt begins.

6. Counselor: OK, let's begin. Now I'll be Mr. _____ and you get up out of your seat with the problem.

Client: Mr. _____, I don't quite understand this problem.

Counselor (as Mr. _____): Well, let me just give you the answer; you'll have one less problem to do then.

Client: Well, uh, I'm not sure the answer is what I need.

Counselor (as Mr. _____): Well, what do you mean?

Debbie (intervenes to prompt): Joan, you might want to indicate you would prefer to work out the answer yourself, but you do need another explanation of the formula.

Client: Well, I'd like to find the answer myself. I do need another explanation of the formula.

Counselor (as Mr. _____): OK. Well, it goes like this . . . .

Client: OK, thanks.

Debbie: Now be sure you end the conversation there and go back to your seat.

The counselor will assess Joan's reactions to the practice.

7. Counselor: OK, what did you think about that, Joan?

Client: It went pretty well. It *was* a help to have Debbie here. That is a good idea.

In the next response, the counselor provides positive feedback to Debbie and to Joan. Another practice is initiated; this also serves as an induction aid.

8. Counselor: I think she helps, too. You seemed to be able to start the conversation very well. You did need a little help in explaining to him what you wanted and didn't want. Once Debbie cued you, you were able to use her cue very effectively. Perhaps it would be a good idea to try this again. Debbie will only prompt this time if she really needs to.

(Second practice ensues; Debbie's amount of prompting is decreased.)

The counselor explores the idea of a self-directed practice.

9. Counselor: That seemed to go very smoothly. I think you are ready to do this again without any assistance. How does that sound?

Client: I think so, too.

After obtaining an affirmative response from Joan, the counselor asks Debbie to leave the room. Just Debbie's physical presence could be a protective condition for Joan, which is another induction aid, so Debbie leaves to make sure the self-directed practice occurs.

10. Counselor: I'm going to ask Debbie to leave the room so you'll be completely on your own this time.
(Self-directed practice ensues.)
Next the counselor cues Joan to provide herself with feedback about her self-directed practice.
11. Counselor: How did you feel about that practice, Joan?
Client: Well, I realized I was relying a little on Debbie. So I think it was good to do it by myself.
The counselor notes the link between self-directed performance and confidence, and starts to work on "success experiences" outside counseling.
12. Counselor: Right. At first it does help to have someone there. Then it builds your confidence to do it by yourself. At this point, I think we're ready to discuss ways you might actually use this in your class. How does that sound?
Client: Fine. A little scary, but fine.
The counselor introduces the idea of Debbie's assistance as an initial aid in Joan's practice outside the session.
13. Counselor: It's natural to feel a little apprehensive at first, but one thing we will do to help you get started on the right foot is to use Debbie again at first.
Client: Oh, good. How will that work?
In response 14, the counselor identifies a hierarchy of situations in Joan's math class. Joan's first attempts will be assisted by Debbie to ensure success at each step.
14. Counselor: Well, apparently math is the only class where you have difficulty doing this, so we want to work on your using this in math class successfully. Since Debbie is in the class with you, instead of going up to Mr. _____ initially by yourself, first you can go with her. In fact, she could initiate the request for help the first time. The next time you could both go up and you could initiate it. She could prompt you or fill in. Gradually, you would get to the point where you would go up by yourself. But we will take one step at a time.
Client: That really does help. I know the first time it would turn out better if she was there, too.
15. Counselor: Right. Usually in doing anything . new, it helps to start slowly and feel good each step of the way. So maybe Debbie can come in now and we can plan the first step.

Debbie will model and guide Joan in using these responses in their math class. Next, the entire procedure will be repeated to work with the other three responses in Joan's hierarchy.

Learning Activity: Participant Modeling

Instructions: Listed below are 14 examples of counselor leads associated with participant modeling. Take some paper and identify in writing: (1) which of the four participant modeling *components* and (2) which of the associated *steps* are presented in each lead. The first one is completed for you as an example. Feedback follows. You may wish to use the Interview Checklist for Participant Modeling at the end of the chapter as a guide.
Example
1. "Ms. Weare, there are three things involved in this procedure. First, I'll show you a way to talk to Freddie. Next you will practice this with my assistance; then we'll have you try this out with Freddie, first with my help, so you will feel pretty good about the results." The *component* is a verbal *set*; the step is an overview of the strategy.
2. "This is a way to help you learn how and what to say to Freddie—first with me in a safe, practice situation."
3. "You say there are several things you want to do and say to Freddie—first to have him talk to you, then to explain you are not going to remind him of the time in the morning or help him dress."
4. "I will help you learn to express these things first by showing you and then by guiding you through it. First, I'll take your part and show you."
5. "Could you take these behaviors and arrange them in an order? Perhaps let's start with the first things you want to say to Freddie."
6. "As I do this, notice I am speaking in a calm but firm voice."
7. "Let me repeat this demonstration for you."
8. "Why don't you try this yourself now while I take the part of Freddie?"
9. "That was good. You spoke in a firm but calm voice. Also, remember to look at me."
10. "Try this again in another practice."
11. "Now remember, don't raise your voice as you talk. Keep it firm but calm."
12. "This time I believe you can practice this scene entirely on your own."
13. "OK, now let's go over the actual situation in which you want this to happen."
14. "On your first attempt, I will come to your house with you and we can conduct a joint conference with Freddie."

Summary

The three modeling strategies presented in this chapter can be used to help clients acquire new responses or to extinguish fears. These modeling strategies promote learning by providing a model to demonstrate the goal behaviors for the client. The way the model is presented differs slightly among the modeling procedures. Symbolic modeling and self-modeling use media for modeled presentations; participant modeling usually employs a live modeling demonstration. Modeling also can be carried out via the client's imagination. Two therapeutic strategies based on imagery, emotive imagery and covert modeling, are described in the next chapter.

Post Evaluation

Part One

Objective 1 asks you to develop a script for a symbolic model. Your script should contain:

a. examples of the modeled dialogue
b. opportunities for practice
c. feedback
d. summarization

Part Two

In the case of Mr. Brown, one of his concerns was not being able to initiate social contacts with his boss. Describe how you would use the five components of the self-as-a-model procedure to help Mr. Brown initiate social contacts with his boss (Objective 2). The five components are: (1) verbal set, (2) recording the desired behavior, (3) editing the tape, (4) demonstrating with the edited tape, and (5) homework: client self-observation and practice.

Part Three

Objective 3 asks you to demonstrate at least 13 out of 16 steps associated with the self-as-a-model strategy with a role-play interview. Assess yourself or have someone else assess you, using the Interview Checklist for Self-as-a-Model at the end of the chapter.

Feedback: Participant Modeling

The numbers in parentheses indicate items on the Interview Checklist for Participant Modeling at the end of the chapter.

1. Verbal set, overview of strategy (2)
2. Verbal set, rationale (1)
3. Modeling, dividing target behaviors into sub-skills (4)
4. Modeling, selection of model (6)
5. Modeling, arrangement of hierarchy (5)
6. Modeling, instructions (7)
7. Modeling, repeated demonstrations (8)
8. Guided participation, client performs target response (9)
9. Guided participation, counselor feedback (10)
10. Guided participation, use of induction aid —repeated practice (11c)
11. Guided participation, use of induction aid —verbal coaching (11b)
12. Guided participation, client self-directed practice (13)
13. Success experiences, identifying "in vivo" situations (14)
14. Success experiences, modeling and guided practice in "in vivo" environment (16)

Part Four

Objective 4 asks you to describe how you would apply the four components of participant modeling with a hypothetical client case. Using the case of Mr. Brown, describe how you would use the four components of participant modeling (verbal set, modeling, guided practice, and success experiences) to help Mr. Brown acquire verbal and nonverbal skills necessary to initiate social contacts with his boss.

Part Five

Objective 5 asks you to demonstrate 14 out of 17 steps of participant modeling with a role-play client. The client might take the role of someone who is afraid to perform certain responses or activities in certain situations. You can assess yourself, using the Interview Checklist for Participant Modeling at the end of the chapter. Feedback for the Post Evaluation follows.

Feedback: Post Evaluation

Part One

Check the contents of your script outline with item 4 on the Checklist for Developing Symbolic Models at the end of the chapter.

Part Two

1. *Purpose or verbal set*
   First, you explain to Mr. Brown what the self-as-a-model procedure consists of and how it could help him practice and gain confidence in his skills of initiating social contacts with his boss.
2. *Recording of behavior*
   After a practice attempt and some coaching of the behaviors required in initiating a contact, have Mr. Brown practice initiating a social contact with you role-playing the part of his boss. You would record these practices until you have obtained an adequate sample of his behavior.
3. *Editing the tape*
   After the practice tape has been made, you would edit the tape so that any inappropriate behaviors are deleted; only appropriate behaviors are left on the tape.
4. *Demonstrating with the tape*
   The edited tape would be used as the model for Mr. Brown, who would hear it replayed. Following the playback, you might suggest additional practice.
5. *Homework*
   Mr. Brown would arrange to listen to or view the tape daily, followed by role-play or covert (mental) practice of the behaviors involved in initiating social contacts with his boss.

Part Three

Rate your taped interview or have someone else rate you using the Interview Checklist for Self-as-a-Model.

Part Four

Here is a brief description of how you might use participant modeling to help Mr. Brown.

Verbal set
First you would explain to Mr. Brown that the procedure can help him acquire the kinds of skills he will need to initiate social contacts with his boss. Also, you would tell him that the procedure involves modeling, guided practice, and success experiences. You might emphasize that the procedure is based on the idea that change can occur when the desired activities are learned in small steps with successful performance emphasized at each step. This successful performance will help Mr. Brown do what he wants to do but presently avoids.

Modeling
You and Mr. Brown would explore the verbal and nonverbal responses that might be involved in Mr. Brown's approaching his boss and asking him out to lunch, for a drink, and so on. For example, these skills might be divided into: direct eye contact, making a verbal request, speaking without hesitation or errors, and speaking in a firm, strong voice. After specifying all the components of the desired response, these should be arranged in a hierarchy according to order of difficulty for Mr. Brown. If there are any other situations in which he has trouble making a request, these also could be included.

You and Mr. Brown would select the appropriate model—either yourself, an aide, or possibly one of Mr. Brown's colleagues. The model selected would demonstrate the first response in the hierarchy (followed by all the others) to Mr. Brown. Repeated demonstrations of any response may be necessary.

Guided participation
After the modeled demonstration of a response, you would ask Mr. Brown to perform it. His first attempts would be assisted with induction aids administered by you or the model. For example, you might verbally coach him, or start with a short message and gradually increase it. After each practice, you would give Mr. Brown feedback, being sure to encourage his positive performance and make suggestions for improvement. Generally, Mr. Brown would practice each response several times, and the number of induction aids would be reduced gradually. Before moving on to practice a *different* response, Mr. Brown should be able to perform the response in a self-directed manner without your presence or support.

Success experiences
You and Mr. Brown would identify situations in his environment in which he would like to use the skills he has learned. In his case, most of the situations would center around social situations with his boss. For example, some of the situations for Mr. Brown might include visiting his boss in his boss's office; going over to speak to his boss during a break or at lunch; asking his boss to accompany him on a coffee break; asking his boss out for lunch; inviting his boss to his home for dinner or drinks. As you may note, some of these situations involve more risk than others. The situations should be arranged in order, from the least to the most risky. Mr. Brown would work on the least risky situation until he was able to do that easily and successfully before going on. Ideally, it would help to have the counselor or model go along with Mr. Brown to model and guide. If the model was one of his colleagues, this would be possible. If this was not possible, Mr. Brown could telephone the counselor just before his "contact" to rehearse and to receive coaching and encouragement.

Part Five

Use the Interview Checklist for Participant Modeling to assess your performance or to have someone else rate you.

Checklist for Developing Symbolic Models

Instructions: Determine whether the following guidelines have been incorporated into the construction of your symbolic model.

Check if completed:

____ 1. Determine what consumers will use the symbolic-modeling procedure and identify their characteristics.
     ____ Age
     ____ Sex
     ____ Ethnic origin, cultural practices, and/or race
     ____ Coping or mastery model portrayed
     ____ Possesses similar concern or problem as client group or population
____ 2. Goal behaviors to be modeled by client have been enumerated.
____ 3. Medium is selected (for example, written script, audio tape, video tape, film, slide tape).
____ 4. Script includes the following ingredients:
     ____ Instructions
     ____ Modeled dialogue
     ____ Practice
     ____ Written feedback
     ____ Written summarization of what has been modeled, with its importance for client
____ 5. Written script has been field-tested.

Interview Checklist for Self-as-a-Model

Instructions: Indicate with a check which of the following leads were used by the counselor in the interview. Some examples of possible leads are provided in the right column; however, these are only suggestions.

Checklist	*Examples of Counselor Leads*
I. *Verbal Set about Strategy*	
____ 1. Counselor provides rationale about strategy.	"This procedure can help you improve your communication with each other using yourselves. We'll use your own examples of good interactions to help you learn these skills."

Checklist	Examples of Counselor Leads

_____ 2. Counselor provides overview of strategy.

"We'll have you practice communicating with each other and we'll tape-record your interactions. Then I'll edit the tape. You'll have a tape that consists of only positive examples of communication. You'll use the tape for homework and practice."

_____ 3. Counselor checks client's willingness to try strategy.

"How willing would you be to try this process to help you learn these communication skills?"

II. *Recording the Desired Behavior*

_____ 4. Counselor and client break down desired behaviors into subskills.

"There are several things we can work on to improve your communication with each other. One thing we might start with is to help you learn to express your feelings to each other about the other person and his or her behavior."

_____ 5. For each subskill, counselor coaches client as to ways to perform skill successfully.

"The basic idea here is to use an 'I' message, coupled with a word that describes how you feel, such as 'I feel angry' or 'I feel happy,' instead of 'You made me angry.' "

_____ 6. Client performs a dry run of skill, using counselor or tape for feedback.

"Let's try this out in a short role-play. Just try to express a feeling you have right now to your spouse using an 'I' message."

_____ 7. Client demonstrates skill while being recorded on video or audio tape.

_____ a. recording took place in the interview.

"This time while you're practicing this with each other, I'm going to tape it."

_____ b. recording took place in "in vivo" situations outside the session.

"In addition to the tape we made today, I'd like you to tape some of your interactions you have at home with each other."

_____ c. recording is repeated until sample of desired behavior is obtained.

"Remember, start with 'I feel.' Let's try this again."

III. *Editing the Tape*

_____ 8. Counselor edits tape so that a clear picture of client's desired behavior is evident and instances of undesired behavior are deleted.

"I'm going to take the tape we made in our session and the one you made at home and edit them before our next session. Basically, I'm going to edit the tape so only your best interactions are left. This gives you a chance to hear yourselves communicating with each other the way you'd like to."

IV. *Demonstrating with the Edited Tape*

_____ 9. Counselor instructs client about what to look or listen for during tape playback.

"While we play this tape, listen to all the times you were able to say 'I feel _____' to each other."

_____ 10. Counselor initiates playback of edited tape for client observation.

"OK, we'll spend some time now listening to these tapes."

Checklist	Examples of Counselor Leads
_____ 11. Counselor provides positive feedback to client for demonstration of desired behavior on tape.	"The tapes show clearly that you are both able to express your feelings to each other in this constructive way."
_____ 12. Counselor initiates client practice of taped behaviors; successes are rewarded and errors corrected.	"Now that you've heard yourselves do this on the tape, let's work on it here."

V. *Homework: Client Self-Observation and Practice*

_____ 13. Using model tape, counselor assigns homework: _____ a. by asking client to observe or listen to model tape and to practice goal responses overtly or covertly ("do" statement) _____ b. daily for a designated period of time (quantity statement)	"I'd like you to take these tapes home and set aside a period of time each day when you can go over and listen to them. After you listen to the tapes, I'd like you to practice this with each other."
_____ 14. Counselor provides some sort of self-directed prompts such as cue cards.	"To help you remember this, I'll give you this card. The card tells you to start each expression of feeling with 'I feel,' then to stop and listen for the other person's response."
_____ 15. Counselor asks client to record number of practice sessions and to rate performance of goal behaviors on a homework log sheet.	"I'd like you to use these log sheets and mark down each time you practice these skills—with or without the tape. Also, try to rate how well you think you demonstrated these skills at each practice on a 1-to-5 scale, with 1 being very poor and 5 being excellent."
_____ 16. Counselor initiates a face-to-face or telephone follow-up to assess client's use of homework and to provide encouragement.	"Why don't you give me a call in 3 or 4 days and check in?"

Consultant Comments:

Interview Checklist for Participant Modeling

Instructions: Determine which of the following leads were used by the counselor in the interview. Check the leads used.

Checklist	Examples of Counselor Leads
I. *Verbal Set about Strategy* _____ 1. Counselor provides rationale about participant-modeling strategy.	"This procedure has been used with other people who have concerns similar to yours. It is a way to help you overcome your fear of _____ or to help you acquire these skills."

Checklist	Examples of Counselor Leads
_____ 2. Counselor provides brief description of components of participant modeling.	"It involves three things. I'll model what you want to do, you'll practice this with my assistance, and then you'll try this out in situations that at first will be pretty easy for you so you can be successful."
_____ 3. Counselor asks for client's willingness to use strategy.	"Would you be willing to try this now?"

II. *Modeling*

_____ 4. Counselor and client decide whether to divide goal behaviors into a series of subtasks or skills.	"Well, let's see. . . . Right now you hardly ever go out of the house. You say it bothers you even to go out in the yard. Let's see if we can identify different activities in which you would gradually increase the distance away from the house, like going to the front door, going out on the porch, out in the yard, out to the sidewalk, to the neighbor's house, and so on."
_____ 5. If goal behaviors were divided (step 4), these subskills are arranged by counselor and client in a hierarchy according to order of difficulty.	"Perhaps we can take our list and arrange it in an order. Start with the activity that is easiest for you now, such as going to the door. Arrange each activity in order of increasing difficulty."
_____ 6. Counselor and client determine and select appropriate model.	"I could help you learn to do this or we could pick someone whom you know or someone similar to yourself to guide you through this. What are your preferences?"
_____ 7. Counselor provides instructions to client prior to demonstration about what to look for.	"Notice that, when the doorbell rings, I will go to the door calmly and quickly and open it without hesitation. Also notice that, after I go to the door, I'm still calm; nothing has happened to me."
_____ 8. Model demonstrates target response at least once; more demonstrations are repeated if necessary.	"OK, let me show this to you again."
_____ If hierarchy is used, first skill is modeled, followed successively by all others, concluding with demonstration combining all subskills.	"Now that I've done the first scene, next I'll show you stepping out on the porch. Then we'll combine these two scenes."

III. *Guided Participation*

_____ 9. Client is asked to perform target response. If a hierarchy is used, first skill in hierarchy is practiced first, successfully followed by second, third, and so on.	"This time you try going to the door when the doorbell rings. I will assist you as you need help."
_____ 10. After each practice, model or counselor provides feedback consisting of positive feedback and error corrections.	"That was quite smooth. You were able to go to the door quickly. You still hesitated a little once you got there. Try to open the door as soon as you see who is there."

Checklist	Examples of Counselor Leads
_____ 11. Initial practice attempts of each skill by client include a number of induction aids, such as:	"I'm going to assist you in your first few practices."
_____ a. joint practice with model or counselor	"Let's do it together. I will walk with you to the door."
_____ b. verbal and/or physical coaching or guiding by model or counselor	"Let me give you a suggestion here. When you open the door, greet the person there. Find out what the person wants."
_____ c. repeated practice of one subtask until client is ready to move on to another	"Let's work on this a few more times until you feel really comfortable."
_____ d. graduated time intervals for practice (short to long duration)	"This time we'll increase the distance you have to walk to the door. Let's start back in the kitchen."
_____ e. arrangement of protective conditions for practice to reduce likelihood of feared or undesired consequences	"We'll make sure someone else is in the house with you."
_____ f. graduated levels of severity of threat or complexity of situation	"OK, now we've worked with opening the door when a good friend is there. This time let's pretend it's someone you are used to seeing but don't know as a friend, like the person who delivers your mail."
_____ 12. In later practice attempts, number of induction aids is gradually reduced.	"I believe now that you can do this without my giving you so many prompts."
_____ 13. Before moving on, client is able to engage in self-directed practice of all desired responses.	"This time I'm going to leave. I want you to do this by yourself."

IV. _Success Experiences (Homework)_

_____ 14. Counselor and client identify situations in client's environment in which client desires to perform target responses.	"Let's list all the actual times and places where you want to do this."
_____ 15. Situations are arranged in hierarchy from easy with least risk to difficult with greater risk.	"We can arrange these in an order. Put the easiest one first, and follow it by ones that are successively harder or more threatening for you."
_____ 16. Starting with easiest and least risky situation, counselor (or model) and client use live or symbolic modeling and guided practice in client's real-life environment. Steps 4–11 are repeated outside session until gradually counselor (or model) reduces level of assistance.	"Starting with the first situation, we're going to work with this when it actually occurs. At first I'll assist you until you can do it on your own."

Checklist	Examples of Counselor Leads

_____ 17. Client is assigned a series of related tasks to carry out in a self-directed manner.

"Now you're ready to tackle this situation without my help. You have shown both of us you are ready to do this on your own."

Suggested Readings

Symbolic Modeling

Edelstein, B., & Eisler, R. Effects of modeling and modeling with instructions and feedback on the behavioral components of social skills. *Behavior Therapy*, 1976, 7, 382–389.

Glasgow, R., & Rosen, G. Behavioral bibliotherapy: A review of self-help behavior therapy manuals. *Psychological Bulletin*, 1978, 85, 1–23.

Melamed, B., & Siegel, L. Reduction of anxiety in children facing hospitalization and surgery by use of filmed modeling. *Journal of Consulting and Clinical Psychology*, 1975, 43, 511–521.

Prentice, N. The influence of live and symbolic modeling on promoting moral judgment of adolescent delinquents. *Journal of Abnormal Psychology*, 1972, 80, 157–161.

Reeder, C., & Kunce, J. Modeling techniques, drug-abstinence behavior, and heroin addicts: A pilot study. *Journal of Counseling Psychology*, 1976, 23, 560–562.

Self-as-a-Model

Hosford, R. *Counseling techniques: Self-as-a-model film.* Washington, D.C.: American Personnel and Guidance Press, 1974.

Hosford, R., & de Visser, L. *Behavioral approaches to counseling: An introduction.* Washington, D.C.: American Personnel and Guidance Press, 1974. Unit 6, Determining and implementing appropriate counseling strategies, 95–139.

Hosford, R., Moss, C., & Morrell, G. The self-as-a-model technique: Helping prison inmates change. In J. D. Krumboltz & C. E. Thoresen (Eds.), *Counseling methods*. New York: Holt, Rinehart & Winston, 1976.

Participant Modeling

Bandura, A. Effecting change through participant modeling. In J. D. Krumboltz & C. E. Thoresen (Eds.), *Counseling methods*. New York: Holt, Rinehart & Winston, 1976.

Bandura, A., Jeffery, R. W., & Gajdos, E. Generalizing change through participant modeling with self-directed mastery. *Behaviour Research and Therapy*, 1975, 13, 141–152.

Bandura, A., Jeffery, R., & Wright, C. Efficacy of participant modeling as a function of response induction aids. *Journal of Abnormal Psychology*, 1974, 83, 56–64.

Jeffery, R. W. Reducing fears through participant modeling and self-directed practice. In J. D. Krumboltz & C. E. Thoresen (Eds.), *Counseling methods*. New York: Holt, Rinehart & Winston, 1976.

Lewis, S. A comparison of behavior therapy techniques in the reduction of fearful avoidance behavior. *Behavior Therapy*, 1974, 5, 648–655.

Smith, G. P., & Coleman, R. E. Processes underlying generalization through participant modeling with self-directed practice. *Journal of Behavior Therapy and Experimental Psychiatry*, 1977, 15, 204–206.

Chapter 17
Emotive Imagery and Covert Modeling

With some client problems, a counselor may find that it is impossible or unrealistic to provide live or symbolic models or to have the client engage in overt practice of the goal behaviors. In these cases, it may be more practical to employ strategies that use the client's imagination for the modeling or rehearsal. This chapter describes two therapeutic procedures that rely heavily on client imagery: emotive imagery and covert modeling. In both of these strategies, scenes are developed that the client visualizes or rehearses by imagination. It has been assumed that the client must be able to generate strong, vivid images to use these procedures, but we do not know at present to what extent the intensity of the client's imagery correlates with therapeutic outcomes (M. J. Mahoney, 1974).

Objectives

1. Given seven examples of counselor leads, identify which of the five steps of the emotive-imagery procedure are presented in each counselor lead. You should be able to identify accurately at least six out of seven examples.
2. Demonstrate 10 out of 13 steps of emotive imagery with a role-play client, using the Interview Checklist for Emotive Imagery at the end of the chapter to assess your performance.
3. Describe how you would apply the five components of covert modeling given a simulated client case.
4. Demonstrate at least 22 out of 27 steps associated with covert modeling with a role-play client, using the Interview Checklist for Covert Modeling at the end of the chapter to assess your use of this strategy.

Assessment of Client Imagery

In both emotive imagery and covert modeling, it is essential to assess the client's potential for engaging in imagery or fantasy. To some extent, the success of these two strategies may depend upon the client's capacity to generate vivid images. As Kazdin (1976b) points out, "presumably, the effect of treatment is influenced by the extent to which the client is imagining the material presented by the therapist" (p. 480). Some clients may be "turned off" by imagery; others may find it difficult to picture vivid scenes in their minds.

There are several ways the counselor can assess the intensity and clarity of client images. First, the client's level of imagery could be assessed before using emotive imagery or covert modeling with a self-report questionnaire such as the Visual and Auditory Imagery parts of the Imaginal Processes Inventory (Singer & Antrobus, 1972), the Betts QMI (Sheehan, 1967), the Imagery Survey Schedule (Cautela & Tondo, 1971), or other such measures as reviewed by White, Sheehan, and Ashton (1977). Also, the counselor and client can develop practice scenes that the client can use to generate images. For example, the counselor might instruct the client to "visualize a scene or event that makes you feel relaxed and pleasant—select a scenario that you really enjoy and feel good about—try to be aware of all your sensations while in the scene." Kazdin (1976b) suggests that the client can narrate aloud the events in the practice scene as they are imagined. Or, after 30 seconds to a minute of imagery, the counselor can ask the client to describe the scene in detail. After the client's description, the counselor might probe about the colors, sounds, movement, temperature, or smell reflected in the scene. The idea is to ascertain how vividly the client imagined the scene. Also, the counselor might ask how the client was feeling during the imagined scene. This question helps the counselor get an impression of how much the client can "get into," or become involved in, the scene.

If a client has some difficulty imagining specific details, the counselor can train the client to engage in more detailed imagery (Phillips, 1971). If this seems too time-consuming, or if the client is reluctant or uninterested in using imagery, a strategy that does not involve imagery may be more appropriate. If a client has good feelings about imagery and can "get into" the practice scene, then the counselor and client may decide to continue with either emotive imagery or covert modeling, depending upon the client's problem and goal behavior.

Emotive Imagery

In using the emotive-imagery procedure, a person focuses on positive thoughts or images while imagining a discomforting or anxiety-arousing activity or situation. By focusing on positive and pleasant images, the person is able to "block" the painful, fearful, or anxiety-provoking situation. One can think of blocking in emotive imagery as a process in which it is difficult for a person to focus on pleasant

thoughts and on anxiety, pain, or tension at the same time. These emotions are incompatible.

Several studies have reported the use of emotive imagery as a therapeutic strategy. Lazarus and Abramovitz (1962) were among the first to report such a study. Children with phobias were instructed to engage in enjoyable fantasies while experiencing phobic stimuli. For example, a child's school phobia was eliminated by introducing imagery scenes about school centered around a fictional character, Noddy. As these authors point out, "the essence of this procedure was to create imagined situations where Noddy played the role of a truant and responded fearfully to the school setting. The patient (child) would then protect him, either by active reassurance or by 'setting a good example'" (pp. 191–195). Lazarus (1968) has used relaxing images to enhance muscle relaxation. The client selects any imagined scene that she or he finds relaxing and focuses on the scene while engaging in deep muscle relaxation. Lazarus claims that he can obtain deeper and more satisfying levels of relaxation with the use of relaxing images. Horan (1973) has used emotive imagery with pregnant women to reduce the discomfort and anxiety associated with childbirth. C. I. Stone, D. A. Demchik-Stone, and J. J. Horan (1977) found that emotive imagery was as effective as the Lamaze method of prophylactic childbirth in controlling pain-tolerance levels of pregnant women. In an analogue study, Horan and Dellinger (1974) found that people who listened to tape-recorded relaxation-producing images were able to hold their hands immersed in ice water more than twice as long as people who did not use relaxing images. Horan, Layng, and Pursell (1976) reported that heart rates of women who experienced discomfort while having their teeth cleaned declined, on the average, from 77 beats per minute to 65 beats after 5 minutes of tape-recorded relaxation-producing emotive images. A novel use of imagery has been applied to cancer patients (Simonton & Simonton, 1975). These researchers found that some terminal cancer patients instructed to imagine their disease and their body's own immune mechanisms (white blood cells) attacking the diseased and weakened cancer cells extended their lives past the predicted life expectancy.

Emotive imagery can be applied to a variety of client concerns and problems. Horan (1976) indicates that such problems as "receiving injections, minor surgery and chronic recurring pain are examples of situations" in which positive images can be used concurrently to reduce discomfort (p. 318). Emotive imagery is also applicable to situations in which people experience boredom or tension created by daily routine. This use of the procedure can be viewed as a cognitive "time-out" or a "rest-and-recuperation" (R-and-R) strategy. "In vivo" emotive imagery can be applied as a single strategy or used with other procedures to increase relaxation and to reduce discomfort or tension. Finally, emotive imagery can be used to counteract phobic responses by developing scenes in which clients imagine themselves coping satisfactorily or behaving effectively.

Emotive imagery involves five steps: a verbal set, assessment of the client's imagery potential, development of imagery scenes, practice of scenes, and homework. See the Interview Checklist for Emotive Imagery at the end of the chapter for some examples of counselor leads associated with these steps.

Verbal Set

The following illustration of the purpose and overview of emotive imagery has been given to pregnant women about the procedure for reducing childbirth anxiety and for relieving discomfort during labor (Horan, 1976):

Here is how *in vivo* emotive imagery works: In this culture women often learn to expect excruciating pain in childbirth. Even intelligent sophisticated women have a hard time shaking this belief. Consequently, the prospect of childbirth is often fraught with considerable anxiety. In the labor room, early contractions are seen as signals for unbearable pain to follow. The result is that even more anxiety occurs.

Now, since anxiety has a magnifying effect on childbirth discomfort, the more anxious you become the more actual pain you will probably

experience. This "vicious circle" happens all too frequently.

The process of *in vivo* emotive imagery involves having you focus on scenes or events which please you or make you feel relaxed, while the contractions are occurring. You simply cannot feel calm, happy, secure—or whatever other emotion the scenes engender—and anxious at the same time. These opposing emotions are incompatible with each other.

So, *in vivo* emotive imagery blocks the anxiety which leads to increased childbirth discomfort. There is also some evidence which suggests that the holding of certain images can raise your pain threshold. Thus, *in vivo* emotive imagery not only eliminates anxiety-related discomfort, but it also has a dulling effect on what might be called real pain! [pp. 317–318].*

The verbal set ends with a request for the client's willingness to try the strategy.

Assessment of Client's Imagery Potential

Because the success of the emotive-imagery procedure may depend on the amount of positive feelings and calmness a client can derive from visualizing a particular scene, it is important for the counselor to get a feeling for the client's potential for engaging in imagery. The counselor can assess the client's imagery potential by the methods discussed at the beginning of this chapter: a self-report questionnaire, or a practice scene with client narration, or counselor "probes" for details.

Development of Imagery Scenes

If the decision is made to continue with the emotive-imagery procedure, the client and counselor will then develop imagery scenes. They should develop at least two, although one scene might be satisfactory for some clients. The exact number and type of scenes developed will

*From "Coping with Inescapable Discomfort through In Vivo Emotive Imagery," by J. J. Horan. In J. D. Krumboltz and C. E. Thoresen (Eds.), *Counseling Methods*. Copyright 1976 by Holt, Rinehart & Winston. Reprinted by permission.

depend on the nature of the concern and the individual client.

Two basic ingredients should be included in the selection and development of the scene. First, the scenario should promote calmness, tranquility, or enjoyment for the client. Examples of such client scenes might include skiing on a beautiful slope, hiking on a trail in a large forest, sailing on a sunny lake, walking on a secluded beach, listening to and watching a symphony orchestra perform a favorite composition, or watching an athletic event. The scenes can involve the client as an active participant or as a participant observer or spectator. For some clients, the more active they are in the scene, the greater the degree of their involvement.

The second ingredient of the scene should be as much sensory detail as possible, such as sounds, colors, temperature, smell, touch, and motion. There may be a high positive correlation between the degree and number of sensations a scene elicits for the client and the amount or intensity of pleasant and enjoyable sensations the client experiences in a particular situation. The counselor and client should decide on the particular senses that will be incorporated into the imagery scenes.

As an example, the following imagery scene was used by Horan (1976) for people who experience discomfort having their teeth cleaned. Note the sensations described in the scene instructions:

Now close your eyes, sit back, and relax. Eyes closed, sitting back in the chair, relaxing. Now visualize yourself standing by the shore of a large lake, looking out across an expanse of blue water and beyond to the far shore. Immediately in front of you stretches a small beach, and behind you a grassy meadow. The sun is bright and warm. The air is fresh and clean. It's a gorgeous summer day. The sky is pale blue with great billowy clouds drifting by. The wind is blowing gently, just enough to make the trees sway and make gentle ripples in the grass. It's a perfect day. And you have it entirely to yourself, with nothing to do, nowhere to go. You take from your car a blanket, towel, and swimsuit, and walk off through the meadow. You find a spot, spread the blanket, and lie down on

it. It's so warm and quiet. It's such a treat to have the day to yourself to just relax and take it easy. Keep your eyes closed, thinking about the warm, beautiful day. You're in your suit now, walking toward the water, feeling the soft, lush grass under your feet. You reach the beach and start across it. Now you can feel the warm sand underfoot. Very warm and very nice. Now visualize yourself walking out into the water up to your ankles; out farther, up to your knees. The water's so warm it's almost like a bath. Now you're moving faster out into the lake, up to your waist, up to your chest. The water's so warm, so comfortable. You take a deep breath and glide a few feet forward down into the water. You surface and feel the water run down your back. You look around; you're still all alone. You still have this lovely spot to yourself. Far across the lake you can see a sailboat, tiny in the distance. It's so far away you can just make out the white sail jutting up from the blue water. You take another breath and kick off this time toward the shore swimming with long easy strokes. Kicking with your feet, pulling through with your arms and hands. You swim so far that when you stop and stand the water's only up to your waist, and you begin walking toward the beach, across the warm sand to the grass. Now you're feeling again the grass beneath your feet. Deep, soft, lush. You reach your blanket and pick up the towel, and begin to dry yourself. You dry your hair, your face, your neck. You stretch the towel across your shoulders, dry your back, your legs. You can feel the warm sun on your skin. It must be ninety degrees, but it's clear and dry. The heat isn't oppressive; it's just nice and warm and comfortable. You lie down on the blanket and feel the deep, soft grass under your head. You're looking up at the sky, seeing those great billowy clouds floating by, far, far, above [Horan, 1976, p. 319].*

Practice of Imagery Scenes

After the imagery scenes have been developed, the client is instructed to practice using them. There are two types of practice. In the first

*From "Coping with Inescapable Discomfort through In Vivo Emotive Imagery," by J. J. Horan. In J. D. Krumboltz and C. E. Thoresen (Eds.), *Counseling Methods*. Copyright 1976 by Holt, Rinehart & Winston. Reprinted by permission.

type, the client is instructed to focus on one of the scenes for about 30 seconds and to picture as much detail as was developed for that scene and feel all the sensations associated with it. The counselor cues the client after the time has elapsed. After the client uses the scene, the counselor obtains an impression of the imagery experience—the client's feelings and sensory details of the scene. If other scenes are developed, the client can be instructed to practice imagining them. Variations on this type of practice might be to have the client use or hold a scene for varying lengths of time.

The second type of practice is to have the client use the scenes in simulated anxious, tense, fearful, or painful situations. The counselor and client should simulate the problem situations while using the imagery scenes. Practice under simulated conditions permits the counselor and client to assess the effectiveness of the scenes for blocking out the discomfort or for reducing the anxiety or phobic reaction. Simulated situations can be created by describing vividly the details of an anxiety-provoking situation while the client uses a scene. For example, the counselor can describe the pleasant scene while interweaving a description of the discomforting situation (Lazarus & Abramovitz, 1962). The counselor can simulate painful situations by squeezing the client's arm while the client focuses on one of the scenes. Or, to simulate labor contractions, the labor coach squeezes the woman's thigh while she focuses on a pleasant image. Another simulation technique is to have clients hold their hands in ice water for a certain length of time. Simulated practice may facilitate generalization of the scene application to the actual problem situation. After the simulated practices, the counselor should assess the client's reactions to using the scene in conjunction with the simulated discomfort or anxiety.

Homework

The client is instructed to apply the emotive imagery "in vivo"—that is, to use the scenes in the fearful, painful, tense, or anxious situation. The client can use a homework log to record the day, time, and situation in which emotive imagery was used. The client also can note reactions before and after using emotive imagery with a five-point scale, with 1 representing minimum discomfort and 5 indicating maximum discomfort. The client should be instructed to bring the homework log to the next session or to a follow-up session.

Model Example: Emotive Imagery

In this model example, we are going to deviate from our usual illustrations of hypothetical cases and present a narrative account of how the two of us used emotive imagery before and during labor for the birth of our first child.

1. *Verbal set*
   First, we discussed a rationale for using emotive imagery during labor in conjunction with the breathing and relaxation techniques (see Chapter 20) we had learned in our prepared-childbirth class. We decided before labor started that we would try emotive imagery at a point during labor when the breathing needed to be supplemented with something else. We also worked out a finger-signaling system to use during contractions so Sherry could inform Bill whether to continue or stop with the imagery scenes, depending upon their effectiveness.
2. *Assessment of imagery potential*
   We also discussed whether or not Sherry was able to use fantasy effectively enough to concentrate during something like a labor contraction. We tested this out by having Bill describe imagery stimuli and having Sherry imagine these and try to increase use of all sensations to make the imagery scenes as vivid as possible.
3. *Development of imagery scenes*
   Together we selected two different scenes to practice with before labor and to use during labor. One scene involved being on our sailboat on a sunny, warm day and sailing quite fast with a good breeze. We felt this scene would be effective because it produced enjoyment and also because it seemed to evoke a lot of sensory experience. The second scene involved being anchored at night on the boat with a full moon, a soft breeze, and some wine. Since both of these scenes represented actual experiences,

we felt they might work better than sheer fantasy.

4. *Practice of imagery scenes*

We knew that much of the success of using emotive imagery during labor would depend upon the degree to which we worked with it before labor. We practiced with our imagery scenes in two ways. First, Sherry imagined these scenes on her own, sometimes in conjunction with her self-directed practice in breathing and relaxation, and sometimes just as something to do —for instance, in a boring situation. Second, Sherry evoked the scenes deliberately while Bill simulated a contraction by squeezing tightly the inside of her thigh.

5. *Homework: In vivo*

We had a chance to apply emotive imagery during labor itself. We started to use it during the active phase of labor—about midway through the time of labor, when the contractions were coming about every 2 minutes. In looking back, we felt it was a useful supplement to the breathing and relaxation typically taught in the Lamaze childbirth method. Sherry felt that a lot of the effectiveness had to do with the soothing effect of hearing Bill's vocal description of the scenes—in addition to the images she produced during the scene descriptions.

Learning Activity: Emotive Imagery

This learning activity is designed to help you learn the process of emotive imagery. It will be easier to do this with a partner, although you can do it alone if a partner is not available. You may wish to try it with a partner first and then just by yourself.

Instructions for Dyadic Activity

1. In dyads, one of you can take the helper role; the other takes the part of the helpee. Switch roles after the first practice with the strategy.
2. The helper should give an explanation about the emotive-imagery procedure.
3. The helper should determine the helpee's potential for imagination: ask the helpee to imagine several pleasant scenes and then probe for details.
4. The helper and helpee together should develop two imagery scenes the helpee can vividly imagine. Imagination of these scenes should produce pleasant, positive feelings.

5. The helpee should practice imagining these scenes—as vividly and as intensely as possible.
6. The helpee should practice imagining a scene while the helper simulates a problem situation. For example, the helper can simulate an anxiety-provoking situation by describing it while the helpee engages in imagery, or the helper can simulate pain by squeezing the helpee's arm during the imagination.

Instructions for Self-Activity

1. Think of two scenes you can imagine very vividly. These scenes should produce positive or pleasant feelings for you. Supply as many details to these scenes as you can.
2. Practice imagining these scenes as intensely as you can.
3. Next, practice imagining one of these scenes while simulating a problem (discomforting) situation such as holding a piece of ice in your hands or running your hands under cold water. Concentrate very hard on the imagery as you do so.
4. Practice this twice daily for the next 3 days. See how much you can increase your tolerance for the cold temperature with daily practice of the imagery scene.

Covert Modeling

Covert modeling is a procedure in which the client imagines a model performing behaviors via instructions. The procedure was developed by Cautela (1971). The covert-modeling procedure assumes that a live or symbolic performance by a model is not necessary. Instead, the client is directed to imagine someone demonstrating the desired behavior. Flannery (1972) used covert modeling as part of a treatment strategy with a college dropout. Cautela, Flannery, and Hanley (1974) compared covert and overt (live) modeling in reducing avoidance behaviors of college students; both procedures were effective. In the last few years, most of the supportive data for the covert-modeling procedure have resulted from studies conducted by Kazdin (1973a, 1974a, 1974b, 1974c, 1974d, 1975, 1976a, 1976b, 1976c). Rosenthal and Reese (1976) explored the effectiveness of covert modeling in developing assertive behaviors. The procedure also has been used to treat alcoholism and obsessive-compulsive behaviors (Hay, Hay, & Nelson, 1977) and to decrease smoking (Nesse & Nelson, 1977). L. Watson (1976) found that covert modeling was effective in helping prison inmates acquire job-interview skills. Covert modeling also has been used to decrease test anxiety (Gallagher & Arkowitz, 1978).

There are several advantages of covert modeling: the procedure does not require elaborate therapeutic or induction aids; scenes can be developed to deal with a variety of problems; the scenes can be individualized to fit the unique concerns of the client; the client can practice the imagery scenes alone; the client can use the imagery scenes as a self-control procedure in problem situations; and covert modeling may be a good alternative when live or filmed models cannot be used or when it is difficult to use overt rehearsal in the interview.

Some questions about certain aspects of covert modeling remain unanswered, such as the importance of the identity of the model, the role of reinforcing consequences, and the type and duration of imagery scenes best used in the procedure. We have attempted to point out the possible alternatives in our description of the components of the covert-modeling strategy. Our description is based not only on our own experience with it, but also on the pioneering efforts of Cautela (1971) and Kazdin (1976b). The five major components of covert modeling are a verbal set about the strategy, practice scenes, developing treatment scenes, applying treatment scenes, and homework. Within each of these five components are several substeps. If you would like an overview of the procedure, see the Interview Checklist for Covert Modeling at the end of the chapter.

Verbal Set

After the counselor and client have reviewed the problem behaviors and the goal behaviors for counseling, the counselor presents the rationale for covert modeling. Here is

Kazdin's (1976b) explanation of a treatment rationale for using covert modeling in assertiveness training:

> In developing behavior such as assertive skills, it is essential to rehearse or practice elements of the skills. Specifically, it is important to rehearse the situations in which assertiveness is the appropriate response. Numerous situations in life require an assertive response of some sort. Learning what these situations are and being able to discriminate appropriate responses are important. People can rehearse situations in their imagination. Imagining certain selected situations can alter one's behavior in those actual situations. For example, to get rid of one's fear, one can imagine carefully selected scenes related to fear and remove the fear. So imagination can strongly influence behavior [p. 477].

The verbal set also should provide a brief description of the process of covert modeling. Cautela (1976) provides an illustration of the way he describes the covert-modeling process to a client:

> In a minute, I'll ask you to close your eyes and try to imagine, as clearly as possible, that you are observing a certain situation. Try to use all the senses needed for the particular situation, e.g. try to actually hear a voice or see a person very clearly. After I describe the scene, I will ask you some questions concerning your feelings about the scene and how clearly you imagined it [p. 324].

Practice Scenes

After providing a verbal set to the client, the counselor may decide to try out the imagery process with several practice scenes. For most clients, imagining a scene may be a new experience and may seem foreign. Kazdin (1976b) suggests that practice scenes may help to familiarize clients with the procedure and sensitize them to focus on specific details of the imagery (p. 478). The use of practice scenes also helps the counselor to assess the client's potential for carrying out instructions in the imagination.

The practice scenes usually consist of simple straightforward situations that are unrelated to the goal behaviors. For example, if you are using covert modeling to help a client acquire job-interview skills, the practice scenes would be unrelated to job-seeking responses. You might use some of the following as practice scenes:

1. Imagine a person in a library checking out a book.
2. Imagine someone lying on the beach in the hot sun.
3. Imagine someone eating a gourmet meal at an elegant restaurant.
4. Imagine someone being entertained at a night spot.

In using practice scenes with a client, the counselor usually follows six steps.

1. The counselor instructs the client to close his or her eyes and to sit back and relax. The client is instructed to tell the counselor when he or she feels relaxed. If the client does not feel relaxed, the counselor may need to decide whether relaxation procedures (Chapter 20) should be introduced. The effect of relaxation on the quality of imagery in covert modeling has not been evaluated. However, research on live and symbolic modeling suggests that modeling may be facilitated when the client is relaxed (Bandura, Blanchard, & Ritter, 1969).

2. The counselor describes a practice scene and instructs the client to imagine the scene and to raise an index finger when the scene has been imagined vividly. The practice scenes are similar to the four previous examples. The counselor reads the scene or instructs the client about what to imagine.

3. The counselor instructs the client to open his or her eyes after the scene is vividly imagined (signal of index finger) and asks the client to describe the scene or to narrate the imagined events.

4. The counselor probes for greater details about the scene—the clothes or physical features of a person in the imagery, the physical setting of the situation, the amount of light, colors of the furniture, decorative features, noises, or smells. This probing may encourage the client to focus on details of the imagery scene.

5. The counselor may suggest additional details for the client to imagine during a subsequent practice. Working with practice scenes first can facilitate the development of the details in the actual treatment scenes.

6. Usually each practice scene is presented several times. The number of practice scenes used before moving on to developing and applying treatment scenes will depend on several factors. If the client feels comfortable with the novelty of the imagined scenes after several presentations, the counselor might consider this a cue to stop using the practice scenes. Also, if the client can provide a fairly detailed description of the imagery after several practice scenes, this may be a good time to start developing treatment scenes. If a client reports difficulty in relaxing, the counselor may need to introduce relaxation training before continuing. For a client who cannot generate images during the practice scenes, another modeling strategy may be needed in lieu of covert modeling.

Developing Treatment Scenes

The treatment scenes used in covert modeling are developed in conjunction with the client and grow out of the desired client outcomes or goals. The scenes consist of a variety of situations in which the client wants to perform the target response in the real-life environment. If the client wants to develop assertion skills, the treatment scenes represent different situations requiring assertive responses. If a client wants to acquire effective job-interview skills, the treatment scenes are developed around job-interview situations.

Five things should be considered in the development of treatment scenes: the model characteristics, whether to use individualized or standardized scenes, whether to use vague or specific scenes, the ingredients of the scenes, and the number of scenes. It is important for the client to help in the development of treatment scenes because client participation can provide many specifics about situations in which the goal behavior is to be performed.

Model Characteristics. As you may recall from Chapter 15, research about model characteristics in live and symbolic modeling indicates that similarity between the model and the client contributes to client change (Bandura, 1971a). Kazdin (1974b) found that, in covert modeling, the use of a same-sex and similar-age model resulted in greater avoidance reduction with college students than an older model or a model of the opposite sex. Also, clients who imagined several (multiple) models showed more change than clients who imagined only one model (Kazdin, 1974a, 1976c). Coping models also seemed to be generally more effective in covert modeling than mastery models (Kazdin, 1973a; Meichenbaum, 1971).

One of the most interesting questions about the covert model is the identity of the model. Kazdin (1974a) found no differences between college-age subjects who imagined *themselves* as the model and subjects who imagined *another person* as the model. Using a somewhat different population, incarcerated youth offenders, L. Watson (1976) found that covert self-modeling (imagining oneself) was superior to covert modeling (imagining someone else) on some measures. As Krumboltz and Thoresen (1976) point out, no one is more similar to the client than the client! (p. 484). At the present time, there are not sufficient data to indicate who the model should be in the covert-modeling procedure. We suspect this may vary with clients and suggest that you give clients the option of deciding whether to imagine themselves or another person as the model. One key factor may involve the particular identity the client can imagine most easily and comfortably. For clients who feel some stress at first in imagining themselves as models, imagining someone else might be introduced first and later replaced with self-modeling.

Individualized versus Standardized Scenes.

The treatment scenes used in covert modeling can be either standardized or individualized. Standardized scenes cover different situations in everyday life and are presented to a group of clients or to all clients with the same target responses. For example, Kazdin (1976b) used a series of standardized scenes describing situations requiring assertive responses for nonassertive clients. Individualized scenes represent situations specifically tailored to suit an individual client. For example, one nonassertive client may need scenes developed around situations with strangers; another may need scenes that involve close friends. Generally, treatment scenes should be individualized for those who have unique concerns and who are counseled individually, since some standardized scenes may not be relevant for a particular client.

Degree of Specificity of Scenes. Another consideration in developing treatment scenes is the degree of specificity of instruction that should be included. Some clients may benefit from very specific instructions about the details of what to imagine. Other clients may derive more gains from covert modeling if the treatment scenes are more general, allowing the client to supply the specific features. A risk of not having detailed instructions is that some clients will introduce scene material that is irrelevant or detracts from the desired outcomes. Kazdin (1976b) has explored clients' imagery during the treatment scenes and found that clients do make some changes. However, he indicates that such changes appear to be infrequent and that there do not seem to be any particular features of a scene introduced by a client that are consistently related to treatment outcome (p. 481). At this point, the data regarding the necessary degree of specificity of a treatment scene are limited. Again, we suggest this decision should consider the client's preferences.

Here is an example of a fairly general treatment scene for a prison inmate about to be released on parole who is seeking employment:

''Picture yourself (or someone else like you) in a job interview. The employer asks why you didn't complete high school. You tell the employer you got in some trouble, and the employer asks what kind of trouble. You feel a little uptight but tell her you have a prison record. The employer asks why you were in prison and for how long. The employer then asks what makes you think you can stay out of trouble and what you have been doing while on parole. Imagine yourself saying that you have been looking for work while on parole and have been thinking about your life and drugs."

The generality of the treatment scene in this example assumes that the client knows what type of response to make and what details to supply in the scene.

A more detailed treatment scene would specify more of the actual responses. For example:

"Picture yourself (or someone else) in a job interview and imagine the following dialogue. The employer says, 'I see that you have only finished three years of high school. You don't intend to graduate?' Picture yourself saying (showing some anxiety): 'Well, no, I want to go to vocational school while I'm working.' The employer asks: 'What happened? How did you get so far behind in school?' Imagine yourself (or someone else) replying: 'I've been out of school for awhile because I've been in some trouble.' Now imagine the employer is showing some alarm and asks: 'What kind of trouble?' You decide to be up front as you imagine yourself saying: 'I want you to know that I have a prison record.' As the employer asks: 'Why were you in prison?' imagine yourself feeling a little nervous but staying calm and saying something like: 'I guess I was pretty immature. Some friends and I got involved with drugs. I'm on parole now. I'm staying away from drugs and I'm looking hard for a job. I really want to work'" [L.. Watson, 1976].

Remember, the degree of specificity of each scene will depend largely on the client, the problem or concern, and the goals for counseling.

Ingredients for the Scene. Three ingredients are required for a treatment scene in the covert-modeling procedure. The first is a de-

scription of the situation or context in which the behavior is to occur. The second is a description of the model demonstrating the behavior to be acquired. The third is a depiction of some favorable outcome or result of the goal behavior. Kazdin (1976b) gives an example of a covert-modeling scene for assertive behavior in which the situation and the goal behavior are illustrated:

Situation: Imagine the person (model) is staying at a hotel. After one night there, he (she) notices that the bed springs must be broken. The bed sags miserably and was very uncomfortable during the night.
Model Demonstrating the Behavior: In the morning, the person goes to the clerk at the desk and says: "The bed in my room is quite uncomfortable. I believe it is broken. I wish you would replace the bed or change my room" [p. 485].

Hay, Hay, and Nelson (1977) developed covert-modeling scenes that included a favorable outcome for an adult male alcoholic. An example of one of the scenes for their client is:

Imagine yourself walking in town and running into a group of your old drinking buddies. They have already been drinking heavily and ask you to join them. They are drinking white lightning. They look happy and you are alone. In the past you would have taken a drink and probably have become drunk. Now cope with the situation. Imagine yourself feeling the "urge" to drink, but refusing and slowly turning and walking down the street [p. 71].

Here the model (the client) is depicted as coping with a situation and then refusing to drink and walking away, which is a favorable or positive outcome.

The inclusion of a favorable consequence as a scene ingredient is based on research indicating that, if a client sees a model rewarded for the behavior, the client is more likely to perform or acquire the response (Bandura, 1976b). Also, specifying a possible favorable outcome to imagine may prevent a client from inadvertently imagining an unfavorable consequence. Kazdin (1974c, 1976c) found that clients who received covert-modeling treatment scenes in which the scene was resolved favorably were more assertive than clients who imagined scenes without any positive consequences or results.

We believe that the favorable outcome in the scene should take the form of some action initiated by the client or of covert self-reinforcement or praise. For example, the favorable outcome illustrated in the scene for the alcoholic client was the client's self-initiated action of walking away from the alcohol (Hay, Hay, & Nelson, 1977). We prefer that the action be initiated or delivered by the client or model instead of someone else in the scene because, in a real situation, it may be too risky to have the client rely on someone else to deliver a favorable outcome in the form of a certain response. We cannot guarantee that clients always will receive favorable responses from someone else in the actual situation.

In some previous reports of covert modeling, nonassertive clients experienced a favorable response from another person through the person's compliance. But as Nietzel, Martorano, and Melnick (1977) point out, using compliance of someone else as a favorable outcome might reinforce inaccurate client expectations and also could fail to help a client learn how to respond to noncompliance. These authors compared the effectiveness of covert modeling with and without "reply training." In other words, some clients were trained to visualize (1) an initial assertive response by the model; (2) another person's noncomplying response; and (3) a second assertive counterreply by the model. The clients who received the extra "reply training" were more assertive and more persevering in their assertions than the clients who were trained only to make an initial assertive response that was followed by compliance from the other person. Reply training to noncompliance may be more realistic and provide more response alternatives than training someone to receive automatic compliance as a positive consequence.

Another way to incorporate a favorable outcome or consequence in a treatment scene is to include an example of client (or model) self-reinforcement or praise. For instance, models might congratulate themselves by saying: "That is terrific. I am proud of myself for what I said to the _____." A favorable consequence in the form of model or client self-praise also is self-administered. Again, in a real-life situation, it may be better for clients to learn to reward themselves than to expect external encouragement that might not be forthcoming.

The person who experiences the favorable outcomes will be the same person the client imagines as the model. If the client imagines someone else as the model, then the client would also imagine that person initiating a favorable outcome or reinforcing himself or herself. Clients who imagine themselves as the models would imagine themselves receiving the positive consequences. There is very little actual evidence on the role of reinforcement in covert modeling. Some of the effectiveness of adding favorable consequences to the treatment scene may depend upon the identity of the covert model and the particular value of the consequences for the client (L. Watson, 1976).

Number of Scenes. The counselor and client can develop different scenes that portray the context or situation in which the client experiences difficulty or wants to use the newly acquired behavior. Multiple scenes can depict different situations in which assertive behavior is generally appropriate. Although there is no set number of scenes that should be developed, certainly several scenes provide more variety than only one or two.

Applying Treatment Scenes

After all the scenes have been developed, the counselor can apply the treatment scenes by having the client imagine each scene. The basic steps involved in applying the treatment scenes include:

1. arranging the scenes in a hierarchy
2. instructing the client before scene presentation
3. presenting one scene at a time from the hierarchy
4. presenting a scene for a specified duration

5. obtaining client reactions to the imagined scene
6. presenting each scene at least twice with the aid of the counselor or tape-recorder
7. having the client imagine each scene at least twice while directing himself or herself
8. selecting and presenting scenes from the hierarchy in a random order

Hierarchy. The scenes developed by the counselor and client should be arranged in a hierarchy for scene presentation (Rosenthal & Reese, 1976). The hierarchy is an order of scenes beginning with one that is relatively easy for the client to imagine with little stress. More difficult or stressful scenes would be ranked by the client.

Instructions. It may be necessary to repeat instructions about imagery to the client if a great amount of time has elapsed since using the practice scenes. The counselor might say:

> In a minute I will ask you to close your eyes and to sit back and relax. I want you to try to imagine as vividly and clearly as possible that you are observing a certain scene. Try to use *all* the senses needed for the particular situation—for example, try to actually hear the voice(s), see the colors, and picture features of a person (or people). After I describe the scene, I will ask you some questions concerning your feelings about the scene and how clearly you imagined it [Cautela, Flannery, & Hanley, 1974].

If a person other than the client is the model, the client is instructed to picture someone his or her own age and sex whom he or she may know. The client is told that the person who is pictured as the model will be used in all the treatment scenes. The counselor also instructs the client to signal by raising an index finger as soon as the scene is pictured clearly and to hold the scene in imagery until the counselor signals to stop.

Sequence of Scene Presentation. Initially, the first scene in the hierarchy is presented to the client. Each scene is presented alone. When one scene has been covered sufficiently, the next scene in the hierarchy is presented. This process continues until all scenes in the hierarchy have been covered.

Duration of Scenes. There are no general ground rules for the amount of time to hold the scene in imagery once the client signals. In Kazdin's (1976c) research, the client held the imagery for 15 seconds after signaling; in another study, the scene duration was 30 seconds (Nesse & Nelson, 1977). We do not know whether this duration is optimal. For some clients, a longer duration may be more beneficial; for others, a shorter duration may be more helpful. We feel that the choice will depend on the counselor's personal preference and experience with the covert-modeling procedure, the nature of the client's problem, the goal behavior for counseling, and—perhaps most important—the client's input about the scene duration. After one or two scenes have been presented, the counselor can query the client about the suitability of the scene duration. Generally, a scene should be held long enough for the client to imagine the three scene ingredients vividly without rushing.

Client Reactions about the Scene. After the client has imagined a particular scene, the counselor queries the client about how clearly it was imagined. The client is asked to describe feelings during particular parts of the scene. The counselor also should ask whether the scene was described too rapidly or the duration of the scene was adequate for the client to imagine the scene ingredients clearly. These questions enable the counselor and client to modify aspects of a scene before it is presented the second time. Client input about possible scene revision can be very helpful. If particular episodes of the scene elicit intense feelings of anxiety, the content of the scene or the manner of presentation can be revised. Perhaps the order of the scenes in the hierarchy needs rearrangement.

Another way to deal with the client's unpleasant feeling or discomfort with a scene is to talk it over. If the client feels stressful when the model (or the self) is engaging in the behavior or activity in the scene, examine with the client what episode in the scene is producing the discomfort. Also, if the client is the model and has difficulty in performing the behavior or activity, discuss and examine the block. Focus on the adaptive behavior or the coping with the situational ingredient of the scene, rather than on the anxiety or discomfort.

After each scene presentation, the counselor should assess the rate of delivery for the scene description, the clarity of the imagery, and the degree of unpleasantness of the scene for the client. Perhaps if the client has a great deal of input in developing the scenes, the level of discomfort produced will be minimized.

Counselor-Directed Scene Repetitions. In the analogue studies of Kazdin (1976b, 1976c), each scene is presented twice by the counselor or on a tape-recording. However, Cautela (1976) recommends that, after presenting the first scene and making any necessary revisions, the counselor repeat the scene four times. The number of scene repetitions may be dictated by the degree of comfort the client experiences while imagining the scene and the complexity of the activities or behaviors the client is to acquire. A complex series of motor skills, for example, may require more repetitions. Also, engaging in some situations may require more repetition until the client feels reasonably comfortable. Again, make the decision about the number of scene repetitions on the basis of client input: ask the client.

Client-Directed Scene Repetition. In addition to counselor-directed scene practice, the client should engage in self-directed scene practice. Again, the number of client practices is somewhat arbitrary, although perhaps two is a minimum. Generally, the client can repeat imagining the scenes alone until he or she feels comfortable in doing so.

Random Presentation of Scenes. After all the scenes in the hierarchy have been presented adequately, the counselor can check out the client's readiness for self-directed homework practice by presenting some of the scenes in random order. This random presentation guards against any "ordering" effect that the

hierarchy arrangement may have had in the scene presentation.

Homework

Self-directed practice in the form of homework is perhaps the most important therapeutic ingredient for generalization. If a person can apply or practice the procedure outside the counseling session, the probability of using the "new" behavior or of coping in the actual situation is greatly enhanced. For example, Cautela (1976) recommends that the counselor instruct the client to practice each scene at home *at least* ten times a day. Nesse and Nelson (1977) also recommend to their clients that they rehearse the scenes ten times daily. They found that most clients did rehearse scenes about eight times per day.

Some clients may find it difficult to practice the scenes at home this frequently. The counselor might encourage more frequent and more reliable home practice by providing the client with a "phone-mate" on a clinic phone. With a phone-mate, clients can call and verbalize their practice imagery over the phone. This procedure not only creates a demand characteristic to facilitate client practice, but also enables the helper to assess the quality of the client's use of the homework. A client also could rehearse the treatment scenes at home with the aid of a tape-recorder (Hay, Hay, & Nelson, 1977). In arranging the homework tasks, the counselor and client should specify how often, how long, what times during the day, and where practice should occur. The counselor should also instruct the client to record the daily use of the modeling scenes on log sheets. The counselor should verify whether the client understands the homework and should arrange for a follow-up after some portion of the homework is completed.

Model Dialogue: Covert Modeling

Here is an example of a covert-modeling dialogue with our client, Joan, to help her acquire participation skills in her math class.

In response 1, the counselor gives Joan a verbal set about covert modeling by briefly describing the rationale used and an overview of the strategy.

1. Counselor: Joan, one way we can help you increase your participation in math class is to help you learn the participation skills you want through practice. In this procedure, you will practice using your imagination. I will describe situations to you and ask you to imagine yourself or someone else participating in the way described in the situation. How does that sound?

   Client: OK. You mean I imagine things like daydreaming?

Further instructions about the strategy are provided in counselor response 2.

2. Counselor: It has some similarities. Only instead of just letting your mind wander, you will imagine some of the skills you want to use to improve your participation in your math class.

   Client: Well, I'm a pretty good daydreamer, so if this is similar I will probably learn from it.

In response 3, the counselor initiates the idea of using practice scenes to determine Joan's level and style of imagery.

3. Counselor: Well, let's see. I think it might help to see how easy or hard it is for you to actually imagine a specific situation as I describe it to you. So maybe we could do this on a try-out basis to see what it feels like for you.

   Client: OK, what happens?

In response 4, the counselor instructs Joan to sit back and relax before imagining the practice scene.

4. Counselor: First of all, just sit back, close your eyes, and relax. (Gives Joan a few minutes to do this.) You look pretty comfortable. How do you feel?

   Client: Fine. It's never too hard for me to relax.

In response 5, the counselor instructs Joan to imagine the scene vividly and to indicate this by raising her finger.

5. Counselor: OK now, Joan, I'm going to describe a scene to you. As I do so, I want you to imagine the scene as vividly as possible. When you feel you have a very strong picture, then raise your index finger. Does that seem clear?

   Client: Yes.

The counselor will offer a practice scene next. Note that the practice scene is simple, relatively mundane, and asks Joan only to imagine another person.

6. Counselor: OK, imagine that someone is about to offer you a summer job. Just picture a person who might offer you a job like this. (Gives Joan time until Joan raises her index finger.)

In response 7, the counselor asks Joan to describe what she did imagine.

7. Counselor: OK, Joan, now open your eyes. Can you tell me what you just imagined?

   Client: Well, I pictured myself with a middle-aged man who asked me if I wanted to lifeguard this summer. Naturally I told him yes.

Joan's imagery report was specific in terms of the actions and dialogue, but she didn't describe too much about the man, so the counselor will probe for more details.

8. Counselor: OK, fine. What else did you imagine about the man? You mentioned his age. What was he wearing? Any physical characteristics you can recall?

   Client: Well, he was about 35 [a 16-year-old's impression of "middle age" is different from a 30-, 40-, or 50-year-old person's definition], he was wearing shorts and a golf shirt—you see, we were by the pool. That's about it.

Joan was able to describe the setting and the man's dress, but no other physical characteristics, so the counselor will suggest that Joan add this to the next practice attempt.

9. Counselor: OK, so you were able to see what he was wearing and also the setting where he was talking to you. I'd like to try another practice with this same scene. Just imagine everything you did before, only this time try to imagine even more details about how this man actually looks. (Counselor presents the same scene, which goes on until Joan raises her finger.)

In response 10, the counselor will again query Joan about the details of her imagery.

10. Counselor: OK, let's stop. What else did you imagine this time about this person or the situation?

    Client: Well, he was wearing white shorts and a blue shirt. He was a tall man, and very tanned. He had dark hair, blue eyes, and had sunglasses on. He was also barefoot. We were standing on the pool edge. The water was blue and the sun was out and it felt hot.

In response 11, the counselor will try to determine how comfortable Joan is with imagery and whether more practice scenes are necessary.

11. Counselor: OK, that's great. Looks like you were able to imagine colors and temperature

—like the sun feeling hot. How comfortable do you feel now with this process?

Client: Oh, I like it. It was easier the second time you described the scene. I put more into it. I like to imagine this anyway.

In response 12, the counselor decides Joan can move ahead and initiates development of treatment scenes.

12. Counselor: Well, I believe we can go on now. Our next step is to come up with some scenes that describe the situations you find yourself in now with respect to participation in math class.

Client: And then I'll imagine them in the same way?

The counselor sets the stage to obtain all the necessary information to develop treatment scenes. Note the emphasis in response 13 on Joan's participation in this process.

13. Counselor: That's right. Once we work out the details of these scenes, you'll imagine each scene as you just did. Now we have sort of a series of things we need to discuss in setting up the scenes in a way that makes it easiest for you to imagine, so I'll be asking you some questions. Your input is very valuable here to both of us.

Client: OK, shoot.

In response 14, the counselor asks Joan whether she would rather imagine herself or someone else as the model.

14. Counselor: Well, first of all, in that practice scene I asked you to imagine someone else. Now you did that, but you were also able to picture yourself from the report you gave me. In using your class scenes, which do you feel would be easiest and least stressful for you to imagine—yourself going through the scene or someone else, maybe someone similar to you, but another person? (Gives Joan time to think.)

Client (pauses): Well, that's hard to say. I think it would be easier for me to imagine myself, but it might be a little less stressful to imagine someone else . . . (pauses again). I think I'd like to try using myself.

In the next response, the counselor reinforces Joan's choice and also points out the flexibility of implementing the procedure.

15. Counselor: That's fine. And besides, as you know, nothing is that fixed. If we get into this and that doesn't feel right and you want to imagine someone else, we'll change.

Client: Okey dokey.

In response 16, the counselor introduces the idea of a coping model.

16. Counselor: Also, sometimes it's hard to imagine yourself doing something perfectly to start with, so when we get into this, I might describe a situation where you might have a little trouble but not much. That may seem more realistic to you. What do you think?

Client: That seems reasonable. I know what you mean. It's like learning to drive a car. In Driver's Ed, we take one step at a time.

In response 17, the counselor will pose the option of individualizing the scenes or using standardized scenes.

17. Counselor: You've got the idea. Now we have another choice also in the scenes we use. We can work out scenes just for you that are tailored to your situation or we can use scenes on a cassette tape I have that have been standardized for many students who want to improve their class-participation skills. Which sounds like the best option to you?

Client: I really don't know. Does it really make a difference?

It is not that uncommon for a client not to know which route to pursue. In the next response, the counselor will indicate a preference and check it out with Joan.

18. Counselor: Probably not, Joan. If you don't have a choice at this point, you might later. My preference would be to tailor-make the scenes we use here in the session. Then, if you like, you could use the taped scenes to practice with at home later on. How does that sound to you?

Client: It sounds good, like maybe we could use both.

In responses 19 and 20, the counselor asks Joan to identify situations in which Joan desires to improve her class participation. Note this is somewhat a review of goal behavior described in Chapter 12.

19. Counselor: Yes, I think we can. Now let's concentrate on getting some of the details we need to make up the scenes we'll use in our sessions. First of all, let's go over the situations in which you want to improve or increase your class participation.

Client: Well, it's mainly in math class—some of those things we talked about earlier, like being called on, going to the board, and so on.

20. Counselor: OK, so you don't notice you need to work on this in any other classes?

Client: No, not really.

Next the counselor explores whether Joan prefers a very general description or a very specific one. Sometimes this makes a difference in how the person imagines.

21. Counselor: OK, Joan, how much detail would you like me to give you when I describe a scene—a little detail, to let you fill in the rest, or do you want me to describe pretty completely what you should imagine?

    Client: Maybe somewhere in between. I can fill in a lot, but I need to know what to fill in.

In response 22, the counselor is asking about the specific situations in which Joan has trouble participating in her math class.

22. Counselor: OK, let's fill out our description a little more. We're talking about situations you confront in your math class. I remember four situations in which you want to increase your participation—you want to answer more when Mr. _____ calls on you, volunteer more answers, go to the board, and tell Mr. _____ you want to work the problems yourself after you ask for an explanation. Any others, Joan?

    Client: I can't think of any offhand.

In responses 23 through 28, the counselor asks Joan to identify the desired behaviors for these situations. Again, much of this is a review of identifying outcome goals (Chapter 12).

23. Counselor: OK, so we've got about four different situations. Let's take each of these separately. For each situation can we think of what you would like to do in the situation—like when Mr. _____ calls on you, for instance?

    Client: Well, I'd like to give him the answer instead of saying nothing or saying "I don't know."

24. Counselor: OK, good. And if you did give him the answer—especially when you do know it—how would you feel?

    Client: Good, probably relieved.

25. Counselor: OK. Now what about volunteering answers?

    Client: Well, Mr. _____ usually asks who has the answer to this; then he calls on people who raise their hand. I usually never raise my hand even when I do know the answer, so I need to just raise my hand and when he calls on me give the answer. I need to speak clearly, too. I think sometimes my voice is too soft to hear.

26. Counselor: OK, now how could you tell Mr.

_____ to let you work out the problems yourself?

    Client: Well, just go up to him when we have a work period and tell him the part I'm having trouble with and ask him to explain it.

27. Counselor: So you need to ask him for just an explanation, and let him know you want to do the work.

    Client: Yup.

28. Counselor, OK, now what about going to the board?

    Client: Well, I do go up. But I always feel like a fool. I get distracted by the rest of the class so I hardly ever finish the problem. Then he lets me go back to my seat even though I didn't finish it. I need to concentrate more so I can get through the entire problem on the board.

Now that the content of the scenes has been developed, the counselor asks Joan to arrange the four scenes in a hierarchy.

29. Counselor: OK, so we've got four different situations in your math class where you want to improve your participation in some way. Let's take these four situations and arrange them in an order. Could you select the situation that right now is easiest for you and least stressful to you, and rank the rest in terms of difficulty and degree of stress?

    Client: Sure, let me think . . . . Well, the easiest thing to do out of all of these would be to tell Mr. _____ I want to work out the problems myself. Then I guess it would be answering when he calls on me and then going to the board. I have a lot of trouble with volunteering answers, so that would be hardest for me.

The counselor emphasizes the flexibility of the hierarchy and provides general instructions to Joan about how they will work with these scenes.

30. Counselor: OK. Now this order can change. At any point you feel it isn't right, we can reorder these situations. What we will do is to take one situation at a time, starting with the easiest one, and I'll describe it to you in terms of the way you want to handle it and ask you to imagine it. So the first scene will involve you telling Mr. _____ what you need explained in order to work the problems yourself.

    Client: So we do this just like we did at the beginning?

Emotive Imagery and Covert Modeling

317

The counselor will <u>precede the scene presentation with very specific instructions</u> to Joan.

31. Counselor: Right. Just sit back, close your eyes, and relax . . . (gives Joan a few minutes to do so). Now remember, as I describe the scene, you are going to imagine yourself in the situation. Try to use all your senses in your imagination—in other words, get into it. When you have a very vivid picture, raise your index finger. Keep imagining the scene until I give a signal to stop. OK?

    Client: Yeah.

The counselor <u>presents the first scene in Joan's hierarchy slowly</u> and with ample pauses to give Joan time to generate the images.

32. Counselor: OK, Joan, picture yourself in math class . . . (pause). Mr. _____ has just finished explaining how to solve for X and Y . . . . Now he has assigned problems to you and has given you a work period . . . . You are starting to do the problems and you realize there is some part of the equation you can't figure out. You take your work-sheet and get up out of your seat and go to Mr. _____'s desk. You are telling Mr. _____ what part of the equation you're having trouble with. You explain to him you don't want him to solve the problem, just to explain the missing part. Now you're feeling good that you were able to go up and ask him for an explanation.
    (The counselor waits for about 10 seconds after Joan signals with her finger.)

The counselor <u>signals Joan to stop</u> and in responses 33 through 36 <u>solicits Joan's reactions</u> about the imagery.

33. Counselor: OK, Joan, open your eyes now. What did you imagine?

    Client: Well, it was pretty easy. I just imagined myself going up to Mr. _____ and telling him I needed more explanation but that I wanted to find the answers myself.

34. Counselor: OK, so you were able to get a pretty vivid picture?

    Client: Yes, very much so.

35. Counselor: What were your feelings during this —particularly as you imagined yourself?

    Client: I felt pretty calm. It didn't really bother me.

36. Counselor: OK, so imagining yourself wasn't too stressful. Did I give you enough time before I signaled to stop?

    Client: Well, probably. Although I think I could have gone on a little longer.

Based on Joan's response about the length of the first scene, the counselor <u>will modify the length during the next presentation</u>.

37. Counselor: OK, I'll give you a little more time the next time.

The counselor <u>presents the same scene again</u>. Usually each scene is presented <u>a minimum of two times</u> by the counselor or on a tape-recorder.

38. Counselor: Let's try it again. I'll present the same scene and I'll give you more time after you signal to me you have a strong picture.
    (Presents the same scene again and checks out Joan's reactions after the second presentation.)

After the counselor-presented scenes, the counselor <u>asks Joan to self-direct her own practice</u>. This also occurs a minimum of two times on each scene.

39. Counselor: You seem pretty comfortable now in carrying out this situation the way you want to. This time instead of my describing the scene orally to you, I'd like you just to go through the scene on your own—sort of a mental practice without my assistance.

    Client: OK. (Pauses to do this for several minutes.)

40. Counselor: OK, how did that feel?

    Client: It was pretty easy even without your instructions, and I think I can see where I can actually do this now with Mr. _____.

The other scenes in the hierarchy are worked through in the same manner.

41. Counselor: Good. Now we will work through the other three scenes in the same manner, sticking with each one until you can perform your desired behaviors in your imagination pretty easily.
    (The other three situations in the hierarchy are worked through.)

42. Counselor: Well, how do you feel now that we've gone over every scene?

    Client: Pretty good. I never thought that my imagination would help me in math class!

After the hierarchy has been completed, the <u>counselor picks scenes to practice at random</u>. This is a way to see how easily the client can perform the scene when it is not presented in the order of the hierarchy.

43. Counselor: Well, sometimes imagining yourself doing something helps you learn how to do it in the actual situation. Now I'd like to just pick a scene here at random and present it to you and have you imagine it again.
    (Selects a scene from the hierarchy at random and describes it.)

    Client: That was pretty easy, too.

The counselor initiates homework practice for Joan.

44. Counselor: OK, I just wanted to give you a chance to imagine a scene when I took something out of the order we worked with today. I believe you are ready to carry out this imagination practice on your own during the week.

    Client: Is this where I use the tapes?

The purpose of homework is explained to Joan.

45. Counselor: Sure. This tape has a series of scenes dealing with verbal class participation. So instead of needing me to describe a scene, the tape can do this. I'd like you to practice with this daily, because daily practice will help you learn to participate more quickly and easily.

    Client: So I just go over a scene the way we did today?

The counselor instructs Joan on how to complete the homework practice. These instructions include a "do" statement, a "quantity" statement, and a method for self-observing homework completion.

46. Counselor: Go over the scenes one at a time —maybe about four times for each scene. Make your imagination as vivid as possible. Also, each time you go over a scene, make a check on your log sheets. Indicate the time of day and place where you use this—also, the length of each practice. And after each practice session, rate the vividness of your imagery on this scale: 1 is not vivid and 5 is very vivid. How about summarizing what you will do for your homework?

    Client: Yes. I just do what we did today and check the number of times I practice each scene and assign a number to the practice according to how strongly I imagined the scene.

At the termination of the session, the counselor indicates a follow-up on the homework will occur at their next meeting.

47. Counselor: Right. And bring your log sheets in at our next meeting and we'll go over this homework then. OK? We had a really good session today. You worked hard. I'll see you next Tuesday.

Learning Activity: Covert Modeling

As you may recall from reading the goals and subgoals of Ms. Weare (Chapter 12), one of her subgoals was to arrange a school conference with Freddie's teacher. Ms. Weare was going to use the conference to explain her new strategy in dealing with Freddie and request help and cooperation from the school. Specifically, Ms. Weare might point out that one of the initial consequences of her strategy might be an increase in Freddie's tardiness at school. Assume that Ms. Weare is hesitant to initiate the conference because she is unsure about what to say during the meeting. Describe how you could use covert modeling to help Ms. Weare achieve this subgoal. Describe specifically how you would use (1) a verbal set; (2) practice scenes; (3) development of treatment scenes; (4) application of treatment scenes; and (5) homework to help Ms. Weare in this objective. Feedback is provided; see if some of your ideas are similar.

Summary

Emotive imagery and covert modeling are two procedures that may be useful when media and live modeling are not feasible. These two strategies can be employed without elaborate therapeutic aids or expensive equipment. Both strategies involve imagery, which makes the procedures quite easy for a client to practice in a self-directed manner. The capacity of clients to generate vivid images may be important for the overall effectiveness of emotive imagery and covert modeling. Assessment of client potential to engage in imagery is a necessary prerequisite before employing either of these procedures. Assuming that clients can produce clear images, counselors may use emotive imagery to deal with fears or discomfort or covert modeling to promote desired responses.

Post Evaluation

Part One

According to Objective 1, you should be able to identify accurately the steps of emotive imagery represented in written examples of counselor leads. For each of the following seven counselor leads, write on a piece of paper which part of emotive imagery the counselor is implementing. There may be more than one counselor lead associated with any part of the procedure. Also, the leads given here are not in any

Feedback: Covert Modeling

1. *Verbal Set*

   First you would explain that covert modeling could help Ms. Weare find the ways to express herself and could help her to practice expressing herself before initiating the actual conference. Second, you would briefly describe the strategy, emphasizing that she will be practicing her role and responses in the school conference using her imagination.

2. *Practice Scenes*

   You would explain that it is helpful to see how she feels about practicing through her imagination. You would select several unrelated scenes, such as imagining someone coming to her home, imagining an old friend calling her, or imagining a new television show about a policewoman. You would present one practice scene and instruct Ms. Weare first to close her eyes, imagine the scene intensely, and to signal to you with her finger when she has a strong picture in her mind. After this point, you could tell her to open her eyes and to describe the details of what she imagined. You might suggest additional details and present the same scene again or present a different scene. If Ms. Weare is able to use imagery easily and comfortably, you could move on to developing the actual treatment scenes.

3. *Developing Treatment Scenes*

   At this point, you would seek Ms. Weare's input about certain aspects of the scenes to be used as treatment scenes. Specifically, you would decide who would be used as the model, whether individualized or standardized scenes would be used, and whether Ms. Weare felt she could benefit from general or specific scenes. Our preference would be to use pretty specific, individualized scenes in which Ms. Weare imagines herself as the model, since she will ultimately be carrying out the action. Next, you should specify the three ingredients of the scenes: (1) the situation in which the behaviors should occur, (2) the behaviors to be demonstrated, and (3) a favorable outcome. For example, the scenes could include Ms. Weare calling the teacher to set up the conference, beginning the conference, explaining her strategy in the conference, and ending the conference. Specific examples of things she could say would be included in each scene. Favorable outcomes might take the form of covert self-praise.

4. *Applying Treatment Scenes*

   After all the treatment scenes have been developed, Ms. Weare would arrange them in a hierarchy from least to most difficult. Starting with the first scene in the hierarchy, you would again instruct Ms. Weare about how to imagine. After the first scene presentation, you would obtain Ms. Weare's reactions to the clearness of her imagery, the duration of the scene, and so on. Any needed revisions could be incorporated before a second presentation of the same scene. You would present each scene to Ms. Weare several times; then have her self-direct her own scene-imagining several times. After all the scenes in the hierarchy had been covered adequately, Ms. Weare would be ready for homework.

5. *Homework*

   You would instruct Ms. Weare to continue to practice the scenes in her imagination outside the session. A follow-up should be arranged. You should be sure that Ms. Weare understands how many times to practice and how such practice can benefit her. Ms. Weare might record her practice sessions on log sheets. Also, she could call in and verbalize the scenes using a phone-mate.

particular order. The five major parts of emotive imagery are:

1. Verbal set
2. Determining the client's potential to use imagery
3. Developing imagery scenes
4. Imagery scene practice training
5. Homework and follow-up

Feedback follows the evaluation.

1. "Can you think of several scenes you could imagine that give you calm and positive feelings? Supply as many details as you can. You

can use these scenes later to focus on instead of the anxiety."
2. "It's important that you practice with this. Try to imagine these scenes at least several times each day."
3. "This procedure can help you control your anxiety. By imagining very pleasurable scenes you can block out some of the fear."
4. "Let's see if you feel that it's easy to imagine something. Close your eyes, sit back, and visualize anything that makes you feel relaxed."
5. "Now, select one of these scenes you've practiced. Imagine this very intensely. I'm going to apply pressure to your arm, but just focus on your imaginary scene."
6. "What we will do, if you feel that imagination is easy for you, is to develop some scenes that are easy for you to visualize and that make you feel relaxed. Then we'll practice having you focus on these scenes while also attempting to block out fear."
7. "Now I'd like you just to practice these scenes we've developed. Take one scene at a time, sit back, and relax. Practice imagining this scene for about 30 seconds. I will tell you when the time is up."

Part Two

Objective 2 asks you to demonstrate 10 out of 13 steps of emotive imagery with a role-play client. You or an observer can rate your performance assisted by the Interview Checklist for Emotive Imagery following on pp. 322–325.

Part Three

Objective 3 asks you to describe how you would use the five components of covert modeling with a simulated client case. Use the case of Mr. Brown and his stated goal of wanting to decrease his worrying about retirement and increase his positive thoughts about retiring, particularly in his work setting. Describe how you would use a verbal set, practice scenes, developing treatment scenes, applying treatment scenes, and homework to help Mr. Brown do this. Feedback follows the evaluation.

Part Four

Objective 4 asks you to demonstrate at least 22 out of 27 steps associated with covert modeling with a role-

play client. The client might take the part of someone who wants to acquire certain skills or to perform certain activities. Use the Interview Checklist for Covert Modeling at the end of the chapter to help you assess your interview.

Feedback: Post Evaluation

Part One

1. Instructing the client to *develop imagery scenes*. These are used as the scenes to focus on to block the unpleasant sensation.
2. Part of *homework*, "in vivo" application of imagery.
3. *Verbal set*—giving the client a rationale for emotive imagery.
4. The counselor is *determining the client's potential to use imagery*.
5. *Imagery scene practice*—with a pain-provoking situation.
6. *Verbal set*—the counselor is explaining an overview of the procedure.
7. *Imagery scene practice*—the client is trained to imagine the scenes very vividly before using them in simulation of anxiety-provoking situations.

Part Two

Rate your performance with the Interview Checklist for Emotive Imagery found on pp. 322–325.

Part Three

Verbal Set
First you would give Mr. Brown a verbal set about covert modeling. You would briefly describe the process to him and explain how using his imagination to "see" someone doing something can help him perform his desired responses.

Practice Scenes
Next you would present a couple of unrelated practice scenes. You would instruct Mr. Brown to close his eyes, relax, and imagine the scene as you describe it. When Mr. Brown signals he is imagin-

---

ing the scene, you would stop and query him about what he imagined. You might suggest additional details for him to imagine during another practice scene. Assuming Mr. Brown feels relaxed and can generate vivid images, you would go on to develop treatment scenes.

Developing Treatment Scenes

You and Mr. Brown would specify certain components to be included in the treatment scenes, including the identity of the model (Mr. Brown or someone else), type of model (coping or mastery), single or multiple models, and specific characteristics of the model to maximize client-model similarity. Next you would decide whether to use individualized or standardized scenes; perhaps in Mr. Brown's case, his own scenes might work best. You would also need to decide how detailed the scene should be. In Mr. Brown's case, a scene might include some examples of positive thoughts and allow room for him to add his own. You and Mr. Brown would generate a list of scenes to be used, specifying:

1. the situation (which for him would be at work when the negative thoughts crop up)
2. the behavior and coping methods he would acquire (stopping interfering thoughts, generating positive thoughts about retirement, and getting back to his project at work)
3. favorable outcomes (for Mr. Brown, this might be being able to get his work done on time)

Applying Treatment Scenes

You and Mr. Brown would arrange the scenes in order—starting first with a work situation in which his thoughts are not as interfering, to situations in which they are most interfering. Starting with the first scene, you would give Mr. Brown specific instructions on imagining. Then you would present the scene to him and have him hold the scene in imagination for a few seconds after he signaled a strong image. Following the scene presentation, you would get Mr. Brown's reactions to the scene and make any necessary revisions in duration, scene content, order in the hierarchy, and so on. The same scene would be presented to Mr. Brown at least one more time, followed by several practices in which he goes through the scene without your assistance. After you had worked through all scenes in the hierarchy, you would present scenes to him in a random order.

Homework

After each scene presentation in the session, you would instruct Mr. Brown to practice the scenes daily outside the session. A follow-up on this homework should be arranged.

Part Four

Assess your interview or have someone else assess it using the Interview Checklist for Covert Modeling at the end of the chapter.

Interview Checklist for Emotive Imagery

Instructions: In a role-play counselor-client interview, determine which of the following counselor leads or questions were demonstrated. Indicate by a check the leads used by the counselor. A few examples of counselor leads are presented in the right column.

Checklist	*Examples of Counselor Leads*

I. *Verbal Set*

_____ 1. Counselor describes purpose of emotive imagery.

"The procedure is called emotive imagery because you can emote pleasant thoughts or images in situations that evoke fear, pain, tension, anxiety, or routine boredom. The procedure helps you block your discomfort or reduce the anxiety that you experience

Checklist	Examples of Counselor Leads
	in the problem situation. The technique involves focusing on imaginary scenes that please you and make you feel relaxed while in the uncomfortable situation. It is extremely difficult for you to feel pleasant, calm, happy, secure, or whatever other emotion is involved in the scene and anxious (tense, fearful, stressed) at the same time. These emotions are incompatible.''
_____ 2. Counselor gives an overview of procedure.	"What we will do is first see how you feel about engaging in imagery and look at the details of the scene you used. Then, we will decide whether emotive imagery is a procedure we want to use. If we decide to use it, we will develop scenes that make you feel calm, good, and generate positive feelings for you. We will practice using the scenes we have developed and try to rehearse using those scenes in a simulated fashion. Later, you will apply and practice using the scene in the real situation. Do you have any questions about my explanation?''
_____ 3. Counselor assesses client's willingness to try strategy.	"Would you like to go ahead and give this a try now?"
II. *Assessment of Client's Imagery Potential*	
_____ 4. Counselor instructs client to engage in imagery that elicits good feelings and calmness.	"Close your eyes, sit back, and relax. Visualize a scene or event that makes you feel relaxed and pleasant. Select something you really enjoy and feel good about. Try to be aware of all your sensations in the scene."
_____ 5. After 30 seconds to a minute, the counselor probes to ascertain the sensory vividness of the client's imagined scene (colors, sounds, movement, temperature, smell). Counselor asks client's feelings about imagery and about "getting into" the scene (feeling good with imaginal process).	"Describe the scene to me." "What sensations did you experience while picturing the scene?" "What temperature, color, sounds, smell, and motions did you experience in the scene?" "How do you feel about the imagery?" "How involved could you get with the scene?"

Checklist	Examples of Counselor Leads
_____ 6. Counselor discusses with client the decision to continue or discontinue with emotive imagery. Decision is based on client's attitude (feelings about imagery) and imaginary vividness.	"You seem to feel good with the imagery and are able to picture a scene vividly. We can go ahead now and develop some scenes just for you." "Perhaps another strategy that would reduce tension without imagery would be better since it is hard for you to 'get into' a scene."

III. *Develop Imagery Scenes*
_____ 7. Counselor and client develop at least two scenes that promote positive feelings for client and involve many sensations (sound, color, temperature, motion, and smell).

"What I would like to do now is to develop or build an inventory of scenes or situations that promote calmness, tranquility, and enjoyment for you. We want to have scenes that will have as much sensory detail as possible for you, so that you can experience color, smell, temperature, touch, sound, and motion. Later, we will use the scenes to focus on instead of anxiety. What sort of scenes can you really get into?"

IV. *Practice of Imagery Scene*
_____ 8. Counselor instructs client to practice focusing on the scene for about 30 seconds.

"Take one of the scenes, close your eyes, sit back, and relax. Practice or hold this scene for about 30 seconds, attempting to picture as much sensory detail as possible. I will cue you when the time is up."

_____ 9. Counselor instructs client to practice focusing on scene with simulated discomfort or anxiety.

"Let us attempt to simulate or create the problem situation and to use the scenes. While I squeeze your arm to have you feel pain, focus on one of the imagery scenes we have developed."

"While I describe the feared situation or scene to you, focus on the scene."
"How did that feel?"

_____ 10. Counselor assesses client's reaction after simulated practice.

"What effects did my describing the discomforting situation (my application of pain) have on your relaxation?"

"Rate your ability to focus on the scene with the discomfort."

"How comfortable did you feel when you imagined this fearful situation then?"

Checklist	Examples of Counselor Leads

V. *Homework and Follow-Up*

_____ 11. Counselor instructs client to apply emotive imagery "in vivo."

"For homework, apply the emotive-imagery scenes to the discomforting situation. Focus on the scene as vividly as possible while you are experiencing the activity or situation."

_____ 12. Counselor instructs client to record use of emotive imagery and to record level of discomfort or anxiety on log sheets.

"After each time you use emotive imagery, record the situation, day, time, and your general reaction on this log. For each occasion that you use imagery, record also your level of discomfort or anxiety using a five-point scale with 5 equal to maximum discomfort and 1 equal to minimum discomfort."

_____ 13. Counselor arranges a follow-up session.

"Let's get together again in 2 weeks to see how your practice is going and to go over your homework log."

Interview Checklist for Covert Modeling

Instructions: Determine which of the following leads were used by the counselor in the interview. Check the leads used.

Checklist	Examples of Counselor Leads

I. *Verbal Set about Strategy*

_____ 1. Counselor provides rationale about strategy.

"This strategy can help you learn how to discuss your prison record in a job interview. I will coach you on some things you could say. As we go over this, gradually you will feel as if you can handle this situation when it comes up in an actual interview."

_____ 2. Counselor provides overview of strategy.

"We will be relying on your imagination a lot in this process. I'll be describing certain scenes and asking you to close your eyes and imagine that you are observing the situation I describe to you as vividly as you can."

_____ 3. Counselor confirms client's willingness to use strategy.

"Would you like to give this a try now?"

II. *Practice Scenes*

_____ 4. Counselor instructs client to sit back, close eyes, and relax in preparation for imagining practice scenes.

"Just sit back, relax, and close your eyes."

_____ 5. Counselor describes a practice scene unrelated to goal and instructs client to imagine scene as counselor describes it and to raise index finger when scene is vividly imagined.

"As I describe this scene, try to imagine it very intensely. Imagine the situation as vividly as possible. When you feel you have a vivid picture, raise your index finger."

Checklist	*Examples of Counselor Leads*

_____ 6. After client indicates vivid imagery, counselor instructs client to open eyes and describe what was imagined during scene.

"OK, now let's stop—you can open your eyes. Tell me as much as you can about what you just imagined."

_____ 7. Counselor probes for additional details about scene to obtain a very specific description from client.

"Did you imagine the color of the room? What did the people look like? Were there any noticeable odors around you? How were you feeling?"

_____ 8. Counselor suggests ways for client to attend to additional details during subsequent practice.

"Let's do another scene. This time try to imagine not only what you see, but what you hear, smell, feel, and touch."

_____ 9. Counselor initiates additional practices of one scene or introduces practice of new scene until client is comfortable with the novelty and is able to provide a detailed description of imagery.

"Let's go over another scene. We'll do this for a while until you feel pretty comfortable with this."

_____ 10. After practice scenes, counselor:

  _____ a. decides to move on to developing treatment scenes

"OK, this seems to be going pretty easily for you, so we will go on now."

  _____ b. decides that relaxation or additional imagery training is necessary

"I believe before we go on it might be useful to try to help you relax a little more. We can use muscle relaxation for this purpose."

  _____ c. decides to terminate covert modeling because of inadequate client imagery.

"Based on this practice, I believe another approach would be more helpful where you can actually see someone do this."

III. *Developing Treatment Scenes*

_____ 11. Counselor and client decide on appropriate characteristics of model to be used in treatment scenes, including:

  _____ a. identity of model (client or someone else)

"As you imagine this scene, you can either imagine yourself or someone else in this situation. Which would be easier for you to imagine?"

  _____ b. coping or mastery model

"Sometimes it's easier to imagine someone who doesn't do this perfectly. What do you think?"

  _____ c. single or multiple models

"We can have you imagine just one other person—someone like yourself—or several other people."

  _____ d. specific characteristics of model to maximize client-model similarity.

"Let's talk over the specific type of person you will imagine."

Checklist	Examples of Counselor Leads

_____ 12. Counselor and client specify:
    _____ a. individualized scenes
    _____ b. standardized scenes.

"We have two options in developing the scenes you will imagine. We can discuss different situations and develop the scenes just to fit you, or else we can use some standardized scenes that might apply to anyone going through a job interview with a prison record. What is your preference?"

_____ 13. Counselor and client decide to use either:
    _____ a. general descriptions of scenes
    _____ b. specific, detailed descriptions of scenes.

"Based on these situations you've just described, I can present them to you in one of two ways. One way is to give you a general description and leave it up to you to fill in the details. Or I can be very detailed and tell you specifically what to imagine. Which approach do you think would be best for you?"

_____ 14. Counselor and client develop specific ingredients to be used in scenes. Ingredients include:
    _____ a. situations or context in which behaviors should occur

"Let's decide the kinds of things that will go in each scene."

"In the scene in which you are interviewing for a job, go over the type of job you might seek and the kind of employer who would be hard to talk to."

    _____ b. behaviors and coping methods to be demonstrated by model

"Now what you want to do in this situation is to discuss your record calmly, explaining what happened and emphasizing that your record won't interfere with your job performance."

    _____ c. favorable outcome of scene, such as:
        _____ 1. favorable client self-initiated action

"At the end of the scene you might want to imagine you have discussed your record calmly without getting defensive."

        _____ 2. client self-reinforcement.

"At the end of the scene, congratulate yourself or encourage yourself for being able to discuss your record."

_____ 15. Counselor and client generate description of multiple scenes.

"OK, now, the job interview is one scene. Let's develop other scenes where you feel it's important to be able to discuss your record. For example, in establishing a closer relationship with a friend."

IV. _Applying Treatment Scenes_
_____ 16. Counselor and client arrange multiple scenes in a hierarchy for scene presentation according to:
    _____ a. client degree of discomfort in situation
    _____ b. degree of difficulty or complexity of situation.

"Based on these six different scenes we've developed, I'd like you to arrange them in an order. Start with the situation that you feel most comfortable with and that is easiest for you to discuss your record in now. End with the situation that is most difficult and gives you the most discomfort or tension."

_____ 17. Counselor precedes scene presentation with instructions to client, including:

    _____ a. instructions to sit back, relax, close eyes

    _____ b. instructions on whom to imagine

    _____ c. instructions to imagine intensely using as many senses as possible

    _____ d. instructions to raise index finger when vivid imagery occurs

    _____ e. instructions to hold imagery until counselor signals to stop.

"I'm going to tell you now what to do when the scene is presented."
"First, just sit back, close your eyes, and relax."
"Now come up with an image of the person you're going to imagine."
"As I describe the scene, imagine it as vividly as possible. Use all your senses—sight, smell, touch, and so on."
"When you start to imagine very vividly, raise your finger."
"And hold that vivid image until I tell you when to stop."

_____ 18. Counselor presents one scene at a time, by describing the scene orally to client or via a tape-recorder.

"Here is the first scene. . . . Imagine the employer is now asking you why you got so far behind in school. Imagine that you are explaining what happened in a calm voice."

_____ 19. Duration of each scene is determined individually for client and is held until client imagines model performing desired behavior as completely as possible (perhaps 20–30 seconds).

"You should be able to imagine yourself saying all you want to about your record before I stop you."

_____ 20. After first scene presentation, counselor solicits client reactions about:

    _____ a. rate of delivery and duration of scene

    _____ b. clearness and vividness of client imagery

    _____ c. degree of discomfort or pleasantness of scene.

"How did the length of the scene seem to you?"
"How intense were your images? What did you imagine?"
"How did you feel while doing this?"

_____ 21. Based on client reactions to first scene presentation:

    _____ a. scene is presented again as is

    _____ b. scene or manner of presentation is revised before second presentation

    _____ c. scene order in hierarchy is changed and another scene is presented next

    _____ d. relaxation or discussion of client discomfort precedes another presentation of scene.

"I'm going to present this same scene again."
"Based on what you've said, let's change the type of employer. Also, I'll give you more time to imagine this the next time."
"Perhaps we need to switch the order of this scene and use this other one first."
"Let's talk about your discomfort."

_____ 22. Each scene is presented a minimum of two times by counselor or on tape-recorder.

_____ 23. Following counselor presentations of scene, client repeats scene at least twice in a self-directed manner.

"OK, now I'm going to present the same scene one or two more times."
"This time I'd like you to present the scene to yourself while imagining it, without relying on me to describe it."

Checklist	Examples of Counselor Leads

_____ 24. After each scene in hierarchy is presented and imagined satisfactorily, counselor presents some scenes to client in a random order, following steps 18–20.

"Now I'm just going to pick a scene at random and describe it while you imagine it."

V. *Homework*

_____ 25. Counselor instructs client to practice scenes daily outside session and explains purpose of daily practice.

"During the week, I'd like you to take these cards where we've made a written description of these scenes and practice the scenes on your own. This will help you acquire this behavior more easily and quickly."

_____ 26. Instructions for homework include:

_____ a. a "do" statement

"Just go over one scene at a time—make your imagination as vivid as possible."

_____ b. a "quantity" statement
_____ c. a method for self-observation of homework completion.

"Go over this five times daily."
"Each time you go over the scene, make a tally on your log sheet. Also, after each practice session, rate the intensity of your imagery on this scale."

_____ 27. Counselor arranges for a follow-up after completion of some amount of homework.

"Bring these sheets next week so we can discuss your practices and see what we need to do as the next step."

Suggested Readings

Emotive Imagery

Horan, J. J. "In vivo" emotive imagery: A technique for reducing childbirth anxiety and discomfort. *Psychological Reports*, 1973, *32*, 1328.

Horan, J. J. Coping with inescapable discomfort through in vivo emotive imagery. In J. D. Krumboltz & C. E. Thoresen (Eds.), *Counseling methods*. New York: Holt, Rinehart & Winston, 1976.

Lazarus, A. A., & Abramovitz, A. The use of "emotive imagery" in the treatment of children's phobias. *Journal of Mental Science*, 1962, *108*, 191–195.

Simonton, O. C., & Simonton, S. S. Belief systems and management of the emotional aspects of malignancy. *Journal of Transpersonal Psychology*, 1975, *7*, 29–47.

Covert Modeling

Cautela, J. R. The present status of covert modeling. *Journal of Behavior Therapy and Experimental Psychiatry*, 1976, *6*, 323–326.

Cautela, J., Flannery, R., & Hanley, S. Covert modeling: An experimental test. *Behavior Therapy*, 1974, *5*, 494–502.

Flannery, R. B. Use of covert conditioning in the behavioral treatment of a drug-dependent college dropout. *Journal of Counseling Psychology*, 1972, *19*, 547–550.

Hay, W., Hay, L., & Nelson, R. The adaptation of covert modeling procedures to the treatment of chronic alcoholism and obsessive-compulsive behavior: Two case reports. *Behavior Therapy*, 1977, *8*, 70–76.

Kazdin, A. E. Covert modeling and the reduction of avoidance behavior. *Journal of Abnormal Psychology*, 1973, *81*, 87–95.

Kazdin, A. E. Comparative effects of some variations of covert modeling. *Journal of Behavior Therapy and Experimental Psychiatry*, 1974, *5*, 225–231.

Kazdin, A. E. Effects of covert modeling and model reinforcement on assertive behavior. *Journal of Abnormal Psychology*, 1974, *83*, 240–252.

Kazdin, A. E. The effect of model identity and fear-relevant similarity on covert modeling. *Behavior Therapy*, 1974, *5*, 624–635.

Kazdin, A. E. Covert modeling, imagery assessment, and assertive behavior. *Journal of Consulting and Clinical Psychology*, 1975, *43*, 716–724.

Kazdin, A. E. Assessment of imagery during covert modeling of assertive behavior. *Journal of Behavior Therapy and Experimental Psychiatry*, 1976, 7, 213–219.

Kazdin, A. E. Developing assertive behavior through covert modeling. In J. D. Krumboltz & C. E. Thoresen (Eds.), *Counseling methods*. New York: Holt, Rinehart & Winston, 1976.

Kazdin, A. E. Effects of covert modeling, multiple models, and model reinforcement on assertive behavior. *Behavior Therapy*, 1976, 7, 211–222.

Nesse, M., & Nelson, R. Variations of covert modeling on cigarette smoking. *Cognitive Therapy and Research*, 1977, 1, 343–353.

Nietzel, M., Martorano, R., & Melnick, J. The effects of covert modeling with and without reply training on the development and generalization of assertive responses. *Behavior Therapy*, 1977, 8, 183–192.

Rosenthal, T. L., & Reese, S. L. The effects of covert and overt modeling on assertive behavior. *Behaviour Research and Therapy*, 1976, 14, 463–469.

Suinn, R. M. Removing emotional obstacles to learning and performance by visuo-motor behavior rehearsal. *Behavior Therapy*, 1972, 3, 308–310.

Suinn, R. M. Visuo-motor behavior rehearsal for adaptive behavior. In J. D. Krumboltz & C. E. Thoresen (Eds.), *Counseling methods*. New York: Holt, Rinehart & Winston, 1976.

Thase, M. E., & Moss, M. K. The relative efficacy of covert modeling procedures and guided participant modeling on the reduction of avoidance behavior. *Journal of Behavior Therapy and Experimental Psychiatry*, 1976, 7, 7–12.

Chapter 18
Cognitive Modeling and Thought-Stopping

Most systems of therapy recognize the importance of overt behavior change *and* cognitive and affective, or covert, behavior change. In recent years, more attention and effort have been directed toward developing and evaluating procedures that are aimed at modifying thoughts, attitudes, and beliefs. These procedures come under the broad umbrella of cognitive therapy (Beck, 1970) or cognitive behavior modification (M. J. Mahoney, 1974; Meichenbaum, 1977). Several assumptions are made about cognitive-change procedures. One of the basic assumptions is that a person's thoughts and beliefs can contribute to maladaptive behavior. Another is that maladaptive behaviors can be altered by dealing directly with the person's beliefs, attitudes, or thoughts (Beck, 1970). Krumboltz and Thoresen (1976) point out that, in many instances, a client's unreasonable self-standards and negative self-thoughts can diminish the power of a treatment program. Attention to the client's beliefs and expectations may be necessary in order for other therapeutic strategies to be successful.

Conceptualizing Client Cognitive Problems

There are many ways to conceptualize cognitive problems. Lazarus (1971) finds that clients who think in extremes, who over-generalize, who attempt to please everyone, and who regard cultural values as absolutes are prone to cognitive disorders (pp. 167–171). Beck (1976) asserts that people who distort or misperceive reality and who engage in illogical thinking are more likely to create problems for themselves. M. J. Mahoney (1974) categorizes cognitive problems into the following five areas:

1. Selective inattention—attending to irrelevant cues and ignoring relevant cues
2. Misperception—mislabeling cues (external or internal)
3. Maladaptive focusing—focusing on irrelevant *external* stimuli or events
4. Maladaptive self-arousal—focusing on irrelevant *internal* stimuli or cues
5. Repertory deficiencies—limited or inadequate behavior due to a deficit in cognitive or overt skills

Although the categorization of problems into these areas is helpful for conceptualization, these categories are not mutually exclusive. In the clinical world, it is more common to see a client who has trouble in several of these areas, all of which interact. For example, a client may feel anxious in social situations with strangers partially because of deficits in certain skills, such as initiating conversations and listening to someone else's message. At the same time, the person may feel anxious because she or he doesn't feel that strangers are receptive. In this case, the client could be misperceiving the situation or ignoring "approach" cues on the part of the stranger. Also, some of the stress may result from focusing on internal arousal cues that contribute to even greater stress. With this client, all these areas would become targets for change. Exploration of the client's problem (Chapters 9 and 10) might reveal that the client misperceives or ignores cues in other types of situations as well. It is likely that any cognitive-change procedure will be directed toward altering multiple rather than single contributing problem factors.

Four cognitive-change procedures are presented in this chapter and in Chapter 19. This chapter describes cognitive modeling and thought-stopping, and Chapter 19 describes cognitive restructuring and stress inoculation. All four of these procedures can attempt to eliminate "cognitive pollution."

Objectives

1. Using a simulated client case, describe how you would apply the seven components of cognitive modeling and self-instructional training.
2. Demonstrate 16 out of 21 steps of the cognitive self-instructional modeling with a role-play client, using the Interview Checklist for Cognitive Modeling at the end of the chapter to rate your performance.
3. Using a counselor-client dialogue, identify the six steps of the thought-stopping strategy reflected in at least 20 out of 25 counselor responses.
4. Demonstrate 21 out of 26 steps of thought-stopping in a role-play interview, using the Interview Checklist for Thought-Stopping at the end of the chapter to assess your performance.

Cognitive Modeling with Self-Instructional Training

Cognitive modeling is a procedure in which counselors show people what to say to themselves while performing a task. Sarason (1973), who used cognitive modeling to decrease test anxiety in college students, views the procedure as "efforts by the model to make explicit for observers the process by which he arrives at the overt responses he makes" (p. 58). Sarason points out that the uniqueness of cognitive modeling is that "the implicit or covert responses related to performance" are modeled (p. 58). These implicit factors may be just as important as the specific overt responses of a modeled display.

Meichenbaum and Goodman (1971) used cognitive modeling to develop self-control in young, impulsive children. The children saw a person model a set of verbalizations and behaviors that characterized a strategy they could use in performing a task. For example, the model verbalized:

> I have to remember to go slowly to get it right. Look carefully at this one (the standard), now look at these carefully (the variants). Is this one different? Yes, it has an extra leaf. Good, I can eliminate this one. Now, let's look at this one (another variant). I think it's this one, but let me first check the others. Good. I'm going slow and carefully. Okay, I think it's this one [p. 121].

The performance of the children exposed to this cognitive model was compared to that of a group in which the children received cognitive modeling plus self-instructional training (Meichenbaum & Goodman, 1971). In the latter group, in addition to viewing the model, the children were trained to produce the self-instructions the model emitted while performing the task. The children performed the task while instructing themselves as the model had done. Over the course of the practice trials, the children's self-verbalizations were faded from an overt to a covert level (p. 122). This group not only decreased decision time, but also significantly reduced performance errors.

The cognitive modeling plus self-instructional training also was used effectively to train hospitalized schizophrenics to alter their thinking, attention, and language behaviors (self-talk) while performing tasks (Meichenbaum & Cameron, 1973b). According to these authors, cognitive modeling with self-instructional training strategy consists of five steps:

1. The counselor serves as the model and first performs the task while talking aloud to himself or herself.
2. The client performs the same task (as modeled by the counselor) while the counselor instructs the client aloud.
3. The client is instructed to perform the same task again while instructing himself or herself aloud.
4. The client whispers the instructions while performing the task.
5. Finally, the client performs the task while instructing himself or herself covertly.

Note that cognitive modeling is reflected in step 1, whereas steps 2 through 5 consist of client practice of self-verbalizations while performing a task or behavior. Also, the client's verbalizations are faded from an overt to a covert level.

We propose that cognitive modeling and self-instructional training should be implemented with seven steps as guidelines:

1. a verbal set about the procedure
2. cognitive modeling of the task and of the self-verbalizations

Client practice in the form of:

3. overt external guidance
4. overt self-guidance
5. faded overt self-guidance
6. covert self-guidance
7. homework

Each of these steps will be explained in the following section. Illustrations also are provided in the Interview Checklist for Cognitive Modeling at the end of the chapter.

Verbal Set

An example of a verbal set for cognitive modeling might be:

"It has been found that some people have difficulty in performing certain kinds of tasks. Often the difficulty is not because they don't have the ability to do it, but because of what they say or think to themselves while doing it. In other words, a person's 'self-talk' can get in the way or interfere with performance. For instance, if you get up to give a speech and you're thinking 'What a flop I'll be,' this sort of thought may affect how you deliver your talk. This procedure can help you perform something the way you want to by examining and coming up with some helpful planning or self-talk to use while performing [rationale]. I'll show what I am saying to myself while performing the task. Then I'll ask you to do the task while I guide or direct you through it. Next, you will do the task again and guide yourself aloud while doing it. The end result should be your performing the task while thinking and planning about the task to yourself [overview]. How does this sound to you? [client willingness]."

After the rationale has been presented and any questions have been clarified, the counselor begins by presenting the cognitive model.

Model of Task and Self-Guidance

First, the counselor instructs the client to listen to what the counselor says to herself or himself while performing the task. Next, the counselor models performing a task while talking aloud. Meichenbaum and Goodman (1971) describe an example of the modeled self-instructions that were given to train impulsive children to copy line patterns:

Nature of Self-Guidance

Questions	Dialogue
1. What has to be done?	"Okay, what is it I have to do?"
2. Answers question in form of planning what to do.	"You want me to copy the picture with different lines."

3. Self-guidance and focused attention.	"I have to go slow and be careful. Okay, draw the line down, down, good; then to the right, that's it; now down some more and to the left."
4. Self-reinforcement.	"Good. Even if I make an error I can go on slowly and carefully. Okay, I have to go down now." "Finished. I did it."
5. Coping self-evaluative statements with error correction options.	"Now back up again. No, I was supposed to go down. That's okay. Just erase the line carefully" [p. 8].

As this example indicates, the counselor's modeled self-guidance should include five parts. The first part of the verbalization asks a question about the nature and demands of the task to be performed. The purposes of the question are to compensate for a possible deficiency in comprehending what to do, to provide a general orientation, and to create a cognitive set. The second part of the modeled verbalization answers the question about what to do or to perform. The answer is designed to model cognitive rehearsal and planning in order to focus the client's attention on relevant task requirements. Self-instruction in the form of self-guidance while performing the task is the third part of the modeled verbalization. The purpose of self-guidance is to facilitate attention to the task and to inhibit any possible overt or covert distractions or task irrelevancies. In the example, modeled self-reinforcement is the fourth part and is designed to maintain task perseverance and to reinforce success. The last part in the modeled verbalization contains coping self-statements to handle errors and frustration, with an option for correcting errors. The example of the modeled verbalization used by Meichenbaum and Goodman depicts a coping model. In other words, the model does make an error in performance, but corrects it and does not give up at that point. See if you can identify these five parts of modeled self-guidance in the following learning activity.

Learning Activity: Modeled Self-Guidance

The following counselor verbalization is a cognitive model for a rehabilitation client who is learning how to use a wheelchair. Identify the five parts of the message: (1) questions of what to do, (2) answers to the question in the form of planning, (3) self-guidance and focused attention, (4) coping self-evaluative statements, and (5) self-reinforcement. Feedback for this activity follows.

> "What is it that I have to do to get from the parking lot over the curb onto the sidewalk and then to the building? I have to wheel my chair from the car to the curb, get over the curb and onto the sidewalk, and then wheel over to the building entrance. Okay, wheeling the chair over to the curb is no problem. I have to be careful now that I am at the curb. Okay, now I've just got to get my front wheels up first. They're up now. So now I'll pull up hard to get my back wheels up. Whoops, didn't quite make it. No big deal. I'll just pull up very hard again. Good. That's better, I've got my chair on the sidewalk now. I did it! I've got it made now."

Overt External Guidance

After the counselor models the verbalizations, the client is instructed to perform the task (as modeled by the counselor) while the counselor instructs or coaches. The counselor coaches the client through the task or activity, substituting the personal pronoun *you* for *I* (for example, "What is it that *you* . . . , *you* have to wheel your chair . . . , *you* have to be careful"). The counselor should make sure that the coaching contains the same five parts of self-guidance that were previously modeled: question, planning, focused attention, coping self-evaluation, and self-reinforcement. Sometimes in the client's real-life situation, other people may be watching when the client performs the task—as could be the case whenever the wheelchair client appears in public. If the presence of other people appears to interfere with the client's performance, the counselor might say, "Those people may be distracting you. Just pay attention to what you are doing." This type of coping statement can be included in the counselor's verbalizations when using overt external guidance in order to make this part of the procedure resemble what the client actually will encounter.

Overt Self-Guidance

The counselor next instructs the client to perform the task while instructing or guiding himself or herself aloud. The purpose of this step is to have the client practice the kind of self-talk that will strengthen attention to the demands of the task and will minimize outside distractions. The counselor should attend carefully to the content of the client's self-verbalizations. Again, as in the two preceding steps, these verbalizations should include the five component parts, and the client should be encouraged to use his or her own words. If the client's self-guidance is incomplete, or if the client gets stuck, the counselor can intervene and coach. If necessary, the counselor can return to the previous steps—either modeling again or coaching the client while the client performs the task (overt external guidance). After the client completes this step, the counselor should provide feedback about parts of the practice the client completed adequately and about any errors or omissions. Another practice might be necessary before moving on to the next step, faded overt self-guidance.

Faded Overt Self-Guidance

The client next performs the task while whispering (lip movements). This part of cognitive modeling serves as an intermediate step between having the client verbalize aloud, as in overt self-guidance, and having the client verbalize silently, as in the next step of covert

Feedback: Modeled Self-Guidance

Question: "What is it that I have to do to get from the parking lot over the curb onto the sidewalk and then to the building?"

Answers with planning: "I have to wheel my chair from the car to the curb, get onto the curb and onto the sidewalk, and then wheel over to the building entrance."

Self-guidance and focused attention: "Okay, wheeling the chair over to the curb is no problem. I have to be careful now that I am at the curb. Okay, now I've just got to get my front wheels up first. They're up now. So now I'll pull up hard to get my back wheels up.

Coping self-evaluation and error-correction option: "Whoops, didn't quite make it. No big deal—I'll just pull up very hard again.

Self-reinforcement: "Good. That's better. I've got my chair on the sidewalk now. I did it! I've got it made now."

self-guidance. In other words, whispering the self-guidance is a way for the client to approximate successively the end result of the procedure: thinking to oneself while performing. In our own experience with this step, we have found that it is necessary to explain this to an occasional client who seems hesitant or concerned about whispering. If a client finds the whispering too foreign or aversive, it might be more beneficial to repeat overt self-guidance several times and finally move directly to covert self-guidance. If the client has difficulty in performing this step or leaves out any of the five parts, an additional practice may be required before moving on.

Covert Self-Guidance

Finally, the client performs the task while guiding or instructing covertly or "in one's head." It is very important for clients to instruct themselves covertly after practicing the self-instructions overtly. After the client does this, the counselor might ask for a description of the covert self-instructions. If distracting or inhibiting self-talk has occurred, the counselor can offer suggestions for more appropriate verbalizations or self-talk and can initiate additional practice. Otherwise, the client is ready to use the procedure outside the session.

Homework

Assigning the client homework is essential for generalization to occur from the interview to the client's environment. The counselor should instruct the client to use the covert verbalizations while performing the desired behaviors alone, outside the counseling session. The homework assignment should specify what the client will do (a "do" statement) and how much or how often (a "quantity" statement). The counselor should also provide a way for the client to monitor and reward himself or herself for completion of homework. A follow-up on the homework task also should be scheduled.

These seven components of cognitive modeling are modeled for you in the following dialogue with our client, Joan. Again, this strategy is used as one way to help Joan achieve her goal of increasing her verbal participation in math class.

Model Dialogue: Cognitive Modeling and Self-Instructional Training

In response 1, the counselor introduces the possible use of cognitive modeling to help Joan acquire the goal of increasing participation in her math class. The counselor is giving a rationale or verbal set about the strategy.

1. Counselor: One of the goals we developed was to help you increase your participation level in your math class. One of the ways we might help you do that is to use a procedure in which I demonstrate the kinds of things you want to do—and also I will demonstrate a way to think or talk to yourself about these tasks. So this procedure will help you develop a plan for car-

rying out these tasks, as well as showing you a way to participate. How does that sound?
Client: OK. Is it hard to do?

In response 2, the counselor provides an overview of the procedure, which is also a part of the verbal set.

2. Counselor: No, not really, because I'll go through it before you do. And I'll sort of guide you along. The procedure involves my showing you a participation method and, while I'm doing that, I'm going to talk out loud to myself to sort of guide myself. Then you'll do that. Gradually, we'll go over the same participation method until you do it on your own and can think to yourself how to do it. We'll take one step at a time. Does that seem clear to you?
Client: Well, pretty much. I've never done anything like this, though.

In response 3, the counselor determines Joan's willingness to try out the procedure.

3. Counselor: Would you like to give it a try?
Client: Sure—I'm willing.

In responses 4 and 5, the counselor sets the stage for modeling of the task and accompanying self-guidance, and instructs the client as to what will be done and what to look for in this step.

4. Counselor: We mentioned there were at least four things you could do to increase your class participation level—asking Mr. _____ for an explanation only, answering more of Mr. _____'s questions, going to the board to do problems, and volunteering answers. Let's just pick one of these to start with. Which one would you like to work with first?
Client: Going to the board to work algebra problems. If I make a mistake there, it's visible to all the class.

5. Counselor: Probably you're a little nervous when you do go to the board. This procedure will help you concentrate more on the task than on yourself. Now in the first step, I'm going to pretend I'm going to the board. As I move out of my chair and up to the board, I'm going to tell you what I'm thinking that might help me do the problems. Just listen carefully to what I say, because I'm going to ask you to do the same type of things afterwards. Any questions?
Client: No, I'm just waiting to see how you handle this. I'll look like Mr. _____. His glasses are always down on his nose and he stares right at you. It's unnerving.

In responses 6 and 7, the counselor initiates and demonstrates the task with accompanying self-guidance. Note, in the modeled part of response 7, the five components of the self-guidance process. Also note that a simple problem has been chosen for illustration.

6. Counselor: OK, you do that. That will help set the scene. Why don't you start by calling on me to go to the board?

   Client (as teacher): Joan, go to the board now and work this problem.

7. Counselor (gets out of seat, moves to imaginary board on the wall, picks up the chalk, verbalizing aloud): What is it I need to do? He wants me to find Y. OK, I need to just go slowly, be careful, and take my time. OK, the problem here reads $4X + Y = 10$, and X is 2.8. OK, I can use X to find Y. [Counselor asks *question* about task.] OK, I'm doing fine so far. Just remember to go slowly. OK, Y has to be $10 - 4X$. If X is 2.8, then Y will be $10 - 4$ multiplied by 2.8. [Counselor focuses *attention* and uses *self-guidance*.] Let's see, 4×2.8 is 10.2. Oops, is this right? I hear someone laughing. Just keep on going. Let me refigure it. No, it's 11.2. Just erase 10.2 and put in $Y = 10 - 11.2$. OK, good. If I keep on going slowly, I can catch any error and redo it. [Counselor uses *coping self-evaluation* and makes *error correction*.] Now it's simple. $10 - 11.2$ is -1.2 and Y is -1.2. Good, I did it, I'm done now and I can go back to my seat. [Counselor *reinforces self*.]

In responses 8 and 9, the counselor initiates <u>overt external guidance</u>: the client performs the task while the counselor continues to verbalize aloud the self-guidance, substituting you *for* I *as used in the previous sequence.*

8. Counselor: OK, that's it. Now let's reverse roles. This time I'd like you to get up out of your seat, go to the board, and work through the problem. I will coach you about what to plan during the process. OK?

   Client: Do I say anything?

9. Counselor: Not this time. You just concentrate on carrying out the task and thinking about the planning I give you. In other words, I'm just going to talk you through this the first time.

   Client: OK, I see.

In response 10, the counselor <u>verbalizes self-guidance while the client performs</u> the problem.

10. Counselor: OK, I'll be Mr. _____. I'll ask you to go to the board and then you go and I'll start coaching you. (As teacher): Joan, I want you to go to the board now and work out this problem: If $2X + Y = 8$ and $X = 2$, what does Y equal? (Joan gets up from chair, walks to imagi-

nary board and picks up chalk.) (As counselor): OK, first you write the problem on the board. $2X + Y = 8$ and $X = 2$. Now ask yourself "What is it I have to do with this problem?" OK, now answer yourself [question].

You need to find the value of Y [answer to question]. OK, just go slowly, be careful, and concentrate on what you're doing. You know $X = 2$, so you can use X to find Y. Your first step is to subtract $8 - 2X$. You've got that up there. OK, you're doing fine—just keep going slowly [focuses attention and uses self-guidance].

$8 - 2$ multiplied by 2 you know is $8 - 4$. Someone is laughing at you. But you're doing fine, just keep thinking about what you're doing. $8 - 4$ is 4, so $Y = 4$ [coping self-evaluation].

Now you've got Y. That's great. You did it. Now you can go back to your seat [self-reinforcement].

In response 11, the counselor <u>assesses the client's reaction</u> before moving on to the next step.

11. Counselor: OK, let's stop. How did you feel about that?

    Client: Well, it's such a new thing for me. I can see how it can help. See, usually when I go up to the board I don't think about the problem. I'm usually thinking about feeling nervous or about Mr. _____ or the other kids watching me.

In response 12, the counselor reiterates the <u>rationale</u> for the cognitive modeling procedure.

12. Counselor: Yes, well, those kinds of thoughts distract you from concentrating on your math problems. That's why this kind of practice may help. It gives you a chance to work on concentrating on what you want to do.

    Client: I can see that.

In responses 13 and 14, the counselor instructs the client to perform the task while verbalizing to herself (<u>overt self-guidance</u>).

13. Counselor: This time I'd like you to go through what we just did—only on your own. In other words, you should get up, go to the board, work out the math problem, and as you're doing that, plan what you're going to do and how you're going to do it. Tell yourself to take your time, concentrate on what you're doing, and give yourself a pat on the back when you're done. How does that sound?

    Client: OK, I'm just going to say something similar to what you said the last time—is that it?

14. Counselor: That's it. You don't have to use the same words. Just try to plan what you're doing.

If you get stuck, I'll step in and give you a cue. Remember, you start by asking yourself what you're going to do in this situation and then answering yourself. This time let's take the problem $5X + Y = 10$; with $X = 2.5$, solve for Y.

Client (gets out of seat, goes to board, writes problem): What do I need to do? I need to solve for Y. I know $X = 2.5$. Just think about this problem. My first step is to subtract $10 - 5X$. 5 multiplied by 2.5 is 12.5. So I'll subtract $10 - 12.5$. (Counselor laughs, Joan turns around.) Is that wrong?

Counselor: Check yourself but stay focused on the problem, not on my laughter.

Client: Well, $10 - 12.5$ is -2.5. $Y = -2.5$. Let's see if that's right. $5 \times 2.5 = 12.5 - 2.5 = 10$. I've got it. Yea.

In response 15, the counselor gives feedback to Joan about her practice. Note the use of "sandwich" feedback, discussed in Chapter 15—a positive comment, followed by a suggestion or criticism, followed by a positive comment.

15. Counselor: That was really great. You only stumbled one time—when I laughed. I did that to see if you would still concentrate. But after that, you went right back to your work and finished the problem. It seemed pretty easy for you to do this. How did you feel?

Client: It really was easier than I thought. I was surprised when you laughed. But then, like you said, I just tried to keep going.

In responses 16, 17, and 18, the counselor instructs Joan on how to perform the problem while whispering instructions to herself (faded overt self-guidance).

16. Counselor: This time we'll do another practice. It will be just like you did the last time with one change. Instead of talking out your plan aloud, I just want you to whisper it. Now you probably aren't used to whispering to yourself, so it might be a little awkward at first.

Client (laughs): Whispering to myself? That seems sort of funny.

17. Counselor: I can see how it does. But it is just another step in helping you practice this to the point where it becomes a part of you—something you can do naturally and easily.

Client: Well, OK. I guess I can see that.

18. Counselor: Well, let's try it. This time let's take a problem with more decimals since you get those, too. If it seems harder, just take more time to think and go slowly. Let's take $10.5X + Y = 25$, with $X = 5.5$.

Client (gets out of seat, goes to board, writes on board, whispers): OK, what do I need to do with this problem? I need to find Y. This has more decimals so I'm just going to go slowly. Let's see, $25 - 10.5X$ is what I do first. I need to multiply 10.5 by 5.5. I think it's 52.75. (Counselor laughs.) Let's see, just think about what I'm doing. I'll redo it. No it's 57.75. Is that right? I'd better check it again. Yes, it's OK. Keep going. $25 - 57.75$ is equal to -32.75, so $Y = -32.75$. I can check it—yes, 10.5×5.5 is $57.75 - 32.75 = 25$. I got it!

Counselor gives feedback in response 19.

19. Counselor: That was great, Joan—very smooth. When I laughed you just redid your arithmetic rather than turning around or letting your thoughts wander off the problem.

Client: It seems like it gets a little easier each time. Actually this is a good way to practice math, too.

In responses 20 and 21, the counselor gives Joan instructions on how to perform the problem while instructing herself covertly (covert self-guidance).

20. Counselor: That's right. Not only for what we do in here, but even when you do your math homework. Now, let's just go through one more practice today. You're really doing this very well. This time I'd like you to do the same thing as before—only this time I'd like you to just think about the problem. In other words, instead of talking out these instructions, just go over them mentally. Is that clear?

Client: You just want me to think to myself what I've been saying?

21. Counselor: Yes—just instruct yourself in your head. Let's take the problem $12X - Y = 36$, with $X = 4$. Solve for Y.

(Joan gets up, goes to the board, and takes several minutes to work through this.)

In response 22, the counselor asks the client to describe what happened during covert self-guidance practice.

22. Counselor: Can you tell me what you thought about while you did that?

Client: Well, I thought about what I had to do, then what my first step in solving the problem would be. Then I just went through each step of the problem and then after I checked it, I thought I was right.

In response 23, the counselor checks to see whether another practice is needed or if they can move on to homework.

23. Counselor: So it seemed pretty easy. That is what we want you to be able to do in class—to instruct yourself mentally like this while you're

working at the board. Would you like to go through this type of practice one more time, or would you rather do this on your own during the week?

Client: I think on my own would help right now.

In response 24, the counselor sets up Joan's homework assignment for the following week.

24. Counselor: OK. I think it would be helpful if you could do this type of practice on your own this week—where you instruct yourself as you work through math problems.

Client: You mean my math homework?

In response 25, the counselor instructs Joan on how to do homework, including what to do (a "do" statement) and how much to do (a "quantity" statement).

25. Counselor: Well, that would be a good way to start. Perhaps you could take seven problems a day. As you work through each problem, go through these self-instructions mentally. Does that seem clear?

Client: Yes, I'll just work out seven problems a day the way we did here for the last practice.

In response 26, the counselor instructs Joan to observe her homework completion on log sheets and arranges for a follow-up of homework at their next session.

26. Counselor: Right. One more thing. On these blank log sheets, keep a tally of the number of times you actually do this type of practice on math problems during the day. This will help you keep track of your practice. And then next week bring your log sheets with you and we can go over your homework.

Learning Activity: Cognitive Modeling

You may recall from the case of Ms. Weare and Freddie that Ms. Weare wanted to eliminate the assistance she gave Freddie in getting ready for school in the morning. One of Ms. Weare's concerns is to find a successful way to instruct Freddie about the new ground rules—mainly that she will not help him get dressed and will not remind him when the bus is 5 minutes away. Ms. Weare is afraid that, after she delivers her instructions, Freddie will either pout or talk back to her. She is concerned that she will not be able to follow through with her plan or else will not be firm in the way she delivers the ground rules to him. (a) Describe how you would use the seven major components of cognitive modeling and self-instructional training to help Ms. Weare to do this; and (b) write out an example of a cognitive-modeling dialogue Ms. Weare could use to accomplish this task. Make sure that this dialogue contains the five neces-

sary parts of the self-guidance process: question, answer, focused attention, self-evaluation, and self-reinforcement. Feedback follows.

Thought-Stopping

Thought control was introduced as early as 1928 by Bain. The thought-control procedure of thought-stopping was developed by J. G. Taylor (1963) and described by both Wolpe (1969) and Lazarus (1971). A recent elaboration of the procedure, which includes the addition of covert assertion, has been described by Rimm and Masters (1974).

Thought-stopping is used to help a client control unproductive or self-defeating thoughts and images by suppressing or eliminating these negative cognitions. Thought-stopping is particularly appropriate with a client who ruminates about a past event that cannot be eliminated or changed ("crying over spilled milk"), with a client who ruminates about an event that is unlikely to occur (what Lazarus [1971, p. 230] calls "a low probability catastrophe"), or with a client who engages in repetitive, unproductive, negative thinking or repetitive anxiety-producing or self-defeating images. The bothersome cognitions may take the form of thoughts or visual images. For example, a person who is always bothered with the idea of his or her spouse having an affair may engage in repetitive thoughts such as "What if this happens to me?" or "It would be my luck to have _____ cheat on me." Another client, concerned over the same event, might report repetitive images such as visualizing the spouse with another person.

Olin (1976) suggests that thought-stopping may not be appropriate for clients who have such intense troubling thoughts that they cannot control them. In our own counseling experience, we have found that thought-stopping works better with clients who are troubled by intermittent rather than continuous self-defeating thoughts. Of course, thought-stopping should be used only with clients whose thoughts are clearly counterproductive.

Feedback: Cognitive Modeling

a. Description of the seven components
   1. *Verbal set*. First, you would explain to Ms. Weare how cognitive modeling could help her in instructing Freddie and what the procedure would involve. You might emphasize that the procedure would be helpful to her in both prior *planning* and *practice*.
   2. *Model of task and self-guidance*. In this step, you would model a way Ms. Weare could talk to Freddie. Your modeling would include both the task (what Ms. Weare could say to Freddie) and the five parts of the self-guidance process.
   3. *Overt external guidance*. Ms. Weare would practice giving her instructions to Freddie while you coach her on the self-guidance process.
   4. *Overt self-guidance*. Ms. Weare would perform the instructions while verbalizing aloud the five parts of the self-guidance process. If she gets stuck, or if she leaves out any of the five parts, you can cue her. This step also may need to be repeated before moving on.
   5. *Faded overt self-guidance*. Assuming Ms. Weare is willing to complete this step, she would perform the instructions to give Freddie while whispering the self-guidance to herself.
   6. *Covert self-guidance*. Ms. Weare would practice giving the instructions to Freddie while covertly guiding herself. When she is able to do this comfortably, you would assign homework.
   7. *Homework*. You would assign homework by asking Ms. Weare to practice the covert self-guidance daily and arranging for a follow-up after some portion had been completed.

b. Example of a model dialogue:

"OK, what is it I want to do in this situation? [question]. I want to tell Freddie that he is to get up and dress himself without my help. That I will no longer come up and help him even when it's time for the bus to come [answer]. OK, just remember to take a deep breath and talk firmly and slowly. Look at Freddie. Say "Freddie, I am not going to help you in the morning. I've got my own work to do. If you want to get to school on time, you'll need to decide to get yourself ready" [focused attention and self-guidance]. Now if he gives me flack, just stay calm and firm. I won't back down [coping self-evaluation]. That should be fine. I can handle it [self-reinforcement].

Wolpe (1971) distinguishes between problem-solving thoughts that lead to action—desirable thoughts—and those that lead to a dead end —negative thoughts.

Thought-stopping has been used in a number of clinical cases. It has been used to reduce hallucinatory images (Bucher & Fabricatore, 1970; Samaan, 1975), to reduce fantasies of dressing in clothes of the opposite sex (Gershman, 1970), to reduce obsessive and self-critical thoughts (M. J. Mahoney, 1971), to eliminate repetitive images of colors (Yamagami, 1971), to reduce anxiety attacks about epileptic seizures (Anthony & Edelstein, 1975), and to eliminate a husband's constant thoughts and images of his wife's past extramarital affair (R. C. Rosen & B. J. Schnapp, 1974). Although the clinical case reports of thought-stopping indicate encouraging results, there is very little evidence available from controlled investigations to lend empirical support to the procedure. Thought-stopping was effective in reducing smoking behavior (Wisocki & Rooney, 1974) and helpful in reducing obsessive thinking of ten outpatients (Hackmann & McLean, 1975). Because of the limited amount of data, a number of questions about the rationale and the mechanism for thought-stopping remain unanswered. Nevertheless, thought-stopping continues to be used frequently, often in conjunction with other strategies. As Wisocki and Rooney point out, there are several advantages of thought-stopping: it is administered easily, it is usually understood by a client, and it is readily employed by the client in a self-regulatory manner (p. 192).

There are six major components of the

thought-stopping strategy: a verbal set, counselor-directed thought-stopping (overt interruption), client-directed thought-stopping (overt interruption), client-directed thought-stopping (covert interruption), a shift to assertive, positive, or neutral thoughts, and homework and follow-up. Some of these steps have been described in case examples (Gershman, 1970; Hackmann & McLean, 1975; Rimm, 1973; Rimm & Masters, 1974; Yamagami, 1971). The specific steps associated with each component can be found in the Interview Checklist for Thought-Stopping at the end of the chapter.

Verbal Set

First, the counselor will explain the rationale for thought-stopping. Before using the strategy, clients should be aware of the nature of their self-defeating thoughts or images. Wolpe (1971) suggests that the counselor should point out how the client's thoughts are futile and in what ways the client would be better off without being plagued by such thoughts or images. Here is an example of a way the counselor might explain the purpose of thought-stopping:

> "You say you are bothered by constant thoughts that you might die in some horrible way. These thoughts take up a lot of energy and really are unnecessary. You would feel better if you weren't constantly thinking about this or having images of a horrible death scene flash through your mind. This procedure can help. You learn to break this habit of thinking. How does this sound to you?"

If the client agrees to try to work with thought-stopping, the counselor should describe the procedure without displaying too graphically the way in which the thoughts are stopped, because the initial surprise is very effective. The counselor might say:

> "I will ask you to sit back and just let thoughts come into your mind. When you tell me you have a thought or an image related to this horrible death scene, I will interrupt you. Then I will teach you how to break this chain of thoughts

yourself so you can do this whenever these thoughts crop up."

Counselor-Directed Thought-Stopping: Overt Interruption

In this first phase of thought-stopping, the counselor assumes the responsibility for interrupting the thoughts. The interruption is overt, consisting of a loud *Stop!* that can be accompanied by a noise such as a hand clap, a ruler hitting a desk, or a whistle. In the first counselor-directed sequence, the client is instructed to verbalize all thoughts and images aloud. The verbalization enables the counselor to determine the precise point when the client shifts from positive thinking to negative thinking.

This sequence goes like this:

1. The counselor instructs the client to sit back and let any thoughts come to mind: "Sit back, relax, and just let thoughts and images flow into your mind."
2. The counselor instructs the client to verbalize aloud these thoughts or images as they occur: "Whenever you start to think about anything or you see an image, just share with me verbally what you're thinking or seeing."
3. At the point where the client verbalizes a self-defeating thought or image, the counselor interrupts with a loud *Stop!* Sometimes, in addition, a loud noise stimulus such as a hand clap, a whistle, or a ruler hitting the desk is used.
4. The counselor points out whether the unexpected interruption was effective in terminating the client's negative thoughts or images: "Perhaps you realize that as soon as I said *Stop!* and interrupted you, your self-defeating thought stopped and didn't go on as often happens."

After this sequence, the counselor directs another thought-stopping sequence in which the client does not verbalize thoughts aloud but uses a hand signal to inform the counselor of the onset of a self-defeating thought or image. This sequence is similar to the first one with the exception of the hand signal:

1. The counselor asks the client to sit back and let thoughts come naturally to mind.
2. The counselor instructs the client to signal with a raised hand or finger when the client notices thinking about the self-defeating or negative ideas.
3. When the client signals, the counselor interrupts with *Stop!*

These three steps are repeated within the session as often as necessary—generally until a pattern of inhibiting the client's self-defeating thoughts by the counselor's command is established.

Client-Directed Thought-Stopping: Overt Interruption

After the client has learned to control negative thoughts in response to the counselor's interruption, the client assumes responsibility for the interrupting. At first the client directs himself or herself in the thought-stopping sequence with the same overt interruption used by the counselor—a loud *Stop!* Here is the way this step might proceed:

1. The client deliberately evokes thinking about something and lets all kinds of thoughts come to mind.
2. The counselor instructs the client to say aloud *Stop!* whenever the client notices a self-defeating thought or image: "This time you can direct yourself in thought-stopping. When you first notice you're thinking about a horrible way of dying, interrupt yourself with a loud *Stop!*"

These two steps are repeated until the client is able to suppress self-defeating thoughts by overt self-interruption. Sometimes a client may report that even the word *Stop* or a clap is not a strong enough stimulus to help actually terminate the undesired thought. In these cases, a snap of a rubber band worn on the wrist at least

for a short time may add to the potential of these stimuli to stop the negative thoughts (M. J. Mahoney, 1971).

Client-Directed Thought-Stopping: Covert Interruption

In many cases, it would be impractical and unwise for clients to interrupt themselves overtly. Imagine what might happen if a client was riding on an airplane, bus, or subway and suddenly yelled *Stop!* Because of this, in the next sequence of thought-stopping, the client substitutes a covert interruption for the overt one. The same two-step sequence occurs:

1. The client lets any thoughts or images come to mind.
2. When the client notices a self-defeating thought, the client stops by covertly saying *Stop!*

These two steps are repeated until the client is able to terminate the self-defeating thoughts with only the covert interruption.

Shift to Assertive, Positive, or Neutral Thoughts

In some instances, a client's negative thoughts may contribute to a greater level of anxiety. In other cases, the client's thought patterns may be cued by some preceding anxiety or tension. In both cases, some degree of anxiety or arousal may be present in addition to the ruminative thinking patterns. In order to reduce any residual anxiety, Rimm and Masters (1974) suggest that the client learn to think assertive thoughts after the self-defeating thoughts are interrupted. Since assertive behavior inhibits anxiety, it is assumed that assertive thoughts also will inhibit any anxiety or arousal that may occur even after the client has learned to suppress the undesired thoughts. Essentially, the client is taught to shift thoughts to assertive responses following the interruption. These responses may either contradict the content of the negative thoughts or be unrelated. For example, in working with a client who was constantly worrying about having a nervous breakdown, Rimm and Masters helped the client learn to think "Screw it. I'm OK. I'm normal." This assertive thought clearly contradicts the nature of the client's self-defeating thoughts. An example of an unrelated, yet still assertive, thought this same client could use might be "Some of the new things I'm going to start in my job this week are . . . " or "I've got some important ideas to express the next time I . . . . "

Rimm and Masters (1974) point out that the assertive thoughts should be realistic and geared toward any actual danger in a situation. For example, if a client is in police work and is constantly thinking about the hazards of the job, it would be unrealistic for this client to use an assertive response that denies real hazards, such as "Being a police officer is a very safe job." However, the client could think about skills and past successes in coping with apparent hazards, such as "When something comes up, I know how to handle it." Although Rimm and Masters refer to these kinds of thoughts as *assertive*, there is a great deal of similarity between these thoughts and the coping thoughts the client is taught in cognitive restructuring (see Chapter 19).

Not all counselors who use thought-stopping have the client shift from self-defeating thoughts to assertive ones. In lieu of using assertive thoughts, the client can be asked to focus on a pleasurable or reinforcing scene (Anthony & Edelstein, 1975; Gershman, 1970; Yamagami, 1971) or a neutral scene, such as an object in the environment (Wolpe, 1971). In an interesting report of thought-stopping, clients who were constantly engaging in self-degrading thoughts were taught to stop the chain of thoughts and replace them with a variety of self-reinforcing thoughts (Hays & Waddell, 1976). For example, someone who catches herself or himself thinking "I'll never be a superstar. What do I have to offer anyway?" stops these thoughts and shifts to thoughts such as "I'm a really good piano player" or "In my own quiet way I can contribute." In our opinion, it is important to have the client learn to shift to

other kinds of thoughts after the self-defeating ones are stopped. However, the particular kinds of thoughts that are substituted should be adapted for the client and the nature of the self-defeating thoughts.

Here are the steps involved in teaching the client to shift from self-defeating to assertive, positive, or neutral thoughts:

1. The counselor explains the purpose of substituting different thoughts for the negative or unproductive ones: "In addition to stopping yourself from ruminating over all the horrible ways you might die, it's helpful to substitute different kinds of thoughts that are unrelated to death. This part of the procedure will help you learn to shift to different thoughts after you stop yourself from the self-defeating thinking."

2. The counselor models the type of thoughts the client could substitute after terminating the self-defeating ones and gives some examples. The client is asked to identify others and to practice using these aloud: "After you signal *Stop!* to yourself, shift your thoughts to something positive, like a beautiful sunset, something fun you did during the day, or an interesting object in the room, like a picture on the wall. See if you can think of several things like this you could think about from time to time. Then just practice saying these things aloud."

3. Next, the client is asked to practice this shift after another sequence of self-directed thought-stopping with overt interruption. As soon as the client says *Stop!* the shift to another kind of thought should be made. The client should verbalize aloud the specific thought used: "This time, repeat the thought-stopping where you stop your negative thoughts by saying *Stop!* aloud. Then practice substituting one of these thoughts you've picked, like thinking about what a good movie you saw last night. Share these positive thoughts aloud."

4. After this practice, the client engages in another practice which is done covertly. The client stops covertly and substitutes different thoughts without verbalizing them aloud:

"Now we'll do the same type of thing—only all in your head. When you notice any thoughts related to a horrible death popping into your mind, think *Stop!* and then think about lying on the beach on a warm day."

5. The client should be encouraged to practice substituting assertive, positive, or neutral thoughts several different times. Each time, the client should use a different thought so that satiation from constant repetition of only one thought does not occur (Rimm & Masters, 1974).

If a client has difficulty making the shift from the negative thoughts to other ones, a cueing device might help. For example, the client can write positive or assertive responses on small note cards and carry these around. Or the client can wear a wrist golf counter and click it as a cue for making the shift in thoughts.

Homework and Follow-Up

Once the client learns the thought-stopping procedure, it is time to use it outside the interview. At first, the client should be instructed to practice the thought-stopping sequence several times each day. This homework practice strengthens the client's control over stopping a chain of self-defeating thoughts as they occur. Samaan (1975) had a client use a tape-recording of his *Stop!* messages in the initial phase of homework practice to strengthen thought control. Gradually, the client's use of the tape-recorded messages with daily practice was eliminated.

In addition to daily practice, clients can initiate thought-stopping whenever they notice they are engaging in negative or self-defeating thinking. The client should be cautioned about the amount of time that often is necessary to break a well-learned habit of thinking a certain way. The client can keep track of the daily practice and the number of times thought-stopping was used "in vivo" on a log sheet. And, as with the application of any counseling strategy, a later follow-up session should be arranged.

How Does Thought-Stopping Actually Work?

There is no single explanation to account for what the client learns when using the thought-stopping strategy. It is assumed that the strategy produces some sort of control over obsessive or repetitive thinking. There are at least four ways in which thought-stopping may help a person learn to control and reduce unwanted thoughts and images. These explanations are not mutually exclusive; to some degree each may contribute to the learning that occurs when thought-stopping is used.

1. The word *stop* (or the loud noise) may be an aversive stimulus that punishes the client's self-defeating thoughts or images. As a result, the maladaptive thoughts are suppressed.
2. The word *stop* and any other accompanying stimulus may be a distraction that breaks the chain of maladaptive thoughts. Campbell (1973) found that thought-stopping accompanied by the distractor of counting backwards reduced obsessional thinking; however, M. J. Mahoney (1971) reported that the same distractor seemed to increase obsessional thinking.
3. The word *stop* has an assertive quality. If this is the case, Rimm and Masters (1974) suggest, the subvocalized *stop* will, like any overt assertive response, inhibit anxiety that may trigger the negative or repetitive thoughts. To the extent that this explanation has merit, the use of covert assertion or positive thoughts to replace the chain of negative thoughts is a very important part of the strategy. Indeed, as M. J. Mahoney (1974) suggests, perhaps thought *substitution* may be even more beneficial than thought *termination*.
4. M. J. Mahoney (1974) indicates that the subvocalized self-instruction *stop* may be incompatible with the maladaptive subvocalized thoughts and images the client is trying to eliminate. The result is that the maladaptive thoughts are replaced by the incompatible self-instruction.

Model Dialogue: Thought-Stopping

As you may recall, one of Joan's goals was to develop positive thoughts about her ability to do well in math. Her two subgoals were to stop negative or self-degrading thoughts about her potential, and to replace these with more realistic, positive thoughts. Also, Joan wanted to decrease the nervous feelings she had before and during math class. Her dialogue with the counselor illustrates a combination of thought-stopping, cognitive restructuring, and stress inoculation. As you will see from the explanations that precede the counselor's responses, thought-stopping is used to help Joan stop her negative thoughts, cognitive restructuring is used to help her learn to replace the self-defeating thoughts with coping thoughts, and stress inoculation is used to help her decrease the tension and nervousness she experiences before and during math class. Thought-stopping is illustrated in session 1. Cognitive restructuring and stress inoculation dialogues are presented in Chapter 19.

Session 1

In this session, the counselor will give Joan a rationale and an overview of all three strategies and teach Joan how to use thought-stopping to stop her negative thoughts about math.

In responses 1 and 2, the counselor reviews the things Joan wants to change and emphasizes that cognitive change requires practice in addition to willpower.

1. Counselor: Joan, we've talked about how you constantly put yourself down about your ability to do well in math—even though you know you have the ability. You know that thinking you can't do math doesn't really reflect your ability, but you find yourself thinking this way anyway. These kinds of thoughts also probably add to the nervousness you feel before and during math class.
   Client: I know what you're saying and I agree. I just can't seem to make myself think I can do it.
2. Counselor: Right. Well, thinking about a situation in a certain way is something you learn like a habit and it takes time to change it. It's not changed easily by just willpower—but by systematic practice of new, more productive ways of thinking.

Client: And you think if I could think about my ability positively that this will help?

Joan, like many clients, is questioning how changing her thoughts can help. The counselor will respond to her concern by pointing out the difference between self-defeating and self-enhancing thoughts and how these different ways of thinking can affect performance.

3. Counselor: Well, let's look at it this way. Whenever you think "I'm a girl, I can't do math" or "This problem is too hard for me, I'll give up" that is just one way to think about math—and it's negative. If you think something like "Girls can do well in math if they want to" or "Being a girl doesn't mean I'm dumb in math" or "I know I have the ability so I'm going to work at it," these thoughts are more positive. The negative thoughts can interfere with your doing OK in math, because you start to convince yourself it's useless. Also, when you think you can't do it, you get nervous and want to give up or get out of the situation. But the positive thoughts give you a way to cope with the situation and help you feel more relaxed. Both of these things can help you improve your performance in math class.
   Client: That makes some sense. I guess it's hard to realize that you can change how you think. I mean, I've had such bad thoughts about math for a while.

Joan understandably is still concerned about how her habitual thinking can be changed. The counselor will deal with this in response 4 by pointing out that it takes time, and in response 5 by describing to Joan how this can be accomplished.

4. Counselor: It is hard at first to realize that you can change the way you think. And it does take time. Would you like to give it a try?
   Client: Yes. I think I'll have to get into it to see how it works.
5. Counselor: OK. Well, let me explain a little about what we will do so you can see exactly how this can help. First, I'll ask you to tell me the specific kinds of things you're usually thinking about yourself and your capacity in math. For any of these thoughts that are negative or self-defeating, I'll teach you a way to stop these kinds of thoughts so they don't just continue [thought-stopping]. Then after you feel you have some control in stopping these thoughts, we'll learn some more positive thoughts. We call these *coping thoughts* because they help you cope with the situation. We'll practice these so you get used to using coping thoughts instead of the negative thoughts [cognitive restruc-

turing]. Then I'll help you learn some body relaxation, which is a way to cope with the nervousness you feel before and during math class. We'll help you practice using your coping thoughts and relaxation in stressful situations [stress inoculation]. How does this sound?

Client: Well, I think it gives me an idea. It sounds like it will take a while.

Joan is continuing to express some concern about the idea so, in response 6, the counselor will respond to this before going ahead with the strategies.

6. Counselor: It will take some time. We'll need to spend some time learning these things, and then it will be important for you to practice what you learn on your own. I'm wondering if you're concerned about the time it might take or about what we might do?

Client: No, not really. Actually it sounds like it has to help. I guess I'm still just getting used to the idea that you can change the way you think.

The counselor realizes that, especially for young people, the idea of thought control may seem foreign. The counselor will attempt to make this more understandable to Joan by pointing out some situations and books using thought control that a client of Joan's age can relate to.

7. Counselor: I realize that often the idea does sound a little unfamiliar. Have you heard of any of the popular books out like _____ or _____ that teach mind control? These books work with the idea that you can have control over the way you think and that your thinking can influence you. For example, the way athletes or musicians perform in the Olympics or a concert to some extent depends upon the way they think about themselves and their ability.

Client: That's true. I hadn't made a connection between that and myself, but I can see where it's the same idea.

Up to this point, the counselor has been working with a verbal set (rationale and overview of strategies) and with information-giving about how Joan's thoughts affect her performance. This verbal set and the information given are common to thought-stopping, cognitive restructuring, and stress inoculation, since all three strategies emphasize the effects of self-defeating thinking on one's feelings and behaviors. In the next sequence, the counselor will work on helping Joan identify and stop the kinds of self-defeating thoughts she has about math. This part of the strategy is primarily the "nuts and bolts" of thought-stopping, although it is also part of cognitive restructuring. In response 8, the counselor asks Joan to describe aloud

her typical thoughts about math; as soon as she describes a chain of negative thoughts, the counselor interrupts her with a loud Stop! in response 9.

8. Counselor: Why don't you sit back now and just think about math class. Then tell me what you're thinking.

Client: Well, I'm thinking how hard math is for me. I'm dumb in it and I'm a girl and that doesn't help and . . .

9. Counselor: *Stop!*

Client (startled): Wow, you surprised me!

In responses 10 and 11, the counselor points out how the unexpected interruption stopped Joan's negative thoughts, emphasizing the potential control Joan has over her thoughts.

10. Counselor: I can see I did. Joan, what happened when I did that?

Client: Well, I was startled. I stopped thinking about how dumb I am in math.

11. Counselor: Right. You were starting to tell me some very negative thoughts about math and your ability—so I stopped you. Then you shut those thoughts off. The interruption like that is startling but it shows you that you don't *have* to let these kinds of thoughts go on.

Client: I can see what you mean, but can I do the same thing?

Next the counselor shows Joan how she controls her thoughts by having Joan interrupt herself with a loud Stop!

12. Counselor: Yes, with lots of practice. And that's what I'll show you now—how to interrupt yourself. This time, think about math class again. Whenever you start to think these things like "You can't do it" or "You're dumb," shout *Stop!*

Client (thinks, then): *Stop!*

13. Counselor: OK—what happened?

Client: Well, I stopped. Of course it seems a little strange.

14. Counselor: It will at first and gradually we'll get to the point where you can stop yourself by *thinking* the word *stop*. But for now let's do this several times until you get used to it.

(Client-directed overt interruption is repeated as necessary.)

Next, the counselor introduces covert interruption; Joan practices interrupting her negative thoughts with a subvocal Stop!

15. Counselor: OK, I'd like you to try the same thing. Only this time when you notice the self-defeating thoughts, stop these just by saying *Stop!* to yourself so no one can hear you.

(Joan does this and practices repeatedly until she

feels she has control over stopping these thoughts.)

16. Counselor: That's really good. It seems like you're able to cut off the thoughts pretty well.
    Client: I can. But will I forget how to do this?

The counselor responds to Joan's concern by emphasizing the importance of practice. A <u>daily homework assignment</u> is given. Also, to get an idea of how often Joan needs to use thought-stopping, the counselor asks her to record other instances of usage in her log.

17. Counselor: Not if you practice at it. What I'd like you to do before our next meeting is to practice these at least three times each day just like you've done today. Then, as you need to, if these thoughts crop up at other times, you can use the thought-stopping then, too. Could you keep track of your daily practices, and the number of other times you do this, on these log sheets and bring these next week?
    Client: Sure. Just write down each practice and each other time I do this—right?

18. Counselor: Right. Remember to put down how often, where, and how long you work with this. Have a good week.

Learning Activities: Thought-Stopping

I. Listed below are four client descriptions. Read each and, on the basis of the description, determine whether thought-stopping would be an appropriate strategy to use with the client. Write on a piece of paper why or why not. You may wish to distinguish between problem-solving thoughts and "dead-end" thoughts in your analysis. Feedback is given on p. 348.

1. The client is unhappy with her or his present job and reports spending a great deal of time thinking about various job alternatives.
2. The clients, a retired couple, are unsure whether their health and age permit them to stay in their large house. They are spending a lot of time trying to decide whether they should move and, if so, what options are available.
3. The client is a young woman whose first baby died several years ago soon after birth. The client reports spending a great deal of time thinking about what she did or didn't do that may have contributed to the baby's death.
4. The client is afraid to go out of her house because she is worried that something bad will happen to her.

II. This learning activity is designed for you to use

thought-stopping with yourself as a kind of self-management procedure.

1. Identify some pervasive "dead-end" thoughts you have about a situation. Make sure the thoughts are self-defeating or unproductive. Perhaps you are even faced with ruminating over some "what if's" about being a helper, such as "What if I don't say the right thing" or "What if I don't help the client" or "What if the client doesn't come back."
2. Sit back and think about the situation—let any thoughts flow into your mind. As soon as you notice a self-defeating thought, say *Stop!* very loudly. Repeat this step about five times.
3. This time, think about the situation and, when you become aware of a self-defeating thought, say *Stop!* subvocally so no one can hear you. Repeat this step about five times.
4. Identify some assertive or positive thoughts you could substitute for the self-defeating ones. If, for example, you wish to eliminate self-defeating thoughts about not being a good helper, some assertive thoughts might be "I will do my best," or "There will always be times when I don't say the best thing," or "My attitude toward clients is one of caring."
5. Now think again about the situation. Stop any self-defeating thoughts subvocally. Then concentrate on an assertive or positive thought. Repeat this about five times, using a different assertive or positive thought each time.
6. Practice this every day for a week or two. Also, use this whenever the self-defeating thoughts you are trying to eliminate appear spontaneously.

Summary

Both cognitive modeling and thought-stopping involve helping a client terminate distracting or self-defeating ruminations. In the next chapter we will see how clients can be taught to stop self-defeating thoughts and to replace these with incompatible coping thoughts and skills. Both the strategies of cognitive restructuring and stress inoculation, presented in Chapter 19, are directed toward *replacement*, not merely elimination, of self-defeating cognitions.

Part One

Describe how you would use the seven components of cognitive modeling and self-instructional training to help Mr. Brown initiate social contacts with his boss (Objective 1). The seven components are:

1. Verbal set
2. Model of task and self-guidance
3. Overt external guidance
4. Overt self-guidance
5. Faded overt self-guidance
6. Covert self-guidance
7. Homework

Feedback follows the evaluation.

Part Two

Objective 2 asks you to demonstrate at least 16 out of 21 steps of the cognitive self-instructional modeling procedure with a role-play client. You can audio-tape your interview or have an observer assess your performance using the Interview Checklist for Cognitive Modeling at the end of the chapter.

Part Three

Objective 3 asks you to identify the components of thought-stopping used by the counselor in a counselor-client dialogue. As you may recall from the goals of the case of Mr. Brown (Chapter 12), Mr. Brown wanted to decrease his negative, self-defeating thoughts about retirement and increase his positive thoughts about retirement. In the following dialogue, the counselor uses thought-stopping to help Mr. Brown achieve these two goals. Your task is to identify each counselor lead by writing down which particular component of thought-stopping it illustrates. The six major parts of the thought-stopping strategy are:

1. Verbal set about strategy
2. Counselor-directed thought-stopping: overt interruption
3. Client-directed thought-stopping: overt interruption
4. Client-directed thought-stopping: covert interruption

Feedback: Thought-Stopping

1. We would not select thought-stopping for this client because the thoughts are related to a realistic present problem of job dissatisfaction. This is a situation the client may be able to change. In order to do so, she or he would need to spend some time thinking about different employment alternatives.
2. We would not use thought-stopping with this couple. They also are faced with a realistic decision and must first think about their options before making a final decision.
3. Although some ruminating over the death of a loved one is natural and realistic, this client is continuing to do so several years after the baby's death. Also the client's thoughts are centered primarily around trying to reconstruct what she did or didn't do—something which, in actuality, she cannot change. Thought-stopping could be used with her.
4. This is a good example of a client whose behavior is influenced by thoughts that reflect a "low probability catastrophe." Although there are reasonable cautions she could take, such as not going out alone at night, her thoughts about something happening to her at other times are unrealistic and interfering. Thought-stopping could be used with her.

5. Shift from self-defeating to assertive, positive, or neutral thoughts
6. Homework and follow-up

Remember, there may be more than one counselor lead associated with each of these parts of the strategy. Feedback is provided at the end of the evaluation.

1. Counselor: I'm glad to see you today, Mr. Brown. Last week we talked about some of the ways we might work together to reach your counseling goals. You indicated an interest in learning a procedure we call thought-stopping. I'm wondering whether you have thought of any questions about this or if you'd like me to review how this might help you.
   Client: No, I really don't have any questions, but it might help if you could just tell me again exactly what we would be doing.
2. Counselor: Sure. First, we talked before about

how your negative thoughts about retirement interfere with your work. You'd like to be able to stop these, but you haven't been able to do so just by willpower. Thought-stopping is a way to hand over the responsibility to you for gaining control of these thoughts, so they don't remain in control of you.

Client: Is it sort of like telling yourself to stop these thoughts?

3. Counselor: Well, it helps you learn to stop your thoughts by using the word *stop* to interrupt your thoughts. However, it is a matter of not only telling yourself, but practicing—to the point where, upon your own command, you can break this habit of continually ruminating at work about the terrible aspects of retirement. Anything else that doesn't seem clear?

Client: No. I think I'd like to give it a try.

4. Counselor: OK. Now first I am going to show you how your negative thoughts can be interrupted. Then I'll show you how to interrupt your thoughts in a way that you can use at work, when you need to. Are you ready?

Client: Yes.

5. Counselor: OK, Mr. Brown. Can you imagine you're at your desk now, working on one of your car projects. As you notice any thoughts that you think of, just share these with me aloud.

Client: Well, I'm thinking that I need to get busy on this design. It's a neat design. What a car. But hell, I won't even be around when it comes out, why can't I . . .

6. Counselor (loudly): *Stop!*

Client: Wow! I stopped. I wasn't expecting that.

7. Counselor: The surprise element sometimes helps even though I realize it is startling. Do you see how you stopped thinking about not being around to see that car when I interrupted you that way?

Client: Yes, I do. It was quite effective.

8. Counselor: What does this suggest to you?

Client: Well, that I don't have to let my thoughts like this go on and on.

9. Counselor: Right. With enough practice, you can learn to stop your thoughts in this sort of way. Now I'd like you to try something similar. Imagine again that you are at your desk. This time, as you become aware of any thoughts, just keep them to yourself. But as soon as you notice that you are starting to get into those negative thoughts, signal this to me by raising your hand. OK?

Client: Yes. (Closes his eyes, pauses, then signals.)

10. Counselor (loudly): *Stop!*

Client: I stopped. I sure did.

11. Counselor: You seem to be working really well with this. I think it would help if we went over this several more times now. (Additional practice ensues.)

12. Counselor: Do you feel that you're at the point where you now automatically stop when you hear this word, or do you think more practice like this is needed before you learn to do this yourself?

Client: I think I'm ready to go on.

13. Counselor: OK. This time I'd like you to interrupt yourself the way I just did. Sit back and imagine you're at your desk working on this car design. When you notice a self-defeating thought, say *Stop!* loudly.

Client (pauses): *Stop!*

14. Counselor: Well, what happened?

Client: Well, it felt strange to say that, but I did stop.

15. Counselor: It does seem strange at first. But if it works, that's what counts. As you practice this it won't seem as strange as it does now. I'd like you to practice this more. (Additional practice.)

16. Counselor: How do you feel about this now?

Client: Pretty good. It's not as strange. Of course it does seem a little like talking to yourself.

17. Counselor: True, and in a sense you are. Of course it wouldn't always be possible for you to actually yell *Stop!* like this, especially if you weren't alone. So what we'll do is practice the same sort of thing again. Only this time you will keep the signal to yourself. Just imagine again that you're at your desk with this project. Let any thoughts come into your mind. This time when you notice a self-defeating thought, just say *Stop!* to yourself subvocally—so no one else hears.

(Client pauses, mouths *Stop!*)

18. Counselor: OK. Now this is the way that you will use thought-stopping when you need to in your office. Let's work with this until you feel there's a pattern established when you mouth or think the word *stop*. (More practice.)

Client: I feel pretty comfortable with this now. I believe I've got this under control.

19. Counselor: OK, good. Now so far we've practiced helping you decrease or stop your negative thoughts about retirement. In this next part of thought-stopping, you can learn to shift to

some positive thoughts about retirement after you stop the negative ones. This helps you replace the interfering thoughts with other ones that are realistic yet positive. Does this seem clear?

Client: Yes, I think so.

20. Counselor: The first thing we need to do is to find some things about retirement that you feel are positive that you can start thinking about. For example, retirement brings some advantages, such as having time to spend with your family, or having time to travel somewhere. Perhaps becoming active in an organization or a group you enjoy is an advantage. Maybe entertaining more or engaging in your woodworking hobby is another advantage. What other positive things about retirement could you think of?

Client: Well, some of the things you mentioned. I've never had enough time to do things I enjoy or to spend time with my family. I guess having more free time is one positive aspect of retirement. Actually I believe retirement will have some pluses for my marriage. It will be good for my wife to see more of me. I've never been home as much as I'd like or she'd like.

21. Counselor: OK, so those are at least two positive things—having free time and enhancing your marriage. Maybe during the week you can think of a few more. What might be helpful now is for you to practice with these positive thoughts. Imagine you're at your desk and use the word *stop* by thinking it if you start those self-defeating thoughts. This time, right after you stop these thoughts, start thinking about one of the positive things about retirement, like having more time. Share with me aloud what your positive thought is.

Client: OK. (Pauses and reflects.) Well, I'm thinking about all the things I will do with some free time.

22. Counselor: OK. Now let's try this again. This time, after you signal *Stop!* to yourself, substitute a different positive thought, like the pluses this will have for your marriage. And this time you don't need to share these thoughts with me—just spend time concentrating on them to yourself.

Client (pauses and reflects): OK.

23. Counselor: Now that is how you can use thought-stopping at work. You'll stop a self-defeating thought and substitute some of these positive thoughts. How about doing this a little more? (Repeated practice.)

24. Counselor: You've really done a good job with

learning this. As you know, it will take some time and practice, so during the next week I'd like you to practice what you just did about three times each day. OK?

Client: Yes, I think practice will help me remember this.

25. Counselor: It will also help you use it when you need to. Keep track of each of your practices on your log and we'll go over this again next week.

Part Four

Objective 4 asks you to demonstrate 21 out of 26 steps associated with the thought-stopping strategy in a role-play interview. You can audio-tape your interview or have an observer rate it using the Interview Checklist for Thought-Stopping at the end of the chapter.

Feedback: Post Evaluation

Part One

1. *Verbal set*

   First, you would explain the steps of cognitive modeling and self-instructional training to Mr. Brown. Then you would explain how this procedure could help him practice and plan the way he might approach his boss.

2. *Model of task and self-guidance*

   You would model for Mr. Brown a way he could approach his boss to request a social contact. You would model the five parts of the self-guidance process: (1) the question about what he wants to do; (2) the answer to the question in the form of planning; (3) focused attention on the task and guiding himself through it; (4) evaluating himself and correcting errors or making adjustments in his behavior in a coping manner; and (5) reinforcing himself for adequate performance.

3. *Overt external guidance*

   Mr. Brown would practice making an approach or contact while you coach him through the five parts of self-guidance as just described.

4. *Overt self-guidance*

   Mr. Brown would practice making a social contact while verbalizing aloud the five parts of the self-guidance process. If he got stuck, you could prompt him or else you could have him repeat this step or recycle step 3.

5. *Faded overt self-guidance*

   Mr. Brown would engage in another practice attempt, only this time he would whisper the five parts of the self-guidance process.

6. *Covert self-guidance*

   Mr. Brown would make another practice attempt while using the five parts of the self-guidance process covertly. You would ask him afterwards to describe what happened. Additional practice with covert self-guidance or recycling to step 4 or 5 may be necessary.

7. *Homework*

   You would instruct Mr. Brown to practice the self-guidance process daily before actually making a social contact with his boss.

Part Two

Rate an audio tape of your interview or have an observer rate you using the Interview Checklist for Cognitive Modeling found on p. 352.

Part Three

1. Verbal set. The counselor reviews the strategy and clarifies Mr. Brown's questions about it.
2. Verbal set. The counselor explains the purpose or rationale of thought-stopping.
3. Verbal set. The counselor explains what thought-stopping is and how it works.
4. Verbal set. The counselor gives a brief overview of what will happen.
5. Counselor-directed thought-stopping: overt interruption. The counselor asks Mr. Brown to imagine the problem situation and report any thoughts.
6. Counselor-directed overt interruption. The loud *Stop! is* the overt interruption. In this first sequence, it is administered by the counselor as a demonstration of how thoughts can be interrupted or terminated.
7. Counselor-directed overt interruption. The counselor points out how the interruption terminates the self-defeating thoughts.
8. Counselor-directed overt interruption. The counselor gets the client to acknowledge potential control over terminating the self-defeating thoughts.
9. Counselor-directed overt interruption. The counselor asks the client to signal a self-defeating thought that the counselor then interrupts overtly.
10. Overt interruption directed by the counselor.
11. Counselor-directed overt interruption. The counselor initiates repetitive practice until the word *stop* exerts control over the client's self-defeating thoughts.
12. Counselor-directed overt interruption. The counselor checks out Mr. Brown's use of this part of thought-stopping before going on.
13. Client-directed overt interruption. Mr. Brown is instructed to terminate his self-defeating thoughts by interrupting them with the word *stop*.
14. Client-directed overt interruption. The counselor queries Mr. Brown about his reaction to this practice attempt.

15. Client-directed overt interruption. The counselor initiates additional practices in which Mr. Brown interrupts his self-defeating thoughts overtly.
16. Client-directed overt interruption. The counselor assesses Mr. Brown's reactions to these practices.
17. Client-directed covert interruption. This time Mr. Brown will interrupt his self-defeating thoughts covertly with a subvocal *Stop!*
18. Client-directed covert interruption. The counselor initiates additional practices where Mr. Brown interrupts his negative thoughts covertly.
19. Shift from self-defeating to positive thoughts. The counselor explains the purpose of this part of the strategy to Mr. Brown.
20. Shift from self-defeating to positive thoughts. The counselor gives some examples of positive thoughts and asks Mr. Brown to identify some he can use.
21. Shift from self-defeating to positive thoughts. The counselor asks Mr. Brown to prac-

tice covert interruption of self-defeating thoughts, followed by substituting a positive thought. This first time, Mr. Brown verbalizes the positive thought aloud.
22. Shift from self-defeating to positive thoughts. The counselor instructs Mr. Brown to practice this covertly, this time using a different positive response. A variety of positive responses should be used by the client to prevent satiation.
23. Shift from self-defeating to positive thoughts. The counselor instructs Mr. Brown to engage in additional practice of the shift.
24. Homework and follow-up. The counselor assigns daily homework practice of the procedure.
25. Follow-up.

Part Four

Rate an audio tape of your interview or have someone else rate it using the Interview Checklist for Thought-Stopping.

Interview Checklist for Cognitive Modeling

Instructions: Determine which of the following leads were used by the counselor in the interview. Check each of the leads used. Some examples of counselor leads are provided in the right column; however, these are only suggestions.

Checklist	*Examples of Counselor Leads*
I. *Verbal Set about Strategy*	
＿＿＿ 1. Counselor provides rationale about strategy.	"This strategy is a way to help you do this task and also plan how to do it. The planning will help you perform better and more easily."
＿＿＿ 2. Counselor provides overview of strategy.	"We will take it step by step. First, I'll show you how to do it and I'll talk to myself aloud while I'm doing it so you can hear my planning. Then you'll do that. Gradually, you'll be able to perform the task while thinking through the planning to yourself at the same time."
＿＿＿ 3. Counselor checks client's willingness to use strategy.	"Would you like to go ahead with this now?"
II. *Model of Task and Self-Guidance*	
＿＿＿ 4. Counselor instructs client what to listen and look for during modeling.	"While I do this, I'm going to orally tell you my plans for doing it. Just listen closely to what I say as I go through this."

Checklist	Examples of Counselor Leads
____ 5. Counselor engages in modeling of task, verbalizing self-guidance aloud.	"OK, I'm walking in for the interview [counselor walks in]. I'm getting ready to greet the interviewer and then wait for his cue to sit down [sits down]."
____ 6. Self-guidance demonstrated by counselor includes five components:	
____ a. *question* about demands of task	"Now what is it I should be doing in this situation?"
____ b. *answers* question by planning what to do	"I just need to greet the person, sit down upon cue, and answer the questions. I need to be sure to point out why they should take me."
____ c. *focused attention* to task and *self-guidance* during task	"OK, just remember to take a deep breath, relax, and concentrate on the interview. Just remember to discuss my particular qualifications and experiences and try to answer questions completely and directly."
____ d. *coping self-evaluation* and, if necessary, *error correction*	"OK, now if I get a little nervous, just take a deep breath. Stay focused on the interview. If I don't respond too well to one question, I can always come back to it."
____ e. *self-reinforcement* for completion of task.	"OK, doing fine. Things are going pretty smoothly."

III. *Overt External Guidance*

____ 7. Counselor instructs client to perform task while counselor coaches.	"This time you go through the interview yourself. I'll be coaching you on what to do and on your planning."
____ 8. Client performs task while counselor coaches by verbalizing self-guidance, changing *I* to *you*. Counselor's verbalization includes the five components of self-guidance:	"Now just remember you're going to walk in for the interview. When the interview begins, I'll coach you through it."
____ a. question about task	"OK, you're walking into the interview room. Now ask yourself what it is you're going to do."
____ b. answer to question	"OK, you're going to greet the interviewer [client does so]. Now he's cueing you to sit down [client sits]."
____ c. focused attention to task and self-guidance during task	"Just concentrate on how you want to handle this situation. He's asking you about your background. You're going to respond directly and completely."
____ d. coping self-evaluation and error correction	"If you feel a little nervous while you're being questioned, just take a deep breath. If you don't respond to a question completely, you can initiate a second response. Try that now."
____ e. self-reinforcement.	"That's good. Now remember you want to convey why you should be chosen. Take your time to do that [client does so]. Great. Very thorough job."

Checklist	*Examples of Counselor Leads*

IV. *Overt Self-Guidance*

___ 9. Counselor instructs client to perform task and instruct self aloud.

"This time I'd like you to do both things. Talk to yourself as you go through the interview in the same way we have done before. Remember, there are five parts to your planning. If you get stuck, I'll help you."

___ 10. Client performs task while simultaneously verbalizing aloud self-guidance process. Client's verbalization includes five components of self-guidance:

___ a. question about task

"Now what is it I need to do?"

___ b. answer to question

"I'm going to greet the interviewer, wait for the cue to sit down, then answer the questions directly and as completely as possible."

___ c. focused attention and self-guidance

"Just concentrate on how I'm going to handle this situation. I'm going to describe why I should be chosen."

___ d. coping self-evaluation and error correction

"If I get a little nervous, just take a deep breath. If I have trouble with one question, I can always come back to it."

___ e. self-reinforcement.

"OK, things are going smoothly. I'm doing fine."

___ 11. If client's self-guidance is incomplete or if client gets stuck, counselor either:

___ a. intervenes and cues client

"Let's stop here for a minute. You seem to be having trouble. Let's start again and try to. . . ."

___ b. recycles client back through step 10.

"That seemed pretty hard, so let's try it again. This time you go through the interview and I'll coach you through it."

___ 12. Counselor gives feedback to client about overt practice.

"That seemed pretty easy for you. You were able to go through the interview and coach yourself. The one place you seemed a little stuck was in the middle, when you had trouble describing yourself. But overall, it was something you handled well. What do you think?"

V. *Faded Overt Self-Guidance*

___ 13. Counselor instructs client on how to perform task while whispering.

"This time I'd like you to go through the interview and whisper the instructions to yourself as you go along. The whispering may be a new thing for you, but I believe it will help you learn to do this."

___ 14. Client performs task and whispers simultaneously.

"I'm going into the room now, waiting for the interviewer to greet me and to sit down. I'm going to answer the questions as completely as possible. Now I'm going to talk about my background."

Checklist	Examples of Counselor Leads
_____ 15. Counselor checks to determine how well client performed.	
_____ a. If client stumbled or left out some of the five parts, client engages in faded overt practice again.	"You had some difficulty with _____. Let's try this type of practice again."
_____ b. If client performed practice smoothly, counselor moves on to next step.	"You seemed to do this easily and comfortably. The next thing is. . . . "
VI. *Covert Self-Guidance*	
_____ 16. Counselor instructs client to perform task while covertly (thinking only) instructing.	"This time while you practice, simply *think* about these instructions. In other words, instruct yourself mentally or in your head as you go along."
_____ 17. Client performs task while covertly instructing.	Only client's actions are visible at this point.
_____ 18. After practice (step 17), counselor asks client to describe covert instructions.	"Can you tell me what you thought about as you were doing this?"
_____ 19. Based on client report (step 18):	
_____ a. Counselor asks client to repeat covert self-guidance.	"It's hard sometimes to begin rehearsing instructions mentally. Let's try it again so you feel more comfortable with it."
_____ b. Counselor moves on to homework.	"OK, you seemed to do this very easily. I believe it would help if you could apply this to some things that you do on your own this week. For instance. . . ."
VII. *Homework*	
_____ 20. Counselor instructs client on how to carry out homework. Instructions include:	"What I'd like you to do this week is to go through this type of mental practice on your own."
_____ a. a "do" statement	"Specifically, go through a simulated interview where you mentally plan your responses as we've done today."
_____ b. a "quantity" statement	"I believe it would help if you could do this two times each day."
_____ c. a method for self-monitoring during completion of homework.	"Each time you do this, make a check on this log sheet. Also, write down the five parts of the self-instructions you used."
_____ 21. Counselor arranges for a face-to-face or telephone follow-up after completion of homework assignment.	"Bring in your log sheets next week or give me a call at the end of the week and we'll go over your homework then."

Consultant Comments: _____

Interview Checklist for Thought-Stopping

Instructions: Determine whether the counselor did or did not demonstrate each of the following leads in the application of the thought-stopping strategy. Check each lead demonstrated by the counselor.

Checklist	Examples of Counselor Leads
I. *Verbal Set about Strategy*	
____ 1. Counselor explains purpose of thought-stopping to client.	"We've agreed that you are bothered by constant thoughts when you're left alone that are upsetting, self-defeating, and cannot be supported by evidence. This procedure is a way for you to learn to inhibit these kinds of thoughts."
____ 2. Counselor gives brief description of strategy.	"First I will ask you to imagine being alone in your hospital room and to tell me what you usually think about then. As soon as you mention a self-defeating thought, I will interrupt you. Then I will teach you how to interrupt yourself and shift your thoughts to something else."
____ 3. Counselor asks client to try strategy.	"Would you like to try it now?"
II. *Counselor-Directed Thought-Stopping: Overt Interruption*	
____ 4. Counselor instructs client to imagine specific problem situation in which chronic, self-defeating thoughts occur, or just to sit back and let any thoughts come to mind.	"Just close your eyes and imagine now that you are all alone in your room. No one is around. It is very quiet. Just let any thoughts you have come into your mind."
____ 5. Counselor asks client to verbalize aloud typical thoughts (both positive and negative) while imagining situation.	"Now as you start to think about anything, share with me whatever you are thinking about."
____ 6. When client verbalizes a self-defeating thought, counselor loudly says *Stop!* (may be accompanied by a hand clap or some other noise, such as a ruler hitting a desk or a whistle).	"OK, *Stop!*" (with a hand clap or noise).
____ 7. After counselor's overt interruption, counselor points out that the unexpected interruption terminated client's self-defeating chain of thoughts.	"Did you notice that as soon as I said *Stop!* you didn't think about being alone anymore?"
____ 8. Counselor instructs client to imagine the situation and to concentrate covertly on any thoughts client has.	"This time just imagine again being alone in your room, and notice but don't verbalize any thoughts you have while you're imagining this."
____ 9. Counselor instructs client to signal with a raised hand or finger whenever client first notices a self-defeating thought.	"When you first start to notice that you're thinking about hearing all these noises, signal to me by raising your hand."
____ 10. As soon as client signals, counselor says *Stop!*	Client raises hand. "*Stop!*"

Checklist	Examples of Counselor Leads

____ 11. Steps 8 through 10 are repeated until a pattern of inhibiting self-defeating thoughts at counselor's command is established.

"Let's try this again. The idea is to get a pattern established so that upon hearing *Stop!* you discontinue these negative thoughts."

III. *Client-Directed Thought-Stopping: Overt Interruption*

____ 12. Counselor instructs client to sit back and notice any thoughts that come to mind.

"Just imagine you're all alone in your room now; imagine what you would be thinking in this situation."

____ 13. Counselor instructs client to say aloud *Stop!* whenever client first notices a self-defeating thought while imagining the situation.

"When you notice a self-defeating thought, say *Stop!* aloud. This time you'll interrupt yourself by saying *Stop!* This gives you control over interrupting this chain of thought."

____ 14. Steps 12 and 13 are repeated until client feels comfortable interrupting overtly.

"Why don't you try this another time or two until you feel very comfortable interrupting yourself like this."

IV. *Client-Directed Thought-Stopping: Covert Interruption*

____ 15. Counselor instructs client to imagine situation and to notice covertly any thoughts during this time.

"Just imagine the same situation and what your thoughts are."

____ 16. Counselor instructs client to *subvocally* say *Stop!* when a self-defeating thought occurs.

"This time, when you are aware of a negative thought, just say *Stop!* to yourself. Say it silently so no one can hear you."

____ 17. Counselor instructs client to repeat steps 15 and 16 until client feels comfortable using covert interruption.

"Let's do this again until you feel this is very natural."

V. *Shift from Self-Defeating to Assertive, Positive, or Neutral Thoughts*

____ 18. Counselor explains purpose of shifting from self-defeating to assertive, positive, or neutral thoughts

"So far we've practiced helping you keep these negative thoughts from getting out of hand by interrupting yourself. Now we're going to learn something that should help you even more. In addition to stopping a thought, you can learn to shift to a very different kind of thought. This helps you manage your feelings of anxiety and gives you a more constructive thing to think about."

____ 19. Counselor models assertive, positive, or neutral thoughts. Client is asked to identify others and to verbalize aloud at least three thoughts client could think about after stopping a negative thought.

"An assertive thought is something you might do or think about in the situation that is realistic and focuses on a rational part of the situation, like 'I've been alone before and I've been able to handle whatever has come up.' Or you could think about something positive, like something you enjoy doing, or you could just concentrate on an object in the room. I'd like you to think of thoughts similar to these and just to get a feel for them. Practice saying these aloud."

Cognitive Modeling and Thought-Stopping

Checklist	Examples of Counselor Leads

_____ 20. Counselor asks client to engage in steps 12 and 13 (client-directed overt interruption) again, and to follow overt interruption by verbalizing aloud a different thought.

"This time I'd like you to imagine the situation again and verbally tell yourself to stop when you notice a self-defeating thought. In addition, after you say _Stop!_ verbalize aloud one of the thoughts you just selected to substitute for the negative thoughts."

_____ 21. Step 20 is repeated with client using a different assertive, positive, or neutral thought with each practice.

"Let's do this a couple of times. Each time after you say _Stop!_ use a different assertive or positive thought. This gives you more options and prevents you from getting tired of just one idea."

_____ 22. Counselor instructs client to engage in steps 15 and 16 (client-directed covert interruption) again, and to follow covert interruption with _covert_ use of an assertive, positive, or neutral thought.

"Now we're going to do the same type of thing—this time all covertly. You'll say _Stop!_ only to yourself —then shift by thinking to yourself a different thought."

_____ 23. Counselor instructs client to repeat step 22 several times, using a different assertive or positive thought after each covert interruption.

"Let's do this another time so you can try out substituting a different thought than you used the last time."

VI. _Homework and Follow-Up_

_____ 24. Counselor instructs client to practice using thought-stopping several times daily and any time self-defeating thoughts occur outside the session.

"You've done a really great job teaching this to yourself here. Now you are ready to use it when you need it outside our session. You should practice this three times each day. You'll also be able to use this procedure whenever a self-defeating thought comes up. It will take time, because you're breaking an old habit, so don't get discouraged or expect too much too fast."

_____ 25. Counselor instructs client to record on a log daily practices and number of times thought-stopping is used "in vivo."

"Record each practice session on your log sheet. Each time you use thought-stopping for these negative thoughts as they crop up, write it down on your log. You'll write down the situation you used it for, the time and place, and the specific assertive or positive thought you used after you stopped the negative thought."

_____ 26. Counselor arranges for follow-up session.

"I'd like to see you in 2 weeks to see how this has helped. We can go over your log data then."

Consultant Comments: _____

Suggested Readings

Cognitive Conceptualization of Client Problems

Beck, A. T. *Cognitive therapy and the emotional disorders.* New York: International Universities Press, 1976.

Dyer, W. *Your erroneous zones.* New York: Funk & Wagnalls, 1976.

Dyer, W. *Pulling your own strings.* New York: Funk & Wagnalls, 1978.

Mahoney, M. J. *Cognition and behavior modification.* Cambridge, Mass.: Ballinger, 1974.

Meichenbaum, D. *Cognitive behavior modification: An integrative approach.* New York: Plenum Press, 1977.

Cognitive Modeling and Self-Instructional Training

Bruch, M. Type of cognitive modeling, imitation of modeled tactics, and modification of test anxiety. *Cognitive Therapy and Research*, 1978, 2, 147–164.

Meichenbaum, D., & Cameron, R. Training schizophrenics to talk to themselves: A means of developing attentional controls. *Behavior Therapy*, 1973, 4, 515–534.

Meichenbaum, D., & Goodman, J. Training impulsive children to talk to themselves: A means of developing self-control. *Journal of Abnormal Psychology*, 1971, 77, 115–126.

Sarason, I. G. Test anxiety and cognitive modeling. *Journal of Personality and Social Psychology*, 1973, 28, 58–61.

Thought-Stopping

Anthony, J., & Edelstein, B. Thought-stopping treatment of anxiety attacks due to seizure-related obsessive ruminations. *Journal of Behavior Therapy and Experimental Psychiatry*, 1975, 6, 343–344.

Hackmann, A., & McLean, C. A comparison of flooding and thought stopping in the treatment of obsessional neurosis. *Behaviour Research and Therapy*, 1975, 13, 263–269.

Rimm, D. C., & Masters, J. C. *Behavior therapy: Techniques and empirical findings.* New York: Academic Press, 1974. Chap. 10, Cognitive methods, 416–449.

Samaan, M. Thought-stopping and flooding in a case of hallucinations, obsessions, and homicidal-suicidal behavior. *Journal of Behavior Therapy and Experimental Psychiatry*, 1975, 6, 65–67.

Chapter 19
Cognitive Restructuring and Stress Inoculation

Risley and Hart (1968) suggest that "much of psychotherapy . . . is based on the assumption that reorganizing and restructuring a patient's verbal statements about himself and his world will result in a corresponding reorganization of the patient's behavior with respect to that world" (p. 107). Cognitive restructuring and stress inoculation both assume that maladaptive emotions and overt responses are influenced or mediated by one's beliefs, attitudes, and expectations—one's "cognitions." Both these procedures help clients to determine the relationship between their cognitions and the resulting emotions and behaviors, to identify faulty or self-defeating cognitions, and to replace these cognitions with self-enhancing or positive thoughts. In both strategies, clients learn how to cope; indirect benefits may include an increase in feelings of resourcefulness, ability to handle a problem, and enhancement of self-concept.

Although the cognitive-restructuring and stress-inoculation procedures described in this chapter reflect a behavioral perspective, no description of these strategies would be complete without some discussion of a major historical antecedent, rational-emotive therapy, or RET. RET, which was developed by Ellis (1975), assumes that all problems are the result of "magical" thinking or irrational beliefs. According to Morris and Kanitz (1975), some of the irrational ideas discussed by Ellis lead to self-condemnation or anger, and others lead to a low tolerance for frustration. The RET therapist helps clients identify which of the irrational ideas are evidenced by their belief systems and emotional reactions.

Ten major irrational ideas cited by Ellis (1974) are:

1. The idea that it is a dire necessity for an adult to be loved or approved by virtually every significant person in his or her community.
2. The idea that one should be thoroughly competent, adequate, and achieving in all possible respects if one is to consider oneself worthwhile.
3. The idea that human unhappiness is externally caused and that people have little or no ability to control their sorrows and disturbances.
4. The idea that one's past history is an all-important determinant of one's present behavior and that because something once strongly affected one's life, it should indefinitely have a similar effect.
5. The idea that there is invariably a right, precise, and perfect solution to human problems and that it is catastrophic if this perfect solution is not found.

6. The idea that if something is or may be dangerous or fearsome, one should be terribly concerned about it and should keep dwelling on the possibility of its occurring.
7. The idea that certain people are bad, wicked, or villainous and that they should be severely blamed and punished for their villainy.
8. The idea that it is awful and catastrophic when things are not the way one would very much like them to be.
9. The idea that it is easier to avoid than to face certain life difficulties and self-responsibilities.
10. The idea that one should become quite upset over other people's problems and disturbances [Ellis, 1974, pp. 152–153].*

According to RET, it is possible to resolve a client's problems by "cognitive control of illogical emotional responses" (Morris & Kanitz, 1975, p. 8). In RET, such control is achieved primarily by reeducating the client through the use of what Ellis (1975) refers to as the "ABCDE model." This model involves showing the client how irrational beliefs (B) about an activity or action (A) result in irrational or inappropriate consequences (C). The client is then taught to dispute (D) the irrational beliefs (B) which are not facts and have no supporting evidence, and then to recognize the effects (E). Usually, the effects (E) are either cognitive effects (cE) or behavioral effects (bE).

As you may realize, one of the major assumptions that RET, cognitive restructuring, and stress inoculation share is that a person's beliefs and thoughts can create emotional distress and maladaptive responding. Another shared assumption is that a person's cognitive system can be changed directly and that such change results in different, and presumably more appropriate, consequences. Ullmann and Krasner (1969) note that any cognitive-change approach involves punishing a client's emo-

tional labels and reinforcing more appropriate evaluations of a situation.

As you will note in this chapter's discussion of cognitive restructuring and stress inoculation, there are some differences between RET and cognitive behavior-modification procedures. One difference is that cognitive-behavioral procedures do not assume that certain irrational ideas are generally held by all. In cognitive restructuring and stress inoculation, each client's *particular* irrational thoughts are identified and are assumed to be idiosyncratic, although some elements may be shared by others as well. A second difference involves the method of change. In RET, the therapist attempts to help the client alter irrational beliefs by verbal persuasion and teaching. Emphasis is placed on helping the client discriminate between irrational beliefs, which have no evidence, and rational beliefs, which can be supported by data. In cognitive restructuring and stress inoculation, in addition to these kinds of discriminations, the client is taught the skill of using coping cognitions in stressful or distressing situations.

Objectives

1. Identify and describe the six components of cognitive restructuring from a written case description.
2. Teach the six major components of cognitive restructuring to another person, or demonstrate these components in a role-play interview.
3. Using a simulated client case, describe how the seven components of stress inoculation would be used with a client.
4. Demonstrate 17 out of 21 steps of stress inoculation in a role-play interview.

Cognitive Restructuring

Although cognitive restructuring was described earlier by Lazarus (1971) and has its roots in rational-emotive therapy (Ellis, 1975), more recently it has been developed by Meichenbaum (1972) under the name *cognitive behavior modifica-*

*From *Humanistic Psychotherapy*, by A. Ellis. Copyright 1974 by McGraw-Hill, Inc. Reprinted by permission of the publisher, McGraw-Hill Book Company, and the author.

tion and by Goldfried, Decenteceo, and Weinberg (1974) under the name *systematic rational restructuring*. Much of the supporting data for cognitive restructuring has come from a series of recent studies conducted by Fremouw and associates (Fremouw & Harmatz, 1975; Fremouw & Zitter, 1978; Glogower, Fremouw, & McCroskey, 1978). Cognitive restructuring has been used to help anxious clients cope with test anxiety (Goldfried, Linehan, & Smith, 1978; Meichenbaum, 1972), speech anxiety (Fremouw & Harmatz, 1975; Fremouw & Zitter, 1978; Thorpe, Amatu, Blakey, & Burns, 1976), and social-interpersonal anxiety (Elder, 1978; Glass, Gottman, and Shmurak, 1976; Kanter & Goldfried, 1979). In related areas, cognitive restructuring has been used to treat depression (F. G. Taylor & W. L. Marshall, 1977) and pain-related stress (Langer, Janis, & Wolfer, 1975; Turk, 1975). Goldfried and Davison (1976) recommend the use of cognitive restructuring for problems related to unrealistically high self-standards. Cognitive restructuring is often a major component of assertion training (Thorpe, 1975). This procedure also is used in conjunction with other therapeutic strategies when the client's belief system becomes part of the change target.

Our presentation of cognitive restructuring reflects these sources and our own adaptations of it based on clinical usage. We present cognitive restructuring in six major parts:

1. Verbal set: rationale and overview of the procedure
2. Identification of client thoughts during problem situations
3. Introduction and practice of coping thoughts
4. Shifting from self-defeating to coping thoughts
5. Introduction and practice of positive or reinforcing self-statements
6. Homework and follow-up.

Each of these parts will be described in this section. A detailed description of these six components can be found in the Interview Checklist for Cognitive Restructuring at the end of the chapter.

Verbal Set

The verbal set used in cognitive restructuring attempts to strengthen the client's belief that "self-talk" can influence performance and particularly that self-defeating thoughts or negative self-statements can cause emotional distress and can interfere with performance.

Rationale. Meichenbaum (1974) has provided a verbal set he used in training test-anxious and speech-anxious college students to use cognitive restructuring. His example of a *rationale* for treatment follows; the language can be adapted.

> One goal of treatment is for each member to become aware of the factors which are maintaining his test (speech) anxiety. Once we can determine what these factors are, then we can change or combat them. One of the surprising things is that the factors contributing to anxiety are not something secretive, but seem to be the thinking processes you go through in evaluative situations. Simply, there seems to be a correlation between how anxious and tense people feel and the kinds of thoughts they are experiencing. For example, the anxiety you experienced in the test (speech) situation may be tied to the kinds of thoughts you had, what you chose to think about, or how you chose to focus your attention. Somehow your thinking gets all tied up with how you are feeling [pp. 9–10].

Overview. Here is an example of an overview of the procedure:

> We will learn how to control our thinking processes and attention. The control of our thinking, or what we say to ourselves, comes about by first becoming aware of when we are producing negative self-statements, catastrophizing, being task-irrelevant, etc. (Once again, give examples of the clients' thinking styles.) The recognition that we are in fact doing this will be a step forward in changing. This recognition will also act as a reminder, a cue, a bell-ringer for us to produce different thoughts and self-instructions, to challenge our thinking styles and to produce incompatible, task-relevant self-instructions and incompatible behaviors. We will learn how to control our thinking processes in our group discussion, by some specific

techniques which I will describe a bit later on. (Pause.) I'm wondering about your reactions to what I have described. Do you have any questions? [pp. 11–12].*

Contrast Self-Defeating and Self-Enhancing Thoughts. In addition to providing a standard verbal set such as the one just illustrated, the cognitive-restructuring procedure should be prefaced by some contrast between self-enhancing or rational thoughts and self-defeating or irrational thoughts. This explanation may help clients discriminate between their own self-enhancing and self-defeating thoughts during treatment. Many clients who could benefit from cognitive restructuring are all too aware of their self-defeating thoughts and are unaware of or unable to generate self-enhancing thoughts. Providing a contrast may help them see that more realistic thinking styles can be developed.

Although some therapists describe beliefs as either rational or irrational (Ellis, 1975; Goldfried, Decenteceo, & Weinberg, 1974), we prefer to label them positive, self-enhancing thoughts or negative, self-defeating ones. In our opinion, this description is less likely to confuse clients who have trouble distinguishing between their *thoughts* as irrational and *themselves* as irrational or "crazy." Also, as Thorpe (1973) points out, the aim of cognitive restructuring is to show clients how negative thoughts are unproductive, how they defeat purposes or goals, rather than that clients' ideas are irrational and wrong.

One way to contrast these two types of thinking is to model some examples of both positive, enhancing self-talk and negative, defeating self-talk. These examples can come out of your personal experiences or can relate to the client's problem situations. The examples might occur *before, during,* or *after* a problem situation (Fremouw, 1977). For example, you might say to the client that in a situation that makes you a little uptight, such as meeting a person for the

first time, you could get caught up in very negative thoughts:

Before meeting:
"What if I don't come across very well?"
"What if this person doesn't like me?"
"I'll just blow this chance to establish a good relationship."

During meeting:
"I'm not making a good impression on this person."
"This person is probably wishing our meeting was over."
"I'd just like to leave and get this over with."
"I'm sure this person won't want to see me after this."

After meeting:
"Well, that's a lost cause."
"I can never talk intelligently with a stranger."
"I might as well never bother to set up this kind of meeting again."
"How stupid I must have sounded."

In contrast, you might demonstrate some examples of positive, self-enhancing thoughts about the same situation:

Before meeting:
"I'm just going to attempt to get to know this person."
"I'm just going to be myself when I meet this person."
"I'll find something to talk about that I enjoy."
"This is only an initial meeting. We'll have to get together more to see how the relationship develops."

During meeting:
"I'm going to try to get something out of this conversation."
"This is a subject I know something about."
"This meeting is giving me a chance to talk about _____."
"It will take some time for me to get to know this person, and vice versa."

After meeting:
"That went OK; it certainly wasn't a flop."
"I can remember how easy it was for me to discuss topics of interest to me."
"Each meeting with a new person gives me a chance to see someone else and explore new interests."
"I was able just to be myself then."

Influence of Self-Defeating Thoughts on Performance. The last part of the verbal set for cognitive restructuring should be an *explicit* attempt to

*From *Therapist Manual for Cognitive Behavior Modification,* by D. Meichenbaum. Unpublished manuscript, 1974. Reprinted by permission of the author.

point out how self-defeating thoughts or negative self-statements are unproductive and can influence emotions and behavior. You are attempting to convey to the client that, whatever we tell ourselves, we are likely to believe it and to act on that belief. However, it is also useful to point out that, in some situations, people don't *literally* tell themselves something. In many situations, our thoughts are so well learned that they are automatic (Goldfried, Decenteceo, & Weinberg, 1974, p. 250). For this reason, you might indicate that you will often ask the client to monitor or log what happens during actual situations between counseling sessions.

Thorpe (1973) has provided an example of a description for nonassertive clients about how unproductive thinking can influence emotions and behavior:

> Many difficulties in social situations are simply based on the way in which we think about them. In other words, it is not that a certain situation is really, in itself, difficult, anxiety-provoking, or uncomfortable, but that we simply look on it that way. What usually happens is that we spend so much time telling ourselves negative things, that we are bound to fail, that we are no good, etc., that we cannot possibly handle the situation well. What we will be doing in therapy is to examine some of the unproductive trains of thought that we have when in a demanding situation. Research has shown that if we can only learn to get rid of such unproductive, self-defeating thoughts, and replace them with realistic, sensible ones, then difficult situations become much easier, simply by looking on them in a more positive way [p. 3].

The importance of providing an adequate rationale for cognitive restructuring cannot be overemphasized. If one begins implementing the procedure too quickly, or without the client's agreement, the process can backfire. Some research indicates that people may be more resistant to changing beliefs if they are pushed or coerced to abandon them and adopt those of someone else (Brehm, 1966; Watts, Powell, & Austin, 1973). As Goldfried, Decenteceo, and Weinberg (1974) point out, the procedure should be implemented slowly "by having clients gradually agree to the underlying rationale" (p. 249). The counselor should not move ahead until the client's commitment to work with the strategy is obtained.

Identifying Client Thoughts in Problem Situations

Assuming that the client accepts the rationale provided about cognitive restructuring, the next step involves an analysis of the client's thoughts in anxious or distressing situations. Both the range of situations and the content of the client's thoughts in these situations should be explored (Meichenbaum, 1974).

Description of Thoughts in Problem Situations. Within the interview, the counselor should query the client about the specific distressing situations encountered and the things the client thinks about before, during, and after these situations. The counselor might say something like "Sit back and think about the situations that are really upsetting to you. What are they?" and then "Can you identify exactly what you are thinking about or telling yourself before you go to _____? What are you thinking during the situation? And afterwards?"

In identifying negative or self-defeating thoughts, the client might be aided by a description of possible cues that compose a self-defeating thought. The counselor can point out that a negative thought may have a "worry quality" such as "I'm afraid . . . ," or a "self-oriented quality" such as "I won't do well" (Meichenbaum, 1974, p. 16). Negative thoughts also may include elements of catastrophizing ("If I fail, it will be awful") or exaggerating (I *never* do well" or "I *always* blow it"). Goldfried (1976b) suggests that clients can identify the extent to which unrealistic thinking contributes to situational anxiety by answering three questions about each anxiety-provoking situation:

Do I make unreasonable demands of myself?
Do I feel that others are approving or disapproving of my actions?
Do I often forget that this situation is only one part of my life?

Modeling of Links between Events and Emotions. If the client has trouble identifying negative thoughts, Meichenbaum (1974) suggests asking the client to recall the situation as if running a movie through his or her head. The counselor may need to point out that the thoughts are the link between the situation and the resulting emotion and ask the client to notice explicitly what this link seems to be. If the client is still unable to identify thoughts, the counselor can model this link, using either the client's situations or situations from the counselor's life. For example, the counselor might say:

> "Here is one example that happened to me. I was a music major in college, and several times a year I had to present piano recitals that were graded by several faculty members and attended by faculty, friends, and strangers. Each approaching recital got worse—I got more nervous and more preoccupied with failure. Although I didn't realize it at the time, the link between the event of the recital and my resulting feelings of nervousness was things I was thinking that I can remember now—like "What if I get out there and blank out?" or "What if my arms get so stiff I can't perform the piece?" or "What if my shaking knees are visible?" Now can you try to recall the specific thoughts you had when you felt so upset about _____?"

Client Modeling of Thoughts. The counselor also can have the client identify situations and thoughts by monitoring and recording events and thoughts outside the interview in the form of homework. For example, Fremouw (1977) suggests that an initial homework assignment might be to have the client observe and record at least three negative self-statements a day in the stressful situation for a week (p. 3). For each day of the week, the client could record the negative self-statements and the situations in which these statements were noted on a daily log (see Figure 19-1).

Using the client's data, the counselor and client can determine which of the thoughts were self-enhancing or productive and which were self-defeating or unproductive. The counselor should attempt to have the *client* discriminate between the two types of statements and identify why the negative ones are self-defeating or unproductive. The identification serves several purposes. First, it is a way to determine whether the client's present repertory consists of both positive and negative self-statements, or whether the client is generating or recalling only negative thoughts. These data also may provide information about the degree of distress in a particular situation. If some self-enhancing thoughts are identified, the client becomes aware that alternatives are already present in his or her thinking style. If no self-enhancing thoughts are reported, this is a cue that some specific attention may be needed in this area. The counselor can demonstrate how the client's unproductive thoughts can be changed by showing how self-defeating thoughts can be restated more constructively (Fremouw, 1977, p. 3).

Introduction and Practice of Coping Thoughts

At this point in the procedure, there is a shift in focus from the client's negative self-statements or self-defeating thoughts to other

Name: _____   Week: _____
Date: _____

Negative Self-Statements: Situations:

1. _____   1. _____
2. _____   2. _____
3. _____   3. _____

Figure 19-1. Example of Daily Log (From *A Client Manual for Integrated Behavior Treatment of Speech Anxiety* by W. Fremouw. Copyright © 1977 by American Psychological Association (JSAS Catalogue of Selected Documents in Psychology). Reprinted by permission.)

kinds of thoughts that are incompatible with the self-defeating ones. These incompatible thoughts may be called coping thoughts, coping statements, or coping self-instructions; and they are developed for each client. There is no attempt to have all clients accept a common core of rational beliefs, as is often done in rational-emotive therapy (Meichenbaum, 1974).

The introduction and practice of coping statements is, as far as we know, crucial to the overall success of the cognitive-restructuring procedure. As Meichenbaum (1974) observes, "it appears that the awareness of one's self-statements is a necessary but *not* sufficient condition to cause behavior change. One needs to produce incompatible self-instructions and incompatible behaviors" (p. 51). A well-controlled investigation of the components of cognitive restructuring conducted by Glogower et al. (1978) seems to support Meichenbaum's contention. These authors found that, with communication-anxious college students, simply identifying negative self-statements was no more effective than extinction (repeated exposure to anxious feelings). The crucial component appeared to be the learning and rehearsal of coping statements, which, by itself, was almost as effective as the combination of identifying negative statements and replacing these with incompatible coping thoughts.

Explanation and Examples of Coping Thoughts. The purpose of coping thoughts should be explained clearly. The client should understand that it is difficult to think of failing at an experience (a self-defeating thought) while at the same time concentrating on just doing one's best, regardless of the outcome (a coping thought). The counselor could explain the purpose and use of coping thoughts like this:

> "So far we've worked at identifying some of the self-defeating things you think during _____. As long as you're thinking about those kinds of things, they can make you feel anxious. But as soon as you replace these with coping thoughts, then the coping thoughts take over, because it is almost impossible to concentrate on both failing at something and coping with the situation at the same time. The coping

thoughts help you to manage the situation and to cope if you start to feel overwhelmed."

The counselor also should model some examples of coping thoughts so that the client can clearly differentiate between a self-defeating and a coping thought. Some examples of coping thoughts to use *before* a situation might be:

"I've done this before and it never is as bad as I think."
"Stay calm in anticipating this."
"Do the best I can. I'm not going to worry how people will react."
"This is a situation which can be a challenge."
"It won't be bad—only a few people will be there."

Some examples of coping thoughts to use *during* a situation include:

"Focus on the task."
"Just think about what I want to do or say."
"What is it I want to accomplish now?"
"Relax so I can focus on the situation."
"Step back a minute, take a deep breath."
"Take one step at a time."
"Slow down, take my time, don't rush."
"OK, don't get out of control. It's a signal to cope."

If you go back and read over these lists of coping examples, you may note some subtle differences among them. Some of them refer to the nature of the situation itself, such as "It won't be too bad," "It can be a challenge," or "Only a few people will be watching me." Fremouw (1977) refers to these as *context-* or *situation-oriented coping statements*. These coping statements help the client reduce the potential level of threat or severity of the anticipated situation. Other coping statements refer more to the plans, steps, or behaviors the person will need to demonstrate during the stressful situation, such as "Concentrate on what I want to say or do," "Think about the task," or "What do I want to accomplish?" These may be called *task-oriented coping statements* (Fremouw, 1977). Another set of coping thoughts can be used to help the client stay calm and relaxed at tense moments. Meichenbaum (1974) refers to these as *coping with being overwhelmed*. These statements include such self-instructions as "Keep cool," "Stay calm," or "Relax, take a deep breath." A fourth type of coping statement, which we call *positive self-statements*, is used to have clients reinforce or encourage themselves for having coped. These can be used during a stressful situation and especially after the situation. The use of positive self-statements in cognitive restructuring is described in more detail later in this chapter.

The point is that a variety of potentially useful coping statements are available to teach clients. For some clients, a particular type of coping response may be most useful; other clients may prefer another kind of coping statement. At this time, we know very little about the specific effects of each of these kinds of coping thoughts. Glogower et al. (1978) found that even clients who were not trained to use coping statements did report some spontaneous (although inconsistent) use of situation-oriented coping thoughts when confronted with anxiety-provoking speech situations. Perhaps further investigations will yield more data about the specific effects of different types of coping statements on the reduction and control of self-defeating emotions and behaviors.

Client Examples of Coping Thoughts. After providing some examples, the counselor should ask the client to think of additional coping statements. The client may select some of the counselor's examples or may come up with self-enhancing or positive statements she or he has used in other situations. The client should be encouraged to select coping statements that feel most natural. Goldfried (1976b) recommends that clients identify coping thoughts by discovering convincing counterarguments for their unrealistic thoughts.

Client Practice. Using these client-selected coping statements, the counselor should ask the client to practice verbalizing coping statements aloud. This is very important, because most clients are not accustomed to using coping statements. Such practice may reduce some of the client's initial discomfort and can strengthen confidence in being able to produce different "self-talk." Also, clients who are "formally" trained to practice coping statements systematically may use a greater variety of coping thoughts, may use more specific coping thoughts, and may report more consistent use of coping thoughts "in vivo" (Glogower et al., 1978).

At first, the client can practice verbalizing the individual coping statements she or he selected to use before and during the situation. Gradually, as the client gets accustomed to coping statements, the coping thoughts should be practiced in the natural sequence in which they will be used. First, the client would anticipate the situation and practice coping statements before the situation to prepare for it, followed by practice of coping thoughts during the situation—focusing on the task and coping with feeling overwhelmed.

It is important for the client to become actively involved in these practice sessions. The counselor should try to ensure that the client does not simply rehearse the coping statements mechanically, by rote. Instead, the client should use these practices to try to internalize the meaning of the coping statements (Meichenbaum, 1977, p. 89).

Shifting from Self-Defeating to Coping Thoughts

After the client has identified negative thoughts and has practiced alternative coping thoughts, the counselor introduces rehearsal of a shift from self-defeating to coping thoughts during stressful situations. Practice of this shift helps the client to use a self-defeating thought as a cue for an immediate switch to coping thoughts.

Counselor Demonstration of Shift. The counselor should model this process before asking the client to try it. This gives the client an accurate idea of how to practice this shift. Here is an example of a counselor modeling for a high school student who constantly "freezes up" in competitive situations.

"OK, I'm sitting here waiting for my turn to try out for cheerleader. Ooh, I can feel myself getting very nervous [anxious feeling]. Now wait, what am I so nervous about? I'm afraid I'm going to make a fool of myself [self-defeating thought]. Hey, that doesn't help [cue to cope]. It will only take a few minutes, and it will be over with before I know it. Besides, only the faculty sponsors are watching. It's not like the whole school [situation-oriented coping thoughts]."

"Well, the person before me is just about finished. Oh, they're calling my name. Boy, do I feel tense [anxious feelings]. What if I don't execute my jumps? [self-defeating thought]. OK, don't think about what I'm not going to do. OK, start out, it's my turn. Just think about my routine—the way I want it to go [task-oriented coping thoughts]."

Client Practice of the Shift. After the counselor demonstration, the client should practice identifying and stopping self-defeating thoughts and replacing them with coping thoughts. The counselor can monitor the client's progress and coach if necessary. The rehearsal of this shift involves four steps:

1. The client imagines the stressful situation or carries out his or her part in the situation via a role-play.
2. The client is instructed to recognize the onset of any self-defeating thoughts and to signal this by raising a hand or finger.
3. Next, the client is told to stop these thoughts. If the client cannot stop these thoughts covertly, a hand clap by the counselor after the signal may work (see thought-stopping in Chapter 18).
4. After the self-defeating thought is stopped, the client immediately replaces it with the coping thoughts. The client should be given some time to concentrate on the coping thoughts. Initially, it may be helpful for the client to verbalize coping thoughts; later, this can occur covertly.

As the client seems able to identify, stop, and replace the self-defeating thoughts, the counselor gradually can decrease the amount of assistance. Before homework is assigned, the client should be able to practice and carry out this shift in the interview setting in a completely self-directed manner.

Introduction and Practice of Positive or Reinforcing Self-Statements

The last part of cognitive restructuring involves teaching clients how to reinforce themselves for having coped. This is accomplished by counselor modeling and client practice of positive or reinforcing self-statements. Many clients who could benefit from cognitive restructuring report not only frequent self-defeating thoughts, but also few or no positive or rewarding self-evaluations. Some clients may learn to replace self-defeating thoughts with task-oriented coping ones and feel better but not satisfied with their progress (K. Mahoney & M. J. Mahoney, 1976). The purpose of including positive or reinforcing self-statements in cognitive restructuring is to help clients learn to praise or congratulate themselves for signs of progress. Although the counselor can provide social reinforcement in the interview, the client cannot always be dependent on encouragement from someone else when confronted with a stressful situation.

Purpose and Examples of Positive Self-Statements. The counselor should explain the purpose of reinforcing self-statements to the client and provide some examples. An explanation might sound like this:

"You know, Joan, you've really done very well in handling these situations and learning to stop those self-defeating ideas and to use some coping thoughts. Now it's time to give yourself credit for your progress. I will help you learn to encourage yourself by using positive or rewarding thoughts, so that each time you're in this situation and you cope, you also give yourself a pat on the back for handling the situation and not getting overwhelmed by it. This kind of self-encouragement helps you to note your progress and prevents you from getting discouraged."

Then the counselor can give some examples of reinforcing self-statements:

"Gee, I did it."
"Hey, I handled that OK."
"I didn't let my emotions get the best of me."
"I made some progress and that feels good."
"See, it went pretty well after all."

Client Selection of Positive Self-Statements. After providing examples, the counselor should ask the client for additional positive statements. The client should select those statements that feel suitable. This is particularly important in using reinforcing statements, because the reinforcing value of a statement may be very idiosyncratic.

Counselor Demonstration of Positive Self-Statements. The counselor should demonstrate how the client can use a positive self-statement after having coped with a situation. Here is an example of a counselor modeling the use of positive self-statements during and after a stressful situation. In this case, the client was an institutionalized adolescent who was confronting her parents in a face-to-face meeting.

> "OK, I can feel them putting pressure on me. They want me to talk. I don't want to talk. I just want to get the hell out of here [self-defeating thought]. Slow down, wait a minute. Don't pressure yourself. Stay cool [coping with being overwhelmed]. Good. That's better [positive self-statement].
> "Well, it's over. It wasn't too bad. I stuck it out. That's progress [positive self-statement]."

Client Practice of Positive Self-Statements. The client should be instructed to practice using positive self-statements during and after the stressful situation. The practice occurs first within the interview and gradually outside the interview with "in vivo" assignments. K. Mahoney and M. J. Mahoney (1976) reported an ingenious type of daily self-directed

practice to help increase the frequency of a client's positive self-evaluations. The client was taught to cue positive self-statements, to practice these by calling a telephone-answering device, and to verbalize self-praise for her efforts at having modified and coped with negative thoughts. These recordings were reviewed by both the client and her counselor. This review served as another way to strengthen the client's positive self-evaluative thoughts (p. 104).

Homework and Follow-Up

Although homework is an integral part of every step of the cognitive-restructuring procedure, the client ultimately should be able to use cognitive restructuring whenever it is needed in actual distressing situations. The client should be instructed to use cognitive restructuring "in vivo" but cautioned not to expect instant success (Goldfried & Davison, 1976). The client can monitor and record the instances in which cognitive restructuring was used over several weeks.

The counselor can facilitate the written recording by providing a homework log sheet that might look something like the one presented in Figure 19-2. The client's log data can be reviewed at a follow-up session to determine the number of times the client is using cognitive restructuring and the amount of progress that has occurred. Also, the counselor can use the follow-up session to encourage the client to apply the procedure to stressful situations that could arise in the future. This may encourage the client to generalize the use of cognitive restructuring to situations other than those that are presently considered problematic.

Occasionally, a client's level of distress may not diminish even after repeated practice of restructuring self-defeating thoughts. In some cases, negative self-statements do not precede or contribute to the person's strong feelings. Some emotions may be classically conditioned and therefore treated more appropriately by a counterconditioning procedure such as systematic desensitization (see Chapter 21). How-

DAILY RECORD OF USE OF COGNITIVE RESTRUCTURING					
Date: _____				Record of: _____	
Description of Situation	Initial Level of Emotion (1 to 5)	Coping Thoughts Used	Positive Self-Statements Used	Terminal Level of Emotion (1 to 5)	Date and Time

Figure 19-2. Homework Log Sheet

ever, even in classically conditioned fears, cognitive processes also may play some role in maintaining or reducing the fear (Davison & Wilson, 1973).

When cognitive restructuring does not reduce a client's level of distress, depression, or anxiety, the counselor and client may need to redefine the problem and goals. As Goldfried and Davison (1976) observe, the therapist should "consider the possibility that his assessment has been inaccurate and that there are, in fact, no internal sentences which are functionally tied to this particular client's problem" (p. 174). Remember that problem definition is analogous to hypothesis-testing, and the counselor's first analysis does not always turn out to be accurate.

Assuming that the original problem as-

sessment is accurate, perhaps a change in parts of the cognitive-restructuring procedure is necessary. Here are some possible revisions:

1. The amount of time the client uses to shift from self-defeating to coping thoughts and to imagine coping thoughts can be increased.
2. The nature of the particular coping statements selected by the client may not be that helpful; a change in the type of coping statements may be beneficial.
3. Cognitive restructuring may need to be supplemented with either additional coping skills such as deep breathing or relaxation or with skill training [Goldfried & Davison, 1976, p. 174].

The use of additional coping skills to deal

with stress and discomfort is described in the next strategy presented in this chapter—stress inoculation.

___

Model Dialogue: Cognitive Restructuring

Session 2

In session 2, the counselor will follow up and review the thought-stopping Joan learned the previous week (see Chapter 18). The rest of the interview will be directed toward helping Joan replace self-defeating thoughts with coping thoughts. This is the "nuts and bolts" of cognitive restructuring; it is similar to the substitution of assertive or positive thoughts in thought-stopping and also is a major part of stress inoculation.

1. Counselor: Good to see you again, Joan. How did your week go?
   Client: Pretty good. I did a lot of practice. I also tried to do this in math class. It helped some, but I still felt nervous. Here are my logs.
In response 2, the counselor reinforces Joan for completing her logs and her daily practice. Joan is usually good at completing these; nevertheless, such work on the client's part should not go unnoticed.
2. Counselor: OK, these look good. Let's go over them. Looks like you did a lot of daily practice. This is terrific. Now, according to your log, you needed to use the thought-stopping prior to your class and several times during the class.
   Client: Right. Especially when we had a test or I had to go to the board. You know how that makes me feel—nervous.
The counselor uses this opportunity to reiterate how Joan's negative thoughts can, to some extent, contribute to her nervous feelings and explains that the physical sensations of nervousness will be dealt with later and cautions Joan not to expect too much change all at once.
3. Counselor: Yes, and some of the nervousness is created by the negative thoughts. However, you've indicated you feel nervous physically, so we'll work with this in another way later on. So it's understandable if you still feel nervous this week. It won't be an overnight change —just one step at a time.
   Client: Yes. Well, I could definitely tell that I cut off these thoughts sooner than I used to.

In response 4, the counselor gives a verbal set for cognitive restructuring; explains the purpose of "coping" thoughts to Joan; and gives an overview of the strategy.
4. Counselor: That's great. And I bet your daily practice helped you do that when you needed to. Today we're going to go one step further. In addition to having you stop the negative thoughts, we're going to work on having you learn to use some more constructive thoughts. I call these *coping thoughts*. You can replace the negative thoughts with coping thoughts that will help you when you're anticipating your class, in your class itself, and when things happen in your class that are especially hard for you—like taking a test or going to the board. What questions do you have about this?
   Client: I don't think any—although I don't know if I know exactly what you mean by a coping thought.
The counselor, in response 5, will explain and give some examples of coping thoughts and particular times or phases when Joan might need to use them.
5. Counselor: OK, let me explain about these and give you some examples. Then perhaps you can think of your own examples. The first thing is that there are probably different times when you could use coping thoughts—like before math class when you're anticipating it. Only, instead of worrying about it, you can use this time to prepare to handle it. For example, some coping thoughts you might use before math class are "No need to get nervous. Just think about doing OK," or "You can manage this situation," or "Don't worry so much—you've got the ability to do OK." Then, during math class, you can use coping thoughts to get through the class and to concentrate on what you're doing, such as "Just psych yourself up to get through this," or "Look at this class as a challenge, not a threat," or "Keep your cool, you can control your nervousness." Then, if there are certain times during math class that are especially hard for you, like taking a test or going to the board, there are coping thoughts you can use to help you deal with really hard things, like "Think about staying very calm now," or "Relax, take a deep breath," or "Stay as relaxed as possible. This will be over shortly." After math class, or after you cope with a hard situation, then you can learn to encourage yourself for having coped by thinking things like "You did it," or "You were able

to control your negative thoughts," or "You're making progress." Do you get the idea?

Client: Yes, I think so.

Next, in responses 6 through 9, the counselor will instruct Joan to select and practice coping thoughts at each critical phase, first starting with preparing for class.

6. Counselor: Joan, let's take one thing at a time. Let's work just with what you might think before your math class. Can you come up with some coping thoughts you could use when you're anticipating your class?

Client: Well (pauses), I could think about just working on my problems and not worrying about myself. I could think that, when I work at it, I usually get it even if I'm slow.

7. Counselor: OK, good. Now just to get the feel for these, practice using them. Perhaps you could imagine you are anticipating your class—just say these thoughts aloud as you do.

Client: Well, I'm thinking that I could look at my class as a challenge. I can think about just doing my work. When I concentrate on my work, I usually do get the answers.

8. Counselor: OK—good! How did that feel?

Client: Well, OK. I can see how this might help. Of course I don't usually think these kinds of things.

9. Counselor: I realize that, and later on today we will practice actually having you use these thoughts after you use the thought-stopping you learned last week. You'll get to the point where you can use your nervousness as a signal to cope. You can stop the self-defeating thoughts and use these coping thoughts instead. Let's practice this some more.

(Additional practice ensues.)

In responses 10, 11, and 12, the counselor asks Joan to select and practice verbalizing coping thoughts she can use during class.

10. Counselor: OK, Joan, now you seem to have several kinds of coping thoughts that might help you when you're anticipating math class. What about some coping thoughts you could use during the class? Perhaps some of these could help you concentrate on your work instead of your tenseness.

Client: Well, I could tell myself to think about what I need to do—like to get the problems. Or I could think—just take one situation at a time. Just psych myself up 'cause I know I really can do well in math if I believe that.

11. Counselor: OK, it sounds like you've already thought of several coping things to use during class. This time, why don't you pretend you're

sitting in your class. Try out some of these coping thoughts. Just say them aloud.

Client: OK. Well, I'm sitting at my desk, my work is in front of me. What steps do I need to take now? Well, I could just think about one problem at a time, not worry about all of them. If I take it slowly, I can do OK.

12. Counselor: OK, that seemed pretty easy for you. Let's do some more practice like this just so these thoughts don't seem unfamiliar to you. As you practice, try hard to think about the meaning of what you're saying to yourself. (More practice occurs.)

Next, Joan selects and practices coping thoughts to help her deal with especially stressful or critical situations that come up in math class (responses 13, 14, and 15).

13. Counselor: This time, let's think of some particular coping statements that might help you if you come up against some touchy situations in your math class—things that are really hard for you to deal with—like taking a test, going to the board, or being called on. What might you think at these times that would keep the lid on your nervousness?

Client: Well, I could think about just doing what is required of me—maybe, as you said earlier, taking a deep breath and just thinking about staying calm, not letting my anxiety get the best of me.

14. Counselor: OK, great. Let's see—can you practice some of these aloud as if you were taking a test, or had just been asked a question, or were at the board in front of the class?

Client: OK. Well, I'm at the board, I'm just going to think about doing this problem. If I start to get really nervous I'm going to take a deep breath and just concentrate on being calm as I do this.

15. Counselor: OK, let's practice this several times. Maybe this time you might use another tense moment like being called on by your teacher. (Further practice goes on.)

Next the counselor points out how Joan may discourage or punish herself after class (responses 16 and 17). Joan selects and practices encouraging or self-rewarding thoughts (responses 18, 19, and 20).

16. Counselor: OK, Joan, there's one more thing I'd like you to practice. After math class, what do you usually think?

Client: I feel relieved. I think about how glad I am it's over. Sometimes I think about the fact that I didn't do well.

17. Counselor: Well, those thoughts are sort of dis-

couraging, too. What I believe might help is if you could learn to encourage yourself as you start to use these coping thoughts. In other words, instead of thinking about not doing well, focus on your progress in coping. You can do this during class, or after class is over. Can you find some more positive things you could think about to encourage yourself—like giving yourself a pat on the back?

Client: You mean like I didn't do as bad as I thought?

18. Counselor: Yes, anything like that.

Client: Well, it's over, it didn't go too badly. Actually I handled things OK. I can do this if I believe it. I can see progress.

19. Counselor: OK, now, let's assume you've just been at the board. You're back at your seat. Practice saying what you might think in that situation that would be encouraging to you.

Client: Well, I've just sat down. I might think that it went fast and I did concentrate on the problem, so that was good.

20. Counselor: OK. Now let's assume class is over. What would you say would be positive, self-encouraging thoughts after class?

Client: Well, I've just gotten out. Class wasn't that bad. I got something out of it. If I put my mind to it, I can do it.

(More practice of positive self-statement occurs.)

In response 21, the counselor instructs Joan to practice the entire sequence of stopping a self-defeating thought and using a coping thought before, during, and after class. Usually the client practices this by imagining the situation.

21. Counselor: So far we've been practicing these coping thoughts at the different times you might use them so you can get used to these. Now let's practice this in the sequence that it might actually occur—like before your class, during the class, coping with a tough situation, and encouraging yourself after class. We can also practice this with your thought-stopping. If you imagine the situation and start to notice any self-defeating thoughts, you can practice stopping these. Then switch immediately to the types of coping thoughts that you believe will help you most at that time. Concentrate on the coping thoughts. How does this sound?

Client: OK, I think I know what you mean (looks a little confused).

Sometimes long instructions are confusing. Modeling may be better. In responses 22 and 23, the counselor

demonstrates how Joan can apply thought-stopping and coping thoughts in practice.

22. Counselor: Well, I just said a lot and it might make more sense if I showed this to you. First, I'm going to imagine I'm in English class. It's almost time for the bell, then it's math class. Wish I could get out of it. It's embarrassing. Stop! That's a signal to use my coping thoughts. No—I need to think about math class as a challenge. Something I can do OK if I work at it. (Pauses.) Joan, do you get the idea?

Client: Yes, now I do.

23. Counselor: OK, I'll go on and imagine now I'm actually in the class. He's given us a worksheet to do in 30 minutes. Whew. How will dumb me ever do that! Stop! I know I can do it, but I need to go slowly and concentrate on the work, not on me. Just take one problem at a time.

Well, now he wants us to read our answers. What if he calls on me? I can feel my heart pounding. Stop! If I get called on, just take a deep breath and answer. If it turns out to be wrong, it's not the end of the world.

Well, the bell rang. I am walking out. I'm glad it's over. Now wait a minute—it didn't go that badly. Actually I handled it pretty well.

Client: I'm seeing now how this fits together with thought-stopping. After you stop a negative thought, you go to a coping thought.

Next, the counselor encourages Joan to try this out in practice attempts.

24. Counselor: That's it. The idea is to stop the negative thoughts and use more constructive ones. Now why don't you try this?

(Joan practices the sequence of thought-stopping and shifting to coping thoughts several times, first with the counselor's assistance, gradually in a completely self-directed manner.)

Before terminating the session, the counselor assigns daily homework practice.

25. Counselor: This week I'd like you to practice this several times each day—just like you did now. Keep track of your practices on your log. Also, you can use this whenever you feel it would be good to cope—before, during, or after math class. Jot these times down too, and we'll go over this next week.

Learning Activities: Cognitive Restructuring

I. Listed below are eight statements. Read each statement carefully and decide whether it is a self-defeating or a self-enhancing statement. Remember, a self-defeating thought is a negative, unproductive way to view a situation; a self-enhancing thought is a realistic, productive interpretation of a situation or of oneself. Write your answers on a piece of paper. Feedback is given on p. 375.

1. "I'll never be able to pass this test."
2. "How can I ever give a good speech when I don't know what I want to say."
3. "What I can do is to take one thing at a time."
4. "I know I'm going to blow it with all those people looking at me."
5. "What I need to think about is what I *want* to say, not what I think I *should* say."
6. "What if I'm imposing? Maybe I'm just wasting their time."
7. "Why bother. She probably wouldn't want to go out with me anyway."
8. "I may not win, but I'll do my best."

I. This learning activity is designed to help you personalize cognitive restructuring in some way by using it yourself.

1. Identify a problem situation for yourself— a situation in which you don't do what you want to, not because you don't have the skills, but because of your negative or self-defeating thoughts. Some examples might be:
   a. You need to approach your boss about a raise, promotion, or change in duties. You know what to say, but you are keeping yourself from doing it because you aren't sure it would have any effect and you aren't sure how the person might respond.
   b. You have the skills to be an effective helper, yet you constantly think that you aren't.
   c. You continue to get positive feedback about the way you handle or respond in a certain situation, yet you constantly are thinking you don't do this very well.
2. For about a week, every time this situation comes up, monitor all the thoughts you have *before, during,* and *after* the situation. Write these thoughts on a log. At the end of the week:
   a. Identify which of the thoughts are self-defeating.
   b. Identify which of the thoughts are self-enhancing.
   c. Determine whether the greatest number of self-defeating thoughts occurs before, during, or after the situation.

3. In contrast to the self-defeating thoughts you have, identify some possible coping or self-enhancing thoughts you could use. On a piece of paper, list some you could use before, during, and after the situation, with particular attention to the time period when you tend to use almost all self-defeating thoughts. Make sure that you include in your list some positive or self-rewarding thoughts, too—for coping!
4. Imagine the situation—before, during, and after it. As you do this, stop any self-defeating thoughts and replace them with coping and self-rewarding thoughts. You can even practice this in role-play. This step should be practiced until you really can feel your coping and self-rewarding thoughts taking hold.
5. Construct a homework assignment for yourself that encourages you to apply this as needed when the self-defeating thoughts occur.

Stress Inoculation

Stress inoculation is an approach to teaching both physical and cognitive coping skills. The procedure was developed by Meichenbaum and Cameron (1973a), who used it to help clients with several phobic reactions to manage anxiety in stressful situations. Meichenbaum and Turk (1976) describe stress inoculation as a type of psychological protection that functions in the same way as a medical inoculation that provides protection from disease. According to these authors, stress inoculation gives the person "a prospective defense or set of skills to deal with future stressful situations. As in medical inoculations, a person's resistance is enhanced by exposure to a stimulus strong enough to arouse defenses without being so powerful that it overcomes them" (p. 3). Although the procedure has been used as remediation, as the name implies, it also can be used for prevention.

Stress inoculation involves three major components: educating the client about the nature of stressful reactions; having the client rehearse various physical and cognitive coping skills; and helping the client apply these skills during exposure to stressful situations. Of these three components, the second, which provides coping-skills training, seems to be the most important (Horan, Hackett, Buchanan, Stone, & Demchik-Stone, 1977). Stress inoculation has been used to help people manage anxiety reactions (Meichenbaum & Cameron, 1973a), to aid abusive clients in anger control (Novaco, 1975), to teach anger management to law-enforcement personnel (Novaco, 1977); and to help people learn how to tolerate and cope with physiological pain (Levendusky & Pankratz, 1975; Turk, 1975) and tension headaches (Holroyd, Andrasik, & Westbrook, 1977). Meichenbaum and Cameron (1973a) found that stress inoculation was superior to systematic desensitization and two other anxiety-relief treatments in reducing avoidance behavior and in promoting treatment generalization of multiphobic clients. Novaco (1975) found that, for anger control, the entire stress-inoculation procedure was more effective than the use of only coping thoughts or physical relaxation. One of the advantages of stress inoculation compared to either cognitive restructuring or relaxation (Chapter 20) is that both relaxation and cognitive coping skills are learned and applied as part of the stress-inoculation procedure.

We wish to acknowledge the work of Meichenbaum and Cameron (1973a), Novaco (1975), and Meichenbaum and Turk (1976) in our presentation of stress inoculation. We describe the procedure in seven major components:

1. Verbal set
2. Information-giving
3. Acquisition and practice of direct-action coping skills
4. Acquisition and practice of cognitive coping skills
5. Application of all coping skills to problem-related situations
6. Application of all coping skills to potential problem situations
7. Homework and follow-up.

A detailed description of each step associated with these seven parts can be found in the Interview Checklist for Stress Inoculation at the end of this chapter.

Feedback: Cognitive Restructuring

I. 1. Self-defeating: the word *never* indicates the person is not giving himself or herself any chance for passing.
2. Self-defeating: the person is doubting both the ability to give a good speech and knowledge of the subject.
3. Self-enhancing: the person realistically is focusing on one step at a time.
4. Self-defeating: the person is saying with certainty, as evidenced by the word *know*, that there is no chance to do well; this is said without supporting data or evidence.
5. Self-enhancing: the client is realistically focusing on his or her own opinion, not on the assessment of others.
6. Self-defeating: the person is viewing the situation only from a negative perspective, as if rejection is expected and deserved.
7. Self-defeating: the person anticipates a negative reaction without any supporting evidence.
8. Self-enhancing: the person recognizes a win may not occur yet still concentrates on doing the best job.

Verbal Set

Here is an example of a verbal set a counselor might use for stress inoculation.

Rationale. The counselor might explain the purpose of stress inoculation for a client having trouble with anger control as follows:

"You find yourself confronted with situations in which your temper gets out of hand. You have trouble managing your anger, especially when you feel provoked. This procedure can help you learn to cope with provoking situations and can help you manage the intensity of your anger when you're in these situations so it doesn't control you."

Overview. Then the counselor can give the client a brief overview of the procedure:

"First, we will try to help you understand the nature of your feelings and how certain situations may provoke your feelings. Next you will learn some ways to manage your anger and to cope with situations in which you feel angry. After you learn these coping skills, we will set up situations where you can practice using these skills to help you control your anger. How does this sound to you?"

Information-Giving

In this procedure, before learning and applying various coping strategies, it is important that the client be given some information concerning the nature of a stressful reaction and the possible coping strategies that might be used. Most clients view stress as something that is automatic and difficult to overcome. It is helpful for the client to understand the nature of a stressful reaction and how various coping strategies can help manage the stress. It appears that this education phase of stress inoculation is "necessary but insufficient for improvement" (Horan et al., 1977, p. 219). As these authors indicate, "the other components of stress inoculation are built on the education framework and cannot be logically examined or clinically administered in isolation" (p. 219).

Three specific things should be explained to the client: a framework for the client's emotional reaction; information about the phases of reacting to stress; and examples of possible types of coping skills.

Framework for Client's Reaction. First, the counselor should explain the nature of the client's reaction to a stressful situation. Although understanding one's reaction may not be sufficient for changing it, the conceptual framework lays some groundwork for beginning the change process. Usually an explanation of some kind of stress (anxiety, anger, pain) involves describing the stress as having two components: physiological arousal, and covert self-statements or thoughts that provoke anxiety, anger, or pain. This explanation may help the client realize that coping strategies must be directed toward the arousal behaviors *and* the

cognitive processes. For example, to describe this framework to a client who has trouble controlling anger, the counselor could say something like:

> "Perhaps you could think about what happens when you get very angry. You might notice that certain things happen to you physically—perhaps your body feels tight, your face may feel warm, you may experience more rapid breathing, or your heart may pound. This is the physical part of your anger. However, there is another thing that probably goes on while you're very angry—that is, what you're thinking. You might be thinking such things as 'He had no right to attack me; I'll get back at him; Boy, I'll show him who's boss; I'll teach her to keep her mouth shut,' and so on. These kinds of thoughts only intensify your anger. So the way you interpret and think about an anger-provoking situation also contributes to arousing hostile feelings."

Phases of Stress Reactions. After explaining a framework for emotional arousal, it is helpful to describe the possible times or phases that the client's arousal level may be heightened. Meichenbaum and Turk (1976) point out that anxious or phobic clients tend to view their anxiety as one "massive panic reaction" (p. 4). Similarly, clients who are angry, depressed, or experiencing pain may interpret their feelings as one large, continuous reaction that has a certain beginning and end. Clients who interpret their reactions this way may perceive the reaction as too difficult to change because it is so massive and overwhelming.

One way to help the client see the potential for coping with feelings is to describe the feelings by specific stages or phases of reacting to a situation. Meichenbaum and Cameron (1973a), Novaco (1975), and Turk (1975) all used four similar stages to help the client conceptualize the various critical points of a reaction: (1) preparing for a stressful, painful, or provoking situation; (2) confronting and handling the situation or the provocation; (3) coping with critical moments or with feelings of being overwhelmed or agitated during the situation; and (4) rewarding oneself after the stress for using coping skills in the first three phases. Explanation of these stages in the preliminary part of stress inoculation helps the client understand the sequence of coping strategies to be learned. To explain the client's reaction as a series of phases, the counselor might say:

"When you think of being angry, you probably just think of being angry for a continuous period of time. However, you might find that your anger is probably not just one big reaction, but comes and goes at different points during a provoking situation. The first critical point is when you anticipate the situation and start to get angry. At this point you can learn to prepare yourself for handling the situation in a manageable way. The next point may come when you're in the middle of the situation and you're very angry. Here you can learn how to confront a provoking situation in a constructive way. Also, there might be times when your anger really gets intense and you can feel it starting to control you—and perhaps feel yourself losing control. At this time, you can learn how to cope with intense feelings of agitation. Then, after the situation is over, instead of getting angry with yourself for the way you handled it, you can learn to encourage yourself for trying to cope with it. In this procedure, we'll practice using the coping skills at these especially stressful or arousing times."

Information about Coping Strategies. Finally, the counselor should provide some information about the kinds of coping strategies that can be used at these critical points. The counselor should emphasize that there are a *variety* of potentially useful coping skills; clients' input in selecting and tailoring these for themselves is *most* important. Some research has indicated that coping strategies are more effective when clients choose those that reflect their own preferences (Chaves & Barber, 1974). In using stress inoculation, both "direct-action" and "cognitive" coping skills are taught (Meichenbaum & Turk, 1976). Direct-action coping strategies are designed to help the client use coping behaviors to handle the stress; cognitive skills are used to give the client coping thoughts (self-statements)

to handle the stress. The client should understand that *both* kinds of coping skills are important and serve different functions. To provide the client with information about the usefulness of these coping skills, the counselor might explain:

"In the next phase of this procedure, you'll be learning a lot of different ways to prepare for and handle a provoking situation. Some of these coping skills will help you learn to cope with provoking situations by your actions and behaviors; others will help you handle these situations by the way you interpret and think about the situation. Not all of the strategies you learn may be useful or necessary for you, so your input in selecting the ones you prefer to use is important."

Acquisition and Practice of Direct-Action Coping Skills

In this phase of stress inoculation, the client acquires and practices some direct-action coping skills. Horan et al. (1977) found that coping-skills training was highly effective in helping people deal with the type of pain they were trained to cope with. The counselor first discusses and models possible action strategies; the client selects some to use and practices them with the counselor's encouragement and assistance. As you may recall, direct-action coping skills are designed to help the client acquire and apply coping behaviors in stressful situations. The most commonly used direct-action coping strategies include:

1. collecting objective or factual information about the stressful situation
2. identifying short-circuit or escape routes, or ways to decrease the stress
3. mental-relaxation methods
4. physical-relaxation procedures.

Information Collection. Collecting objective or factual information about a stressful situation may help the client evaluate the situation more realistically. Also, information about a situation may reduce the ambiguity for the client and indirectly reduce the level of threat. For example, for a client who may be confronted with physical pain, some information about the source and expected timing of pain can reduce stress. This coping method is widely used in childbirth classes. The women and their "labor coaches" are taught and shown that the experienced pain is actually a uterine contraction. They are given information about the timing and stages of labor and the timing and intensity of contractions so that, when labor occurs, their anxiety will not be increased by misunderstanding or lack of information about what is happening to their bodies.

Collecting information about the nature of an anxiety- or anger-engendering situation serves the same purpose. For example, in using stress inoculation to help clients control anger, collecting information about the people who typically provoke them may help. Also, clients can collect information that can help them view provocation as a *task* or a problem to be solved, rather than as a threat or a personal attack (Novaco, 1975).

Identification of Escape Routes. Identifying escape routes is a way to help the client cope with stress before it gets out of hand. The idea of an escape route is to short-circuit the explosive or stressful situation, or to deescalate the stress, before the client behaves in a way that may "blow it." This coping strategy may help abusive clients learn to identify cues that elicit their physical or verbal abuse and to take some preventive action before "striking out." This is similar to the stimulus-control self-management strategy discussed in Chapter 23. These escape or prevention routes can be very simple things that the client can *do* to prevent losing control or losing face in the situation. An abusive client could perhaps avoid striking out by counting to 60, leaving the room, or talking about something humorous.

Mental Relaxation. Mental relaxation can also help clients cope with stress. Mental relaxa-

tion may involve attention-diversion tactics: angry clients can control their anger by concentrating on a problem to solve, by counting floor tiles in the room, by thinking about a funny or sexy joke, or by thinking about something positive about themselves. Attention-diversion tactics are commonly used to help people control pain. Instead of focusing on the pain, the person may concentrate very hard on an object in the room, or on the repetition of a word (a mantra) or a number. Again, in the Lamaze method of childbirth, the women are taught to concentrate on a "focal point" such as an object in the room or, as we used, a picture of a sailboat. In this way, the woman's attention is directed to an object instead of to the tightening sensations in her lower abdomen.

Some people find that mental relaxation is more successful when they use imagery or fantasy. People who enjoy daydreaming or who report a vivid imagination may find imagery a particularly useful way to promote mental relaxation. Generally, imagery as a coping method helps the client focus or go on a fantasy trip instead of focusing on the stress, the provocation, or the pain. For example, instead of thinking about how anxious or angry she or he feels, the client might learn to fantasize about lying on a warm beach, being on a sailboat, making love, or eating a favorite food (see emotive imagery in Chapter 17). For pain control, the person can imagine different things about the pain. A woman in labor can picture the uterus contracting like a wave instead of thinking about pain. Or a person who experiences pain from a routine source, such as extraction of a wisdom tooth, can use imagery to change the circumstances producing the pain. Instead of thinking about how terrible and painful it is to have a tooth pulled, the person can imagine that the pain is only the aftermath of intense training for a marathon race or is from being the underdog who was hit in the jaw during a fight with the world champion (Knox, 1972).

Physical Relaxation. Physical-relaxation methods are particularly useful for clients who report physiological components of anxiety and anger, such as sweaty palms, rapid breathing or heartbeat, or nausea. Physical relaxation is also a very helpful coping strategy for pain control, because body tension will heighten the sensation of pain. Physical relaxation may consist of muscle relaxation or breathing techniques. A more detailed description of these procedures is provided in Chapter 20.

Each direct-action strategy should first be explained to the client with discussion of its purpose and procedure. Several sessions may be required to discuss and model all the possible direct-action coping methods. After the strategies have been described and modeled, the client should select the particular methods to be used. The number of direct-action strategies used by a client will depend on the intensity of the reaction, the nature of the stress, and the client's preferences. With the counselor's assistance, the client should practice using each skill in order to be able to apply it in simulated and "in vivo" situations.

Acquisition and Practice of Cognitive Coping Skills

This part of stress inoculation is very similar to the cognitive-restructuring strategy described earlier in this chapter. The counselor models some examples of coping thoughts the client can use during stressful phases of problem situations, and the client practices substituting coping thoughts for negative or self-defeating thoughts.

Description of Four Phases of Cognitive Coping. As you remember from our discussion of information-giving, the counselor helps the client to understand the nature of an emotional reaction by conceptualizing the reaction by phases. In helping the client acquire cognitive coping skills, the counselor may first wish to review the importance of learning to cope at crucial times. The counselor can point out that the client can learn a set of cognitive coping skills

for each important phase: preparing for the situation, confronting and handling the situation, coping with critical moments in the situation, and stroking oneself after the situation. Note that the first phase refers to coping skills *before* the situation; the second and third phases involve coping *during* the situation; and the fourth phase refers to coping *after* the situation. The counselor can describe these four phases to the client with an explanation similar to this:

"Earlier we talked about how your anger is not just one giant reaction, but something that peaks at certain stressful points when you feel provoked or attacked. Now you will learn a method of cognitive control that will help you control any negative thoughts that may make you more angry and also help you use coping thoughts at stressful points. There are four times that are important in your learning to use coping thoughts, and we'll work on each of these four phases. First is how you interpret the situation initially, and how you think about responding or preparing to respond. Second is actually dealing with the situation. Third is coping with anything that happens during the situation that *really* provokes you. After the situation, you learn to encourage yourself for keeping your anger in control."

Modeling Coping Thoughts. After explaining the four phases of using cognitive coping skills to the client, the counselor would model possible examples of coping statements that are especially useful for each of the four phases.

Meichenbaum and Turk (1976) have provided an excellent summary of the coping statements used by Meichenbaum and Cameron (1973a) for anxiety control, by Novaco (1975) for anger control, and by Turk (1975) for pain control. These statements, presented in Table 19-1, are summarized for each of the four coping phases: preparing for the situation, confronting the situation, coping with critical moments, and reinforcing oneself for coping. The counselor would present examples of each phase.

Table 19-1. Examples of Coping Thoughts Used in Stress Inoculation

1. Preparing for a Stressor (Meichenbaum & Cameron, 1973a)

   What is it you have to do?

   You can develop a plan to deal with it.

   Just think about what you can do about it. That's better than getting anxious.

   No negative self-statements; just think rationally.

   Don't worry; worry won't help anything.

   Maybe what you think is anxiety is eagerness to confront it.

   Preparing for a Provocation (Novaco, 1975)

   What is it that you have to do?

   You can work out a plan to handle it.

   You can manage this situation. You know how to regulate your anger.

   If you find yourself getting upset, you'll know what to do.

   There won't be any need for an argument.

   Time for a few deep breaths of relaxation. Feel comfortable, relaxed and at ease.

   This could be a testy situation, but you believe in yourself.

   Preparing for the Painful Stressor (Turk, 1975)

   What is it you have to do?

   You can develop a plan to deal with it.

   Just think about what you have to do.

   Just think about what you can do about it.

   Don't worry; worrying won't help anything.

   You have lots of different strategies you can call upon.

2. Confronting and Handling a Stressor (Meichenbaum & Cameron, 1973a)

   Just "psych" yourself up—you can meet this challenge.

   One step at a time; you can handle the situation.

   Don't think about fear; just think about what you have to do. Stay relevant.

   This anxiety is what the doctor said you would feel. It's a reminder to use your coping exercises.

   This tenseness can be an ally, a cue to cope.

   Relax; you're in control. Take a slow deep breath. Ah, good.

   Confronting the Provocation (Novaco, 1975)

   Stay calm. Just continue to relax.

   As long as you keep your cool, you're in control here.

   Don't take it personally.

   Don't get all bent out of shape; just think of what to do here.

   You don't need to prove yourself.

   There is no point in getting mad.

   You're not going to let him get to you.

   Don't assume the worst or jump to conclusions. Look for the positives.

   It's really a shame that this person is acting the way she is.

   For a person to be that irritable, he must be awfully unhappy.

   Confronting and Handling the Pain (Turk, 1975)

   You can meet the challenge.

   One step at a time; you can handle the situation.

   Just relax, breathe deeply and use one of the strategies.

   Don't think about the pain, just what you have to do.

   This tenseness can be an ally, a cue to cope.

   Relax. You're in control; take a slow deep breath. Ah. Good.

   This anxiety is what the trainer said you might feel. That's right; it's the reminder to use your coping skills.

If you start to get mad, you'll just be banging your head against the wall. So you might as well just relax.

There's no need to doubt yourself. What he says doesn't matter.

3. Coping with the Feeling of Being Overwhelmed (Meichenbaum & Cameron, 1973a)

When fear comes, just pause.

Keep the focus on the present; what is it you have to do?

Label your fear from 0 to 10 and watch it change.

You should expect your fear to rise.

Don't try to eliminate fear totally; just keep it manageable.

You can convince yourself to do it. You can reason your fear away.

It will be over shortly.

It's not the worst thing that can happen.

Just think about something else.

Do something that will prevent you from thinking about fear.

Describe what is around you. That way you won't think about worrying.

Coping with Arousal and Agitation (Novaco, 1975)

Your muscles are starting to feel tight. Time to relax and slow things down.

Getting upset won't help.

It's just not worth it to get so angry.

You'll let him make a fool of himself.

It's reasonable to get annoyed, but let's keep the lid on.

Time to take a deep breath.

Your anger is a signal of what you need to do. Time to talk to yourself.

You're not going to get pushed around, but you're not going haywire either.

Try a cooperative approach. Maybe you are both right.

He'd probably like you to get really angry. Well, you're going to disappoint him.

You can't expect people to act the way you want them to.

Coping with Feelings at Critical Moments (Turk, 1975)

When pain comes just pause; keep focusing on what you have to do.

What is it you have to do?

Don't try to eliminate the pain totally; just keep it manageable.

You were supposed to expect the pain to rise; just keep it under control.

Just remember, there are different strategies; they'll help you stay in control.

When the pain mounts you can switch to a different strategy; you're in control.

4. Reinforcing Self-Statements (Meichenbaum & Cameron, 1973a)

Self-Reward (Novaco, 1975)

Reinforcing Self-Statements (Turk, 1975)

It worked; you did it.	It worked!	Good, you did it.
Wait until you tell your therapist about this.	That wasn't as hard as you thought.	You handled it pretty well.
It wasn't as bad as you expected.	You could have gotten more upset than it was worth.	You knew you could do it!
You made more out of the fear than it was worth.	Your ego can sure get you in trouble, but when you watch that ego stuff you're better off.	Wait until you tell the trainer about which procedures worked best.
Your damn ideas—that's the problem. When you control them, you control your fear.	You're doing better at this all the time.	
It's getting better each time you use the procedures.	You actually got through that without getting angry.	
You can be pleased with the progress you're making.	Guess you've been getting upset for too long when it wasn't even necessary.	
You did it!		

From "The Cognitive-Behavioral Management of Anxiety, Anger, and Pain," by D. Meichenbaum and D. Turk. In P. O. Davidson (Ed.), *The Behavioral Management of Anxiety, Depression and Pain.* Copyright 1976 by Brunner/Mazel, Inc. Reprinted by permission.

Client Selection of Coping Thoughts. After the counselor models some possible coping thoughts for each phase, the client should add some or select those that fit. The counselor should encourage the client to "try on" and adapt the thoughts in whatever way feels most natural. The client might look for coping statements he or she has used in other stress-related situations. At this point in the procedure, the counselor should be helping to tailor a coping program *specifically* for this client. If the client's self-statements are too general, they may lead only to "rote-repetition" and not function as effective self-instructions (Meichenbaum, 1977, p. 160). The counselor might explain this to the client in this way:

"You know, your input in finding coping thoughts that work for you is very important. I've given you some examples. Some of these you might feel comfortable with, and there may be others you can think of too. What we want to do now is to come up with some specific coping thoughts you can and will use during these four times that fit for *you*, not me or someone else."

Client Practice of Coping Thoughts. After the client selects coping thoughts to use for each phase, the counselor will instruct the client to practice these self-statements by saying them aloud. This verbal practice is designed to help the client become familiar with the coping thoughts and accustomed to the words. After this practice, the client also should practice the selected coping thoughts in the sequence of the four phases. This practice helps the client learn the timing of the coping thoughts in the application phase of stress inoculation.

The counselor can say something like:

"First I'd like you to practice using these coping thoughts just by saying them aloud to me. This will help you get used to the words and ideas of coping. Next, let's practice these coping thoughts in the sequence that you would use them when applying them to a real situation. Here, I'll show you. OK, first I'm anticipating the situation, so I'm going to use coping statements that help me prepare for the situation, like 'I know this type of situation usually upsets me, but I have a plan now to handle it,' or 'I'm going to be able to control my anger even if this situation is rough.' Next, I'll pretend I'm actually into the situation. I'm going to cope so I can handle it. I might say something to myself like 'Just stay calm. Remember who I'm dealing with. This is their style. Don't take it personally,' or 'Don't overreact. Just relax.'

"OK, now the person's harassment is continuing. I am going to cope with feeling more angry. I might think 'I can feel myself getting more upset. Just keep relaxed. Concentrate on this,' or 'This is a challenging situation. How can I handle myself in a way I don't have to apologize for.' OK, now I haven't gotten abusive or revengeful. So I'll think something to encourage myself, like 'I did it,' or 'Gee, I really kept my cool.'

"OK, now you try it. Just verbalize your coping thoughts in the sequence of preparing for the situation, handling it, coping with getting really agitated, and then encouraging yourself."

Application of All Coping Skills to Problem-Related Situations

The next part of stress inoculation involves having the client apply both the direct-action and the cognitive coping skills in the face of stressful, provoking, or painful situations. Before the client is instructed to apply the coping skills "in vivo," she or he practices applying coping skills under simulated conditions with the counselor's assistance. The application phase of stress inoculation appears to be important for the overall efficacy of the procedure. As Meichenbaum and Cameron (1973a) point out, simply having a client rehearse coping skills *without* opportunities to apply them in stressful situations seems to result in an improved but limited ability to cope.

The application phase involves providing the client with exposure to simulations of problem-related situations. For example, the client who wanted to control anger would have opportunities to practice coping in a variety of anger-provoking situations. During this application practice, it is important that the client be faced with a stressful situation and also that the client practice the skills in a coping manner. In other words, the application should be arranged and conducted as realistically as possible. The angry client can be encouraged to practice feeling very agitated and to rehearse even starting to lose control—but then applying the coping skills to gain control (Novaco, 1975). This type of application practice is viewed as the client's providing a self-model of how to behave in a stressful situation. By imagining faltering or losing control, experiencing anxiety, and then coping with this, the person practices the thoughts and feelings as they are likely to occur in a real-life situation (Meichenbaum, 1977, p. 178). In the application phase of stress inoculation, the client's anxiety or anger is used as a cue or reminder to cope.

Modeling of Application of Coping Skills. The counselor should first model how the client can apply the newly acquired skills in a coping manner when faced with a stressful situation. Here is an example of a counselor demonstration of this process with a client who is working toward anger control (in this case, with his family):

"I'm going to imagine that the police have just called and told me that my 16-year-old son was just picked up again for breaking and entering. I can feel myself start to get really hot. Whoops, wait a minute. That's a signal [arousal cue for coping]. I'd better start thinking about using my relaxation methods to stay calm and using my coping thoughts to prepare myself for handling this situation constructively.

"OK, first of all, sit down and relax. Let those muscles loosen up. Count to ten. Breathe deeply [direct-action coping methods]. OK, now I'll be seeing my son shortly. What is it I have to do? I know it won't help to lash out or to hit him. That won't solve anything. So I'll work out another plan. Let him do most of the talking. Give him the chance to make amends or find a solution [cognitive coping: preparing for the situation]. OK, now I can see him walking in the door. I feel sort of choked up. I can feel my fists getting tight. He's starting to explain. I want to interrupt and let him have it. But wait [arousal cue for coping]. Concentrate on counting and on breathing slowly [direct-action coping]. Now just tell myself—keep cool. Let him talk. It won't help now to blow up [cognitive coping: confronting situation]. Now I can imagine myself thinking back to the last time he got arrested. Why in the hell doesn't he learn? No son of mine is going to be a trouble-maker [arousal]. Whew. I'm pretty damn angry. I've got to stay in control, especially now [cue for coping]. Just relax, muscles! Stay loose [direct-action coping]. I can't expect him to live up to my expectations. I can tell him I'm disappointed, but I'm not going to blow up and shout and hit [cognitive coping: feelings of greater agitation]. OK, I'm doing a good job of keeping my lid on [cognitive coping: self-reinforcement]."

Client Application of Coping Skills in Imaginary and Role-Play Practice. After the counselor modeling, the client should practice a similar sequence of both direct-action and cognitive coping skills. The practice can occur in two ways: imagination and role-play. We find it is often useful to have the client first practice the coping skills while imagining problem-related situations. This practice can be repeated until the client feels very comfortable in applying the coping strategies to imagined situations. Then the client can practice the coping skills with the counselor's aid in a role-play of a problem situation. The role-play practice should be similar to the "in vivo" situations the client encounters. For instance, our angry client could identify specific situations and people with whom he or she is most likely to blow up or lose control. The client can imagine each situation (starting with the most manageable one) and imagine using the coping skills. Then, with the counselor taking the part of a provoker, the client can practice the coping skills in role-play.

Application of All Coping Skills to Potential Problem Situations

Any therapeutic procedure should be designed not only to help clients deal with current problems but also to help them anticipate con-

structive handling of potential problems. In other words, an adequate therapeutic strategy should prevent future problems as well as resolve current ones. The prevention aspect of stress inoculation is achieved by having clients apply the newly learned coping strategies to situations that may not be problematic now but could be stressful in the future. If this phase of stress inoculation is ignored, the effects of the inoculation may be very temporary. In other words, if clients do not have an opportunity to apply the coping skills to situations other than the current problem-related ones, their coping skills may not generalize beyond the present problem situations.

Application of coping skills to other potentially stressful situations is accomplished in the same way as application to the *specific* problem areas. First, after explaining the usefulness of coping skills in other areas of the client's life, the counselor demonstrates the application of coping strategies to a potential, hypothetical stressor. The counselor might select a situation the client has not yet encountered, although the situation would require active coping for anyone who might encounter it. Such situations could include not receiving a desired job promotion or raise, facing a family crisis, moving to a new place, anticipating retirement, being very ill, and so on. After the counselor has modeled application of coping skills to these sorts of situations, the client would practice applying the skills in these or in similar situations that she or he identifies. The practice can occur in imagination or in role-play enactments. Turk (1975) used a novel method of role-play to provide clients with opportunities to apply coping skills. The counselor or trainee role-played a novice, while the client took the part of a trainer or helper. The client's task in the role-play was to train the novice in how to cope with stress—in this case, the stress of experiencing pain. Although Turk did not specifically assess the effects of this particular type of application practice, Fremouw and Harmatz (1975) found that speech-anxious students who acted as helpers and taught anxiety-reduction procedures to other speech-anxious students showed more improvement than other speech-anxious students who learned how to help but were not given an opportunity to do so (latent helpers). Putting the client in the role of a helper or a trainer may provide another kind of application opportunity that also may have benefits for the client's acquisition of coping strategies.

Homework and Follow-Up

When the client has learned and used stress inoculation within the interviews, she or he is ready to use coping skills "in vivo." The counselor and client should discuss the potential application of coping strategies to actual situations. The counselor might caution the client not to expect to cope beautifully with every problematic situation initially. The client should be encouraged to use a daily log to record the specific situations and the number of times the coping strategies are used. The log data can be used in a subsequent follow-up as one way to determine the client's progress.

In our opinion, stress-inoculation training is one of the most comprehensive therapeutic treatments presently in use. Teaching clients both direct-action and cognitive coping skills that can be used in current and potential problematic situations provides skills that are under the clients' own control and are applicable to future as well as current situations. Stress inoculation deserves much more empirical investigation than it has yet received, but the results of the limited previous investigations point to its clinical potential.

Model Dialogue: Stress Inoculation

Session 3

In this session, the counselor will teach Joan some direct-action coping skills for mental and physical relaxation to help her cope with her physical sensations of nervousness about her math class. Imagery manipulations and slow, deep breathing will be used.

First, the counselor reviews the work of the previous session.

1. Counselor: Hi, Joan. How was your week?
   Client: Pretty good, you know this, well, whatever you call it, it's starting to help. I took a test this week and got an 85—I usually get a 70 or 75.
2. Counselor: That really is encouraging. And that's where the effects of this count—on how you do in class. About how many times did you use the coping thoughts this week?
   Client (gets out log): Well, at least once before class, and once during class, and once afterwards. Some days—more often. The hard times still seem to be some of those situations where I feel I might goof. Like when I took this test, I still felt queasy in my stomach.

The counselor introduces the idea of other coping skills to deal with Joan's nervousness.

3. Counselor: Well the coping thoughts will help you control your anxiety but may not eliminate it. Since what we did last week went well for you, I believe today we might work with some other coping skills. These might help you decrease your nervous feelings even more.
   Client: What would this be?

In responses 4 and 5, the counselor explains and models possible direct-action coping skills.

4. Counselor: Well, one thing we might do is to help you learn how to imagine something that gives you very calm feelings, and while you're doing this to take some slow, deep breaths—like this (counselor models closing eyes, breathing slowly and deeply). When I was doing that, I thought about curling up in a chair with my favorite book—but there are many different things you could think of. For instance, to use this in your math class, you might imagine that you are doing work for which you will receive some prize or award. Or you might imagine that you are learning problems so you'll be in a position to be a helper for someone else. Do you get the idea?
   Client: I think so. I guess it's like trying to imagine or think about math in a pretend kind of way.
5. Counselor: Yes—and in a way that reduces rather than increases the stress of it for you.
   Client: I think I get the idea. It's sort of like when I imagine that I'm doing housework for some famous person instead of just at my house—it makes it more tolerable.

In response 6, the counselor asks Joan to find some helpful imagery manipulations to promote calm feelings.

6. Counselor: That's a good example. You imagine that situation to prevent yourself from getting

too bored. Here, you find a scene or scenes to think about to prevent yourself from getting too nervous. Can you take a few minutes to think about one or two things you could imagine —perhaps about math—that would help you to feel calm instead of nervous?

Client (pauses): Well, maybe I could pretend that the math class is part of some training I need in order to do something exciting, like being one of the females in the space program.

In responses 7 and 8, the counselor instructs Joan to practice *these* direct-action coping skills.

7. Counselor: OK, good. We can work with that, and if it doesn't help, we can come up with something else. Why don't you try first to practice imagining this while you also breathe slowly and deeply as I did a few minutes ago. (Joan practices.)

8. Counselor: OK. How did that feel?

Client: OK—it was sort of fun.

In response 9, the counselor gives homework—asks Joan to engage in self-directed practice *of these coping skills before the next session.*

9. Counselor: Good. Now this week I'd like you to practice this in a quiet place two or three times each day. Keep track of your practice sessions in your log and also rate your tension level before and after you practice. Next week we will go over this log and then work on a way you can apply what we did today—and the thought-stopping and coping thoughts we learned in our two previous sessions. So I'll see you next week.

Session 4

In this session, the counselor helps Joan integrate the strategies of the other three sessions (thought-stopping, coping thoughts, and imagery and breathing coping skills). Specifically, Joan learns to apply all these coping skills in imagery and role-play practices of some stressful situations related to math class. Application of coping skills to problem-related situations is a part of stress inoculation and helps the client to generalize the newly acquired coping skills to "in vivo" situations as they occur.

In responses 1 and 2, the counselor will review Joan's use of *the* direct-action skills homework.

1. Counselor: How are things going, Joan?

Client: OK. I've had a hard week—one test and two pop quizzes in math. But I got 80s. I also did

my imagination and breathing practice. You know, that takes a while to learn.

2. Counselor: That's natural. It does take a lot of practice before you really get the feel of it. So it would be a good idea if you continued the daily practice again this week. How did it feel when you practiced?

Client: OK—I think I felt less nervous than before.

The counselor introduces the idea of applying all the coping skills in practice situations *and* presents a rationale *for this application phase.*

3. Counselor: That's good. As time goes on, you will notice more effects from it. Up to this point, we've worked on some things to help you in your math class—stopping self-defeating thoughts, and using imagination and slow breathing to help you cope and control your nervousness. What I think might help now is to give you a chance to use all these skills in practices of some of the stressful situations related to your math class. This will help you use the skills when you need to during the class or related situations. Does this sound OK?

Client: Yes.

Next, the counselor demonstrates (models) how Joan can practice her skills *in an* imaginary practice.

4. Counselor: What I'd like you to do is to imagine some of the situations related to your math class and try to use your coping thoughts *and* the imagination scene and deep breathing to control your nervousness. Let me show you how you might do this. OK, I'm imagining that it's almost time for math class. I'm going to concentrate on thinking about how this class will help me train for the space program. If I catch myself thinking I wish I didn't have to go, I'm going to use some coping thoughts. Let's see—class will go pretty fast. I've been doing better. It can be a challenge. Now, as I'm in class, I'm going to stop thinking about not being able to do the work. I'm going to just take one problem at a time. One step at a time. Oops. Mr. _____ just called on me. Boy, I can feel myself getting nervous. Just take a deep breath . . . . Do the best you can. It's only one moment anyway. Well, it went pretty well. I can feel myself starting to cope when I need to. OK, Joan, why don't you try this several times now?

(Joan practices applying coping thoughts and direct action with different practice situations in imagination.)

In response 5, the counselor checks out Joan's reaction *to applying the skills in practice via imagination.*

5. Counselor: Are you able to really get into the situation as you practice this way?

Client: Yes, although I believe I have to use my coping even more when it really happens.

Sometimes role-play makes the practice more real. The counselor introduces this next. Note that the counselor will add a stress element by calling on Joan at unannounced times.

6. Counselor: That's right. This kind of practice can help you apply the coping when you need to. Maybe it would help if we did some role-play practice. I'll be your teacher this time. Just pretend to be in class. I'll be talking, but at an unannounced time, I'm going to call on you to answer a question. Just use your coping thoughts and your slow breathing as you need to when this happens. (Role-play practice of this and related scenarios occurs.)

The counselor assesses Joan's reaction to role-play practice and asks Joan to rate her level of nervousness during the practice.

7. Counselor: How comfortable do you feel with these practices? Could you rate the nervousness you feel as you do this on a 1-to-5 scale, with 1 being not nervous and 5 being very nervous?

Client: Well, about a 2.

The counselor encourages Joan to apply coping statements in the math-related problem situations as they occur, assigns homework, and schedules a follow-up.

8. Counselor: Well, I think you are ready to use this as you need to during the week. Remember, any self-defeating thought or body tenseness is a cue to cope, using your coping thoughts and imagination and breathing skills. I'd like you to keep track of the number of times you use this on your log sheets. Also rate your level of nervousness before, during, and after math class on the log sheet. How about coming back in 2 weeks to see how things are going?

Client: Fine.

Learning Activities: Stress Inoculation

I. Listed below are eight examples of various direct-action coping skills. Using the coding system, identify on a piece of paper the *type* of direct-action coping skill displayed in each example. Feedback is given on p. 388.

Code

Information (I)
Escape route (ER)
Attention-diversion (AD)
Imagery manipulations (IM)
Muscle relaxation (MR)
Breathing techniques (B)

Examples

1. "Learn to take slow, deep breaths when you feel especially tense."
2. "Instead of thinking just about the pain, try to concentrate very hard on one spot on the wall."
3. "Imagine that it's a very warm day and the warmth makes you feel relaxed."
4. "If it really gets to be too much, just do the first part only—leave the rest for a while."
5. "You can expect some pain, but it is really only the result of the stitches. It doesn't mean that something is wrong."
6. "Just tighten your left fist. Hold it and notice the tension. Now relax it—feel the difference."
7. "Try to imagine a strong, normal cell attacking the weak, confused cancer cells when you feel the discomfort of your treatment."
8. "When it gets very strong, distract yourself—listen hard to the music or study the picture on the wall."

II. Listed below are eight examples of cognitive coping skills used at four different phases: preparing for a situation, confronting or handling the situation, dealing with critical moments in the situation, and self-encouragement for coping. On a piece of paper, identify which phase is represented by each example. Feedback follows.

1. "By golly, I did it."
2. "What will I need to do?"
3. "Don't lose your cool. Take a deep breath."
4. "Think about what you want to say—not how people are reacting to you now."
5. "Relax, it will be over shortly."
6. "Can you feel this—the coping worked!"
7. "When you get in there, just think about the situation, not your anxiety."
8. "That's a signal to cope now. Keep your mind on what you're doing."

Summary

The four cognitive-change procedures of cognitive modeling, thought-stopping, cognitive restructuring, and stress inoculation are being used more frequently in counseling and therapy—even to the point of achieving acceptance, notoriety, and "best-seller" status (Dyer, 1976). Yet thorough investigative efforts into the components and effects of these strategies have only just begun. We wholeheartedly agree with the Mahoneys' plea: "As clinical scientists, our research has only recently begun to examine the functional role of cognitive processes in maladjustment and therapeutic behavior change. Our understanding of the 'inside story' needs rigorous cultivation" (K. Mahoney & M. J. Mahoney, 1976, p. 105).

Post Evaluation

Part One

Objective 1 asks you to identify and describe the six major components of cognitive restructuring in a client case. Using the case described here, explain briefly the way in which you would use the steps and components of cognitive restructuring with *this* client. You can use the seven questions following the client case to describe your use of this procedure. Feedback follows the evaluation.

Description of client: The client is a female, currently a junior in college, majoring in education and getting very good grades. She reports that she has an active social life and has some good close friendships with both males and females. Despite obvious "pluses," the client reports constant feelings of being worthless and inadequate. Her standards for herself seem to be unrealistically high: although she has almost a straight "A" average, she still chides herself that she does not have all "A's." Although she is attractive and has an active social life, she thinks that she should be more attractive and more talented.

1. How would you explain the rationale for cognitive restructuring to this client?
2. Briefly give an overview of the cognitive-restructuring procedure as you might explain it to the client.
3. Give an example you might use with this client to point out the difference between a self-defeating and a self-enhancing thought. Try to base your example on the client's description.
4. How would you have the client identify her

Feedback: Stress Inoculation

I. 1. B
   2. AD
   3. IM
   4. ER
   5. I
   6. MR
   7. IM
   8. AD

If this was difficult for you, you might review the direct-action coping skills.

II. 1. encouraging phase
    2. preparing for the situation
    3. dealing with a critical moment
    4. confronting the situation
    5. dealing with a critical moment
    6. encouragement for coping
    7. preparing for the situation
    8. confronting the situation

If you had trouble identifying the four phases of cognitive coping skills, you may want to review Table 19-1.

thoughts about herself—her grades, appearance, social life, and so on?
5. What are some possible coping thoughts this client might use?
6. Explain how, in the session, you would help the client practice shifting from self-defeating to coping thoughts.
7. What kind of homework assignment would you use to help the client increase her use of coping thoughts about herself?

Part Two

Objective 2 asks you to teach the six components of cognitive restructuring to someone else or to demonstrate these components with a role-play client. Use the Interview Checklist for Cognitive Restructuring at the end of the chapter as a teaching and evaluation guide.

Part Three

Objective 3 asks you to describe how you would apply the major components of stress inoculation with a client case. Using the client description below, respond to the five questions following the case description as if you were using stress inoculation with this client. Feedback follows the evaluation.

Description of client: The client has been referred to you by Family Services. He is unemployed, receiving welfare support, and has three children. He is married to his second wife; the oldest child is hers by another marriage. He has been referred because of school complaints that the oldest child, a seventh-grader, has arrived at school several times with obvious facial bruises and cuts. The oldest child has implicated the stepfather in this matter. After a long period of talking, the client reports that he has little patience with this boy and sometimes does strike him in the face as his way of disciplining the child. He realizes that maybe, on occasion, he has gone too far. Still he gets fed up with the boy's "irresponsibility" and "lack of initiative" for his age. At these times, he reports, his impatience and anger get the best of him.

1. Explain the purpose of stress inoculation as you would to this client.
2. Briefly give an overview of the stress-inoculation procedure.
3. Describe and explain one example of each of the following kinds of direct-action coping skills that might be adopted for or useful to this client.
   a. information about the situation
   b. an escape route
   c. an attention-diversion tactic
   d. an imagery manipulation
   e. physical relaxation
4. Explain, as you might to this client, the four phases of an emotional reaction and of times for coping. For each of the four phases, give two examples of cognitive coping skills (thoughts) that you would give to this client. The four phases are: preparing for a disagreement or argument with the boy; confronting the situation; dealing with critical, very provoking times; and encouraging himself for coping.
5. Describe how you would set up practice opportunities in the interview with this client to help him practice applying the direct-action and cognitive coping skills in simulated practices of the provoking situations.

Part Four

Objective 4 asks you to demonstrate 17 out of 21 steps of the stress-inoculation procedure with a role-play client. Assess this activity using the Interview Checklist for Stress Inoculation at the end of the chapter.

Feedback: Post Evaluation

Part One

1. You might emphasize that the client thinks of herself as inadequate although there are, in actuality, many indications of adequacy. You can explain that CR would help her identify some of her thoughts about herself that are beliefs, not facts, and are unrealistic thoughts, leading to feelings of depression and worthlessness. In addition, CR would help her learn to think about herself in more realistic, self-enhancing ways. See the Interview Checklist for Cognitive Restructuring at the end of the chapter for another example of the CR rationale (p. 391).
2. See lead 2 on the checklist for a description of an overview of CR.
3. Self-enhancing or realistic thoughts for this client would be thinking that an almost straight "A" average is good. A self-defeating thought is that this average is not good enough. In this case, almost any self-degrading thought is self-defeating because, for this client, these thoughts are only beliefs. Thinking that she is not good enough is self-defeating. Self-enhancing or positive thoughts about herself are more realistic interpretations of her experiences—good grades, close friends, active social life, and so on. Recognition that she is intelligent and attractive is a self-enhancing thought.
4. You could ask her to describe different situations and the thoughts she has about herself in them. She could also observe this during the week. You could model some possible thoughts she might be having. See leads 6, 7, 8, and 9, in the checklist that is given on p. 392.
5. There are many possible coping thoughts she could use. Here are some examples: "Hey, I'm doing pretty well as it is." "Don't be so hard on yourself. You aren't perfect." "That worthless feeling is a sign to cope—recognize my assets." "What's more attractive anyway? I am attractive." "Don't let that one 'B' get me down. It's not the end of the world."
6. See leads 13 through 16 on the checklist.
7. Many possible homework assignments might help. Here are a few examples:

Cognitive Restructuring and Stress Inoculation

a. Every time she uses a coping thought, she could record it on her log.
b. She could cue herself to use a coping thought by writing these down on note cards and reading a note before doing something else, like getting a drink or making a phone call, or by using a phone-answering device to report and verbalize coping thoughts.
c. She could enlist the aid of a close friend or roommate. If the roommate notices that the client starts to "put herself down," she could interrupt her. The client could then verbalize a coping statement.

Part Two

Use the Interview Checklist for Cognitive Restructuring at the end of the chapter to assess your teaching or counseling demonstration of this procedure.

Part Three

1. Your rationale to this client might sound something like this:

   "You realize that there are times when your anger and impatience do get the best of you. This procedure can help you learn to control your feelings at especially hard times— when you're very upset with this child —so that you don't do something you will regret later."

2. Here is a brief overview of stress inoculation:

   "First, we'll look at the things the child can do that really upset you. When you realize you're in this type of situation, you can learn to control how upset you are—through keeping yourself calm. This procedure will help you learn different ways to keep calm and not let these situations get out of hand."

3. Information—See lead 7, part a, on the Interview Checklist for Stress Inoculation at the end of the chapter for some examples (see p. 396).

   Escape route—See lead 7, part b.
   Attention-diversion—See lead 7, part c.

Imagery manipulations—See lead 7, part d.
Physical relaxation—See lead 7, parts e and f.

4. Here are some examples of a possible explanation of the four coping phases and of cognitive coping skills you might present to this client.

Phase	Explanation	Cognitive Coping
Preparing for a provoking situation	Before you have a disagreement or discussion, you can plan how you want to handle it.	"What do I want to say to him that gets my point across?" "I can tell him how I feel without shouting."
Confronting a provoking situation	When you're talking to him, you can think about how to stay in control.	"Just keep talking in a normal voice, no yelling." "Let him talk, too. Don't yell a lot; it doesn't help."
Dealing with a very provoking moment	If you feel very angry, you really need to think of some things to keep you from blowing your cool.	"Wait a minute. Slow down. Don't let the lid off." "Keep those hands down. Stay calm now."
Encouraging self for coping	Recognize when you do keep your cool. It's important to do this, to give yourself a pat on the back for this.	"I kept my cool that time!" "I could feel myself getting angry, but I kept in control then."

5. Practice opportunities can be carried out by the client in imagination or by you and the client in role-play. In a role-play practice, you could take the part of the child. See leads 14, 15, and 16 on the Interview Checklist for Stress Inoculation for some examples of this type of practice.

Part Four

Use the Interview Checklist for Stress Inoculation to assess your role-play interview.

Interview Checklist for Cognitive Restructuring

Instructions to observer: Identify whether the counselor demonstrated the lead listed in the checklist. Check which leads the counselor used.

Checklist	Examples of Counselor Leads
I. *Rationale and Overview: Verbal Set*	
_____ 1. Counselor explains purpose and rationale of cognitive restructuring.	"You've reported that you find yourself getting anxious and depressed during and after these conversations with the people who have to evaluate your work. This procedure can help you identify some things you might be thinking in this situation that are just beliefs, not facts, and are unproductive. You can learn more realistic ways to think about this situation that will help you cope with it in a way that you want to."
_____ 2. Counselor provides brief overview of procedure.	"There are three things we'll do in using this procedure. *First,* this will help you identify the kinds of things you're thinking before, during, and after these situations that are self-defeating. *Second,* this will teach you how to stop a self-defeating thought and replace it with a coping thought. *Third,* this will help you learn how to give yourself credit for changing these self-defeating thoughts."
_____ 3. Counselor explains difference between rational or self-enhancing thoughts (facts) and irrational or self-defeating thoughts (beliefs) and provides examples of each.	"A self-defeating thought is one way to interpret the situation, but it is usually negative and unproductive, like thinking that the other person doesn't value you or what you say. In contrast, a self-enhancing thought is a more constructive and realistic way to interpret the situation—like thinking that what you are talking about has value to you."
_____ 4. Counselor explains influence of irrational and self-defeating thoughts on emotions and performance.	"When you're constantly preoccupied with yourself and worried about how the situation will turn out, this can affect your feelings and your behavior. Worrying about the situation can make you feel anxious and upset. Concentrating on the situation and not worrying about its outcome can help you feel more relaxed, which helps you handle the situation more easily."
_____ 5. Counselor confirms client's willingness to use strategy.	"Are you ready to try this now?"

II. *Identifying Client Thoughts in Problem Situations*
____ 6. Counselor asks client to
describe problem situations and
identify examples of rational and
self-enhancing thoughts and
of irrational and self-defeating
thoughts client typically
experiences in these situations.

"Think of the last time you were in this situation. Describe for me what you think before you have a conversation with your evaluator. . . . What are you usually thinking during the conversation? . . . What thoughts go through your mind after the conversation is over? Now, let's see which of those thoughts are actual facts about the situation or are constructive ways to interpret the situation. Which ones are your beliefs about the situation that are unproductive or self-defeating?"

____ 7. If client is unable to complete
step 6, counselor models possible
examples of thoughts or "links" between
event and client's emotional
response.

"OK, think of the thoughts that you have while you're in this conversation as a link between this event and your feelings afterward of being upset and depressed. What is the middle part? For instance, it might be similar to 'I'll never have a good evaluation, and I'll lose this position,' or 'I always blow this conversation and never make a good impression.' Can you recall thinking anything like this?"

____ 8. Counselor instructs client
to monitor and record content of
thoughts *before, during,* and
after stressful or upsetting situations
prior to next session.

"One way to help you identify this link or your thoughts is to keep track of what you're thinking in these situations as they happen. This week I'd like you to use this log each day. Try to identify and write down at least three specific thoughts you have in these situations each day and bring this in with you next week."

____ 9. Using client's monitoring,
counselor and client identify
client's self-defeating thoughts.

"Let's look at your log and go over the kinds of negative thoughts that seem to be predominant in these situations. We can explore how these specific thoughts affect your feelings and performance in this situation—and whether you feel there is any evidence or rational basis for these."

III. *Introduction and Practice of Coping Thoughts*
____ 10. Counselor explains purpose
and potential use of "coping
thoughts" and gives some examples of
coping thoughts to be used:
    ____ a. before the situation—
        preparing for it
    ____ b. during the situation
        ____ 1. focusing on task
        ____ 2. dealing with feeling
            overwhelmed

"Up to this point, we've talked about the negative or unproductive thoughts you have in these situations and how they contribute to your feeling uncomfortable, upset, and depressed. Now we're going to look at some alternative, more constructive ways to think about the situation—using coping thoughts. These thoughts can help you prepare for the situation, handle the situation, and deal with feeling upset or overwhelmed in the situation. As long as you're using some coping thoughts, you avoid giving up control and letting the old self-defeating thoughts take over. Here are some examples of coping thoughts."

Checklist	Examples of Counselor Leads
____ 11. Counselor instructs client to think of additional coping thoughts client could use or had used before.	"Try to think of your own coping thoughts— perhaps ones you can remember using successfully in other situations, ones that seem to fit for you."
____ 12. Counselor instructs client to practice verbalizing selected coping statements.	"At first you will feel a little awkward using coping statements. It's like learning to drive a stick shift after you've been used to driving an automatic. So one way to help you get used to this is for you to practice these statements aloud."
____ a. Counselor instructs client first to practice coping statements individually. Coping statements to use before a situation are practiced, then coping statements to use during a situation.	"First just practice each coping statement separately. After you feel comfortable with saying these aloud, practice the ones you could use before this conversation. OK, now practice the ones you could use during this conversation with your evaluator."
____ b. Counselor instructs client to practice sequence of coping statements as they would be used in actual situation.	"Now let's put it all together. Imagine it's an hour before your meeting. Practice the coping statements you could use then. We'll role-play the meeting. As you feel aroused or overwhelmed, stop and practice coping thoughts during the situation."
____ c. Counselor instructs client to become actively involved and to internalize meaning of coping statements during practice.	"Try to really put yourself into this practice. As you say these new things to yourself, try to think of what these thoughts really mean."

IV. *Shifting from Self-Defeating to Coping Thoughts*

____ 13. Counselor models shift from recognizing a self-defeating thought and stopping it to replacing it with a coping thought.	"Let me show you what we will practice today. First, I'm in this conversation. Everything is going OK. All of a sudden I can feel myself starting to tense up. I realize I'm starting to get overwhelmed about this whole evaluation process. I'm thinking that I'm going to blow it. No, I stop that thought at once. Now, I'm just going to concentrate on calming down, on taking a deep breath, and thinking only about what I have to say."

Checklist	Examples of Counselor Leads

_____ 14. Counselor helps client practice shift from self-defeating to coping thought. Practice consists of four steps:
   _____ a. having client imagine situation or carry it out in a role-play (behavior rehearsal)
   _____ b. recognizing self-defeating thought (which could be signaled by a hand or finger)
   _____ c. stopping thought (which could be supplemented with hand clap)
   _____ d. replacing thought with coping thought (and possibly supplemented with deep breathing).
	"Now let's practice this. You will imagine the situation. As soon as you start to recognize the onset of a self-defeating thought, stop it. Verbalize the thought aloud, and tell yourself to stop. Then verbalize a coping thought in place of it and imagine carrying on with the situation."

_____ 15. Counselor helps client practice using shift for each problem situation until anxiety or stress felt by client while practicing situation is decreased to a reasonable or negligible level and client can carry out practice and use coping thoughts in self-directed manner.	"Let's keep working with this situation until you feel pretty comfortable with it and can shift from self-defeating to coping thoughts without my help."

V. _Introduction and Practice of Positive or Reinforcing Self-Statements_

_____ 16. Counselor explains purpose and use of positive or reinforcing self-statements and gives some examples of these to client.	"You have really made a lot of progress in learning to use coping statements before and during these situations. Now it's time to learn to reward or encourage yourself. After you've coped with a situation, you can pat yourself on the back for having done so by thinking a positive or rewarding thought like 'I did it,' or 'I really managed that pretty well.'"
_____ 17. Counselor instructs client to think of additional positive self-statements and to select some to try out.	"Can you think of some things like this that you think of when you feel good about something or when you feel like you've accomplished something? Try to come up with some of these thoughts that seem to fit for you."
_____ 18. Counselor models application of positive self-statements as self-reinforcement for shift from self-defeating to coping thoughts.	"OK, here is the way you can reward yourself for having coped. You recognize the self-defeating thought. Now you're in the situation using coping thoughts, and you're thinking things like 'Take a deep breath,' or 'Just concentrate on this task.' Now the conversation is finished. You know you were able to use coping thoughts and you reward yourself by thinking 'Yes, I did it,' or 'I really was able to manage that.'"

Checklist	Examples of Counselor Leads
___ 19. Counselor instructs client to practice use of positive self-statements in interview following practice of shift from self-defeating to coping thoughts. This should be practiced in sequence (coping *before* and *during* situation and reinforcing oneself *after* situation).	"OK, let's try this out. As you imagine the conversation, you're using the coping thoughts you will verbalize. . . . Now, imagine the situation is over, and verbalize several reinforcing thoughts for having coped."

VI. *Homework and Follow-Up*

Checklist	Examples of Counselor Leads
___ 20. Counselor instructs client to use cognitive-restructuring procedure (identifying self-defeating thought, stopping it, shifting to coping thought, reinforcing with positive self-statement) in situations outside the interview.	"OK, now you're ready to use the entire procedure whenever you have these conversations in which you're being evaluated— or any *other* situation in which you recognize your negative interpretation of the event is affecting you. In these cases, you recognize and stop any self-defeating thoughts, use the coping thoughts before the situation to prepare for it, and use the coping thoughts during the situation to help focus on the task and deal with being overwhelmed. After the situation is over, use the positive self-thoughts to reward your efforts."
___ 21. Counselor instructs client to monitor and record on log sheet number of times client uses cognitive restructuring outside the interview.	"I'd like you to use this log to keep track of the number of times you use this procedure and to jot down the situation in which you're using it. Also rate your tension level on a 1 to 5 scale before and after each time you use this."
___ 22. Counselor arranges for follow-up.	"Do this recording for the next two weeks. Then, let's get together for a follow-up session."

Consultant Comments: _____

___

Interview Checklist for Stress Inoculation

Instructions to observer: Determine which of the following steps were demonstrated by the counselor in using stress inoculation with a client or in teaching stress inoculation to another person. Check any step the counselor demonstrated in the application of the procedure.

Checklist	Example of Counselor Lead
I. *Verbal Set*	
___ 1. Counselor explains purpose of stress inoculation.	"Stress inoculation is a way to help you cope with feeling anxious so that you can manage your reactions when you're confronted with these situations."

Cognitive Restructuring and Stress Inoculation

Checklist	Example of Counselor Lead
_____ 2. Counselor provides brief description of stress-inoculation procedure.	"First we'll try to understand how your anxious feelings affect you now. Then you'll learn some coping skills that will help you relax physically—and help you use coping thoughts instead of self-defeating thoughts. Then you'll have a chance to test out your coping skills in stressful situations we'll set up."
_____ 3. Counselor checks to see whether client is willing to use strategy.	"How do you feel now about working with this procedure?"

II. *Information-Giving*

_____ 4. Counselor explains nature of client's emotional reaction to a stressful situation.	"Probably you realize that, when you feel anxious, you are physically tense. Also, you may be thinking in a worried way—worrying about the situation and how to handle it. Both the physical tenseness and the negative or worry thoughts create stress for you."
_____ 5. Counselor explains possible *phases* of reacting to a stressful situation.	"When you feel anxious, you probably tend to think of it as one giant reaction. Actually, you're probably anxious at certain times or phases. For example, you might feel very uptight just anticipating the situation. Then you might feel uptight during the situation, especially if it starts to overwhelm you. After the situation is over, you may feel relieved—but down on yourself, too."
_____ 6. Counselor explains specific kinds of coping skills to be learned in stress inoculation and importance of client's input in tailoring coping strategies.	"We'll be learning some action kinds of coping strategies—like physical or muscle relaxation, mental relaxation, and just common-sense ways to minimize the stress of the situation. Then also you'll learn some coping ways to view and think about the situation. Not all of these coping strategies may seem best for you, so your input in selecting the ones you feel are best for you is important."

III. *Acquisition and Practice of Direct-Action Coping Skills*

_____ 7. Counselor discusses and models direct-action coping strategies (or uses a symbolic model):	"First, I'll explain and we can talk about each coping method. Then I'll demonstrate how you can apply it when you're provoked."
_____ a. collecting objective or factual information about stressful situation	"Sometimes it helps to get any information you can about things that provoke and anger you. Let's find out the types of situations and people that can do this to you. Then we can see whether there are other ways to view the provocation. For example, what if you looked at it as a situation to challenge your problem-solving ability rather than as a personal attack?"
_____ b. identifying short-circuit or escape routes; alternative ways to deescalate stress of situation	"Suppose you're caught in a situation. You feel it's going to get out of hand. What are some ways to get out of it or to deescalate it *before* you strike out? For example, little things like counting to 60, leaving the room, using humor, or something like that."

Checklist	Example of Counselor Lead

mental relaxation:
_____ c. attention-diversion

"OK, one way to control your anger is to distract yourself—take your attention away from the person whom you feel angry with. If you have to stay in the same room, concentrate very hard on an object in the room. Think of all the questions about this object you can."

_____ d. imagery manipulations

"OK, another way you can prevent yourself from striking out is to use your imagination. Think of something very calming and very pleasurable like your favorite record or like being on the beach with the hot sun."

physical relaxation:
_____ e. muscle relaxation

"Muscle relaxation can help you cope whenever you start to feel aroused and feel your face getting flushed or your body tightening up. It can help you learn to relax your body, which can in turn help you control your anger."

_____ f. breathing techniques

"Breathing is also important in learning to relax physically. Sometimes, in a tight spot, taking slow, deep breaths can give you time to get yourself together before saying or doing something you don't want to."

_____ 8. Client selects most useful coping strategies and practices each under counselor's direction.

"We've gone over a lot of possible methods to help you control your anger so it doesn't result in abusive behavior. I'm sure that you have some preferences. Why don't you pick the methods that you think will work best for you, and we'll practice with these so you can get a feel for them."

IV. *Acquisition and Practice of Cognitive Coping Skills*

_____ 9. Counselor describes four phases of using cognitive coping skills to deal with a stressful situation.

"As you may remember from our earlier discussion, we talked about learning to use coping procedures at important points during a stressful or provoking situation. Now we will work on helping you learn to use coping thoughts during these four important times—preparing for the situation, handling the situation, dealing with critical moments during the situation, and encouraging yourself after the situation."

_____ 10. For each phase, counselor models possible examples of coping statements.

"I'd like to give you some ideas of some possible coping thoughts you could use during each of these four important times. For instance, when I'm trying to prepare or psych myself up for a stressful situation, here are some things I think about."

_____ 11. For each phase, client selects most natural coping statements.

"The examples I gave may not feel natural for you. What I'd like you to do is to pick or add ones that you could use comfortably, that wouldn't seem foreign to you."

_____ 12. Counselor instructs client to practice using these coping statements for each phase.

"Sometimes, because you aren't used to concentrating on coping thoughts at these important times, it feels a little awkward at first. So I'd like you to get a feel for these just by practicing aloud the ones you selected. Let's work first on the ones for preparing for a provoking situation."

Checklist	Example of Counselor Lead
___ 13. Counselor models and instructs client to practice sequence of all four phases and verbalize accompanying coping statements.	"OK, next I'd like you to practice verbalizing the coping thoughts aloud in the sequence that you'll be using when you're in provoking situations. For example [counselor models]. Now you try it."

V. *Application of All Coping Skills to Problem-Related Situations*

___ 14. Using coping strategies and skills selected by client, counselor models how to apply these in a coping manner while imagining a stressful (problem-related) situation.	"Now you can practice using all these coping strategies when confronted with a problem situation. For example, suppose I'm you and my boss comes up to me and gives me criticism based on misinformation. Here is how I might use my coping skills in that situation."
___ 15. Client practices coping strategies while imagining problem-related stressful situations. (This step is repeated as necessary.)	"OK, this time why don't you try it? Just imagine this situation—and imagine that each time you start to lose control, that is a signal to use some of your coping skills."
___ 16. Client practices coping strategies in role-play of problem-related situation. (This step is repeated as necessary.)	"We could practice this in role-play. I could take the part of your boss and initiate a meeting with you. Just be yourself and use your coping skills to prepare for the meeting. Then, during our meeting, practice your skills whenever you get tense or start to blow up."

VI. *Application of All Coping Skills to Potential Problem Situations (Generalization)*

___ 17. Counselor models application of client-selected coping strategies to non-problem-related or other potentially stressful situations.	"Let's work on some situations now that aren't problems for you but could arise in the future. This will give you a chance to see how you can apply these coping skills to other situations you encounter in the future. For instance, suppose I just found out I didn't get a promotion that I believe I really deserved. Here is how I might cope with this."
___ 18. Client practices, as often as needed, applying coping strategies to potentially stressful situations by:	"OK, you try this now."
___ a. imagining potentially stressful situation	"Why don't you imagine you've just found out you're being transferred to a new place. You are surprised by this. Imagine how you would cope."
___ b. taking part in a role-play practice	"This time let's role-play a situation. I'll be your husband and tell you I've just found out I am very ill. You practice your coping skills as we talk."
___ c. taking part of a teacher in a role-play and teaching a novice how to use coping strategies for stressful situations	"This time I'm going to pretend that I have chronic arthritis and am in constant pain. It's really getting to me. I'd like you to be my trainer or helper and teach me how I could learn to use some coping skills to deal with this chronic discomfort."

Checklist	*Example of Counselor Lead*

VII. *Homework and Follow-Up*

—— 19. Counselor and client discuss application of coping strategies to "in vivo" situations.

"I believe now you could apply these coping skills to problem situations you encounter during a typical day or week. You may not find that these work as quickly as you'd like, but you should find yourself coping more and not losing control as much."

—— 20. Counselor instructs client how to use log to record uses of stress inoculation for "in vivo" situations.

"Each time you use the coping skills, mark it down on the log and briefly describe the situation in which you used this."

—— 21. Counselor arranges for a follow-up.

"We could get together in several weeks and go over your logs and see how you're doing."

Consultant Comments: _____

Suggested Readings

Cognitive Restructuring

Beck, A. T. *Cognitive therapy and the emotional disorders.* New York: International Universities Press, 1976.

Fremouw, W. J., & Zitter, R. E. A comparison of skills training and cognitive restructuring-relaxation for the treatment of speech anxiety. *Behavior Therapy,* 1978, *9,* 248–259.

Glogower, F. D., Fremouw, W. J., & McCroskey, J. C. A component analysis of cognitive restructuring. *Cognitive Therapy and Research,* 1978, *2,* 209–223.

Goldfried, M. R., & Davison, J. C. *Clinical behavior therapy.* New York: Holt, Rinehart, & Winston, 1976. Chap. 8, Cognitive relabeling, 158–185.

Goldfried, M. R., Linehan, M. M., & Smith, J. L. Reduction of test anxiety through cognitive restructuring. *Journal of Consulting and Clinical Psychology,* 1978, *46,* 32–39.

Meichenbaum, D. Cognitive modification of test anxious students. *Journal of Consulting and Clinical Psychology,* 1972, *39,* 370–380.

Meichenbaum, D. *Cognitive-behavior modification: An integrative approach.* New York: Plenum Press, 1977. Chap. 6, Cognitive restructuring techniques, 183–199.

Schmidt, J. Cognitive restructuring: The art of talking to yourself. *The Personnel and Guidance Journal,* 1976, *55,* 71–74.

Taylor, F. G., & Marshall, W. L. Experimental analysis of a cognitive-behavioral therapy for depression. *Cognitive Therapy and Research,* 1977, *1,* 59–72.

Wein, K. S., Nelson, R. O., & Odom, J. V. The relative contributions of reattribution and verbal extinction to the effectiveness of cognitive restructuring. *Behavior Therapy,* 1975, *6,* 459–474.

Stress Inoculation

Holroyd, K. A., Andrasik, F., & Westbrook, T. Cognitive control of tension headache. *Cognitive Therapy and Research,* 1977, *1,* 121–133.

Horan, J. J., Hackett, G., Buchanan, J. D., Stone, C. I., & Demchik-Stone, D. Coping with pain: A component analysis of stress inoculation. *Cognitive Therapy and Research,* 1977, *1,* 211–221.

Langer, E. J., Janis, I. L., & Wolfer, J. A. Reduction of psychological stress in surgical patients. *Journal of Experimental Social Psychology,* 1975, *11,* 155–165.

Levendusky, P., & Pankratz, L. Self-control techniques as an alternative to pain medication. *Journal of Abnormal Psychology,* 1975, *85,* 165–168.

Meichenbaum, D. *Cognitive-behavior modification: An integrative approach.* New York: Plenum Press, 1977. Chap. 5, Stress-inoculation training, 143–182.

Meichenbaum, D., & Turk, D. The cognitive-behavioral management of anxiety, anger, and pain. In P. O. Davidson (Ed.), *The Behavioral management of anxiety, depression and pain.* New York: Brunner/Mazel, 1976.

Novaco, R. W. *Anger control: The development and evaluation of an experimental treatment.* Lexington, Mass.: Heath, 1975.

Novaco, R. W. A stress inoculation approach to anger management in the training of law enforcement officers. *American Journal of Community Psychology,* 1977, 5, 327–346.

Chapter 20
Meditation and Muscle Relaxation

Feeling uptight? stressful? anxious?
Does your blood pressure zoom up at certain times or in certain situations?
Having trouble sleeping at night?
Does your head pound and ache at the end of the day?

A great number of people would respond affirmatively to these four questions. Anxiety is one of the most common problems reported by clients; stress is related to physiological discomfort such as headaches and indigestion. Stress is also correlated with heart disease, cancer, and other serious diseases. Perhaps as a consequence of the "stress syndrome," the last few years have produced an explosion in procedures for stress or anxiety management, originally introduced in 1929 as "progressive relaxation" (Jacobson, 1929). Related books have appeared on nonfiction best-seller lists (Benson, 1976; Bloomfield, Cain, Jaffe, & Kory, 1975; Denniston & McWilliams, 1975), and a flurry of research endeavors has explored the relative strengths and weaknesses of stress-management approaches (Nicassio & Bootzin, 1974; Shoemaker & Tasto, 1975; J. C. Smith, 1975). Two stress-management or relaxation strategies are presented in this chapter: meditation and muscle relaxation. They are typically used to treat both cognitive and physiological indexes of stress, including anxiety, anger, and pain. The two strategies differ somewhat in that meditation is primarily a cognitive-relaxation procedure, whereas muscle relaxation focuses on physical sensations (Marlatt & Marques, 1977, p. 131). The benefits of both procedures may not be realized unless they are used to prevent, as well as to remediate, stress-related symptoms.

Objectives

1. Identify which step of meditation (the relaxation response) is reflected by each of ten counselor responses. You should be able to identify accurately eight out of ten examples.
2. Teach the process of meditation (the relaxation response) to another person. Audio-tape your teaching and assess your steps with the Interview Checklist for Meditation, or have an observer evaluate you on the checklist while you teach the procedure to someone else.
3. Describe how you would apply the seven major components of the muscle-relaxation procedure, given a simulated client case.
4. Demonstrate 13 out of 15 steps of muscle relaxation with a role-play client, using the Interview Checklist for Muscle Relaxation to assess your performance.

Meditation (The Relaxation Response)

Meditation is a cognitive exercise conducted in a quiet, calm environment in which a person focuses on breathing by using a mental device. *The relaxation response* is the label Benson (1974, 1976) gives this technique. The word *meditation* is associated with the mystical traditions of the East. For example, Zen (Zazen) breath meditation was developed many centuries ago as a technique for attaining religious insight (D. H. Shapiro & S. M. Zifferblatt, 1976). Transcendental Meditation (TM) is another procedure used to turn one's attention inward toward more subtle levels of thought. In a review of meditation as psychotherapy, J. C. Smith (1975) states that the "term *meditation* refers to a family of mental exercises that generally involve calmly limiting thought and attention. Such exercises vary widely and can involve sitting still and counting breaths, attending to a repeated thought, or focusing on virtually any simple external or internal stimulus" (p. 558).

Several studies have reported on the effectiveness of meditation as a therapeutic strategy. J. C. Smith's (1975) review of research about meditation as a therapeutic procedure yielded three general findings. First, experienced meditators who volunteer without pay for meditation research appear "healthier" than nonmeditators. Second, people who are beginners and who practice meditation for 4 to 10 weeks show more "improvement" on a variety of tests than nonmeditators measured for the same period of time. Third, 4 to 10 weeks of regular practice of meditation is associated with greater decrements in "psychopathology" than those experienced by control nonmeditators. However, Smith points out that the expectation of relief (I want to and will get better) and the regular practice of sitting quietly were not controlled for by any of the studies reviewed.

In other studies, Boudreau (1972) found that TM relieved symptoms associated with claustrophobia in one case and excessive perspiration in another. Girodo (1974) found that people with a short history of anxiety neurosis effectively reduced their anxiety symptoms with meditation. Zen breath meditation and self-management techniques were applied to reduce methadone dosage of two drug addicts (D. H. Shapiro & S. M. Zifferblatt, 1976) and to treat generalized anxiety (D. H. Shapiro, in press). Attention-focusing techniques derived from meditation procedures were as effective as progressive relaxation in treating 24 insomniacs to reduce latency of sleep onset (Woolfolk, Carr-Kaffashan, McNulty, & Lehrer, 1976). Breath meditation was effective in reducing systolic and diastolic blood pressure of a 71-year-old hypertensive from 170/105 before treatment to 135/90 several months after treatment (Rappaport & Cammer, 1977). Both the relaxation response and muscle relaxation significantly decreased alcohol consumption of many clients (Marlatt & Marques, 1977).

D. H. Shapiro and S. M. Zifferblatt (1976) have described the process of Zen meditation in five overlapping steps:

1. There is a reactive effect when a person begins to focus on breathing. For example, breathing may be faster.
2. Later, the person's attention wanders from the breathing and he or she becomes habituated in the exercise.
3. The person is taught to catch himself or herself whenever attention wanders and return to breathing. Either this process may cause another reactive effect or, with practice, one may learn to breathe effortlessly.
4. The person is able to continue to focus on breathing while at the same time passively observing new thoughts as they come into his or her awareness.
5. The last process (Step 4) can have two functions: (a) the person becomes desensitized to distracting thoughts, and (b) the person eventually removes thoughts by focusing on breathing [p. 522].

Benson (1974, 1976) has described meditation, or the relaxation response, as a counterbalancing technique for alleviating the environmental effects of stress. Often, when people feel stress, "fight-or-flight" is the coping response used. Regular practice or elicitation of the relaxation response can stimulate the area of·

the hypothalamus in the brain that can decrease systolic and diastolic blood pressure, heart rate, respiratory rate, and oxygen consumption. The fight-or-flight response to stress can raise these physiological rates (Benson, 1976). According to Benson (1974, 1976), four basic elements are needed to elicit the relaxation response: a quiet environment, a mental device, a passive attitude, and a comfortable position.

Meditation can be used alone or in conjunction with other procedures (see D. H. Shapiro & S. M. Zifferblatt, 1976). The elements listed by Benson (1976) for eliciting the relaxation response and the processes described by Shapiro and Zifferblatt have been interwoven into the following description of the steps for meditation.

Steps for Meditation

We describe the meditation procedure in eight steps:

1. The counselor gives the client a verbal set for the procedure.
2. The counselor and client select a mental device.
3. The counselor instructs the client about body comfort.
4. The counselor instructs the client about breathing and use of a mental device.
5. The counselor instructs the client about a passive attitude.
6. The client tries to meditate for 10 to 20 minutes.
7. The counselor probes the client about the meditative experience.
8. Finally, the client is assigned homework and is instructed to keep a daily log of meditative experiences.

The Interview Checklist for Meditation at the end of the chapter summarizes these steps.

Verbal Set. Here is an example of a *rationale* for meditation used by D. H. Shapiro (1978b):

Meditation is nothing magical. It takes patience and practice; you have to work at it; and, just by meditating, all life's problems will not be solved. On the other hand, meditation is potentially a very powerful tool, and it is equally important to suggest what you might be able to expect from meditation the first month you practice it. Studies have shown that Zen meditation can have a strong effect within the first two to four weeks. Some of these effects can be measured physiologically—e.g., brain wave states, slower breathing, slower heart rate. These all contribute to a state of relaxation and inner calm. Meditation may help you become more aware, both of what is going on outside you, and what is happening within you—your thoughts, feelings, hopes, fears. Thus, although meditation won't solve all your problems, it can give you the calmness, the awareness, and the self-control to actively work on solving those problems.*

Here is an illustration of an *overview* of the strategy:

"What we will do first is select a focusing or mental device. You will then get in a relaxed and comfortable position. Afterwards, I will instruct you about focusing on your breathing and using your mental device. We will talk about a passive attitude while meditating. You will meditate about 10 to 20 minutes. Then we will talk about the experience."

Selecting a Mental Device. Most forms of meditation can be referred to as "concentrative" meditation, in which one tries to clear one's mind of intruding thoughts by focusing for a time on a single stimulus (Ornstein, 1972). Often this stimulus takes the form of a mental device. A mental device, or "mantra," is usually a single-syllable sound or word such as *in, out, one,* or *zum,* although concentration on a mental riddle also is possible. The client repeats the syllable or word silently or in a low tone while

---

*This and all other quotations from this source are from "Instructions for a Training Package Combining Formal and Informal Zen Meditation with Behavioral Self-Control Strategies," by D. H. Shapiro. From *Psychologia.* Copyright 1978 by Kyoto University. Reprinted by permission of the publisher.

meditating. The rationale for the repetition of the syllable or word is to free the client from focusing on logical and externally oriented thought. Instead, the client focuses on a constant stimulus—the word, sound, syllable, or phrase. Repetition of the word assists in breaking the stream of distracting thoughts (Benson, 1976). The mental device is used to help the client focus on breathing. The counselor should describe the rationale for the mental device to the client and give examples of possible options for a mental device. Benson (1974) suggests the use of the word *one* "because of its simplicity and neutrality" (p. 54). The client then selects his or her own mental device to use while meditating.

Instructions about Body Comfort. The first prerequisite for body comfort is a quiet environment in which to meditate. The counselor should create a quiet, calm environment that is as free of distractions as possible. Benson (1976) claims that some background noise may prevent the relaxation response. A quiet environment is less distracting and may facilitate elimination of intrusive thoughts. The counselor tells the client that there are several ways to meditate or to elicit the relaxation response and says that he or she will show the client one way. Then the counselor instructs the client to get in a comfortable position. This can be sitting in a comfortable chair with the head and arms supported, or the person might wish to sit on the floor, assuming a semilotus position (this is particularly good for "private" practice sessions). As in muscle relaxation, the client should wear comfortable clothing. Getting into a comfortable position minimizes muscular effort. After getting into a comfortable position, the client is instructed to close her or his eyes and to relax all muscles deeply. The counselor might name a few muscle groups—"relax your face, your neck, your head, shoulders, chest, your lower torso, your thighs, going to your calves, and to your feet." The muscle groups described in Table 20-1 later in this chapter can be used at this point. After the client is relaxed, the counselor gives instructions about breathing and using the mental device.

Instructions about Breathing and Use of the Mental Device. The counselor instructs the client to breathe through the nose and to focus on or become aware of breathing. It is believed that the focused-breathing component of meditation helps a person learn to relax and to manage tension (D. H. Shapiro, 1978a). At first, it may be difficult for some people to be natural when focusing on breathing. The counselor should encourage the client to breathe easily and naturally with a suggestion to "allow the air to come to you" on each inhalation. For each exhalation, the client is instructed to exhale slowly, letting all the air out of the lungs. While focusing on breathing, the client uses the mental device by saying it silently. Clients are instructed to repeat the mental device silently for each inhalation and each exhalation and are encouraged to keep their attention on the breathing and the mental device.

Instructions about a Passive Attitude. The counselor instructs the client to maintain a passive attitude and to allow relaxation to occur at its own pace. Also, the client is instructed, if attention wanders and distracting images or thoughts occur, not to dwell on them and to return to repeating the mental device or word. The client should allow the distracting thoughts to pass through cognition or the mind and just be passive. If distracting thoughts occur for several minutes, instruct the client not to be evaluative and to return to repeating the mental device. As Benson (1974) states, "the purpose of the response is to help one rest and relax, and this requires a completely passive attitude. One should not scrutinize his performance or try to force the response, because this may well prevent the response from occurring. When distracting thoughts enter the mind, they should simply be disregarded" (p. 54). The relaxation response is not an occasion for thinking things over or for problem-solving. D. H. Shapiro (1978a) hypothesizes that this emphasis in meditation on the "ongoing present" may alert people to notice when they become distracted from tasks and also may represent a way to return to the present, or the "here and now."

Meditate 10 to 20 Minutes. The client is instructed to meditate for about 10 to 20 minutes. The counselor tells the client to open her or his eyes to check the time if desired. A clock or watch that the client can see easily should be provided. Also, the counselor instructs the client what to do after the meditative session. For example, some clients may wish to keep their eyes closed for a couple of minutes before opening them—or just to sit quietly for several minutes.

Probe about the Meditative Experience. The counselor asks the client about the experience with meditation. For example, the counselor should ask how the client felt, how the mental device was used, what happened to any distracting thoughts, and whether the client was able to maintain a passive attitude.

Homework and Follow-Up. As homework, the counselor asks the client to practice the relaxation response once or twice a day at home or at work. Each practice session may last 10 to 15 minutes. Practice should not occur within 2 hours after any meal, because the digestive processes appear to interfere with relaxation. Practice should occur in a quiet environment free from distractions or interruptions. Also, for some people, practice several hours before bedtime can interfere with going to sleep. The client should be instructed to keep a daily log of each time the relaxation response is used. The log might include the time of day meditation was used, the setting, the period of time spent in practice, and the client's reaction to the experience or level of relaxation as rated on a five-point scale.

Another homework assignment proposed by D. H. Shapiro and S. M. Zifferblatt (1976) is *informal meditation.* This requires that a person be conscious and aware, and observe or attend very closely to ordinary daily activities (pp. 521–522). A client could be instructed simply to observe all events and behaviors that occur throughout the day. This type of informal meditation is similar to what Ornstein (1972) describes as "opening up"—meditative exercises

in which the person simply focuses on whatever is happening as it occurs, in the "here and now." Informal meditation may be used more frequently as homework than formal meditation because it is somewhat easier, less structured, and takes less time.

Another way to use informal meditation as homework is to ask the client to observe some selected problem or stress-related environmental event in a detached, nonevaluative fashion. For such events that might produce tension, anxiety, anger, fear, or pain, the client could be instructed to focus on breathing and to initiate calmness and relaxation. Here is an example of this type of assignment developed by D. H. Shapiro (1978b), which he refers to as "contingent informal meditation":

> *Awareness.* List below current problems, difficulties, or concerns which you are having or have had that cause you to become tense and anxious:
>
> a. _____
> b. _____
> c. _____
>
> Let's pick a situation *a*, now, and see if we can make it as specific as possible. Who is present; where are you; what kinds of things are you doing, saying, thinking. Now close your eyes and imagine yourself in that situation, and allow yourself to experience the tension that you normally feel.
>
> *Interruption of sequence and competing response.* Once you have observed these thoughts and actions, say to yourself "Stop!" as you clench your fist and your jaw. Then relax your fingers and your jaw and imagine yourself beginning to do an informal breath meditation: you are closing your eyes and beginning to focus on your breathing. Now, actually take two deep breaths through your nose, and as you exhale let your "center" sink into your stomach. Say to yourself:
>
> 1. Your name: "I am _____."
> 2. "I am breath" (and take another deep breath).
> 3. "I am calm and relaxed and am in control" (and take two more deep breaths, letting

your "center" sink to your stomach as you exhale).

Now imagine yourself becoming more and more relaxed; imagine yourself meditating, feeling calm, and in control. At the count of ten you may open your eyes, and you will feel calm, relaxed, and wide awake. [Repeat this process for situations *b* and *c*.]

In addition to the formal practice of the relaxation response twice daily, informal meditation could be assigned as an "in vivo" application of the procedure. The client can also be instructed to keep a log of informal meditation applied "in vivo" to stressful situations. After the client has used the meditation homework for about a month, a follow-up session should be scheduled. This session can use the client's log data to check on the frequency of use of the homework, the client's reactions to the homework, and the client's recorded stress level.

Learning Activities: Meditation

I. Teaching meditation to a client is an informational process. The counselor provides the instructions, and the client engages in meditation in a self-directed manner. To practice giving instructions to someone about meditation, select a partner or a role-play client and give instructions as described in the Interview Checklist for Meditation at the end of the chapter. Then assess how well your partner was able to implement your instructions. If you wish, reverse roles so that you can experience being instructed by another person.

II. This learning activity provides you with an opportunity to try out formal meditation. Do this in a quiet, restful place when you will not be interrupted for 20 minutes. Do *not* do this within 2 hours *after* a meal or within 2 hours of going to sleep.

   1. Get in a comfortable sitting position and close your eyes.
   2. Relax your entire body. Think about all of the tension draining out of your body.
   3. Meditate for about 15 to 20 minutes.

     a. Breathe easily and naturally through your nose.
     b. Focus on your breathing with the thought of a number (one) or a word. Say (think) your word silently each time you inhale and exhale.
     c. If other thoughts or images appear, don't dwell on them but don't force them away. Just relax and focus on your word or breathing.
   4. Try to assess your reactions to your meditative experience:

     How do you feel about it?
     How do you feel afterwards?
     What sorts of thoughts or images come in your mind?
     How much difficulty did you have with distractions?

   5. Practice the relaxation response systematically—twice daily for a week, if possible.

III. To experience "informal meditation," we suggest you follow the homework assignment developed by Shapiro described on pp. 405–406. Try to do this daily for at least a week.

Muscle Relaxation

In muscle relaxation, a person is taught to relax by becoming aware of the sensations of tensing and relaxing major muscle groups. Take a few moments to feel and to become aware of some of these sensations. Make a fist with your preferred or dominant hand. Clench your fist of that hand. Clench it tightly and study the tension in your hand and forearm. Become aware and feel those sensations of tension. Now let the tension go in your fist, hand, and forearm. Relax your hand and rest it. Note the difference between the tension and the relaxation. Do the exercise once more, only this time close your eyes. Clench your fist tightly; become aware of the tension in your hand and forearm; then relax your hand and let the tension flow out. Note the different sensations of relaxing and tensing your fist. Try it.

If you did this exercise, you may have

noticed that your hand and forearm *cannot* be tense and relaxed at the same time. In other words, relaxation is incompatible with tension. You may also have noted that you instructed your hand to tense up and then to relax. You sent messages from your head to your hand to impose tension and then to create relaxation. You can cue a muscle group (the hand and forearm, in this case) to perform or respond in a particular manner (tense up and relax). This exercise was perhaps too brief for you to notice changes in other bodily functions. For example, tension and relaxation can affect one's blood pressure, heart rate, and respiration rate and can also influence covert processes and the way one performs or responds overtly.

Relaxation training is not new, but it has recently become a popular technique to deal with a variety of client concerns. Jacobson (1929; 1964) developed an extensive procedure called progressive relaxation. Later, Wolpe (1958) described muscle relaxation as an anxiety-inhibiting procedure with his systematic-desensitization strategy (see Chapter 21). Bernstein and Borkovec (1973) wrote a thorough relaxation manual entitled *Progressive Relaxation Training.* Goldfried and Davison (1976) have described relaxation training in their book about behavior therapy.

Relaxation training has been used with clients who have insomnia (Knapp, Downs, & Alperson, 1976; Nicassio & Bootzin, 1974), high blood pressure (Shoemaker & Tasto, 1975), with a child having epileptic seizures (Ince, 1976), with a male adult compulsively engaging in ritualistic checking (Alban & Nay, 1976), as a health-promoting technique with geriatric clients (Andréoli, Picot, & Richard, 1974), with asthma sufferers (Alexander, 1972; Sirota & Mahoney, 1974), with people who have tension headaches (Tasto & Hinkle, 1973), and as an anxiety-reduction procedure (Deffenbacher, 1976; Goldfried & Trier, 1974; R. K. Russell, J. F. Sipich, & J. Knipe, 1976). The Lamaze (1958) method of childbirth uses relaxation training to facilitate a more relaxed and less painful labor and delivery.

Studies also have investigated the relative effectiveness of relaxation training administered in person versus a tape-recording. In a comparison study, Paul and Trimble (1970) found little success with relaxation administered by a tape-recorder; training in person was more effective. However, Israel and Beiman (1977) found that tape-recorded relaxation was as effective as "live" training for reductions in tonic heart rate, respiration rate, and muscle tension. Our preference is to have a counselor administer relaxation training within the interview. Tape-recorded instructions can be used for homework or outside practice sessions.

Some of these studies on the effects of muscle relaxation are analogue investigations that have solicited volunteer clients from newspaper ads and posters. Volunteer clients may or may not respond to treatment or training in the same fashion as clients. Our point is one that we have stressed often: the effects of muscle relaxation, like those of any other strategy, are related to satisfactory problem identification, the client, and the ability of the counselor to apply the procedure or strategy competently and confidently. These are precautions counselors should heed; one should not apply relaxation training indiscriminately.

Some Cautions in Using Muscle Relaxation

There are two areas the counselor should assess before applying muscle relaxation (Bernstein & Borkovec, 1973). First, make sure the client is medically cleared to engage in muscle relaxation (p. 12). For example, a person who suffers headaches or lower-back pain may have an organic basis for these complaints. Also, a person may be taking a drug that is incompatible with the purposes of muscle relaxation. For some clients, tensing certain muscle groups may have detrimental effects. The counselor should obtain a medical clearance from the client's physician or encourage the client to have a physical examination if there is a complaint that might be organically caused. Relaxation exercises may have to be adjusted for handicapped clients or for clients who cannot perform exercises for particular muscle groups.

The next caution is to discover the causes

of the client's reported tension (Bernstein & Borkovec, 1973, p. 12). The counselor would probably have achieved this during problem definition (see Chapters 9 and 10). For example, is muscle relaxation a reasonable strategy for alleviation of the client's problem? If the client is experiencing tension in a job situation, the counselor and client may prefer to deal first with the client's external situation (the job). Bernstein and Borkovec point out that there is a difference between dealing with the tension of daily problems and handling the tension of someone who is on the verge of financial disaster. In the latter case, combinations of therapeutic strategies may be necessary. As Goldfried (1977b) notes, relaxation training may be more effective on a short-term basis and when supplemented with other therapeutic strategies. Also, the clinical potential of relaxation may be enhanced when the procedure is presented to clients as a coping skill (p. 84).

Steps of Muscle Relaxation

Muscle relaxation consists of the following seven steps:

1. Verbal set
2. Instructions about dress
3. Creation of a comfortable environment
4. Counselor modeling of the relaxation exercises
5. Instructions for muscle relaxation
6. Posttraining assessment
7. Homework and follow-up.

These steps are described in detail in the Interview Checklist for Muscle Relaxation at the end of the chapter.

Verbal Set. Here is an example of one way a counselor might explain the purpose of relaxation: "This process, if you practice it regularly, can help you become relaxed. The relaxation benefits you derive can help you sleep better at night." An overview of the procedure might be: "This procedure involves learning to tense and relax different muscle groups in your body. By doing this, you can contrast the difference between tenseness and relaxation. This will help you to recognize tension so you can instruct yourself to relax."

In addition, the counselor should explain that muscle relaxation is a skill. The process of learning will be gradual and will require regular practice. Finally, the counselor might explain that some discomfort may occur during the relaxation process. If so, the client can just move his or her body to a more comfortable position. Also, the client may experience some floating, warming, or heavy sensations typical for some people learning muscle relaxation. The counselor should inform the client about these possible sensations. The verbal set for muscle relaxation should be concluded by asking the client about willingness to try the procedure.

Instructions about Dress. Before the actual training session, the client should be instructed about appropriate clothing. The client should wear comfortable clothes such as slacks, a loose-fitting blouse or shirt, or any apparel that will not be distracting during the exercises. Also, clients who wear contact lenses should be instructed to wear their regular glasses for the training. They can take off the glasses while going through the exercises. It is uncomfortable to wear contact lenses when your eyes are closed.

Creation of a Comfortable Environment. A comfortable environment is necessary for effective muscle-relaxation training. The training environment should be quiet and free of distracting noises such as telephone rings, workers outside breaking up the street, and airplane sounds. A padded recliner chair should be used if possible. If the counseling facility cannot afford one, an aluminum lawn chair or recliner covered with a foam pad may be satisfactory. If relaxation training is to be applied to groups, pads or blankets can be placed on the floor with pillows used to support the head (Gershman & Clouser, 1974). The clients can lie on the floor on their backs, with their legs stretched out and their arms along their sides with palms down.

Counselor Modeling of the Relaxation Exercises. Immediately before the relaxation training begins, the counselor should model briefly at least a few of the muscle exercises that will be used in training. The counselor can start with either the right or left hand (make a fist, then relax the hand, opening the fingers; tense and relax the other hand; bend the wrists of both arms and relax them; shrug the shoulders and relax them) and continue demonstrating some of the rest of the exercises. The counselor should tell the client that the demonstration is going at a much faster rate than the speed at which the client will perform the exercises. Also, the counselor should punctuate the demonstration with comments like "When I clench my biceps like this, I feel the tension in my biceps muscles, and now, when I relax and drop my arms to my side, I notice the difference between the tension that was in my biceps and the relative relaxation I feel now." The counselor uses these comments to model discriminating the contrast between tension and relaxation.

Instructions for Muscle Relaxation. Muscle-relaxation training can start after the counselor has given the client the rationale for the procedure, answered any questions about relaxation training, instructed the client about what to wear, created a comfortable environment for the training, and modeled some of the various muscle-group exercises. In delivering (or reading) the instructions for the relaxation-training exercises, the counselor's voice should be conversational, not dramatic. Goldfried and Davison (1976) recommend that the counselor practice along with the client during the beginning exercises. Practicing initial relaxation exercises with the client can provide the counselor with a sense of timing for delivering the verbalizations of relaxing and tension. Also, accompanying counselor practice may decrease any awkwardness the client feels about doing "body type" exercises.

In instructing the client to tense and relax muscles, remember that you do *not* want to instruct the client to tense up as hard as possible. You do not want the client to strain a muscle. Be careful of your vocabulary when giving instruc-tions. Do not use phrases like "hard as you can," "sagging or drooping muscles," or "tense the muscles until they feel like they could snap." Sometimes you can supplement instructions to tense and relax with comments about the client's breathing or the experiencing of warm or heavy sensations. These comments may help the client to relax.

The various muscle groups used for client training can be categorized into 17 groups, 7 groups, or 4 groups. These sets of muscle groups, adapted from Bernstein and Borkovec (1973), are listed in Table 20-1. Generally, in initial training sessions, the counselor instructs the client to go through all 17 muscle groups. When the client can alternately tense and relax any of the 17 muscle groups upon command, you can abbreviate this somewhat long procedure and train the client in relaxation using seven muscle groups. After this process, the client can practice relaxation using only four major muscle groups. Start with either 17 or 7 muscle groups. This may help the client to discriminate sensations of tension and relaxation in different parts of the body. Then the number of muscle groups involved in the relaxation can be reduced gradually. When the client gets to the point of using the relaxation "in vivo," 4 muscle groups are much less unwieldy than 17!

The following section illustrates how the counselor can instruct the client in relaxation using all 17 muscle groups. First, the counselor instructs the client to settle back as comfortably as possible—either in the recliner chair or on the floor with the head on a pillow. The arms can be alongside the body, resting on the arms of the chair or on the floor with the palms of the hands down. The counselor then instructs the client to close her or his eyes. In some instances, a client may not wish to do this; at other times, the counselor and the client may decide that it might be more therapeutic to keep the eyes open during the training. In such cases, the client can focus on some object in the room or on the ceiling. Tell the client to *listen* and to *focus* on your instructions. The following model instructions and the examples for the training exercises for the 17 muscle groups were adapted from a relaxation tape-recording by Lazarus (1970).

17 Muscle Groups	7 Muscle Groups	4 Muscle Groups
1. Clenching *fist* of dominant *hand*. 2. Clenching *fist* of non-dominant *hand*. 3. Bending *wrist* of one or both arms. 4. Clenching *biceps* (one at a time or together). 5. Shrugging *shoulders* (one at a time or together). 6. Wrinkling *forehead*. 7. Closing *eyes* tightly. 8. Pressing *tongue* or clenching *jaws*. 9. Pressing *lips* together. 10. Pressing *head* back (on chair or pillow). 11. Pushing *chin* into chest. 12. Arching *back*. 13. Inhaling and holding *chest muscles*. 14. Tightening *stomach* muscles. 15. Contracting *buttocks*.* 16. Stretching *legs*. 17. Pointing *toes* toward head.	1. Hold *dominant arm* in front with elbow bent at about 45-degree angle while making a fist (hand, lower arm, and biceps muscles). 2. Same exercise with *nondominant arm*. 3. Facial muscle groups. Wrinkle *forehead* (or frown), squint *eyes*, wrinkle up *nose*, clench *jaws* or press *tongue* on roof of mouth, press *lips* or pull corners of mouth back. 4. Press or bury *chin* in chest (neck and throat). 5. *Chest, shoulders, upper back*, and *abdomen*. Take deep breath, hold it, pull shoulder blades back and together, while making stomach hard (pulling in). 6. *Dominant thigh, calf, and foot*. Lift foot off chair or floor slightly while pointing toes and turning foot inward. 7. Same as 6, with *nondominant thigh, calf, and foot*.	1. Right and left *arms, hands*, and *biceps* (same as 1 and 2 in 7-muscle group). 2. *Face* and *neck* muscles. Tense all *face* muscles (same as 3 and 4 in the 7-muscle group) while 3. *Chest, shoulders, back* and *stomach* muscles (same as 5 in 7-muscle group). 4. Both left and right upper *leg, calf*, and *foot* (combines 6 and 7 in 7-muscle group).

*This muscle group can be eliminated; its use is optional.

Begin this way: "Now get as comfortable as you can. Close your eyes and listen to what I'm going to tell you. I'm going to make you aware of certain sensations in your body and then show you how you can reduce these sensations to increase feelings of relaxation."

After the client is in a comfortable position, the counselor can begin to have the client alternately tense and relax each of the 17 muscle groups, starting with the fist of the nondominant or dominant hand. The counselor should proceed slowly and provide ample time for the client to tighten and to relax each muscle. Also, the counselor should build in pauses between the presentations of the muscle groups. Usually in initial training sessions, each muscle group is presented twice. Bernstein and Borkovec (1973) note that, in teaching muscle relaxation to a client, a series of events must occur for each muscle group. This includes the following five things:

1. First the client's attention should be directed to the muscle group.

2. Secondly, at a verbal cue from the counselor (such as "tighten your fist"), the muscle group is tensed.
3. Third, the client usually holds the tension for a time period of five to seven seconds.
4. Upon a verbal cue from the counselor (such as "relax now"), the muscle group is relaxed.
5. The client's attention is directed toward the feelings of relaxation [p. 25].

This five-step process, in which relaxation is induced by alternately tensing and relaxing muscle groups, is used during initial instruction to assist the client in making clear discriminations about these two sensations. Once this is established, the client can use a verbal or mental cue to induce relaxation independently.

Here is a way the counselor might proceed with initial training in muscle relaxation, using the list of 17 muscle groups in Table 20-1.

1. *Fist of dominant hand.* "First think about your right arm, your right hand in particular. Clench your right fist. Clench it tightly and study the tension in the hand and in the forearm. Study those sensations of tension. (Pause.) Now let go. Just relax the right hand and let it rest on the arm of the chair (or floor). (Pause.) And note the difference between the tension and the relaxation. (10-second pause.)"
2. *Fist of nondominant hand.* "Now we'll do the same with your left hand. Clench your left fist. Notice the tension (5-second pause) and now relax. Enjoy the difference between the tension and the relaxation. (10-second pause.)"
3. *Wrist of one or both arms.* The counselor can instruct the client to bend the wrists of both arms at the same time or to bend each separately. You might start with the dominant arm if you instruct the client to bend the wrists one at a time.
"Now bend both hands back at the wrists so that you tense the muscles in the back of the hand and in the forearm. Point your fingers toward the ceiling. Study the tension, and now relax. (Pause.) Study the difference be-

tween tension and relaxation. (10-second pause.)"
4. *Biceps.* The counselor can instruct the client to work with both biceps or just one at a time. If you train the client to do one at a time, start with the dominant biceps. The instructions for this exercise are:
"Now clench both your hands into fists and bring them toward your shoulders. As you do this, tighten your biceps muscles, the ones in the upper part of your arm. Feel the tension in these muscles. (Pause.) Now relax. Let your arms drop down to your sides. See the difference between the tension and the relaxation. (10-second pause.)"
5. *Shoulders.* Usually the client is instructed to shrug both shoulders. However, the client could be instructed to shrug one shoulder at a time.
"Now we'll move to the shoulder area. Shrug your shoulders. Bring them up to your ears. Feel and hold the tension in your shoulders. (Pause.) Now, let both shoulders relax. Note the contrast between the tension and the relaxation that's now in your shoulders. (10-second pause.)"
6. *Forehead.* This and the next three exercises are for the facial muscles. The instructions for the forehead are:
"Now we'll work on relaxing the various muscles of the face. First, wrinkle up your forehead and brow. Do this until you feel your brow furrow. (Pause.) Now relax. Smooth out the forehead. Let it loosen up. (10-second pause.)"
7. *Eyes.* The purpose of this exercise is for the client to contrast the difference between tension and relaxation for the muscles that control the movements of the eyes.
"Now close your eyes tightly. Can you feel tension all around your eyes? (5-second pause.) Now relax those muscles, noting the difference between the tension and the relaxation. (10-second pause.)"
8. *Tongue or jaws.* You can instruct some clients to clench their jaws:
"Now clench your jaws by biting your teeth together. Pull the corners of your mouth back. Study the tension in the jaws. (5-

second pause.) Relax your jaws now. Can you tell the difference between tension and relaxation in your jaw area? (10-second pause.)"

This exercise may be difficult for some clients who wear dentures. An alternative exercise is to instruct them: "Press your tongue into the roof of your mouth. Note the tension within your mouth. (5-second pause.) Relax your mouth and tongue now. Just concentrate on the relaxation. (10-second pause.)"

9. *Pressing the lips together.* The last facial exercise involves the mouth and chin muscles.

"Now press your lips together tightly. As you do this, notice the tension all around the mouth. (Pause.) Now relax those muscles around the mouth. Enjoy this relaxation in your mouth area and your entire face. (Pause.)"

10. *The head.* The model instructions for this exercise are:

"Now we'll move to the neck muscles. Press your head back against your chair. Can you feel the tension in the back of your neck and in your upper back? Hold the tension. (Pause.) Now let your head rest comfortably. Notice the difference. Keep on relaxing. (Pause.)"

11. *Chin in chest.* This exercise focuses on the muscles in the neck, particularly the front of the neck.

"Now continue to concentrate on the neck area. Bring your head forward. See if you can bury your chin into your chest. Note the tension in the front of your neck. Now relax and let go. (10-second pause.)"

12. *The back.* Be careful here—you don't want the client to get a sore back.

"Now direct your attention to your upper back area. Arch your back like you're sticking out your chest and stomach. Can you feel tension in your back? Study that tension. (Pause.) Now relax. Note the difference between the tension and the relaxation. (10-second pause.)"

13. *Chest muscles.* Inhaling (filling the lungs) and holding the breath focuses the client's attention on the muscles in the chest and down into the stomach area.

"Now take a deep breath, filling your lungs, and hold it. Feel the tension all through your chest and into your stomach area. Hold that tension. (Pause.) Now relax and let go. Let your breath out naturally. Enjoy the pleasant sensations. (10-second pause.)"

14. *Stomach muscles.* "Now think about your stomach. Tighten up the muscles in your abdomen. Hold this. Make the stomach like a knot. Now relax. Loosen those muscles now. (10-second pause.)"

An alternative instruction is to tell the client to "pull in your stomach" or "suck in your stomach."

15. *The buttocks.* Moving down to other areas of the body, the counselor instructs or coaches the client to tighten the buttocks. This muscle group is optional; with some clients, the counselor may delete it and move on to the legs. The model instructions are:

"Now tighten (tense or contract) your buttocks by pulling them together and pushing them into the floor (or chair). Note the tension. And now relax. Let go and relax. (10-second pause.)"

16. *Legs.* "I'd like you now to focus on your legs. Stretch both legs. Feel tension in the thighs. (5-second pause.) Now relax. Study the difference again between tension in the thighs and the relaxation you feel now. (10-second pause.)"

17. *Toes.* "Now concentrate on your lower legs and feet. Tighten both calf muscles by pointing your toes toward your head. Pretend a string is pulling your toes up. Can you feel the pulling and the tension? Note that tension. (Pause.) Now relax. Let your legs relax deeply. Enjoy the difference between tension and relaxation. (10-second pause.)"

After each muscle group has been tensed and relaxed twice, the counselor usually concludes relaxation training with a summary and review. The counselor goes through the review by listing each muscle group and asking the client to dispel any tension that is noted as the counselor names the muscle area. Here is an example:

> "Now, I'm going to go over once more the muscle groups that we've covered. As I name each group, try to notice whether there is any tension in those muscles. If there is any, try to concentrate on those muscles and tell them to relax. Think of draining the tension completely out of your body as we do this. Now relax the muscles in your feet, ankles, and calves. (Pause.) Get rid of tension in your knees and thighs. (5-second pause.) Loosen your hips. (Pause.) Let the muscles of your lower body go. (Pause.) Relax your abdomen, waist, lower back. (Pause.) Drain the tension from your upper back, chest, and shoulders. (Pause.) Relax your upper arms, forearms, and hands. Loosen the muscles of your throat and neck. (Pause.) Relax your face. (Pause.) Let all the tension drain out of your body. (Pause.) Now just sit quietly with your eyes closed."

The counselor can conclude the training session by evaluating the client's level of relaxation on a scale from 0 to 5 or by counting aloud to the client to instruct him or her to become successively alert. For example:

> "Now I'd like you to think of a scale from 0 to 5, where 0 is complete relaxation and 5 is extreme tension. Tell me where you would place yourself on that scale now."
> "I'm going to count from 5 to 1. When I reach the count of 1, open your eyes. 5 . . . 4 . . . 3 . . . 2 . . . 1. Open your eyes now."

Posttraining Assessment. After the session of relaxation training has been completed, the counselor asks the client about the experience. The counselor can ask "What is your reaction to the procedure?" "How do you feel?" "What reaction did you have when you focused on the tension?" "What about relaxation?" or "How did the contrast between the tension and relaxation feel?" The counselor should be encouraging about the client's performance, praise the client, and build a positive expectancy set about the training and practice.

Bernstein and Borkovec (1973) suggest that people experiencing relaxation training may have several problems. Some of these potential problem areas are cramps, excessive laughter or talking, spasms or tics, intrusive thoughts, falling asleep, inability to relax specific muscle groups during relaxation, and unfamiliar sensations. If the client experiences muscle cramps, possibly too much tension is being created in the particular muscle group. In this case, the counselor can instruct the client to decrease the amount of tension. If spasms and tics occur in certain muscle groups, the counselor can mention that these occur commonly, as in one's sleep, and possibly the reason that the client is aware of them now is that he or she is awake. Excessive laughter or talking would most likely occur in group-administered relaxation training. Possibly the best solution is to ignore it or to discuss how such behavior can be distracting.

The most common problem is for the client to fall asleep during relaxation training. The client should be informed that continually falling asleep can impede learning the skills associated with muscle relaxation. By watching the client throughout training, the counselor can confirm whether the client is awake.

If the client has difficulty or is unable to relax a specific muscle group, the counselor and client might work out an alternative exercise for that particular muscle group. If intrusive client thoughts become too distracting, the counselor might suggest changing the focus of the thought to something less distracting or to more positive or pleasant thoughts. It might be better for some clients to gaze at a picture of their choosing placed on the wall or ceiling throughout the training. Another strategy for dealing with interfering or distracting thoughts is to help the client to use task-oriented coping statements or thoughts (see Chapter 19), which would facilitate focusing on the relaxation training.

The last potential problem is the occurrence of unfamiliar sensations, such as floating, warmth, and headiness. The counselor should point out that these sensations are common and that the client should not fear them. A more detailed discussion of these potential problems and their possible solutions is provided by

Bernstein and Borkovec (1973). The counselor need not focus on these problems unless they are reported by the client or noted by the counselor during a training session.

Homework and Follow-Up. The last step in muscle relaxation is assigning homework. The counselor should inform the client that relaxation training, like learning any skill, requires a great deal of practice. The more the client practices the procedure, the more proficient he or she will become in gaining control over tension, anxiety, or stress. The client should be instructed to select a quiet place for practice, free from distracting noise. The client should be en-

couraged to practice the muscle-relaxation exercises about 15 to 20 minutes twice a day. The relaxation exercises should be done when there is no time pressure. They can be done in a recliner chair or on the floor with a pillow supporting the head. The client should be encouraged to complete the homework log after each practice. An example of a homework log appears in Figure 20-1. Clients can rate their reactions on a scale from 1 (little or no tension) to 5 (extremely tense) before and after each practice. They can practice the relaxation exercises using a tape-recording of the relaxation instructions or from memory. After client homework practices, a follow-up session should be scheduled.

HOMEWORK LOG SHEET					
Date	Practice Session	Location of Session	Number of Muscle Groups Exercised	Level of Tension	
				Before Practice (1 to 5)	After Practice (1 to 5)

Note: 1 = little or no tension; 2 = some tension; 3 = moderately tense;
4 = very tense; 5 = extremely tense

Figure 20-1. Example Homework Log Sheet for Relaxation Training

Variations of Muscle-Relaxation Procedure

There are several variations of the muscle-relaxation training procedure as we've described it. These variations, which include recall, counting, and differential relaxation, are arranged and designed in successive approximations from the counselor assisting the client to acquire the skills to the client applying the relaxation skills in real-life situations. The four-muscle-group exercises listed in Table 20-1 can be used in combination with the recall and counting procedures described by Bernstein and Borkovec (1973).

Recall. Recall proceeds according to the relaxation exercises for the four muscle groups (Table 20-1) without muscular tension. The counselor first instructs the client about the rationale for using this variation of relaxation training: "to increase your relaxation skills without the need to tense up the muscles." The client is asked to focus on each muscle group. Then the counselor instructs the client to focus on one of the four muscle groups (arms; face and neck; chest, shoulders, back, and stomach; legs and feet) and to relax and just recall what it was like when the client released the tension (in the previous session) for that particular muscle group. The counselor might suggest that, if there is tension in a particular muscle group, the client should just relax or send a message for the muscle to relax, and allow what tension there is to "flow out." The counselor gives similar instructions for all four muscle groups. Again, the client is to recall what the relaxation felt like for each muscle group. Recall can generally be used after first using the tension-relaxation contrast procedure for the four muscle groups. Gradually, the client can use recall to induce relaxation in self-directed practices. Recall also can be used in combination with counting. See Bernstein and Borkovec (1973) for a more detailed discussion of this variation.

Counting. The rationale for counting is that it helps the client to become very deeply relaxed. Again, the counselor explains the rationale for using counting. The counselor says that she or he will count from one to ten and that this will help the client to become more relaxed after each number. The counselor might say slowly:

> "One—you are becoming more relaxed; two —notice that your arms and hands are becoming more and more relaxed; three—feel your face and neck becoming more relaxed; four, five—more and more relaxed are your chest and shoulders; six—further and further relaxed; seven—back and stomach feel deeply relaxed; eight—further and further relaxed; nine—your legs and feet are more and more relaxed; ten —just continue to relax like you are—relax more and more."

The counselor can use this counting procedure with recall. Also, the client can be instructed to use counting in real situations that provoke tension. For a more detailed presentation of counting, see Bernstein and Borkovec (1973) and Goldfried and Davison (1976). As you may remember from Chapter 19, counting is one type of direct-action coping skill used in stress inoculation. Counting can increase relaxation and decrease tension, and the client should be encouraged to practice it outside the session.

Differential Relaxation. This variation may contribute to generalization of the relaxation training from the treatment session to the client's world. The idea of differential relaxation is to help the client recognize what muscles are needed in various situations, body positions, and activities in order to differentiate which muscle groups are used and which are not. Table 20-2 illustrates some possible levels for the differential-relaxation procedure.

Table 20-2. Levels of Differential-Relaxation Procedure

Situation	Body Position	Activity Level
Quiet	Sitting	Low—inactive
Noisy	Standing	High—routine movements

As an example of differential relaxation, the counselor might have the client sit down in a regular chair (not a recliner) and ask the client to identify which muscles are used and which are not when sitting. If tension is felt in muscles that are not used (face, legs, and stomach), the client is instructed to induce and to maintain relaxation in the muscles not required for what the client is doing (sitting). The counselor can instruct the client to engage in different levels of the differential-relaxation procedure—for example, standing up in a quiet place, inactive, or standing up. After several practice sessions, the client can be assigned homework to engage in various levels of these activities. Examples might be sitting in a quiet cafeteria, sitting in a noisy cafeteria while eating, standing in line for a ticket to some event, or walking in a busy shopping center. In practicing differential relaxation, the client tries to recognize whether any tension exists in the nonessential muscle groups. If there is tension in the nonengaged muscles, the client concentrates on dispelling it.

Model Dialogue: Muscle Relaxation

In this dialogue, the counselor demonstrates relaxation training to help Joan deal with her physical sensations of nervousness.

First, the counselor gives Joan a verbal set for relaxation. The counselor explains the purpose of muscle relaxation and gives Joan a brief overview of the procedure.

1. Counselor: Basically, we all learn to carry around some body tension. Some is OK. But in a tense spot, usually your body is even more tense, although you may not realize this. If you can learn to recognize muscle tension and relax your muscles, this state of relaxation can help to decrease your nervousness or anxiety. What we'll do is to help you recognize when your body is relaxed and when it is tense, by deliberately tensing and relaxing different muscle groups in your body. We should get to the point where, later on, you can recognize the sensations that mean tension and use these as a signal to yourself to relax. Does this make sense?

Client: I think so. You'll sort of tell me how to do this?

Next, the counselor will "set up" the relaxation by attending to details about the room and the client's comfort.

2. Counselor: Yes. At first I'll show you so you can get the idea of it. One thing we need to do before we start is for you to get as comfortable as possible. So that you won't be distracted by light, I'm going to turn off the light. If you are wearing your contact lenses, take them out if they're uncomfortable, because you may feel more comfortable if you go through this with your eyes closed. Also, I use a special chair for this. You know the straight-backed chair you're sitting on can seem like a rock after a time. That might distract, too. So I have a padded chaise you can use for this. (Gets lounge chair out.)

Client (sits in chaise): Umm. This really is comfortable.

Next the counselor begins to model the muscle relaxation for Joan. This shows Joan how to do it and may alleviate any embarrassment on her part.

3. Counselor: Good. That really helps. Now I'm going to show you how you can tense and then relax your muscles. I'll start first with my right arm. (Clenches right fist, pauses and notes tension, relaxes fist, pauses and notes relaxation; models several other muscle groups.) Does this give you an idea?

Client: Yes. You don't do your whole body?

The counselor provides further information about muscle relaxation, describes sensations Joan might feel, and checks to see whether Joan is completely clear on the procedure before going ahead.

4. Counselor: Yes, you do. But we'll take each muscle group separately. By the time you tense and relax each muscle group, your whole body will feel relaxed. You will feel like you are "letting go," which is very important when you tense up—to let go rather than to tense even more. Now you might not notice a lot of difference right away—but you might. You might even feel like you're floating. This really depends on the person. The most important thing is to remain as comfortable as possible while I'm instructing you. Do you have any questions before we begin, anything you don't quite understand?

Client: I don't think so. I think that this is maybe a little like yoga.

The counselor proceeds with instructions to alternately tense and relax each of 17 muscle groups.

5. Counselor: Right. It's based on the same idea —learning to have control over body tension.

OK, get very comfortable in your chair and we'll begin. (Gives Joan several minutes to get comfortable, then uses the relaxation instructions. The majority of the session is spent in instructing Joan in muscle relaxation as illustrated on pp. 411–412.)

After the relaxation, the counselor queries Joan about her feelings during and after the relaxation. It is important to find out how the relaxation affected the client.

6. Counselor: OK, Joan, how do you feel now?
   Client: Pretty relaxed.
7. Counselor: How did the contrast between the tensed and relaxed muscles feel?
   Client: It was pretty easy to tell. I guess sometimes my body is pretty tense and I don't think about it.

The counselor assigns relaxation practice to Joan as daily homework.

8. Counselor: As I mentioned before, this takes regular practice in order for you to use it when you need it—and to really notice the effects. I have put these instructions on this audio tape, and I'd like you to practice with this tape two times each day during the next week. Do the practice in a quiet place at a time when you don't feel pressured, and use a comfortable place when you do practice. Do you have any questions about the practice?
   Client: No, I think I understand.

Counselor explains the use of the log.

9. Counselor: Also, I'd like you to use a log sheet with your practice. Mark down where you practice, how long you practice, what muscle groups you use, and your tension level before and after each practice on this six-point scale. Remember, 0 is complete relaxation and 6 is complete or extreme tension. Let's go over an example of how you use the log. . . . Now, any questions?
   Client: No. I can see this will take some practice.

Finally, the counselor arranges a follow-up.

10. Counselor: Right—it really is like learning any other skill—it doesn't just come automatically. Why don't you try this on your own for 2 weeks and then come back. OK?

Learning Activity: Muscle Relaxation

Because muscle relaxation involves the alternate tensing and relaxing of a variety of muscle groups, it is sometimes hard to learn the procedure well enough to use it with a client. We have found that the easiest way to learn this is to do muscle relaxation yourself.

Using it not only helps you learn what is involved, but also may have some indirect benefits for you —increased relaxation!

This learning activity is designed for you to apply the muscle-relaxation procedure you've just read about to yourself. You can do this by yourself or with a partner. You may wish to try it out alone and then with someone else.

By Yourself

1. Get in a comfortable position, wear loose clothing, and remove your glasses or contact lenses.
2. Use the written instructions in this chapter to practice muscle relaxation. This can be done by putting the instructions on tape, or by reading the instructions to yourself. In this case, go through the procedure quickly to get a feel for the process; then do it again slowly without trying to rely too much on having to read the instructions. As you go through the relaxation, study the differences between tension and relaxation.
3. Try to assess your reactions after the relaxation. On a scale from 0 to 5 (0 being very relaxed and 5 being very tense), how relaxed do you feel? Were there any particular muscle groups that were hard for you to contract or relax?
4. One or two times through muscle relaxation is not enough to learn it or to notice any effects. Try to practice this procedure on yourself once or twice daily over the next 3 to 7 days.

With a Partner

One of you can take the role of a helper; the other can be the person learning relaxation. Switch roles so you can practice helping someone else through the procedure and trying it out on yourself.

1. The helper should begin by giving an explanation and a rationale for muscle relaxation and any instructions about it before you begin.
2. The helper can read the instructions on muscle relaxation to you. The helper should give you ample time to tense and relax each muscle group and should encourage you to note the different sensations associated with tension and relaxation.
3. After going through the process, the helper should query you about your relaxation level and your reactions to the process.

Summary

The two strategies presented in this chapter, meditation and muscle relaxation, often are used as a single treatment to prevent stress and to deal with stress-related situations. In addition, both of these strategies may be used to countercondition anxiety as part of another therapeutic procedure known as systematic desensitization. Desensitization, and the role of meditation and relaxation with it, are explored in the next chapter.

Post Evaluation

Part One

For objective 1, you should identify accurately the steps of the meditation procedure represented by examples of counselor instructive responses. On a piece of paper, for each of the following ten counselor responses, identify which part of the meditation procedure is being implemented. There may be more than one counselor response associated with a part. Also, these examples are not in any particular order. The eight major parts of meditation are:

1. Verbal set
2. Selection of a mental device
3. Instructions for body comfort
4. Breathing and word instruction
5. Instruction about passive attitude
6. Meditating for 10 to 20 minutes
7. Probing about the meditative experience
8. Homework and practice.

Feedback follows the evaluation.

1. "It is very important that you practice this at home regularly. Usually there are no effects without regular practice—about twice daily."
2. "One position you may want to use is to sit on the floor Indian-style—crossing your legs and keeping your back straight. If this feels uncomfortable, then just assume any sitting position that is comfortable for you."
3. "This procedure has been used to help people with high blood pressure, people who have trouble sleeping at night, and just as a general stress-reduction process."
4. "Breathe through your nose and focus on your breathing. If you can concentrate on one word as you do this, it may be easier."
5. "Be sure to practice at a quiet time when you don't think you'll be interrupted. Also, do not practice within 2 hours after a meal or within 2 hours before going to sleep at night."
6. "Just continue now to meditate like this for 10 or 15 minutes. Sit quietly then for several minutes after you're finished."
7. "The procedure involves learning to focus on your breathing while sitting in a quiet place. Sometimes concentrating on just one word may help you do this. You continue to do this for about 15 minutes each time."
8. "How easy or hard was this for you to do?"
9. "There may be times when other images or thoughts come into your mind. Try to just maintain a passive attitude. If you're bothered by other thoughts, don't dwell on them, but don't force them away. Just focus on your breathing and your word."
10. "Pick a word like *one* or *zum* that you can focus on—something neutral to you."

Part Two

Objective 2 asks you to teach the process of meditation to another person. You can have an observer evaluate you, or you can audio-tape your teaching session and rate yourself. You can use the Interview Checklist for Meditation at the end of the chapter as a teaching guide and evaluation tool (see p. 420).

Part Three

Objective 3 asks you to describe how you would apply the major parts of the muscle-relaxation procedure. Using this client description and the six questions following it, describe how you would use certain parts of the procedure with this person. You can check your responses with the feedback that follows the evaluation.

Description of client: The client is a middle-aged man who is concerned about his inability to sleep at night. He has tried sleeping pills but does not want to rely on medication.

1. Give an example of a verbal set you could use about the procedure. Include a rationale and an overview.
2. Give a brief example of instructions you might give this client about appropriate dress for relaxation training.

---

3. List any special environmental factors that may affect the client's use of muscle relaxation.
4. Describe some of the important muscle groups that you would instruct the client to tense and relax alternately.
5. Give two examples of probes you might use with the client after relaxation to assess his use of and reactions to the process.
6. What instructions about a homework assignment (practice of relaxation) would you give to this client?

Part Four

Objective 4 asks you to demonstrate 13 out of 15 steps of muscle relaxation with a role-play client. An observer or the client can assess your performance, or you can assess yourself, using the Interview Checklist for Muscle Relaxation at the end of the chapter.

Feedback: Post Evaluation

Part One

1. homework (practice)
2. instruction about body comfort
3. verbal set—telling the client how this is used
4. instruction about breathing and mental device
5. homework—giving the client instructions about how to carry out the practice
6. instructing the client to meditate for 10 to 20 minutes
7. verbal set—providing a brief overview of the procedure
8. probing about the meditative experience—assessing the client's reactions
9. instruction about a passive attitude
10. selection of a mental device such as a syllable or a number.

Part Two

Use the Interview Checklist for Meditation as a teaching and evaluation guide.

Part Three

1. Verbal set for client:
   a. Rationale: "This process, if you practice it regularly, can help you become relaxed. The relaxation benefits you derive can help you sleep better at night."
   b. Overview: "This procedure involves learning to tense and relax different muscle groups in your body. By doing this, you can contrast the difference between tenseness and relaxation. This will help you to recognize tension so you can instruct yourself to relax."
2. Instructions about dress: "You don't want anything to distract you, so wear comfortable, loose clothes for training. You may want to remove your glasses or contact lenses."
3. Environmental factors:
   a. Quiet room with reclining chair
   b. No obvious distractions or interruptions
4. Muscle groups used in the procedure include:
   a. fist of each arm
   b. wrist of each arm
   c. biceps of each arm
   d. shoulders
   e. facial muscles—forehead, eyes, nose, jaws, lips
   f. head, chin, and neck muscles
   g. back
   h. chest
   i. stomach
   j. legs and feet
5. Some possible probes are:
   a. On a scale from 0 to 100, with 0 being very relaxed and 100 very tense, how do you feel now?
   b. What is your overall reaction to what you just did?
   c. How did the contrast between the tensed and relaxed muscles feel?
   d. How easy or hard was it for you to do this?
6. Homework instructions should include:
   a. practice twice daily
   b. practice in a quiet place; avoid interruptions
   c. use a reclining chair, the floor, or a bed with pillow support for your head

Part Four

Use the Interview Checklist for Muscle Relaxation to assess your performance.

Interview Checklist for Meditation

Instructions: Determine which of the following counselor leads or questions were demonstrated in the interview. Check each of the leads used by the counselor. Some examples of counselor leads are provided in the right column.

Checklist	*Examples of Counselor Leads*
I. *Verbal Set*	
_____ 1. Counselor describes purpose of procedure.	"I would like to teach you a mental exercise called the relaxation response, or meditation. The relaxation response has been used to relieve fatigue caused by anxiety, to decrease stress that can lead to high blood pressure, and to help people who have difficulty getting to sleep at night. It can be used to have you become more relaxed. It desensitizes some people to their fears, concerns, or thoughts. The procedure helps you become more relaxed and deal more effectively with your tension and stress. It may give you a new awareness."
_____ 2. Counselor gives client overview.	"What we will do first is select a focusing or mental device. You will then get in a relaxed and comfortable position. Afterwards, I will instruct you about focusing on your breathing and using your mental device. We will talk about a passive attitude while meditating. You will meditate about 10 to 20 minutes. Then, we will talk about the experience."
_____ 3. Counselor confirms client's willingness to use strategy.	"How do you feel now about working with meditation?"
II. *Selecting a Mental Device*	
_____ 4. Counselor provides rationale for mental device.	"First, we want to select a mental device or a focusing device. It is a word, syllable, or phrase that helps you focus on breathing, and by repeating it you can become free of distracting thoughts or images."
_____ 5. Counselor gives examples of mental devices.	"Examples of a mental device are *one, zum, in, Rama*. Think of something you can say to yourself that is easy and that will be fairly neutral to you."
III. *Instructions about Body Comfort*	
_____ 6. Counselor conducts meditation training in quiet environment.	"We want to meditate in a quiet environment, free of distractions and interruption."
_____ 7. Counselor tells client to close eyes and get in comfortable position.	"There are several ways to meditate. I'll show you one. I want you to get in a comfortable position while you are sitting there. Now, close your eyes."
_____ 8. Counselor instructs client to relax major muscle groups.	"Relax all the muscles in your body—relax (said slowly) your head, face, neck, shoulders, chest, your torso, thighs, calves, and your feet. Keep all your muscles relaxed."

Checklist	Examples of Counselor Leads

IV. *Instructions about Breathing and Use of Mental Device*

_____ 9. Counselor instructs client to focus on breathing and to use mental device with each inhalation and exhalation.

"Breathe through your nose and focus on (or become aware of) your breathing. It is sometimes difficult to be natural when you are doing this. Just let the air come to you. Breathe easily and naturally. As you do this, say your mental device for each inhalation and exhalation. Say your mental device silently to yourself each time you breathe in and out."

V. *Instructions about Passive Attitude*

_____ 10. Counselor instructs client to maintain passive attitude and to allow relaxation to occur at its own pace. Also, client is instructed, if attention wanders and unrelated images and thoughts occur that take away from breathing, not to dwell on them but return to repeating mental device.

"Be calm and passive. If distracting thoughts or images occur, attempt to be passive about them by not dwelling on them. Return to repeating the mental device. Try to achieve effortless breathing. After more practice, you will be able to examine these thoughts or images with greater detachment."

"After a while, you may become aware that you were busy with distracting thoughts or images and you have not said your mental device for a couple of minutes. When this happens, just return to saying your word. Do not attempt to keep the thoughts out of your mind; just let them pass through. Keep your mind open—don't try to solve problems or think things over. Allow the thoughts to flow smoothly into your mind and then drift out. Say your mental device and relax. Don't get upset with distracting thoughts. Just return to your mental device."

VI. *Meditate for 10 to 20 Minutes*

_____ 11. Client is instructed to meditate for 10 to 20 minutes. Counselor instructs client on what to do after mediative session.

"Continue to meditate for about 10 (15 or 20) minutes. You can open your eyes to check on the time. After you have finished, sit quietly for several minutes. You may wish to keep your eyes closed for a couple of minutes and later open them. You may not want to stand up for a few minutes."

VII. *Probe about the Meditative Experience*

_____ 12. Counselor asks client about experience with meditation.

"How did you feel about the experience?"

"What sort of thoughts or images flowed through your mind?"

"What did you do when the distracting thoughts drifted in?"

"How did you feel about your mental device?"

Meditation and Muscle Relaxation

Checklist	*Examples of Counselor Leads*

VIII. *Homework and Follow-Up*

_____ 13. Formal meditation:
Counselor instructs client
to practice formal meditation
(relaxation response) once or
twice a day at home or at work.
Counselor cautions client not
to meditate within 2 hours
after a meal or within a couple
of hours before bedtime.

"Practice meditation (relaxation response) two
times a day. Like anything else we are trying
to learn, you will become better with practice.
You can do it at work or at home. Get comfortable
in your meditative (relaxation-response) position.
Practice in a quiet place away from noise and
interruptions. Do not use meditation (relaxation
response) as a substitute for sleep. Usually,
meditation before sleep might make you feel very
awake. Also, do not meditate within 2 hours
after a meal or within a couple of hours before
bedtime. Keep a log for each meditative experience,
where it was used, time of day used, and
rate each use on a five-point scale."

_____ 14. Informal meditation:
Counselor instructs client to apply
informal meditation "in vivo."

"Also, I think it would be helpful for you to
apply an informal meditation in problem or
stressful situations that may occur daily. The
way you can do this is, when in the situation,
be detached and passive. Observe yourself and
focus on being calm and on your breathing. Be
relaxed in those situations that evoke stress.
How does that sound?"

_____ 15. Counselor schedules follow-up
session.

"After you have practiced the homework daily for
the next 2 weeks, bring in your logs and we'll
see what has happened."

Consultant Comments: _____

Interview Checklist for Muscle Relaxation

Instructions: Indicate by a checkmark each counselor lead demonstrated in the checklist. Some model counselor leads are included for each item on the checklist.

Checklist	Counselor Leads
I. Verbal Set	
_____ 1. Counselor provides explanation of purpose of muscle relaxation.	"The name of the strategy that I believe will be helpful is *muscle relaxation*. Muscle relaxation has been used very effectively to benefit people who have a variety of concerns like insomnia, high blood pressure, anxiety, or stress, or for people who are bothered by everyday tension. Muscle relaxation will be helpful in decreasing your tension. It will benefit you because you will be able to control and to dispel tension that interferes with your daily activities."
_____ 2. Counselor gives overview of how muscle relaxation works.	"What we will do is that I will ask you to tense up and relax various muscle groups. All of us have some tensions in our bodies—otherwise we could not stand, sit, or move around. Sometimes we have too much tension. By tensing and relaxing, you will become aware of and contrast the feelings of tension and relaxation. Later we will train you to send a message to a particular muscle group to relax when nonessential tension creeps in. You will learn to control your tension and relax when you feel tension."
_____ 3. Counselor describes muscle relaxation as a skill.	"Muscle relaxation is a skill. And, like learning any skill, it will take a lot of practice to learn it well—a lot of repetition and training are needed to acquire the muscle-relaxation skill."
_____ 4. Counselor instructs client about moving around if uncomfortable and informs client of sensations that may feel unusual.	"At times during the training and muscle exercises, you may want to move while you are on your back on the floor (or on the recliner). Just feel free to do this so that you can get more comfortable. Also, you may feel heady sensations as we go through the exercise. These sensations are not unusual. Do you have any questions concerning what I just talked about? If not, do you want to try this now?"
II. Client Dress	
_____ 5. Counselor instructs client about what to wear for training session.	"For the next session, wear comfortable clothing." "Wear regular glasses instead of your contact lenses."

Checklist	Counselor Leads

III. Comfortable Environment

_____ 6. Counselor uses quiet environment, padded recliner chair, or floor with a pillow under client's head.

"During training, I'd like you to sit in this recliner chair. It will be more comfortable and less distracting than this wooden chair."

IV. Counselor Models the Exercises

_____ 7. Counselor models some exercises for muscle groups.

"I would like to show you (some of) the exercises we will use in muscle relaxation. First, I make a fist to create tension in my right hand and forearm and then relax it. . . ."

V. Instructions for Muscle Relaxation

_____ 8. Counselor reads or recites instructions from memory in conversational tone and practices along with client.

_____ 9. Counselor instructs client to get comfortable, close eyes, and listen to instructions.

"Now, get as comfortable as you can, close your eyes, and listen to what I'm going to be telling you. I'm going to make you aware of certain sensations in your body and then show you how you can reduce these sensations to increase feelings of relaxation."

_____ 10. Counselor instructs client to tense and relax alternately each of the 17 muscle groups (_two_ times for each muscle group in initial training).

_____ a. Fist of dominant hand

"First study your right arm, your right hand in particular. Clench your right fist. Clench it tightly and study the tension in the hand and in the forearm. Study those sensations of tension. (Pause.) And now let go. Just relax the right hand and let it rest on the arm of the chair. (Pause.) And note the difference between the tension and the relaxation. (10-second pause.)"

_____ b. Fist of nondominant hand

"Now we'll do the same with your left hand. Clench your left fist. Notice the tension (5-second pause) and now relax. Enjoy the difference between the tension and the relaxation. (10-second pause.)"

_____ c. One or both wrists

"Now bend both hands back at the wrists so that you tense the muscles in the back of the hand and in the forearm. Point your fingers toward the ceiling. Study the tension, and now relax. (Pause.) Study the difference between tension and relaxation. (10-second pause.)"

Checklist	Counselor Leads
____ d. Biceps of one or both arms	"Now, clench both your hands into fists and bring them toward your shoulders. As you do this, tighten your biceps muscles, the ones in the upper part of your arm. Feel the tension in these muscles. (Pause.) Now relax. Let your arms drop down again to your sides. See the difference between the tension and the relaxation. (10-second pause.)"
____ e. Shoulders	"Now we'll move to the shoulder area. Shrug your shoulders. Bring them up to your ears. Feel and hold the tension in your shoulders. Now, let both shoulders relax. Note the contrast between the tension and the relaxation that's now in your shoulders. (10-second pause.)"
____ f. Forehead	"Now we'll work on relaxing the various muscles of the face. First, wrinkle up your forehead and brow. Do this until you feel your brow furrow. (Pause.) Now relax. Smooth out the forehead. Let it loosen up. (10-second pause.)"
____ g. Eyes	"Now close your eyes tightly. Can you feel tension all around your eyes? (5-second pause.) Now relax those muscles, noting the difference between the tension and the relaxation. (10-second pause.)"
____ h. Tongue or jaw	"Now clench your jaw by biting your teeth together. Pull the corners of your mouth back. Study the tension in the jaws. (5-second pause.) Relax your jaws now. Can you tell the difference between tension and relaxation in your jaw area? (10-second pause.)"
____ i. Lips	"Now, press your lips together tightly. As you do this, notice the tension all around the mouth. (Pause.) Now relax those muscles around the mouth. Just enjoy the relaxation in your mouth area and your entire face. (Pause.)"
____ j. Head backward	"Now we'll move to the neck muscles. Press your head back against your chair. Can you feel the tension in the back of your neck and in the upper back? Hold the tension. Now let your head rest comfortably. Notice the difference. Keep on relaxing. (Pause.)"
____ k. Chin in chest	"Now continue to concentrate on the neck area. See if you can bury your chin into your chest. Note the tension in the front of your neck. Now relax and let go. (10-second pause.)"
____ l. Back	"Now direct your attention to your upper back area. Arch your back like you're sticking out your chest and stomach. Can you feel tension in your back? Study that tension. (Pause.) Now relax. Note the difference between the tension and the relaxation."

Meditation and Muscle Relaxation

Checklist	Counselor Leads
____ m. Chest muscles	"Now take a deep breath, filling your lungs, and hold it. See the tension all through your chest and into your stomach area. Hold that tension. (Pause.) Now relax and let go. Let your breath out naturally. Enjoy the pleasant sensations. (10-second pause.)"
____ n. Stomach muscles	"Now think about your stomach. Tighten the abdomen muscles. Hold this tension. Make your stomach like a knot. Now relax. Loosen these muscles now. (10-second pause.)"
____ o. Buttocks	"Focus now on your buttocks. Tense your buttocks by pulling them in or contracting them. Note the tension that is there. Now relax—let go. (10-second pause.)"
____ p. Legs	"I'd like you now to focus on your legs. Stretch both legs. Feel tension in the thighs. (5-second pause.) Now relax. Study the difference again between the tension in the thighs and the relaxation you feel now. (10-second pause.)"
____ q. Toes	"Now concentrate on your lower legs and feet. Tighten both calf muscles by pointing your toes toward your head. Pretend a string is pulling your toes up. Can you feel the pulling and the tension? Note that tension. (Pause.) Now relax. Let your legs relax deeply. Enjoy the difference between tension and relaxation. (10-second pause.)"
____ 11. Counselor instructs client to review and relax all muscle groups.	"Now, I'm going to go over again the different muscle groups that we've covered. As I name each group, try to notice whether there is any tension in those muscles. If there is any, try to concentrate on those muscles and tell them to relax. Think of draining any residual tension out of your body. Relax the muscles in your feet, ankles, and calves. (Pause.) Let go of your knee and thigh muscles. (Pause.) Loosen your hips. (Pause.) Loosen the muscles of your lower body. (Pause.) Relax all the muscles of your stomach, waist, lower back. (Pause.) Drain any tension from your upper back, chest, and shoulders. (Pause.) Relax your upper arms, forearms, and hands. (Pause.) Let go of the muscles in your throat and neck. (Pause.) Relax your face. (Pause.) Let all the muscles of your body become loose. Drain all the tension from your body. (Pause.) Now sit quietly with your eyes closed."
____ 12. Counselor asks client to rate relaxation level following training session.	"Now I'd like you to think of a scale from 0 to 5, where 0 is complete relaxation and 5 extreme tension. Tell me where you would place yourself on that scale now."

Checklist	Counselor Leads
VI. *Posttraining Assessment*	
____ 13. Counselor asks client about first session of relaxation training, discusses problems with training if client has any.	"How do you feel?" "What is your overall reaction to the procedure?" "Think back about what we did—did you have problems with any muscle group?" "What reaction did you have when you focused on the tension? What about relaxation?" "How did the contrast between the tension and relaxation feel?"
VII. *Homework and Follow-Up*	
____ 14. Counselor assigns homework and requests that client complete homework log for practice sessions.	"Relaxation training, like any skill, takes a lot of practice. I would like you to practice what we've done today. Do the exercise twice a day for about 15 to 20 minutes each time. Do the exercises in a quiet place in a reclining chair, on the floor with a pillow, or on your bed with a head pillow. Also, try to do the relaxation at a time when there is no time pressure—like after work, before dinner, or before your bedtime. Try to avoid any interruptions, like telephone calls and people wanting to see you. Complete the homework log I have given you. Make sure you fill it in for each practice session. Do you have any questions?"
____ 15. Counselor arranges for follow-up session.	"Why don't you practice with this over the next 2 weeks and come back then."

Notations for Problems Encountered or Variations Used: _____

Suggested Readings

Meditation

Benson, H. Your innate asset for combating stress. *Harvard Business Review*, July–August 1974, *52*, 49–60.

Benson, H. *The relaxation response*. New York: Avon, 1976.

Marlatt, G. A., & Marques, J. K. Meditation, self-control and alcohol use. In R. B. Stuart (Ed.), *Behavioral self-management: Strategies, techniques, and outcomes*. New York: Brunner/Mazel, 1977.

Shapiro, D. H. Behavioral and attitudinal changes resulting from a "Zen experience" workshop and Zen meditation. *Journal of Humanistic Psychology*, 1978, *18*, 21–29. (a)

Shapiro, D. H. Instructions for a training package combining formal and informal Zen meditation with behavioral self-control strategies. *Psychologia*, 1978, *31*, 70–76. (b)

Shapiro, D. H., & Zifferblatt, S. M. Zen meditation and behavioral self-control: Similarities, differences, and clinical applications. *American Psychologist*, 1976, *31*, 519–532.

Smith, J. C. Meditation as psychotherapy: A review of the literature. *Psychological Bulletin*, 1975, *82*, 558–564.

Woolfolk, R. L., Carr-Kaffashan, L., McNulty, T. F., & Lehrer, P. M. Meditation training as a treatment for insomnia. *Behavior Therapy*, 1976, *7*, 359–365.

Muscle Relaxation

Bernstein, D. A., & Borkovec, T. D. *Progressive relaxation training: A manual for the helping professions.* Champaign, Ill.: Research Press, 1973.

Borkovec, T., Grayson, J., & Cooper, K. Treatment of general tension: Subjective and physiological effects of progressive relaxation. *Journal of Consulting and Clinical Psychology*, 1978, *46*, 518–528.

Goldfried, M. R. The use of relaxation and cognitive relabeling as coping skills. In R. B. Stuart (Ed.), *Behavioral self-management: Strategies, techniques, and outcomes.* New York: Brunner/Mazel, 1977.

Goldfried, M. R., & Davison, G. C. *Clinical behavior therapy.* New York: Holt, Rinehart & Winston, 1976. Chap. 5, Relaxation training, 81–111.

Goldfried, M. R., & Trier, C. S. Effectiveness of relaxation as an active coping skill. *Journal of Abnormal Psychology*, 1974, *83*, 348–355.

Shoemaker, J. E., & Tasto, D. L. The effects of muscle relaxation on blood pressure of essential hypertensives. *Behaviour Research and Therapy*, 1975, *13*, 29–43.

Chapter 21
Systematic Desensitization

Consider the following cases:

A man has been a successful high school teacher. He is teaching while plagued with a personal problem: he is married yet is in love with another person. One day at school he is overcome with anxiety. He leaves school to go home; the next day, the thought of school elicits so much anxiety he feels sick. For the last few months, he has not returned to school. Also, because of this, he is convinced he is "going crazy."

A high school student gets good grades on homework and self-study assignments. Whenever he takes a test, he "freezes." Some days, if he can, he avoids or gets out of the class because he feels so anxious about the test even the day before. When he takes a test, he feels overcome with anxiety, he cannot remember very much, and his resulting test grades are quite low.

These two case descriptions reflect instances in which a person learned an anxiety response to a situation. According to Bandura (1969), anxiety is a persistent, learned maladaptive response resulting from stimuli that have acquired the capacity to elicit very intense emotional reactions. In addition, both people described in these cases felt fear in situations where there was no obvious external danger (sometimes referred to as a *phobia*; R. J. Morris, 1975, p. 229). Also, to some degree, each person

managed to avoid the nondangerous feared situation (sometimes referred to as a *phobic reaction*; Morris, p. 229). These people will probably require counseling or therapy.

In contrast, in the next two cases, a person is prevented from learning an anxiety response to a certain situation.

A child is afraid to learn to swim because of a prior bad experience with water. The child's parent or teacher gradually introduces the child to swimming, first by visiting the pool, dabbling hands and feet in the water, getting in up to the knees, and so on. Each approach to swimming is accompanied by a pleasure—being with a parent, having a toy or an inner tube, or playing water games.

A person has been in a very bad car accident. The person recovers and learns to get back in a car by sitting in it, going for short distances first, often accompanied by a friend or the music on the radio.

In the two descriptions you just read, the situation never got out of hand; that is, it never acquired the capacity to elicit a persistent anxiety response, nor did the people learn to avoid the situation continually. Why? See if you can identify common elements in these situations that prevented these two people from becoming therapy candidates. Go over these last two cases again. Do you notice that, in each case, there was some type of stimulus or emotion present that counteracted the fear or anxiety? The parent used pleasurable activities to create enjoyment for the child while swimming; the person in the car took a friend or listened to music. Also, these people learned to become more comfortable with a potentially fearful situation gradually. Each step of the way represented a larger or more intense dose of the feared situation.

In a simplified manner, these elements reflect some of the processes that seem to occur in the procedure of *systematic desensitization*, a widely used anxiety-reduction strategy. According to Wolpe (1973):

> Systematic desensitization is one of a variety of methods for breaking down neurotic anxiety-response habits in piecemeal fashion . . . a physiological state inhibitory of anxiety is induced in the patient by means of muscle relaxation, and he is then exposed to a weak anxiety-evoking stimulus for a few seconds. If the exposure is repeated several times, the stimulus progressively loses its ability to evoke anxiety. Then successively "strange" stimuli are introduced and similarly treated [p. 95].

Objectives

1. Write in at least six out of seven major components of systematic desensitization on a blank flow chart.
2. Using written examples of four sample hierarchies, identify at least three hierarchies by type (spatio-temporal, thematic, personal).
3. Given a written client case description, identify and describe at least 9 of the following 11 procedural steps of desensitization:
   a. a rationale
   b. an overview
   c. a method for identifying client emotion-provoking situations
   d. a type of hierarchy appropriate for this client
   e. a method of ranking hierarchy items the client could use
   f. an appropriate counterconditioning or coping response
   g. a method of imagery assessment
   h. a method of scene presentation
   i. a method of client signaling during scene presentation
   j. a written notation method to record scene-presentation progress
   k. an example of a desensitization home-work task.
4. Demonstrate at least 22 out of 28 steps of systematic desensitization in several role-play interviews.

Reported Uses of Desensitization

Systematic desensitization was used widely as early as 1958 by Wolpe. In 1961, Wolpe reported its effectiveness in numerous case reports, which also were substantiated by successful case reports cited by Lazarus (1967). Since 1963, when Lang and Lazovik conducted the first controlled study of systematic desensitization, its use as a therapy procedure has been the subject of numerous empirical investigations and case reports.

As an anxiety-reduction strategy, it has been used to treat test anxiety (Cornish & Dilley, 1973; J. Mann, 1972; Osterhouse, 1976), speech anxiety (Russell & Wise, 1976; Woy & Efran, 1972; Zemore, 1975), and interpersonal-social anxiety (Dua, 1972; Fry, 1973; Kanter & Goldfried, 1979), to name just a few. Boudreau and Jeffery (1973) successfully treated stuttering in eight male clients with desensitization. Also, it has been used extensively with common phobias, including acrophobia (fear of heights), agoraphobia (fear of open places), and claustrophobia (fear of enclosed places). It has been used to treat fear of flying, fear of death, fear of criticism or rejection—and, after the stimulus movie *Jaws*, fear of sharks. Of course, one should not apply desensitization automatically whenever a client reports "anxiety." In some cases, the anxiety may be the logical result of another problem. For example, a person who continually procrastinates on work deadlines may feel anxious. Using this procedure would only help the person become desensitized or numb to the possible consequences of continued procrastination. A more logical approach might be to help the client reduce the procrastination behavior that is clearly the antecedent for the experienced anxiety. This illustration reiterates the importance of thorough problem definition (Chapters 9 and 10) as a prerequisite for selecting and implementing counseling strategies.

Generally, desensitization is appropriate when a client has the capability or the skills to handle a situation or perform an activity but avoids the situation or performs less than adequately because of anxiety. For example, in the two cases described at the beginning of this chapter, the teacher had a history of successful teaching yet persistently avoided school (or related thoughts) because of the associated anxiety. The high school student had the ability to do well and adequate study skills, yet his performance on tests was not up to par because of his response. In contrast, if a person avoids a situation because of skill deficits, then desensitization is inadequate and probably inappropriate (Rimm & Masters, 1974). As you may recall from Chapter 16, modeling procedures work very well with many kinds of skill-deficit problems. People with many fears or with general, pervasive anxiety may benefit more from cognitive-change strategies (Chapters 18 and 19) or from combinations of strategies in which desensitization may play some role. Also, some anxiety may be maintained by the client's maladaptive self-verbalizations. In these instances, cognitive restructuring or stress inoculation (Chapter 19) may be a first treatment choice or may be used in conjunction with desensitization.

At the same time, desensitization should not be overlooked as a possible treatment strategy for client problems that do not involve anxiety. Marquis, Morgan, and Piaget (1973) suggest that desensitization can be used with any conditioned emotion. It has been used to reduce anger (Hearn & Evans, 1972) and to increase tolerance of White students toward Black peers (Cotharin & Mikulas, 1976). Dengrove (1966) reports the use of desensitization to treat situations of loss and grief, such as separation from a loved one or loss of a valued job or object.

Comparison to Other Treatment Approaches

Desensitization also has been the subject of a great many studies that compare it to other therapy methods on certain dependent measures. In the treatment of test anxiety, desensitization has been compared to covert positive reinforcement (Kostka & Galassi, 1974), hypnosis (Melnick & Russell, 1976), cognitive therapy (Holroyd, 1976), cue-controlled relaxation (R. K. Russell, F. Wise, & J. P. Stratoudakis, 1976), and modeling, flooding, and study-skills training (Horne & Matson, 1977). In treating speech anxiety, it has been compared to an insight treatment focusing on maladaptive self-verbalizations (Meichenbaum, Gilmore, & Fedoravicius, 1971) and to cue-controlled relaxation (R. K. Russell & R. Wise, 1976). Shaw and Thoresen (1974) compared desensitization to modeling in treating dental phobia; Curran (1975) compared desensitization with skills training consisting of modeling and behavior rehearsal on social-anxiety measures. Rudestam and Bedrosian (1977) compared flooding and desensitization in anxiety reduction of animal phobias and social phobias of college students.

Despite the fact that desensitization has enjoyed substantial empirical support, a great deal of controversy surrounds its current status. There is general agreement that desensitization is effective in reducing fears and neurotic behavior. The controversy centers around how and why the procedure works, or the processes surrounding desensitization that are responsible for its results (Kazdin & Wilcoxon, 1976).

Theoretical Explanations of Desensitization

We will briefly summarize some of the possible theoretical explanations of the desensitization procedure. This will help you understand both the counterconditioning and the self-control models for implementing desensitization.

Desensitization by Reciprocal Inhibition

In 1958, Wolpe explained the way in which desensitization ostensibly works with the principle of *reciprocal inhibition*. When reciprocal inhibition occurs, a response such as fear is inhibited by another response or activity that is stronger than and incompatible with the fear response (or any other response to be inhibited). In other words, if an incompatible response occurs in the presence of fear of a stimulus situation, and if the incompatible response is stronger than the fear, desensitization occurs, and the stimulus situation loses its capacity to evoke fear. The reciprocal-inhibition theory is based on principles of classical or instrumental conditioning. In order for desensitization to occur, according to the reciprocal-inhibition principle, three processes are required:

1. A strong anxiety-competing or counterconditioning response must be present. Usually this competing or inhibiting response is deep muscle relaxation. Although other responses (such as eating, assertion, and sexual ones) can be used, Wolpe (1973) feels that relaxation is most helpful.
2. A graded series of anxiety-provoking stimuli is presented to the client. These stimulus situations are typically arranged in a hierarchy with low-intensity situations at the bottom and high-intensity situations at the top.
3. Contiguous pairing of one of these aversive stimulus situations and the competing or counterconditioning response (relaxation) must occur. This is usually accomplished by having the client achieve a state of deep relaxation and then imagine an aversive stimulus (presented as a hierarchy item) while relaxing. The client stops imagining the situation whenever anxiety (or any other emotion to be inhibited) occurs. After additional relaxation, the situation is re-presented several times.

In recent years, some parts of the reciprocal-inhibition principle have been challenged, both by personal opinion and by empirical explorations. There is some doubt that relaxation functions in the manner suggested by Wolpe—as a response that is inherently antagonistic to anxiety (Lang, 1969). As Kazdin and Wilcoxon (1976) observe, some research indicates that desensitization is not dependent on muscle relaxation, or a hierarchical arrangement of anxiety-provoking stimuli, or the pairing of these stimuli with relaxation as an incompatible response (p. 731). These research results have led some people to abandon a reciprocal-inhibition explanation for desensitization.

Desensitization by Extinction

Lomont (1965) proposed that extinction processes account for the results of desensitization. In other words, anxiety responses diminish as a result of presenting conditioned stimuli without reinforcement. This theory is based on principles of operant conditioning. Wolpe (1976) agrees that desensitization falls within this operational definition of extinction and that extinction may play a role in desensitization. Similarly, Wilson and Davison (1971) have argued that desensitization reduces a client's anxiety level sufficiently that she or he gradually approaches the feared stimuli and the fear is then extinguished.

Some studies indicate that other factors, including habituation (Mathews, 1971; van Egeren, 1971), gender of the counselor and the client (Geer & Hurst, 1976), and reinforcement and instructions (Leitenberg, Agras, Barlow, & Oliveau, 1969) may be at least partially responsible for the results of desensitization.

Nonspecific Factors and Desensitization

After a critical review of the literature, Kazdin and Wilcoxon (1976) conclude that it is not now possible to rule out nonspecific treatment factors such as client expectancy as a plausible reason for the therapeutic effects of desensitization. Although many studies of desensitization have included a placebo group to control for nonspecific treatment effects, many of these control groups did not generate the same expectancy for improvement as the treatment groups. According to Kazdin and Wilcoxon, there are only five studies in which both desensitization and the control conditions gave comparable expectancy sets to the subjects. Of these five studies, only one (Gelder, Bancroft, Gath, Johnston, Mathews, & Shaw, 1973) found that desensitization was superior to the comparable control conditions (Kazdin & Wilcoxon, p. 745). Therefore, the effectiveness of the desensitization procedure may be, to some extent, the result of additive factors such as the therapeutic relationship, the rationale presented to the client, and the client's expectancy of change.

Desensitization as Self-Control Training

In 1971, Goldfried challenged the idea that desensitization was a relatively passive process of deconditioning. Goldfried proposed that desensitization involved learning a general anxiety-reducing skill, rather than mere desensitization to some specific aversive stimulus (p. 228). According to this self-control explanation, the client learns to use relaxation as a way to cope with anxiety or to bring anxiety under control, not simply to replace anxiety. Eventually, the client learns to identify the cues for muscular tension, to respond by relaxing away the tension, and to relabel the resulting emotion (p. 229). As learning occurs, Goldfried hypothesized, the relaxation responses may become "anticipatory," having the effect of partially or completely "short circuiting" the anxiety or fear (p. 229).

Goldfried (1971) suggested certain modifications in the desensitization procedure that are more consistent with his view of the process. The client is told that desensitization involves learning the skill of relaxation as a way to cope with anxiety. During relaxation training, emphasis is placed on having the client become aware of sensations associated with tension and

learning to use these sensations as a cue to relax. Since emphasis is placed on training the client to cope with anxiety cues and responses, the situations that elicit the anxiety are less important. Therefore, a single hierarchy can be used that reflects a variety of stimulus situations, not just those involving one theme (the latter is the procedure advocated by Wolpe, 1973). According to the reciprocal-inhibition theory, the relaxation response must be stronger than the anxiety response. Therefore, the client is taught to stop visualizing the anxiety-provoking situation when anxious and to relax. In Goldfried's model, the client is instructed to maintain the image even though anxious and to relax away the tension. Finally, the client is taught to apply the skill to "in vivo" situations (pp. 231–232).

These procedural aspects of the self-control desensitization model were compared to the traditional (reciprocal-inhibition) procedure of desensitization for the treatment of speech and test anxiety in college students (Zemore, 1975). Both methods produced improvements in treated *and* untreated fears of clients. Another study comparing these two methods of desensitization as a test-anxiety treatment found that they were comparable on the dependent measures, with the self-control model showing significantly greater anxiety reduction on one test-anxiety self-report measure (Spiegler, Cooley, Marshall, Prince, Puckett, & Skenazy, 1976). These authors noted that, in the self-control model, only 4 of the 21 hierarchy items used dealt specifically with test-anxiety situations, supporting Goldfried's (1971) assumption that not all situations in the problem area need be included in the hierarchy for desensitization to occur (Spiegler et al., 1976). Further support for this position was reported by Goldfried and Goldfried (1977), who found no difference between speech-anxious subjects desensitized with a hierarchy relevant to speech anxiety and other speech-anxious people desensitized with a hierarchy totally unrelated to speech anxiety. In another study, test-anxious students treated by self-control desensitization did better on both self-report and performance measures than students receiving standardized desensitization from a reciprocal-inhibition framework (Denney & Rupert, 1977).

Given the controversy surrounding the process of desensitization, what conclusions can be drawn about the possible ways to implement the procedure? First of all, perhaps there is no single right way to proceed with desensitization. A variety of procedural steps may be effective. Second, the specific ways in which desensitization is used will reflect the counselor's biases and preferences. To the extent that you believe a particular way of using desensitization works, this belief will only enhance the outcomes. Third, the specifics of the desensitization procedure should be adapted to each client. Very few studies have explored possible interactions between procedural varia-

tions in desensitization and client characteristics. Individual clients may respond differently to the particular rationale they receive or to the particular way in which a hierarchy is used. The counselor should always attempt to implement desensitization in a way that is likely to produce the best results for each client. Finally, perhaps the overall procedure of desensitization should integrate a variety of components from several theoretical explanations to ensure that no important contributing variable is overlooked. We have attempted to do this in our presentation of the procedural aspects of desensitization in the following section. The seven major components of systematic desensitization are presented in Figure 21-1. A summary of the procedural steps associated with each com-

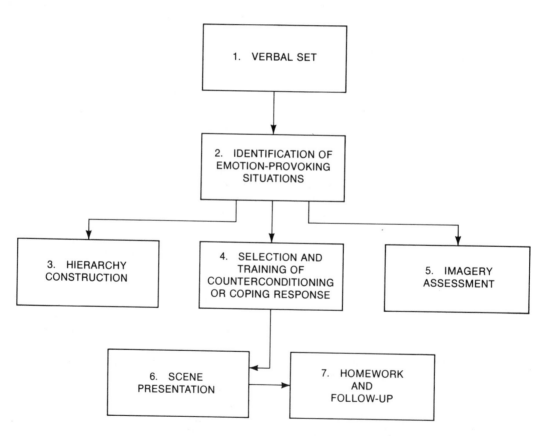

Figure 21-1. Components of Systematic-Desensitization Procedure

ponent is found in the Interview Checklist for Systematic Desensitization at the end of the chapter.

Components of Desensitization

Verbal Set

The rationale and overview given to the client in the verbal set about desensitization are very important for several reasons. First, the rationale and overview establish the particular model or way in which the counselor plans to implement the procedure. The client is therefore informed of the principles of desensitization. Second, the outcomes of desensitization may be enhanced when the client is given very clear instructions and a positive expectancy set (Leitenberg et al., 1969). The *particular* rationale and overview you present to the client depend on the actual way you plan to implement desensitization.

Rationale and Overview of Counterconditioning Model. If you plan to use a counterconditioning model, you would present a rationale that explains how the client's fear or other conditioned emotion can be counterconditioned using desensitization. Your overview of the procedure would emphasize the use of an anxiety-free response to replace the conditioned emotion, the construction of a hierarchy consisting of a graduated series of items representing the emotion-provoking situations, and the pairing of these hierarchy items with the anxiety-free response (such as relaxation).

One rationale and overview based on a counterconditioning model has been used by Osterhouse (1976) in group-administered desensitization for test anxiety. Portions of this rationale are reprinted below:

The procedure we will use to help you overcome any unusually strong fears of examinations is called desensitization. . . . This approach is based upon the fact that it is impossible to be afraid and relaxed at the same time. For example, a student might want to

ask a professor a question, or perhaps criticize something the professor has said. He may find, however, when he starts to speak that he experiences shortness of breath, his heart pounds, or his hands perspire. He is unable to make his point. These are anxiety reactions and don't occur when the student is relaxed. Therefore, an important part of the method involves teaching you to relax as completely as possible. You may think that you don't have to be taught how to relax, but the fact is that most people are frequently unaware of their tensions.

Once you have learned how to relax, then this group will develop a list of situations in which the anxiety occurs. This list will be made up so that it contains items representing many different degrees of anxiety. . . . This list is called a hierarchy. . . .

One of the most interesting aspects of this procedure is that it tends to generalize to real life situations. Even though the procedure only requires you to imagine yourself in situations related to fear of examinations, there is a strong tendency for fear to decrease in the actual situation [p. 270].*

Rationale and Overview of Self-Control Model. If you plan to implement desensitization by emphasizing coping and self-control skills for tension management, your rationale and overview should reflect this emphasis. Goldfried (1971) suggests the following rationale and overview for explaining desensitization as training in self-control:

There are various situations where, on the basis of your past experience, you have learned to react by becoming tense (anxious, nervous, fearful). What I plan to do is help you to learn how to cope with these situations more successfully, so that they do not make you as upset. This will be done by taking note of a number of those situations which upset you to varying degrees, and then having you learn to cope with the less stressful situations before moving on to the more difficult ones. Part of the treatment involves learning how to relax so that in

*From "Group Systematic Desensitization of Test Anxiety," by R. A. Osterhouse. In J. D. Krumboltz and C. E. Thoresen (Eds.), *Counseling Methods*. Copyright 1976 by Holt, Rinehart and Winston. Reprinted by permission.

---

situations where you feel yourself getting nervous you will be better able to eliminate this tenseness. Learning to relax is much like learning any other skill. When a person learns to drive, he initially has difficulty in coordinating everything, and often finds himself very much aware of what he is doing. With more and more practice, however, the procedures involved in driving become easier and more automatic. You may find the same thing occurring to you when you try to relax in those situations where you feel yourself starting to become tense. You will find that as you persist, however, it will become easier and easier [p. 231].

In one study, test-anxious students who received this sort of active coping rationale for desensitization achieved significantly better grade-point averages than students who received a rationale explaining desensitization according to the principle of classical conditioning (Denney & Rupert, 1977).

Model Dialogue: Verbal Set

Here is an example of a verbal set the counselor could use to explain to Joan how desensitization can help her with her fear and avoidance of math class:

"Joan, we've talked about how you get very nervous before and during your math class. Sometimes you try to skip it. But you realize you haven't always felt this way about math. You've *learned* to feel this way. There is a procedure called desensitization that can help you replace your tension with relaxation. Eventually, the things about math class you now fear will not be tense situations for you. This procedure has been used very successfully to help other people reduce their fear of a certain situation.

"In desensitization, you will learn how to relax. After you're relaxed, I'll ask you to imagine some things about your math class— starting first with not too stressful things, and gradually working with more stressful things. As we go along, the relaxation will start to replace the anxiety. These stressful situations then will no longer seem so stressful to you.

"What questions do you have about this?"

Identification of Emotion-Provoking Situations

If the counselor and client have defined the problem thoroughly, there already will be some indications about the dimensions or situations that provoke anxiety (or any other emotional arousal) in the client. However, the counselor and client must be sure to isolate the most crucial situations in which the client should become less anxious or upset (Goldfried & Davison, 1976, p. 114). This is not always an easy task, as first appearances can be deceiving. Wolpe (1973) cites cases where the initial problem seemed to indicate fear of open places (agoraphobia); yet the complaint was related to difficult unresolved situations in the client's marriage. Goldfried and Davison recommend that counselors ask themselves and their clients what the consequences may be of desensitization to one thing or another (p. 115).

The emotion-provoking situations must be defined idiosyncratically for each client. Marquis et al. (1973) observe that, even among clients who have the same type of fear or phobia, the specific anxiety-provoking situations associated with the fear can vary greatly.

There are at least three ways in which the counselor can try to identify past and present situations that are anxiety-provoking to the client. These three methods include the interview assessment, client self-monitoring, and client completion of related self-report questionnaires.

Interview Assessment. The interview assessment will be similar to the interview assessment we proposed in Chapters 9 and 10 on problem definition. The counselor should use leads that will establish the specific circumstances and situations that elicit the conditioned emotion. For instance, does the client feel anxious in all social situations or only those with strangers present? Does the client's anxiety vary with the number of people present, or with whether the client is accompanied or alone? Does the client experience more anxiety with people of the same or opposite sex? These are examples of the kinds of information the interview assessment could provide about a client's anxiety in certain social situations.

Client Self-Monitoring. In addition to the information obtained during the session, the counselor may obtain even more data by having the client observe and record on a log the emotion-provoking situations as they occur during the week. The log sheet illustrated in Chapter 10 can be used for this purpose. The client would observe and note what was going on, where, with whom, and when the emotion, such as anxiety, was detected. The client also might rate the level of anxiety felt during the situation on a scale of 1 (low) to 10 (high) or on a scale of 0 (no anxiety) to 100 (panic).*

Self-Report Questionnaires. Some counselors find that additional data about specific emotion-provoking situations can be gained by having the client complete one or more self-report questionnaires. A commonly used questionnaire is the Wolpe-Lang (1964) Fear Survey Schedule (FSS). Descriptions of other self-report measures of fear and anxiety are presented in Lick and Katkin (1976).

The counselor should persist in this identification process until specific emotion-provoking situations are identified. Marquis et al. (1973) indicate that information-gathering is not complete until the counselor knows the factors related to the onset and maintenance of the client's problem and until the client believes that all pertinent information has been shared with the counselor (p. 2). At this point, the counselor and client are ready to construct a hierarchy.

*Although 1–5 and 1–7 rating scales are recommended in Chapter 13, the 0–100 rating scale is typically used in desensitization because it corresponds to the Suds scaling method described on p. 442 of this chapter.

Model Dialogue: Identifying Emotion-Provoking Situations

Counselor: Joan, we've already discussed some of the situations about your math class that make you feel anxious. What are some of these?

Client: Well, before class, just thinking about having to go bothers me. Sometimes at night I get anxious—not so much doing math homework but studying for tests.

Counselor: OK. Can you list some of the things that happen during your math class that you feel anxious about?

Client: Well, always when I take a test. Sometimes when I am doing problems and don't know the answers—having to ask Mr. _____ for help. And, of course, when he calls on me or asks me to go to the board.

Counselor: OK, good. And I believe you said before that you feel nervous about volunteering answers, too.

Client: Right—that, too.

Counselor: And yet these sorts of situations don't seem to upset you in your other classes?

Client: No. And really math class has never been as bad as it is this year. I guess part of it is the pressure of getting closer to graduating and, well, my teacher makes me feel dumb. I felt scared of him the first day of class. Yet I've always felt somewhat nervous about working with numbers.

Counselor: So some of your fear centers around your teacher, too—and then perhaps there's some worry about doing well enough to graduate.

Client: Right. Although I know I won't do *that* badly.

Counselor: OK, good. You realize that, even with not liking math and worrying about it, you won't get a bad grade.

Client: Not worse than a "C."

Counselor: There's one thing I'd like you to do this week. Could you make a list of anything about the subject of math—and your math class—that has happened and has made you nervous? Also, write down anything about math or your class that *could* happen that you would feel anxious about. Then, if you think it's a situation that makes you a little anxious, mark *L* by it. If it's average, mark *A*. If it does or could make you very nervous, mark *V*.

Client: OK.

Hierarchy Construction

A hierarchy is a list of stimulus situations to which the client reacts with graded amounts of anxiety or some other emotional response (Wolpe, 1958). Hierarchy construction can consume a good deal of interview time because of the various factors involved in constructing an adequate hierarchy. These factors include selection of a type of hierarchy, the number of hierarchies (single or multiple), identification of hierarchy items, identification of control items, and ranking and spacing of items.

Types of Hierarchies. Based on the stimulus situations that evoke anxiety (or any emotion to be counterconditioned), the counselor should select an appropriate type of hierarchy in which to cast specific items or descriptions of the aversive situations. Marquis et al. (1973) describe three possible kinds of hierarchies: spatio-temporal, thematic, and personal (pp. 3–4). Spatio-temporal and thematic hierarchies are used more commonly than personal ones and an occasional hierarchy may be a combination of any of these three types. The particular type used will depend on the client's problem, the counselor's preferences, and the client's preferences.

A spatio-temporal hierarchy is developed by using items that represent physical or time dimensions, such as distance from one's house or time before taking an exam. In either case, anxiety, for example, seems to vary with proximity to the feared object or situation. Someone who is afraid to leave the house will get more anxious as the distance away from home increases. A client who has "exam panic" will get more anxious as the exam draws closer. Therefore, in developing a spatio-temporal hierarchy, usually more items are put at the high end of the scale than at the low end, so the space or time differences at the high end of the scale are smaller.

Here is an example of a spatio-temporal hierarchy used with a client who was very fearful of taking tests. The items are arranged in terms of time:

1. Your instructor announces on the first day of class that the first exam will be held in one month. You know that the month will go quickly.
2. A week before the exam, you are sitting in class and the instructor reminds the class of the exam date. You realize you have a lot of studying to do during the week.
3. You are sitting in the class and the instructor mentions the exam, scheduled for the next class session, 2 days away. You realize you still have a lot of pages to read.
4. Now it is 1 day before the exam. You are studying in the library. You wonder whether you have studied as much as everyone else in the class.
5. It is the night before the test. You are in your room studying. You think about the fact that this exam grade is one-third of your final grade.
6. It is the night before the exam—late evening. You have just finished studying and have gone to bed. You're lying awake going over your reading in your mind.
7. You wake up the next morning and your mind flashes to this being exam day. You wonder how much you will remember of what you read the night and day before.
8. It is later in the day, 1 hour before the exam. You do some last-minute scanning of your lecture notes. You start to feel a little hassled—even a little sick. You wish you had more time to prepare.
9. It is 15 minutes before the class—time to walk over to the classroom. As you're walking over, you realize how important this grade will be. You hope you don't "blank out."
10. You go into the building, stop to get a drink of water, then enter the classroom. You look around and see people laughing. You think that they are more confident and better prepared than you.
11. The instructor is a little late. You are sitting in class waiting for the teacher to come and pass out the tests. You wonder what will be on the test.
12. The instructor has just passed out tests. You

receive your copy. Your first thought is that the test is so long—will you finish in time?

13. You start to work on the first portion of the test. There are some questions you aren't sure of. You spend time thinking, then see that people around you are writing. You skip these questions and go on.

14. You look at your watch. The class is half over—only 25 minutes left. You feel like you have dawdled on the first part of the test. You wonder how much your grade will be pulled down if you don't finish.

15. You continue to work as fast as you can; occasionally you worry about the time. You glance at your watch—5 minutes left. You still have a lot of unanswered questions.

16. Time is just about up. There are some questions you had to leave blank. You worry again about this test being one-third of your grade.

A thematic hierarchy consists of items exposing the client to various components or parameters of feared objects, activities, or situations. For example, a client who is afraid of criticism or disapproval may find that the fear varies, depending on who criticizes, what is criticized, and how the criticism is delivered. Here is an example of a thematic hierarchy used with a person who found criticism very stressful:

1. A classmate that you don't especially respect tells you you're too quiet and asks "What's the matter with you?"

2. A casual friend tells you that you look tired today.

3. A good friend points out that the color of your attire isn't really "your best color."

4. Your tennis date, a person you consider to be just "OK," tells you that you need to improve your tennis game.

5. You're in class and the teacher assigns a group project. Your group is meeting and you offer an idea for the project—no one responds to it.

6. You run into a person you used to date regularly; he or she avoids speaking to you.

7. Your sister comes in and complains you've been too busy to pay much attention to her.

8. Your best friend comments that you seem moody today and aren't too much fun to be around.

9. Your mother suggests you're putting on a little weight and need to exercise more.

10. You meet someone you like and ask him or her to go to a game with you. The person turns down your invitation.

11. You get a paper back that you worked hard on. You only get a "C." The teacher writes across the top "Some good ideas, but you didn't develop them at all."

12. You are in front of the class making an individual presentation. Several people in the class are talking and laughing as you speak.

13. Your father complains that your grades aren't as good as they should be and implies that you're lazy.

14. You're in your honors class. The class is engaged in a big discussion. You offer one idea. Someone responds with "That's dumb."

A personal hierarchy is not used as often as the other two types, but it is very useful with clients who are persistently bothered by thoughts or memories of a certain individual. Dengrove (1966) recommends the use of a personal hierarchy to desensitize anxiety related to the separation or termination of a relationship. Items at the bottom of the hierarchy may consist of blissful or pleasant scenes or memories progressing toward items at the top of the hierarchy representing painful or anxiety-provoking memories or thoughts (Marquis et al., 1973).

Here is an example of a personal hierarchy used with a male client who was bothered by painful memories of the termination of a close relationship:

1. You have been with Susie every day for the last month. You're sitting holding her in your arms and feeling like she's the only woman you'll ever love like this.

2. You and Susie are sitting on the floor in your

apartment, drinking wine and listening to records.

3. You've just returned from taking Susie to her first race. She's ecstatic about the experience.
4. You and Susie are studying together in the library.
5. You and Susie are drinking beer at the local pub.
6. You and Susie aren't spending every day together. Sometimes she wants to study alone now. You're in the library by yourself studying.
7. You call Susie up late at night. The phone rings continuously without any answer. You wonder where she is.
8. You call Susie to ask her out for dinner and she turns you down—says she doesn't feel well.
9. You're walking down the street by the tennis court. You see Susie playing there with another person. You wonder why she hasn't told you about him.
10. You go over to Susie's. She isn't there. You wait until she comes. She sees you, goes back to her car, and drives away.
11. You call Susie on the phone. She says she doesn't want to see you anymore, that she never has really loved you, and hangs up on you.

Number of Hierarchies. Whether you use one or several hierarchies also depends on the client's problem and preferences, and your preferences. Some therapists believe separate hierarchies should be constructed for different themes or different parameters of one theme (Marquis et al., 1973; Wolpe & Lazarus, 1966). Using multiple hierarchies may be less confusing but can require more time for hierarchy construction and presentation. Goldfried (1971) asserts that establishing separate hierarchies for carefully determined themes is not essential. He recommends constructing a single hierarchy composed of situations eliciting increasing amounts of tension, regardless of whether the hierarchy items represent any particular theme (p. 232). According to Gold-

fried, construction of a single hierarchy with items reflecting a variety of anxiety-provoking situations may facilitate generalization of the desensitization process from the session to the client's environment. Whether to use one or several hierarchies is a choice you will need to make during the process of hierarchy construction.

Identification of Hierarchy Items. The counselor must initiate a method of generating the specific items for the hierarchy. The client's role in this process is extremely important. Generally, the counselor can ask the client to aid in identifying hierarchy items by interview questions or by a homework assignment. The counselor can question the client about specific emotion-provoking scenes during the interview. Goldfried and Davison (1976) instruct clients to think of a large balloon and to draw items from different parts of the balloon that represent all the elements in the balloon. However, questioning the client about the scenes should not occur simultaneously with relaxation training. If the client is queried about hierarchy items after engaging in a period of deep relaxation, her or his responses may be altered.

If the client has difficulty responding concretely to interview questions, the counselor can assign homework for item identification. The counselor can give the client a stack of blank 3 × 5 index cards. The client is asked to generate items during the week and to write down each item on a separate note card. Often this homework assignment is useful even with clients who respond very thoroughly to the interview questions. During the week, the client has time to add items that were not apparent during the session.

The counselor should continue to explore and generate hierarchy items until a number have been identified that represent a range of aversive situations and varying degrees of emotional arousal. A hierarchy typically contains 10 to 20 items but occasionally may have fewer than 10 or more than 20. Goldfried and Davison (1976) and Marquis et al. (1973) suggest some criteria to use to construct adequate hierarchy items:

1. Some of the items should represent situations that, if carried out by the client "in vivo," are under the client's control (do not require instigation from others).
2. An item must be concrete and specific. Embellishing the item description with sufficient details may help the client obtain a clear and vivid visualization of the item during scene presentation. As an example, an item that reads "Your best friend disapproves of you" is too general. A more concrete item would be "Your best friend disapproves of your boyfriend and tells you that you are stupid for going out with him."
3. Items should be similar to or represent actual situations the client has faced or may have to confront in the future. If dialogue is written into an item, the language used should be adapted to the client.
4. Items selected should reflect a broad range of situations in which the client's fear (or other emotion) does or could occur.
5. Items should be included that reflect all different levels of the emotion, ranging from low to high intensity.

After the hierarchy items are identified, the client and counselor can identify several control items.

Identification of Control Items. A control item consists of a relaxing or neutral scene to which the client is not expected to have any strong emotional reaction. Control scenes are placed at the bottom of the hierarchy and represent a zero or "no anxiety" ranking. Some examples of control items might be to "imagine a colored object," "imagine you're sitting in the sun on a day with a completely blue sky," or "imagine you're looking at a field of vivid yellow daffodils." A control item often is used to test the client's ability to visualize anxiety-free material and to give the client a relaxing or pleasant scene to imagine during scene presentation in order to enhance the level of relaxation.

After all the hierarchy and control items have been identified, the client can arrange the items in order of increasing emotional arousal through a ranking method.

Ranking and Spacing of Hierarchy Items. The counselor and client work together to identify an appropriate order for the items in the hierarchy. Generally, the client plays the major role in ranking, but the counselor must ensure that the spacing between items is satisfactory. The hierarchy items are ranked in order of increasing difficulty, stress, or emotional arousal. The control items are placed at the lowest end of the hierarchy, and each item that represents more difficulty or greater anxiety is placed in a successively higher position in the hierarchy. Items at the highest end of the hierarchy represent the situations that are most stressful or anxiety-producing for the client.

The counselor should explain how the hierarchy items are arranged before asking the client to rank them. The counselor also should explain the purpose of this type of hierarchy arrangement so that the client fully understands the necessity of spending time to rank the items. The counselor can point out that desensitization occurs gradually and that the function of a hierarchy is to identify low-stress items to which the client will be desensitized before higher-stress items. The client's learning to face or cope with a feared situation will begin with more manageable situations first and gradually extend to more difficult situations. The counselor may emphasize that at no point will the client be asked to imagine or cope with a scene or situation that is very stressful before learning to deal successfully with less stressful scenes. This point is often reassuring to an occasional client whose anxiety is so great that the desensitization procedure itself is viewed with great trepidation.

There are several methods the client can use to order the hierarchy items. Three methods that are commonly used include: rank-ordering; "suds" scaling; and low, medium, and high ordering. Rank-ordering is the simplest method. Each hierarchy item is written on a 3 × 5 note card (this note card is also useful later for the counselor to make notations about the item presentation). The client takes the stack of note cards and rank-orders the cards, with the least stressful situations at the bottom and successively more stressful items in an appropriate ascending order. The bottom item, a control item, can be assigned a 1; each successive item can be assigned one higher number. These numbers can be written at the top of each card in pencil, since the order of the items may change. After the client has rank-ordered the cards, the counselor can go over the order to determine whether there are too many or too few gaps between items. Items should be graduated evenly, with a fairly equal amount of difference between them. If items are bunched together, a few can be deleted. If there are large spaces between items, new ones can be added.

In the "suds" scaling method, items are arranged according to a point system in which the various points represent levels of the emotion referred to as "suds," or "subjective units of disturbance" (Wolpe & Lazarus, 1966). The most common scale is 100 points, where 0 suds represents complete relaxation and 100 suds indicates panic or an extremely stressful reaction. However, occasionally a 10-point suds scale is used, with 0 representing relaxation and 10 indicating panic. We think that the 100-point scale is simpler to use, because the greater range of points makes adequate spacing between items easier. If a client uses the suds scale to arrange items, each item is assigned a number representing the amount of stress it generates for the client. If the item doesn't generate much stress, the client may assign it 10, 15, or 20 suds; average amounts of stress might be assigned 35, 40, 45, or 50; whereas 85, 90, 95, and 100 suds represent situations that produce much anxiety or stress. (This hierarchy scaling method should not be confused with assessment of behavior with a rating scale, described in Chapter 13.)

After the items are arranged according to the assigned suds, the counselor should make sure that no item is separated from the previous item by more than 10 suds; at the high end of the scale, spacing of no more than 5 suds between items often is necessary (Marquis et al., 1973). If there are large gaps (greater than 10 or 5 suds), the counselor and client should write additional, intermediate items to fill in. If there are too many items around the same level, particularly at the lower end of the hierarchy, some of these items may be deleted. The suds system may require more explanation to the client and more time for item arrangement. However, it has several advantages. First, the point system makes it easy to determine whether there is too much or too little space between items. Second, the use of the suds scale at this point in desensitization introduces the client to a way to discriminate and label varying degrees of relaxation and tension. Often this kind of labeling system is useful during relaxation training and scene presentation.

If the client has difficulty assigning specific suds ratings, a "low, medium, high" ranking method can be used instead. In this method, suggested by Goldfried and Davison (1976), the client rates items that produce little anxiety, which represent the bottom one-third of the hierarchy, or 0 to 33 suds; then rates average anxiety-producing items, which make up the middle of the hierarchy, or 34 to 66 suds; and finally the items that produce much anxiety, which compose the top end of the hierarchy, or 67 to 100 suds. After the items are sorted into these three groups, the client can rank-order items within each group. Then the counselor can go over the items to make sure the spacing is reasonable.

Whichever ranking method is used, the counselor should emphasize that it is flexible and subject to change. Any type of hierarchy or order of items is useful only to the degree that it helps desensitize the emotion or helps the client to cope. Many times, a carefully constructed hierarchy will require some change during scene presentations.

Although we have described how to construct a hierarchy for an individual client, hierarchy construction also can be adapted for groups of clients. For some clients standardized hierarchies may work as well as individualized ones (Emery & Krumboltz, 1967; McGlynn, Wilson, & Linder, 1970; Nawas, Fishman, &

Pucel, 1970). For a description of hierarchy construction with a group of clients, see Osterhouse (1976).

Model Dialogue: Hierarchy Construction

Counselor: Hi, Joan. I see you brought your list with you. That's great, because today we're going to work on a list that's called a hierarchy. In your case, it will center around the theme or the idea of math anxiety. It's a list of all the situations about math that are anxiety-producing for you. We'll list these situations and then I'll ask you to rank them, starting with the less stressful ones. Does this seem clear?

Client: Yes. Actually I did something like that this week in making my list, didn't I?

Counselor: Right, you did. Now what we want to do is take your list, add any other situations that are stressful that aren't on here, and make sure each item on this list is specific. We may need to add some details to some of the items. The idea is to get a close description of the way the situation actually is or actually does or could happen. Let's take a look at your list now.

1. Sitting in English thinking about math class (L)
2. On way to math class (L)
3. At home, doing math homework (L)
4. At home, studying for a math test (A)
5. In math class, teacher giving out test (V)
6. In math class, taking test (V)
7. In math class, teacher asks me question (V)
8. In math class, at board, having trouble (V)
9. In math class, working problems at desk, don't know some answers (A)
10. Asking teacher for help (A)
11. Volunteering an answer (V)
12. Getting test or assignment back with low grade (V)
13. Teacher telling me I'll flunk or barely pass (V)
14. Doing anything with numbers, even outside math class, like adding up a list of numbers (A)
15. Talking about math with someone (A)

Counselor: Well, it looks like you've really worked hard at putting down some math situations that are stressful for you and indicating just how stressful they are. OK, let's go over this list and fill in some details. For each item here, can you write in 1 or 2 more details about the situation? What exactly happens that you feel nervous about? For instance, when you're sitting in English, what is it you're thinking that makes you nervous?

Client: OK, I see what you mean.

Counselor: Let's go over each item here and, as you tell me the details, I'll jot these down.
(This step proceeds until a concrete description is obtained for each item. Counselor checks them to see what items meet necessary criteria which, with added details, these do. Criteria include: some items are under client's control; items are concrete; items represent past, present, or future anxiety-provoking scenes; items sample a broad range of situations; items represent varying levels of anxiety.)

Counselor: What else can you think of about math that is or could be stressful?

Client: Nothing right now. Not everything on my list has happened, but like if my teacher did tell me I was going to flunk, that would be very tense.

Counselor: You've got the idea. Now can you think of something not related to math that would be pleasant or relaxing for you to think about—like skiing down a slope or lying on the beach?

Client: Well, what about sitting in front of a campfire roasting marshmallows?

Counselor: Good. Now later on, as we proceed, I might ask you to relax by imagining a pleasant scene. Then you could imagine something like that.

Client: OK.

Counselor: I'd like you now to take these items we've listed on these cards and rank-order each item. We're going to put this pleasant item having to do with the campfire at the bottom of the list. Then go through the cards and put each card in an order from the least stressful to the most stressful situation. Is that clear?

Client: You mean the thing that bothers me least to the thing that makes me most nervous?

Counselor: Exactly. Each item as you go up the stack of cards should be a little more stressful than the previous item.

Client: OK. (Takes about 10 minutes to rank-order the 16 cards.)

Counselor: OK. I'm going to lay each card out to see what you've got here, starting at the bottom.

Card 1: Sitting in front of a campfire on a cool

night with friends, singing songs and roasting marshmallows (control item).

Card 2: Sitting in my room at my desk doing routine math homework over fairly easy material.

Card 3: Sitting in English about 10 minutes before the bell. Thinking about going to math class next and wondering if I can hide or if I'll get called on.

Card 4: Walking down the hall with a couple of classmates to math class. Walking in the door and seeing the teacher looking over our homework. Wondering how I did.

Card 5: A girlfriend calls up and talks about our upcoming test in math—wonder if I'll pass it.

Card 6: Seeing a big list of numbers, like on a store receipt, and having to check the total to make sure it's OK.

Card 7: In math class, sitting at my desk; having to work on problems and coming across some that are confusing. Don't have much time to finish.

Card 8: Working on problems at my desk. I'm stumped on a couple. Nothing I try works. Having to go up and ask Mr. _____ for help. He tries to do it for me; I feel dumb.

Card 9: Sitting in my room at home the night before a big math test; studying for the test and wondering if I'll blank out on it.

Card 10: In math class taking a test and coming across some problems I don't know how to do.

Card 11: Waiting to get a test or an assignment back and worrying about a low grade.

Card 12: Sitting in math class and the teacher asks for the answer; raising my hand to volunteer it; wonder if it's right.

Card 13: Sitting in math class waiting for a big test to be passed out. Wondering what's on it and if I'll be able to remember things.

Card 14: Sitting in math class and suddenly the teacher calls on me and asks me for an answer. I feel unprepared.

Card 15: Sitting in math class and the teacher sends me to the board. I'm at the board trying to work a problem in front of the class. I'm getting stuck.

Card 16: The teacher calls me in for a confer-ence after school. Mr. _____ is telling me I'm in big trouble and barely passing. There's a good chance I could flunk math.

Counselor: OK, now it seems like each of these items represents a somewhat more stressful situation. Do you feel that there are any large jumps between items—like going from a very low-stress situation to a higher-stress one suddenly?

Client (looks over list): No, I don't think so.

Counselor: OK, we'll stick with this list and this order for now. Of course this is tentative. Later on, if we feel something needs to be moved around or added, we will do so.

Learning Activity: Hierarchy Construction

This learning activity is designed to give you some practice in constructing different kinds of hierarchies. You can do this activity by yourself or with another person.

Part One: Spatio-Temporal Hierarchy

Think of for yourself, or have your partner identify, a situation you fear and avoid. This situation should be something where the fear increases as the distance or time proximity toward the feared object or situation gets closer. For example, you might fear and avoid approaching certain kinds of animals or high places (distance). Or you might get increasingly anxious as the time before an exam, a speech, or an interview diminishes (time). For this situation, identify the specific situations that are anxiety-provoking. Try to identify all the relevant parameters of the situation. For example, does your anxiety vary if you're alone or with another person, if you're taking a midterm or a quiz, if you're speaking before a large or a small group? List each anxiety-provoking situation that could be a hierarchy item on a separate index card. Also list one control (pleasant) item on a card. After you or your partner believes all the relevant items are listed, you or your partner should take the cards and rank-order them. The control item will be at the bottom, followed by items that evoke successively greater anxiety. Check the rank order to make sure items are equally spaced. Add or delete items as necessary.

Part Two: Thematic Hierarchy

This time, you or your partner should identify a situation you fear and avoid that is related to a certain theme: fear of being rejected or criticized, fear of engaging in risk-taking situations, fear of failure, fear of losing control, fear of getting ill or of death, and so on. Identify the specific anxiety-provoking situations associated with this theme, ones that have made or could make you anxious. Identify all the relevant parameters: does your fear vary with what you do? who is with you? List each anxiety-provoking situation that could represent a hierarchy item on a card or a piece of paper. After all the relevant items are listed, rank-order each item using the suds scale. Assign each item a number from 0 (no anxiety) to 100 (panic), depending on the intensity and amount of anxiety it provokes. Then arrange the items in order of increasing suds. Check to make sure there are no more than 10 suds between each item and 5 suds between high-intensity items. Add or delete items as necessary.

Part Three: Personal Hierarchy

See if you or your partner can identify a situation about which you have painful or unpleasant memories. Such situations might include loss of a prized object, loss of a job or friend, or termination of a close relationship. Generate emotion-provoking situations related to this loss, including situations associated with pleasant memories and unpleasant memories. List each situation on a separate card. When all items are identified and listed, rank-order the cards into low, medium, and high groupings. Pleasant memories would constitute the low grouping, less pleasant in the middle grouping, and very unpleasant in the high grouping. Then, within each group, you can arrange the cards in another order from most pleasant at the bottom of the hierarchy to most painful at the top.

Selection and Training of Counterconditioning or Coping Response

According to the principles of reciprocal inhibition and counterconditioning, for desensitization to take place, the client must respond in a way that inhibits (or counterconditions) the anxiety or other conditioned emotion. A self-control model of desensitization emphasizes the client's learning of a skill to use to cope with the anxiety. In either model, the counselor should select and train the client to use a response that may be considered either an alternative to anxiety or incompatible with anxiety.

Selection of a Response. The counselor's first task is to select an appropriate counterconditioning or coping response for the client to use. Typically, the anxiety-inhibiting or counterconditioning response used in desensitization is deep muscle relaxation (Marquis et al., 1973; Wolpe, 1973). Muscle relaxation also is recommended by Goldfried (1971) for use as the coping response. Muscle relaxation has some advantages. As you may remember from Chapter 20, its use in anxiety reduction and management is well documented. Wolpe (1973) prefers muscle relaxation because it doesn't require any sort of motor activity to be directed from the client toward the sources of anxiety (p. 98). Muscle relaxation is easily learned by most clients and easily taught in the interview. It is also adaptable for client daily practice. However, an occasional client may have difficulty engaging in relaxation. Also, relaxation is not always applicable to "in vivo" desensitization, in which the client carries out rather than imagines the hierarchy items (Marquis et al., 1973).

When deep muscle relaxation cannot be used as the counterconditioning or coping response, the counselor may decide to proceed without this sort of response or to substitute an alternative response. In some cases, clients have been desensitized without relaxation (Daniels, 1974; Rachman, 1968). However, with a client who is very anxious, it may be risky to proceed without any response to counteract the anxiety. Many other examples of counterconditioning and coping responses have been used in desensitization, including emotive imagery and meditation (Boudreau, 1972), assertion responses, feeding responses, ginger ale (Mogan & O'Brien, 1972), music (Lowe, 1973), laughter (Ventis, 1973), sexual responses (Bass, 1974), anger (A. J. Goldstein, M. Serber, & G. Piaget, 1970), kung fu (Gershman & Stedman, 1976), and coping thoughts (Weissberg, 1975). Some of these responses quite obviously are less easily applied in an office setting but may be suitable for certain cases of "in vivo" or self-administered desensitization.

If muscle relaxation is not suitable for a client, emotive imagery (Chapter 17), meditation (Chapter 20), and coping thoughts (Chapter 19) may be reasonable substitutes that are practical to use in the interview and easy to teach. For example, if the counselor selects emotive imagery, the client can focus on pleasant scenes during desensitization. If meditation is selected, the client can focus on breathing and counting. In the case of coping thoughts, the client can whisper or subvocalize coping statements.

Explanation of Response to the Client. Whatever counterconditioning or coping response is selected, its use and purpose in desensitization should be explained to the client. The client will be required to spend a great deal of time in the session and at home learning the response. Usually a large amount of client time will result in more pay-offs if the client understands how and why this sort of response should be learned.

In emphasizing that the response is for counterconditioning, the counselor can explain that one of the ways desensitization can help the client is by providing a substitute for anxiety (or other emotions). The counselor should emphasize that this substitute response is incompatible with anxiety and will minimize the felt anxiety so that the client does not continue to avoid the anxiety-provoking situations.

Goldfried (1971) recommends that explanations of relaxation as a coping response should inform clients that they will be made aware of sensations associated with tension and will learn to use these sensations as a signal to cope and to relax away the tension. After the client indicates understanding of the need for learning another response, the counselor can begin to teach the client how to use the selected response.

Training in the Response. The counselor will need to provide training for the client in the particular response to be used. The training

in muscle relaxation or any other response may require at least portions of several sessions to complete. The training in a counterconditioning or coping response can occur simultaneously with hierarchy construction. Half of the interview can be used for training; the other portion can be used for hierarchy construction. Remember, though, that identifying hierarchy items should not occur simultaneously with relaxation. The counselor can follow portions of the interview protocol for cognitive restructuring (Chapter 19) for training in coping statements; the interview checklists for emotive imagery (Chapter 17), muscle relaxation, and meditation (Chapter 20) can be used to provide training in these responses.

Before and after each training session, the counselor should ask the client to rate the felt level of stress or anxiety. This is another time when the suds scale is very useful. The client can use the 0-to-100 scale and assign a numerical rating to the level of anxiety. Generally, training in the counterconditioning or coping response should be continued until the client can discriminate different levels of anxiety and can achieve a state of relaxation after a training session equivalent to 10 or less on the 100-point suds scale (Marquis et al., 1973). If, after successive training sessions, the client has difficulty using the response in a nonanxious manner, another response may need to be selected.

After the client has practiced the response with the counselor's direction, daily homework practice should be assigned. An adequate client demonstration of the counterconditioning or coping response is one prerequisite for actual scene presentation. A second prerequisite involves a determination of the client's capacity to use imagery.

Model Dialogue: Selection of and Training in Counterconditioning or Coping Response

Counselor: Perhaps you remember when I explained desensitization to you I talked about replacing anxiety with something else like relaxation. What I'd like to do today is show you a relaxation method you can learn. How does that sound?

Client: OK, is it like yoga?

Counselor: Well, it's carried out differently than yoga, but it is a skill you can learn with practice and it has effects similar to yoga. This is a process of body relaxation. It involves learning to tense and relax different muscle groups in your body. Eventually you will learn to recognize when a part of you starts to get tense, and you can signal to yourself to relax.

Client: Then how do we use it in desensitization?

Counselor: After you learn this, I will ask you to imagine the items on your hierarchy—but only when you're relaxed, like after we have a relaxation session. What happens is that you're imagining something stressful, only you're relaxed. After you keep working with this, the stressful situations become less and less anxiety-provoking for you.

Client: That makes sense to me, I think. The relaxation can help the situation to be less tense.

Counselor: Yes, it plays a big role—which is why I consider the time we'll spend on learning the relaxation skill so important. Now one more thing, Joan. Before and after each relaxation session, I'll ask you to tell me how tense or how relaxed you feel at that moment. You can do this by using a number from 0 to 100—0 would be total relaxation and 100 would be total anxiety or tenseness. How do you feel right now, on that scale?

Client: Well, not totally relaxed, but not real tense. Maybe around a 30.

Counselor: OK. Would you like to begin with a relaxation-training session now?

Client: Sure. (Training in muscle relaxation following the interview checklist presented in Chapter 20 is given to Joan. An abbreviated version of this is also presented in the model dialogue of scene presentation on pp. 455–456).

Imagery Assessment

The typical administration of desensitization relies heavily on client imagery. The relearning or counterconditioning that is achieved in desensitization occurs during the client's visualization of the hierarchy items. This, of course, assumes that imagination of a situation is equivalent to a real situation and that the learning that occurs in the imagined situation generalizes to the real situation (Goldfried & Davison, 1976, p. 113). M. J. Mahoney (1974) points out that recent evidence indicates there may be considerable variability in the degree to which these assumptions about imagery really operate. Still, if desensitization is implemented, the client's capacity to generate images is vital to the way in which this procedure typically is used.

Explanation to the Client. The counselor can explain that the client will be asked to imagine the hierarchy items as if the client were a participant in the situation. The counselor might indicate that imagining a feared situation can be very similar to actually being in the situation. If the client becomes desensitized while imagining the aversive situations, then the client also will experience less anxiety when actually in the situation. The counselor can suggest that, because people respond differently to using their imagination, it is a good idea to practice visualizing several situations.

Assessment of Client Imagery. The client's capacity to generate clear and vivid images can be assessed by use of practice (control) scenes or by a questionnaire, as described in Chapter 17. Generally, it is a good idea to assess the client's imagery for desensitization at two different times—when the client is deliberately relaxed and when the client is not deliberately relaxed. According to Wolpe (1973), imagery assessment of a scene under relaxation conditions serves two purposes. First, it provides the counselor with information about the client's ability to generate anxiety-free images. Second, it suggests whether any factors are present that may inhibit the client's capacity to imagine anxiety-free material. For example, a client who is concerned about losing self-control may have trouble generating images of a control item (Wolpe, 1973, p. 122). After each visualization, the counselor can ask the client to describe the details of the imagined scene aloud.

Criteria for Effective Imagery. Remember

that, in the typical administration of desensitization, the client's use of imagery plays a major role. A client who is unable to use imagery may not benefit from a hierarchy that is presented via imagination. Based on the results of the client's imagery assessment, the counselor should determine whether the client's images meet the criteria for effective therapeutic imagery. These four criteria have been proposed by Marquis et al. (1973):

1. The client must be able to imagine a scene concretely, with sufficient detail, and evidence of touch, sound, smell, sight sensations.
2. The scene should be imagined in a way that the client is a participant, not an observer.
3. The client should be able to switch a scene image on and off upon instruction.
4. The client should be able to hold a particular scene as instructed without drifting off or changing the scene [p. 10].

If these or other difficulties are encountered during imagery assessment, the counselor may decide to continue to use imagery and provide imagery training, or to add a dialogue or a script; to present the hierarchy in another manner (slides, role-plays, or "in vivo"); or to terminate desensitization and use an alternative therapeutic strategy. Whenever the client is able to report clear, vivid images that meet most of the necessary criteria, the counselor can initiate the "nuts and bolts" of desensitization—presentation of the hierarchy items.

Model Dialogue: Imagery Assessment

The following assessment should be completed two different times: once after a relaxation session and once when Joan is not deliberately relaxed.

Counselor: Joan, I will be asking you in the procedure to imagine the items we've listed in your hierarchy. Sometimes people use their imagination differently, so it's a good idea to see how you react to imagining something. Could you just sit back and close your eyes and relax? Now get a picture of a winter snow scene in your mind. Put yourself in the picture, doing something. (Pauses.) Now, can you describe exactly what you imagined?

Client: Well, it was a cold day, but the sun was shining. There was about a foot of snow on the ground. I was on a toboggan with two friends going down a big hill very fast. At the bottom of the hill we rolled off and fell in the snow. That was cold!

Counselor: So you were able to imagine sensations of coldness. What colors do you remember?

Client: Well, the hill of course was real white and the sky was blue. The sun kind of blinded you. I had on a bright red snow parka.

Counselor: OK, good. Let's try another one. I'll describe a scene and ask you to imagine it for a certain amount of time. Try to get a clear image as soon as I've described the scene. Then, when I say "Stop the image," try to erase it from your mind. OK, here's the scene. It's a warm, sunny day with a good breeze. You're out on a boat on a crystal-clear lake. OK—now imagine this—put in your own details. (Pauses.) OK, Joan, stop the image. Can you tell me what you pictured? (Joan describes the images.) How soon did you get a clear image of the scene after I described it?

Client: Oh, not long. Maybe a couple seconds.

Counselor: Were you able to erase it when you heard me say *stop*?

Client: Pretty much. It took me a couple of seconds to get completely out of it.

Counselor: Did you always visualize being on a boat, or did you find your imagination wandering or revising the scene?

Client: No, I was on the boat the entire time.

Counselor: How do you feel about imagining a scene now?

Client: These are fun. I don't think imagination is hard for me anyway.

Counselor: Well, you do seem pretty comfortable with it, so we can go ahead.

(Joan's images meet the criteria for effective imagery: the scenes are imagined concretely; she sees herself in a scene as a participant; she is able to turn the image on and off fairly well upon instruction; she holds a scene constant; there is no evidence of any other difficulties.)

Hierarchy Scene Presentation

Scenes in the hierarchy are presented after the client has been given training in a counterconditioning or coping response and after the client's imagery capacity has been assessed. Each scene presentation is paired with the counterconditioning or coping response so that the client's anxiety (or other emotion) is counterconditioned or decreased. There are several possible ways that scenes can be presented to the client. Our discussion of this component of desensitization reflects some of the possible variations of scene presentation. The counselor must select a method for presenting scenes and a method for client signaling before progressing with actual scene presentation. Scene presentations follow a certain format and usually are concluded after 15 to 20 minutes.

Identify and Explain a Method of Scene Presentation. The counselor will first need to decide upon the method of scene presentation to use and explain it in detail to the client before proceeding. There are three possible methods of scene presentation; the alphabetical labels for these methods (R, H, and A) were coined by Evans (1974).

Method R is used primarily when implementing desensitization according to a traditional model based on the principles of reciprocal inhibition or counterconditioning. In method R, when the client visualizes an item and reports anxiety associated with the visualization, the client is instructed to *remove* or stop the image, then to relax. According to Wolpe (1973), the timing of scene presentation should maximize the amount of time the client imagines a situation without anxiety and minimize the amount of time the client imagines a scene eliciting anxiety.

There are several reasons for having the client remove the image when anxiety occurs. First, the principle of reciprocal inhibition assumes that, for a response such as anxiety to be successfully counterconditioned, the relaxation (or other counterconditioning) response must be stronger than the anxiety response. This principle is applied to scene presentation, so

that the reaction any given item elicits from the client is never stronger than the nonanxiety response being used. In the presence of anxiety, the client is told to stop the image to prevent the anxiety from escalating to the point where it might be stronger than the client's state of relaxation. According to Wolpe (1973), continued exposure to a disturbing scene may even increase the client's sensitivity to it. This is an added reason to terminate the scene when it evokes a strong client reaction. However, some studies have indicated that sensitivity to a scene does not increase when clients are asked to hold the image in spite of tension (Zemore, 1975; Spiegler et al., 1976). These findings have lent some credence to a method of scene presentation based on a self-control model of desensitization. This has been identified by Evans (1974) as method H.

In method H, when the client indicates anxiety associated with any given scene, the counselor asks the client to *hold* the image, to continue with the visualization, and to relax away the tension. Goldfried (1971) asserts that this is a more realistic method of scene presentation, since in real life, the client can't "eliminate" a situation upon becoming tense. This method of scene presentation was used successfully in three studies (Denney & Rupert, 1977; Spiegler et al., 1976; Zemore, 1975).

A third method of scene presentation may be referred to as method A (Evans, 1974). In method A, when the client indicates tension, he or she is instructed to switch the image to an *"adaptive alternative"* (p. 45). This might consist of an appropriate response in the feared situation or a coping response, similar to the coping thoughts taught to clients in cognitive restructuring and stress inoculation (Chapter 19). For example, a client who feared losing control of his temper with his children might be presented with the hierarchy item: "It is 5:00 at night. You are trying to fix dinner. Your three children are running underfoot and screaming. The telephone and doorbell both ring at the same time." If this item is tension-producing for the client (what parent wouldn't be tense!), he would be instructed to switch off this image and to visualize an adaptive coping response, something he can do that is under his control, such as "think of staying calm and collected. Ask one child to get the door, the other to answer the phone. Make sure things in the oven are under control before going to the phone or to the door." These coping scenes should be worked out with the client before the hierarchy items are actually presented. This method also has some empirical support (Meichenbaum, 1972). According to Meichenbaum, having the client use coping imagery is based on the premise that, when clients imagine hierarchy items, they are providing themselves with "a model for their own behavior" (p. 372). After explaining the scene-presentation method, the counselor also will need to explain the use of a signaling process.

Identify and Explain a Signaling System. During the presentation of hierarchy items, there are several times when the counselor and client need to communicate. In order not to interrupt the client's achievement of a relaxed state, it is useful to work out a signaling system the client can use in a relatively nondistracting manner. To prevent the signals from "getting crossed," it is a good idea to identify and explain a signaling system to the client before actually starting to present the hierarchy items.

There is no one right signaling method, and several can be used. You should select one that is clear to both you and the client to prevent any confusion. One signaling method advocated by Wolpe (1973) is to instruct the client to raise the left index finger 1 inch as soon as a clear image of the item is formed. Wolpe presents the item for a specified time (usually about 7 seconds) and then asks the client to stop or remove the image and to rate the level of anxiety felt during the visualization with a number on the 0-to-100 suds scale. This signaling method allows the counselor to determine if and when the visualization begins. Also, this provides immediate feedback about the client's suds level of disturbance.

An alternative signaling method is to ask the client to imagine the scene and to indicate whether any anxiety is felt by raising an index finger. This signaling system has the advantage of letting the counselor know the time when the client started to notice the tension. However, with this method, the counselor cannot be sure when the visualization began, nor does the counselor obtain a specific rating of the client's anxiety.

Another signaling method used to indicate quantitative changes in anxiety is to instruct the client to raise a hand as the anxiety goes up (say, above 10 suds) and to lower it as the anxiety decreases (Marquis et al., 1973). This signaling method might be advantageous when the counselor asks the client to hold a scene image and to relax away the tension. The counselor could determine when the client did successfully lower the tension level.

A fourth method of signaling involves the use of the words *tense* and *calm* in lieu of hand or finger signals. The client is instructed to say "tense" when anxiety is noticed and "calm" when relaxation is achieved. Marquis et al. (1973) point out that this method may be slightly more disruptive of relaxation than hand or finger signals, but it may be clearer and prevent misunderstanding of signals (p. 9).

None of these methods needs to be used arbitrarily. The counselor may wish to discuss possible signaling methods and encourage the client to choose one. Such choices strengthen the client's belief that she or he is an active, responsible participant in the treatment process. If one signaling method is used initially and seems distracting or confusing, it can be changed. As soon as the scene-presentation and signaling methods are determined, the counselor can initiate scene presentation. Scene presentation follows a fairly standardized format.

Format of a Scene-Presentation Session. Each scene-presentation session should be preceded by a training session involving the designated counterconditioning or coping. As you will recall, the idea is to present the hierarchy items concurrently with some counterconditioning or coping response. For example, the counselor can inform the client that they will go through a period of relaxation, after which the counselor will ask the client to imagine a scene from the hierarchy. Depending on the particular counter-conditioning or coping response to be used, the client should engage in a brief period of muscle relaxation, meditation, or emotive imagery. The client's relaxation rating following this period should be 10 or less on the 100-point suds scale before the counselor presents a hierarchy item.

At this point, the counselor begins by describing a hierarchy item to the client and instructing the client to evoke the scene in imagination. The initial session begins with the first, or least anxiety-provoking, item in the hierarchy. Successive scene presentations always begin with the last item successfully completed at the preceding session. This helps to make a smooth transition from one session to the next and checks on learning retention. Also, starting with the last successfully completed item may prevent spontaneous recovery of the anxiety response (Marquis et al., 1973, p. 11). Sometimes relapse between two scene-presentation sessions does occur (Agras, 1965; Rachman, 1966), and this procedure is a way to check for it.

In presenting the item, the counselor should describe it and ask the client to imagine it. Usually the counselor presents an item for a specified amount of time before asking the client to stop the image. There is no set duration for scene presentation. Marquis et al. (1973) point out that typically the client is asked to visualize the scene for 20 seconds. Even clients who signal anxiety before 20 seconds are up may be asked to continue to picture the scene for the full time. Clients are then asked to remove the image and relax (the R method), to hold the image and relax (the H method), or to switch to an adaptive alternative (the A method).

There are several reasons why a visualization period of at least 20 (and perhaps up to 40) seconds may be important. First, if the client signals anxiety before this time and the counselor immediately instructs the client to stop the image, some avoidance responses may be inadvertently reinforced (H. R. Miller & M. M. Nawas, 1970). Second, some recent evidence indicates that both physiological and self-report indexes of anxiety show greater reduction with a longer scene duration, such as 30 seconds per scene (Eberle, Rehm, & McBurney, 1975; Ross &

Proctor, 1973; Rudestam & Bedrosian, 1977). Longer scene presentation may result in even greater anxiety reduction for high-intensity items (Eberle et al., 1975), and faster desensitization of high-intensity items (Watts, 1973, 1974). Watts also found that a longer scene presentation of 30 to 45 seconds tended to prevent spontaneous recovery of previously desensitized items.

If the client holds the scene for the specified duration and does not report any tension, the counselor can instruct the client to stop the scene and to take a little time to relax. This relaxation time serves as a breather between item presentations. During this time, the counselor can cue the onset of relaxation with descriptive words such as "let all your muscles relax" or with the presentation of a control item. There is no set time for a pause between items. Generally a pause of 30 to 60 seconds is sufficient, although some clients may need as much as 2 or 3 minutes (Marquis et al., 1973).

If the client indicates that anxiety was experienced during the visualization, the counselor will instruct the client to remove the image and relax (method R), hold the image and relax away the tension (method H), or switch the image to an adaptive or coping alternative (method A). Generally, the counselor will pause for 30 to 60 seconds and then present the same item again. Successful coping or anxiety reduction with one item is required before presenting the next hierarchy item. Marquis et al. (1973) indicate that an item can be considered successfully completed with two successive no-anxiety presentations (p. 11). However, items that are very anxiety-arousing, such as those at the high end of the hierarchy, may require three or four successive no-anxiety repetitions.

If an item continues to elicit anxiety after three presentations, this may indicate some trouble and a need for adjustment. Continued anxiety for one item may indicate a problem in the hierarchy or in the client's visualization. There are at least three things a counselor can try to alleviate continual anxiety resulting from the same item: a new, less anxiety-provoking item can be added to the hierarchy; the same item can be presented to the client more briefly; or the client's visualization can be assessed to determine whether the client is drifting from or revising the scene.

The counselor should be careful to use standardized instructions at all times during scene-presentation sessions. Standardized instructions are important regardless of whether the client signals anxiety or reports a high or a low anxiety rating on the suds scale. Rimm and Masters (1974) observe that a counselor can inadvertently reinforce a client for not signaling anxiety by saying "good." The client, often eager to please the counselor, may learn to avoid giving reports of anxiety because these are not similarly reinforced.

Each scene-presentation session should end with an item that evokes no anxiety or receives a low suds rating, since the last item of a series is well remembered (Lazarus & Rachman, 1957). At times, the counselor may need to return to a lower item on the hierarchy so that presentation of a non-anxiety-provoking scene can end the session. Generally, any scene-presentation session should be terminated when three to five hierarchy items have been completed successfully, or at the end of 15 to 30 minutes, whichever comes first. A session may be terminated with completion of fewer items or in a shorter time if the client seems restless. Desensitization requires a great deal of client concentration, and the counselor should not attempt to extend a session beyond the client's concentration limits.

Identify Notation Method. Desensitization also requires some concentration and attention on the counselor's part! Just think about the idea of conducting perhaps four or five scene-presentation sessions with one client and working with one or more hierarchies with 10 to 20 items per hierarchy! The counselor has a great deal of information to note and recall. Most counselors use some written recording or notation method during the scene-presentation sessions. There are several possible ways to make notations of the client's progress in each scene-presentation session. We will describe three possible recording methods. These methods are only suggestions;

you may discover a notation system that parallels more closely your own procedural style of desensitization.

Marquis et al. (1973) use a "Desensitization Record Sheet" to record the hierarchy item numbers and the anxiety or suds rating associated with each item presentation. Their record sheet is exhibited in Figure 21-2, with a sample notation provided at the top of the sheet.

Goldfried and Davison (1976) use a notation system written on the 3 × 5 index card that contains the description of the hierarchy item and the item number. Underneath the item description is space for the counselor to note the duration of the item presentations and whether item presentation did or did not elicit anxiety. An example is presented in Figure 21-3. In this example, the numbers refer to the time in seconds that the client visualized each presentation of the item. The plus sign indicates a no-anxiety or low-suds visualization, and the minus sign indicates an anxiety or high-suds visualization. Note that there were two successive no-anxiety visualizations (+30 and +40) before the item was terminated.

One of the most comprehensive notation methods has been developed by Evans (1974), using the front and back of a pre-printed 4 × 6 index card. Notations about the client's progress in scene presentation are made on categories listed on the back of the card.

The front of this record is shown in Figure 21-4. On this side of the card, the hierarchy scene itself is described. If, during scene presentation, any variations or revisions are made, these can be recorded below the scene description. A sample hierarchy item has been completed.

The back of the card, used to complete details about the scene-presentation session, is presented in Figure 21-5. Sample descriptions have been completed on this card. The back includes a place at the top of the card for the client's anxiety or suds rating of the item (Anxiety Rating) and the order of the item in the hierarchy (Rank Order). Each item also can be numbered (Item #) and identified by the theme of the hierarchy (Theme). If the counselor plans to incorporate coping images in the scene pre-

Subject's Name:	Jane Doe			Time needed to relax at the beginning of the session: 15 minutes
Theme of Hierarchy:	Criticism			Time needed to visualize the scene presented: 10 sec. /8 sec. /9 sec. /5 sec.

Date and Total Time Spent in Session	Item Hierarchy Number	Anxiety + or − or Suds Rating		Time between Items	Comments, Observations, Changes in Procedure, or Other Special Treatment
7-14-77 45 minutes	4	+8 +20	−15 +30	60 sec./ 60 sec./ 30 sec./ 60 sec./	

Figure 21-2. Desensitization Record Sheet. (From *A Guidebook for Systematic Desensitization* (3rd ed.), by J. Marquis, W. Morgan, and G. Piaget. 1973, Veterans' Workshop, Palo Alto, California. Reprinted by permission.)

Item No. 6
Date 7-14-77

ITEM DESCRIPTION

You are walking to class thinking about the upcoming exam. Your head feels crammed full of details. You are wondering whether you've studied the right material.

+5 −9 +10 −15 +20 −25 +30 +40

Figure 21-3. Notation Card (Adapted from *Clinical Behavior Therapy,* by Marvin R. Goldfried and Gerald C. Davison. Copyright © 1976 by Holt, Rinehart and Winston. Reprinted by permission of Holt, Rinehart and Winston.

```
┌──────────────────────────────────────────────────────┐
│                                                        │
│   HIERARCHY SCENE                                      │
│     1.  You are walking to class thinking about the    │
│   upcoming exam. Your head feels crammed full of       │
│   details. You are wondering whether you've studied the│
│   right material.                                      │
│                                                        │
│   VARIATIONS                                           │
│     2.                                                 │
│                                                        │
│     3.                                                 │
│                                                        │
│     4.                                                 │
│                                                        │
│                                                        │
│                                                        │
│                                                        │
│                                                        │
│                                                        │
│                                                        │
└──────────────────────────────────────────────────────┘
```

Figure 21-4. Front of Record Card. (From "A Handy Record-Card for Systematic Desensitization Hierarchy Items," by I. M. Evans, *Journal of Behavior Therapy and Experimental Psychiatry,* 1974, 5, 43–46. Copyright 1974 by Pergamon Press, Inc. Reprinted by permission.)

sentation, these can be discussed and noted next to "Adaptive Alternative."

In the righthand column of this card, there is a place to indicate the client's suds rating after relaxation at the beginning of the session (this should be 10 or less). Any problems encountered in the session can be recorded under "Difficulties." Signs of client anxiety can be noted under "Physiological." The date each hierarchy item is successfully completed is noted under "Date Completed," and the date the client reports an anxiety-free experience of the item in real life can be noted with "Success *In Vivo*."

The items in the lefthand column of the card under "Presentation" refer to methods of scene presentation and, as Evans (1974) points out, were designed to reflect the major variations in this part of the procedure. The counselor can record the version of the hierarchy item used (from the front of the card), the time required for the client to obtain a clear image (Image La-

tency), the duration of the scene held by the client (Duration Held), and, if necessary, a rating of the image clarity from 1 (not clear) to 10 (very clear). If the client reports anxiety during the scene visualization, the time at which this is reported after the image is obtained can be noted (Anxiety Latency). Once the client indicates anxiety, the counselor can instruct the client to remove the scene (method R), hold the scene (method H), or switch to the adaptive alternative (method A). The particular method used can be recorded next to "Strategy: R/H/A." If you ask the client to indicate when the anxiety diminishes, the length of time this takes is noted after "Anxiety Decrease." If you ask the client to continue to hold an image despite anxiety, this duration can be noted after "Duration Held." A report of the client's suds level of anxiety during the scene presentation can be noted after "Anxiety Suds." Although this recording system does take more time to complete, its comprehensive-

Item: 6	Theme: Test anxiety	Anxiety Rating: 70 Suds	Rank Order: 6

Adaptive Alternative: Concentrate on what you've studied, not whether it is right or wrong.

PRESENTATION:	1	2	3	4	5	
Version	#1					Starting Suds: 5
						Difficulties:
Image Latency	8 sec.					
Duration Held	15 sec.					
Image Clarity	8					
Anxiety Latency	10 sec.					Physiological:
Strategy: R/H/A/	A					Some flushing of neck.
Anxiety Decrease	25 sec.					Date Completed:
Duration Held	5 sec.					7-14-77
Anxiety Suds	45 suds					Success *In Vivo:* 7-28-77

Figure 21-5. Back of Record Card. (From "A Handy Record-Card for Systematic Desensitization Hierarchy Items," by I. M. Evans, *Journal of Behavior Therapy and Experimental Psychiatry*, 1974, 5, 43–46. Copyright 1974 by Pergamon Press, Inc. Reprinted by permission.)

ness can aid the progress of a given session and can pinpoint trouble spots as they occur.

Model Dialogue: Scene Presentation

Counselor: Joan, after our relaxation session today, we're going to start working with your hierarchy. I'd like to explain how this goes. After you've relaxed, I'll ask you to imagine the first item on the low end of your hierarchy. That is, the pleasant one. It will help you relax even more. Then I'll describe the next item. I will show you a way to let me know if you feel any anxiety while you're imagining it. If you do, I'll ask you to stop or erase the image and to relax. You'll have some time to relax before I give you an item again. Does this seem clear?

Client: I believe so.

Counselor: One more thing. If at any point during the time you're imagining a scene you feel nervous or anxious about it, just raise your finger. This will signal that to me. OK?

Client: OK.

Counselor: Just to make sure we're both on the same track, could you tell me what you believe will go on during this part of desensitization?

Client: Well, after relaxation you'll ask me to imagine an item at the bottom of the hierarchy. If I feel any anxiety, I'll raise my finger and you'll ask me to erase the scene and relax.

Counselor: Good. And even if you don't signal anxiety after a little time of imagining an item, I'll tell you to stop and relax. This gives you a sort of breather. Ready to begin?

Client: Yep.

Counselor: OK, first we'll begin with some relaxation. Just get in a comfortable position and close your eyes and relax. . . . Let the tension drain out of your body. . . . Now, to the word *relax*, just let your arms go limp. . . . Now relax your face. . . . Loosen up your face and neck muscles. . . . As I name each muscle group, just use the word *relax* as the signal to let go of all the tension. . . .

Now, Joan, you'll feel even more relaxed by thinking about a pleasant situation. . . . Just imagine you're sitting around a campfire on a cool winter night. . . . You're with some good friends, singing songs and roasting marshmallows [presentation of item 1, or control item]. (Gives Joan about 40 seconds for this image.) Now I'd like you to imagine you're sitting in your room at your desk doing math homework that's pretty routine and is fairly easy [presentation of item 2 in hierarchy]. (Counselor notes duration of presentation on stopwatch. At 25 seconds Joan has not signaled. Counselor records "+25" for item 2.) OK, Joan, stop that image and erase it from your mind. Just concentrate on feeling very relaxed. (Pauses 30 to 60 seconds.) Now I'd like you to again imagine you're in your room sitting at your desk doing math homework that is routine and fairly simple [second presentation of item 2]. (Counselor notes 35 seconds and no signal. Records "+35" on card for item 2.) OK, Joan, now just erase the image from your mind and relax. Let go of all your muscles. (Pause of 40 seconds. Since two successive presentations of this item did not elicit any anxiety, the counselor will move on to item 3.)

Now I'd like you to imagine you're sitting in English class. It's about 10 minutes before the bell. Your mind drifts to math class. You wonder if anything will happen like getting called on [presentation of item 3 in hierarchy]. (Counselor notes duration of presentation with stopwatch. At 12 seconds, Joan's finger goes up. Counselor records "−12" on card for item 3. Waits 3 more seconds.) OK, Joan, just erase that image from your mind. . . . Now relax. Let relaxation flood your body. . . . Think again about being in front of a campfire. (Pauses for about 40 seconds for relaxation.)

Now I'd like you to again imagine you're sitting in English class. It's almost time for the bell. You think about math class and wonder if you'll be called on [second presentation of item 3 in the hierarchy]. (Counselor notes duration with stopwatch. At 30 seconds, Joan has not signaled. Counselor notes "+30" on card.) OK, Joan, now just erase that image and concentrate on relaxing. (Pauses about 40 seconds.) OK,

again imagine yourself sitting in English class. It's just a few minutes before the bell. You think about math class and wonder if you'll be called on [third presentation of item 3]. (At 30 seconds, no signal. Notation of "+30" recorded on card. Since the last two presentations of this item did not evoke anxiety, the counselor can move on to item 4 or can terminate this scene-presentation session on this successfully completed item if time is up or if Joan is restless.)

OK, Joan, stop imagining that scene. Think about a campfire. . . . Just relax. (Another control item can be used for variation. After about 30 to 40 seconds, item 4 is presented or session is terminated.)

If this session had been terminated after the successful completion of item 3, the next scene-presentation session would begin with item 3. Other hierarchy items would be presented in the same manner as in this session. If Joan reported anxiety for three successive presentations of one item, the session would be interrupted, and an adjustment in the hierarchy would be made.

Learning Activity: Scene Presentation

This learning activity is designed to familiarize you with some of the procedural aspects of scene presentation. You can complete this activity by yourself or with a partner who can serve as your client.

Part One

1. Select one of the hierarchies you or your partner developed in the learning activity on hierarchy construction.
2. Select a counterconditioning or coping response to use, such as muscle relaxation or imagery.
3. Administer relaxation or imagery to yourself or to your partner.
4. If you have a partner, explain the use of method R of scene presentation and the signaling system where the person raises a finger when anxiety is noticed or reports a suds rating after the scene is terminated.
5. By yourself, or with your partner, start by presenting the lowest item in the hierarchy. If no anxiety is signaled after a specified duration, instruct your partner to remove the image and relax; then re-present the same scene. Re-

member, two successive no-anxiety presentations are required before presenting the next item. If anxiety is signaled, instruct yourself or your partner to remove the image and relax. After about 30 to 60 seconds, re-present the same item.

6. Select a notation system to use. Record at least the number of times each item was presented, the duration of each presentation, and whether each presentation did or did not evoke anxiety (or the anxiety rating if suds is used).

Part Two

1. Complete the activity again. This time, for step 4, substitute the following: Explain the use of method H of scene presentation and the signaling method where the client raises a finger when anxiety is increased and lowers it when anxiety is decreased.
2. For step 5: Present the next item in the hierarchy. If no anxiety is indicated by a raised finger after about a 30-second presentation, instruct the person to relax; then present the same item again before moving on.
3. If anxiety is indicated, instruct yourself or the person to hold the scene and try to relax away the tension, indicating decreased tension by a lowered finger.

Part Three

1. Again, with yourself or a partner, complete Part One. This time, for step 4, do the following. Instruct the person in method A of scene presentation. Identify one or two coping images you or the person could use. Instruct the person in the signaling method where the word *tense* is used to indicate anxiety and *calm* is used to indicate relaxation.
2. For step 5: Present an item. When you or the person says "tense," instruct yourself or the person to switch to the adaptive alternative (the coping image) and to report relaxation by saying "calm."

Part Four

Reflect on or discuss with your partner the different methods of scene presentation and signaling used in this activity. Which ones did you or your partner feel comfortable or uncomfortable using? Did any method seem less confusing or easier than another? If so, why?

Homework and Follow-Up

Homework is essential to the successful completion of desensitization! Homework may include daily practice of the selected relaxation procedure, visualization of the items completed in the previous session, and exposure to "in vivo" situations.

Assignment of Homework Tasks. Most counselors instruct clients to practice the relaxation method being used once or twice daily. This is especially critical in the early sessions, in which training in the counterconditioning or coping response occurs. In addition, a counselor can assign the client to practice visualizing the items covered in the last session after the relaxation session. Goldfried and Davison (1976) record three to five items on a cassette tape so that clients can administer this assignment themselves. Gradually, "in vivo" homework tasks can be added. As desensitization progresses, the client should be encouraged to participate in real-life situations that correspond to the situations covered in hierarchy-item visualization during the sessions. This is very important in order to facilitate generalization from imagined to real anxiety-producing situations. However, there may be some risk in the client's engaging in a real situation corresponding to a hierarchy item that has not yet been covered in the scene-presentation sessions (Rimm & Masters, 1974).

Homework Log Sheets and Follow-Up. The client should record completion of all homework assignments on daily log sheets. After all desensitization sessions are completed, a follow-up session or contact should be arranged.

Model Dialogue: Homework and Follow-Up

Counselor: Joan, you've been progressing through the hierarchy items very well in our session. I'd like you to try some practice on your own similar to what we've been doing.
Client: OK, what is it?
Counselor: Well, I'm thinking of a hierarchy item

that's near the middle of your list. It's something you've been able to imagine last week and this week without reporting any nervousness. It's the one on your volunteering an answer in class.

Client: You think I should do that?

Counselor: Yes, although there is something I'd like to do first. I will put this item and the two before it on a tape. Each day after you practice your relaxation, I'd like you to use the tape and go over these three items just as we do here. If this goes well for you, then next week we can talk about your actually starting to volunteer a bit more in class.

Client: OK with me.

Counselor: One more thing. Each time you use the tape this week, write it down on a blank log sheet. Also note your tension level before and after the practice with the tape on the 0-to-100 scale. Then I'll see you next week.

All the components of systematic desensitization are summarized in Figure 21-6. You may find this to be a useful review of procedural aspects of this strategy.

Problems Encountered during Desensitization

Although desensitization can be a very effective therapeutic procedure, occasionally problems are encountered that make it difficult or impossible to administer. Sometimes these problems can be minimized or alleviated. At other times, a problem may require the counselor to adopt an alternative strategy.

Wolpe (1973) and Marquis et al. (1973) discuss some of the problems that may be barriers to effective implementation of desensitization. Some of the more common difficulties include problems in relaxation, imagery, and hierarchy arrangement and presentation. An occasional client may not be able to relax. Wolpe treats this problem by hypnosis. Sometimes relaxation can be enhanced with additional training or with a gradual shaping process (R. J. Morris, 1973). An alternative method of relaxation can be used, or a different type of counterconditioning response

can be selected. Another source of difficulty may be the client's inability to generate vivid, clear images. Marquis et al. report that a counselor may be able to strengthen a client's imagery by adding dialogue or a script to the item descriptions. Phillips (1971) has proposed a method of imagery training used to heighten a person's ability to imagine scenes. If imagery continues to be a problem, then "in vivo" desensitization that does not require imagery may be used. Also, the hierarchy may be presented by other means, such as slides (O'Neil & Howell, 1969), video cassette tapes (Caird & Wincze, 1974), or role-play (Hosford, 1969).

An inaccurate hierarchy arrangement, the selection of the wrong theme, and inadequacies in the method of hierarchy presentation also can be trouble spots. Sometimes these problems can be alleviated by reordering the hierarchy, reanalyzing the client's fear, or using some possible variations in the method of scene presentations. Occasionally, clients will benefit from a different form of desensitization. Some of the possible variations of desensitization are discussed in the next section.

Variations of Systematic Desensitization

The desensitization procedure described in this chapter reflects the traditional procedure applied over a series of sessions to an individual client by a counselor, using an individualized hierarchy imagined by the client. The many possible variations of this method of desensitization are described briefly in this section. For more detailed information, we encourage you to consult the references mentioned in this section and those listed in the suggested readings at the end of the chapter.

Massed Desensitization

Desensitization does not have to be administered over a series of spaced sessions in order to be effective. In an attempt to speed up the treatment procedure, some recent investigations have explored the effectiveness of desensitization administered in massed intervals of

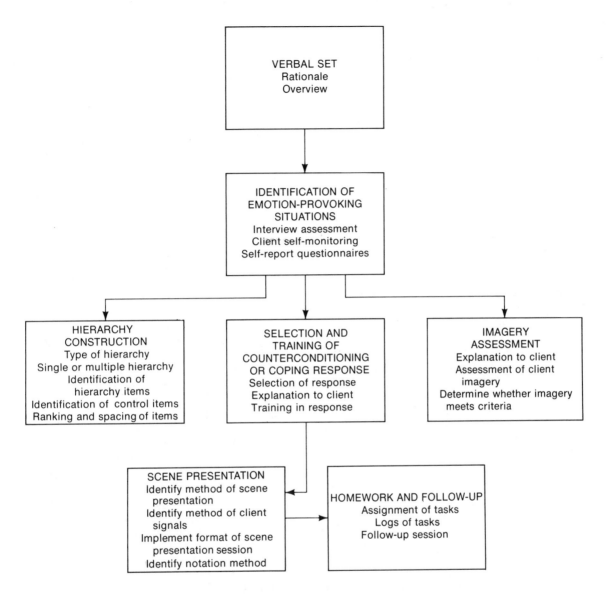

Figure 21-6. Components of Systematic Desensitization

time (Hall & Hinkle, 1972). In massed desensitization, relaxation training may be administered in 1 hour, with hierarchy presentation occurring for 2 to 4 hours (Richardson & Suinn, 1973; Suinn, Edie, & Spinelli, 1970). In some forms of massed desensitization, the clients complete only the highest items in the hierarchy (Richard-

son & Suinn). Desensitization also can be administered in time blocks over a very short span of time, such as 12 hours or 5 days (Dua, 1972). Further investigation is needed to determine the specific potentialities of massed desensitization for different types of clients and varying levels of anxiety (W. H. Cormier & L. S. Cormier, 1975).

Group-Administered Desensitization

Administration of desensitization to a group of clients who share similar concerns or fears also is effective and is more efficient than individual administration. For example, Osterhouse (1976) administered desensitization to a group of test-anxious college students. Other examples of group-administered desensitization have been reported by Paul and Shannon (1966) and Denholtz and Mann (1974). Group-administered desensitization often follows a specific treatment protocol. Standardized relaxation instructions are given to the entire group. Also, a standardized hierarchy is administered to the group en masse.

Self-Administered Desensitization

Some studies of desensitization have indicated that the presence of a counselor is not critical to the effectiveness of the strategy (Cornish & Dilley, 1973; Nawas, Fishman, & Pucel, 1970). G. M. Rosen, R. E. Glasgow, and M. Barrera (1976) found that clients who administered desensitization to themselves continued to improve after posttesting more than clients who were administered desensitization by a counselor. In self-administered desensitization, the client administers the procedure with the assistance of written instructions, audio tapes (Cornish & Dilley, 1973), or a treatment manual such as the one developed by Dawley and Wenrich (1973). Recent evidence has suggested that self-administered desensitization may incur more dropouts than counselor-administered desensitization (Marshall, Presse, & Andrews, 1976). However, this problem seems to be eliminated by even minimal counselor contact, such as a weekly telephone call to the client.

"In Vivo" Desensitization

"In vivo" desensitization involves actual client exposure to the situations in the hierarchy. The client performs or engages in the graded series of situations instead of imagining each item. This variation is used when a client has difficulty using imagery or does not experience anxiety during imagery, or when a client's actual exposure to the situations will have more therapeutic effects. If it is possible actually to expose the client to the feared stimuli, then "in vivo" desensitization is preferable to imagined exposure because it will produce more rapid results and will foster greater generalization. At times, the counselor may accompany the client to the feared situation (Sherman, 1972). "In vivo" desensitization resembles participant modeling (Chapter 16), in which the client performs a graduated series of difficult tasks with the help of induction aids. MacDonald and Bernstein (1974) and Turnage and Logan (1974) have reported clinical cases involving "in vivo" desensitization. O'Neil and Howell (1969) found that snake-phobic clients who were exposed to "in vivo" desensitization achieved greater anxiety reduction at follow-up than clients who imagined hierarchy items or clients who saw the items portrayed on color slides.

The primary procedural problem associated with "in vivo" desensitization involves adequate use and control of a counterconditioning response (Marquis et al., 1973). Sometimes it is difficult for a client to achieve a state of deep relaxation while simultaneously performing an activity. However, it is not always necessary to use a counterconditioning response to decrease the client's anxiety in threatening situations. Often exposure alone will result in sufficient anxiety reduction, particularly if the exposure occurs in graduated amounts and with induction aids.

Summary

Historically, desensitization probably has the longest track record of any of the therapeutic strategies presented in this book. Its results are well and frequently documented. Yet there is far more controversy surrounding its use than existed 10 years ago, primarily because of alternative explanations to account for its results. We do not believe that desensitization has outlived its usefulness as a method for reducing extreme anxiety or conditioned emotional reactions. But today, desensitization does not occupy a singular place in many practitioners' repertoires of possible anxiety-reduction methods. Its use as an anxiety-management strategy currently may be supplemented with or replaced by a variety of other methods for reducing and coping with fears and tension. And, as Krumboltz and Thoresen (1976) assert, the aim of *any* anxiety-reduction strategy should be to teach a client self-control skills so that future

stress does not push the client's anxiety beyond "tolerable limits" (p. 247).

Part One

Objective 1 asks you to fill in six out of seven major components of systematic desensitization on a blank flow chart. Use this flow chart to identify these components.

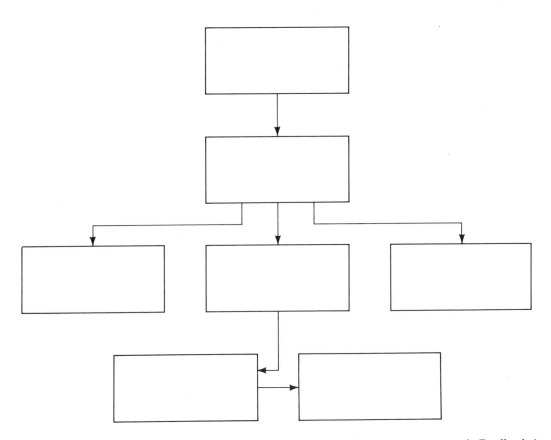

Feedback follows the evaluation.

Part Two

Objective 2 states that you should be able to identify accurately at least three out of four hierarchies by type. Read each hierarchy carefully, then identify on a piece of paper whether the hierarchy is spatio-

temporal, thematic, or personal. Feedback is provided at the end of the evaluation.

Hierarchy 1 (fear of heights)
1. You are walking along the sidewalk. It is on a completely level street.
2. You are walking along the sidewalk, ascending. At the top of the street, you look down and realize you've climbed a hill.

3. You are climbing a ladder up to a second-story window.
4. You are riding in a car, and the road curves higher and higher.
5. You are riding in a car and you look outside. You notice you are driving on the edge of a good-sized hill.
6. You are starting to climb up to the top of a fire tower. You are halfway up. You look down and see how far you've climbed.
7. You are climbing a ladder up to the roof of a three-story house.
8. You have climbed to the top of a fire tower and look down.
9. You are riding in a car and are at the edge of a cliff on a mountain.
10. You are at the very top of a mountain, looking down into the surrounding valley.

Hierarchy 2 (fear of being rejected)
1. You speak to a stranger on the street. He doesn't hear you.
2. You go into a department store and request some information from one of the clerks. The clerk snaps at you in response.
3. You ask a stranger to give you change. She gives you a sarcastic reply.
4. You ask a casual acquaintance to lend you a book. He refuses.
5. You ask a friend over to dinner. The friend is too busy to come.
6. You apply for a membership in a social club, and your application is denied.
7. You are competing for a job. You and another person are interviewed; the other person is hired, you are not chosen.
8. You have an argument with your best friend. She leaves suddenly. You don't hear from her for a while.
9. You have an argument with your husband. Your husband says he would rather do things alone than with you.
10. Your husband asks you for a divorce and says he doesn't love you any more.

Hierarchy 3 (loss of a close relationship)
1. You remember a warm, starry night. You ask this woman you love to marry you. She accepts. You are very happy.
2. The two of you are traveling together soon after your marriage, camping out and traveling around in a van.
3. The two of you are running in the water together at the beach and having a good time being together.

4. You and this person are eating dinner together at home.
5. The two of you are disagreeing over how to spend money. She wants to save it; you are arguing to use some of it for camping supplies.
6. The two of you are arguing over your child. She wants the child to go with you on all trips; you want a babysitter occasionally.
7. The two of you are starting to eat some meals apart. You are working late to avoid coming home for dinner.
8. She is wrapped up in her social activities; you, in your work. On the weekends you go your separate ways.
9. You have a discussion about your relationship and separate activities. You start sleeping on the couch.
10. The two of you go to see a lawyer to initiate discussion about a separation.

Hierarchy 4 (fear of giving speeches)
1. Your instructor casually mentions a required speech to be given by the end of the course.
2. Your instructor passes around a sign-up sheet for the speeches. You sign up.
3. You talk about the speech with some of your classmates. You aren't sure what to say.
4. You go to the library to look up some resource material for your speech. You don't find too much.
5. Some of your classmates start to give speeches. You think about how good their speeches are and wonder how yours will be.
6. It is a week before the speech. You're spending a lot of time working on it.
7. It is the day before the speech. You're going over your notes religiously.
8. It is the night before the speech. You lie awake thinking about it.
9. It is the next morning. You wake up and remember it is speech day. You don't feel hungry at breakfast.
10. Later that morning you're walking to speech class. A classmate comes up and says, "Well, I guess you're on today."
11. You're sitting in speech class. The instructor will call on you any moment. You keep going over your major points.

Part Three

Objective 3 asks you to identify and describe at least 9 out of 11 procedural steps of desensitization using a written client case description. Read this case description carefully; then respond by identifying and describing the 11 items listed after the description.

Your client is a fifth-grade boy at a local elementary school. This year, the client's younger sister has entered first grade at the same school. After a few weeks at school, your client, Ricky, began to complain about school to his teacher and parents. He would come to school and get sick. His parents would come and take him home. After a medical check-up, the doctor can find nothing physically wrong with Ricky. Yet Ricky continues either to get sick at school or to wake up sick in the morning. He appears to be better on weekends. He says he hates school and it makes him sick to his stomach to have to go. On occasion, he has vomited in the morning. The parents report that it is getting harder and harder to get Ricky to attend school. Suppose you were to use desensitization as one strategy in this case to help Ricky overcome his tension and avoidance of school. Identify and describe how you would implement the following 11 steps of desensitization with Ricky. Adapt your language to words that a 10-year-old could understand.

1. your rationale of desensitization
2. your description of an overview of desensitization
3. a method for helping Ricky identify the anxiety-provoking situations about school
4. the type of hierarchy that would be used with Ricky
5. a ranking method Ricky could use to arrange the hierarchy items
6. an appropriate counterconditioning or coping response you could train Ricky to use
7. a method of assessing Ricky's imagery capacity
8. a method of scene presentation you would use with Ricky
9. a method Ricky could use for signaling during scene presentation
10. a notation method you might use to keep track of hierarchy presentation
11. an example of one homework task associated with desensitization you might assign to Ricky to complete

Feedback follows the evaluation.

Part Four

Objective 4 asks you to demonstrate at least 22 out of 28 steps of systematic desensitization with a role-play client. Several role-play interviews may be required in order for you to include all the major procedural components of desensitization. Use the Interview Checklist for Systematic Desensitization at the end of the chapter as an assessment tool.

Feedback: Post Evaluation

Part One

Refer back to the flow chart of the seven major components of systematic desensitization found in Figure 21-1 on p. 434.

Part Two

1. Spatio-temporal. The items are arranged by increasing distance (height) off the ground.
2. Thematic. The items are arranged around the theme of rejection.
3. Personal. The items are arranged from pleasant to unpleasant memories of an ex-spouse.
4. Spatio-temporal. The items are arranged by time; as the time approaching the situation diminishes, the fear intensifies.

Part Three

Here are some possible descriptions of the 11 procedural steps of desensitization you were asked to identify and describe. See if your responses are in some way similar to these.

1. Rationale: "Ricky, it seems like it's very hard for you to go to school now or even think about school without feeling sick. There are some things about school that upset you this much. We can work together to find out what bothers you, and I can help you learn to be able to go to school without feeling so upset or sick to your stomach, so you can go to school again and feel OK about it. How does that sound?"
2. Overview: "There are several things you and I will do together. First we'll talk about the things about school that upset you. I'll ask you to think about these situations, only instead of feeling upset when you do, I'll show you a way to stay calm and keep the butterflies out of your stomach. It will take a lot of practice in this room, but after a while you will be able to go back to your class and feel calm and OK about it!"
3. Method for identifying the anxiety-provoking situations:
    a. use of interview leads such as "Ricky, what do you do in school that makes you feel sick? What about school makes you want to stay at home? What happens at school that bothers you? When do you feel most upset about school?"
    b. use of client self-monitoring: "Ricky, could you keep a chart for me this week? Each time you feel upset about school, mark down what has happened or what you're thinking about that makes you feel upset or sick."
4. Type of hierarchy: A thematic hierarchy would be used. One hierarchy might consist of school-related anxiety-provoking situations. Depending on the anxiety-provoking situations identified, another thematic hierarchy may emerge, dealing with jealousy. It is possible that the avoidance of school is a signal that Ricky really fears being upstaged by his younger sister.
5. Ranking method: Because of Ricky's age, an easy ranking method should be used. Probably it would be easiest to start with the low, medium, high method. You would ask Ricky to sort the cards of the hierarchy items into three piles: a low pile (things that only upset him a little), a medium pile (things that upset him somewhat), and a high pile (things that really upset him). You might give him a pictorial or visual "anchor point" to describe the three different piles. The low pile is like going to the dentist to have your teeth examined. The middle pile is like going to the dentist to have your teeth cleaned. The high pile is like going to the dentist to have a cavity in your tooth filled.
6. Counterconditioning or coping response: Muscle relaxation can be used easily with a child Ricky's age as long as you just show him (by modeling) the different muscle groups and the way to tighten and let go of a muscle.
7. Method of imagery assessment: Ask Ricky to tell you some daydreams he has, or some things he loves to do. Before and after a relaxation-training session, ask him to imagine or pretend he is doing one of these things. Then have him describe the details of his imagined scene. Children often have a capacity for more vivid and descriptive imagery than adults.

8. Method of scene presentation: We would probably try method R or method A. Method R is simple to use and easily understood (stop imagining _____; now relax). Method A could be useful, since Ricky is legally required to attend school and does need to learn to cope with it. Method H may be less easily understood by a child, who might find it difficult to know what is meant by "hold the image and relax away the tension."

9. Signaling method: Again, you want to suggest something that is easily understood and used by Ricky. Perhaps the use of *word* signals might minimize any confusion. You would instruct him to say "tense" when he's upset or anxious and "calm" when he's less bothered or more relaxed.

10. Notation method: The easiest notation method might be to use each hierarchy card and note the number of times each item is presented, the duration of each presentation, and an indication of whether Ricky did or did not report being "tense" during or after the item. This notation system looks like this:

Item No. _____ Date _____
Item description
+ 10 − 15 + 15 + 20

The item was presented 4 times; the numbers 10, 15, 15, and 20 refer to the duration of each presentation; the + indicates no anxiety report; the − indicates a "tense" signal.

11. Examples of possible·homework tasks:
   a. a list of anxiety-related situations
   b. practice of muscle relaxation
   c. practice of items covered in the interview, possibly with the use of coping imagery
   d. exposure to certain school-related "in vivo" situations

Part Four

You or an observer can rate your desensitization interviews using the Interview Checklist for Systematic Desensitization that follows.

Interview Checklist for Systematic Desensitization

Instructions to observer: Listed below are some procedural steps of systematic desensitization. Check which of these steps were used by the counselor in implementing this procedure. Some possible examples of these leads are described in the right column of the checklist.

Checklist	Examples of Counselor Leads
I. *Verbal Set*	
_____ 1. Counselor gives client rationale for desensitization, clearly explaining how it works.	"This procedure is based on the idea that you can learn to replace your fear (or other conditioned emotion) in certain situations with a better or more desirable response, such as relaxation or general feelings of comfort."
	"You have described some situations where you have learned to react with fear (or some other emotion). This procedure will give you skills to help you cope with these situations so they don't continue to be so stressful."

Checklist	*Examples of Counselor Leads*
_____ 2. Counselor describes brief overview of desensitization procedure.	"There are three basic things that will happen—first, training you to relax, next, constructing a list of situations in which you feel anxious, and finally, having you imagine scenes from this list, starting with low-anxiety scenes, while you are deeply relaxed."
	"First you will learn how to relax, and to notice tension so you can use it as a signal to relax. Then we'll identify situations that, to varying degrees, upset you or make you anxious. Starting with the least discomforting situations, you will practice the skill of relaxation as a way to cope with the stress."
_____ 3. Counselor checks to see whether client is willing to use strategy.	"Are you ready to try this now?"
II. *Identification of Emotion-Provoking Situations* _____ 4. Counselor initiates at least one of the following means of identifying anxiety-provoking stimulus situations:	
_____ a. interview assessment through problem leads	"When do you notice that you feel most _____?"
	"Where are you when this happens?"
	"What are you usually doing when you feel _____?"
	"What types of situations seem to bring on this feeling?"
_____ b. client self-monitoring	"This week I'd like you to keep track of any situation that seems to bring on these feelings. On your log, write down where you are, what you're doing, who you're with, and the intensity of these feelings."
_____ c. self-report questionnaires	"One way that we might learn more about some of the specific situations that you find stressful is for you to complete this short questionnaire. There are no right or wrong answers—just describe how you usually feel or react in the situations presented."

Checklist	Examples of Counselor Leads
_____ 5. Counselor continues to assess anxiety-provoking situations until client identifies some specific situations.	"Let's continue with this exploration until we get a handle on some things. Right now you've said that you get nervous and upset around certain kinds of people. Can you tell me some types or characteristics of people that bother you or make you anxious almost always?" "OK, good, so you notice you're always very anxious around people who can evaluate or criticize you, like a boss or teacher."

III. *Hierarchy Construction*

_____ 6. Counselor identifies a type of hierarchy to be constructed with client:	"Now we're going to make a list of these anxiety-provoking situations and fill in some details and arrange these in an order, starting with the least anxiety-provoking situation all the way to the most anxiety-provoking one."
_____ a. spatio-temporal	"Since you get more and more anxious as the time for the speech gets closer and closer, we'll construct these items by closer and closer times to the speech."
_____ b. thematic	"We'll arrange these items according to the different kinds of situations in which people criticize you—depending on who does it, what it's about, and so on."
_____ c. personal	"We'll construct a hierarchy of items that represent your memories about her, starting with pleasant memories and proceeding to unpleasant or painful memories."
_____ d. combination	
_____ 7. Counselor identifies the number of hierarchies to be developed:	
_____ a. single hierarchy	"We will take all these items that reflect a number of different situations that are anxiety-producing for you and arrange them in one list."
_____ b. multiple hierarchies	"Since there are a number of different types of situations you find stressful, we'll construct one list for situations involving criticism and another list for situations involving social events."
_____ 8. Counselor initiates identification of hierarchy items through one or more methods:	"I'd like us to write down some items that describe each of these anxiety-provoking scenes with quite a bit of detail."
_____ a. interview questions (*not* when client is engaged in relaxation)	"Describe for me what your mother could say that would bother you most. How would she say it? Now who, other than your mother, could criticize you and make you feel worse? What things are you most sensitive to being criticized about?"

Checklist	Examples of Counselor Leads

_____ b. client completion of note cards (homework)

"This week I'd like you to add to this list of items. I'm going to give you some blank index cards. Each time you think of another item that makes you get anxious or upset about criticism, write it down on one card."

_____ 9. Counselor continues to explore hierarchy items until items are identified that meet the following criteria:

    _____ a. Some items, if carried out "in vivo," are under client's control (do not require instigation from others).

"Can you think of some items that—if you actually were to carry them out—would be things you could initiate without having to depend on someone else to make the situation happen?"

    _____ b. Items are concrete and specific.

"OK, now just to say that you get nervous at social functions is a little vague. Give me some details about a social function in which you might feel pretty comfortable and one that could make you feel extremely nervous."

    _____ c. Items are similar to or represent past, present, or future situations that _have_ or _could_ provoke the emotional response from client.

"Think of items that represent things that have made you anxious before or currently— and things that could make you anxious if you encountered them in the future."

    _____ d. Items have sampled broad range of situations in which emotional response occurs.

"Can you identify items representing different types of situations that seem to bring on these feelings?"

    _____ e. Items represent different levels of emotion aroused by representative stimulus situations.

"Let's see if we have items here that reflect different amounts of the anxiety you feel. Here are some items that don't make you too anxious. What about ones that are a little more anxiety-provoking, up to ones where you feel panicky?"

_____ 10. Counselor asks client to identify several control items (neutral, non-emotion-arousing).

"Sometimes it's helpful to imagine some scenes that aren't related to things that make you feel anxious. Could you describe something you could imagine that would be pleasant and relaxing?"

_____ 11. Counselor explains purpose of ranking and spacing items according to increasing levels of arousal.

"It may take a little time, but you will rank these hierarchy items from least anxiety-producing to most anxiety-producing. This gives us an order to the hierarchy that is gradual, so we can work just with more manageable situations before moving on to more stressful ones."

_____ 12. Counselor asks client to arrange hierarchy items in order of increasing arousal, using one of the following ranking methods, and explains method to client:

"Now I would like you to take the items and arrange them in order of increasing anxiety, using the following method."

Checklist	Examples of Counselor Leads
_____ a. rank-ordering	"We have each hierarchy item written on a separate note card. Go through the cards and rank-order them according to increasing levels of anxiety. Items that don't provoke much anxiety go on the bottom, followed by items that are successively more anxiety-producing."
_____ b. "suds"	"I'd like you to arrange these items using a 0-to-100 scale. 0 represents total relaxation and 100 is comparable to complete panic. If an item doesn't give you any anxiety, give it a 0. If it is just a little stressful, maybe a 15 or 20. Very stressful items would get a higher number, depending on how stressful."
_____ c. Low, medium, high ordering	"Take the items written on these cards and sort them into one of three groups. One group, small amounts of anxiety. The second group would consist of items provoking an average amount of anxiety. The third group would consist of items which are very or intensely anxiety-producing for you."
_____ 13. Counselor adds or deletes items if necessary in order to achieve reasonable spacing of items in hierarchy.	"Let's see, at the lower end of the hierarchy you have many items. We might drop out a few of these. But you only have three items at the upper end, so we have some big gaps here. Can you think of a situation provoking a little bit more anxiety than this item but not quite as much as this next one? We can add that in here."

IV. *Selection and Training of Counterconditioning or Coping Response*

_____ 14. Counselor selects appropriate counterconditioning or coping response to use to countercondition or cope with anxiety (or other conditioned emotion):	"Now I believe it would help to find a response to help you counteract the anxiety, such as _____."
_____ a. deep muscle relaxation	(contrasting tensed and relaxed muscles)
_____ b. emotive imagery	(evoking pleasurable scenes in imagination)
_____ c. meditation	(focusing on breathing and counting)
_____ d. coping thoughts or statements	(concentrating on coping or productive thoughts incompatible with self-defeating ones)
_____ 15. Counselor explains purpose of particular response selected and describes its role in desensitization.	"This response is like a substitute for anxiety. It will take time to learn it, but it will help to decrease your anxiety so that you can face rather than avoid these feared situations."
	"This training will help you recognize the onset of tension. You can use these cues you learn as a signal to relax away the tension."

Checklist	Examples of Counselor Leads

_____ 16. Counselor trains client in use of counterconditioning or coping response. Daily practice of this response also is suggested.

"We will spend several sessions learning this so you can use it as a way to relax. This relaxation on your part is a very important part of this procedure. After you practice this here, I'd like you to do this at home two times each day over the next few weeks. Each practice will make it easier for you to relax."

_____ 17. Counselor asks client before and after each training session to rate felt level of anxiety or arousal.

"Using a scale from 0 to 100, with 0 being complete relaxation and 100 being intense anxiety, where would you rate yourself now?"

_____ 18. Counselor continues with training until client can discriminate different levels of anxiety and can use nonanxiety response to achieve 10 or less rating on 0-to-100 scale.

"Let's continue with this until you feel this training really has an effect on your relaxation state after you use it."

V. _Imagery Assessment_

_____ 19. Counselor explains use of imagery in desensitization.

"In this procedure, I'll ask you to imagine each hierarchy item as if you were actually there. We have found that imagining a situation can be very similar to actually being in the situation. Becoming desensitized to anxiety you feel while imagining an unpleasant situation will transfer to the real situations, too."

_____ 20. Counselor assesses client's capacity to generate vivid images by:

"It might be helpful to see how you react to using your imagination."

_____ a. presenting control items when client is using a relaxation response

"Now that you're relaxed, get a picture in your mind of sitting in the sun on a warm day. The sky is very blue, not a cloud in it. The grass and trees are green. You can feel the warmth of the sun on your body."

_____ b. presenting hierarchy items when client is not using a relaxation response

"OK, just imagine that you're at this party. You don't know anyone. Get a picture of yourself and the other people there. It's a very large room."

_____ c. asking client to describe imagery evoked in a and b.

"Can you describe what you imagined? What were the colors you saw? What did you hear or smell?"

_____ 21. Counselor, with client's assistance, determines whether client's imagery meets the following criteria and, if so, decides to continue with desensitization:

_____ a. Client is able to imagine scene concretely with details.

"Were you able to imagine the scene clearly? How many details can you remember?"

Checklist	Examples of Counselor Leads

_____ b. Client is able to imagine scene as participant, not onlooker.

"When you imagined the scene, did you feel as if you were actually there and involved— or did it seem like you were just an observer, perhaps watching it happen to someone else?"

_____ c. Client is able to switch scene on and off upon instruction.

"How soon were you able to get an image after I gave it to you? When did you stop the image after I said _Stop_?"

_____ d. Client is able to hold scene without drifting off or revising it.

"Did you ever feel like you couldn't concentrate on the scene and started to drift off?"

"Did you ever change anything about the scene during the time you imagined it?"

_____ e. Client shows no evidence of other difficulties.

"What else did you notice that interfered with getting a good picture of this in your mind?"

VI. _Hierarchy Scene Presentation_

_____ 22. Counselor identifies and explains method of scene presentation to be used:

"I'd like to explain exactly how we will proceed. I'm going to present an item in the hierarchy to you after we go through relaxation. Here is what I'll instruct you to do."

_____ a. Method R—client will be instructed to stop image when anxiety is felt and to relax.

"When you tell me that you feel some anxiety while imagining the scene, I'll ask you to stop or remove the scene from your mind. Then I'll instruct you to relax. You'll have some time to relax before I ask you to imagine the scene another time."

_____ b. Method H—client will be instructed to hold image when anxiety is felt and to relax away tension.

"When you indicate that you feel some anxiety while you're imagining a scene, I'll ask you to continue to visualize the scene, but to relax away the tension as you do so."

_____ c. Method A—client will be instructed to switch image to coping image when anxiety is felt.

"When you indicate that you feel some anxiety while you're imagining the scene, I'll ask you to switch the scene to a type of coping scene and to concentrate for a few minutes on the coping image."

_____ 23. Counselor identifies and explains method of signaling to be used:

"It's very important that we work out a signaling system for you to use when I present the hierarchy items to you. I'll explain how you can signal. Make sure to tell me if it doesn't seem clear."

_____ a. Client is instructed to raise index finger when clear image is visualized.

"When I present an item, I'd like you to raise your index finger slightly at the point when you obtain a clear picture of the scene in your mind."

Checklist	Examples of Counselor Leads
_____ b. Client is instructed to raise index finger when anxiety is noticed while visualizing.	"I'll ask you to imagine an item. If, at any point during this imagination, you feel tension, signal this by raising your index finger."
_____ c. Client is instructed to raise finger to signal increased anxiety and to lower finger to indicate decreased anxiety.	"When you feel anxiety building up as you imagine the item, signal this by raising your finger. As the anxiety decreases and calmness takes over, signal this by lowering your finger."
_____ d. Client is instructed to indicate anxiety with the word *tense* and to signal relaxation with the word *calm*.	"When, during the visualization of an item, you notice anxiety, say 'tense.' When you feel calmer and more relaxed, say 'calm.'"
_____ 24. For each session of scene presentation:	
_____ a. Counselor precedes scene presentation with muscle relaxation or other procedures to help client achieve relaxation before scenes are presented.	"Let your whole body become heavier and heavier as all your muscles relax. . . . Feel the tension draining out of your body. . . . Relax the muscles of your hands and arms. . . ."
_____ b. Counselor begins initial session with lowest (least anxiety-provoking) item in hierarchy and for successive sessions begins with last item successfully completed at previous session.	"I'm going to start this first session with the item that is at the bottom of the hierarchy." "Today we'll begin with the item we ended on last week for a review."
_____ c. Counselor describes item and asks client to imagine it for 20 to 40 seconds.	"Just imagine you are sitting in the classroom waiting for the test to be passed to you, wondering how much you can remember." (Counts 20 to 40 seconds, then instructs client in either R, H, or A method.)
_____ (1.) If client held image and did not signal anxiety, counselor instructs client to stop image and relax for 30 to 60 seconds.	"Now, stop visualizing this scene and just take a little time to relax. Think of sitting in the sun on a warm day, with blue sky all around you."
_____ (2.) If client indicated anxiety during or after visualizing scene, counselor uses method R, H, or A, selected in no. 22.	(R) "Now remove the image and just relax." (H) "Now hold the image but relax away the tension." (A) "Switch the image to the coping one we discussed earlier."
_____ d. After pause of 30 to 60 seconds between items, counselor presents each item to client a second time.	"Now I want you to imagine the same thing. Concentrate on being very relaxed, then imagine that you are sitting in the classroom waiting for the test to be passed to you, wondering how much you can remember."

_____ e. Each item is successfully completed (with no anxiety) at least two successive times (more for items at top of hierarchy) before new item is presented.	"I'm going to present this scene to you once more now. Just relax, then imagine that. . . ."
_____ f. If an item elicits anxiety after three presentations, counselor makes some adjustments in hierarchy or in client's visualization process.	"Let's see what might be bogging us down here. Do you notice that you are drifting away from the scene while you're imagining it— or revising it in any way? Can you think of a situation we might add here that is just a little bit less stressful for you than this one?"
_____ g. Standardized instructions are used for each phase of scene presentation; reinforcement of *just* the no-anxiety items is avoided.	"OK, I see that was not stressful for you. Just concentrate on relaxing a minute." "What was your feeling of anxiety on the 0-to-100 scale? 20. OK, I want you to just relax for a minute, then I'll give you the same scene."
_____ h. Each scene-presentation session ends with a successfully completed item (no anxiety for at least two successive presentations).	"OK, let's end today with this item we've just been working on, since you reported 5 suds during the last two presentations."
_____ i. Each session is terminated:	"We've done quite a bit of work today. Just spend a few minutes relaxing, and then we will stop."
_____ (1.) when three to five items are completed	
_____ (2.) after 15 to 20 minutes of scene presentation	
_____ (3.) after indications of client restlessness or distractibility.	
_____ 25. Counselor uses written recording method during scene presentation to note client's progress through hierarchy.	"As we go through this session, I'm going to make some notes about the number of times we work with each item and your anxiety rating of each presentation."

VII. *Homework and Follow-Up*

_____ 26. Counselor assigns homework tasks that correspond with treatment progress of desensitization procedure:	"There is something I'd like you to do this week on a daily basis at home."
_____ a. daily practice of selected relaxation procedure	"Practice this relaxation procedure two times each day in a quiet place."
_____ b. visualization of items successfully completed at previous session	"On this tape there are three items we covered this week. Next week at home, after your relaxation sessions, practice imagining each of these three items."

Checklist	Examples of Counselor Leads
_____ c. exposure to "in vivo" situations corresponding to successfully completed hierarchy items	"You are ready now to actually go to a party by yourself. We have gotten to a point where you can imagine doing this without any stress."
_____ 27. Counselor instructs client to record completion of homework on daily log sheets.	"Each time you complete a homework practice, record it on your log sheets."
_____ 28. Counselor arranges for follow-up session or check-in.	"Check in with me in 2 weeks to give me a progress report."

Consultant Comments: _____

Suggested Readings

Reported Uses of Desensitization

Boudreau, L., & Jeffery, C. Stuttering treated by desensitization. *Journal of Behavior Therapy and Experimental Psychiatry*, 1973, *4*, 209–212.

Cotharin, R., & Mikulas, W. Systematic desensitization of racial emotional responses. *Journal of Behavior Therapy and Experimental Psychiatry*, 1975, *6*, 347–348.

Furst, J. B., & Cooper, A. Combined use of imaginal and interoceptive stimuli in desensitizing fear of heart attacks. *Journal of Behavior Therapy and Experimental Psychiatry*, 1970, *1*, 87–89.

Hearn, M., & Evans, D. Anger and reciprocal inhibition therapy. *Psychological Reports*, 1972, *30*, 943–948.

Wish, P., Hasazi, J., & Jurgela, A. Automated direct conditioning of a childhood phobia. *Journal of Behavior Therapy and Experimental Psychiatry*, 1973, *4*, 279–284.

Comparison of Desensitization to Other Approaches

Curran, J. P. Social skills training and systematic desensitization in reducing dating anxiety. *Behaviour Research and Therapy*, 1975, *13*, 65–68.

Horne, A. M., & Matson, J. L. A comparison of modeling, desensitization, flooding, study skills, and control groups for reducing test anxiety. *Behavior Therapy*, 1977, *8*, 1–8.

Kanter, N. J., & Goldfried, M. R. Relative effectiveness of rational restructuring and self-control desensitization in the reduction of interpersonal anxiety. *Behavior Therapy*, 1979, *10*, 472–490.

Meichenbaum, D., Gilmore, J., & Fedoravicius, A. Group insight versus group desensitization in treating speech anxiety. *Journal of Consulting and Clinical Psychology*, 1971, *36*, 410–421.

Russell, R. K., & Wise, F. Treatment of speech anxiety by cue-controlled relaxation and desensitization with professional and paraprofessional counselors. *Journal of Counseling Psychology*, 1976, *23*, 583–586.

Shaw, D. W., & Thoresen, C. E. Effects of modeling and desensitization in reducing dentist phobia. *Journal of Counseling Psychology*, 1974, *21*, 415–420.

Theoretical Explanations of Desensitization

Davison, G. C., & Wilson, G. T. Processes of fear-reduction in systematic desensitization: Cognitive and social reinforcement factors in humans. *Behavior Therapy*, 1973, *4*, 1–21.

Denney, D. R., & Rupert, P. Desensitization and self-control in the treatment of test anxiety. *Journal of Counseling Psychology*, 1977, *24*, 272–280.

Goldfried, M. R. Systematic desensitization as training in self-control. *Journal of Consulting and Clinical Psychology*, 1971, *37*, 228–234.

Kazdin, A. E., & Wilcoxon, L. A. Systematic desensitization and nonspecific treatment effects: A methodological evaluation. *Psychological Bulletin*, 1976, *83*, 729–758.

Lomont, J. F. Reciprocal inhibition or extinction? *Behaviour Research and Therapy*, 1965, *3*, 209–219.

Spiegler, M., Cooley, E., Marshall, G., Prince, H., Puckett, S., & Skenazy, J. A self-control versus a counterconditioning paradigm for systematic desensitization: An experimental comparison. *Journal of Counseling Psychology*, 1976, *23*, 83–86.

Tori, C., & Worell, L. Reduction of human avoidant behavior: A comparison of counterconditioning, expectancy, and cognitive information approaches. *Journal of Consulting and Clinical Psychology*, 1973, *41*, 269–278.

van Egeren, L. F. Psychophysiological aspects of systematic desensitization: Some outstanding issues. *Behaviour Research and Therapy*, 1971, *9*, 65–77.

Wolpe, J. *Psychotherapy by reciprocal inhibition*. Stanford, Calif.: Stanford University Press, 1958.

Wolpe, J. *Theme and variations: A behavior therapy casebook*. New York: Pergamon Press, 1976. Chap. 2, The reciprocal inhibition theme and the emergence of its role in psychotherapy, 11–30.

Components of Desensitization

Evans, I. M. A handy record-card for systematic desensitization hierarchy items. *Journal of Behavior Therapy and Experimental Psychiatry*, 1974, *5*, 43–46.

Goldfried, M. R. Systematic desensitization as training in self-control. *Journal of Consulting and Clinical Psychology*, 1971, *37*, 228–234.

Marquis, J., Morgan, W., & Piaget, G. *A guidebook for systematic desensitization* (3rd ed.). Palo Alto, Calif.: Veterans' Workshop, 1973.

Morris, R. J. Fear reduction methods. In F. H. Kanfer & A. P. Goldstein (Eds.), *Helping people change*. New York: Pergamon Press, 1975.

Rimm, D. C., & Masters, J. C. *Behavior therapy: Techniques and empirical findings*. New York: Academic Press, 1974. Chap. 2, Systematic desensitization, 43–80.

Wolpe, J. *The practice of behavior therapy* (2nd ed.). New York: Pergamon Press, 1973. Chap. 6, Systematic desensitization, 95–140.

Problems Encountered during Desensitization

Marquis, J., Morgan, W., & Piaget, G. *A guidebook for systematic desensitization* (3rd ed.). Palo Alto, Calif.: Veterans' Workshop, 1973. Troubleshooting, 14–17.

Variations in Systematic Desensitization

Dawley, H. H., & Wenrich, W. W. *Patient's manual for systematic desensitization*. Palo Alto, Calif.: Veterans' Workshop, 1973.

Denholtz, M., & Mann, E. An audiovisual program for group desensitization. *Journal of Behavior Therapy and Experimental Psychiatry*, 1974, *5*, 27–29.

Donner, L., & Guerney, B. Automated group desensitization for test anxiety. *Behaviour Research and Therapy*, 1969, *7*, 1–13.

Dua, P. S. Group desensitization of a phobia with three massing procedures. *Journal of Counseling Psychology*, 1972, *19*, 125–129.

Marshall, W., Presse, L., & Andrews, W. A self-administered program for public speaking anxiety. *Behaviour Research and Therapy*, 1976, *14*, 33–39.

McGlynn, F., Wilson, A., & Linder, L. Systematic desensitization of snake-avoidance with individualized and non-individualized hierarchies. *Journal of Behavior Therapy and Experimental Psychiatry*, 1970, *7*, 201–204.

O'Neil, D., & Howell, R. Three modes of hierarchy presentation in systematic desensitization therapy. *Behaviour Research and Therapy*, 1969, *7*, 289–294.

Osterhouse, R. A. Group systematic desensitization of test anxiety. In J. D. Krumboltz & C. E. Thoresen (Eds.), *Counseling methods*. New York: Holt, Rinehart & Winston, 1976.

Richardson, F. C., & Suinn, R. M. A comparison of traditional systematic desensitization, accelerated massed desensitization, and anxiety management training in the treatment of mathematics anxiety. *Behavior Therapy*, 1973, *4*, 212–218.

Sherman, A. R. Real-life exposure as a primary therapeutic factor in the desensitization treatment of fear. *Journal of Abnormal Psychology*, 1972, *79*, 19–28.

Wolpe, J. *The practice of behavior therapy* (2nd ed.). New York: Pergamon Press, 1973. Chap. 7, Variants of systematic desensitization, 141–162.

Chapter 22
Self-Management Programs and Self-Monitoring

Self-management is a process in which clients direct their own behavior change with any one therapeutic strategy or a combination of strategies. For self-management to occur, the client must take charge of manipulating either internal or external variables to effect a desired change. Although a counselor may instigate self-management procedures and train the client in them, the client assumes the control for carrying out the process. Kanfer (1975) distinguishes between therapist-managed procedures, in which a majority of the "therapeutic work" occurs *during* the interviews, and self-managed (or client-managed) procedures, in which most of the work takes place *between* the sessions (p. 310).

Self-management is a relatively recent phenomenon in counseling, and reports of clinical applications and theoretical descriptions have burgeoned since 1970. During this time, definitions of self-management have remained unclear, partly because of terminological confusion. Self-change methods have been referred to as self-control (Cautela, 1969; Thoresen & Mahoney, 1974); self-regulation (Kanfer, 1970, 1975); and self-management (M. J. Mahoney, 1971, 1972). We prefer the label *self-management* because it suggests conducting and handling one's life in a somewhat skilled manner. Also, the term *self-management* avoids the concepts of inhibition and restraint that often are associated

with the words *control* and *regulation* (Thoresen & Mahoney).

In using self-management procedures, a client directs change efforts by modifying aspects of the environment or by manipulating and administering consequences (Jones, Nelson, & Kazdin, 1977, p. 151). Four self-management strategies are described in this chapter and in Chapter 23: self-monitoring, stimulus control, self-reward, and self-contracting. These four strategies typically are classified as self-management because in each procedure the client, in a self-directed fashion, alters or controls antecedents and consequences to produce the desired behavioral changes. However, none of these strategies is entirely independent of environmental variables and external sources of influence (Jones et al., 1977).

In addition to these four self-management procedures, it should be noted that a client can use virtually any helping strategy in a self-directed or self-administered manner. For example, a client could apply relaxation training to manage anxiety by using a relaxation-training audio tape without the assistance of a counselor. In fact, some degree of client self-management may be a necessary component of every successful therapy case. For example, in all the other helping strategies described in this book, some elements of self-management are suggested in the procedural guidelines for strategy implementation. These self-managed aspects of any therapy procedure typically include:

1. client self-directed practice in the interview
2. client self-directed practice in the "in vivo" setting (often through homework tasks)
3. client self-observation and recording of target behaviors or of homework
4. client self-reward (verbal or material) for successful completion of action steps and homework assignments.

Objectives

1. Identify and describe the five characteristics of an effective self-management program.
2. Given a written client case description, describe the use of the five components of self-monitoring for this client.
3. Teach another person how to engage in self-monitoring as a self-change strategy.

Characteristics of an Effective Self-Management Program

Well-constructed and well-executed self-management programs have some advantages that are not so apparent in counselor-administered procedures. For instance, use of a self-management procedure may increase a person's perceived control over the environment and decrease dependence on the counselor or others. Perceived control over the environment often motivates a person to take some action (Rotter, Chance, & Phares, 1972). Second, self-management approaches are practical—inexpensive and portable (Thoresen & Mahoney, 1974, p. 7). Also, self-management strategies are usable. By this we mean that occasionally a person will refuse to go "into therapy" to stop drinking or to lose weight (for example), but will agree to use the self-administered instructions that a self-management program provides. In fact, one study found that people who had never received counseling were more agreeable than clients to the idea of using self-management (Williams, Canale, & Edgerly,

1976). Finally, self-management strategies may enhance generalization of learning—both from the interview to the environment and from problematic to nonproblematic situations (Thoresen & Mahoney, 1974, p. 7). These are some of the possible advantages of self-management that have spurred both researchers and practitioners to apply and explore some of the components and effects of successful self-management programs. Although many questions remain unanswered, we can say tentatively that the following factors may be important in an effective self-management program:

1. A combination of strategies, some focusing on antecedents of behavior and others on consequences
2. Consistent use of strategies over a period of time
3. Evidence of client self-evaluation, goal-setting with fairly high standards
4. Use of covert, verbal, or material self-reinforcement
5. Some degree of external or environmental support

Combination of Strategies

A combination of self-management strategies is usually more useful than a single strategy. In a weight-control study, M. J. Mahoney, N. G. Moura, and T. C. Wade (1973) found that the addition of self-reward significantly enhanced the procedures of self-monitoring and stimulus control. Also, people who combined self-reward and self-punishment lost more weight than those who used just one of the procedures. Greiner and Karoly (1976) found that students who used self-monitoring, self-reward, and planning strategies improved their study behavior and academic performance more than students who used only one strategy. Mitchell and White (1977) found that the frequency of clients' reported migraine headaches was reduced in direct proportion to the number of self-management skills they used. Similarly, Perri and Richards (1977) discovered that successful self-controllers reported using a greater number of techniques for a longer time than unsuccessful self-controllers. In this study, successful self-controllers were those persons who had increased or decreased the target behavior at least 50% and had maintained this level after a period of several months. Examples of problem areas for which comprehensive self-management programs have been developed include weight control (Heckerman & Prochaska, 1977; K. Mahoney & M. J. Mahoney, 1976; Penick, Filion, Fox, & Stunkard, 1971; Polly, Turner, & Sherman, 1976); exercise (Turner, Polly, & Sherman, 1976); study behavior (Groverman, Richards, & Caple, 1975); and insomnia (Bootzin, 1977).

Consistent Use of Strategies

Consistent, regular use of the strategies is a very important component of effective self-management. Seeming ineffectiveness may be due, not to the impotence of the strategy but to its inconsistent or sporadic application (Thoresen & Mahoney, 1974, p. 107). Perri and Richards (1977) found that successful self-controllers reported using methods more frequently and more consistently than unsuccessful self-controllers. Similarly, another investigation noted that the "failures" in a self-management smoking-reduction program cheated in using the procedures and their contracts, whereas the "successes" did not (Hackett, Horan, Stone, Linberg, Nicholas, & Lukaski, 1976). In a case study of self-management, Greenberg and Altman (1976) found that smoking decrements occurred quite slowly (2 to 4 months). If self-management efforts are not used over a certain period of time, their effectiveness may be too limited to produce any change.

Self-Evaluation and Standard-Setting

Self-evaluation in the form of standard-setting (or goal-setting) and intention statements seems to be an important component of a self-management program. Spates and Kanfer (1977) found that children's performance on a learning task was enhanced only after the children had been trained to set standards or performance criteria. Greiner and Karoly (1976) also reported the importance of standard-setting in a self-management program designed to improve the study behavior of college students. Some evidence also suggests that self-selected stringent standards affect performance more positively than lenient standards (Bandura, 1971b; Brownell, Colletti, Ersner-Hershfield, Hershfield, & Wilson, 1977). Perri and Richards (1977) described successful self-controllers as setting higher goals and criteria for change than unsuccessful self-controllers. However, the standards set should be realistic and within reach, or it is unlikely that self-reinforcement will ever occur.

Use of Self-Reinforcement

Self-reinforcement, either covert, verbal, or material, appears to be an important ingredient of an effective self-management program. Being able to praise oneself covertly or to note positive improvement seems to be correlated with self-change (Perri & Richards, 1977). In contrast, self-criticism (covert and verbal) seems to mitigate against change (Hackett et al., 1976; K. Mahoney & M. J. Mahoney, 1976). M. J. Mahoney, N. G. Moura, and T. C. Wade (1973) found that a material self-reward (such as money) was more effective than either self-monitoring or self-punishment in a weight-reduction program. And, across four different problem areas of college students (eating, smoking, studying, and dating), successful self-controllers reported using self-reward far more frequently (67%) than unsuccessful self-controllers (19%) (Perri & Richards, 1977).

Environmental Support

Some degree of environmental or external support is necessary to effect and maintain the changes resulting from a self-management program. For example, public display of self-monitoring data and the help of another person provide opportunities for social reinforcement that often augment behavior change (Rutner & Bugle, 1969; Van Houten, Hill, & Parsons, 1975). Successful participants in a smoking-reduction program reported effective use of environmental contracts, whereas "failures" reported sabotage of the contracts by significant others (Hackett et al., 1976). Similarly, Perri and Richards (1977) observed that successful self-controllers reported receiving more positive feedback from others about their change efforts than the unsuccessful self-controllers. To maintain any self-managed change, there must be some support from the social and physical environment (Kanfer, 1975; Thoresen & Mahoney, 1974).

Steps in Developing a Client Self-Management Program

We have incorporated these five characteristics of effective self-management into a description of the steps associated with a self-management program. These steps are applicable to any program in which the client uses stimulus control, self-contracting, self-monitoring, or self-reward. Figure 22-1 summarizes the steps associated with developing a self-management program; the characteristics of effective self-management reflected in the steps are noted in the left column of the figure.

In developing a self-management program, steps 1 and 2 both involve aspects of standard-setting and self-evaluation. In step 1, the client identifies and records the target behavior and its antecedents and consequences. This step involves self-monitoring in which the client collects baseline data about the behavior to be changed. If baseline data have not been collected as part of problem definition (Chapter 10), it is imperative that such data are collected now, before using any self-management strategies. In step 2, the client explicitly identifies the desired behavior, conditions, and level of change. As you may remember from Chapter 12, the behavior, condition, and level of change are the three parts of a counseling outcome goal. De-

fining the goal is an important part of self-management because of the possible motivating effects of standard-setting. Establishing goals may interact with some of the self-management procedures and contribute to part of the desired effects (Jones et al., 1977).

Steps 3 and 4 are directed toward helping the client select a combination of self-management strategies to use. The counselor will need to explain all the possible self-management strategies to the client (step 3). The counselor should emphasize that the client should select some strategies that involve prearrangement of the antecedents and some that involve manipulation and self-administration of consequences. Ultimately, the client is responsible for selecting which self-management strategies should be used (step 4). Client selection of the strategies is an important part of the overall *self-directed* nature of self-management.

Steps 5 through 9 all involve procedural considerations that may strengthen client commitment and may encourage consistent use of the strategies over time. First, the client sets up a contract with himself or herself that specifies what and how much change is desired and the action steps (strategies) the client will take to produce the change (step 5). (The counselor and client can refer to the guidelines on p. 507 for developing a self-contract.) Next, the counselor will instruct the client how to carry out the selected strategies (step 6). (The counselor can follow the guidelines listed in Table 23-1 for stimulus control, those listed in Table 22-1 for self-monitoring, and the ones presented for self-reward on p. 502.) Explicit instructions and modeling by the counselor may encourage the client to use a procedure more accurately and effectively. The instructional set given by a counselor may contribute to some degree to the overall treatment outcomes (Jones et al., 1977). The client also may use the strategies more effectively if there is an opportunity to rehearse the procedures in the interview under the counselor's direction (step 7). Finally, the client applies the strategies "in vivo" (step 8) and records (monitors) the frequency of use of each strategy and the level of the target behavior (step 9). Some of the treatment effects of self-

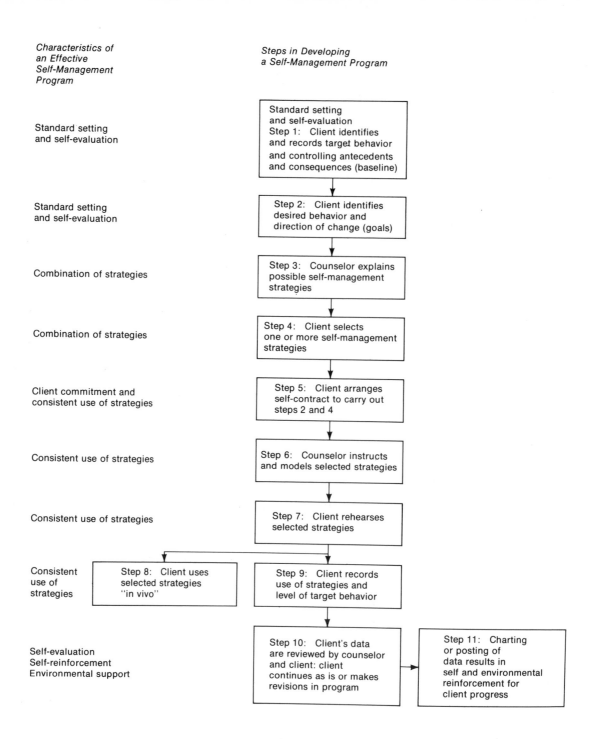

Characteristics of an Effective Self-Management Program	Steps in Developing a Self-Management Program
Standard setting and self-evaluation	Standard setting and self-evaluation Step 1: Client identifies and records target behavior and controlling antecedents and consequences (baseline)
Standard setting and self-evaluation	Step 2: Client identifies desired behavior and direction of change (goals)
Combination of strategies	Step 3: Counselor explains possible self-management strategies
Combination of strategies	Step 4: Client selects one or more self-management strategies
Client commitment and consistent use of strategies	Step 5: Client arranges self-contract to carry out steps 2 and 4
Consistent use of strategies	Step 6: Counselor instructs and models selected strategies
Consistent use of strategies	Step 7: Client rehearses selected strategies
Consistent use of strategies	Step 8: Client uses selected strategies "in vivo" Step 9: Client records use of strategies and level of target behavior
Self-evaluation Self-reinforcement Environmental support	Step 10: Client's data are reviewed by counselor and client: client continues as is or makes revisions in program Step 11: Charting or posting of data results in self and environmental reinforcement for client progress

Figure 22-1. Developing an Effective Self-Management Program

management also may be a function of the client's self-recording (Jones et al.).

Steps 10 and 11 involve aspects of self-evaluation, self-reinforcement, and environmental support. The client has an opportunity to evaluate progress toward the goal by reviewing the self-recorded data collected during strategy implementation (step 10). Review of the data may indicate that the program is progressing smoothly or that some adjustments are needed. When the data suggest that some progress toward the goal is being made, the client's self-evaluation may set the occasion for self-reinforcement. Charting or posting of the data (step 11) can enhance self-reinforcement and can elicit important environmental support for long-term maintenance of client change.

The following section describes how self-monitoring can be used to record the target behavior. Such recording can occur initially for problem definition and goal-setting, or it can be introduced later as a self-change strategy. We will discuss specifically how self-monitoring can be used to promote behavior change.

Self-Monitoring

Purposes of Self-Monitoring

In Chapter 10, we defined self-monitoring as a process in which clients observe and record specific things about themselves and their interactions with environmental situations. Self-monitoring is a useful adjunct to problem definition because the observational data can verify or change the client's verbal report about the problem behavior. We recommend that clients record their daily self-observations over a designated time period on a behavior log. Usually the client observes and records the problem behavior, controlling antecedents, and resulting consequences. Thoresen and Mahoney (1974) assert that self-monitoring is a major *first* step in any self-change program (as in any change program!). The client must be able to discover what is happening *before* implementing a self-change strategy, just as the counselor must know what is going on before using any other

therapeutic procedure. In other words, any self-management strategy, like any other strategy, should be preceded by a baseline period of self-observation and recording. During this period, the client collects and records data about the behavior to be changed (B), the antecedents (A) of the behavior, and the consequences (C) of the behavior. In addition, the client may wish to note how much or how often the behavior occurs. For example, a client might record the daily amount of study time or the number of times he or she left the study time and place to do something else. The behavior log presented in Chapter 10 for problem-identification data also can be used by a client to collect baseline data before implementing a self-management program. If self-management strategies are being introduced by the counselor *after* problem definition, these self-observation data already should be available.

As we discussed in Chapter 13, self-monitoring is very useful for assessment and evaluation. When a client self-monitors the target behavior either before or during a treatment program, "the primary utility of self-monitoring lies in its assessment or data collection function" (Ciminero, Nelson, & Lipinski, 1977, p. 196). However, in recent years, practitioners and researchers have realized that the mere act of self-observation can produce change. As one collects data about oneself, the data collection may influence the behavior being observed. We now know that self-monitoring is useful not only to collect data but also to promote client change. If properly structured and executed, self-monitoring can be used as one type of self-management strategy.

Clinical Uses of Self-Monitoring

A number of research reports and clinical case studies have explored self-monitoring as the major treatment strategy. In many cases, a self-monitoring procedure alone has been sufficient to produce at least short-term changes in the behavior being observed. McFall (1970), one of the first to investigate self-monitoring, found that college students who monitored their urge to smoke decreased the number of cigarettes smoked and the time spent smoking per cigarette. Gottman and McFall (1972) found that verbal classroom participation of high school sophomores was influenced by self-monitoring. M. J. Mahoney, B. S. Moore, T. C. Wade, and N. G. Moura (1973) reported that students who self-monitored, either continuously or intermittently, increased their review time for an exam when compared to students who did not engage in monitoring. The influence of self-monitoring on study behavior was examined in a single case study of an eighth-grade girl (Broden, Hall, & Mitts, 1971) and in a group-comparative study using college students (Richards, 1976). A number of people have examined the role of self-monitoring as the predominant therapeutic strategy used for weight reduction (Bellack, Rozensky, & Schwartz, 1974; Fisher, Green, Friedling, Levonkron, & Porter, 1976; Romanczyk, 1974). Self-monitoring also was used effectively by institutionalized juvenile girls to increase their work behavior (Seymour & Stokes, 1976).

Self-monitoring has been used to modify covert behaviors as well as overt responses. For example, Rutner and Bugle (1969) found that self-monitoring and public display of the monitoring data dramatically decreased the hallucinations of a hospitalized schizophrenic woman. Frederiksen (1975) reported that intensive self-monitoring of the antecedents, consequences, and frequency of episodes of ruminative thinking of a 25-year-old housewife decreased these episodes significantly. The decline was maintained at a 6-month follow-up. Other studies have found self-monitoring to be effective only when used with another self-management procedure (M. J. Mahoney, 1974; M. J. Mahoney, N. G. Moura, & T. C. Wade, 1973).

Factors Influencing the Reactivity of Self-Monitoring

As you may recall from Chapter 13, two issues involved in self-monitoring are the reliability of the self-recording and its reactivity. Reliability refers to the accuracy of the self-recorded data and is important when self-monitoring is used to evaluate the goal behaviors. However, as a change strategy, the accuracy of the data is not that crucial. From a counseling perspective, the reactivity of self-monitoring makes it suitable for a change strategy. McFall (1970) explains the potential reactivity of self-monitoring this way: "When an individual begins paying unusually close attention to one aspect of his behavior, that behavior is likely to change, even though no change may be intended or desired" (p. 140). As an example of reactivity, Kanfer (1975) noted that a married couple using self-monitoring to observe their frequent arguments reported that, whenever the monitoring device (a tape-recorder) was turned on, the argument was avoided. Although the reactivity of self-monitoring can be a problem in data collection, it can be an asset when self-monitoring is used intentionally as a helping strategy. In using self-monitoring as a change strategy, it is important to try to maximize the reactive effects of self-monitoring—at least to the point of producing desired behavioral changes.

A number of factors seem to influence the reactivity of self-monitoring. A summary of these factors suggests that self-monitoring "is most likely to produce positive behavioral changes when change-motivated subjects continuously monitor a limited number of discrete, positively-valued target behaviors; when performance feedback and goals or standards are made available and are unambiguous; and when the monitoring act is both salient and closely related in time to the target behaviors" (McFall, 1977b, p. 208).

Nelson (1977) has identified eight variables that seem to be related to the occurrence, intensity, and direction of the reactive effects of self-monitoring:

1. Motivation. Clients who are interested in changing the self-monitored behavior are more likely to show reactive effects when they self-monitor.
2. Valence of target behaviors. Behaviors a person values positively are likely to increase

with self-monitoring; negative behaviors are likely to decrease; neutral behaviors may not change.

3. Type of target behaviors. The type and nature of the behavior that is being monitored may affect the degree to which self-monitoring procedures effect change.

4. Standard-setting (goals), reinforcement, and feedback. Reactivity is enhanced for people who self-monitor in conjunction with goals and the availability of performance reinforcement or feedback.

5. Timing of self-monitoring. The time when the person self-records can influence the reactivity of self-monitoring. Self-monitoring before a response occurs may produce different results than monitoring after the occurrence of the target response.

6. Devices used for self-monitoring. More obtrusive or visible recording devices seem to be more reactive than unobtrusive devices.

7. Number of target responses monitored. Self-monitoring of only one response increases reactivity. As more responses are concurrently monitored, the reactivity decreases.

8. Schedule of self-monitoring. The frequency with which a person self-monitors can affect reactivity. Continuous self-monitoring may result in more behavior change than intermittent self-recording.

Steps of Self-Monitoring

The effectiveness of self-monitoring seems to vary with several parameters, including the characteristics of the client and of the target behavior (Lipinski, Black, Nelson, & Ciminero, 1975; Nelson, Lipinski, & Black, 1976a); the demand characteristics of the situation (Kazdin, 1974e); and the various components of the monitoring procedure (Bellack et al., 1974; Kanfer, 1975; M. J. Mahoney & C. E. Thoresen, 1974). Some of the important steps of self-monitoring will be explored in this section.

Self-monitoring involves at least five important steps: *discrimination* of a response, *recording* of a response, *charting* of a response,

display of data, and *analysis* of data (Thoresen & Mahoney, 1974, pp. 43–44). Each of these five steps and guidelines for their use will be discussed, and they are summarized in Table 22-1. However, remember that the steps are all interactive, and the presence of all of them may be required for a person to use self-monitoring effectively.

Discrimination of a Response

When a client engages in self-monitoring, first an observation or discrimination of a response is required. For example, a client who is monitoring fingernail-biting must be able to discriminate instances of nail-biting from instances of other behavior. Discrimination of a response occurs whenever the client is able to identify the presence or absence of the behavior, whether overt like nail-biting or covert like a positive self-thought. Thoresen and Mahoney (1974) point out that making behavioral discriminations can be thought of as the "awareness" facet of self-monitoring (p. 43).

Discrimination of a response involves helping the client to identify *what* to monitor. Often this decision will require counselor assistance. There is some evidence that the type and valence of the monitored response affects the results of self-monitoring. For example, Romanczyk (1974) found that self-monitoring produced greater weight loss for people who recorded their daily weight and daily caloric intake than for those who recorded only daily body weight. As McFall (1977b) has observed, it is not very clear why some target responses seem to be better ones to self-monitor than others. At this point, the selection of target responses remains a pragmatic choice (McFall, 1977b). M. J. Mahoney (1977) points out that there may be times when self-monitoring of certain responses could detract from therapeutic effectiveness, as in asking a suicidal client to monitor depressive thoughts (pp. 244–245).

The effects of self-monitoring also vary with the valence of the target response. As M. J. Mahoney and C. E. Thoresen (1974)

Table 22-1. Steps of Self-Monitoring

1. *Discrimination* of a response	A. selection of target response to monitor
	  1. type of response
	  2. valence of response
	  3. number of responses

2. *Recording* of a response	A. timing of recording
	  1. prebehavior recording to decrease a response; postbehavior recording to increase a response
	  2. immediate recording
	  3. recording when no competing responses distract recorder
	B. method of recording
	  1. frequency counts
	  2. duration measures
	    a. continuous recording
	    b. time-sampling
	C. devices for recording
	  1. portable
	  2. accessible
	  3. economical
	  4. somewhat obtrusive

3. *Charting* of a response	A. charting and graphing of daily totals of recorded behavior
4. *Displaying* of data	A. public display of chart for environmental support
5. *Analysis* of data	A. accuracy of data interpretation B. knowledge of results for self-evaluation and self-reinforcement

indicate, there are always "two sides" of a behavior that could be monitored—the positive and the negative (p. 37). There seem to be times when one side is more important for self-monitoring than the other (Kanfer, 1970; Mahoney & Thoresen, p. 37).

Most of the evidence indicates that self-monitoring of positive responses increases these responses. In contrast, self-monitoring decreases the frequency of negative behaviors (Broden, Hall, & Mitts, 1971; Cavior & Marabotto, 1976; Nelson, Lipinski, & Black,

1976a). Unfortunately, there are very few data to guide a decision about the specific type and valence of responses to monitor. Because the reactivity of self-monitoring is affected by the value assigned to a behavior (D. L. Watson & R. G. Tharp, 1977), one guideline might be to have the client monitor the behavior that she or he cares *most* about changing. Generally, it is a good idea to encourage the client to limit monitoring to only one response, at least initially. If the client engages in self-monitoring of one behavior with no problems, then more items can be added.

Recording of a Response

After the client has learned to make discriminations about a response, the counselor can provide instructions and examples about the method for recording the observed response. Most clients have probably never recorded their behavior *systematically*. Systematic recording is crucial to the success of self-monitoring, so it is imperative that the client understand the importance and methods of recording. The client needs instructions in when and how to record, and devices for recording. The timing, method, and recording devices all can influence the effectiveness of self-monitoring.

Timing of Self-Monitoring: When to Record. One of the least understood processes of self-monitoring involves timing, or the point when the client actually records the target behavior. Instances have been reported of both pre-behavior and postbehavior monitoring. In pre-behavior monitoring, the client records the intention or urge to engage in the behavior *before* doing so. In postbehavior monitoring, the client records each completed instance of the target behavior—*after* the behavior has occurred. Kazdin (1974f) points out that the precise effects of self-monitoring may depend upon the point at which monitoring occurs in the chain of responses relative to the response being recorded (p. 239). Kanfer (1975) concludes that existing data are insufficient to judge whether pre- or postbehavior monitoring will have maximal effects. Nelson (1977) indicates that the effects of the timing of self-monitoring may depend partially on whether other responses are competing for the person's attention at the time the response is recorded. Another factor influencing the timing of self-monitoring involves the amount of time between the response and the actual recording. Most people agree that delayed recording of the behavior weakens the efficacy of the monitoring process (Kanfer, 1975; Kazdin, 1974f).

We suggest four guidelines that may help the counselor and client decide when to record. First, if the client is using monitoring as a way to *decrease* an undesired behavior, prebehavior monitoring may be more effective, as this seems to interrupt the response chain early in the process. An example of the rule of thumb for self-monitoring an undesired response would be: "Record whenever you have the urge to smoke or to eat." McFall (1970) found that prebehavior monitoring did reduce smoking behavior. Similarly, Bellack et al. (1974) found that prebehavior monitoring resulted in more weight loss than postbehavior monitoring. If the client is using self-monitoring to *increase* a desired response, then postbehavior monitoring may be more helpful. As Bellack et al. observe, postbehavior monitoring can make a person more aware of a "low frequency, desirable behavior" (p. 529). Third, recording instances of a desired behavior as it occurs or immediately after it occurs may be most helpful. The rule of thumb is to "record *immediately* after you have the urge to smoke—or *immediately* after you have covertly praised yourself; do not wait even for 15 or 20 minutes, as the impact of recording may be lost." Fourth, the client should be encouraged to self-record the response when not distracted by the situation or by other competing responses.

Method of Self-Monitoring: How to Record. The counselor also needs to instruct the client in a *method* for recording the target responses. McFall (1977b) points out that the method of recording can vary in a number of ways. As he notes:

> It can range from a very informal and unstructured operation, as when subjects are asked to make mental notes of any event that seems related to mood changes, to something fairly formal and structured, as when subjects are asked to fill out a mood-rating sheet according to a time-sampling schedule. It can be fairly simple, as when subjects are asked to keep track of how many cigarettes they smoke in a given time period; or it can be complex and time-consuming, as when they are asked to record not only how many cigarettes they smoke, but also the time, place, circumstances, and affective response associated with lighting each cigarette. It can be a relatively objective matter, as when counting the calories consumed each day; or it can be a very subjective matter, as when recording the number of instances each

day when they successfully resist the temptation to eat sweets [p. 197].

Ciminero et al. (1977) suggest that the recording method should be "easy to implement, must produce a representative sample of the target behavior, and must be sensitive to changes in the occurrence of the target behavior" (p. 198).

For therapy purposes, there are two methods a client can use to record data: a frequency count and a duration count. Selection of one of these methods will depend primarily upon the type of target response and its frequency. To record the *number* of target responses, the client can use a frequency count. Frequency counts are most useful for monitoring responses that are discrete, do not occur all the time, and are of short duration (Ciminero et al., 1977, p. 190). For instance, clients might record the number of times they had an urge to smoke or the number of times they praised or complimented themselves covertly.

Other kinds of target responses are recorded more easily and accurately with a duration count. Any time a client wants to record the amount or length of a response, a duration count can be used. Ciminero et al. (1977) recommend the use of a duration measure whenever the target response is not discrete and varies in length (p. 198). For example, a client might use a duration count to note the amount of time spent reading textbooks or practicing a competitive sport. Or a client might want to keep track of the length of time spent in a "happy mood."

Sometimes a client may want to record two different responses and use both the frequency and duration methods. For example, a client might use a frequency count to record each urge to smoke and a duration count to monitor the time spent on smoking a cigarette. D. Watson and R. Tharp (1972) suggest that the counselor can recommend frequency counts whenever it is easy to record clearly separate occurrences of the behavior, and duration counts whenever the behavior continues for long periods.

As you may remember from our description of self-monitoring in Chapter 13, both fre-

quency and duration counts can be recorded with either a continuous recording or a time-sampling method.

Devices for Self-Monitoring. Often clients report that one of the most intriguing aspects of self-monitoring involves the device or mechanism used for recording. In order for recording to occur systematically and accurately, the client must have access to some recording device or instrument. A variety of devices have been used to help clients keep accurate records. Note cards, daily log sheets, and diaries can be used to make written notations. A popular self-recording device is a wrist counter, such as a golf counter. Lindsley (1968) adapted the golf counter for self-recording in different settings. If several behaviors are being counted simultaneously, the client can wear several wrist counters or use knitting tallies. K. Mahoney (1974) describes a wrist counter with rows of beads that permits the recording of several behaviors. Audio and video tapes, toothpicks, or small plastic tokens also can be used as recording devices. D. L. Watson and R. G. Tharp (1977) report the use of pennies to count: a client can carry pennies in one pocket and transfer one penny to another pocket each time a behavior occurs. Children can record frequencies by pasting stars on a chart or by using a "countoon" (Kunzelmann, 1970), which has pictures and numbers for three recording columns: "what do I do," "my count," and "what happens." Clocks, watches, and kitchen timers can be used for duration counts.

The counselor and client select a recording device. Here is an opportunity to be inventive! From a practical standpoint, there are several criteria to consider in helping a client to select an adequate recording device. The device should be portable and accessible so that it is present whenever the behavior occurs (D. L. Watson & R. G. Tharp, 1977). The device should be easy and convenient to use, and economical. Also, the obtrusiveness of the device should be considered. The recording device can function as a cue (discriminative stimulus) for the client to self-monitor, so it should be noticeable enough to remind the client to engage in self-monitoring. However, a device that is too obtrusive may draw attention from others who could reward or punish the client for self-monitoring (Ciminero et al., 1977, p. 202). Finally, the device should be capable of giving cumulative frequency data so that the client can chart daily totals of the behavior (Thoresen & Mahoney, 1974).

After the client has been instructed in the timing and method of recording, and after a recording device has been selected, the client should practice using the recording system. Breakdowns in self-monitoring often occur because a client did not understand the recording process clearly. Rehearsal of the recording procedures may ensure that the client will record accurately. Generally, a client should engage in self-recording for 3 to 4 weeks. Usually the effects of self-monitoring are not apparent in only 1 or 2 weeks' time.

Charting of a Response

The data recorded by the client with the aid of a recording device should be translated onto a more permanent storage record such as a chart or graph that enables the client to inspect the self-monitored data visually. This type of visual guide may provide the occasion for client self-reinforcement (Kanfer, 1975) which, in turn, can influence the reactivity of self-monitoring. The data can be charted by days, using a simple line graph. For example, a client counting the number of urges to smoke a cigarette could chart these by days as in Figure 22-2. A client recording the amount of time spent studying daily could use the same sort of line graph to chart duration of study time. The vertical axis would be divided into time intervals such as 15 minutes, 30 minutes, 45 minutes, or 1 hour.

The client should receive either verbal or written instructions on a way to chart and graph the daily totals of the recorded response. The counselor can assist the client in interpreting the chart in the sessions on data review and analysis. If a client is using self-monitoring to increase a behavior, the line on the graph should go up gradually if the self-monitoring is having the desired effect. In contrast, if self-monitoring is influencing an undesired response to decrease, the line on the graph should go down gradually.

Display of Data

After the graph has been made, the counselor should encourage the client to display the completed chart. If the chart is displayed in a "public" area, this display may prompt environmental reinforcement, a necessary part of an effective self-management program. Several studies have found that the effects of self-monitoring are augmented when the data chart is displayed as a public record (McKenzie & Rushall, 1974; Rutner & Bugle, 1969; Van Houten, Hill, & Parsons, 1975).

Analysis of Data

If the client's recording data are not reviewed and analyzed, the client may soon feel like he or she was told to make a graph just for the practice of drawing straight lines! A very important facet of self-monitoring is the information it can provide to the client. There is some evidence that people who receive feedback about their self-recording change more than those who do not (Kazdin, 1974e). The recording and charting of data should be used *explicitly* to provide the client with knowledge of results about behavior or performance. Specifically, the client should bring the data to weekly counseling sessions for review and analysis. In these sessions, the counselor can encourage the client to compare the data with the desired goals and standards. The client can use the recorded data for self-evaluation and determine whether the data indicate that the behavior is within or outside the desired limits. The counselor also can aid in data analysis by helping the client to interpret the data correctly. As Thoresen and Mahoney (1974) observe, "errors about what the charted data represent can seriously hinder success in self-control" (p 44).

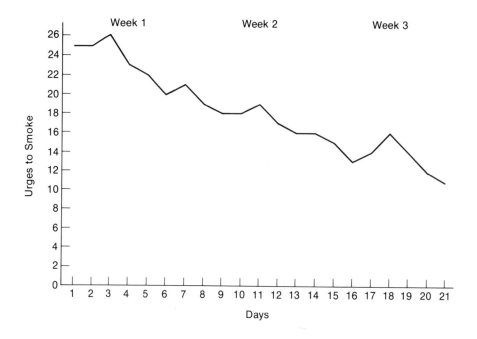

Figure 22-2. Self-Monitoring Chart

Model Example: Self-Monitoring

As you may recall from Joan's goal chart in Chapter 12, one of Joan's goals was to increase her positive thoughts (and simultaneously decrease her negative thoughts) about her ability to do well with math. This goal lends itself well to application of self-management strategies for several reasons. First, the goal represents a covert behavior (positive thoughts) which is observable only by Joan. Second, the "flip side" of the goal (the negative thoughts) represents a very well-learned habit. Probably most of these negative thoughts occur *outside* the counseling sessions. In order to change this thought pattern, Joan will need to use strategies she can apply frequently (as needed) "in vivo." Also, she will need to use strategies she can administer to herself.

Here is a description of the way self-monitoring could be used to help Joan achieve this goal.

1. *Discrimination of a response.* The counselor would need to help Joan define the target response specifically. One definition could be: "Anytime I think about myself doing math or working with numbers successfully." The counselor should provide some possible examples of this response, such as "Gee, I did well on my math homework today" or "I was able to balance the checkbook today." Joan also should be encouraged to identify some examples of the target response. Since Joan wants to increase this behavior, the target response would be stated in the "positive."

2. *Recording of a response.* The counselor should instruct Joan in timing, a method, and a device for recording. In this case, because Joan is using self-monitoring to increase a desired behavior, she would use postbehavior monitoring. Joan should be instructed to record *immediately* after a target thought has occurred. She is interested in recording the *number* of such thoughts, so she could use a frequency count. A tally on a note card or a wrist counter could be selected as the device for recording. After these instructions, Joan should practice recording before actually doing it. She should be instructed to engage in self-monitoring for about 4 consecutive weeks.

3. *Charting of a response.* After each week of self-monitoring, Joan can add her daily frequency

totals and chart them by days on a simple line graph.

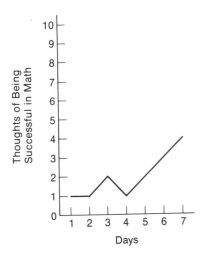

Days

Joan is using self-monitoring to increase a behavior; as a result, if the monitoring has the desired effect, the line on her graph should gradually rise. It is just starting to do so here; additional data for the next few weeks should show a greater increase if the self-monitoring is influencing the target behavior in the desired direction.

4. *Display of data.* After Joan has made a data chart, she may wish to post it in a place such as her room, where her friends could see it and encourage her for progress. Public posting also may cue Joan to reinforce herself for progress.

5. *Analysis of data.* During the period of self-monitoring, Joan should bring in her data for weekly review sessions with the counselor. The counselor can provide reinforcement and help Joan interpret the data accurately. Joan can use the data for self-evaluation by comparing the "story" of the data to her stated desired behavior and level of change.

Learning Activity: Self-Monitoring

This learning activity is designed to help you use self-monitoring yourself. The instructions describe a self-monitoring plan for you to try out.

1. Discrimination of a target response:

a. Specify one target behavior you would like to change. Pick either the positive or negative side of the behavior to monitor—depending on which you value most and whether you want to increase or decrease this response.

b. Write down a definition of this behavior. How clear is your definition?

c. Can you write some examples of this behavior? If you had trouble with these, try to "tighten up" your definition—or else contrast positive and negative instances of the behavior.

2. Recording of the response:

a. Specify the *timing* of your self-recording. Remember the "rules of thumb":
   1. prebehavior monitoring to decrease an undesired response
   2. postbehavior monitoring to increase a desired response
   3. record immediately—don't wait
   4. record when there are no competing responses.
   Write down the timing you choose.

b. Select a *method* of recording (frequency, duration, interval). Remember:
   1. frequency counts for clearly separate occurrences of the response
   2. duration measures for responses that occur for a period of time.

c. Select a *device* to assist you in recording. Remember that the device should be:
   1. portable
   2. accessible
   3. economical
   4. obtrusive enough to serve as a reminder to self-record.

d. After you have made these determinations, engage in self-monitoring for at least a week (preferably 2). Then complete steps 3, 4, and 5.

3. Charting of response: Take your daily self-recording data and chart them on a simple line graph for each day that you self-monitored.

4. Displaying of data: Arrange a place to display your chart where it may elicit strokes from others.

5. Analysis of data: Compare your chart to your stated desired behavior change. What has happened to the behavior?

Summary

Thoresen and Mahoney (1974) suggest that "self-monitoring provides a method by which a person can become quantifiably more aware of both his own behavior and the factors that influence it'' (p. 64). As a measurement device used to define problems and to collect evaluative data, self-monitoring is indispensable. As a self-change strategy, self-monitoring may help a client to initiate some desired changes. Generally, the effects produced by self-monitoring are temporary (Kanfer, 1975; Lipinski & Nelson, 1974; Thoresen & Mahoney, 1974). For many clients, self-monitoring may be a useful but not a sufficient self-change strategy unless it is used in conjunction with other self-management procedures. Typically, self-monitoring has been combined with stimulus control, self-reward and self-punishment, and self-contracting. As you may remember from our earlier description of self-management programs, employing a combination of strategies is an important part of the overall program. Additional self-management strategies are discussed in Chapter 23.

Post Evaluation

Part One

Objective 1 asks you to identify and describe the five major factors involved in a comprehensive self-management program. You may wish to do this covertly, or write out your descriptions on a piece of paper.

Part Two

Objective 2 asks you to describe the application of the five components of self-monitoring to a written client case. Read the following case carefully. Then respond in writing to the questions listed.

Client Case Description
The client is a 30-year-old woman who has been married for the last 10 years. Over the last 2 years she has been troubled by constant thoughts that her husband will die young and she will be left alone. She realizes there is no basis for these thoughts. Her baseline data indicate that these episodes of ruminative thinking occur anywhere from five to ten times daily.

Suppose you were to use self-monitoring to help this client *decrease* these thoughts.

1. Explain the process of *response discrimination* as it would be used with this client.
2. Give brief examples of the instructions you would give to this client about *response recording*. Include instructions about (a) *timing* of the recording; (b) *method* of recording; and (c) a *device* for recording.
3. Provide an example of a *chart* the client could use to plot the daily totals of the monitored behavior.
4. What are some examples of places where you would instruct this client to *display* the charted data?
5. Describe at least one way the client could engage in *data analysis*.

Part Three

Objective 3 asks you to teach someone else how to engage in self-monitoring. Your teaching should follow the five guidelines listed in Table 22-1. You should teach the person response discrimination, self-recording, data-charting, data display, and data analysis. Feedback follows.

Part One

The five main factors of an effective self-management program are:
1. Combination of strategies
2. Consistent use of strategies
3. Standard-setting and self-evaluation
4. Self-reinforcement
5. Environmental support.

Part Two

1. Response-discrimination training would involve selecting, defining, and giving examples of the response to be monitored. The counselor should model some examples of the defined behavior and elicit some others from the client. Because the client wants to decrease such thoughts, the target response would be stated in the negative form—"I'm afraid my husband will die and leave me alone."

2. *Timing of the recording:* Since this client is using self-monitoring to decrease an undesired behavior, she would engage in prebehavior monitoring; each time she had the urge or started to think about being left alone, she would record.

   Method of recording: The client would be instructed to use a frequency count and record the number of times she started to think about being left alone. If she was unable to discern when these thoughts started and ended, she could record with time-sampling. For example, she could divide a day into equal time intervals using the "all or none" method. If such thoughts occurred during an interval, she would record *yes*; if they did not, she would record *no*. Or, during each interval, she could rate the approximate frequency of these thoughts on a numerical scale such as 0 for "never occurring," 1 for "occasionally," 2 for "often," and 3 for "very frequently."

   Device for recording: There is no one right device to assist this client in recording. She could count the frequency using a tally on a note card or a golf wrist counter. Or she could use a daily log sheet to keep track of interval occurrences.

3. A simple chart might have days along the horizontal axis and frequency of thought urges along the vertical axis.

4. This client may or may not wish to display the data in a public place at home. If not, she could carry the data in her purse or knapsack.

5. The client could engage in data analysis by reviewing the data with the counselor or by comparing the data to the baseline or to her goal (desired level of behavior change). The latter involves self-evaluation and may set the stage for self-reinforcement.

Part Three

Use Table 22-1 as a guide to assist your teaching. You might also determine whether the person you taught implemented self-monitoring accurately.

Suggested Readings

Characteristics of an Effective Self-Management Program

Brownell, K., Colletti, J., Ersner-Hershfield, R., Hershfield, S., & Wilson, G. Self-control in school children: Stringency and leniency in self-determined and externally imposed performance standards. *Behavior Therapy*, 1977, *8*, 442–455.

Greiner, J., & Karoly, P. Effects of self-control training on study activity and academic performance: An analysis of self-monitoring, self-reward, and systematic-planning components. *Journal of Counseling Psychology*, 1976, *23*, 495–502.

Kanfer, F. H. The many faces of self-control, or behavior modification changes its focus. In R. B. Stuart (Ed.), *Behavioral self-management: Strategies, techniques and outcomes.* New York: Brunner/Mazel, 1977.

Mitchell, K. R., & White, R. G. Behavioral self-management: An application to the problem of migraine headaches. *Behavior Therapy*, 1977, *8*, 213–221.

Perri, M. G., & Richards, C. S. An investigation of naturally occurring episodes of self-controlled behaviors. *Journal of Counseling Psychology*, 1977, *24*, 178–183.

Spates, C. R., & Kanfer, F. H. Self-monitoring, self-evaluation, and self-reinforcement in children's learning: A test of a multistage self-regulation model. *Behavior Therapy*, 1977, *8*, 9–16.

Williams, R. L., Canale, J., & Edgerly, J. Affinity for self-management: A comparison between counseling clients and controls. *Journal of Behavior Therapy and Experimental Psychiatry*, 1976, *7*, 231–234.

Williams, R. L., & Long, J. D. *Toward a self-managed life-style*. Boston: Houghton Mifflin, 1975. Part 1, The essence of self-management, 4–51.

Factors Influencing Self-Monitoring

Kanfer, F. H. Self-monitoring: Methodological limitations and clinical applications. *Journal of Consulting and Clinical Psychology*, 1970, *35*, 148–152.

Kazdin, A. E. Self-monitoring and behavior change. In M. J. Mahoney & C. E. Thoresen (Eds.), *Self-control: Power to the person*. Monterey, Calif.: Brooks/Cole, 1974.

Komaki, J., & Dore-Boyce, K. Self-recording: Its effects on individuals high and low in motivation. *Behavior Therapy*, 1978, *9*, 65–72.

Nelson, R. Methodological issues in assessment via self-monitoring. In J. D. Cone & R. P. Hawkins (Eds.), *Behavioral assessment: New directions in clinical psychology*. New York: Brunner/Mazel, 1977.

Nelson, R., Lipinski, D., & Black, J. The relative reactivity of external observations and self-monitoring. *Behavior Therapy*, 1976, *7*, 314–321.

Richards, C. S., McReynolds, W., Holt, S., & Sexton, T. Effects of information feedback and self-administered consequences on self-monitoring study behavior. *Journal of Counseling Psychology*, 1976, *23*, 316–321.

Sieck, W. A., & McFall, R. M. Some determinants of self-monitoring effects. *Journal of Consulting and Clinical Psychology*, 1976, *44*, 958–965.

Clinical Uses of Self-Monitoring

Bellack, A. S., Rozensky, R., & Schwartz, J. A comparison of two forms of self-monitoring in a behavioral weight reduction program. *Behavior Therapy*, 1974, *5*, 523–530.

Broden, M., Hall, R., & Mitts, B. The effect of self-recording on the classroom behavior of two eighth-grade students. *Journal of Applied Behavior Analysis*, 1971, *4*, 191–199.

Frederiksen, L. W. Treatment of ruminative thinking by self-monitoring. *Journal of Behavior Therapy and Experimental Psychiatry*, 1975, *6*, 258–259.

McFall, R. M. Effects of self-monitoring on normal smoking behavior. *Journal of Consulting and Clinical Psychology*, 1970, *35*, 135–142.

McKenzie, T. L., & Rushall, B. S. Effects of self-recording on attendance and performance in a competitive swimming training environment. *Journal of Applied Behavior Analysis*, 1974, *7*, 199–206.

Richards, C. S. Improving study behaviors through self-control techniques. In J. D. Krumboltz & C. E. Thoresen (Eds.), *Counseling methods*. New York: Holt, Rinehart & Winston, 1976.

Seymour, F. W., & Stokes, T. F. Self-recording in training girls to increase work and evoke staff praise in an institution for offenders. *Journal of Applied Behavior Analysis*, 1976, *9*, 41–54.

Components of Self-Monitoring

Ciminero, A., Nelson, R., & Lipinski, D. Self-monitoring procedures. In A. R. Ciminero, K. S. Calhoun, and H. E. Adams (Eds)., *Handbook of behavioral assessment*. New York: John Wiley, 1977.

Mahoney, M. J. Some applied issues in self-monitoring. In J. D. Cone & R. P. Hawkins (Eds.), *Behavioral assessment: New directions in clinical psychology*. New York: Brunner/Mazel, 1977.

Mahoney, M. J., & Thoresen, C. E. (Eds.). *Self-control: Power to the person*. Monterey, Calif.: Brooks/Cole, 1974. Chap. 3, Assessment in self-control, 27–38.

McFall, R. M. Parameters of self-monitoring. In R. B. Stuart (Ed.), *Behavioral self-management: Strategies, techniques and outcomes*. New York: Brunner/Mazel, 1977.

Thoresen, C. E., & Mahoney, M. J. *Behavioral self-control*. New York: Holt, Rinehart & Winston, 1974. Chap. 3, Self-observation, 40–64.

Watson, D. L., & Tharp, R. G. *Self-directed behavior: Self-modification for personal adjustment* (2nd ed.). Monterey, Calif.: Brooks/Cole, 1977. Chap. 4, Self-knowledge: Observation and recording, 41–71.

Chapter 23
Stimulus Control, Self-Reward, and Self-Contracting

Four self-management procedures are commonly used in conjunction with self-monitoring:

1. Stimulus control—the prearrangement of antecedents or cues to increase or decrease a target behavior
2. Self-reward—self-presentation of a self-determined positive stimulus following a desired response
3. Self-punishment—self-removal of a positive stimulus following an undesired response
4. Self-contracting—the prearrangement of consequences that will follow execution of a target response.

Some guidelines for developing and implementing these three strategies are presented in this chapter.

Objectives

1. Given a client case description, describe how the client could use stimulus-control methods to reduce or increase the rate of a behavior.
2. Given a written client case description, be able to describe the use of the four components of self-reward for this client.
3. Teach another person how to use self-reward.
4. Serving as a consultant, help another person draw up a written self-contract that includes the six features of a good self-contract.
5. In a role-play interview, demonstrate with another person five out of six steps of implementing a self-contract.

Stimulus Control: Prearrangement of Antecedents

Kanfer (1975) defines stimulus control as the predetermined arrangement of environmental conditions that makes it impossible or unfavorable for an undesired behavior to occur (p. 322). Stimulus-control methods emphasize rearranging or modifying environmental conditions that serve as cues or antecedents of a particular response. As you may recall from the discussion of the ABC model of behavior in Chapter 9, a behavior often is guided by certain things that precede it (antecedents) and is maintained by positive or negative events that follow it (consequences). Also, you may remember that both antecedents and consequences can be external (overt) or internal (covert). For example, an antecedent could be a situation, an emotion, a cognition, or an overt or covert verbal instruction.

How Antecedents Acquire Stimulus Control

When antecedents are consistently associated with a behavior that is reinforced in the *presence* (not the absence) of these antecedent stimuli, they gain control over the behavior. You might think of this as "stimulus control," since an antecedent is a stimulus for a certain response. When an antecedent gains stimulus control over the response, there is a high probability that the response will be emitted in the presence of these particular antecedent events. For example, most of us "automatically" slow down, put our foot on the brake, and stop the car when we see a red traffic light. The red light is a stimulus that has gained control over our stopping-the-car behavior. Generally, the fact that antecedents exert stimulus control is helpful, as it is in driving when we go ahead with a green light and stop at the sight of a red light.

Inappropriate Stimulus Control in Problem Behavior

Client problem behaviors may occur because of *inappropriate* stimulus control. For example, Ferster, Nurnberger, and Levitt (1962) were perhaps the first to note that inappropriate stimulus control was related to obesity. They found that eating responses of overweight people tended to be associated with many environmental cues. If a person eats something not only at the dining table, but also when working in the kitchen, watching television, walking by the refrigerator, and stopping at a Dairy Queen, the sheer number of eating responses could soon result in obesity. Too many environmental cues often are related to other client problems, particularly "excesses" such as smoking and drinking. In these cases, the primary aim of a self-management stimulus-control method is to reduce the number of cues associated with the undesired response, such as eating or smoking.

Other problem behaviors have been observed that seem to involve excessively narrow stimulus control. At the opposite pole from obesity are people who eat so little that their physical and psychological health suffers (a condition referred to as anorexia nervosa). For these people, there are too few eating cues. Lack of exercise can be a function of too narrow stimulus control. For some people, the paucity of environmental cues associated with exercise results in very little physical activity. In these cases, the primary aim of a stimulus-control strategy is to establish or increase the number of cues that will elicit the desired behavior.

To summarize, stimulus-control self-management involves reducing the number of antecedent stimuli associated with an undesirable behavior while simultaneously increasing the antecedent cues associated with a desirable response (M. J. Mahoney & C. E. Thoresen, 1974; Thoresen & Mahoney, 1974). The principal methods of stimulus control and some examples are presented in Table 23-1.

Using Stimulus Control to Decrease Behavior

To decrease the rate of a behavior, the antecedent cues associated with the behavior should be reduced in frequency or prearranged or altered in terms of time and place of occurrence. When cues are separated from the habitual behavior by alteration or elimination, the old, undesired habit can be terminated (M. J. Mahoney & C. E. Thoresen, 1974, p. 42). Many behavioral "excesses," such as eating, smoking, drinking, or self-criticism, are tied to a great number of antecedent situations. Reducing these cues can restrict the occurrence of the undesired behavior. For instance, Nolan (1968) and Roberts (1969) reported case studies in which smoking was restricted to only one special "smoking chair." Existing cues can be prearranged to make the target behavior so hard to execute that the person is unlikely to do it. An example would be altering the place of smoking by moving one's smoking chair to an inconvenient place like the basement. The smoker would have to go downstairs each time she or he wanted a cigarette. Cues also can be prearranged by placing the control of the cues in the hands of another person. Giving a pack of

Table 23-1. Principles and Examples of Stimulus-Control Strategies

Principle of Change	Example
To decrease a behavior:	
Reduce or narrow the frequency of cues associated with the behavior.	
1. Prearrange or alter cues associated with the place of the behavior:	
a. Prearrange cues that make it hard to execute the behavior.	Place fattening foods in high, hard-to-reach places.
b. Prearrange cues so that they are controlled by others.	Ask friends or family to serve you only one helping of food and to avoid serving fattening foods to you.
2. Alter the time or sequence (chain) between the antecedent cues and the resulting behaviors:	
a. Break up the sequence.	Buy and prepare food only on a full stomach.
b. Change the sequence.	Substitute and engage in nonfood activities when you start to move toward snacking (toward refrigerator, cupboard, or candy machine).
c. Build pauses into the sequence.	Delay second helpings of food for a predetermined amount of time.
To increase a behavior:	
Increase or prearrange the cues associated with the response.	
1. Seek out these cues deliberately to perform the desired behavior.	Arrange only one room with a desk to study. When you need to study, go to this place.
2. Concentrate on the behavior when in the situation.	Concentrate only on studying in the room. If you get distracted, get up and leave. Don't mix study with other activities, such as listening to records or talking.
3. Gradually extend the behavior to other situations.	When you have control over studying in one room, extend the behavior to another conducive room or place.
4. Promote the occurrence of helpful cues by others or by self-generated reminders.	Ask your roommate to remind you to leave the desk when talking or when distracted; remind yourself of good study procedures by posting a list over your study desk or by using verbal or covert self-instructions.

cigarettes to a friend is an example of this method. The friend should agree to help you reduce smoking and should agree not to reinforce or punish any instances of your smoking behavior (the undesired response).

A behavior can also be reduced through stimulus control by interrupting the learned pattern or sequence that begins with one or more antecedent cues and results in the undesired response. This sequence may be referred to as a *chain*. A problem behavior often is the result of a long chain of events. For example, a variety of behaviors make up the sequence of smoking. Before puffing on a cigarette, a person has to go to a cigarette machine, put money in the machine, take out a pack of cigarettes, take out one cigarette from the pack, and light the cigarette.

This chain might be interrupted in one of three ways: breaking up the chain of events, changing the chain, or building pauses into the chain (D. L. Watson & R. G. Tharp, 1977, pp. 161–163). All these methods involve prearranging or altering the time of occurrence of the behavior. A chain of events can be broken up by discovering and interrupting an event early in the sequence or by scrambling or mixing up the typical order of events. For example, the smoker could break up the chain by not carrying the change required for a cigarette machine. Or, if the smoker typically smokes at certain times, the usual order of events leading up to smoking could be mixed up or scrambled. The smoker also could change the typical chain of events. A person who starts to light up a cigarette whenever bored, tense, or lacking something to do with his or her hands could perform a different activity at this point, such as calling a friend when bored, relaxing when tense, or knitting or playing cards to provide hand activity. Finally, the smoker could interrupt the chain by deliberately building pauses into the chain. As you may recall, when antecedents exert control over a behavior, the behavior occurs almost automatically. As Watson and Tharp point out, one way to deal with this automatic quality is to pause before responding to a cue (p. 163). For instance, whenever the smoker has an urge to light up in response to a stress cue, a deliberate pause of 10 minutes can be built in before the person actually does light up. Gradually this time interval can be increased. Sometimes you can even strengthen the pause procedure by covertly instructing yourself on what you want to do or by thinking about the benefits of not smoking. The pause itself can then become a new antecedent "for a more desirable link in the chain of events" (Watson & Tharp, p. 164).*

Using Stimulus Control to Increase Behavior

Stimulus-control methods also can be used to increase a desired response. As noted in Table 23-1, to increase the rate of a response, a person increases or prearranges the antecedent cues as-

*This and all other quotations from this source are from *Self-Directed Behavior: Self-Modification for Personal Adjustment* (2nd ed.), by D. L. Watson and R. G. Tharp. Copyright © 1977 by Wadsworth Publishing Company, Inc. Reprinted by permission of the publisher, Brooks/Cole Publishing Company, Monterey, California.

sociated with the desired behavior. The person deliberately seeks out these cues to perform the behavior and concentrates only on this behavior when in the situation. Competing or distracting responses must be avoided. Gradually, as stimulus control over the behavior in one situation is achieved, the person can extend the behavior by performing it in another, similar situation. This process of stimulus generalization means that a behavior learned in one situation can be performed in different, but similar, situations (D. L. Watson & R. G. Tharp, 1977, p. 167). The person can promote the occurrence of new antecedent cues by using reminders from others, self-reminders, or overt or covert self-instructions (Watson & Tharp). The rate of a desired response is increased by increasing the times and places in which the person performs the response.

As an example, suppose you are working with a client who wants to increase his or her amount of daily exercise. First, more cues would be established to which the person would respond with isometric or physical activity. For example, the person might perform isometric activities whenever sitting in a chair or waiting for a traffic light. Or the person might perform physical exercises each morning and evening on a special exercise mat. The client would seek out these prearranged cues and concentrate on performing the activity while in the situation. Other behaviors should not be performed while in these situations, since a competing response could interfere with the exercise activity (D. L. Watson & R. G. Tharp, 1977, p. 165). Gradually, the client could extend the exercise activities to new, but similar, situations—for example, doing isometrics while sitting on the floor or waiting for a meeting to start. The person can also promote exercise behavior in these situations by reminders—posting an exercise chart on the wall or carrying it around in a pocket or wallet, displaying an exercise list, and so forth.

According to Kanfer (1975), one advantage of stimulus control is that only minimal self-initiated steps are required to trigger environmental changes that effect desired or undesired responses (p. 322). Blechman, Olson, and Hellman (1976) found that one exposure to a family contract game was sufficient to achieve stimulus control over the family's discussion behavior. The participation in the game accelerated family problem-solving behavior and decreased their antagonistic, off-task discussion. However, stimulus-control methods often are insufficient to modify behavior without the support of other strategies. As M. J. Mahoney and C. E. Thoresen (1974) observe, stimulus-control methods are not usually sufficient for long-term self-change unless accompanied by other self-management methods that exert control over the *consequences* of the target behavior. Two self-management methods that involve self-presented consequences are discussed in the following section.

Model Example: Stimulus Control

This model example will illustrate how stimulus control can be used as *one way* to help Joan achieve her goal of increasing positive thoughts about her math ability. The stimulus-control methods she uses also will be incorporated in her self-contract as action steps (see pp. 510–511). Joan's stated goal is to increase positive thoughts about her math ability. Recall that the principle of change in using stimulus control to increase a behavior is to increase the cues associated with the behavior. Here's how we would implement this principle with Joan.

1. Establish at least one cue Joan could use as an antecedent for positive thoughts. We might suggest something like putting a piece of tape over her watch.
2. Develop a list of several positive thoughts about math. Each thought could be written on a blank card that Joan could carry with her.
3. Instruct Joan to read or think about a thought on one card *each* time she looks at her watch. Instruct her to seek out the opportunity deliberately by looking at her watch frequently and then concentrating on one of these positive thoughts.
4. When Joan gets to the point where she automatically thinks of a positive thought after looking at her watch, other cues can be established that she can use in the same way. For instance, she can put a ☺ on her math book. Each time she gets

out her math book and sees the "smiley face," she can use this cue to concentrate on another positive thought.
5. She can promote more stimulus control over these thoughts by using reminders. For instance, Joan could put a list of positive thoughts on the mirror or the closet door in her room. Each time she sees the list, it serves as a reminder. Or she can ask a friend or classmate to remind her to "think positively" whenever the subject of math or math class is being discussed.

Learning Activity: Stimulus Control

Since the emphasis in this chapter is on self-management, the learning activities in this chapter are designed to help you use these strategies yourself! The purpose of this learning activity is to help you reduce an unwanted behavior using stimulus-control methods.

1. Specify a behavior that you find undesirable and that you wish to decrease. It can be an overt one, such as smoking, eating, biting your nails, or making sarcastic comments, or it can be a covert behavior, such as thinking about yourself in negative ways or thinking how great food or smoking tastes.
2. Select one or more stimulus-control methods to use for behavior reduction from the list and examples given in Table 23-1. Remember, you will be reducing the number of cues or antecedent events associated with this behavior by altering the times and places.
3. Implement these stimulus-control methods daily for 2 weeks.
4. During the 2 weeks, engage in self-monitoring. Record the type and use of your method and the amount of your target behavior, using frequency or duration methods of recording.
5. At the end of 2 weeks, review your recording data. Did you use your selected method consistently? If not, what contributed to your infrequent use? If you used it consistently, did you notice any gradual reduction in the target behavior by the end of 2 weeks? What problems did you encounter in applying a stimulus-control method with yourself? What did you learn about stimulus control that might help you when using it with clients?

Self-Reward: A Definition

Self-reward procedures are used to help clients regulate and strengthen their behavior with the aid of self-produced consequences. Many actions of an individual are controlled by self-produced consequences as much as by external consequences (Bandura, 1974, 1976b). As Bandura (1974) explains, "people typically set themselves certain standards of behavior and self-administer rewarding or punishing consequences depending on whether their performances fall short of, match, or exceed their self-prescribed demands" (p. 87). There is evidence that most patterns of self-reinforcement and self-punishment are acquired and modified by learning (Bandura, 1971b).

According to Bandura (1971b), there are several necessary conditions of self-reinforcement or self-reward:

1. The individual (rather than someone else) determines the criteria for adequacy of her or his performance and for resulting reinforcement.
2. The individual (rather than someone else) controls the access to the reward.
3. The individual (rather than someone else) is his or her own reinforcing agent and administers the rewards.

Note that self-reward involves *both* the self-determination and the self-administration of a reward. This distinction has, at times, been overlooked in self-reinforcement research and application. The characteristics of self-reward proposed by Bandura (1971b) suggest that the person has free access to the rewards; this is considered an essential feature of self-reward processes.

As a self-management procedure, self-reward is used to strengthen or increase a desired response. It is assumed that the operations involved in self-reward parallel those that occur in external reinforcement. In other words, a self-presented reward, like an externally administered reward, is defined by the function it exerts on the target behavior. A reinforcer (self- or external) is something that, when ad-

ministered following a target response, tends to maintain or increase the probability of that response in the future. A major advantage of self-reward over external reward is that a person can use and apply this strategy independently.

Self-reward can be classified into two categories: positive self-reward and negative self-reward. In positive self-reward, one presents oneself with a positive stimulus (to which one has free access) *after* engaging in a specified behavior. Examples of positive reward include praising yourself after you have completed a long and difficult term paper, buying yourself a new record after you have engaged in a specified amount of piano practice, or imagining that you are resting on your favorite beach after you have completed your daily exercises. Negative self-reward involves the removal of a negative stimulus after execution of a target response. For example, obese clients removed portions of suet from their refrigerators after certain amounts of weight loss (Penick, Filion, Fox, & Stunkard, 1971). Taking down an uncomplimentary picture or chart from your wall after performing the target response is another example of negative self-reward.

Our discussion of self-reward as a therapeutic strategy is limited to the use of positive self-reward for several reasons. First, there has been very little research to validate the negative self-reward procedure. Second, by definition, negative self-reward involves an aversive activity. It is usually unpleasant for a person to keep suet in the refrigerator or to put an ugly picture on the wall. Many people will not use a strategy that is aversive. Also, we do not recommend that counselors suggest strategies that seem aversive, because the client may feel that terminating the counseling is preferable to engaging in an unpleasant change process.

Clinical Uses of Self-Reward

Self-reward has been explored as a convenient and effective classroom-management procedure (Bolstad & Johnson, 1972; McLaughlin, 1976). It has been used as a major component in comprehensive self-change programs involving weight control (K. Mahoney & M. J. Mahoney, 1976; Polly, Turner, & Sherman, 1976) and exercise programming (Turner, Polly, & Sherman, 1976). Jackson (1972) used self-reward to treat a woman who was depressed and very critical of herself. Self-reinforcement decreased the client's depressive moods, as indicated by daily self-ratings.

Self-reward has been investigated in several controlled studies that have presented evidence for the utility of self-reinforcement as a clinical treatment strategy. For example, M. J. Mahoney, N. G. Moura, and T. C. Wade (1973) found that self-reward was a more effective weight-reduction strategy than self-monitoring, self-punishment, or stimulus control. In this study, self-reward consisted of having the people give themselves money to purchase desired items after certain amounts of weight loss. M. J. Mahoney (1974) also found that self-reward strategies resulted in more weight loss than self-monitoring, especially when the clients made the rewards contingent on improved eating habits rather than weekly weight losses. Bellack (1976) reported that self-reward was more effective than self-monitoring in producing weight reduction, even without therapist contacts. He concluded that self-reward may substantially augment the role of self-monitoring in effecting behavior change.

Both the case studies and controlled investigations of self-reward indicate that this strategy has a promising place in clinical treatment programs. In a review of self-reinforcement, Jones, Nelson, and Kazdin (1977) note that "overall, self-reinforcement has been shown to be a viable technique in treating a plethora of both clinical and educational problems" (p. 160). However, these authors point out that some of the clinical effects typically attributed to the self-reinforcement procedure also may be a function of certain external factors, including a client's previous reinforcement history, client goal-setting, the role of client self-monitoring, surveillance by another person, external contingencies in the client's environment, and the instructional set given to the client about the self-reward procedure. The specific role these external variables may play in self-reward is still relatively little known. However, a counselor should acknowledge and perhaps try to capitalize on some of these factors to heighten the clinical effects of a self-reward strategy.

Components of Self-Reward

Self-reward involves planning by the client of appropriate rewards and of the conditions in which they will be used. Self-reward can be described by four major components: (1) selection of appropriate self-rewards, (2) delivery of self-rewards, (3) timing of self-rewards, and (4) planning for self-change maintenance. These components are described in this portion of the chapter and are summarized in the following list. Although these components are discussed separately, remember that all of them are integral parts of an effective self-reward procedure.

1. Selection of appropriate rewards
   a. individualize the reward
   b. use accessible rewards
   c. use several rewards
   d. use different types of rewards (verbal-symbolic, material, imaginal, current, potential)
   e. use potent rewards
   f. use rewards that are not punishing to others
   g. match rewards to target response
2. Delivery of self-rewards
   a. self-monitor for data of target response
   b. specify what and how much is to be done for a reward
   c. specify frequent reinforcement in small amounts for different levels of target response
3. Timing of self-reward
   a. reward should come after, not before, behavior
   b. rewards should be immediate
   c. rewards should follow performance, not promises
4. Planning for self-change maintenance
   a. enlist help of others in sharing or dispensing rewards
   b. review data with counselor

Selection of Appropriate Rewards

In helping a client to use self-reward effectively, some time and planning must be devoted to selecting rewards that are appropriate for the client and the desired target behavior. Selecting rewards can be time-consuming. However, effective use of self-reward is somewhat dependent on the availability of events that are truly reinforcing to the client. The counselor can assist the client in selecting appropriate self-rewards; however, the client should have the major role in determining the specific contingencies.

Rewards can take many different forms. A self-reward may be verbal-symbolic, material, or imaginal. One verbal-symbolic reward is self-praise, such as thinking or telling oneself "I did a good job." A material reward is something tangible—an event (such as a movie), a purchase (such as a banana split), or a token or point that can be exchanged for a reinforcing event or purchase. An imaginal reinforcer is the covert visualization of a scene or situation that is pleasurable and produces good feelings. Imaginal reinforcers might include picturing yourself as a thin person after losing weight or imagining that you are water-skiing on a lake you have all to yourself.

Self-rewards also can be classified as current or potential. A current reward is something pleasurable that happens routinely or occurs daily, such as eating, smoking, or reading a newspaper. A potential reward is something that would be new and different if it happened, something a person does infrequently or anticipates doing in the future. Examples of potential rewards include going on a vacation or purchasing a "luxury" item (something you love but rarely buy for yourself, not necessarily something expensive). Engaging in a "luxury" activity—something you rarely do—can be a potential reinforcer. For a person who is very busy and constantly working, "doing nothing" might be a luxury activity that is a potential reinforcer.

In selecting appropriate self-rewards, a client should consider the availability of these various kinds of rewards. We believe that a well-balanced self-reward program involves a *variety* of different types of self-rewards. A counselor might encourage a client to select *both* verbal-symbolic and material rewards. Relying only on material rewards may ignore the important role of positive self-evaluations in a self-change program. Also, material rewards have been criticized for overuse and misuse (O'Leary, Poulos, & Devine, 1972). Imaginal reinforcers may not be so powerful as verbal-symbolic and material ones. However, they are completely portable and can be used to supplement verbal-symbolic and material rewards when it is impossible for an individual to use these other types (D. L. Watson & R. G. Tharp, 1977).

In selecting self-rewards, a client should also consider the use of both current and potential rewards. One of the easiest ways for a client to use current rewards is to observe what daily thoughts or activities are reinforcing and then to rearrange these so that they are used in contingent rather than noncontingent ways (Kanfer, 1975; D. L. Watson & R. G. Tharp, 1977). However, whenever a client uses a current reward, some deprivation or self-denial is involved. For example, agreeing to read the newspaper only after cleaning the kitchen involves initially denying oneself some pleasant, everyday event in order to use it to reward a desired behavior. As Thoresen and Mahoney (1974) point out, this initial self-denial introduces an aversive element into the self-reward strategy. Some people do not respond well to any aversiveness associated with self-change or self-directed behavior. One of us, in fact, consistently "abuses" the self-reward principle by doing the reward before the response (reading the paper before cleaning the kitchen)—precisely as a reaction against the aversiveness of this "programmed" self-denial. One way to prevent self-reward from becoming too much like programmed abstinence is to have the client select novel or potential reinforcers to use in addition to current ones.

There are several ways a counselor can help a client identify and select various kinds of self-rewards. One way is simply with verbal report. The counselor and client can discuss current self-reward practices and desired luxury items and activities (Kanfer, 1975). The client also can identify rewards by using "in vivo" observation. The client should be instructed to observe and list current consequences that seem to maintain some behaviors. Finally, the client can identify and select rewards by completing preference and reinforcement surveys. A preference survey is designed to help the client identify preferred and valued activities. Here is an example of one that D. L. Watson and R. G. Tharp (1977) recommend:

1. What kinds of things do you like to have?
2. What are your major interests?
3. What are your hobbies?
4. What people do you like to be with?
5. What do you like to do with those people?
6. What do you do for fun?
7. What do you do to relax?
8. What do you do to get away from it all?
9. What makes you feel good?
10. What would be a nice present to receive?
11. What kinds of things are important to you?
12. What would you buy if you had an extra $10? $50? $100?
13. On what do you spend your money each week?
14. What behaviors do you perform every day? (Don't overlook the obvious or the commonplace.)
15. Are there any behaviors that you usually perform instead of the target behavior?
16. What would you hate to lose?
17. Of the things you do every day, which would you hate to give up? [p. 97].

The client can complete this sort of preference survey in writing or in a discussion. Clients who find it difficult to identify rewarding events might also benefit from completing a more formalized reinforcement survey, such as the Reinforcement Survey Schedule written by Cautela and Kastenbaum (1967). The client can be given homework assignments to identify possible verbal-symbolic and imaginal reinforcers. For instance, the client might be asked to make a daily list for a week of positive self-thoughts or of the positive consequences of desired change. Or the client could make a list of all the things about which she or he likes to daydream or of some imagined scenes that would be pleasurable (Watson & Tharp, 1977).

Sometimes a client may seem thwarted in initial attempts to use self-reward because of difficulties in identifying rewards. D. L. Watson and R. G. Tharp (1977) note that people whose behavior consumes the reinforcer (such as smoking or eating), whose behavior is reinforced intermittently, or whose avoidance behavior is maintained by negative reinforcement may not be able to identify reinforcing consequences readily. Individuals who are "locked into" demanding schedules cannot find daily examples of reinforcers. Sometimes depressed people have trouble identifying reinforcing events. In these cases, the counselor and client have several options that can be used to overcome difficulties in selecting effective self-rewards.

A client who does not have the time or money for material rewards might use imaginal rewards. Imagining pleasant scenes following a target response has been described by Cautela (1970) as *covert positive reinforcement* (CPR). In the CPR procedure, the client usually imagines performing a desired behavior, followed by imagination of a reinforcing scene. In one example, dieters imagined more positive body images as their reinforcing scene (Horan, Baker, Hoffman, & Shute, 1975). D. L. Watson and R. G. Tharp (1977) recommend that a client use imaginal reinforcers only when other kinds are not available, since some of the research on the CPR procedure has produced very mixed results. As an example, in at least one study (Bajtelsmit & Gershman, 1976), having the person imagine the reinforcer *before* the desired behavior was just as effective in reducing test anxiety as having the person imagine the reinforcer *after* the desired behavior. For these reasons, some people have questioned the exact method by which CPR really operates (Ladouceur, 1974).

A second available option for problem cases is to use a client's everyday activity as a self-reward. Some clinical cases have used a mundane activity such as answering the phone (Lawson & May, 1970) or opening the daily mail (Spinelli & Packard, 1975) as the self-reward. (Actually, such an activity may work more as a cueing device than a reinforcer; see Thoresen and Mahoney, 1974.) If a frequently occurring behavior is used as a self-reward, it should be a desirable or at least a neutral activity. As D. L. Watson and R. G. Tharp (1977) note, a client should not use as a self-reward any high-frequency behavior that they would stop immediately if they could. Using a negative high-frequency activity as a reward may seem more like punishment than reinforcement.

With depressed clients, selecting self-rewards is often difficult, because many events lose their reinforcing value for someone who is depressed. Before using self-reward with a depressed client, it might be necessary to increase the reinforcing value of certain events. Anton, Dunbar, and Friedman (1976) describe the procedure of "anticipation training" designed to increase depressed clients' positive anticipations of events. In anticipation training, a client identifies and schedules several pleasant events to perform and then constructs three positive anticipation statements for each activity. The client imagines engaging in an activity and imagines the anticipation statements associated with the activity. An example adapted from Anton et al. of some anticipation statements for one activity might be:

Activity planned: *Spending an afternoon at the lake*
Date to be carried out: *Tuesday; Wednesday if it rains Tuesday*
I will enjoy: *sitting on the beach reading a book*
I will enjoy: *getting in the water on a hot day*
I will enjoy: *getting a suntan*

No thought, event, or imagined scene is reinforcing for everyone. Often what one person finds rewarding is very different from the rewards selected by someone else. In using self-reward, it is important to help clients choose rewards that will work well for *them*—not for the counselor, a friend, or a spouse. Kanfer (1975) notes that "it is crucial that the selected reinforcers relate to the client's personal history. They must be acceptable to him as something he wants, could easily acquire or do, and that would make him feel good" (pp. 338–339).

The counselor should use the following guidelines to help the client determine some self-rewards that might be used effectively.

1. *Individualize* the reward to the client (Homme, Csanyi, Gonzales, & Rechs, 1969).
2. The reward should be *accessible* and *convenient* to use after the behavior is performed.
3. *Several* rewards should be used interchangeably to prevent satiation (a reward can lose its reinforcing value because of repeated presentations).
4. Different *types* of rewards should be selected (verbal-symbolic, material, imaginal, current, potential).
5. The rewards should be *potent*, but not so valuable that an individual will not use them contingently.
6. The rewards should not be *punishing* to others. D. L. Watson and R. G. Tharp (1977) suggest that, if a reward involves someone else, then the other person's agreement should be obtained.
7. The reward should be *compatible* with the desired response (Kanfer, 1975). For instance, a person losing weight might use new clothing as a reward, or thoughts of a new body image after weight loss. Using eating as a reward is not a good match for a weight-loss target response.

Delivery of Self-Reward

The second part of working out a self-reward strategy with a client involves specifying the conditions and method of delivering the self-rewards. First of all, a client cannot deliver or administer a self-reward without some data base. Self-reward delivery is dependent upon systematic data-gathering; self-monitoring is an essential first step.

Second, the client should determine the precise conditions under which a reward will be delivered. The client should, in other words, state the rules of the game. The client should know *what* and *how much* has to be done before administering a self-reward. Usually, self-reward is more effective when clients reward themselves for small steps of progress (Homme et al., 1969). In other words, performance of a subgoal should be rewarded. Waiting to reward oneself for demonstration of the overall goal usually introduces too much of a delay between responses and rewards.

Finally, the client should indicate how much and what kind of reward will be given for performing various responses or different levels of the goals. The client should specify that doing so much of the response results in one type of reward and how much of it. Usually reinforcement is more effective when broken down into smaller units that are self-administered more frequently (Homme et al., 1969). The use of tokens or points provides for frequent, small units of reinforcement; these can be exchanged for a "larger" reinforcer after a certain number of points or tokens are accumulated.

Timing of Self-Rewards

The counselor also needs to instruct the client about the timing of self-reward—when a self-reward should be administered. There are three ground rules for the timing of a self-reward; most of these have been suggested by Homme et al. (1969):

1. A self-reward should be administered *after* performing the specified response, not before.
2. A self-reward should be administered *immediately* after the response. Long delays may render the procedure ineffective.
3. A self-reward should follow *actual performance*, not promises to perform.

Planning for Self-Change Maintenance

Self-reward, like any self-change strategy, needs environmental support for long-term maintenance of change (Kanfer, 1975; M. J. Mahoney, 1974). The last part of using self-reward involves helping the client find ways to plan for self-change maintenance. First, the counselor can encourage the client to enlist the help of others in a self-reward program. Other people can share in or dispense some of the reinforcement (D. L. Watson & R. G. Tharp, 1977). Some evidence indicates that people who

receive rewards from others at least initially may benefit more from self-reward (M. J. Mahoney & C. E. Thoresen, 1974). Second, the client should plan to review the data collected during self-reward with the counselor. The review sessions give the counselor a chance to reinforce the client and to help the client make any necessary revisions in the use of the strategy. Counselor expectations and approval for client progress may add to the overall effects of the self-reward strategy (Jones et al., 1977).

Some Cautions in Using Rewards

The use of rewards as a motivational and informational device is a controversial issue. Using rewards, especially material ones, as incentives has been criticized on the grounds that tangible rewards are overused, misused, and often discourage rather than encourage the "rewardee" (Levine & Fasnacht, 1974; O'Leary, Poulos, & Devine, 1972). Furthermore, as McKeachie (1974, 1976) observes, high levels of reward (or punishment) are not necessarily optimal for performance (McKeachie, 1976, p. 823).

As a therapy technique, self-reward should not be used indiscriminately. Before suggesting self-reward, the counselor should carefully consider the individual client, the client's previous reinforcement history, and the client's desired change. When a counselor and client do decide to use self-reward, two cautionary guidelines should be followed. First, material rewards should not be used solely or promiscuously. Levine and Fasnacht (1974) recommend that the therapist seek ways to increase a person's intrinsic satisfaction in performance before automatically resorting to extrinsic rewards as a motivational technique. Second, the counselor's role in self-reward should be limited to providing instructions about the procedure and encouragement for progress. The client should be the one who selects the rewards and determines the criteria for delivery and timing of reinforcement. As Jones et al. (1977) observe, when the target behaviors and the contingencies are specified by someone other than the person using self-reward, the procedure can hardly be described accurately as a self-change operation (p. 174).

Model Example: Self-Reward

This example will illustrate how self-reward could be used to help Joan increase her positive thoughts about her ability to do well in math.

1. Selection of appropriate rewards: First the counselor would help Joan select some appropriate rewards to use for reaching her predetermined goal. The counselor would encourage Joan to identify some self-praise she could use to reward herself symbolically or verbally ("I did it"; "I can gradually see my attitude about math changing"). Joan could give herself points for daily positive thoughts. She could accumulate and exchange the points for material rewards, including current rewards (such as engaging in a favorite daily event) and the potential rewards (such as a purchase of a desired item). These are suggestions; Joan should be responsible for the actual selection. The counselor could suggest that Joan identify possible rewards through observation or completion of a preference survey. The counselor should make sure that the rewards Joan selects are accessible and easy to use. Several rewards should be selected to prevent satiation. The counselor also should make sure that the rewards selected are potent, compatible with Joan's goal, and not punishing to anyone else.
2. Delivery of rewards: The counselor would help Joan determine guidelines for delivery of the selected rewards. Joan might decide to give herself a point for each positive thought. This allows for reinforcement of small steps toward the overall goal. A predetermined number of daily points, such as 5, might result in delivery of a current reward, such as watching TV or going over to her friend's house. A predetermined number of weekly points could mean delivery of a potential self-reward, such as shopping or purchasing a new item. Joan's demonstration of her goal beyond the specified level could result in delivery of a bonus self-reward.
3. Timing of rewards: The counselor would instruct Joan to administer the reward *after* the positive thoughts or after the specified number of points is accumulated. The counselor can emphasize that the rewards follow performance, not promises. Also, the counselor should encourage Joan to engage in the rewards as soon as possible after the daily and weekly target goals have been met.
4. Planning for self-change maintenance: The counselor can help Joan find ways to plan for self-change maintenance. One way is to schedule periodic "check-ins" with the counselor. Also, Joan might select a friend who could help her share in the reward by watching TV or going shopping with her or by praising Joan for her goal achievement. Use of a friend in this way is also included in Joan's self-contract (pp. 510–511).

Learning Activity: Self-Reward

This learning activity is designed to have you engage in self-reward.

1. Select a target behavior you want to increase. Write down your goal (the behavior to increase, desired level of increase, and conditions in which behavior will be demonstrated).
2. Select several different types of self-rewards to use and write them on a piece of paper. The types to use are verbal-symbolic, material (both current and potential), and imaginal. See whether your selected self-rewards meet the following criteria:
   a. Individually tailored to you?
   b. Accessible and convenient to use?
   c. Several different self-rewards?
   d. Different types of self-rewards?
   e. Are rewards potent?
   f. Are rewards not punishing to others?
   g. Are rewards compatible with your desired goal?
3. Set up a plan for delivery of your self-reward: What type of reinforcement and how much will be administered? How much and what demonstration of the target behavior are required?
4. When do you plan to administer a self-reward?
5. How could you enlist the aid of another person?
6. Apply self-reward for a specified time period. Did your target response increase? To what extent?
7. What did you learn about self-reward that might help you in suggesting this to a client?

Self-Punishment

Self-punishment is a self-management strategy in which a person attempts to influence the frequency of an undesired behavior by decreasing or weakening the response. Two types of self-punishment can be used. In positive self-punishment, one removes a positive stimulus after a target behavior. Taking away points or tokens and foregoing a pleasant activity are examples of positive self-punishment. In negative self-punishment, one presents oneself with an unpleasant stimulus following the target behavior (Thoresen & Mahoney, 1974, p. 93). An example of negative self-punishment would be covertly criticizing yourself after eating too much, or putting up a picture of yourself in which you look fat after overeating. Most people favor positive rather than negative self-punishment (M. J. Mahoney & C. E. Thoresen, 1974; Thoresen & Mahoney, 1974), primarily because removal of a reinforcer may be more effective and less problematic than presentation of an aversive stimulus (Bandura, 1969).

Clinical Uses of Self-Punishment

Several case studies, but only a few well-controlled investigations, have explored self-punishment as a therapeutic strategy. It has been used to reduce hallucinations (Bucher & Fabricatore, 1970; Weingartner, 1971), self-critical obsessions (M. J. Mahoney, 1971), smoking (Axelrod, Hall, Weis, & Rohrer, 1974), and obesity (M. J. Mahoney, N. G. Moura, & T. C. Wade, 1973; Morganstern, 1974). A majority of the reported clinical uses of self-punishment have involved the negative type: an individual has self-administered an unpleasant stimulus after engaging in the target response.

Self-punishment is used to reduce or to weaken an undesired response. It is assumed that self-punishment operates in a manner that is similar, if not parallel, to externally administered punishment. The punishing contingencies are considered to be punitive if, when administered after a target response, they reduce the probability that the response will occur in the future.

Disadvantages of Self-Punishment

In our opinion, more disadvantages than advantages may result from the use of self-punishment as a *primary* self-management procedure. Self-punishment is a controversial therapy strategy and has a very weak data base to support its use. Studies on positive self-punishment are particularly scarce. Both positive and negative forms of self-punishment involve aversive processes. We doubt that most clients would use self-punishment with the consistency and regularity required of an effective self-management strategy. As D. L. Watson and R. G. Tharp (1977) point out, it is very difficult for most people to do something unpleasant. When one is required to engage in an unpleasant activity frequently, the procedure often will be abandoned after a few short-lived attempts. Even if a client were to administer self-punishment consistently, the procedure might not have the desired effect. As Kanfer (1975) notes, sometimes the use of self-punishment does not decrease the target behavior but simply reduces the guilt or anxiety associated with it.

In our opinion, another disadvantage of suggesting self-punishment to a client is the implicit endorsement of an aversive strategy for changing behavior. There is not much doubt that the counselor can be a very potent model for clients. In recommending and using possible counseling strategies, it is helpful to remember that clients may adapt the application of a recommended procedure for a variety of uses and purposes. If aversive strategies constitute a predominant part of self-change programs, clients may expect change for themselves (and others) to result only under conditions of negative contingencies. In our own counseling, we are reluctant to recommend self-punishment to a client because, in doing so, we are modeling the control of behavior by negative rather than positive contingencies. Unfortunately, we find that, for most clients (and many nonclients as well), self-punitive responses are common. Clients usually know how to criticize themselves or how to influence someone else by removing a positive contingency or administering an unpleasant one. Generally, we feel that clients would benefit more by using procedures in which they learn how to influence change with self-praise, positive self-verbalizations, and administration of positive consequences.

Because of the disadvantages associated with self-punishment, we recommend its use only under very limited conditions and only in cases where behavior reduction is a necessary and viable client goal. First of all, self-punishment should be used only in combination with a self-reward. If a person is going to remove a positive stimulus to reduce an unwanted behavior, it is essential also to administer a positive stimulus to strengthen the desired response. Limited evidence suggests that self-punishment used in conjunction with self-reward is more effective than self-punishment alone (M. J. Mahoney, N. G. Moura, & T. C. Wade, 1973). One way that self-punishment could be combined with self-reward is through the use of predefined sanctions and rewards in a self-contract, as described in the next section.

Self-Contracting

Self-contracting is a self-management strategy that involves determining in advance the external and internal consequences that will follow the execution of the desired or undesired response. Because the terms of the contract are specified and carried out primarily by the client, we refer to this as a *self-contract*. Self-contracting may strengthen a client's commitment to carry out action steps regularly and consistently. Although self-contracting as we describe it is a form of self-management, such a contract can be adopted at any point in the counseling process. As you may recall from Chapter 11, a contract can be useful during the process of establishing counseling goals.

A self-contract may take the form of a contingency contract, in which the target behavior and the contingencies for meeting or not meeting it are specified (Homme, Csanyi, Gonzales,

& Rechs, 1969). The positive contingencies may be referred to as *rewards*; the negative ones may be called *sanctions* (Stuart, 1971). As an example, a smoker could set up a contingency self-contract as follows:

Target Behavior: My goal is to reduce my cigarette-smoking from 200 cigarettes a week (7-day period) to 150 cigarettes a week.
Reward: If, after 7 days, I have not smoked more than 150 cigarettes, I will go out to dinner on the seventh night at my favorite place.
Sanction: If I have smoked more than my limit, I will donate $5 to the Cancer Society.

Some case studies exploring contingency self-contracts involve the client's deposit of a valuable possession or money with the counselor (Boudin, 1972; R. A. Mann, 1972). If the client meets the goal, portions or the entire amount of money or the possession are returned. If the contract terms are not met, the counselor turns over the possession or money to someone else—often a group disliked by the client, such as the opposing political party. M. J. Mahoney and C. E. Thoresen (1974) observe that a client may be reluctant to agree to a contract involving initial deposits of money or possessions because of the possible risk of loss (p. 46).

A self-contract also may prearrange social-environmental consequences. The client can enlist the aid of another person who agrees to do certain things to ensure that the contract contingencies are, in fact, applied. In one investigation using self-contracting to increase study time, 40% of the contracts were "broken" by people who did not administer or withhold reinforcement according to the contract terms (McReynolds & Church, 1973). Employing the services of another person may increase the likelihood that the client will maintain the contract.

In some cases, self-contracts are used as the primary behavior-change strategy. For example, Vance (1976) used self-contracting as a method of improving students' study behavior. Self-contracts often are used in combination with other self-management or therapeutic strategies.

Features of a Good Self-Contract

A good self-contract has six basic features:

1. The contract terms should be clear to all involved parties. The behavior to be achieved and an acceptable criterion level should be specified.
2. The contract should include a balance of rewards and sanctions appropriate to the desired behavior.
3. The contract should emphasize the positive and may include a bonus clause.
4. The contract should include a clause that involves the participation of another person. The person should have a positive rather than a negative role.
5. The contract should be written and include a place for signatures.
6. The contract should include a recording system (a progress log) that specifies the desired behavior to be observed, the amount (frequency or duration) of the behavior, and the rewards and sanctions administered. If possible, the recording system should be verified by one other person.

First, the terms of the self-contract should be stated clearly. They should specify the behavior to be achieved and an acceptable criterion level of performance. For example, a self-contract designed to improve study habits should state something like "Increase study time in a quiet place by 2 hours per day" instead of "study more" or "study better." Weathers and Liberman (1975) point out that "novices in contracting are inclined toward writing vague, general terms using the ambiguity to ease the negotiation. . . . [The result is that] each party can interpret a vague statement in ways agreeable to himself. This serves only to postpone the conflict" (p. 209). Second, the contract contingencies of rewards and sanctions should be appropriate for the contracted behavior. The client always should be rewarded sufficiently for achieving the contract goal. Some sanctions may be necessary to maintain the potency of a contract (R. A. Mann, 1972), although occasionally an effective self-contract may include only re-

wards (Vance, 1976). Whether or not sanctions are included should be determined on an individual basis, since each person responds differently to the use of a sanction as a motivating device. Often the success of a self-contract depends upon the type and timing of the self-administered rewards or sanctions. All the guidelines for determining effective rewards and sanctions presented earlier in this chapter should be considered in drawing up a workable self-contract. The overall flavor of the contract should be positive. The behavior to be achieved should be stated in positive terms. In addition to the stated rewards, a bonus clause may be included to reward nearly flawless demonstration of the contracted behavior (Stuart, 1971).

A good self-contract may be more effective if at least one other person (the counselor or a client's significant other) participates. This person may agree to carry out certain activities or to assist in implementing the contract contingencies. She or he can agree to reinforce the client for instances of the desired behavior and to ignore instances of the undesired behavior. Generally, we do not believe that other people should punish the client (apply aversive stimuli or withdraw pleasant ones) for failure to meet the contract terms. Clients often respond negatively, not positively, to aversive environmental pressure (Hackett, Horan, Stone, Linberg, Nicholas, & Lukaski, 1976). Administering or receiving punishment can have bad overtones and serious side effects, particularly when the two parties are closely or intimately involved with each other. Generally, the role of the significant other in a self-contract should be neutral or positive, not negative.

The contract should be written and should include a place for the signatures of all involved parties. A written contract can minimize ambiguity and may function as a demand characteristic by prompting the client to complete it. Finally, a self-contract should include a recording system. This system can help the client self-monitor the behavior to be observed, the amount of the behavior, and the rewards and sanctions administered. Kanfer (1975) points out that a recording system provides a way to inform the client of progress while carrying out the contractual terms (p. 321). A progress log is one example of a recording system for a self-contract. Vance (1976) used progress logs that people completed daily to monitor their progress in carrying out the terms of their self-contracts for weight control and cardiovascular-fitness activities. If possible, the client's recording data or progress log should be verified by the other person who participates in the self-contract.

We present an example of one possible self-contract and an accompanying log for recording in Figures 23-1 (self-contract) and 23-2 (progress log). The self-contract and log include

Name of person
making contract _____ *Sara* _____

Name of other
persons _____ *Jane (Roommate)* _____

Date _____ *June 10, 1977* _____

Goal of contract:	*To increase my daily exercise at home from zero to 10 minutes daily.*	(Target behavior) (Criterion level)
Action steps carried out by me:	*I agree to do 10 minutes of exercises each day in the morning after getting out of bed and to keep track of the amount of daily exercise on my log sheet.*	(Terms of contract)
Action steps carried out by others:	*Jane will do exercises with me and will verify my log sheet.*	(Participation clause for other persons)
Rewards carried out by me:	*For each day that I do 10 minutes exercise I will either watch 30 extra minutes of TV or read in my favorite book 30 extra minutes.*	(Positive consequences- self-administered)
Carried out by others:	*Jane will give positive feedback after 10 minutes of exercise and will see that I have 30 minutes quiet time to read or watch TV at night.*	(Positive consequences administered by others)
Bonus	*If at the end of one week I have done 10 minutes of exercise each day, I will spend $5.00 any way I want to.*	(Additional positive consequences for nearly flawless completion of contract)
Sanctions (optional) carried out by me:	*For each day that I do not do 10 minutes exercise I will not watch TV or read my favorite book that day.*	(Sanctions—self- administered)
Carried out by others:	*For each day I do not do 10 minutes exercise, Jane will ignore this and say nothing.*	(Sanctions—other administered)

Date contract
will be reviewed: _____ *July 10, 1977* _____

Signed ___ *Sara M.* ___ (Client signature)

_____ *Jane P.* ___ (Other person's signature)

Figure 23-1. Example of a Self-Contract

Name	Sara			
Behavior being observed	_Daily physical exercises_			
Verification source	_Jane_			

Week	Date	Amount/Frequency of Behavior	Reward Used (or) Sanction Used	Verified By
1	June 11	10 min.	30 min. TV	J.P.
1	June 12	10 min.	30 min. reading	J.P.
1	June 13	10 min.	30 min. reading	J.P.
1	June 14	15 min.	30 min. reading	J.P.
1	June 15	10 min.	30 min. reading	J.P.
1	June 16	10 min.	30 min. TV	J.P.
1	June 17	15 min.	30 min. TV plus $5.00 for a record (bonus)	J.P.
2	June 18	10 min.	30 min. TV	J.P.
2	June 19	10 min.	30 min. TV	J.P.
2	June 20	5 min.	no TV	J.P.
2	June 21	10 min.	30 min. reading	J.P.
2	June 22	10 min.	30 min. reading	J.P.
2	June 23	5 min.	no reading	J.P.
2	June 24	10 min.	30 min. reading but no bonus	J.P.

Figure 23-2. Example of Self-Contract Progress Log

the six features of a good self-contract. Each clause is explained in the righthand column of Figure 23-1. The client uses the progress log to keep track of the desired behavior and its duration. Note that the other person assisting with the contract also verifies the progress log (Figure 23-2). Using another person as a verification source can help the client carry out the contract terms and can lend validity to the monitoring system when it is used to collect data for evaluation of counseling (Chapter 13). This "surveillance" by another person also can influence the results of self-contracting (Jones et al., 1977).

Steps in Implementing a Self-Contract

Part of the success of a self-contract may depend on the way the contract is implemented. Here is a summary of the steps of contract implementation:

1. The contract terms should be negotiated, not proclaimed, by all involved parties (client, counselor, significant other).

2. Oral and written client commitment to the contract should be obtained.
3. The behaviors specified in the contract should be rehearsed by the client.
4. The client (and any other person involved) should carry out the contractual procedures systematically and regularly.
5. The contract should be reviewed at a later time and revised if necessary.
6. The counselor should provide reinforcement to the client as the client implements the contractual procedures.

First, all the terms of the contract should be negotiated by all parties involved—client, counselor, and significant other. The central feature of a contract is that _all_ involved parties specify the terms (L. S. Cormier & W. H. Cormier, 1975, p. 10). A contract differs from a rule or a proclamation, where only one person sets the terms. Contract negotiation implies that the contract terms are specified without the threat of explicit or subtle coercion (Weathers & Liberman, 1975). The advantage of a contract is that the terms are more likely to be acceptable to everyone who plays a role in contract implementation (Williams, Long, & Yoakley, 1972). Before the contract is implemented, the counselor should obtain client commitment to the actions, not the promises, specified by the contract (Kanfer & Karoly, 1972). Both oral and written commitment (a signature on the contract) are important. The client also should rehearse the contracted behaviors with the counselor before applying the contract "in vivo." Such rehearsal may help the client to carry out the contracted responses with a minimum of problems. Rehearsal also may motivate the client to implement the contract regularly and systematically. As Kanfer (1975) observes, the effectiveness of a self-contract depends upon the degree to which the contract is used for "everyday conduct" (p. 323).

There are several ways to encourage a client to adhere to contract terms. First, the client may be more likely to use a self-contract if the terms maximize the rewards and minimize the costs for the individual (Weathers & Liberman, 1975, p. 209). As these authors assert, the contract must do more than simply meet the "status quo"; advantages that exceed the status quo must be provided for the user of the contract. Second, the client may use the self-contract more consistently if the contract terms are reasonable and do not require too much time, effort, or achievement of the client. If the contract asks too much or fails to reward the client for small steps of progress, the client may become easily discouraged and abandon the contract. The counselor should help the client develop a self-contract that emphasizes behaviors within the client's capability and that provides reinforcement for gradual levels of improvement (Weathers & Liberman, p. 209). Third, the contract should be reviewed periodically to determine whether it is being carried out or if revisions are necessary. Finally, as with any self-management procedure, the counselor should be sure to encourage or reinforce the client during the time the contract is being used. Support and check-ins by the counselor may strengthen the possibility that the client will maintain the contract terms (Cantrell, Cantrell, Huddleston, & Wooldridge, 1969).

Model Example: Self-Contracting

The previous model examples presented in Chapter 22 and in this chapter illustrated how self-monitoring, stimulus control, and self-reward could be used to help Joan increase positive thoughts about her ability to do well in math class. This model example will present a self-contract arranged by Joan, the counselor, and Joan's best friend, Debbie, to help Joan achieve the same goal. The self-contract and Joan's log sheet are presented on p. 511. The goal of the contract is stated positively and includes a criterion level of performance. Also, the three action steps listed that Joan will carry out include the stimulus-control methods described earlier in the chapter and log recording (self-monitoring). Debbie's first action step is also part of stimulus control. Her second step indicates her role as a verification source to document Joan's use of contract rewards and sanctions. (It would be difficult to document the frequency of the target behavior because it is covert.) In this contract, the rewards are stated as points. Joan can exchange a predetermined number of points for a current material reward (watching TV). For an even greater number of points, she can have another reward or bonus (new nail polish). Failure to meet the predetermined daily number of points results in a sanction, or foregoing the reward. Note that Debbie's role in the sanction is neutral rather than negative; she simply ignores Joan's lack of goal achievement.

Learning Activity: Self-Contracting

Have you ever tried to contract with yourself to do something? If not, here's your opportunity! We suggest you decide on an overt or covert behavior you wish to increase. For example, you might want to do more daily physical activity, to do more reading or studying, to think more positive thoughts about yourself, or to practice a new helping skill. After you've decided on something:

1. Draw up a contract for yourself using the format presented in Figure 23-1.
2. Enlist the aid of one other person to help you carry out the contract and to serve as a verification source.
3. Implement the terms of the contract over a 2-week period.
4. During the 2-week period, also engage in self-monitoring. Observe and record your desired be-

JOAN'S SELF-CONTRACT

Name of person:	_Joan_
Name(s) of other person(s):	_Debbie_
Date:	_June 1, 1977_

Goal of contract

To increase my positive thoughts about my math ability to at least five per day

Action steps carried out by me:

1. I will concentrate on a positive thought on my card each time I look at my watch.
2. I will count and record each positive thought on my progress log.
3. I will look at my reminder list of positive thoughts each time I open my closet door.

Action steps carried out by others:

1. Debbie will remind me to think positively whenever we start to discuss math.
2. Debbie will verify on my log my use of rewards and sanctions.

Rewards
a. Carried out by me:

I will give myself 1 point for each positive thought I count. At the end of a day if I have 5 points total I will watch one hour more of TV.

b. Carried out by others:

Debbie will praise me for reaching my goal.

Bonus:

If I have at least 40 points at the end of the week I will buy new nail polish.

Sanctions
a. Carried out by me:

If I have less than 5 points at the end of a day, I will not watch TV.

b. Carried out by others:

If I have less than 5 points at the end of the day, Debbie will say nothing.

Date of
Contract Review: _July 1, 1977_

Signed:	_Joan Z._
	(client)
	Debbie S.
	(friend)
	_Mr. or Ms. W._
	(counselor)

JOAN'S PROGRESS LOG SHEET

Name: _Joan_

Behavior to
be Recorded: _Positive thoughts about my math ability_

Week	Date	Amount/Frequency of Behavior	Points/Day	Points/Week	Reward or Sanction	Verified by
1	June 2	𝈤𝈤	5		TV	DS
1	June 3	////	4		no TV	DS
1	June 4	///	3		no TV	DS
1	June 5	𝈤𝈤	5		TV	DS
1	June 6	////	4		no TV	DS
1	June 7	///	3		no TV	DS
1	June 8	////	4	28	no nail polish or TV	DS
2	June 9	////	4		no TV	DS
2	June 10	𝈤𝈤	5		TV	DS
2	June 11	𝈤𝈤 /	6		TV	DS
2	June 12	𝈤𝈤 /	6		TV	DS
2	June 13	𝈤𝈤 /	6		TV	DS
2	June 14	𝈤𝈤 /	6		TV	DS
2 DS	June 15	𝈤𝈤 //	7	40	TV and shopping new nail polish (bonus)	DS

Stimulus Control, Self-Reward, and Self-Contracting

havior, the amount of it, and the reward or sanction used on an accompanying progress log, similar to the one presented in Figure 23-2.

5. After the 2-week period, review your log data and the self-contract. Did you increase the desired behavior? If not, what parts of the self-contract need revision? In what ways did this learning activity provide experiential information that might help you use self-contracts with your clients?

Promoting Client Commitment to Use Self-Management Strategies

A critical issue in any self-management strategy that is still unresolved has been termed "the contract problem" (M. J. Mahoney, 1970). Finding ways to strengthen a client's stated commitment to using a self-management strategy consistently is a major challenge to any helper (Kanfer, 1975; Thoresen & Mahoney, 1974). There are several things a counselor might do to increase the probability that a client will use self-management strategies consistently. First, some clients seem to be more hesitant about self-management methods upon first entering therapy (Williams, Canale, & Edgerly, 1976). Perhaps clients who decide to seek the assistance of a helper are discouraged with their own self-change efforts. For this reason, counselors may want to avoid introducing self-management strategies in early counseling sessions (Williams et al., p. 234).

Second, clients' regular use of self-management may depend partially on their motivation to change. People who are very motivated to change a behavior seem to benefit more from self-management than those who aren't interested in modifying the target response (Ciminero, Nelson, & Lipinski, 1977). In view of the importance of the client's desire to change the goal behavior, the counselor might precede initiating a self-management strategy with some assessment of the client's motivation level. J. Brown (1978) recommends that the following questions be answered orally or in writing by the client:

1. How much money would you be willing to spend to do _____? (Put any maximum dollar amount between 0 and 10,000.)
2. If unpleasant activity—real, unpaid, work —were required instead of money, how many *minutes* each day would you be willing to spend to reach your goal? (Put in any maximum number of *minutes* between 0 and 480.)
3. On the following scale, please circle the number that best indicates how motivated you are to make this change.

4—Extremely motivated. . . . Nothing is more important to me.
3—Very motivated. . . .
2—Moderately motivated. . . .
1—Not motivated [p. 127].*

Third, in using self-management programs, the help and support of other people should not be ignored. The use of significant others to aid the client in the use of a strategy may greatly enhance the behavior change. Self-help groups are one example: clients' self-directed change programs are supported by friends or by other clients working toward similar goals (Stuart, 1977).

The helper, too, should maintain at least minimal contact with the client while the self-management strategies are being used. These strategies are an excellent way to bridge the gap from regular weekly counseling sessions to termination of counseling. Use of self-management procedures at this point may promote generalization of client changes from the interview setting to the client's environment. However, the counselor should maintain some contact with the client during this period, even if it involves only informal telephone calls. Employing self-management strategies in the concluding sessions also can help the counselor and client achieve a gradual and successful termination. Some guidelines for termination

*From *An Analysis of Self-Monitoring-Provided Feedback in a Behavioral Weight Reduction Program*, by J. Brown. Unpublished doctoral dissertation, West Virginia University, 1978. Reprinted by permission.

of the helping process are presented in the following section.

Termination of the Helping Relationship

If the data collected before, during, and after the use of counseling strategies reveal that the client is making progress toward the desired outcomes, these data become a source of motivation and encouragement to the client. As strategies are implemented successfully and goals are reached, the counselor and client will either decide to terminate counseling or will negotiate another counseling contract. The counselor ethically should intervene only to the extent requested by the client. Once the initial goals are attained, additional change efforts are not begun unless the client requests or agrees to this explicitly. For example, suppose you are helping a client achieve the goal of making a vocational decision. After this point, if the client wants your assistance to pursue something else, such as improving communication with parents, the process begins all over again. The problem situation is defined, new goals are established, and appropriate means of reaching the goals are implemented. If the client has no other concerns or does not choose to present additional problems, then counseling is ended. According to Eisenberg and Delaney (1977), the counseling process is terminated "when the counselor and client no longer see each other for the purpose of counseling" (p. 199).

The process of termination is not always as simple as it sounds. As Eisenberg and Delaney (1977) observe, "there are important emotional factors involved for both the client and the counselor in the termination stage" (p. 199). If the relationship has developed into a strong one, then both counselor and client have developed warm feelings for each other. Both may approach termination with a sense of loss. In addition, the client has relied on the counselor as a major source of support. It is likely that the client will approach termination with some degree of separation anxiety. Therefore, it is important to give advance notice of termination so that dependence on counseling is gradually reduced and the client's self-directed efforts are maintained and rewarded.

Termination can be spread out over several weeks, but, to avoid reinforcing a client's dependent behavior, it should not be prolonged any more than necessary. If the client seems very insecure about terminating, it may take several sessions to work through such insecurity before the final termination session. It is generally a good idea to terminate with these guidelines in mind:

1. Point out the client's achievements and independence.
2. Share your positive feelings about the client and the relationship.
3. Plan for a follow-up at a future date.
4. "Leave your door open" should the client decide to reinitiate counseling in the future.

A Concluding Comment

It is now time for us to conclude the relationship we have had with each of you as you have read and reacted to this book. For the last six years, one of our goals has been to communicate in a systematic way some of the skills and strategies involved in helping interviews. The completion of this writing endeavor gives us a sense of satisfaction. Our satisfaction is greater if the book has helped you to become the skilled counselor you have the potential to be. Hopefully, the practice you have had in completing this book will enable you to carry out these skills and strategies independently. However, we encourage you to consult any part of the book when necessary.

We hope that, as you gain experience in helping, you can develop your counseling style and apply the strategies we have presented with some ingenuity. Creative application of helping procedures suggests that you are not a slave to the methodology but can adapt, expand, or vary it as the need arises (Egan, 1975, p. 199). Using helping procedures methodically or creatively is like painting by numbers or painting "free style." In the first case you are painting by following the suggestion of someone else. The result is often artificial and stylized. In the latter case, you are painting by following your own interpretation. The result is genuine and individualized—something that characterizes the best helping relationships.

Post Evaluation

Part One

Objective 1 asks you to describe how stimulus-control methods could be used to increase or reduce a behavior for a given client. Using the following case description, describe in writing how you would use stimulus control to reduce the client's eating behavior and to increase her control over her study behavior.

Case Description
The client is a freshman in college, living at home. She is concerned because she is under more pressure and has gained 25 pounds recently. She is having trouble keeping up with her course work because she lacks discipline to study. She wants help in reducing her weight and increasing her studying.

1. Describe how the client could use stimulus control to reduce her eating behavior:
   a. How could she reduce or narrow the cues associated with eating?
   b. How could she prearrange cues that make overeating or eating snacks or fattening foods difficult?
   c. How could she prearrange some cues to be controlled by other people?
   d. How could she break up the sequence or chain of eating behavior?
   e. How could she change the typical sequence or chain resulting in eating?
   f. How could she build pauses into the eating chain?
2. Describe how she could increase control of her study behavior using stimulus control by:
   a. prearranging the cues associated with studying
   b. concentrating on the behavior while in the prearranged situations
   c. promoting the occurrence of helpful cues by reminders.

Part Two

Objective 2 asks you to describe the application of the four components of self-reward for a written client case. Read the following case; then respond in writing to the questions that follow.

Client Case Description
The client is a young man who wants to increase the number of women he asks out for dates; he has set a goal of asking at least three different women out per week. You have instructed the client as to how to self-monitor this target behavior. In addition, you plan to instruct the client to use self-reward. He will count and chart the number of women he actually invites, then administer a self-reward if he met his weekly goal.

Selection of Rewards
1. What would be two examples of a verbal-symbolic reward the client could use? Two examples of a material reward? Two examples of an imaginal reward?
2. List at least three characteristics of an effective self-reward.
3. If the client had trouble identifying material reinforcers, what is one alternative that could be used?

Delivery of Rewards
4. Give an example of how you would instruct the client to administer and deliver a self-reward (for example, what type and how much reinforcement for levels of goal achievement).

Timing of Self-Rewards
5. List at least two instructions you would give the client about *when* to administer the reward.

Planning for Self-Change Maintenance
6. Write at least one thing the client could do to plan for self-change maintenance.

Part Three

Objective 3 asks you to teach someone else how to use a self-reward procedure to increase or strengthen a behavior. You can use the list on p. 499 as a guide. You should teach the person how to select appropriate self-rewards, how to deliver self-reinforcement, when to administer self-rewards, and how to plan for self-change maintenance.

Part Four

Objective 4 asks you to serve as a consultant to help another person write a self-contract. Make sure the contract includes the six features listed on p. 507. Also, a progress log (Figure 23-2) may be necessary for the person to observe and record use of the contract terms.

Part Five

Objective 5 asks you to conduct a role-play interview, demonstrating five out of six steps of implementing a self-contract with another person. You may wish to do this with the person with whom you consulted in Part Three. Use the list on p. 509 as a guide in demonstrating these steps.

Feedback: Post Evaluation

Part One

Refer to Table 23-1 for examples of stimulus control to reduce eating behavior and to increase study behavior.

Part Two

1. The *verbal symbolic rewards* used by this client could consist of self-praise for inviting a woman or could consist of covert verbalizations about the positive consequences of his behavior. Here are some examples:

   "I did it! I asked her out."
   "I did just what I wanted to do."
   "Now that I called her, I've got a great date."
   "Wow! What a good time I'll have with _____."

   Material rewards would be things or events the client indicates he prefers or enjoys. These might include buying a record, eating a snack, smoking, listening to music, or playing ball. Both current and potential rewards should be used. Of course, these activities are only possibilities; the client has to decide whether they are reinforcing.

   Examples of an *imaginal* reward may include either pleasant scenes or scenes related to going out:

   a. Imagining oneself on a raft on a lake.
   b. Imagining oneself on a football field.
   c. Imagining oneself with one's date at a movie.
   d. Imagining oneself with one's date lying on a warm beach.

2. See if you identified at least three of the following seven characteristics of an effective self-reward:

   1. The rewards should be individualized for the client.
   2. The rewards should be accessible and easy to use.
   3. There should be several different rewards.
   4. Different types of rewards should be selected.
   5. The rewards should be potent.
   6. The rewards should not be punishing to others.
   7. The rewards should be compatible with the client's desired goal.

3. If the client had trouble identifying some material reinforcers, here are some possible options:
   a. The client could use high-frequency behaviors as rewards as long as these behaviors were desirable, not aversive.
   b. The client could use imagery to reinforce himself covertly in lieu of material rewards.
   c. The client perhaps could increase the potency of certain material events or activities with the use of "anticipation training." In anticipation training, a client preselects several activities in which to engage and rehearses anticipation statements about each activity.

4. Each woman this client asks out is a step in the desired direction. After the client asks out one woman, he might administer a verbal-symbolic or imaginal reward. When he reaches his desired weekly level of asking out three, he could administer a larger material reward.

5. See whether your instructions about the timing of self-reward included at least two of the following:
   a. The reward should be administered after, not before, the target behavior is carried out.
   b. The reward should be administered immediately and without delay.

---

6. The client could plan for self-change maintenance by holding review sessions with the counselor and by enlisting the aid of another person to share in or dispense the rewards.

Part Three

Use the list on p. 499 as a guide to evaluate your teaching of the self-reward strategy. You also may wish to have your "student" keep data on the use of the procedure and the change in the target behavior.

Part Four

Check your self-contract with the six features listed on p. 507. Does your contract include each feature? Check your contract with the example contract in Figure 23-2 to see whether they are similar.

Part Five

You, the client, or another person can assess your implementation of a self-contract, using the steps listed on p. 509 as a guide.

Suggested Readings

Stimulus Control

Blechman, E., Olson, D., & Hellman, I. Stimulus control over family problem-solving behavior: The family contract game. *Behavior Therapy*, 1976, 7, 686–692.

Bootzin, R. R. Effects of self-control procedures for insomnia. In R. B. Stuart (Ed.), *Behavioral self-management: Strategies, techniques and outcomes*. New York: Brunner/Mazel, 1977.

Ferster, C. B., Nurnberger, J. I., & Levitt, E. B. The control of eating. *Journal of Mathetics*, 1962, 1, 87–109.

Greenberg, I., & Altman, J. Modifying smoking behavior through stimulus control: A case report. *Journal of Behavior Therapy and Experimental Psychiatry*, 1976, 7, 97–99.

Mahoney, M. J., & Jeffrey, D. B. A manual of self-control procedures for the overweight. JSAS *Catalog of Selected Documents in Psychology*, 1974, 4, 129.

Shapiro, D., Turksky, B., Schwartz, G., & Shnidman, S. Smoking on cue: A behavioral approach to smoking reduction. *Journal of Health and Social Behavior*, 1971, 12, 108–113.

Watson, D. L., & Tharp, R. G. *Self-directed behavior: Self-modification for personal adjustment* (2nd ed.). Monterey, Calif.: Brooks/Cole, 1977. Chap. 8, Antecedents, 155–173.

Definitions of Self-Reward

Bandura, A. Vicarious and self-reinforcement processes. In R. Glaser (Ed.), *The nature of reinforcement*. New York: Academic Press, 1971.

Bandura, A. Self-reinforcement processes. In M. J. Mahoney & C. E. Thoresen (Eds.), *Self-control: Power to the person*. Monterey, Calif.: Brooks/Cole, 1974.

Bandura, A. Self-reinforcement: Theoretical and methodological considerations. *Behaviorism*, 1976, 4, 135–155.

Catania, A. C. The myth of self-reinforcement. *Behaviorism*, 1975, 3, 192–199.

Goldiamond, I. Self-reinforcement. *Journal of Applied Behavior Analysis*, 1976, 9, 509–514.

Jones, R. T., Nelson, R. E., & Kazdin, A. E. The role of external variables in self-reinforcement: A review. *Behavior Modification*, 1977, 1, 147–178.

Kanfer, F. H., & Karoly, P. Self-control: A behavioristic excursion into the lion's den. *Behavior Therapy*, 1972, 3, 398–416.

Clinical Uses of Self-Reward

Bellack, A. A comparison of self-reinforcement and self-monitoring in a weight reduction program. *Behavior Therapy*, 1976, 7, 68–75.

Bolstad, O. D., & Johnson, S. M. Self-regulation in the modification of disruptive classroom behavior. *Journal of Applied Behavior Analysis*, 1972, 5, 443–454.

Gulanick, N., Woodburn, L., & Rimm, D. Weight gain through self-control procedures. *Journal of*

Consulting and Clinical Psychology, 1975, 43, 536–539.

Jackson, B. Treatment of depression by self-reinforcement. Behavior Therapy, 1972, 3, 298–307.

Jeffrey, D. A comparison of the effects of external control and self-control on the modification and maintenance of weight. Journal of Abnormal Psychology, 1974, 83, 404–410.

Mahoney, M. J., Moura, N. G., & Wade, T. C. Relative efficacy of self-reward, self-punishment, and self-monitoring techniques for weight loss. Journal of Consulting and Clinical Psychology, 1973, 40, 404–407.

McLaughlin, T. F. Self-control in the classroom. Review of Educational Research, 1976, 46, 631–663.

Components of Self-Reward

Thoresen, C. E., & Mahoney, M. J. Behavioral self-control. New York: Holt, Rinehart & Winston, 1974. Chap. 4, Self-reward, 65–91.

Watson, D. L., & Tharp, R. G. Self-directed behavior: Self-modification for personal adjustment (2nd ed.). Monterey, Calif.: Brooks/Cole, 1977. Chap. 6, Consequences, 91–119.

Cautions in Using Rewards

Levine, F., & Fasnacht, G. Token rewards may lead to token learning. American Psychologist, 1974, 29, 816–820.

McKeachie, W. J. The decline and fall of the laws of learning. Educational Researcher, 1974, 3, March, 7–11.

O'Leary, K., Poulos, R., & Devine, V. Tangible reinforcers: Bonuses or bribes. Journal of Consulting and Clinical Psychology, 1972, 38, 1–8.

Self-Punishment

Axelrod, S., Hall, R., Weis, L., & Rohrer, S. Use of self-imposed contingencies to reduce the frequency of smoking behavior. In M. J. Mahoney & C. E. Thoresen (Eds.), Self-control: Power to the person. Monterey, Calif.: Brooks/Cole, 1974.

Thoresen, C. E., & Mahoney, M. J. Behavioral self-control. New York: Holt, Rinehart & Winston, 1974. Chap. 5, Self-punishment and aversive self-regulation, 92–107.

Self-Contracting

Homme, L., Csanyi, A., Gonzales, M., & Rechs, J. How to use contingency contracting in the classroom. Champaign, Ill.: Research Press, 1969.

McReynolds, W. T., & Church, A. Self-control, study skills development and counseling approaches to the improvement of study behavior. Behaviour Research and Therapy, 1973, 11, 233–235.

Vance, B. Using contracts to control weight and to improve cardiovascular physical fitness. In J. D. Krumboltz & C. E. Thoresen (Eds.), Counseling methods. New York: Holt, Rinehart & Winston, 1976.

Client Commitment to Self-Management

Kanfer, F. H. Self-management methods. In F. H. Kanfer & A. P. Goldstein (Eds.), Helping people change. New York: Pergamon Press, 1975.

Williams, R. L., Canale, J., & Edgerly, J. Affinity for self-management: A comparison between counseling clients and controls. Journal of Behavior Therapy and Experimental Psychiatry, 1976, 7, 231–234.

Termination of Helping

Eisenberg, S., & Delaney, D. J. The counseling process (2nd ed.). Chicago: Rand McNally, 1977. Chapter 11, Termination and follow-up.

Hackney, H., & Cormier, L. S. Counseling strategies and objectives (2nd ed.). Englewood Cliffs, N.J.: Prentice-Hall, 1979. Chapter 6, Beginnings and endings.

References

Agras, W. S. An investigation of the decrements of anxiety responses during systematic desensitization therapy. *Behaviour Research and Therapy,* 1965, *2,* 267–270.

Alban, L. S., & Nay, W. R. Reduction of ritual checking by a relaxation-delay treatment. *Journal of Behavior Therapy and Experimental Psychiatry,* 1976, *7,* 151–154.

Alexander, A. B. Systematic relaxation and flow rates in asthmatic children: Relationship to emotional precipitants and anxiety. *Journal of Psychosomatic Research,* 1972, *16,* 405–410.

American Personnel and Guidance Association. Ethical standards. *The Personnel and Guidance Journal,* 1961, *40,* 206–209.

American Psychological Association. *Ethical standards of psychologists.* Washington, D.C.: Author, 1977.

Andréoli, A., Picot, A., & Richard, J. The bodies of the aged as perceived through relaxation therapy. *Revue de Médecine Psychosomatique et de Psychologie Médicale,* 1974, *16,* 271–282.

Anthony, J., & Edelstein, B. Thought-stopping treatment of anxiety attacks due to seizure-related obsessive ruminations. *Journal of Behavior Therapy and Experimental Psychiatry,* 1975, *6,* 343–344.

Anton, J. L., Dunbar, J., & Friedman, L. Anticipation training in the treatment of depression. In J. D. Krumboltz & C. E. Thoresen (Eds.), *Counseling methods.* New York: Holt, Rinehart & Winston, 1976.

Argyle, M. *Social interaction.* New York: Atherton Press, 1969.

Ascher, L. M., & Phillips, D. Guided behavior rehearsal. *Journal of Behavior Therapy and Experimental Psychiatry,* 1975, *6,* 215–218.

Auerswald, M. C. Differential reinforcing power of restatement and interpretation on client production of affect. *Journal of Counseling Psychology,* 1974, *21,* 9–14.

Auld, F., Jr., & White, A. M. Sequential dependencies in psychotherapy. *Journal of Abnormal and Social Psychology,* 1959, *58,* 100–104.

Axelrod, S., Hall, R., Weis, L., & Rohrer, S. Use of self-imposed contingencies to reduce the frequency of smoking behavior. In M. J. Mahoney & C. E. Thoresen (Eds.), *Self-control: Power to the person.* Monterey, Calif.: Brooks/Cole, 1974.

Baer, D. M., Wolf, M. M., & Risley, T. R. Some current dimensions of applied behavior analysis. *Journal of Applied Behavior Analysis,* 1968, *1,* 91–97.

Bain, J. A. *Thought control in everyday life.* New York: Funk & Wagnalls, 1928.

Bajtelsmit, J., & Gershman, L. Covert positive reinforcement: Efficacy and conceptualization. *Journal of Behavior Therapy and Experimental Psychiatry,* 1976, *7,* 207–212.

Bandura, A. *Principles of behavior modification.* New York: Holt, Rinehart & Winston, 1969.

Bandura, A. Psychotherapy based upon modeling principles. In A. E. Bergin & S. L. Garfield (Eds.), *Handbook of psychotherapy and behavior change: An empirical analysis.* New York: John Wiley, 1971. (a)

Bandura, A. Vicarious and self-reinforcement processes. In R. Glaser (Ed.), *The nature of reinforcement.* New York: Academic Press, 1971. (b)

Bandura, A. Self-reinforcement processes. In M. J.

Mahoney & C. E. Thoresen (Eds.), *Self-control: Power to the person.* Monterey, Calif.: Brooks/Cole, 1974.

Bandura, A. Effecting change through participant modeling. In J. D. Krumboltz & C. E. Thoresen (Eds.), *Counseling methods.* New York: Holt, Rinehart & Winston, 1976. (a)

Bandura, A. Self-reinforcement: Theoretical and methodological considerations. *Behaviorism,* 1976, *4,* 135–155. (b)

Bandura, A. Social learning theory. In J. T. Spence, R. C. Carson, & J. W. Thibaut (Eds.), *Behavioral approaches to therapy.* Morristown, N.J.: General Learning Press, 1976. (c)

Bandura, A., & Adams, N. E. Analysis of self-efficacy theory of behavioral change. *Cognitive Therapy and Research,* 1977, *1,* 287–310.

Bandura, A., Adams, N. E., & Beyer, J. Cognitive processes mediating behavioral change. *Journal of Personality and Social Psychology,* 1977, *35,* 125–139.

Bandura, A., Blanchard, E. B., & Ritter, B. Relative efficacy of desensitization and modeling approaches for inducing behavioral, affective, and attitudinal changes. *Journal of Personality and Social Psychology,* 1969, *13,* 173–199.

Bandura, A., & Jeffery, R. W. Role of symbolic coding and rehearsal processes in observational learning. *Journal of Personality and Social Psychology,* 1973, *26,* 122–130.

Bandura, A., Jeffery, R. W., & Gajdos, E. Generalizing change through participant modeling with self-directed mastery. *Behaviour Research and Therapy,* 1975, *13,* 141–152.

Bandura, A., Jeffery, R., & Wright, C. Efficacy of participant modeling as a function of response induction aids. *Journal of Abnormal Psychology,* 1974, *83,* 56–64.

Bandura, A., & Simon, K. The role of proximal intentions in self-regulation of refractory behavior. *Cognitive Therapy and Research,* 1977, *1,* 177–193.

Barlow, D., & Hersen, M. Single-case experimental designs: Uses in applied clinical research. *Archives of General Psychiatry,* 1973, *29,* 319–325.

Barnabei, F., Cormier, W., & Nye, L. Determining the effects of three counselor verbal responses on client verbal behavior. *Journal of Counseling Psychology,* 1974, *21,* 355–359.

Bass, B. A. Sexual arousal as an anxiety inhibitor. *Journal of Behavior Therapy and Experimental Psychiatry,* 1974, *5,* 151–152.

Bayes, M. Behavioral cues of interpersonal warmth. *Journal of Consulting and Clinical Psychology,* 1972, *39,* 333–339.

Beck, A. T. Cognitive therapy: Nature and relation to behavior therapy. *Behavior Therapy,* 1970, *1,* 184–200.

Beck, A. T. *Depression: Causes and treatment.* Philadelphia: University of Pennsylvania Press, 1972.

Beck, A. T. *Cognitive therapy and the emotional disorders.* New York: International Universities Press, 1976.

Bellack, A. A comparison of self-reinforcement and self-monitoring in a weight reduction program. *Behavior Therapy,* 1976, *7,* 68–75.

Bellack, A. S., & Hersen, M. Self-report inventories in behavioral assessment. In J. D. Cone & R. P. Hawkins (Eds.), *Behavioral assessment: New directions in clinical psychology.* New York: Brunner/Mazel, 1977.

Bellack, A. S., Rozensky, R., & Schwartz, J. A comparison of two forms of self-monitoring in a behavioral weight reduction program. *Behavior Therapy,* 1974, *5,* 523–530.

Benson, H. Your innate asset for combating stress. *Harvard Business Review,* July–August 1974, *52,* 49–60.

Benson, H. *The relaxation response.* New York: Avon, 1976.

Berenson, B. G., & Mitchell, K. M. *Confrontation: For better or worse.* Amherst, Mass.: Human Resource Development Press, 1974.

Bergman, D. V. Counseling method and client responses. *Journal of Consulting Psychology,* 1951, *15,* 216–224

Bernstein, D. A. Manipulation of avoidance behavior as a function of increased or decreased demand on repeated behavioral tests. *Journal of Consulting and Clinical Psychology,* 1974, *42,* 896–900.

Bernstein, D. A., & Borkovec, T. D. *Progressive relaxation training: A manual for the helping professions.* Champaign, Ill.: Research Press, 1973.

Birdwhistell, R. L. *Kinesics and context.* Philadelphia: University of Pennsylvania Press, 1970.

Blechman, E., Olson, D., & Hellman, I. Stimulus control over family problem-solving behavior: The family contract game. *Behavior Therapy,* 1976, *7,* 686–692.

Bloomfield, H. H., Cain, M. P., Jaffe, D. T., & Kory, R. B. *TM: Discovering inner energy and overcoming stress.* New York: Dell, 1975.

Bolstad, O. D., & Johnson, S. M. Self-regulation in the modification of disruptive classroom behavior. *Journal of Applied Behavior Analysis,* 1972, *5,* 443–454.

Bootzin, R. R. Stimulus control treatment for insomnia. *American Psychological Association Proceedings,* 1972, 395–396.

Bootzin, R. R. Effects of self-control procedures for insomnia. In R. B. Stuart (Ed.), *Behavioral self-management: Strategies, techniques and outcomes.* New York: Brunner/Mazel, 1977.

Borkovec, T., Grayson, J., & Cooper, K. Treatment of general tension: Subjective and physiological effects of progressive relaxation. *Journal of Consulting and Clinical Psychology,* 1978, 46, 518–528.

Bornstein, P. H., Hamilton, S. B., Carmody, T. B., Rychtarik, R. G., & Veraldi, D. M. Reliability enhancement: Increasing the accuracy of self-report through mediation-based procedures. *Cognitive Therapy and Research,* 1977, 1, 85–98.

Boudin, H. M. Contingency contracting as a therapeutic tool in the deceleration of amphetamine use. *Behavior Therapy,* 1972, 3, 604–608.

Boudreau, L. Transcendental meditation and yoga as reciprocal inhibitors. *Journal of Behavior Therapy and Experimental Psychiatry,* 1972, 3, 97–98.

Boudreau, L., & Jeffery, C. Stuttering treated by desensitization. *Journal of Behavior Therapy and Experimental Psychiatry,* 1973, 4, 209–212.

Brammer, L. M., & Shostrom, E. L. *Therapeutic psychology: Fundamentals of actualization counseling and psychotherapy.* Englewood Cliffs, N.J.: Prentice-Hall, 1968.

Brehm, J. W. *A theory of psychological reactance.* New York: Academic Press, 1966.

Broden, M., Hall, R., & Mitts, B. The effect of self-recording on the classroom behavior of two eighth-grade students. *Journal of Applied Behavior Analysis,* 1971, 4, 191–199.

Broverman, I., Broverman, D., Clarkson, F., Rosenkrantz, P., & Vogel, S. Sex-role stereotypes and clinical judgments of mental health. *Journal of Consulting and Clinical Psychology,* 1970, 34, 1–7.

Brown, D., & Parks, J. Interpreting nonverbal behavior: A key to more effective counseling: Review of literature. *Rehabilitation Counseling Bulletin,* 1972, 15, 176–184.

Brown, J. *An analysis of self-monitoring-provided feedback in a behavioral weight reduction program.* Unpublished doctoral dissertation, West Virginia University, 1978.

Brownell, K., Colletti, G., Ersner-Hershfield, R., Hershfield, S., & Wilson, G. Self-control in school children: Stringency and leniency in self-determined and externally imposed performance standards. *Behavior Therapy,* 1977, 8, 442–455.

Bruch, M. Type of cognitive modeling, imitation of modeled tactics, and modification of test anxiety. *Cognitive Therapy and Research,* 1978, 2, 147–164.

Bucher, B., & Fabricatore, J. Use of patient-administered shock to suppress hallucinations. *Behavior Therapy,* 1970, 1, 382–385.

Caird, W. K., & Wincze, J. P. Videotaped desensitization of frigidity. *Journal of Behavior Therapy and Experimental Psychiatry,* 1974, 5, 175–178.

Campbell, L. M. A variation of thought-stopping in a twelve-year-old boy: A case report. *Journal of Behavior Therapy and Experimental Psychiatry,* 1973, 4, 69–70.

Canfield, J., & Wells, H. *100 ways to enhance self concept in the classroom: A handbook for teachers and parents.* Englewood Cliffs, N.J.: Prentice-Hall, 1976.

Cantrell, R. P., Cantrell, M. L., Huddleston, C. M., & Wooldridge, R. L. Contingency contracting with school problems. *Journal of Applied Behavior Analysis,* 1969, 2, 215–220.

Carkhuff, R. *Helping and human relations.* Vol. 1: *Selection and training.* New York: Holt, Rinehart & Winston, 1969. (a)

Carkhuff, R. *Helping and human relations.* Vol. 2: *Practice and research.* New York: Holt, Rinehart & Winston, 1969. (b)

Carkhuff, R. *The art of helping.* Amherst, Mass.: Human Resource Development Press, 1972.

Carkhuff, R. R., & Alexik, M. Effect of client depth of self-exploration upon high and low functioning counselors. *Journal of Counseling Psychology,* 1967, 14, 350–355.

Carkhuff, R. R., & Pierce, R. M. *Trainer's guide. The art of helping.* Amherst, Mass.: Human Resource Development Press, 1975.

Carkhuff, R. R., Pierce, R. M., & Cannon, J. R. *The art of helping III.* Amherst, Mass.: Human Resource Development Press, 1977.

Catania, A. C. The myth of self-reinforcement. *Behaviorism,* 1975, 3, 192–199.

Cautela, J. R. Behavior therapy and self-control: Techniques and implications. In C. Franks (Ed.), *Behavior therapy: Appraisal and status.* New York: McGraw-Hill, 1969.

Cautela, J. R. Covert reinforcement. *Behavior Therapy,* 1970, 1, 33–50.

Cautela, J. R. *Covert modeling.* Paper presented at the fifth annual meeting of the Association for Advancement of Behavior Therapy, Washington, D.C., September 1971.

Cautela, J. R. The present status of covert modeling.

Journal of Behavior Therapy and Experimental Psychiatry, 1976, *6*, 323–326.

Cautela, J., Flannery, R., & Hanley, S. Covert modeling: An experimental test. *Behavior Therapy*, 1974, *5*, 494–502.

Cautela, J. R., & Kastenbaum, R. A reinforcement survey schedule for use in therapy, training and research. *Psychological Report*, 1967, *20*, 1115–1130.

Cautela, J. R., & Tondo, T. R. *Imagery survey schedule*. Unpublished. imagery questionnaire, Boston College, 1971.

Cautela, J. R., & Upper, D. The process of individual behavior therapy. In M. Hersen, R. Eisler, & P. Miller (Eds.), *Progress in behavior modification I*. New York: Academic Press, 1975.

Cautela, J. R., & Upper, D. The behavioral inventory battery: The use of self-report measures in behavioral analysis and therapy. In M. Hersen & A. S. Bellack (Eds.), *Behavioral assessment: A practical handbook*. New York: Pergamon Press, 1976.

Cavior, N., & Marabotto, C. M. Monitoring verbal behaviors in a dyadic interaction. *Journal of Consulting and Clinical Psychology*, 1976, *44*, 68–76.

Chassan, J. B. Probability processes in psychoanalytic psychiatry. In J. Scher (Ed.), *Theories of the mind*. New York: Free Press, 1962.

Chaves, J., & Barber, T. Cognitive strategies, experimenter modeling, and expectation in the attenuation of pain. *Journal of Abnormal Psychology*, 1974, *83*, 356–363.

Ciminero, A. R. Behavioral assessment: An overview. In A. R. Ciminero, K. S. Calhoun, & H. E. Adams (Eds.), *Handbook of behavioral assessment*. New York: John Wiley, 1977.

Ciminero, A., Nelson, R., & Lipinski, D. Self-monitoring procedures. In A. R. Ciminero, K. S. Calhoun, & H. E. Adams (Eds.), *Handbook of behavioral assessment*. New York: John Wiley, 1977.

Coe, W. C., & Buckner, L. G. Expectation, hypnosis, and suggestion methods. In F. H. Kanfer & A. P. Goldstein (Eds.), *Helping people change*. New York: Pergamon Press, 1975.

Cone, J. D., & Hawkins, R. P. (Eds.). *Behavioral assessment: New directions in clinical psychology*. New York: Brunner/Mazel, 1977.

Cormier, L. S., & Cormier, W. H. *Behavioral counseling: Operant procedures, self-management strategies, and recent innovations*. Boston: Houghton Mifflin, 1975.

Cormier, L. S., & Cormier, W. H. Developing and implementing self-instructional modules for counselor training. *Counselor Education and Supervision*, 1976, *16*, 37–45.

Cormier, W. H., & Cormier, L. S. *Behavioral counseling: Initial procedures, individual and group strategies*. Boston: Houghton Mifflin, 1975.

Cormier, W. H., Cormier, L. S., Zerega, W. D., & Wagaman, G. L. Effects of learning modules on the acquisition of counseling strategies. *Journal of Counseling Psychology*, 1976, *23*, 136–141.

Cornish, R. D., & Dilley, J. S. Comparison of three methods of reducing test anxiety: Systematic desensitization, implosive therapy, and study counseling. *Journal of Counseling Psychology*, 1973, *20*, 499–503.

Cotharin, R., & Mikulas, W. Systematic desensitization of racial emotional responses. *Journal of Behavior Therapy and Experimental Psychiatry*, 1975, *6*, 347–348.

Cozby, P. C. Self-disclosure: A literature review. *Psychological Bulletin*, 1973, *79*, 73–91.

Cronbach, L. J. *Essentials of psychological testing* (3rd ed.). New York: Harper & Row, 1970.

Cronbach, L. J. Beyond the two disciplines of scientific psychology. *American Psychologist*, 1975, *30*, 116–127.

Crowley, T. J., & Ivey, A. E. Dimensions of effective interpersonal communications: Specifying behavioral components. *Journal of Counseling Psychology*, 1976, *23*, 267–271.

Curran, J. P. Social skills training and systematic desensitization in reducing dating anxiety. *Behaviour Research and Therapy*, 1975, *13*, 65–68.

Daniels, L. K. A single session desensitization without relaxation training. *Journal of Behavior Therapy and Experimental Psychiatry*, 1974, *5*, 207–208.

Danish, S., & Hauer, A. *Helping skills: A basic training program*. New York: Behavioral Publications, 1973.

D'Augelli, A. R. Nonverbal behavior of helpers in initial helping interactions. *Journal of Counseling Psychology*, 1974, *21*, 360–363.

Davison, G. C., & Wilson, G. T. Processes of fear-reduction in systematic desensitization: Cognitive and social reinforcement factors in humans. *Behavior Therapy*, 1973, *4*, 1–21.

Dawidoff, D. J. *The malpractice of psychiatrists*. Springfield, Ill.: Charles C Thomas, 1973.

Dawley, H. H., & Wenrich, W. W. *Patient's manual for systematic desensitization*. Palo Alto, Calif.: Veterans' Workshop (V.A. Hospital), 1973.

Deffenbacher, J. L. Relaxation *in vivo* in the treatment

of test anxiety. *Journal of Behavior Therapy and Experimental Psychiatry*, 1976, *7*, 289–292.

Dengrove, E. *Treatment of non-phobic disorders by the behavioral therapies.* Paper presented at the meeting of the Association for Advancement of Behavior Therapy, New York, December 1966.

Denholtz, M., & Mann, E. An audiovisual program for group desensitization. *Journal of Behavior Therapy and Experimental Psychiatry*, 1974, *5*, 27–29.

Denney, D. R., & Rupert, P. Desensitization and self-control in the treatment of test anxiety. *Journal of Counseling Psychology*, 1977, *24*, 272–280.

Denniston, D., & McWilliams, P. *The TM book.* New York: Warner Books, 1975.

Donner, L., & Guerney, B. Automated group desensitization for test anxiety. *Behaviour Research and Therapy*, 1969, *7*, 1–13.

Doster, J. A. Effects of instructions, modeling, and role rehearsal on interview verbal behavior. *Journal of Consulting and Clinical Psychology*, 1972, *39*, 202–209.

Dua, P. S. Group desensitization of a phobia with three massing procedures. *Journal of Counseling Psychology*, 1972, *19*, 125–129.

Dyer, W. *Your erroneous zones.* New York: Funk & Wagnalls, 1976.

Dyer, W. *Pulling your own strings.* New York: Funk & Wagnalls, 1978.

Dyer, W. W., & Vriend, J. *Counseling techniques that work.* Washington, D.C.: American Personnel and Guidance Association, 1975.

D'Zurilla, T. J., & Goldfried, M. R. Problem solving and behavior modification. *Journal of Abnormal Psychology*, 1971, *78*, 107–126.

Eberle, T., Rehm, L., & McBurney, D. Fear decrement to anxiety hierarchy items: Effects of stimulus intensity. *Behaviour Research and Therapy*, 1975, *13*, 225–261.

Edelstein, B., & Eisler, R. Effects of modeling and modeling with instructions and feedback on the behavioral components of social skills. *Behavior Therapy*, 1976, *7*, 382–389.

Egan, G. *The skilled helper: A model for systematic helping and interpersonal relating.* Monterey, Calif.: Brooks/Cole, 1975.

Egan, G. *Interpersonal living: A skills/contract approach to human-relations training in groups.* Monterey, Calif.: Brooks/Cole, 1976.

Eisenberg, S., & Delaney, D. J. *The counseling process* (2nd ed.). Chicago: Rand McNally, 1977.

Ekman, P. Body position, facial expression and verbal behavior during interviews. *Journal of Abnormal and Social Psychology*, 1964, *68*, 295–301.

Ekman, P., & Friesen, W. Head and body cues in the judgment of emotion: A reformulation. *Perceptual and Motor Skills*, 1967, *24*, 711–724.

Ekman, P., & Friesen, W. Nonverbal leakage and clues to deception. *Psychiatry*, 1969, *32*, 88–106. (a)

Ekman, P., & Friesen, W. The repertoire of nonverbal behavior: Categories, origins, usage, and coding. *Semiotica*, 1969, *1*, 49–98. (b)

Ekman, P., Friesen, W. V., & Ellsworth, P. *Emotion and the human face: Guidelines for research and an integration of findings.* New York: Pergamon Press, 1972.

Elder, J. *Comparison of cognitive restructuring and response acquisition in the enhancement of social competence in college freshmen.* Unpublished doctoral dissertation, West Virginia University, 1978.

Ellis, A. *Humanistic psychotherapy.* New York: McGraw-Hill, 1974.

Ellis, A. *Growth through reason.* North Hollywood, Calif.: Wilshire Book Company, 1975.

Emery, J. R., & Krumboltz, J. D. Standard versus individualized hierarchies in desensitization to reduce test anxiety. *Journal of Counseling Psychology*, 1967, *14*, 204–209.

Epstein, L., Webster, J., & Miller, P. Accuracy and controlling effects of self-monitoring as a function of concurrent responding and reinforcement. *Behavior Therapy*, 1975, *6*, 654–666.

Evans, I. M. A handy record-card for systematic desensitization hierarchy items. *Journal of Behavior Therapy and Experimental Psychiatry*, 1974, *5*, 43–46.

Exline, R. V., & Winters, L. C. Affective relations and mutual glances in dyads. In S. S. Tomkins & C. E. Izard (Eds.), *Affect, cognition, and personality.* New York: Springer, 1965.

Ferster, C. B., Nurnberger, J. I., & Levitt, E. B. The control of eating. *Journal of Mathetics*, 1962, *1*, 87–109.

Fisher, E. B., Green, L., Friedling, C., Levonkron, J., & Porter, F. Self-monitoring of progress in weight reduction: A preliminary report. *Journal of Behavior Therapy and Experimental Psychiatry*, 1976, *7*, 363–365.

Flanders, J. P. A review of research on imitative behavior. *Psychological Bulletin*, 1968, *69*, 316–337.

Flannery, R. B. Use of covert conditioning in the behavioral treatment of a drug-dependent college dropout. *Journal of Counseling Psychology*, 1972, *19*, 547–550.

Flowers, J. V. Simulation and role playing methods.

In F. H. Kanfer & A. P. Goldstein (Eds.), *Helping people change.* New York: Pergamon Press, 1975.

Frank, G. H., & Sweetland, A. A study of the process of psychotherapy: The verbal interaction. *Journal of Consulting Psychology,* 1962, *26,* 135–138.

Frank, J. D. *Persuasion and healing.* Baltimore: Johns Hopkins Press, 1961.

Frederiksen, L. W. Treatment of ruminative thinking by self-monitoring. *Journal of Behavior Therapy and Experimental Psychiatry,* 1975, *6,* 258–259.

Frederiksen, L. W., Epstein, L. H., & Kosevsky, B. P. Reliability and controlling effects of three procedures for self-monitoring smoking. *The Psychological Record,* 1975, *25,* 255–264.

Fremouw, W. J. A client manual for integrated behavior treatment of speech anxiety. JSAS *Catalogue of Selected Documents in Psychology,* 1977, *1,* 14. MS. 1426.

Fremouw, W. J., & Harmatz, M. G. A helper model for behavioral treatment of speech anxiety. *Journal of Consulting and Clinical Psychology,* 1975, *43,* 652–660.

Fremouw, W. J., & Zitter, R. E. A comparison of skills training and cognitive restructuring-relaxation for the treatment of speech anxiety. *Behavior Therapy,* 1978, *9,* 248–259.

Fretz, B. R. Postural movements in a counseling dyad. *Journal of Counseling Psychology,* 1966, *13,* 335–343.

Frey, D. H. The anatomy of an idea: Creativity in counseling. *The Personnel and Guidance Journal,* 1975, *54,* 22–27.

Fry (Dua), P. S. Effects of desensitization treatment on core-condition training. *Journal of Counseling Psychology,* 1973, *20,* 214–219.

Furst, J. B., & Cooper, A. Combined use of imaginal and interoceptive stimuli in desensitizing fear of heart attacks. *Journal of Behavior Therapy and Experimental Psychiatry,* 1970, *1,* 87–89.

Gagné, R. M. *The conditions of learning* (2nd ed.). New York: Holt, Rinehart & Winston, 1970.

Gagné, R., & Briggs, L. *Principles of instructional design.* New York: Holt, Rinehart & Winston, 1974.

Galassi, J. P., DeLo, J. S., Galassi, M. D., & Bastien, S. The college self-expression scale: A measure of assertiveness. *Behavior Therapy,* 1974, *5,* 165–171.

Galassi, M. D., & Galassi, J. P. The effects of role playing variations on the assessment of assertive behavior. *Behavior Therapy,* 1976, *7,* 343–347.

Gallagher, J. W., & Arkowitz, H. Weak effects of

covert modeling treatment of test anxiety. *Journal of Behavior Therapy and Experimental Psychiatry,* 1978, *9,* 23–26.

Gambrill, E. D., & Richey, C. A. An assertion inventory for use in assessment and research. *Behavior Therapy,* 1975, *6,* 550–561.

Gazda, G. M. *Human relations development: A manual for educators.* Boston: Allyn & Bacon, 1973.

Gazda, G., Walters, R., & Childers, W. *Human relations development: A manual for health sciences.* Boston: Allyn & Bacon, 1975.

Geer, C. A., & Hurst, J. C. Counselor-subject sex variables in systematic desensitization. *Journal of Counseling Psychology,* 1976, *23,* 296–301.

Geis, G. L., & Chapman, R. Knowledge of results and other possible reinforcers in self-instructional systems. *Educational Technology,* 1971, *11,* 38–50.

Gelatt, H., Varenhorst, B., Carey, R., & Miller, G. *Decisions and outcomes: A leader's guide.* Princeton, N.J.: College Entrance Examination Board, 1973.

Gelder, M. G., Bancroft, J. H. J., Gath, D. H., Johnston, D. W., Mathews, A. M., & Shaw, P. M. Specific and non-specific factors in behavior therapy. *British Journal of Psychiatry,* 1973, *123,* 445–462.

Gershman, L. Case conference: A transvestite fantasy treated by thought-stopping, covert sensitization and aversive shock. *Journal of Behavior Therapy and Experimental Psychiatry,* 1970, *1,* 153–161.

Gershman, L., & Clouser, R. A. Treating insomnia with relaxation and desensitization in a group setting by an automated approach. *Journal of Behavior Therapy and Experimental Psychiatry,* 1974, *5,* 31–35.

Gershman, L., & Stedman, J. M. Using Kung Fu to reduce anxiety in a claustrophobic male. In J. D. Krumboltz & C. E. Thoresen (Eds.), *Counseling methods.* New York: Holt, Rinehart & Winston, 1976.

Giannandrea, V., & Murphy, K. C. Similarity self-disclosure and return for a second interview. *Journal of Counseling Psychology,* 1973, *20,* 545–548.

Girodo, M. Yoga meditation and flooding in the treatment of anxiety neurosis. *Journal of Behavior Therapy and Experimental Psychiatry,* 1974, *5,* 157–160.

Gladstein, G. Nonverbal communication and counseling/psychotherapy: A review. *Counseling Psychologist,* 1974, *4,* 34–57.

Glasgow, R., & Rosen, G. Behavioral bibliotherapy: A

review of self-help behavior therapy manuals. *Psychological Bulletin*, 1978, *85*, 1–23.

Glass, C. R., Gottman, J. M., & Shmurak, S. H. Response acquisition and cognitive self-statement modification approaches to dating-skills training. *Journal of Counseling Psychology*, 1976, *23*, 520–526.

Glogower, F. D., Fremouw, W. J., & McCroskey, J. C. A component analysis of cognitive restructuring. *Cognitive Therapy and Research*, 1978, *2*, 209–223.

Goldfried, M. R. Systematic desensitization as training in self-control. *Journal of Consulting and Clinical Psychology*, 1971, *37*, 228–234.

Goldfried, M. R. Behavioral assessment. In I. B. Weiner (Ed.), *Clinical methods in psychology*. New York: John Wiley, 1976. (a)

Goldfried, M. R. *Exercise manual and log for self-modification of anxiety: To accompany audio cassette # T44B*. New York: Biomonitoring Applications, 1976. (b)

Goldfried, M. R. Behavioral assessment in perspective. In J. D. Cone & R. P. Hawkins (Eds.), *Behavioral assessment: New directions in clinical psychology*. New York: Brunner/Mazel, 1977. (a)

Goldfried, M. R. The use of relaxation and cognitive relabeling as coping skills. In R. B. Stuart (Ed.), *Behavioral self-management: Strategies, techniques and outcomes*. New York: Brunner/Mazel, 1977. (b)

Goldfried, M. R., & Davison, G. C. *Clinical behavior therapy*. New York: Holt, Rinehart & Winston, 1976.

Goldfried, M. R., Decenteceo, E. T., & Weinberg, L. Systematic rational restructuring as a self-control technique. *Behavior Therapy*, 1974, *5*, 247–254.

Goldfried, M. R., & D'Zurilla, T. J. A behavioral-analytic model for assessing competence. In C. D. Spielberger (Ed.), *Current topics in clinical and community psychology*. New York: Academic Press, 1969.

Goldfried, M. R., & Goldfried, A. P. Cognitive change methods. In F. H. Kanfer & A. P. Goldstein (Eds.), *Helping people change*. New York: Pergamon Press, 1975.

Goldfried, M. R., & Goldfried, A. P. Importance of hierarchy content in the self-control of anxiety. *Journal of Consulting and Clinical Psychology*, 1977, *45*, 124–134.

Goldfried, M. R., Linehan, M. M., & Smith, J. L. The reduction of test anxiety through cognitive restructuring. *Journal of Consulting and Clinical Psychology*, 1978, *46*, 32–39.

Goldfried, M. R., & Trier, C. S. Effectiveness of relaxation as an active coping skill. *Journal of Abnormal Psychology*, 1974, *83*, 348–355.

Goldiamond, I. Self-control procedures in personal behavior problems. *Psychological Reports*, 1965, *17*, 851–868.

Goldiamond, I. A constructional approach to self control. In A. Schwartz & I. Goldiamond, *Social casework: A behavioral approach*. New York: Columbia University Press, 1975.

Goldiamond, I. Self-reinforcement. *Journal of Applied Behavior Analysis*, 1976, *9*, 509–514.

Goldstein, A. J., Serber, M., & Piaget, G. Induced anger as a reciprocal inhibitor of fear. *Journal of Behavior Therapy and Experimental Psychiatry*, 1970, *1*, 67–70.

Goldstein, A. P. *Therapist-patient expectancies in psychotherapy*. New York: Pergamon Press, 1962.

Goldstein, A. P. *Psychotherapeutic attraction*. New York: Pergamon Press, 1971.

Goldstein, A. P. *Structured learning therapy*. New York: Academic Press, 1973.

Goldstein, A. P. Relationship-enhancement methods. In F. H. Kanfer & A. P. Goldstein (Eds.), *Helping people change*. New York: Pergamon Press, 1975.

Goldstein, A. P., & Stein, N. *Prescriptive psychotherapies*. New York: Pergamon Press, 1976.

Goodwin, D. L. Consulting with the classroom teacher. In J. D. Krumboltz & C. E. Thoresen (Eds.), *Behavioral counseling: Cases and techniques*. New York: Holt, Rinehart & Winston, 1969.

Gordon, T. *Parent effectiveness training*. New York: Wyden, 1970.

Gottman, J. M., & Leiblum, S. R. *How to do psychotherapy and how to evaluate it*. New York: Holt, Rinehart & Winston, 1974.

Gottman, J. M., & McFall, R. M. Self-monitoring effects in a program for potential high school dropouts: A time-series analysis. *Journal of Consulting and Clinical Psychology*, 1972, *39*, 273–281

Graves, J. R., & Robinson, J. D. Proxemic behavior as a function of inconsistent verbal and nonverbal messages. *Journal of Counseling Psychology*, 1976, *23*, 333–338.

Greenberg, I., & Altman, J. Modifying smoking behavior through stimulus control: A case report. *Journal of Behavior Therapy and Experimental Psychiatry*, 1976, *7*, 97–99.

Greene, L. Effects of verbal evaluative feedback and interpersonal distance on behavioral compliance. *Journal of Counseling Psychology*, 1977, 24, 10–14.

Greiner, J., & Karoly, P. Effects of self-control training on study activity and academic performance: An analysis of self-monitoring, self-reward and systematic-planning components. *Journal of Counseling Psychology*, 1976, 23, 495–502.

Groverman, A. M., Richards, C. S., & Caple, R. B. Literature review, treatment manuals, and bibliography for study skills counseling and behavioral self-control approaches to improving study behavior. JSAS *Catalog of Selected Documents in Psychology*, 1975, 5, 342–343. (Ms. No. 1128)

Gulanick, N., Woodburn, L., & Rimm, D. Weight gain through self-control procedures. *Journal of Consulting and Clinical Psychology*, 1975, 43, 536–539.

Haase, R. F., & DiMattia, D. J. Spatial environments and verbal conditioning in a quasi-counseling interview. *Journal of Counseling Psychology*, 1976, 23, 414–421.

Haase, R. F., & Tepper, D. Nonverbal components of empathic communication. *Journal of Counseling Psychology*, 1972, 19, 417–424.

Hackett, G., Horan, J. J., Stone, C., Linberg, S., Nicholas, W., & Lukaski, H. *Further outcomes and tentative predictor variables from an evolving comprehensive program for the behavioral control of smoking.* Paper presented at the annual meeting of the American Educational Research Association, San Francisco, April 1976.

Hackmann, A., & McLean, C. A comparison of flooding and thought stopping in the treatment of obsessional neurosis. *Behaviour Research and Therapy*, 1975, 13, 263–269.

Hackney, H. Facial gestures and subject expression of feelings. *Journal of Counseling Psychology*, 1974, 21, 173–178.

Hackney, H., & Cormier, L. S. *Counseling strategies and objectives* (2nd ed.). Englewood Cliffs, N.J.: Prentice-Hall, 1979.

Hackney, H., Ivey, A., & Oetting, E. Attending, island and hiatus behavior: A process conception of counselor and client interaction. *Journal of Counseling Psychology*, 1970, 17, 342–346.

Hackney, H., & Nye, L. S. *Counseling strategies and objectives.* Englewood Cliffs, N. J.: Prentice-Hall, 1973.

Hackstian, A. R., Zimmer, J. M., & Newby, J. F. *A descriptive and comparative study of the dimensions of counselor response* (Tech. Rep. 11). Amherst: University of Massachusetts, School of Education, January 1971.

Hall, E. T. *The hidden dimension.* Garden City, N.Y.: Doubleday, 1966.

Hall, R. A., & Hinkle, J. E. Vicarious desensitization of test anxiety. *Behaviour Research and Therapy*, 1972, 10, 407–410.

Hall, S., Hall, R., DeBoer, G., & O'Kulitch, P. Self and external management compared with psychotherapy in the control of obesity. *Behaviour Research and Therapy*, 1977, 15, 89–95.

Halpern, T. P. Degree of client disclosure as a function of past disclosure, counselor disclosure, and counselor facilitativeness. *Journal of Counseling Psychology*, 1977, 24, 41–47.

Hartley, J., & Davies, I. Preinstructional strategies: The role of pretests, behavioral objectives, overviews and advance organizers. *Review of Educational Research*, 1976, 46, 239–265.

Hawkins, D. Learning the unteachable. In L. Shulman & E. Keislar (Eds.), *Learning by discovery: A critical appraisal.* Chicago: Rand McNally, 1966.

Hawkins, R. P., & Dobes, R. W. Behavioral definitions in applied behavior analysis: Explicit or implicit. In B. C. Etzel, J. M. LeBlanc, & D. M. Baer (Eds.), *New developments in behavioral research: Theory, method, and application.* Hillsdale, N.J.: Lawrence Erlbaum, 1977.

Hay, W., Hay, L., & Nelson, R. The adaptation of covert modeling procedures to the treatment of chronic alcoholism and obsessive-compulsive behavior: Two case reports. *Behavior Therapy*, 1977, 8, 70–76.

Hays, V., & Waddell, K. J. A self-reinforcing procedure for thought stopping. *Behavior Therapy*, 1976, 7, 559.

Hearn, M., & Evans, D. Anger and reciprocal inhibition therapy. *Psychological Reports*, 1972, 30, 943–948.

Heckerman, C. L., & Prochaska, J. O. Development and evaluation of weight reduction procedures in a health maintenance organization. In R. B. Stuart (Ed.), *Behavioral self-management: Strategies, techniques and outcomes.* New York: Brunner/Mazel, 1977.

Helner, P. A., & Jessell, J. Effects of interpretation as a counseling technique. *Journal of Counseling Psychology*, 1974, 21, 475–481.

Hersen, M., & Barlow, D. H. *Single-case experimental designs: Strategies for studying behavior change.* New York: Pergamon Press, 1976.

Hersen, M., & Bellack, A. S. (Eds.). *Behavioral assessment: A practical handbook.* New York: Pergamon Press, 1976.

Hertel, R. K. Application of stochastic process analyses to the study of psychotherapeutic processes. *Psychological Bulletin, 1972, 77,* 421–430.

Highlen, P. S., & Baccus, G. K. Effect of reflection of feeling and probe on client self-referenced affect. *Journal of Counseling Psychology, 1977, 24,* 440–443.

Hill, C. A process approach for establishing counseling goals and outcomes. *The Personnel and Guidance Journal, 1975, 53,* 571–576.

Hill, C. E., & Gormally, J. Effects of reflection, restatement, probe, and nonverbal behaviors on client affect. *Journal of Counseling Psychology, 1977, 24,* 92–97.

Hoffman, M. A., & Spencer, G. P. Effect of interviewer self-disclosure and interviewer-subject sex pairing on perceived and actual subject behavior. *Journal of Counseling Psychology, 1977, 24,* 383–390.

Hoffman-Graff, M. A. Interviewer use of positive and negative self-disclosure and interviewer-subject sex pairing. *Journal of Counseling Psychology, 1977, 24,* 184–190.

Holahan, C. J., & Slaikeu, K. A. Effects of contrasting degrees of privacy on client self-disclosure in a counseling setting. *Journal of Counseling Psychology, 1977, 24,* 55–59.

Holroyd, K. A. Cognition and desensitization in the group treatment of test anxiety. *Journal of Consulting and Clinical Psychology, 1976, 44,* 991–1001.

Holroyd, K. A., Andrasik, F., & Westbrook, T. Cognitive control of tension headache. *Cognitive Therapy and Research, 1977, 1,* 121–133.

Homme, L., Csanyi, A., Gonzales, M., & Rechs, J. *How to use contingency contracting in the classroom.* Champaign, Ill.: Research Press, 1969.

Hoopes, M. H., & Scoresby, A. L. Commitment to change: Structuring the goals and ground rules for counseling. In J. D. Krumboltz & C. E. Thoresen (Eds.), *Behavioral counseling: Cases and techniques.* New York: Holt, Rinehart & Winston, 1969.

Horan, J. J. "In vivo" emotive imagery: A technique for reducing childbirth anxiety and discomfort. *Psychological Reports, 1973, 32,* 1328.

Horan, J. J. Coping with inescapable discomfort through in vivo emotive imagery. In J. D. Krumboltz & C. E. Thoresen (Eds.), *Counseling methods.* New York: Holt, Rinehart & Winston, 1976.

Horan, J. J., Baker, S. B., Hoffman, A. M., & Shute, R. E. Weight loss through variations in the co-vant control paradigm. *Journal of Consulting and Clinical Psychology, 1975, 43,* 68–72.

Horan, J. J., & Dellinger, J. K. "In vivo" emotive imagery: A preliminary test. *Perceptual and Motor Skills, 1974, 39,* 359–362.

Horan, J. J., Hackett, G., Buchanan, J. D., Stone, C. I., & Demchik-Stone, D. Coping with pain: A component analysis of stress inoculation. *Cognitive Therapy and Research, 1977, 1,* 211–221.

Horan, J. J., Hackett, G., Stone, C., Nicholas, W., Linberg, S., & Lukaski, H. *Evaluation of a comprehensive program for the behavioral control of smoking.* Paper presented to the annual meeting of the American Educational Research Association, San Francisco, April 1976.

Horan, J. J., Layng, F. C., & Pursell, C. H. Preliminary study of the effects of "in vivo" emotive imagery on dental discomfort. *Perceptual and Motor Skills, 1976, 42,* 105–106.

Horne, A. M., & Matson, J. L. A comparison of modeling, desensitization, flooding, study skills, and control groups for reducing test anxiety. *Behavior Therapy, 1977, 8,* 1–8.

Hosford, R. E. Overcoming fear of speaking in a group. In J. D. Krumboltz & C. E. Thoresen (Eds.), *Behavioral counseling: Cases and techniques.* New York: Holt, Rinehart & Winston, 1969.

Hosford, R. *Counseling techniques: Self-as-a-model film.* Washington, D.C.: American Personnel and Guidance Press, 1974.

Hosford, R., & de Visser, L. *Behavioral approaches to counseling: An introduction.* Washington, D.C.: American Personnel and Guidance Press, 1974.

Hosford, R., Moss, C., & Morrell, G. The self-as-a-model technique: Helping prison inmates change. In J. D. Krumboltz & C. E. Thoresen (Eds.), *Counseling methods.* New York: Holt, Rinehart & Winston, 1976.

Huck, S. W., Cormier, W. H., & Bounds, W. G. *Reading statistics and research.* New York: Harper & Row, 1974.

Hughes, H., & Haynes, S. Structured laboratory observation in the behavioral assessment of parent-child interactions: A methodological critique. *Behavior Therapy, 1978, 9,* 428–447.

Humphreys, L., & Beiman, I. The application of multiple behavioral techniques to multiple problems of a complex case. *Journal of Behavior Therapy and Experimental Psychiatry, 1975, 6,* 311–315.

Ince, L. P. The use of relaxation training and a conditioned stimulus in the elimination of epileptic seizures in a child: A case study. *Journal of Be-*

havior Therapy and Experimental Psychiatry, 1976, 7, 39–42.

Israel, E., & Beiman, I. Live versus recorded relaxation training: A controlled investigation. *Behavior Therapy*, 1977, 8, 251–254.

Ivey, A. E. *Microcounseling: Innovations in interview training.* Springfield, Ill.: Charles C Thomas, 1971.

Ivey, A., & Gluckstern, N. *Basic attending skills: Participant manual.* Amherst, Mass.: Microtraining Associates, 1974.

Ivey, A., & Gluckstern, N. *Basic influencing skills: Participant manual.* Amherst, Mass.: Microtraining Associates, 1976.

Jackson, B. Treatment of depression by self-reinforcement. *Behavior Therapy*, 1972, 3, 298–307.

Jacobson, E. *Progressive relaxation.* Chicago: University of Chicago Press, 1929.

Jacobson, E. *Anxiety and tension control.* Philadelphia: Lippincott, 1964.

Jeffery, K. M. *The effects of goal-setting on self-motivated persistence.* Unpublished doctoral dissertation, Stanford University, 1977.

Jeffery, R. W. Reducing fears through participant modeling and self-directed practice. In J. D. Krumboltz & C. E. Thoresen (Eds.), *Counseling methods.* New York: Holt, Rinehart & Winston, 1976.

Jeffrey, D. A comparison of the effects of external control and self-control on the modification and maintenance of weight. *Journal of Abnormal Psychology*, 1974, 83, 404–410.

Johnson, D. *Reaching out: Interpersonal effectiveness and self-actualization.* Englewood Cliffs, N.J.: Prentice-Hall, 1972.

Johnston, J. M., & O'Neill, G. The analysis of performance criteria defining course grades as a determinant of college student academic performance. *Journal of Applied Behavior Analysis*, 1973, 6, 261–268.

Jones, R. T., Nelson, R. E., & Kazdin, A. E. The role of external variables in self-reinforcement: A review. *Behavior Modification*, 1977, 1, 147–178.

Jourard, S. M. *The transparent self* (Rev. ed.). New York: Van Nostrand Reinhold, 1971.

Jourard, S. M., & Friedman, R. Experimenter-subject "distance" and self-disclosure. *Journal of Personality and Social Psychology*, 1970, 15, 278–282.

Jourard, S. M., & Jaffe, P. E. Influence of an interviewer's disclosure on the self-disclosing behavior of interviewees. *Journal of Counseling Psychology*, 1970, 17, 252–257.

Kanfer, F. H. Self-monitoring: Methodological limita-

tions and clinical applications. *Journal of Consulting and Clinical Psychology*, 1970, 35, 148–152.

Kanfer, F. H. Self-management methods. In F. H. Kanfer & A. P. Goldstein (Eds.), *Helping people change.* New York: Pergamon Press, 1975.

Kanfer, F. H. The many faces of self-control, or behavior modification changes its focus. In R. B. Stuart (Ed.), *Behavioral self-management: Strategies, techniques and outcomes.* New York: Brunner/Mazel, 1977.

Kanfer, F. H., & Goldstein, A. P. Introduction. In F. H. Kanfer & A. P. Goldstein (Eds.), *Helping people change.* New York: Pergamon Press, 1975.

Kanfer, F. H., & Grimm, L. G. Behavioral analysis: Selecting target behaviors in the interview. *Behavior Modification*, 1977, 1, 7–28.

Kanfer, F. H., & Karoly, P. Self-control: A behavioristic excursion into the lion's den. *Behavior Therapy*, 1972, 3, 398–416.

Kanfer, F. H., & Phillips, J. S. A survey of current behavior therapies and a proposal for classification. In C. M. Franks (Ed.), *Behavior therapy: Appraisal and status.* New York: McGraw-Hill, 1969.

Kanfer, F. H., & Phillips, J. S. *Learning foundations of behavior therapy.* New York: John Wiley, 1970.

Kanfer, F. H., & Saslow, G. Behavioral diagnosis. In C. M. Franks (Ed.), *Behavior therapy: Appraisal and status.* New York: McGraw-Hill, 1969.

Kanter, N. J., & Goldfried, M. R. Relative effectiveness of rational restructuring and self-control desensitization in the reduction of interpersonal anxiety. *Behavior Therapy*, 1979, 10, 472–490.

"Karajan: A new life," *Time*, November 29, 1976. Vol. 108, 81–82.

Karoly, P. Operant methods. In F. H. Kanfer & A. P. Goldstein (Eds.), *Helping people change.* New York: Pergamon Press, 1975.

Kaul, T. J., Kaul, M. A., & Bednar, R. L. Counselor confrontation and client depth of self-exploration. *Journal of Counseling Psychology*, 1973, 20, 132–136.

Kazdin, A. Covert modeling and the reduction of avoidance behavior. *Journal of Abnormal Psychology*, 1973, 81, 89–95. (a)

Kazdin, A. E. Methodological and assessment considerations in evaluating reinforcement programs in applied settings. *Journal of Applied Behavior Analysis*, 1973, 6, 517–531. (b)

Kazdin, A. E. Comparative effects of some variations of covert modeling. *Journal of Behavior Therapy and Experimental Psychiatry*, 1974, 5, 225–231. (a)

Kazdin, A. E. Covert modeling, model similarity,

and reduction of avoidance behavior. *Behavior Therapy*, 1974, *5*, 325–340. (b)

Kazdin, A. Effects of covert modeling and model reinforcement on assertive behavior. *Journal of Abnormal Psychology*, 1974, *83*, 240–252. (c)

Kazdin, A. E. The effect of model identity and fear-relevant similarity on covert modeling. *Behavior Therapy*, 1974, *5*, 624–635. (d)

Kazdin, A. E. Reactive self-monitoring: The effects of response desirability, goal setting, and feedback. *Journal of Consulting and Clinical Psychology*, 1974, *42*, 704–716. (e)

Kazdin, A. E. Self-monitoring and behavior change. In M. J. Mahoney & C. E. Thoresen (Eds.), *Self-control: Power to the person*. Monterey, Calif.: Brooks/Cole, 1974. (f)

Kazdin, A. E. Covert modeling, imagery assessment, and assertive behavior. *Journal of Consulting and Clinical Psychology*, 1975, *43*, 716–724.

Kazdin, A. E. Assessment of imagery during covert modeling of assertive behavior. *Journal of Behavior Therapy and Experimental Psychiatry*, 1976, *7*, 213–219. (a)

Kazdin, A. E. Developing assertive behavior through covert modeling. In J. D. Krumboltz & C. E. Thoresen (Eds.), *Counseling methods*. New York: Holt, Rinehart & Winston, 1976. (b)

Kazdin, A. E. Effects of covert modeling, multiple models, and model reinforcement on assertive behavior. *Behavior Therapy*, 1976, *7*, 211–222. (c)

Kazdin, A. E. Statistical analyses for single-case experimental designs. In M. Hersen & D. H. Barlow, *Single-case experimental designs: Strategies for studying behavior change*. New York: Pergamon Press, 1976. (d)

Kazdin, A. E. Assessing the clinical or applied importance of behavior change through social validation. *Behavior Modification*, 1977, *1*, 427–452.

Kazdin, A. E., & Wilcoxon, L. A. Systematic desensitization and nonspecific treatment effects: A methodological evaluation. *Psychological Bulletin*, 1976, *83*, 729–758.

Kent, R. N., & Foster, S. L. Direct observational procedures: Methodological issues in naturalistic settings. In A. R. Ciminero, K. S. Calhoun, & H. E. Adams (Eds.), *Handbook of behavioral assessment*. New York: John Wiley, 1977.

Kiesler, D. J. Experimental designs in psychotherapy research. In A. Bergin & S. Garfield (Eds.), *Handbook of psychotherapy and behavior change: An empirical analysis*. New York: John Wiley, 1971.

Knapp, M. L. *Nonverbal communication in human interaction*. New York: Holt, Rinehart & Winston, 1972.

Knapp, T. J., Downs, D. L., & Alperson, J. R. Behavior therapy for insomnia: A review. *Behavior Therapy*, 1976, *7*, 614–625.

Knight, P. H., & Bair, C. K. Degree of client comfort as a function of dyadic interaction distance. *Journal of Counseling Psychology*, 1976, *23*, 13–16.

Knox, J. *Cognitive strategies for coping with pain: Ignoring vs. acknowledging*. Unpublished doctoral dissertation, University of Waterloo, 1972.

Komaki, J., & Dore-Boyce, K. Self-recording: Its effects on individuals high and low in motivation. *Behavior Therapy*, 1978, *9*, 65–72.

Kostka, M. P., & Galassi, J. P. Group systematic desensitization versus covert positive reinforcement in the reduction of test anxiety. *Journal of Counseling Psychology*, 1974, *21*, 464–468.

Krause, M. S. Comparative effects on continuance of four experimental intake procedures. *Social Casework*, 1966, *47*, 515–519.

Krumboltz, J. D. Behavioral goals for counseling. *Journal of Counseling Psychology*, 1966, *13*, 153–159.

Krumboltz, J. D., & Thoresen, C. E. (Eds.). *Behavioral counseling: Cases and techniques*. New York: Holt, Rinehart & Winston, 1969.

Krumboltz, J. D., & Thoresen, C. E. (Eds.). *Counseling methods*. New York: Holt, Rinehart & Winston, 1976.

Kunzelmann, H. D. (Ed.). *Precision teaching*. Seattle: Special Child Publications, 1970.

LaCrosse, M. B. Nonverbal behavior and perceived counselor attractiveness and persuasiveness. *Journal of Counseling Psychology*, 1975, *22*, 563–566.

Ladouceur, R. An experimental test of the learning paradigm of covert positive reinforcement in deconditioning anxiety. *Journal of Behavior Therapy and Experimental Psychiatry*, 1974, *5*, 3–6.

Lamaze, F. *Painless childbirth: Psychoprophylactic method*. London: Burke, 1958.

Lang, P. J. The mechanics of desensitization and the laboratory study of human fear. In C. M. Franks (Ed.), *Behavior therapy: Appraisal and status*. New York: McGraw-Hill, 1969.

Lang, P., & Lazovik, A. Experimental desensitization of a phobia. *Journal of Abnormal and Social Psychology*, 1963, *66*, 519–525.

Langer, E. J., Janis, I. L., & Wolfer, J. A. Reduction of psychological stress in surgical patients. *Journal of Experimental Social Psychology*, 1975, *11*, 155–165.

Lavelle, J. Comparing the effects of an affective and a behavioral counselor style on client interview behavior. *Journal of Counseling Psychology*, 1977, 24, 173–177.

Lawson, D. M., & May, R. B. Three procedures for the extinction of smoking behavior. *Psychological Record*, 1970, 20, 151–157.

Lazarus, A. Behavioural rehearsal vs. non-directive therapy vs. advice in effecting behaviour change. *Behaviour Research and Therapy*, 1966, 4, 209–212.

Lazarus, A. A. In support of technical eclecticism. *Psychological Reports*, 1967, 21, 415–416.

Lazarus, A. Variations in desensitization therapy. *Psychotherapy: Theory, Research and Practice*, 1968, 5, 50–52.

Lazarus, A. A. The "inner circle" strategy: Identifying crucial problems. In J. D. Krumboltz & C. E. Thoresen (Eds.), *Behavioral counseling: Cases and techniques*. New York: Holt, Rinehart & Winston, 1969.

Lazarus, A. A. *Daily living: Coping with tension and anxieties*. Chicago: Instructional Dynamics, 1970. (Tape of relaxation exercises)

Lazarus, A. A. *Behavior therapy and beyond*. New York: McGraw-Hill, 1971.

Lazarus, A. A. Multimodal behavior therapy: Treating the "basic id." *Journal of Nervous and Mental Disease*, 1973, 156, 404–411.

Lazarus, A. A., & Abramovitz, A. The use of "emotive imagery" in the treatment of children's phobias. *Journal of Mental Science*, 1962, 108, 191–195.

Lazarus, A., & Rachman, S. The use of systematic desensitization in psychotherapy. *South African Medical Journal*, 1957, 32, 934–937.

Leitenberg, H., Agras, W. S., Barlow, D. H., & Oliveau, D. C. Contribution of selective positive reinforcement and therapeutic instructions to systematic desensitization therapy. *Journal of Abnormal Psychology*, 1969, 74, 113–118.

Levendusky, P., & Pankratz, L. Self-control techniques as an alternative to pain medication. *Journal of Abnormal Psychology*, 1975, 84, 165–168.

Levin, F. M., & Gergen, K. J. Revealingness, ingratiation, and the disclosure of self. *Proceedings of the 77th Annual Convention of the American Psychological Association*, 1969, 4 (Pt. 1), 447–448.

Levine, F., & Fasnacht, G. Token rewards may lead to token learning. *American Psychologist*, 1974, 29, 816–820.

Levy, L. H. *Psychological interpretation*. New York: Holt, Rinehart & Winston, 1963.

Lewis, E. C. *The psychology of counseling*. New York: Holt, Rinehart & Winston, 1970.

Lewis, S. A comparison of behavior therapy techniques in the reduction of fearful avoidance behavior. *Behavior Therapy*, 1974, 5, 648–655.

Lichtenberg, J. W., & Hummel, T. J. Counseling as stochastic process: Fitting a Markov chain model to initial counseling interviews. *Journal of Counseling Psychology*, 1976, 23, 310–315.

Lick, J. R., & Bootzin, R. R. Expectancy factors in the treatment of fear: Methodological and theoretical issues. *Psychological Bulletin*, 1975, 82, 917–931.

Lick, J. R., & Katkin, E. S. Assessment of anxiety and fear. In M. Hersen & A. S. Bellack (Eds.), *Behavioral assessment: A practical handbook*. New York: Pergamon Press, 1976.

Lick, J., & Unger, T. The external validity of behavioral fear assessment: The problem of generalizing from the laboratory to the natural environment. *Behavior Modification*, 1977, 1, 283–306.

Lindsley, O. R. A reliable wrist counter for recording behavior rates. *Journal of Applied Behavior Analysis*, 1968, 1, 77–78.

Linehan, M. Issues in behavioral interviewing. In J. D. Cone & R. P. Hawkins (Eds.), *Behavioral assessment: New directions in clinical psychology*. New York: Brunner/Mazel, 1977.

Lipinski, D. P., Black, J. L., Nelson, R. O., & Ciminero, A. Influence of motivational variables on the reactivity and reliability of self-recording. *Journal of Consulting and Clinical Psychology*, 1975, 43, 637–646.

Lipinski, D., & Nelson, R. The reactivity and unreliability of self-recording. *Journal of Consulting and Clinical Psychology*, 1974, 42, 118–123.

Lomont, J. F. Reciprocal inhibition or extinction? *Behaviour Research and Therapy*, 1965, 3, 209–219.

Lorion, R. P. Patient and therapist variables in the treatment of low-income patients. *Psychological Bulletin*, 1974, 81, 344–354.

Lowe, J. C. Excitatory response to music as a reciprocal inhibitor. *Journal of Behavior Therapy and Experimental Psychiatry*, 1973, 4, 297–299.

MacDonald, M. L., & Bernstein, D. A. Treatment of a spider phobia by *in vivo* and imaginal desensitization. *Journal of Behavior Therapy and Experimental Psychiatry*, 1974, 5, 47–52.

Mager, R. F. *Preparing instructional objectives*. Palo Alto, Calif.: Fearon, 1962.

Mahoney, K. Count on it: A simple self-monitoring device. *Behavior Therapy*, 1974, 5, 701–703.

Mahoney, K., & Mahoney, M. J. Cognitive factors in weight reduction. In J. D. Krumboltz & C. E.

Thoresen (Eds.), *Counseling methods*. New York: Holt, Rinehart & Winston, 1976.

Mahoney, M. J. Toward an experimental analysis of coverant control. *Behavior Therapy*, 1970, *1*, 510–521.

Mahoney, M. J. The self-management of covert behavior: A case study. *Behavior Therapy*, 1971, *2*, 575–578.

Mahoney, M. J. Research issues in self-management. *Behavior Therapy*, 1972, *3*, 45–63.

Mahoney, M. J. *Cognition and behavior modification*. Cambridge, Mass.: Ballinger, 1974.

Mahoney, M. J. Cognitive therapy and research: A question of questions. *Cognitive Therapy and Research*, 1977, *1*, 5–16. (a)

Mahoney, M. J. Reflections on the cognitive-learning trend in psychotherapy. *American Psychologist*, 1977, *32*, 5–13. (b)

Mahoney, M. J. Some applied issues in self-monitoring. In J. D. Cone & R. P. Hawkins (Eds.), *Behavioral assessment: New directions in clinical psychology*. New York: Brunner/Mazel, 1977. (c)

Mahoney, M. J., & Jeffrey, D. B. A manual of self-control procedures for the overweight. *JSAS Catalog of Selected Documents in Psychology*, 1974, *4*, 129, Ms. N. 775.

Mahoney, M. J., Moore, B. S., Wade, T. C., & Moura, N. G. Effects of continuous and intermittent self-monitoring on academic behavior. *Journal of Consulting and Clinical Psychology*, 1973, *41*, 65–69.

Mahoney, M. J., Moura, N. G., & Wade, T. C. Relative efficacy of self-reward, self-punishment, and self-monitoring techniques for weight loss. *Journal of Consulting and Clinical Psychology*, 1973, *40*, 404–407.

Mahoney, M. J., & Thoresen, C. E. (Eds.). *Self-control: Power to the person*. Monterey, Calif.: Brooks/Cole, 1974.

Mann, B., & Murphy, K. C. Timing of self-disclosure, reciprocity of self-disclosure, and reactions to an initial interview. *Journal of Counseling Psychology*, 1975, *22*, 304–308.

Mann, J. Vicarious desensitization of test anxiety through observation of a video-taped treatment. *Journal of Counseling Psychology*, 1972, *19*, 1–7.

Mann, R. A. The behavior-therapeutic use of contingency contracting to control an adult behavior problem: Weight control. *Journal of Applied Behavior Analysis*, 1972, *5*, 99–109.

Marlatt, G. A., & Marques, J. K. Meditation, self-control and alcohol use. In R. B. Stuart (Ed.), *Behavioral self-management: Strategies, techniques and outcomes*. New York: Brunner/Mazel, 1977.

Marlatt, G. A., & Perry, M. A. Modeling methods. In F. H. Kanfer & A. P. Goldstein (Eds.), *Helping people change*. New York: Pergamon Press, 1975.

Marquis, J., Morgan, W., & Piaget, G. *A guidebook for systematic desensitization* (3rd ed.). Palo Alto, Calif.: Veterans' Workshop, 1973.

Marshall, W., Presse, L., & Andrews, W. A self-administered program for public speaking anxiety. *Behaviour Research and Therapy*, 1976, *14*, 33–39.

Martinez, J. A., & Edelstein, B. *The effects of demand characteristics on the assessment of heterosocial competence*. Paper presented at the annual meeting of the Association for the Advancement of Behavior Therapy, Atlanta, December 1977.

Maslin, A., & Davis, J. L. Sex-role stereotyping as a factor in mental health standards among counselors-in-training. *Journal of Counseling Psychology*, 1975, *22*, 87–91.

Maslow, A. H. *The psychology of science: A reconnaissance*. New York: Harper & Row, 1966.

Mathews, A. M. Psychophysiological approaches to the investigation of desensitization and related procedures. *Psychological Bulletin*, 1971, *76*, 73–91.

McDonald, F. J. Behavior modification in teacher education. In *Behavior modification in education: 72nd yearbook of the National Society for the Study of Education*, Part 1. Chicago: University of Chicago Press, 1973.

McFall, R. M. Effects of self-monitoring on normal smoking behavior. *Journal of Consulting and Clinical Psychology*, 1970, *35*, 135–142.

McFall, R. M. Analogue methods in behavioral assessment: Issues and prospects. In J. D. Cone & R. P. Hawkins (Eds.), *Behavioral assessment: New directions in clinical psychology*. New York: Brunner/Mazel, 1977. (a)

McFall, R. M. Parameters of self-monitoring. In R. B. Stuart (Ed.), *Behavioral self-management: Strategies, techniques and outcomes*. New York: Brunner/Mazel, 1977. (b)

McFall, R. M., & Lillesand, D. B. Behavior rehearsal with modeling and coaching in assertion training. *Journal of Abnormal Psychology*, 1971, *77*, 313–323.

McFall, R., & Twentyman, C. Four experiments on the relative contributions of rehearsal, modeling, and coaching to assertion training. *Journal of Abnormal Psychology*, 1973, *81*, 199–218.

McGlynn, F., Wilson, A., & Linder, L. Systematic desensitization of snake-avoidance with individualized and non-individualized hierarchies. *Journal of Behavior Therapy and Experimental Psychiatry*, 1970, *1*, 201–204.

McGuire, D., Thelen, M., & Amolsch, T. Interview self-disclosure as a function of length of modeling and descriptive instructions. *Journal of Consulting and Clinical Psychology*, 1975, *43*, 356–362.

McKeachie, W. J. The decline and fall of the laws of learning. *Educational Researcher*, 1974, *3*, 7–11.

McKeachie, W. J. Psychology in America's bicentennial year. *American Psychologist*, 1976, *31*, 819–833.

McKenzie, T. L., & Rushall, B. S. Effects of self-recording on attendance and performance in a competitive swimming training environment. *Journal of Applied Behavior Analysis*, 1974, *7*, 199–206.

McLaughlin, T. F. Self-control in the classroom. *Review of Educational Research*, 1976, *46*, 631–663.

McReynolds, W. T., & Church, A. Self-control, study skills development and counseling approaches to the improvement of study behavior. *Behaviour Research and Therapy*, 1973, *11*, 233–235.

Meichenbaum, D. H. Examination of model characteristics in reducing avoidance behavior. *Journal of Personality and Social Psychology*, 1971, *17*, 298–307.

Meichenbaum, D. Cognitive modification of test anxious college students. *Journal of Consulting and Clinical Psychology*, 1972, *39*, 370–380.

Meichenbaum, D. *Therapist manual for cognitive behavior modification*. Unpublished manuscript, University of Waterloo, 1974.

Meichenbaum, D. A cognitive-behavior modification approach to assessment. In M. Hersen & A. S. Bellack (Eds.), *Behavioral assessment: A practical handbook*. New York: Pergamon Press, 1976.

Meichenbaum, D. *Cognitive-behavior modification: An integrative approach*. New York: Plenum Press, 1977.

Meichenbaum, D., & Cameron, R. *Stress inoculation: A skills training approach to anxiety management*. Unpublished manuscript, University of Waterloo, 1973. (a)

Meichenbaum, D., & Cameron, R. Training schizophrenics to talk to themselves: A means of developing attentional control. *Behavior Therapy*, 1973, *4*, 515–534. (b)

Meichenbaum, D., Gilmore, J., & Fedoravicius, A. Group insight versus group desensitization in treating speech anxiety. *Journal of Consulting and Clinical Psychology*, 1971, *36*, 410–421.

Meichenbaum, D., & Goodman, J. Training impul-

sive children to talk to themselves: A means of developing self-control. *Journal of Abnormal Psychology*, 1971, *77*, 115–126.

Meichenbaum, D., & Turk, D. The cognitive-behavioral management of anxiety, anger, and pain. In P. O. Davidson (Ed.), *The behavioral management of anxiety, depression and pain*. New York: Brunner/Mazel, 1976.

Melamed, B., & Siegel, L. Reduction of anxiety in children facing hospitalization and surgery by use of filmed modeling. *Journal of Consulting and Clinical Psychology*, 1975, *43*, 511–521.

Melnick, J. A comparison of replication techniques in the modification of minimal dating behavior. *Journal of Abnormal Psychology*, 1973, *81*, 51–59.

Melnick, J., & Russell, R. W. Hypnosis versus systematic desensitization in the treatment of test anxiety. *Journal of Counseling Psychology*, 1976, *23*, 291–295.

Melnick, J., & Stocker, R. An experimental analysis of the behavioral rehearsal with feedback technique in assertiveness training. *Behavior Therapy*, 1977, *8*, 222–228.

Merbaum, M., & Southwell, E. A. Conditioning of affective self-references as a function of the discriminative characteristics of experimenter intervention. *Journal of Abnormal Psychology*, 1965, *70*, 180–187.

Meyer, V., Liddell, A., & Lyons, M. Behavioral interviews. In A. R. Ciminero, K. S. Calhoun, & H. E. Adams (Eds.), *Handbook of behavioral assessment*. New York: John Wiley, 1977.

Miller, B. V., & Bernstein, D. A. Instructional demand in a behavioral avoidance test for claustrophobic fears. *Journal of Abnormal Psychology*, 1972, *80*, 206–210.

Miller, H. R., & Nawas, M. M. Control of aversive stimulus termination in systematic desensitization. *Behaviour Research and Therapy*, 1970, *8*, 57–61.

Miller, S. B. The contribution of therapeutic instructions to systematic desensitization. *Behaviour Research and Therapy*, 1972, *10*, 159–169.

Mischel, W. *Personality and assessment*. New York: John Wiley, 1968.

Mischel, W. *Introduction to personality*. New York: Holt, Rinehart & Winston, 1971.

Mitchell, K. R., & White, R. G. Behavioral self-management: An application to the problem of migraine headaches. *Behavior Therapy*, 1977, *8*, 213–221.

Mogan, J., & O'Brien, J. S. The counterconditioning of a vomiting habit by sips of ginger ale. *Journal* of *Behavior Therapy and Experimental Psychiatry,* 1972, 3, 135–137.

Moos, R. H. Assessment of the psychosocial environments of community-oriented psychiatric treatment programs. *Journal of Abnormal Psychology,* 1972, 79, 9–18.

Morganstern, K. P. Cigarette smoke as a noxious stimulus in self-managed aversion therapy for compulsive eating: Technique and case illustration. *Behavior Therapy,* 1974, 5, 255–260.

Morganstern, K. P. Behavioral interviewing: The initial stages of assessment. In M. Hersen & A. S. Bellack (Eds.), *Behavioral assessment: A practical handbook.* New York: Pergamon Press, 1976.

Morris, K. T., & Kanitz, H. M. *Rational emotive therapy.* Boston: Houghton Mifflin, 1975.

Morris, R. J. Shaping relaxation in the unrelaxed client. *Journal of Behavior Therapy and Experimental Psychiatry,* 1973, 4, 353–354.

Morris, R. J. Fear reduction methods. In F. H. Kanfer & A. P. Goldstein (Eds.), *Helping people change.* New York: Pergamon Press, 1975.

Murphy, K. C., & Strong, S. R. Some effects of similarity self-disclosure. *Journal of Counseling Psychology,* 1972, 19, 121–124.

Murphy, P. Personal communication, October 1976.

National Training Laboratories Institute for Applied Behavioral Science. *Reading book: Laboratories in human relations training.* Washington, D.C.: National Education Association, 1969.

Nawas, M., Fishman, S., & Pucel, J. A standardized desensitization program applicable to group and individual treatments. *Behaviour Research and Therapy,* 1970, 8, 49–56.

Nay, W. R. Analogue measures. In A. R. Ciminero, K. S. Calhoun, & H. E. Adams (Eds.), *Handbook of behavioral assessment.* New York: John Wiley, 1977.

Nelson, R. Methodological issues in assessment via self-monitoring. In J. D. Cone & R. P. Hawkins (Eds.), *Behavioral assessment: New directions in clinical psychology.* New York: Brunner/Mazel, 1977.

Nelson, R. O., Lipinski, D. P., & Black, J. L. The reactivity of adult retardates' self-monitoring: A comparison among behaviors of different valences, and a comparison with token reinforcement. *Psychological Record,* 1976, 26, 189–201. (a)

Nelson, R., Lipinski, D., & Black, J. The relative reactivity of external observations and self-monitoring. *Behavior Therapy,* 1976, 7, 314–321. (b)

Nelson, R. O., Lipinski, D. P., & Boykin, R. A. The effects of self-recorders' training and the obtrusiveness of the self-recording device on the accuracy and reactivity of self-monitoring. *Behavior Therapy,* 1978, 9, 200–208.

Nesse, M., & Nelson, R. O. Variations of covert modeling on cigarette smoking. *Cognitive Therapy and Research.* 1977, 1 343–354.

Nicassio, P., & Bootzin, R. A comparison of progressive relaxation and autogenic training as treatments for insomnia. *Journal of Abnormal Psychology,* 1974, 83, 253–260.

Nietzel, M., Martorano, R., & Melnick, J. The effects of covert modeling with and without reply training on the development and generalization of assertive responses. *Behavior Therapy,* 1977, 8, 183–192.

Nolan, J. D. Self-control procedures in the modification of smoking behavior. *Journal of Consulting and Clinical Psychology,* 1968, 32, 92–93.

Novaco, R. W. *Anger control: The development and evaluation of an experimental treatment.* Lexington, Mass.: Heath, 1975.

Novaco, R. A stress inoculation approach to anger management in the training of law enforcement officers. *American Journal of Community Psychology,* 1977, 5, 327–346.

Nye, L. S. Obtaining results through modeling. *The Personnel and Guidance Journal,* 1973, 51, 380–384.

Okun, B. F. *Effective helping: Interviewing and counseling techniques.* North Scituate, Mass.: Duxbury Press, 1976.

O'Leary, K., Poulos, R., & Devine, V. Tangible reinforcers: Bonuses or bribes. *Journal of Consulting and Clinical Psychology,* 1972, 38, 1–8.

Olin, R. J. Thought-stopping: Some cautionary observations. *Behavior Therapy,* 1976, 7, 706–707.

O'Neil, D., & Howell, R. Three modes of hierarchy presentation in systematic desensitization therapy. *Behaviour Research and Therapy,* 1969, 7, 289–294.

Orne, M. T. Demand characteristics and the concept of quasi-controls. In R. Rosenthal & R. Rownow (Eds.), *Artifact in behavioral research.* New York: Academic Press, 1969.

Ornstein, R. E. *The psychology of consciousness.* New York: Viking, 1972.

Osterhouse, R. A. Group systematic desensitization of test anxiety. In J. D. Krumboltz & C. E. Thoresen (Eds.), *Counseling methods.* New York: Holt, Rinehart & Winston, 1976.

Palisi, A., & Ruzicka, M. Practicum students' verbal responses to different clients. *Journal of Counseling Psychology,* 1974, 21, 87–91.

Passons, W. R. *Gestalt approaches in counseling.* New York: Holt, Rinehart & Winston, 1975.

Paul, G. L. *Insight versus desensitization in psychotherapy: An experiment in anxiety reduction.* Stanford, Calif.: Stanford University Press, 1966.

Paul, G. L. Strategy of outcome research in psychotherapy. *Journal of Consulting Psychology,* 1967, *31,* 109–118.

Paul, G. L., & Shannon, D. T. Treatment of anxiety through systematic desensitization in therapy groups. *Journal of Abnormal Psychology,* 1966, *71,* 124–135.

Paul, G. L., & Trimble, R. W. Recorded vs. "live" relaxation training and hypnotic suggestion: Comparative effectiveness for reducing physiological arousal and inhibiting stress response. *Behavior Therapy,* 1970, *1,* 285–302.

Penick, S. B., Filion, R., Fox, S., & Stunkard, A. J. Behavior modification in the treatment of obesity. *Psychosomatic Medicine,* 1971, *33,* 49–55.

Perez, J. *The initial counseling contact.* Boston: Houghton Mifflin, 1968.

Perls, F. S. Four lectures. In J. Fagan & I. L. Shepherd (Eds.), *Gestalt therapy now.* New York: Harper & Row, 1970.

Perls, F. S. *The Gestalt approach and eyewitness to therapy.* Menlo Park, Calif.: Science and Behavior Books, 1973.

Perri, M. G., & Richards, C. S. An investigation of naturally occurring episodes of self-controlled behaviors. *Journal of Counseling Psychology,* 1977, *24,* 178–183.

Peterson, D. R. *The clinical study of social behavior.* New York: Appleton-Century-Crofts, 1968.

Phillips, L. W. Training of sensory and imaginal responses in behavior therapy. In R. D. Rubin, H. Fensterhein, A. A. Lazarus, & C. M. Franks (Eds.), *Advances in behavior therapy.* New York: Academic Press, 1971.

Platt, J. J., & Spivack, G. Social competence and effective problem-solving thinking in psychiatric patients. *Journal of Clinical Psychology,* 1972, *28,* 3–5.

Polansky, N. A. On duplicity in the interview. *American Journal of Orthopsychiatry,* 1967, *37,* 568–579.

Polly, S., Turner, R. D., & Sherman, A. R. A self-control program for the treatment of obesity. In J. D. Krumboltz & C. E. Thoresen (Eds.), *Counseling methods.* New York: Holt, Rinehart & Winston, 1976.

Prazak, G. Accountability for counseling programs. In J. D. Krumboltz & C. E. Thoresen (Eds.), *Counseling methods.* New York: Holt, Rinehart & Winston, 1976.

Prentice, N. The influence of live and symbolic modeling on promoting moral judgment of adolescent delinquents. *Journal of Abnormal Psychology,* 1972, *80,* 157–161.

Rachman, S. Studies in desensitization—III: Speed of generalization. *Behaviour Research and Therapy,* 1966, *4,* 7–15.

Rachman, S. The role of muscular relaxation in desensitization therapy. *Behaviour Research and Therapy,* 1968, *6,* 159–166.

Rachman, S. Clinical applications of observational learning, imitation and modeling. *Behavior Therapy,* 1972, *3,* 379–397.

Rappaport, A. F., & Cammer, L. Breath meditation in the treatment of essential hypertension. *Behavior Therapy,* 1977, *8,* 269–270.

Raths, L., Harmin, M., & Simon, S. *Values and teaching.* Columbus, Ohio: Charles E. Merrill, 1966.

Rathus, S. A. A 30-item schedule for assessing assertive behavior. *Behavior Therapy,* 1973, *4,* 398–406.

Reeder, C., & Kunce, J. Modeling techniques, drug-abstinence behavior, and heroin addicts: A pilot study. *Journal of Counseling Psychology,* 1976, *23,* 560–562.

Reid, J. B. Reliability assessment of observation data: A possible methodological problem. *Child Development,* 1970, *41,* 1143–1150.

Richards, C. S. Behavior modification of studying through study skills advice and self-control procedures. *Journal of Counseling Psychology,* 1975, *22,* 431–436.

Richards, C. S. Improving study behaviors through self-control techniques. In J. D. Krumboltz & C. E. Thoresen (Eds.), *Counseling methods.* New York: Holt, Rinehart & Winston, 1976.

Richards, C. S., McReynolds, W., Holt, S., & Sexton, T. Effects of information feedback and self-administered consequences on self-monitoring study behavior. *Journal of Counseling Psychology,* 1976, *23,* 316–321.

Richards, C. S., Perri, M. G., & Gortney, C. Increasing the maintenance of self-control treatments through faded counselor contact and high information feedback. *Journal of Counseling Psychology,* 1976, *23,* 405–406.

Richardson, F. C., & Suinn, R. M. A comparison of traditional systematic desensitization, accelerated massed desensitization, and anxiety management training in the treatment of mathematics anxiety. *Behavior Therapy,* 1973, *4,* 212–218.

Rimm, D. C. Thought stopping and covert assertion

in the treatment of phobias. *Journal of Consulting and Clinical Psychology*, 1973, *41*, 466–467.

Rimm, D. C., & Masters, J. C. *Behavior therapy: Techniques and empirical findings*. New York: Academic Press, 1974.

Rinn, R. C., & Vernon, J. C. Process evaluation of outpatient treatment in a community mental health center. *Journal of Behavior and Experimental Psychiatry*, 1975, *6*, 5–11.

Risley, T., & Hart, B. Developing correspondence between the nonverbal and verbal behavior of preschool children. *Journal of Applied Behavior Analysis*, 1968, *1*, 267–281.

Roberts, A. H. Self-control procedures in modification of smoking behavior: Replication. *Psychological Reports*, 1969, *24*, 675–676.

Robin, A. L. Behavioral instruction in the college classroom. *Review of Educational Research*, 1976, *46*, 313–354.

Rogers, C. *Client-centered therapy*. Boston: Houghton Mifflin, 1951.

Rogers, C. R. The necessary and sufficient conditions of therapeutic personality change. *Journal of Consulting Psychology*, 1957, *21*, 95–103.

Rogers, C. R. *On becoming a person*. Boston: Houghton Mifflin, 1961.

Rogers, C. R. (Ed.). *The therapeutic relationship and its impact*. Madison: University of Wisconsin Press, 1967.

Romanczyk, R. G. Self-monitoring in the treatment of obesity: Parameters of reactivity. *Behavior Therapy*, 1974, *5*, 531–540.

Rose, S. D. *Treating children in groups: A behavioral approach*. San Francisco: Jossey-Bass, 1973.

Rosen, G. M. Therapy set: Its effects on subjects' involvement in systematic desensitization and treatment outcome. *Journal of Abnormal Psychology*, 1974, *83*, 291–300.

Rosen, G. M., Glasgow, R. E., & Barrera, M. A controlled study to assess the clinical efficacy of totally self-administered systematic desensitization. *Journal of Consulting and Clinical Psychology*, 1976, *44*, 208–217.

Rosen, R. C., & Schnapp, B. J. The use of a specific behavioral technique (thought-stopping) in the context of conjoint couples therapy: A case report. *Behavior Therapy*, 1974, *5*, 261–264.

Rosenhan, D. L. On being sane in insane places. *Science*, 1973, *179*, 250–258.

Rosenthal, T. Modeling therapies. In M. Hersen, R. Eisler, & P. Miller (Eds.), *Progress in behavior modification*, Vol. 2. New York: Academic Press, 1976.

Rosenthal, T. L., Hung, J. H., & Kelley, J. E. Therapist social influence: Sternly strike while the iron is hot. *Behaviour Research and Therapy*, 1977, *15*, 253–259.

Rosenthal, T. L., & Reese, S. L. The effects of covert and overt modeling on assertive behavior. *Behaviour Research and Therapy*, 1976, *14*, 463–469.

Ross, S. M., & Proctor, S. Frequency and duration of hierarchy item exposure in a systematic desensitization analogue. *Behaviour Research and Therapy*, 1973, *11*, 303–312.

Rotter, J. B., Chance, J. E., & Phares, E. J. (Eds.). *Applications of a social learning theory of personality*. New York: Holt, Rinehart & Winston, 1972.

Rudestam, K., & Bedrosian, R. An investigation of the effectiveness of desensitization and flooding with two types of phobias. *Behaviour Research and Therapy*, 1977, *15*, 23–30.

Russell, M. L. *The decision-making book for children*. Unpublished manuscript, Stanford University, 1974.

Russell, M. L., & Thoresen, C. E. Teaching decision-making skills to children. In J. D. Krumboltz & C. E. Thoresen (Eds.), *Counseling methods*. New York: Holt, Rinehart & Winston, 1976.

Russell, R. K., Sipich, J. F., & Knipe, J. Progressive relaxation training: A procedural note. *Behavior Therapy*, 1976, *7*, 566–568.

Russell, R. K., & Wise, F. Treatment of speech anxiety by cue-controlled relaxation and desensitization with professional and paraprofessional counselors. *Journal of Counseling Psychology*, 1976, *23*, 583–586.

Russell, R. K., Wise, F., & Stratoudakis, J. P. Treatment of test anxiety by cue-controlled relaxation and systematic desensitization. *Journal of Counseling Psychology*, 1976, *23*, 563–566.

Rutner, I. T., & Bugle, C. An experimental procedure for the modification of psychotic behavior. *Journal of Consulting and Clinical Psychology*, 1969, *33*, 651–653.

Salzinger, K. The place of operant conditioning of verbal behavior in psychotherapy. In C. M. Franks (Ed.), *Behavior therapy: Appraisal and status*. New York: McGraw-Hill, 1969.

Samaan, M. Thought-stopping and flooding in a case of hallucinations, obsessions, and homicidal-suicidal behavior. *Journal of Behavior Therapy and Experimental Psychiatry*, 1975, *6*, 65–67.

Sarason, I. G. Test anxiety and cognitive modeling. *Journal of Personality and Social Psychology*, 1973, *28*, 58–61.

Savitsky, J. C., Zarle, T. H., & Keedy, N. S. The effect

of information about an interviewer on interviewee perceptions. *Journal of Counseling Psychology*, 1976, 23, 158–159.

Schmidt, J. Cognitive restructuring: The art of talking to yourself. *The Personnel and Guidance Journal*, 1976, 55, 71–74.

Schmidt, L. D., & Strong, S. R. "Expert" and "inexpert" counselors. *Journal of Counseling Psychology*, 1970, 17, 115–118.

Schofield, W. *Psychotherapy: The purchase of friendship*. Englewood Cliffs, N.J.: Prentice-Hall, 1964.

Schonbar, R. A. Confessions of an ex-nondirectivist. In E. F. Hammer (Ed.), *Use of interpretation in treatments*. New York: Grune & Stratton, 1968.

Schutz, W. *Joy: Expanding human awareness*. New York: Grove Press, 1967.

Schwartz, A., & Goldiamond, I. *Social casework: A behavioral approach*. New York: Columbia University Press, 1975.

Semb, G., Hopkins, B. L., & Hursh, D. E. The effects of study questions and grades on student test performance in a college course. *Journal of Applied Behavior Analysis*, 1973, 6, 631–642.

Seymour, F. W., & Stokes, T. F. Self-recording in training girls to increase work and evoke staff praise in an institution for offenders. *Journal of Applied Behavior Analysis*, 1976, 9, 41–54.

Shapiro, D. H. Behavioral and attitudinal changes resulting from a "Zen experience" workshop and Zen meditation. *Journal of Humanistic Psychology*, 1978, 18, 21–29. (a)

Shapiro, D. H. Instructions for a training package combining formal and informal Zen meditation with behavioral self-control strategies. *Psychologia*, 1978, 31, 70–76. (b)

Shapiro, D. H. Zen meditation and behavioral self-management applied to a case of generalized anxiety. *Psychologia*, in press.

Shapiro, D., Turksky, B., Schwartz, G., & Shnidman, S. Smoking on cue: A behavioral approach to smoking reduction. *Journal of Health and Social Behavior*, 1971, 12, 108–113.

Shapiro, D. H., & Zifferblatt, S. M. Zen meditation and behavioral self-control: Similarities, differences, and clinical applications. *American Psychologist*, 1976, 31, 519–532.

Shapiro, M. B. The single case in clinical-psychological research. *Journal of General Psychology*, 1966, 74, 3–23.

Shaw, D. W., & Thoresen, C. E. Effects of modeling and desensitization in reducing dentist phobia. *Journal of Counseling Psychology*, 1974, 21, 415–420.

Sheehan, P. W. A shortened form of Betts' questionnaire upon mental imagery. *Journal of Clinical Psychology*, 1967, 23, 386–389.

Shelton, J. L., & Ackerman, J. M. *Homework in counseling and psychotherapy*. Springfield, Ill.: Charles C Thomas, 1974.

Sherman, A. R. Real-life exposure as a primary therapeutic factor in the desensitization treatment of fear. *Journal of Abnormal Psychology*, 1972, 79, 19–28.

Sherman, A. R. *Behavior modification: Theory and practice*. Monterey, Calif.: Brooks/Cole, 1973.

Shoemaker, J. E., & Tasto, D. L. The effects of muscle relaxation on blood pressure of essential hypertensives. *Behaviour Research and Therapy*, 1975, 13, 29–43.

Shure, M. B., & Spivack, G. Means-ends thinking adjustment, and social class among elementary-school-aged children. *Journal of Consulting and Clinical Psychology*, 1972, 38, 348–353.

Sieck, W. A., & McFall, R. M. Some determinants of self-monitoring effects. *Journal of Consulting and Clinical Psychology*, 1976, 44, 958–965.

Simkins, L. The reliability of self-recorded behaviors. *Behavior Therapy*, 1971, 2, 83–87.

Simon, S., Howe, L., & Kirschenbaum, H. *Values clarification*. New York: Holt, Rinehart & Winston, 1972.

Simonson, N. The impact of therapist disclosure on patient disclosure. *Journal of Counseling Psychology*, 1976, 23, 3–6.

Simonton, O. C., & Simonton, S. S. Belief systems and management of the emotional aspects of malignancy. *Journal of Transpersonal Psychology*, 1975, 7, 29–47.

Singer, J. L. Navigating the stream of consciousness: Research in daydreaming and related inner experience. *American Psychologist*, 1975, 30, 727–738.

Singer, J. L., & Antrobus, J. S. Daydreaming, imaginal processes, and personality: A normative study. In P. W. Sheehan (Ed.), *The function and nature of imagery*. New York: Academic Press, 1972.

Sirota, A. D., & Mahoney, M. J. Relaxing on cue: The self regulation of asthma. *Journal of Behavior Therapy and Experimental Psychiatry*, 1974, 5, 65–66.

Skinner, B. F. *Science and human behavior*. New York: Macmillan, 1953.

Smith, D., & Peterson, J. Counseling and values in a time perspective. *The Personnel and Guidance Journal*, 1977, 55, 309–318.

Smith, D. L. Goal attainment scaling as an adjunct to

counseling. *Journal of Counseling Psychology*, 1976, *23*, 22–27.

Smith, E. J. Counseling Black individuals: Some stereotypes. *The Personnel and Guidance Journal*, 1977, *55*, 390–396.

Smith, G. P., & Coleman, R. E. Processes underlying generalization through participant modeling with self-directed practice. *Behaviour Research and Therapy*, 1977, *15*, 204–206.

Smith, J. C. Meditation as psychotherapy: A review of the literature. *Psychological Bulletin*, 1975, *82*, 558–564.

Smith-Hanen, S. S. Effects of nonverbal behaviors on judged levels of counselor warmth and empathy. *Journal of Counseling Psychology*, 1977, *24*, 87–91.

Snow, R. E. Representative and quasi-representative designs for research on teaching. *Review of Educational Research*, 1974, *44*, 265–291.

Spates, C. R., & Kanfer, F. H. Self-monitoring, self-evaluation, and self-reinforcement in children's learning: A test of a multistage self-regulation model. *Behavior Therapy*, 1977, *8*, 9–16.

Spiegler, M., Cooley, E., Marshall, G., Prince, H., Puckett, S., & Skenazy, J. A self-control versus a counterconditioning paradigm for systematic desensitization: An experimental comparison. *Journal of Counseling Psychology*, 1976, *23*, 83–86.

Spinelli, P. R., & Packard, T. *Behavioral self-control delivery systems*. Paper presented at the National Conference on Behavioral Self-Control, Salt Lake City, February 1975.

Spivack, G. *A conception of healthy human functioning* (Research and Evaluation Report No. 15). Philadelphia: Hahnemann Medical College and Hospital, Division of Research and Evaluation, Department of Mental Health Sciences, 1973.

Spooner, S. E., & Stone, S. C. Maintenance of specific counseling skills over time. *Journal of Counseling Psychology*, 1977, *24*, 66–71.

Srebalus, D. J. Rethinking change in counseling. *The Personnel and Guidance Journal*, 1975, *53*, 415–421.

Stevens, B. *Don't push the river*. Lafayette, Calif.: Real People Press, 1970.

Stevens, J. O. *Awareness: Exploring, experimenting, experiencing*. Lafayette, Calif.: Real People Press, 1971.

Stone, C. I., Demchik-Stone, D. A., & Horan, J. J. Coping with pain: A component analysis of Lamaze and cognitive-behavioral procedures. *Journal of Psychosomatic Research*, 1977, *21*, 451–456.

Stone, G., & Gotlib, I. Effect of instructions and mod-

eling on self-disclosure. *Journal of Counseling Psychology*, 1975, *22*, 288–293.

Stone, G. L., & Morden, C. J. Effect of distance on verbal productivity. *Journal of Counseling Psychology*, 1976, *23*, 486–488.

Stone, G. L., & Vance, A. Instructions, modeling, and rehearsal: Implications for training. *Journal of Counseling Psychology*, 1976, *23*, 272–279.

Strong, S. Counseling: An interpersonal influence process. *Journal of Counseling Psychology*, 1968, *15*, 215–224.

Strong, S. R., & Dixon, D. N. Expertness, attractiveness, and influence in counseling. *Journal of Counseling Psychology*, 1971, *18*, 562–570.

Stuart, R. B. Behavioral contracting within the families of delinquents. *Journal of Behavior Therapy and Experimental Psychiatry*, 1971, *2*, 1–11.

Stuart, R. B. Self-help group approach to self-management. In R. B. Stuart (Ed.), *Behavioral self-management: Strategies, techniques and outcomes*. New York: Brunner/Mazel, 1977.

Sue, D. W. Counseling and the culturally different. *The Personnel and Guidance Journal*, 1977, *55*, 381–425 (Special Issue). (a)

Sue, D. W. Counseling the culturally different: A conceptual analysis. *The Personnel and Guidance Journal*, 1977, *55*, 422–425. (b)

Sue, D. W., & Sue, D. Barriers to effective cross-cultural counseling. *Journal of Counseling Psychology*, 1977, *24*, 420–429.

Suinn, R. M. Behavior rehearsal training for ski racers. *Behavior Therapy*, 1972, *3*, 519–520. (a)

Suinn, R. M. Removing emotional obstacles to learning and performance by visuo-motor behavior rehearsal. *Behavior Therapy*, 1972, *3*, 308–310. (b)

Suinn, R. M. Visuo-motor behavior rehearsal for adaptive behavior. In J. D. Krumboltz & C. E. Thoresen (Eds.), *Counseling methods*. New York: Holt, Rinehart & Winston, 1976.

Suinn, R. M., Edie, C. A., & Spinelli, P. R. Accelerated massed desensitization: Innovation in short-term treatment. *Behavior Therapy*, 1970, *1*, 303–311.

Sullivan, H. S. *The psychiatric interview*. New York: Norton, 1954.

Swensen, C. H. *An approach to case conceptualization*. Boston: Houghton Mifflin, 1968.

Tasto, D. L. Self-report schedules and inventories. In A. R. Ciminero, K. S. Calhoun, & H. E. Adams (Eds.), *Handbook of behavioral assessment*. New York: John Wiley, 1977.

Tasto, D. L., & Hinkle, J. E. Muscle relaxation treatment for tension headaches. *Behaviour Research and Therapy,* 1973, *11,* 347–349.

Taylor, F. G., & Marshall, W. L. Experimental analysis of a cognitive-behavioral therapy for depression. *Cognitive Therapy and Research,* 1977, *1,* 59–72.

Taylor, J. G. A behavioral interpretation of obsessive-compulsive neurosis. *Behaviour Research and Therapy,* 1963, *1,* 237–244.

Thase, M. E., & Moss, M. K. The relative efficacy of covert modeling procedures and guided participant modeling on the reduction of avoidance behavior. *Journal of Behavior Therapy and Experimental Psychiatry,* 1976, *7,* 7–12.

Thase, M., & Page, R. A. Modeling of self-disclosure in laboratory and nonlaboratory interview settings. *Journal of Counseling Psychology,* 1977, *24,* 35–40.

Thomas, E. J. Social casework and social group work: The behavioral modification approach. In *Encyclopedia of Social Work,* Vol. II. New York: National Association of Social Workers, 1971.

Thomas, E. J. *Marital communication and decision making.* New York: Free Press, 1977.

Thomas, E. J., O'Flaherty, K., & Borkin, J. Coaching marital partners in family decision making. In J. D. Krumboltz & C. E. Thoresen (Eds.), *Counseling methods.* New York: Holt, Rinehart & Winston, 1976.

Thompson, A., & Wise, W. Steps toward outcome criteria. *Journal of Counseling Psychology,* 1976, *23,* 202–208.

Thoresen, C. E., & Mahoney, M. J. *Behavioral self-control.* New York: Holt, Rinehart & Winston, 1974.

Thorpe, G. L. *Short-term effectiveness of systematic desensitization, modeling and behavior rehearsal, and self-instructional training in facilitating assertive-refusal behavior.* Unpublished doctoral dissertation, Rutgers University, 1973.

Thorpe, G. L. Desensitization, behavior rehearsal, self-instructional training and placebo effects on assertive-refusal behavior. *European Journal of Behavioural Analysis and Modification,* 1975, *1,* 30–44.

Thorpe, G., Amatu, H., Blakey, R., & Burns, L. Contributions of overt instructional rehearsal and "specific insight" to the effectiveness of self-instructional training: A preliminary study. *Behavior Therapy,* 1976, *7,* 504–511.

Tori, C., & Worell, L. Reduction of human avoidant behavior: A comparison of counterconditioning, expectancy, and cognitive information approaches. *Journal of Consulting and Clinical Psychology,* 1973, *41,* 269–278.

Trager, G. L. Paralanguage: A first approximation. *Studies in Linguistics,* 1958, *13,* 1–12.

Truax, C. B. Reinforcement and nonreinforcement in Rogerian psychotherapy. *Journal of Abnormal Psychology,* 1966, *71,* 1–9.

Truax, C. B., & Mitchell, K. M. Research on certain therapist interpersonal skills in relation to process and outcome. In A. Bergin & S. Garfield (Eds.), *Handbook of psychotherapy and behavior change: An empirical analysis.* New York: John Wiley, 1971.

Turk, D. *Cognitive control of pain: A skills training approach for the treatment of pain.* Unpublished master's thesis, University of Waterloo, 1975.

Turnage, J. R., & Logan, D. L. Treatment of a hypodermic needle phobia by *in vivo* systematic desensitization. *Journal of Behavior Therapy and Experimental Psychiatry,* 1974, *5,* 67–69.

Turner, R. D., Polly, S., & Sherman, A. R. A behavioral approach to individualized exercise programming. In J. D. Krumboltz & C. E. Thoresen (Eds.), *Counseling methods.* New York: Holt, Rinehart & Winston, 1976.

Uhlemann, M. R., Lea, G. W., & Stone, G. L. Effect of instructions and modeling on trainees low in interpersonal-communication skills. *Journal of Counseling Psychology,* 1976, *23,* 509–513.

Ullmann, L. P., & Krasner, L. *A psychological approach to abnormal behavior.* Englewood Cliffs, N.J.: Prentice-Hall, 1969.

Vance, B. Using contracts to control weight and to improve cardiovascular physical fitness. In J. D. Krumboltz & C. E. Thoresen (Eds.), *Counseling methods.* New York: Holt, Rinehart & Winston, 1976.

van Egeren, L. F. Psychophysiological aspects of systematic desensitization: Some outstanding issues. *Behaviour Research and Therapy,* 1971, *9,* 65–77.

Van Hoose, W. H.; & Kottler, J. A. *Ethical and legal issues in counseling and psychotherapy.* San Francisco: Jossey-Bass, 1977.

Van Houten, R., Hill, S., & Parsons, M. An analysis of a performance feedback system: The effects of timing and feedback, public posting, and praise upon academic performance and peer interaction. *Journal of Applied Behavior Analysis,* 1975, *8,* 449–457.

Ventis, W. Case history: The use of laughter as an alternative response in systematic desensitization. *Behavior Therapy,* 1973, *4,* 120–122.

"Von Stade: Forget the Magic." *Time*, December 13, 1976, Vol. 108, 101–102.

Walls, R. T., Werner, T. J., Bacon, A., & Zane, T. Behavior checklists. In J. D. Cone & R. P. Hawkins (Eds.), *Behavioral assessment: New directions in clinical psychology*. New York: Brunner/Mazel, 1977.

Watson, D., & Friend, R. Measurement of social-evaluative anxiety. *Journal of Consulting and Clinical Psychology*, 1969, 33, 448–457.

Watson, D., & Tharp, R. *Self-directed behavior: Self-modification for personal adjustment*. Monterey, Calif.: Brooks/Cole, 1972.

Watson, D. L., & Tharp, R. G. *Self-directed behavior: Self-modification for personal adjustment* (2nd ed.). Monterey, Calif.: Brooks/Cole, 1977.

Watson, L. *The effects of covert modeling and covert reinforcement on job-interview skills of youth offenders*. Unpublished doctoral dissertation, West Virginia University, 1976.

Watson, O. M. *Proxemic behavior: A cross-cultural study*. The Hague: Mouton, 1970.

Watts, F. N. Desensitization as an habituation phenomenon: I. Stimulus intensity as determinant of the effects of stimulus lengths. *Behaviour Research and Therapy*, 1971, 9, 209–217.

Watts, F. N. The control of spontaneous recovery of anxiety in imaginal desensitization. *Behaviour Research and Therapy*, 1974, 12, 57–59.

Watts, F. N., Powell, G. E., & Austin, S. V. The modification of abnormal beliefs. *British Journal of Medical Psychology*, 1973, 46, 359–363.

Weathers, L., & Liberman, R. P. The family contracting exercise. *Journal of Behavior Therapy and Experimental Psychiatry*, 1975, 6, 208–214.

Wein, K. S., Nelson, R. O., & Odom, J. V. The relative contributions of reattribution and verbal extinction to the effectiveness of cognitive restructuring. *Behavior Therapy*, 1975, 6, 459–474.

Weingaertner, A. H. Self-administered aversive stimulation with hallucinating hospitalized schizophrenics. *Journal of Consulting and Clinical Psychology*, 1971, 36, 422–429.

Weissberg, M. Anxiety-inhibiting statements and relaxation combined in two cases of speech anxiety. *Journal of Behavior Therapy and Experimental Psychiatry*, 1975, 6, 163–164.

Whalen, C. Effects of a model and instructions on group verbal behaviors. *Journal of Consulting and Clinical Psychology*, 1969, 33, 509–521.

White, K., Sheehan, P. W., & Ashton, R. Imagery assessment: A survey of self-report measures. *Journal of Mental Imagery*, 1977, 1, 145–170.

Williams, R. L., Canale, J., & Edgerly, J. Affinity for self-management: A comparison between counseling clients and controls. *Journal of Behavior Therapy and Experimental Psychiatry*, 1976, 7, 231–234.

Williams, R. L., & Long, J. D. *Toward a self-managed life-style*. Boston: Houghton Mifflin, 1975.

Williams, R. L., Long, J. D., & Yoakley, R. W. The utility of behavior contracts and behavior proclamations with advantaged senior high school students. *Journal of School Psychology*, 1972, 10, 329–338.

Wilson, G. T., & Davison, G. C. Processes of fear reduction in systematic desensitization: Animal studies. *Psychological Bulletin*, 1971, 76, 1–14.

Wish, P., Hasazi, J., & Jurgela, A. Automated direct conditioning of a childhood phobia. *Journal of Behavior Therapy and Experimental Psychiatry*, 1973, 4, 279–283.

Wisocki, P. A., & Rooney, E. J. A comparison of thought stopping and covert sensitization techniques in the treatment of smoking: A brief report. *The Psychological Record*, 1974, 24, 191–192.

Wolberg, L. R. *The technique of psychotherapy* (2nd ed.). New York: Grune & Stratton, 1967.

Wolf, M. M. Social validity: The case for subjective measurement or how applied behavior analysis is finding its heart. *Journal of Applied Behavior Analysis*, 1978, 11, 203–214.

Wolpe, J. *Psychotherapy by reciprocal inhibition*. Stanford, Calif.: Stanford University Press, 1958.

Wolpe, J. The systematic desensitization treatment of neuroses. *Journal of Nervous and Mental Disease*, 1961, 132, 189–203.

Wolpe, J. *The practice of behavior therapy*. New York: Pergamon Press, 1969.

Wolpe, J. Dealing with resistance to thought-stopping: A transcript. *Journal of Behavior Therapy and Experimental Psychiatry*, 1971, 2, 121–125.

Wolpe, J. *The practice of behavior therapy* (2nd ed.). New York: Pergamon Press, 1973.

Wolpe, J. *Theme and variations: A behavior therapy casebook*. New York: Pergamon Press, 1976.

Wolpe, J., & Lang, P. J. A fear survey schedule for use in behavior therapy. *Behaviour Research and Therapy*, 1964, 2, 27–30.

Wolpe, J., & Lazarus, A. *Behavior therapy techniques*. New York: Pergamon Press, 1966.

Woolfolk, R. L., Carr-Kaffashan, L., McNulty, T. F., & Lehrer, P. M. Meditation training as a treatment for insomnia. *Behavior Therapy*, 1976, 7, 359–365.

Woy, J. R., & Efran, J. S. Systematic desensitization and expectancy in the treatment of speaking anxiety. *Behaviour Research and Therapy*, 1972, *10*, 43–49.

Yamagami, T. The treatment of an obsession by thought-stopping. *Journal of Behavior Therapy and Experimental Psychiatry*, 1971, *2*, 133–135.

Zemore, R. Systematic desensitization as a method of teaching a general anxiety-reducing skill. *Journal of Consulting and Clinical Psychology*, 1975, *43*, 157–161.

Ziemelis, A. Effects of client preference and expectancy upon the initial interview. *Journal of Counseling Psychology*, 1974, *21*, 23–30.

Zimmer, J. M., & Anderson, S. Dimensions of positive regard and empathy. *Journal of Counseling Psychology*, 1968, *15*, 417–426.

Zimmer, J. M., & Park, P. Factor analysis of counselor communications. *Journal of Counseling Psychology*, 1967, *14*, 198–203.

Zimmer, J. M., & Pepyne, E. W. A descriptive and comparative study of dimensions of counselor response. *Journal of Counseling Psychology*, 1971, *18*, 441–447.

Zimmer, J. M., Wightman, L. E., & McArthur, D. L. *Categories of counselor behavior as defined from cross validated factor structures* (Final report, United States Office of Education Project No. 9-A0003). Amherst: University of Massachusetts, School of Education, 1970.

Author Index

Borkin, J., 114
Borkovec, T. D., 407, 408, 409, 410, 413, 414, 415, 428
Bornstein, P. H., 213, 248
Boudin, H. M., 506
Boudreau, L., 402, 430, 445, 474
Bounds, W. S., 203
Boykin, R. A., 213
Brammer, L. J., 20, 86, 87, 88, 89, 93
Brehm, J. W., 364
Briggs, L., 201
Broden, M., 482, 484, 492
Broverman, D., 16, 28
Broverman, I., 16, 28
Brown, D., 48
Brown, J., 512
Brownell, K., 478, 491
Bruch, M., 359
Buchanan, J. D., 375, 376, 377, 399
Bucher, B., 340, 505
Buckner, L. G., 115, 276
Bugle, C., 479, 482, 487
Burns, L., 362

Cain, M. P., 401
Caird, W. K., 458
Calhoun, K. S., 248, 249, 492
Cameron R., 332, 359, 374, 375, 376, 379, 380, 381, 383
Cammer, L., 402
Campbell, L. M., 344
Canale, J., 477, 492, 512, 517
Canfield, J., 146
Cannon, J. R., 49, 68, 70, 72, 76
Cantrell, M. L., 510
Cantrell, R. P., 510
Caple, R. B., 478
Carey, R., 105, 106, 115
Carkhuff, R. R., 11, 19, 21, 22, 23, 24, 49, 54, 56, 67, 68, 70, 72, 76, 84, 85
Carmody, T. B., 213, 248
Carr-Kaffashan, L., 402, 427
Catania, A. C., 516
Cautela, J. R., 168, 213, 248, 303, 307, 308, 313, 314, 329, 476, 501
Cavior, N., 484
Chance, J. E., 477
Chapman, R., 267
Chassan, J. B., 217
Chaves, J., 377
Childers, W., 106, 115
Church, A., 506, 517
Ciminero, A. R., 206, 207, 208, 211, 212, 248,

249, 481, 483, 486, 487, 492, 512
Clarkson, F., 16, 28
Clouser, R. A., 408
Coe, W. C., 115, 276
Coleman, R. E., 285, 289, 301
Colletti, J. G., 478, 491
Cone, J. D., 137, 163, 248, 249, 492
Cooley, E., 433, 449, 475
Cooper, A., 474
Cooper, K., 428
Cormier, L. S., 8, 49, 60, 65, 68, 76, 79, 83, 93, 251, 263, 459, 509, 517
Cormier, W. H., 8, 56, 60, 203, 263, 459, 509
Cornish, R. D., 430, 460
Cotharin, R., 431, 474
Cozby, P. C., 95, 97, 114
Cronbach, L. J., 208, 213, 214, 221, 222
Crowley, T. J., 94
Csanyi, A., 502, 503, 506, 517
Curran, J. P., 431, 474

Daniels, L. K., 445
Danish, S., 76
D'Augelli, A. R., 43
Davidson, P. O., 382, 399
Davies, I., 9, 104
Davis, J. L., 16
Davison, G. C., 137, 163, 252, 253, 255, 261, 266, 269, 276, 362, 369, 370, 399, 407, 409, 415, 428, 432, 436, 440, 442, 447, 452, 453, 457, 474
Dawidoff, D. J., 171
Dawley, H. H., 460, 475
Decenteceo, E. T., 362, 363, 364
Deffenbacher, J. L., 407
Delaney, D. J., 99, 100, 169, 251, 260, 512, 517
Dellinger, J. K., 303
DeLo, J., 213
Demchik-Stone, D. A., 303, 375, 376, 377, 399
Dengrove, E., 431, 439
Denholtz, M., 460, 475
Denney, D. R., 434, 436, 449, 474
Denniston, D., 401
Devine, V., 500, 503, 517
de Visser, L., 180, 185, 201, 204, 250, 280, 301
Dilley, J. S., 430, 460
DiMattia, D. J., 40, 44
Dixon, D. N., 43
Dobes, R. W., 212
Donner, L., 475
Dore-Boyce, K., 492
Doster, J. A., 102
Downs, D. L., 407
Dua, P. S., 430, 459, 475

Dunbar, J., 502
Dyer, W. W., 8, 124, 146, 359, 388
D'Zurilla, T. J., 105, 115, 206, 254

Eberle, T., 451
Edelstein, B., 205, 215, 301, 340, 343, 359
Edgerly, J., 477, 492, 512, 517
Edie, C. A., 459
Efran, J. S., 205, 430
Egan, G., 8, 19, 21, 28, 49, 56, 62, 67, 68, 77,
    82, 84, 85, 87, 90, 93, 94, 95, 96, 97, 99,
    114, 203, 251, 252, 253, 255, 260, 512
Eisenberg, S., 99, 100, 169, 251, 260, 513, 517
Eisler, R., 301
Ekman, P., 29, 30, 31, 38
Elder, J., 362
Ellis, A., 360, 361, 363
Ellsworth, D., 38
Emery, J. R., 442
Epstein, L. H., 212, 213
Ersner-Hershfield, R., 478, 491
Evans, D., 431, 474
Evans, I. M., 449, 452, 454, 455, 475
Exline, R. V., 38

Fabricatore, J., 340, 505
Fasnacht, G., 503, 517
Fedoravicius, A., 431, 474
Ferster, C. B., 494, 516
Filion, R., 478, 498
Fisher, E. B., 482
Fishman, S., 442, 460
Flannery, R. B., 307, 313, 329
Flowers, J. V., 276
Fox, S., 478, 498
Frank, G. H., 54
Frank, J. D., 205
Franks, C. M., 93, 163
Frederiksen, L. W., 212, 482, 492
Fremouw, W. J., 362, 363, 365, 366, 384, 399
Fretz, B. R., 44
Frey, D. H., 7, 254
Friedling, C., 482
Friedman, L., 502
Friedman, R., 96
Friend, R., 213, 221
Friesen, W., 29, 30, 31, 38
Fry, P. S., 430
Furst, J. B., 474

Gagné, R. M., 187, 201
Gajdos, E., 269, 276, 285, 301
Galassi, J. P., 213, 214, 431
Galassi, M. D., 213, 214

Gallagher, J. W., 308
Gambrill, E. D., 213
Garfield, S. L., 28, 260
Gath, D. H., 433
Gazda, G. M., 28, 43, 48, 68, 106, 115
Geer, C. A., 432
Geis, G. L., 267
Gelatt, H., 105, 106, 115
Gelder, M. G., 433
Gergen, K. J., 97
Gershman, L., 340, 341, 343, 408, 445, 501
Giannandrea, V., 96, 97
Gilmore, J., 431, 474
Girodo, M., 402
Gladstein, G., 48
Glaser, R., 516
Glasgow, R. E., 279, 301, 460
Glass, C. R., 362
Glogower, F. D., 362, 366, 367, 399
Gluckstern, N., 28, 49, 51, 52, 54, 60, 63, 70, 76,
    78, 79, 86, 89, 93, 94, 97, 101, 114
Goldfried, A. P., 7, 433
Goldfried, M. R., 7, 105, 115, 142, 163, 206, 213,
    252, 253, 254, 255, 261, 266, 269, 276, 362,
    363, 364, 367, 369, 370, 399, 407, 408, 409,
    415, 428, 430, 433, 435, 436, 440, 442, 445,
    446, 447, 449, 452, 453, 457, 474, 475
Goldiamond, I., 102, 128, 138, 146, 154, 157, 163,
    187, 201, 516
Goldstein, A. J., 445
Goldstein, A. P., 18, 19, 28, 104, 115, 250, 254,
    260, 276, 475, 517
Goodman, J., 332, 333, 359
Goodwin, D. L., 128
Gordon, T., 19, 20
Gormally, J., 55, 56, 63, 79, 93
Gonzales, M., 502, 503, 506, 517
Gotlib, I., 102, 114
Gottman, J. M., 167, 170, 171, 180, 189, 201, 362,
    482
Graves, J. R., 43, 44, 48
Grayson, J., 428
Green, L., 482
Greenberg, I., 478, 516
Greene, L., 45, 48
Greiner, J., 477, 478, 491
Grimm, L. G., 138, 141, 142, 163
Groverman, A. M., 478
Guerney, B., 475
Gulanick, N., 517

Haase, R. F., 21, 28, 40, 43, 44
Hackett, G., 375, 376, 377, 399, 478, 479, 507

Hackmann, A., 340, 341, 359
Hackney, H., 43, 48, 49, 60, 65, 68, 76, 79, 83, 93, 117, 118, 120, 125, 250, 251, 517
Hall, E. T., 29, 40, 48
Hall, R. A., 459
Hall, R. V., 482, 484, 492, 505, 517
Halpern, T. P., 96
Hamilton, S. B., 213, 248
Hanley, S., 307, 313, 329
Harmatz, M. G., 362, 384
Harmin, M., 15
Hart, B., 360
Hartley, J., 9, 104
Hasazi, J., 474
Hauer, A. L., 76
Hawkins, D., 104
Hawkins, R., 137, 163, 212, 248, 249, 492
Hay, L., 308, 311, 312, 313, 329
Hay, W., 308, 311, 312, 313, 329
Haynes, S., 206, 214, 248
Hays, V., 343
Hearn, M., 431, 474
Hecherman, C. L., 478
Hellman, I., 496, 516
Helner, P. A., 88, 89, 93
Hersen, M., 137, 163, 181, 203, 213, 214, 248
Hershfield, S., 478, 491
Hertel, R. K., 54, 55
Highlen, P. S., 54, 63, 67, 76
Hill, C. E., 55, 56, 63, 79, 93, 165, 180, 184, 201
Hill, S., 479, 487
Hinkle, J. E., 407, 459
Hoffman, M. A., 501
Hoffman-Graff, M. A., 95, 96, 114
Holahan, C. J., 40
Holroyd, K. A., 375, 399, 431
Holt, S., 492
Homme, L., 502, 503, 506, 517
Hoopes, M. H., 202
Hopkins, B. L., 4
Horan, J. J., 303, 304, 305, 329, 375, 376, 377, 399, 478, 479, 501, 507
Horne, A. M., 431, 474
Hosford, R. E., 180, 185, 201, 204, 250, 280, 282, 301, 458
Howe, L., 16, 28
Howell, R., 458, 460, 475
Huck, S. W., 203
Huddleston, C. M., 510
Hughes, H., 206, 214, 248
Hummel, T. J., 54, 55, 56, 60, 125
Humphreys, L., 260
Hung, J. H., 205, 248

Hursh, D. E., 4
Hurst, J. C., 432

Ince, L. P., 407
Israel, E., 407
Ivey, A. E., 28, 43, 49, 51, 52, 54, 60, 63, 70, 76, 78, 79, 86, 89, 93, 94, 97, 101, 114, 120, 125

Jackson, B., 499, 517
Jacobson, E., 401, 407
Jaffe, D. T., 401
Jaffe, P. E., 97
Janis, I. L., 362, 399
Jefferey, C., 430, 474
Jefferey, K. M., 187
Jefferey, R. W., 262, 265, 266, 269, 276, 285, 301
Jeffrey, D. B., 516, 517
Jessell, J., 88, 89, 93
Johnson, D., 85, 93
Johnson, S. M., 498, 517
Johnston, D. W., 433
Johnston, J. M., 4
Jones, R. T., 476, 479, 499, 503, 509, 516
Jourard, S. M., 96, 114
Jurgela, A., 474

Kanfer, F. H., 80, 93, 115, 126, 138, 141, 142, 163, 205, 254, 276, 475, 476, 478, 479, 482, 483, 484, 485, 487, 490, 491, 492, 493, 496, 500, 502, 503, 505, 507, 510, 512, 516, 517
Kanitz, H. M., 360, 361
Kanter, N. J., 362, 430, 474
Karoly, P., 142, 477, 478, 491, 510, 516
Kastenbaum, R., 501
Katkin, E. S., 206, 212, 213, 214, 216, 248, 437
Kaul, M. A., 84
Kaul, T. J., 84
Kazdin, A. E., 203, 205, 211, 212, 215, 249, 263, 276, 302, 303, 307, 308, 310, 311, 313, 314, 329, 330, 431, 432, 433, 475, 476, 479, 483, 485, 487, 492, 499, 503, 509, 516
Keedy, N. S., 96
Kelley, J. E., 205, 248
Kiesler, D. J., 260
Kirschenbaum, H., 16, 28
Knapp, M. L., 29, 30, 31, 38, 43, 45, 48
Knapp, T. J., 407
Knight, P. H., 44
Knipe, J., 407
Knox, J., 378
Komaki, J., 492
Kory, R. B., 401

Kosevsky, B. P., 212
Kostka, M. P., 431
Kottler, J., 171, 181, 253, 254
Krasner, L., 361
Krause, M. S., 104
Krumboltz, J. D., 2, 8, 20, 114, 127, 137, 141,
    165, 170, 180, 182, 185, 202, 253, 267, 301,
    304, 305, 310, 329, 330, 331, 435, 442, 461,
    475, 489, 490, 492, 517
Kunce, J., 278, 301
Kunzelman, H. D., 486

LaCrosse, M. B., 44, 48
Ladouceur, R., 501
Lamaze, F., 407
Lang, P. J., 213, 429, 432, 437
Langer, E. J., 362, 399
Lavelle, J., 51, 53, 54, 60
Lawson, D. M., 501
Layng, F. C., 303
Lazarus, A. A., 141, 147, 250, 266, 303, 306, 329,
    331, 339, 361, 409, 429, 440, 442, 452
Lazovik, A., 429
Lea, G. W., 21
Lehrer, D. M., 402, 427
Leiblum, S. R., 167, 170, 171, 180, 189, 201
Leitenberg, H., 432, 435
Levendusky, P., 375, 399
Levin, F. M., 97
Levine, F., 503, 517
Levitt, E. B., 494, 516
Levonkron, J., 482
Levy, L. H., 93
Lewis, E. C., 105, 106, 115
Lewis, S., 301
Liberman, R. P., 506, 507, 509, 510
Lichtenberg, J. W., 54, 55, 60, 125
Lick, J. R., 206, 211, 212, 213, 214, 215, 216, 248, 437
Liddell, A., 145
Lillesand, D. B., 101, 114
Linberg, S., 478, 479, 507
Linder, L., 442, 475
Lindsley, O. R., 486
Linehan, M. M., 138, 140, 141, 154, 163, 362, 399
Lipinski, D. P., 205, 206, 208, 211, 212, 213, 248,
    481, 483, 484, 486, 487, 490, 492, 512
Logan, D. L., 460
Lomont, J. F., 431, 475
Long, J. D., 492, 510
Lorion, R. P., 18
Lowe, J. C., 445
Lukaski, H., 478, 479, 507
Lyons, M., 145

MacDonald, M. L., 460
Mager, R. F., 201
Mahoney, K., 8, 368, 369, 388, 478, 486, 499
Mahoney, M. J., 8, 128, 130, 131, 203, 204, 208,
    212, 213, 248, 249, 255, 302, 331, 340, 341,
    344, 359, 368, 369, 388, 407, 447, 476, 477,
    478, 479, 481, 482, 483, 484, 487, 492, 494,
    497, 499, 500, 501, 503, 505, 506, 512, 516,
    517
Mann, B., 96, 97, 114
Mann, E., 460, 475
Mann, J., 430
Mann, R. A., 506, 507
Marabotto, C. M., 484
Marlatt, G. A., 263, 276, 277, 401, 402, 427
Marques, J. K., 401, 402, 427
Marquis, J. N., 431, 436, 437, 438, 439, 440, 442,
    445, 446, 448, 450, 451, 452, 453, 458, 460, 475
Marshall, G., 433, 449, 475
Marshall, W. L., 362, 399, 460, 475
Martinez, J. A., 205, 215
Martorano, R., 312, 330
Maslin, A., 16
Maslow, A. H., 253
Masters, J. C., 11, 339, 341, 342, 343, 344, 359,
    431, 452, 457, 475
Mathews, A. M., 432, 433
Matson, J. L., 431, 474
May, R. B., 501
McArthur, D. L., 56
McBurney, D., 451
McCroskey, J. C., 362, 366, 367, 399
McDonald, F. J., 280
McFall, R. M., 101, 114, 211, 212, 213, 214, 248,
    265, 276, 481, 482, 483, 485, 492
McGlynn, F., 442, 475
McGuire, D., 102, 114, 279
McKeachie, W. J., 8, 9, 267, 503, 517
McKenzie, T. L., 487, 492
McLaughlin, T. F., 498, 517
McLean, C., 340, 341, 359
McNulty, T. F., 402, 427
McReynolds, W. T., 492, 506, 517
McWilliams, P., 401
Meichenbaum, D. A., 138, 142, 143, 163, 263,
    310, 331, 332, 333, 359, 361, 362, 363, 364,
    365, 366, 367, 374, 375, 376, 377, 379, 380,
    381, 382, 383, 399, 431, 450, 474
Melamed, B., 301
Melnik, J., 267, 276, 312, 330, 431
Merbaum, M., 205
Meyer, V., 145
Mikulas, W., 431, 474

Miller, B. V., 205
Miller, G., 105, 106, 115
Miller, H. R., 451
Miller, P., 213
Miller, S. B., 104
Mischel, W., 128, 211, 263
Mitchell, K. M., 28, 93
Mitchell, K. R., 477, 491
Mitts, B., 482, 484, 492
Mogan, J., 445
Moore, B. S., 482
Moos, R. H., 213
Morden, C. J., 44, 48
Morgan, W., 431, 436, 437, 438, 439, 440, 442, 445, 446, 448, 450, 451, 452, 453, 458, 460, 475
Morganstern, K. P., 11, 72, 138, 139, 140, 163, 170, 181, 505
Morrell, G., 280, 282, 301
Morris, K. T., 360, 361
Morris, R. J., 429, 458, 475
Moss, C., 280, 282, 301
Moss, M. K., 330
Moura, N. G., 477, 478, 482, 499, 505, 506, 517
Murphy, K. C., 96, 97, 114
Murphy, P., 10

Nawas, M. M., 442, 451, 460
Nay, W. R., 214, 248, 407
Nelson, R. E., 476, 479, 499, 503, 509, 516
Nelson, R. O., 205, 206, 208, 211, 212, 213, 248, 308, 311, 312, 313, 314, 329, 330, 399, 481, 482, 483, 484, 485, 486, 487, 490, 492, 512
Nesse, M., 308, 313, 314, 330
Nicassio, P., 205, 212, 401, 407
Nicholas, W., 478, 479, 507
Nietzel, M., 312, 330
Nolan, J. D., 494
Novaco, R. W., 375, 378, 379, 380, 381, 383
Nurnberger, J. I., 494, 516
Nye, L. S., 56, 60, 117, 118, 250, 262, 279

O'Brien, J. S., 445
Odom, J. V., 399
Oetting, E., 120, 125
O'Flaherty, K., 114
Okun, B. F., 16, 17, 28, 210, 225, 250, 251, 252, 253, 254
O'Leary, K., 500, 503, 517
Olin, R. J., 339
Oliveau, D. C., 432, 435
Olson, D., 496, 516
O'Neil, D., 458, 460, 475

O'Neill, G., 4
Orne, M. T., 205, 215, 248
Ornstein, R. E., 403, 405
Osterhouse, R. A., 430, 435, 443, 460, 475

Packard, T., 501
Page, R. A., 96, 114
Palisi, A., 49
Pankratz, L., 375, 399
Park, P., 56
Parks, J., 48
Parsons, M., 479, 487
Passons, W. R., 28, 30, 31, 41, 42, 48, 52
Paul, G. L., 126, 204, 250, 407, 460
Penick, S. B., 478, 498
Pepyne, E. W., 56, 80
Perez, J., 76
Perls, F. S., 26, 30
Perri, M. G., 477, 478, 491
Perry, M. A., 263, 276, 277
Peterson, D. R., 139
Peterson, J., 16, 28
Phares, E. J., 477
Phillips, D., 269
Phillips, J. S., 80, 93, 126
Phillips, L. W., 458
Piaget, G., 431, 436, 437, 438, 439, 440, 442, 445, 446, 448, 450, 451, 452, 453, 458, 460, 475
Picot, A., 407
Pierce, R. M., 21, 22, 23, 24, 49, 68, 70, 72, 76
Platt, J. J., 105
Polansky, N. A., 96
Polly, S., 478, 499
Porter, F., 482
Poulos, R., 500, 503, 517
Powell, G. E., 364
Prazak, G., 202
Prentice, N., 301
Presse, L., 460, 475
Prince, H., 433, 449, 475
Prochaska, J. O., 478
Proctor, S., 451
Pucel, J., 443, 460
Puckett, S., 433, 449, 475
Pursell, C., 303

Rachman, S., 445, 451, 452
Rappaport, A. F., 402
Raths, L., 15
Rathus, S. A., 213
Rechs, J., 502, 503, 506, 517
Reeder, C., 278, 301
Reese, S. L., 307, 313, 330

Stevens, J. O., 28
Stocker, R., 267, 276
Stokes, T. F., 482, 492
Stone, C. I., 303, 375, 376, 377, 478, 479, 507
Stone, G. L., 21, 44, 48, 101, 114
Stone, S. C., 50
Stratoudakis, J. P., 431
Strong, S. R., 43, 97
Stuart, R. B., 211, 248, 427, 428, 491, 492, 506, 507, 512, 516
Stunkard, A. J., 478, 498
Sue, D., 18, 19, 28, 38, 40, 41, 48
Sue, D. W., 18, 19, 28, 38, 40, 41, 48
Suinn, R. M., 330, 459, 475
Sullivan, H. S., 29
Sweetland, A., 54
Swensen, C. H., 137, 145

Tasto, D. L., 206, 213, 249, 401, 407, 428
Taylor, F. G., 362, 399
Taylor, J. G., 339
Tepper, D., 21, 28, 43, 44
Tharp, R. G., 484, 486, 492, 495, 496, 500, 501, 502, 503, 505, 516, 517
Thase, M. E., 96, 114, 330
Thelen, M., 102, 114, 279
Thomas, E. J., 102, 114, 267
Thompson, A., 196
Thoresen, C. E., 2, 8, 20, 114, 127, 128, 130, 137, 141, 185, 202, 208, 253, 267, 280, 301, 304, 305, 310, 329, 330, 331, 431, 435, 461, 474, 475, 476, 477, 479, 481, 483, 484, 487, 489, 490, 492, 494, 497, 500, 501, 503, 505, 506, 512, 516, 517
Thorpe, G. L., 362, 363, 364
Tondo, T. R., 303
Tori, C., 475
Trager, G. L., 29
Trier, C. S., 407, 428
Trimble, R. W., 407
Truax, C. B., 28, 54, 205
Turk, D., 374, 375, 376, 377, 379, 380, 381, 382, 384, 399
Turksky, B., 516
Turnage, J. R., 460
Turner, R. D., 478, 499
Twentyman, C., 265, 276

Uhlemann, M. R., 21
Ullmann, L. P., 361
Unger, T., 206, 211, 212, 214, 215, 216, 248
Upper, D., 168, 213, 248

Vance, A., 101, 102
Vance, B., 506, 507, 508, 517
van Egeren, L. F., 432, 475
Van Hoose, W. H., 171, 181, 253, 254
Van Houten, R., 479, 487
Varenhorst, B., 105, 106, 115
Ventis, W., 445
Veraldi, D. M., 213, 248
Vernon, J. C., 229, 233, 249
Vogel, S., 16, 28
Vriend, J., 8, 124

Waddell, K. J., 343
Wade, T. C., 477, 478, 482, 499, 505, 506, 517
Wagaman, G. L., 8
Walls, R. T., 209, 249
Walters, R., 106, 115
Watson, D., 213, 221
Watson, D. L., 484, 486, 492, 495, 496, 500, 501, 502, 503, 505, 516, 517
Watson, L., 308, 310, 311, 312
Watson, O. M., 31
Watts, F. N., 364, 451
Weathers, L., 509, 510
Webster, J., 213
Wein, K. S., 399
Weinberg, L., 362, 363, 364
Weingaertner, A. H., 505
Weis, L., 505, 517
Weissberg, M., 445
Wells, H., 146
Wenrich, W. W., 460, 475
Werner, T. J., 209, 249
Westbrook, T., 375, 399
Whalen, C., 102
White, A. M., 54
White, K., 303
White, R. G., 477, 491
Wightman, L. E., 56
Wilcoxon, L. A., 431, 432, 433, 475
Williams, R. L., 477, 492, 510, 512, 517
Wilson, A., 442, 475
Wilson, G. T., 432, 474, 478, 491
Wincze, J. P., 458
Winters, L. C., 38
Wise, F., 430, 431, 474
Wise, W., 196
Wish, P., 474
Wisocki, P. A., 340
Wolberg, L. R., 60
Wolf, M. M., 248, 249
Wolfer, J. A., 362, 399

Wolpe, J., 138, 163, 213, 339, 340, 341, 343, 407,
    430, 432, 433, 436, 437, 438, 440, 442, 445,
    447, 449, 450, 458, 475
Woodburn, L., 517
Wooldridge, R. L., 510
Woolfolk, R. L., 402, 427
Worell, L., 475
Woy, J. R., 205, 430
Wright, C., 266, 285, 301

Yamagami, T., 340, 341, 343
Yoakley, R. W., 510

Zane, T., 209, 249
Zarle, T. H., 96
Zemore, R., 430, 433, 449
Zerega, W. D., 8
Ziemelis, A., 104
Zifferblatt, S. M., 402, 403, 405, 427
Zimmer, J. M., 56, 80
Zitter, R. E., 362, 399

Subject Index

Childbirth, 304, 306–307, 378 (*see also* Lamaze)
 emotive imagery during, 304, 306–307
 information about and coping, 378
Clarification, 62, 63–65
 definition of, 62, 63
 examples of, 62, 63
 learning activity for, 64–65
 purpose of, 63
Coaching, 265–266 (*see also* Induction aids)
 definition of, 265
 in rehearsal, 265–266
Cognitive behavior modification, 331, 361 (*see also* Cognitive therapy, Cognitive restructuring)
Cognitive map, 117–120
 directions for in the interview, 118–119
 model dialogue of, 119–120
Cognitive modeling (and self-instruction), 332–339, 352–355
 definition of, 332
 example of self-guidance, 333–334
 interview checklist of, 352–355
 learning activities for, 334, 339
 model dialogue of, 336–339
 steps in, 333–336
 uses of, 332–333
Cognitive restructuring, 361–374, 391–395
 components of, 362–371
 interview checklist of, 391–395
 learning activities for, 373–374
 model dialogue of, 371–373
 uses of, 361–362
Cognitive therapy, 331–332, 360–361
 assumptions of, 331, 361
 conceptualization of client problems, 331–332
Commitment (involvement), 189, 252, 506, 512
 in action plans, 252
 in contracting, 506
 in establishing goals, 189
 in self-management, 512
Competence (needs), 13, 14–15
 assessment for, 14–15
Conditioning, 432
 classical, 432
 operant, 432
Confrontation, 78, 82–86
 client reactions to, 85–86
 definition of, 78, 82
 for distorted messages, 82–83
 effects of, 84
 examples of, 78, 83–84
 ground rules, 84–85
 learning activity for, 86
 for mixed messages, 83–84

purposes of, 82
Congruence, 20, 41
 as genuineness, 20
 with verbal and nonverbal behavior, 41
Consequences (*see also* Reinforcers and Punishers):
 in covert modeling, 311–312
 definition of, 128
 interview leads to identify consequences, 144–145
 negative (punishers), 130
 overt and covert, 131
 positive (reinforcers), 130
 in self-contracting, 506
 in self-management, 497, 481
 self-produced (determined), 498
 in stimulus control, 493
Consultant (helper), 5
Content (cognitive), 51–52, 65
 cognitive focus, 51–52
 content messages, 65
Contingency contracts, 506 (*see also* Self-contracting)
Continuous recording, 207–208, 483, 486
Control scenes, 308–309, 441
 in covert modeling, 308–309
 in desensitization hierarchies, 441
Conversational style (in helping), 49–51
 inappropriate communication, 50
 learning activities for, 50–51
Coping (slider) models, 263, 310
Coping skills (of client), 145–146, 334, 377–383
 assessment of, 145–146
 cognitive coping, 377, 379–383
 in cognitive modeling, 334
 direct-action coping, 377–379
 information about, 377
Coping thoughts (of client), 366–379, 380–382, 449–450
 coping with being overwhelmed, 366–379
 in desensitization, 443, 445, 446, 449–450
 examples of, 366, 380–382
 positive self-statements, 367, 368–369
 situation-oriented coping, 366–379
 task-oriented coping, 366–379
Counseling process, 7
Counseling relationship, 11, 19–25, 204–205
 components of, 11
 facilitative conditions of (empathy, genuineness, positive regard), 19–22
 learning activities for, 22–25
 as a nonspecific factor in evaluation, 204–205
 in selection of treatment strategies, 251

Counseling strategies (*see* Treatment strategies)
Counterconditioning:
    for conditioned emotions, 369
    in desensitization, 432, 435, 445–447, 449, 460
Covert behavior, 131–132, 143–144
    covert "ABCs," 129, 131–132, 133, 143
    interview leads to identify covert behaviors, 143–144
Covert modeling, 307–319, 325–329
    advantages of, 308
    components of, 308–314
    covert self-modeling, 310
    definition of, 307
    interview checklist of, 325–329
    learning activity for, 319
    model dialogue of, 314–319
    uses of, 307–308
Covert positive reinforcement, 501
Cueing, 55, 494–497

Demand characteristics, 205, 214–215, 483
Desensitization (*see* Systematic desensitization)
Devices (for recording), 483
    for self-monitoring, 486–487
Discrimination, 116–125, 483–484, 494
    definition of, 56, 116
    discriminative stimulus, 55, 494
    of interview, 116–125
    in self-monitoring, 483–484
Duration:
    of covert modeling scenes, 313
    of desensitization scenes, 451
    duration counts, 147, 155, 208, 218, 486

Emotive imagery, 303–307, 322–325
    definition of, 303
    in desensitization, 445, 446
    ingredients in scenes, 305
    interview checklist, 322–325
    learning activity for, 307
    model example of, 306–307
    steps in, 304–306
    uses of, 303–304
Empathy, 20–22, 24
    advanced empathy, 21
    discrimination rating of, 21, 29
    nonverbal behaviors of, 21
    primary empathy, 21
Ethical issues (in helping):
    counselor competency, 253
    information-seeking about client, 139
    reevaluation of client goals, 170–171

referral, 171
termination of helping, 513
value conflict with client, 16
Evaluation (of helping), 2, 4, 116–117, 124–125, 203–249, 513
    of helping outcomes, 206–229
        learning activities for, 209–210, 216, 227–229
        methods of measurement, 210–216
        times of measurement, 216–217
        types of measurement, 206–209
    of helping process 229–235
        definition of, 229
        description of helper's skills, 233–234
        description of helping sessions, 229
        description of treatment strategies, 233
        purpose of, 229
    of interview responses, 116–117, 124–125
    model example of, 235–244
    system for recording data, 234–235
    termination of helping, 513
Expectations, 18–19
    of clients, 104
    of counselors, 18
    in desensitization, 432–433
    learning activity for, 118–119
    as a nonspecific factor, 205
Extinction, 432

Family contract game, 496–497
Feedback, 267–268
    conditions of, 267
    definition of, 267
    feedback rating scale, 25
    in participant modeling, 288
    with rehearsal, 268
    role of in learning activities, 6
    in self-monitoring, 487
    in symbolic modeling, 279
Follow-up, 225–228
    graph of follow-up data, 228
    reasons for, 225–226
    and termination of helping, 513
    types of, 225
    ways to conduct, 226–227
Frequency counts, 147, 155, 207–208, 218, 486
Functional relationship, 54

Genuineness, 20 (*see also* Congruence)
Goals (of helping), 164–181, 182–202, 252, 479
    outcome goals, 182–202, 479
        flexibility in goal-setting, 196–197
        goal chart, 194
        interview checklist of, 199–200

interview leads for defining goals, 183–189
learning activities for, 190, 195–196
model dialogue, 190–194
and selection of treatment strategies, 252
steps in defining goals, 183
three parts of goals, 4, 182, 479
purposes of goals, 165
steps in selecting goals, 165
interview checklist of, 178–180
interview leads for selecting goals, 167–171
learning activities for, 170–171, 175–176
model dialogue of, 172–175
Graphs:
baseline graphs:
of client rating data, 220
of role-play data, 221
of self-monitored data, 218–219
of self-report data, 221–222
graphs of:
follow-up data, 228
posttreatment data, 226
treatment effects, 223, 225
purposes of, 218
in self-monitoring, 487
Group-administered desensitization, 460
Guided participation, 287–289

Helping strategies (see Treatment strategies)
Helping style, 10, 26
checklist for, 27, 112–113, 163, 200–201
Hierarchy:
of covert modeling scenes, 313
in desensitization, 432, 433, 438–445
criteria for hierarchies, 441
identification of hierarchy items, 440–441
personal hierarchy, 439–440
presentation of hierarchy scenes, 449–457
ranking of hierarchy items, 442
spatio-temporal hierarchy, 438–439
standardized hierarchies, 442–443, 460
thematic hierarchy, 439
of goal behaviors, 287
of subgoals, 187
Homework (see also Transfer-of-training):
characteristics of, 269
in cognitive modeling, 336
in cognitive restructuring, 369–370
in covert modeling, 314
in emotive imagery, 306
in meditation, 405–406
in relaxation, 414
in self-as-a-model, 282
self-monitoring of homework, 269

in stress inoculation, 385
in systematic desensitization, 440, 446, 457
in thought-stopping, 344
Hypnosis, 431, 458

Imagery:
assessment of clients, 302–303
as a coping skill, 378
in covert modeling, 307–308
criteria for effective imagery, 448
in desensitization, 447–448
emotive imagery, 303–307
problems in, 458
in self-reward, 500, 501
Imitation (see Modeling)
Immediacy, 98–101
of client, 99
of counselor, 98
definition of, 98
ground rules, 100
learning activities for, 100–101
purposes of, 99–100
of relationship, 99
Induction aids, 265–266, 288–289 (see also Coaching)
definition of, 265
examples of, 265
use of in participant modeling, 288–289
Information (as coping skill), 377–378
Information-giving, 105–106, 376–377
definition of, 105
example of, 106
ground rules, 105–106
in problem-solving, 105
purposes of, 105
in stress inoculation, 376–377
Inner circle strategy, 141–142
Instructions, 101–102
in covert modeling, 313
definition of, 101
in desensitization, 452
ground rules of, 102
as a nonspecific factor, 205
in participant modeling, 287
purposes of, 101
in self-monitoring, 479, 487
in symbolic modeling, 279
three elements of, 102
Interpretation, 78, 86–90
client reactions to, 89
definition of, 78, 86–87
effects of, 88
examples of, 78, 87–88

overt, 5, 265
self-directed, 266, 289, 314
in strategy implementation, 264–265
in cognitive modeling, 333, 335–336
in cognitive restructuring, 366, 367, 368, 369
of contract terms, 510
in covert modeling, 312–314
in emotive imagery, 305–306
in participant modeling, 288
in stress inoculation, 382–383, 384
in symbolic modeling, 279
in thought-stopping, 342–344
Reinforcement (*see also* Consequences):
definition of, 498, 501
reinforcement survey, 501
reinforcing self-statements, 368–369
removal of reinforcement, 505
self-reinforcement (*see also* Self-reward), 334,
478, 481, 487, 498–499
in treatment strategies:
contracting, 506, 507, 510
covert modeling, 311–312
desensitization, 432
thought-stopping, 343
types of reinforcers:
current, 500, 502, 504
high-frequency, 501–502
imaginal, 500, 501, 502
material, 500, 502, 504
potential, 500, 502, 504
verbal-symbolic, 500, 501, 502, 504
verbal interview reinforcement, 54–55
Relaxation:
in covert modeling, 309
in emotive imagery, 303
mental relaxation, 378
in modeling, 262
muscle relaxation, 406–417
cautions, 407–408
in desensitization, 432, 433, 445, 446, 451,
458
interview checklist of, 423–427
learning activity for, 417
model dialogue of, 416–417
steps of, 408–414
uses of, 407
variations in, 415–416
physical relaxation, 378–379
relaxation response, 402–406 (*see also*
Meditation)
Reliability:
definition of, 482
of interview, 210

of observers, 216
of self-monitoring, 212–213
Resistance, 189
definition of, 189
reasons for, 189
Rewards (*see* Reinforcement)
Role-play, 6, 214–215, 220–221 (*see also* Rehearsal)
collection of role-play data during baseline,
220–221
for counseling skills, 6
as a measurement method, 214–215

Sanction, 506, 507, 510 (*see also* Punishers)
Satiation, 502, 504
Self-administered desensitization, 460
Self-as-a-model, 280–285, 296–298, 310
definition of, 280
interview checklist of, 296–298
learning activity for, 284–285
model example of, 282–284
steps in, 280–282
Self-contracting, 479, 506–512
definition of, 506
features of, 507–509
learning activity for, 510–512
model example of, 510–511
steps in implementing, 509–510
Self-control, 433–436, 449, 476 (*see also*
Self-management)
in desensitization, 433–434, 435–436, 449, 476
Self-defeating (irrational) thoughts, 339, 342–344,
363–365, 367–368
Self-development, 1, 2
Self-disclosure, 95–98
definition of, 95
effects of, 96–97
ground rules, 97–98
learning activities for, 98
purposes of, 96
types of:
demographic, 95
negative, 96
personal, 95
positive, 95–96
Self-enhancing (rational) thoughts, 363, 365,
380–382 (*see also* Coping thoughts)
Self-help groups, 512
Self-image, 11–15
learning activity for, 14–15
Self-instruction:
coping self-instructions, 366, 496
self-instructional training, 332–336
in symbolic modeling, 278